Mind and Brain

Principles of Neuropsychology

ilinsky, Ph.D.

or of Psychology

idgeport

PRAEGER

PRAEGER SCIENTIFIC

a • Eastbourne, UK
• Tokyo • Sydney

Library of Congress Cataloging in Publication Data

Gilinsky, Alberta Steinman, 1918–
    Mind and brain.

    Includes bibliographies and index.
    1. Neuropsychology.   2. Mind and body.   I. Title.
[DNLM: 1. Neurophysiology.   2. Psychophysiology. WL 102
G474m]
QP360.G55   1984   612'.82   83-24740
ISBN 0-03-059874-5
ISBN 0-03-059876-1 (pbk.)

Published in 1984 by Praeger Publishers
CBS Educational and Professional Publishing
A Division of CBS, Inc.
521 Fifth Avenue, New York, New York 10175 U.S.A.

456789   052   98765432

Printed in the United States of America

Contents

For my mother

Foreword

In the rapid and spectacular development of neuroscience, there is danger that the major function of the brain, complex behavior, may not receive the scientific attention it deserves. Advances in cellular and molecular neurobiology are so exciting and so technologically elegant that answers to the age-old scientific questions of sensation and perception, learning and memory, motivation and emotion, and thinking and intelligence may seem to be just around the corner. We may hope that they are, and with them the solution to problems of mental retardation, affective disorders, senile dementia, and psychosis. But not without the concomitant development of a scientific basis for psychology and the study of behavior, particularly as they relate to the structure and function of the nervous system.

It is this scientific base in psychology and its relation to the study of the brain that Professor Gilinsky provides in this book. Other monographs and textbooks in neuropsychology and behavioral neuroscience deal with the anatomy of the brain and the physiology and cell biology of neurons. Their relevance for the basic organizing principles of behavior and practical human problems are all too easily lost. This book is different. It is fundamentally concerned with the principles of psychology and the data from experimental psychology, physiological psychology, and clinical neuropsychology that provide a scientific base for the questions we ask about the behavioral functions of the brain.

What Professor Gilinsky does here is to bring classical experimental psychology to bear on the problems of neuropsychology. She builds on the classical contributions of William James, Robert S. Woodworth, Jerzy Konorski, and Donald O. Hebb that are not always remembered in modern neuroscience. She interweaves these with the clinical insights of A.R. Luria, Wilder Penfield, and Norman Geschwind. And most important of all, she brings both the facts of experimental psychology and the insights of clinical neurology into meaningful perspective with the modern neurobiological work of David Hubel and Torsten Wiesel, Eric Kandel, Edward Evarts, Vernon Mountcastle, and Richard Thompson.

Right from the beginning the book addresses the major questions of psychology and the study of behavior: sensation and perception; reflex and voluntary action; motivation, emotion, and reinforcement; attention, learning, and memory; insight, thinking, and judgment; language consciousness, and awareness of self. Behavior is discussed from both the evolutionary and developmental viewpoints, so animal as well as human studies are reviewed and interwoven. The organization of the brain for the management of both affective and cognitive behavior is described, including hemispheric specialization and the lateralization of human brain function as shown in clinical cases with unilateral lesions and in Sperry's work with split brain humans. The nature of the various sensory analyzers (especially the visual) and their neuroanatomical and neurophysiological organization in the cerebral cortex is described, including the central origin of images and hallucinations. So also are the biological substrates for object perception and pattern recognition in the organization of the associative cortex. Mechanisms for reflex and voluntary motor action and their central "scores" or control mechanisms are discussed. The importance of learning, remembering, and forgetting are given extensive attention, and their importance is stressed throughout the book, for it is the plasticity of the nervous system that makes mind and behavior the complex processes that they are. Language and the complex cognitive functions of the brain are given extensive treatment, especially in an excellent chapter on the experience of clinical neurology with aphasia, agnosia, apraxia, and other disorders following brain lesion in humans.

The brain is described not only as hierarchical, but also as heterarchical (with multiple parallel, but integrated, levels of control). The study of psychology tells us that the organization of the brain has to be modular and its function categorical in that it deals with objects that are recognizable from any angle and that belong in a broad class of objects. Similarly, it deals with movements that achieve the same end results regardless of the muscles or even limbs involved. Modern neurophysiological findings fit well with these ideas and lead to the concept that there must be neurons and sets of neurons responsive to such complex features of the environment and in control of complex acts. Professor Gilinsky calls these units "cognons." They are direct theoretical descendants of Konorski's "gnostic units," and evidence for them is appearing in the work of Charles Gross, Vernon Mountcastle, Edward Evarts, and Patricia Goldman-Rakic.

There is a new excitement in this approach to neuropsychology and behavioral neuroscience from the standpoint of the facts, principles, and theories of experimental psychology. A classically trained experimental psychologist, Professor Gilinsky brings important insights for the neurobiologist and presents sound hypotheses for how the brain must be organized to do what it does in expressing complex behavior. In the study of memory, for example, she reminds us not only that there are short-term and long-term memories, but that different processes may be involved when recall, recognition, or relearning are used as the measures of memory.

Physiological psychologists and behavioral neurobiologists have much to be proud of in this book. Their responsibility in the exciting future of neuroscience is made clear in the way questions are posed for the investigation of the functions of the nervous system. Most important of all, students will be given a big boost in their understanding of modern neurobiology as it relates to complex behavior and psychological processes, both normal and abnormal. The advanced undergraduate major in psychology and behavioral neurobiology should have no difficulty mastering this text, and the graduate student in psychology and the neurosciences will find it a remarkable resource of well-documented facts, principles, and theories. Finally, the specialist in psychology who wants to know more about the brain and the neuroscience investigator without background in psychology will have much to learn here.

We all owe Professor Gilinsky a great debt for her remarkable ability to bring us an in-depth study of how the basic facts and principles of psychology fit with what is known about the anatomy, physiology, and chemistry of the brain. We have much to profit from her insights and her sound hypotheses, and, as a consequence, much to gain in our efforts to investigate and understand the complex behavioral and psychological functions of the brain.

Eliot Stellar
Philadelphia

Preface

Neuropsychology has progressed to the point that it can assert that everything human beings can perceive, conceive, or do is a result of the central nervous system's ability to structure and restructure its own activity. Everything mental arises from the functioning of the active nervous system: The central nervous system is the place of mind in nature.

W.B. Weimer, 1976, p. 7

Perhaps the most exciting discovery that you can make about yourself and your world is that all the diverse phenomena of nature are tied together by astonishingly few relations. Surprisingly few general principles are needed to account for the ties between your conscious experience and the underlying neurophysiology of your brain and central nervous system. Yet these ties are far from evident in the functioning of your perceptual mechanisms. The light you see, the sounds you hear, the heat you feel: these reveal more than elementary sensations—what you get are objects: people's faces, familiar voices, music, sunshine. You are generally not aware of the components from which these perceptions are derived. Consider your immediate recognition of a friend or the mistaken identification of a stranger—a true or a false perception. Although one is correct, the other an illusion, both depend upon the identical processes in the cerebral cortex of your brain. How can this be?

This book seeks to reveal the way in which the brain works to integrate elementary sensations into unitary perceptions. It examines the nature of perceiving, starting with selective attention and drives, including curiosity and exploratory behavior, and going on to some questions of central importance in both psychology and neurobiology.

How does the brain work to organize conscious experience so as to construct a workable representation of the physical world? How does experience provide the organism with sufficiently accurate information to enable it to move safely about and secure its biological needs? Why and when does the perceptual process result in error and illusion? What causes hallucinations and dreams? How do we acquire new knowledge and retain it in memory? What do we remember, and why do we forget?

xix

These questions of perception, learning, and memory are the most important—and the most challenging in both neurobiology and psychology. Until very recently these processes took place inside a "black box." Neurobiologists have now opened the "black box" and in the past few years have made enormous advances in the study of perceiving, learning, and memory with the techniques of cell biology. What made this possible was the discovery that, on the cellular level, learning is universal in all nervous systems.

Few general principles are required to relate neurophysiology to behavior. Building on the work of Pavlov, Sherrington, Cajal, Woodworth, Luria, and the more recent research of Mountcastle, Hubel, Wiesel, Sperry, Kandel, Geschwind, and Konorski, this account attempts to come to grips with the problem everyone regards as impossible—the problem of elucidating the relations between the mind and the brain.

First and foremost is the principle of the uniqueness of the nerve cell. Individual neurons connect invariably to the same target cells. Each cell has its own particular job to perform and can react with amazing specificity to selected stimuli. A single "command cell" can exert remarkably powerful control over a complex sequence of behavior. Examples can be found in many different animals. One impulse in a command cell in the goldfish will cause the animal to flee in fear. A dual action command cell in the snail regulates its heart rate. It excites the heart to beat faster while inhibiting the cells that inhibit the heart and that constrict the major blood vessels. This one cell thus raises heart rate and increases circulation. A rhythm generator cell in some insects controls many pairs of muscle in legs or wings to bring about smoothly coordinated patterns of walking or flying.

The realization that the nervous system in all animals has similar properties leads to a simplifying generalization. Perhaps human behavior is also controlled by individual neurons localized in precisely determined regions of the brain. No one has yet identified the particular neuron that recognizes a familiar face or programs a spoken sentence. But neurobiologists are beginning to accept the idea that cells with such precise functions do exist in the human brain. The theory puts the controlling mind back in the center of psychology and locates it in the cerebral cortex or cognitive cortex. The keystone, which I call the *cognon*—the cognitive neuron—is the anatomical and functional substrate of the unitary perception, image, or idea.

This concept of a mental unit provides a powerful tool for unifying the phenomena of perception, conceptual thought, and voluntary action. The cognon has a number of distinctive properties. It can integrate a complex input and quickly decide whether to trigger a response. It has integrity, constancy, stability. Although it represents a stimulus pattern whose constituent impulses vary widely, the cognon does not "know" from what constituents it is composed and cannot be subdivided or merged with other patterns. Like other single cells it obeys the all-or-none law of the nervous impulse. The cognon thus insures for perception the immediate recognition and constancy of familiar objects presented in different settings. You recognize a familiar face at a glance, a friend's voice after hearing one word, the odor of coffee after one whiff.

By combining behavioral, cellular, and biochemical analyses in animal experiments with studies of behavioral disorders in brain-damaged humans, we are coming close to an architectonic mapping of highly specialized human brain functions. Still, consider the fact that our brain contains more than 100 billion nerve cells. Even if we knew what each cell does at any moment, we still would face the difficult task of determining how the intricate circuitry of the central nervous system transmits and integrates nerve impulses.

Here a major advance has been attained with the principle of nerve integration. Sherrington saw that the functional significance of reciprocal innervation in coordinating reflexes was to prevent antagonistic action by causing the activation of one reflex to repress the activity of the other. The facts of inhibitory interaction, expressed by muscles and other effectors, suggested to Sherrington a mechanism for integrating *sensory* information as well as *motor* behavior. He realized that, fundamentally, perception and action are dual representations of the same processes. These give rise to "singleness of action"—the integrative activity of the whole organism.

A single general principle—the antagonistic interaction of opponent neural processes—appears more and more forcible as the universal mechanism of integration of the organism. Whether a given synapse (junction between cells) is excitatory or inhibitory depends upon what chemical transmitter the presynaptic cell releases at the site and its effect on the target cell. It is the sum of their excitatory and inhibitory effects that determine whether the cell will fire and the rate of its response.

The functional significance of opposed excitatory and inhibitory influences is to emphasize the response to differences, to contrasts, to relations, and to ignore absolute properties of stimulation. The nervous system quickly learns to neglect repeated stimuli; a change, however slight, is news and evokes a brisk response—a volley of electrical impulses in the excited nerve cell.

With brilliant inventiveness, Jerzy Konorski, Director of the Nencki Institute and head of its Neurophysiological Laboratory in Warsaw, Poland, tied these ideas to cognitive processes: perception, learning, and memory. He saw that the integrative activity of the brain made use of the convergent and divergent processing of neural signals by single cells arranged in orderly levels in different regions of the cerebral cortex. His model accounted for nonassociative (perceptual) learning resulting from sensitization of potential connections developed in ontogeny. He explained associative learning, expressed in both classical and instrumental conditioning, by temporally paired unit activity under the facilitating influence of drive arousal.

Konorski's recent work has been sadly neglected in this country. His important contributions and our exchanges of visits between Poland and the United States provided the impetus for this book. Jerzy Konorski did not live to see the emerging confirmation of many of his ideas, now beautifully revealed in studies by researchers in widely separated areas, such as cellular biology, biochemistry, electrophysiology, clinical, and cognitive psychology. My aim in this book is to bring together these discoveries to focus on the most important problems in behavioral neuroscience: the neural mechanisms of perception, learning, memory, thought, and voluntary action.

With this approach I hope to clarify and extend Konorski's system and make it available to more students and research investigators in the neural and behavioral sciences. The explosion of studies in this fast-moving group of sciences seems to cry out for a framework of theory into which to fit the bewildering array of facts.

In contrast to other textbooks on physiological psychology, here is an interdisciplinary synthesis based on new discoveries from European and American laboratories and neurological clinics. Electrophysiological, neuropathological, and behavioral studies of animals and humans are used to provide a comprehensive system linking psychology and physiology, thought and action, emotion and cognition. Observations of split brain patients, disorders following damage or injury to the brain, and experiments on intact organisms (children, adults, and nonhuman animals) are brought together here in a unified theory.

A comprehensive treatment of the anatomy and physiology of the central nervous system is beyond the scope of this book. So, too, are details of methods and findings of the studies of neurobiology, experimental, and clinical psychology. Many excellent reviews of these important data are listed at the end of each chapter, and references to key studies appear in the bibliography at the back of the book.

General Organization

The overall structure of the book stresses three themes:

1. Mind is what the brain does, and can be regarded from various perspectives: as overt behaviors, as conscious experiences, as neurophysiological processes, as biochemical or molecular events. No single perspective or level is more real or important than the others—all are valid and equally necessary.

2. Heredity and environment interact to modify behavior at every stage of development. Thus, although we inherit a precise anatomical structure of nerves and synapses, these orderly connections are plastic and modifiable, functionally and morphologically, as the result of learning. We are growing to realize that the traditional distinction between nature and nurture is illusory.

Social and environmental determinants, no less than organic causes, have *biological* consequences.

3. The key to the development of the highest human mental functions is contained in two strategies of nature: modular or categorical organization and overlapping or parallel processing. As a result, the brain constructs many diverse small scale models, internal representations of the outside world in relation to the self. This makes possible the anticipation of future events and ideational testing of potential actions. Thought conserves energy and enables us to avoid pain and the possibly harmful consequence of overt behavior.

The book is divided into five parts. Part One, the *Scope of Neuro-psychology* introduces the main themes and provides a brief overview of the spiral development of ideas about brain localization.

Chapter One discusses the nervous system and its operation and evolution, and leads to a consideration (Chapter Two) of how the basic activities of all organisms are rooted in survival needs to protect and preserve the self and the species. Chapter Three examines the specialized functions of the human brain on the basis of evidence provided by studies of hemispheric lateralization, especially the dramatic experiments on the split brain.

The rest of the book considers in turn the three major functional systems of the brain: afferent systems provide information about the environment and feedback from our own activities; association systems serve learning, imagination, thought, and memory; efferent systems control motor coordination and voluntary or instrumental movement. The problem is to discover how the brain works to regulate overt behavior and convert thought to action. The book concludes with the attempt to bring the various parts together to consider the integrative activity of the brain as a whole. These overarching themes are treated in Parts Two to Five.

Part Two, *Afferent Systems: The Neuropsychology of Perception* deals with the problem of how the senses provide information to the brain about the world outside and also with feedback about the movements produced by the organism itself (Chapter Four). Chapter Five shows how this information is organized into specific perceptual systems or analyzers, giving rise to the formation of neural units called *cognons* that represent biologically meaning-ful objects and events. The psychological evidence for this, and the categories of unitary perceptions represented by cognons in the various analyzers (vision, audition, kinesthesis, etc.) are described in Chapter Six.

Part Three, *Associative Systems: The Neuropsychology of Learning and Cognition* attempts to explain how the theoretical system developed in the preceding chapters accounts for the relations between perception, imagina-tion, hallucination, and dreaming (Chapter Seven). Since cognons can be aroused via associative pathways as well as by direct sensory stimulation, here is the basis for associative learning, including both classical and instrumental conditioning. Their relations to each other, to nonassociative learning, and to insight are considered in Chapter Eight. Fundamental to these processes, drives (emotions) play a dual role, serving both to energize and to direct behavior to achieve the individual's goals. Chapter Nine provides neurophysiological evidence for this approach, based on disorders of cognition, personality, and behavior in human patients following brain damage.

Chapter Ten takes up the problem central to both neurobiology and psychology—the problem that Hebb and Lashley considered to be the most neglected and the most challenging in the attempt to combine the two disciplines into neuropsychology—the problem of directed thought. By approaching the problem through a consideration of the limitations of short-term memory imposed by the constraints of maintaining serial order, we see that the span of attention, the span of memory, and the span of judgment, share common features based on a common modular structure. With the realization that all nervous systems have similar properties, the way in which short-term memory grades into long-term memory is at last becoming accessible to effective study. Chapter Eleven explains how the temporal pairing of two stimuli in classical conditioning and the temporal pairing of stimulus and response in instrumental conditioning establish direct connections between two active centers in the brain (i.e., their neural representations) under the facilitating influence of drive or emotive arousal. The astonishing finding is that remembering and forgetting, two opposing forms of learning, take place at a common locus, the presynaptic terminals of sensory neurons, and are mediated by the same basic mechanism for strengthening or weakening synaptic connections—the amount of biochemical transmitter released by the sensory cells. Indeed, both nonassociative and associative learning can be explained as the result of changes in the strength of already existing contacts between specific neurons, and related to persistent changes in behavior at the psychological level.

Part Four, *Efferent Systems: The Neuropsychology of Motor Behavior* begins with a chapter on action programs and the central control of voluntary movement (Chapter Twelve) and then (Chapter Thirteen) turns to consider a possible common code for perception and action based on topological concepts and the application of Fourier theory to the analysis and synthesis of spatial patterns of form and movement.

Part Five, *Integrative Activity of the Brain* attempts to relate the ideas of the various preceding parts of the book to provide intellectual cohesion and unity. It begins with a consideration of nature and nurture in the development of complex skills (Chapter Fourteen) and then (Chapter Fifteen) concludes with a general summary of the principles and concepts of human neuropsychology with special reference to such controversial problems as the distinctions between the emotive and the cognitive brain, the recovery from brain damage and mental illness, and the functions of consciousness, especially the riddle of self-consciousness.

The higher behavioral functions are localized in different areas of the brain. A picture of the functions of the major divisions of the association cortex is emerging from ablation and electrophysiological studies in animals, and from neurosurgical and clinical observations of human subjects. The book examines the higher brain functions located in specialized regions of the left and right hemispheres. It quickly becomes obvious that each one of these regions subserves many overlapping functions, yet certain distinctions do appear. Thus, almost all significant organic *personality* disorders occur with disease in either the frontal or temporal lobe. While disorders of space perception, language, and memory may result from lesions of the frontal, parietal, occipital, or temporal lobes, the specific nature of the perceptual or cognitive deficit will vary with the locus of the lesion. For example, disorders of short-term memory for spatial directions are related to prefrontal lesions, while disorders of spatial attention that affect reaching for and manipulating objects in extrapersonal space are due largely to parietal lesions. Severe amnesia for newly acquired information follows the bilateral destruction of the temporal lobes and the hippocampal system. Disorders of speech may result from agnosias or disconnections in many parts of the brain, although the localization of the various forms of aphasia in the left hemisphere in the majority of people (and their most probable lesion site) has become more certain. Where localization is certain, I will so specify, but since human pathology is rarely precisely circumscribed, this book will be less concerned with the question *where* than with the questions *how* and *why* certain functions appear or disappear.

A vast literature has grown to bear on neuropathology that is well beyond the scope of this book. My concern in what follows is to emphasize that all mental processes are biological and jointly influenced by heredity and environment. The realization that specialized behavioral functions, motivation, learning, and memory are universal in all nervous systems makes these functions accessible for study by the newly combined techniques of molecular and behavioral analyses. At the level of cellular biology, what we find is that both functional (plastic) and organic processes in brain are precisely localized in specific nerve cells and their synaptic connections.

Is it possible to shift from the neurophysiological to the psychological level in explaining these processes? I have tried to do that in this book. Whenever possible, when introducing a physiological concept like "targeting reflex," I have named its subjective or psychological counterpart, "attention"; I have paired "drive" with "emotion," and "antidrive" with "mood." In the glossary at the end of the book, these physiological and psychological definitions are cross-indexed in a way that I hope will be helpful.

Acknowledgments

I thank the students, friends, and colleagues who helped me with my task, especially Eliot Stellar for understanding extraordinarily well what I was attempting to do and encouraging me. Both he and Eric R. Kandel read all or large parts of earlier drafts of the manuscript and made many valuable suggestions. I cannot express sufficient gratitude to them or to my most endearing taskmaster, research associate, and critic, Armand Gilinsky, for devotion to my project.

I also thank Adam Gilinsky, Armand Gilinsky, Jr., Deborah L. Jans, Helen Kelly, Colleen MacGillvary, Stuart Mayper, Jeddeo Paul, and many students who gave generously of their time and assistance.

I would like to acknowledge the timely and cheerful manuscript preparation provided by Lolly Bassett's *Letter Perfect* service.

Special thanks go to my Praeger senior editor, George Zimmar, whose keen advice and incisive eye never failed at critical periods; to copy editor Gail Hapke, for fine tuning the manuscript and making it into a real book with incredible speed and competence; and to the production staff of Publication Services.

My work was supported in part by the University of Bridgeport. A semester's release time from teaching and a summer research grant helped bring this book to completion.

Most of the original illustrations were drawn by Fran Gaulin. Other figures were drawn by Susan McGoey and Annie Vallotton, who prepared all of the unnumbered drawings.

I am especially grateful to colleagues who contributed photographs: Stuart Anstis, Colin Blakemore, Fergus W. Campbell, Tiffany Field, Patricia Goldman-Rakic, I. Gormezano, David Hubel, Eric R. Kandel, John Robson, Ronald K. Siegel, Eliot Stellar, Peter Thompson, and Richard F. Thompson.

PART ONE

Introduction: The Scope of Neuropsychology

CHAPTER ONE

An Overall View

*Every behavior selected for study, every observation and interpretation,
requires subjective processing by an introspective observer. Logically, there is
no way of circumventing this or the more disturbing conclusion that the cold,
hard facts of science, like the firm pavement under foot, are all derivatives of a
soft brain.*

(Paul MacLean, 1970, p. 337)

INTRODUCTION

This book is directed to the reader who would like to know more about how
the brain functions to control perception, consciousness, language, and
creative thought.

The desire to gain some clear understanding of how the brain works to
control perception and other higher mental processes is difficult to satisfy.
There are three reasons for this. First, research on the nervous system has
followed a molecular analysis using electrophysiological, biochemical, and
anatomical methods. This analytical approach has unearthed minute details
of structure and function of parts and cells, but failed to come to grips with the
single most fundamental aspect of living organisms—their purposive organization.

Second, the more nearly synthetic approaches of the cognitive theorist
and the animal behaviorist have explicitly rejected physiology as belonging to

another scientific discipline. They have not studied the brain, and they have nothing to say about its functioning. The experimental studies of associative learning or conditioning, problem solving, and linguistic functions have led to important findings, but the conclusions based on them are often inconsistent with neurophysiological information.

The third reason is not scientific but philosophical. In the seventeenth century, Descartes sharply separated *res cogitans* (the soul) from *res extensa* (the body). The resulting dualism enabled physiologists to get on with the study of the nervous machinery of the body unencumbered by a theological soul. Rapid progress was thus made possible in studies of anatomy and physiology. The result was a new science based on the spinal reflex and the nervous mechanisms underlying motor and glandular responses to stimuli. This century has, therefore, seen major developments in the behavioral sciences on the one hand and the neural sciences on the other, but with no stable bridge between them. Each field has grown in selective isolation from the other, and, consequently, sterility and artificiality have afflicted psychology.

Students who approach psychology with a curiosity about mind—consciousness, learning, memory, and thought—come away disappointed. They fail to find in current textbooks any adequate physiological explanations of higher mental functions. The Cartesian dichotomy of two distinct substances, mind and body, has been a dilemma for psychologists who have tried to cope with both sides and tie them together in some fashion.

NEUROPSYCHOLOGY: AN INTERDISCIPLINARY SCIENCE

The study of the mind belongs to psychology and the study of the brain to neurobiology. The convergence of the two disciplines in neuropsychology has led to the hope that these different descriptions can be related to each other and that mind can understand itself. *Neuropsychology* may be defined as the study of the relations between the functions of the brain and behavior, including mental reactions and experience.

New tools, combining behavioral study, radioactive selective staining techniques, and cellular analysis, are now employed in studying alert, behaving subjects. The results are giving a new sense of excitement and optimism to behavioral and brain scientists. At last we can begin to explain how the mind works.

Experiments on human patients who have undergone surgical disconnection of the cerebral hemispheres (the split brain operation for the control of epilepsy) have made a major contribution to our knowledge of the specialized functions of the human brain—language, emotional expression, perception, and consciousness. These diverse lines of investigation converge, bringing us a broad new definition of "mind"—helping to bridge the gap between the artificial intelligence specialists who want to build a better "brain" and the neuroscientists who hope to explain the one that nature gives us.

The situation at present is that a large collection of particular facts has been obtained by scientists in many fields of investigation. These data are sometimes taken to mean that the sciences of living organisms—the science of behavior, and neuropsychology in particular—soon will be nothing more than a kind of super physiology-chemistry-physics. In reality they do nothing of the kind. Neuropsychology deals with concepts peculiar to itself—with drives and emotions: fear, hunger, pain, curiosity, sexuality, and pleasure; with learning, memory, and forgetting; with language and its disorders; with images, dreams, delusions, and conflicts; with thinking, and purposive, voluntary attention and action.

These phenomena certainly obey the laws of chemistry and physics; living organisms can do nothing to contravene those laws. But it is a mistake to speak of "reducing" the psychological phenomena that interest us to physics and chemistry. What this book aims to do is just the opposite: its goal is to assemble, to piece together, and to integrate a framework of ideas about the mind from a knowledge of its constituent parts. Such a unifying synthesis is what is most conspicuously lacking in the science of behavior. We are in danger of being lost in minute details—the challenge is to find a systematic theory into which to fit them and which will show us how to frame new questions for future research.

Robert S. Woodworth, late Columbia University professor, and chairman for many years of its graduate department of experimental psychology, arrived at a view that appeals to me—a parallelism of different scientific descriptions of the same process:

> The parallelism is not necessarily between the psychical and physical, but may and does occur whenever different sciences set themselves to the description of the same natural process. The different sciences will employ different techniques, and, in particular, one science will go into finer detail than the other, even as one map goes into more detail than another map of the same country. While the detailed map certainly includes much that does not appear in the comprehensive map of a larger area, it has to leave to the latter the presentation of the broad geographical relationships. Thus the same real object can be given description at two (or more) different "levels" or magnifications. The same parallelism appears between gross and microscopic anatomy, between organ physiology and cellular physiology, between geology and the physics and chemistry of the minute processes that enter into the broad geological processes. (Woodworth, 1939, p. 23)

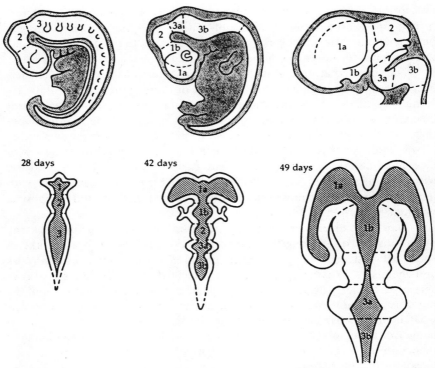

Figure 1.1A. The basic divisions of the human brain: (1) the forebrain, (2) midbrain, and (3) hindbrain undergo further subdivisions with age. Angevine & Cotman, 1981.

The view that science deals with relations between events, relations that can be examined at many different levels, is well based. The hearing of a voice, the image of a smiling face, the idea of the expanding universe—are no less events in the stream of natural events than the flexion of a muscle or the taped recording of action potentials of a sensory neuron.

The value of Woodworth's solution to the mind-body problem is that it provides a place for both conscious experience and behavior, for both psychology and physiology, within the bounds of natural science. Psychologists need not fear that their profession as scientists will vanish as physiology succeeds in further reducing cellular organic processes to their micromolecular constituents. Ever finer analyses need not replace holistic, psychological concepts based on the integrative activity of the intact organism. There is freedom here—the investigator is not restricted to either a reductionist or a holistic approach. Both approaches are needed. What we get are different descriptions of the same process, no one of which can lay claim to a greater reality than another.

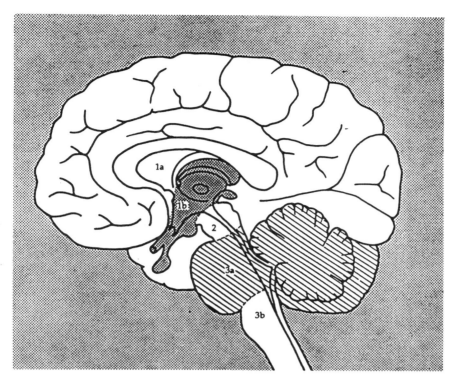

Figure 1.1B. Adult derivatives of the basic subdivisions of the embryonic brain. Angevine & Cotman, 1981.

AN OVERALL VIEW OF THE BRAIN

To get the most out of this book you will need to have some rudimentary knowledge of the anatomy of the human brain. As the brain develops during embryonic and fetal growth, the gross changes are clear. The three main parts of the brain—the forebrain, the midbrain, and the hindbrain—orignate as prominent swellings at the head end of the neural tube. (See Figure 1.1A.)

The largest growth occurs in the forebrain where the cerebral hemispheres overgrow the midbrain and hindbrain. They appear smooth surfaced during the first four or five months of pregnancy and then begin to assume their characteristic convolutions and invaginations. In vertebrates lower than mammals, the cerebrum is small. In higher mammals, and particularly in primates, it increases dramatically in both size and complexity. (See Figure 1.1B.)

In the brain of a mammal the cerebral hemisphere is the largest part. In humans and many mammalian species, the cerebral mantle or neocortex is furrowed into convolutions called *gyri* and fissures called *sulci*. The convolutions are the result of evolution's attempt to fit an expanding volume into a skull still small enough to squeeze through the birth canal. The result for humans is a long period of infant dependence while the nervous system continues to mature. Indeed, the human newborn infant does not possess functioning cerebral hemispheres; behavior at first is largely reflexive and uncoordinated (Peiper, 1963). (See Figure 1.2.)

While psychologists have focused their attention on the cerebral cortex in the forebrain, with its impressive cognitive functions, the other parts of the brain—the midbrain and the hindbrain—are critical for survival and regulate our vital needs, our emotions, and our personality traits.

Together with the spinal cord, the three main parts of the brain comprise the central nervous system. The entire system consists of many smaller structures with distinctive details of anatomy and chemistry, although they are extensively interconnected within and between the major regions. (See Figure 1.3.)

The main features are listed here, but I advise the reader to consult the excellent general references listed at the end of this chapter.

The names (in italics) of the parts of the brain that will be discussed in this book follow:

1. The *hindbrain* (or rhombencephalon—"encephalon"; within the head) contains the *brainstem* (the pons and medulla) and, attached to its lower end, the *cerebellum,* which controls motor coordination. The core of the brain stem contains the *reticular formation*—a dense network of *neurons* (nerve cells) whose central function is the general arousal to activity of all the rest of the brain. This region regulates the circadian (daily) rhythm of sleep and waking and the many degrees of alertness in between. The mobilization that prepares the body for action is stimulated by chemical substances: *adrenalin* and the related substance, *norepinephrine.* Many norepinephrine-containing cells are concentrated in a small cluster here—the *locus coeruleus* (blue place), involved in arousal, dreaming, sleep, and mood. These chemical neurotransmitters belong to a family called *catecholamines.*

2. The *midbrain* (mesencephalon) consists of the tectum and the tegmentum. The tectum includes two elevations known as the *superior colliculus* and the *inferior colliculus* (upper and lower hills). In birds and lower animals these are the visual and auditory brains, respectively. They serve in human beings to direct attention to the location of objects.

3. The *forebrain* (prosencephalon) is complex. It contains the diencephalon (between brains) and the telencephalon (far brain). The diencephalon contains the *thalamus* and its subdivisions in the upper two-thirds, and the *hypothalamus* in the lower third. The telencephalon consists of the paired cerebral hemispheres, capped by the *neocortex,* the convoluted sheet of

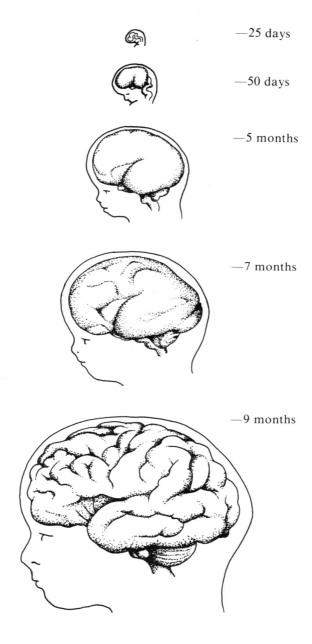

—25 days

—50 days

—5 months

—7 months

—9 months

Figure 1.2. Development of the human brain in ontogeny. Side views of a succession of embryonic and fetal stages drawn to the same scale.

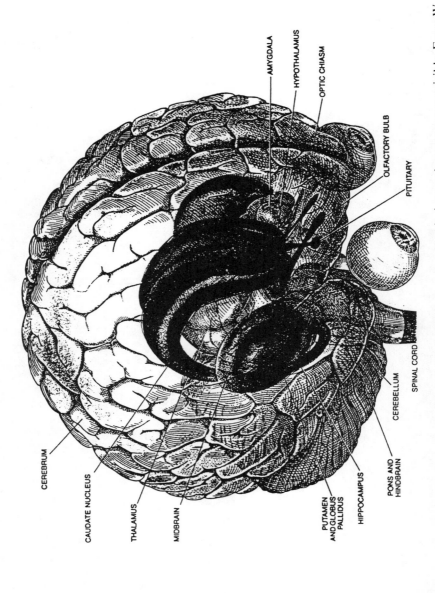

Figure 1.3. The human brain and spinal cord. The brain is drawn so that its internal structures are visible. From W.J.H. Nauta & N. Feirtag, "The Organization of the Brain," *Scientific American*, 1979, *241*, 78–91. Copyright © 1979 by Scientific American, Inc. All rights reserved.

10

the cerebral cortex. Close to the neocortex, one finds the *hippocampus* and the *olfactory* fields. The *amygdala* and the *corpus striatum* are masses of gray matter within the depths of the cerebral hemispheres. The corpus striatum consists of two distinct cell groups: the *basal ganglia* (the caudate nucleus, the putamen, and the globus pallidium) and an outer district known as the *striatum.*

It is tempting to assign a function to each one of these regions and to their subdivisions. But these structures are incredibly complex. They consist of neurons (nerve cells) packed together so intimately that in any one region their branches are densely intertwined.

A discovery by the Italian anatomist Camillio Golgi in 1875 of a method of staining neurons allowed individual cells to be seen in their entirety for the first time. His achievement convinced physiologists that the neuron is the basic unit of nervous tissue.

Following this discovery, the major problem was to determine how these cells communicate with one another. Is there complete continuity of connections—a neural network—or do separated lines form between individual cells?

The Spanish neurophysiologist, Santiago Ramón y Cajal (1908), using Golgi's selective method of staining nerve tissue, found the answer. Cajal compiled massive evidence to show that only certain cells are connected to certain other cells. There is precision wiring: that is, the connections are arranged in a definite, orderly manner. Precision wiring suggests that everything is laid down by genetic inheritance, but learning can take place because the strength of the connections and traffic routes can be changed by experience.

David H. Hubel, 1981 Nobel laureate and professor of neurobiology at the Harvard Medical School, in his introduction to *The Brain* (1979, p. 5), calls Cajal's research "gigantic" and "the most important single work in neurobiology." All of our further understanding of how the brain works is based on this solid foundation. There is no longer any controversy. New advances start from this one fundamental fact: the brain is made up of discrete, well-defined nerve cells communicating at specialized points of contact, the *synapses,* in a highly ordered and precise functional architecture.

In further comments on Cajal, David Hubel writes:

> From his time on it has been clear that to understand the brain the neurologist not only would have to learn how the various subdivisions are constructed, but also they would have to discover their *purposes* and learn in detail how they function as individual structures and as groups. Before that could be done, it would be necessary to find out how a *single neuron* generates its signals and transmits them to the next cell. (1979, p. 5) (Emphasis added.)

NERVE CELLS AND BEHAVIOR

New techniques have led to an explosion of discoveries, making neurobiology one of the most active branches of all sciences. Three tools—the microscope, the selective staining of neural tissue, and the microelectrode—have enabled the neurobiologist to investigate the highly specialized cells that comprise the elementary units of the central nervous system, the spinal cord and the brain.

Estimates place the number of nerve cells, or *neurons, that make up the human brain at about 10^{11}* (one hundred billion) give or take a factor of 10 (Hubel, 1979; Stevens, 1979). Surrounding the neurons, supporting and nourishing them, are almost as many glial cells. It is the neurons that interest us: they are the active, integrating units of the brain and, as we shall see, the elementary units of the mind. (See Figure 1.4.)

Neurons differ from other cells in the body: like the organism itself, they live once and die once. They do not regenerate once destroyed. But, and this is their magic—neurons are modifiable. They change as the result of growth during development or maturation, and they change as the result of experience. Maturation changes them by ensuring that they make highly specific connections with one another and with their targets. They do this by growing axons and sending them in the right direction. Both genetic and epigenetic factors arising in the cell's environment interact to shape their development—to elaborate dendritic processes and form appropriate bio-chemical properties and membrane receptors. Experience changes nervous tissue by inducing changes in the amount of chemical substances—*neuro-transmitters*—to be released at synapses, the junctions between nerve cells. (See Figure 1.5.) Their unique anatomical and physiological features make the brain function in a way that is unlike any other organ in the body. No computer, however swift and cleverly programmed, has yet been able to imitate the human brain.

Neurons transmit signals in the form of brief electrochemical impulses. These transient signals, called *action potentials,* convey information along the cells of the nervous system. (See Figure 1.6.) A nerve cell at rest, not involved in signaling, is positively charged on the outside and negatively charged on the inside. This potential difference (about -70 MV) in electrical charge is respon-sible for the resting membrane potential. If the arrival of a signal reduces this voltage difference to a critical level, the threshold potential difference, the in-side becomes more positive and causes the initiation of an *action potential.* The action potential is the neural impulse. It propagates actively down the entire length of the axon without decrease in amplitude much as a flame travels along the fuse of a firecracker. The action potential is therefore highly effective in signaling over a distance. A stronger stimulus has no effect on the amplitude of the action potential—it results in a greater *frequency* of impulse firing. The frequency of action potentials in a single sensory or motor neuron conveys no information other than the intensity of the stimulus; it indicates

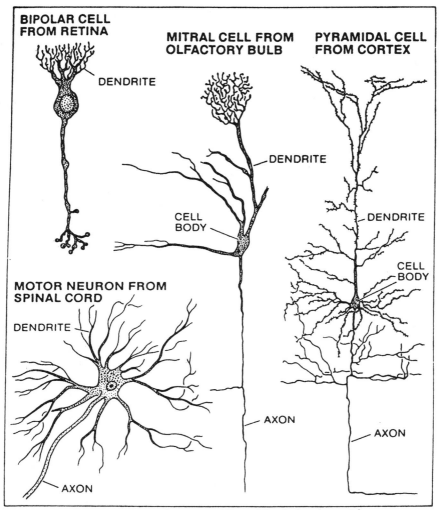

Figure 1.4. Various types of neurons. The cell body has branching processes, the dendrites, that make synaptic contact with other nerve fibers. The axon (often longer than shown) is covered with a segmented myelin sheath. Kuffler & Nicholls, 1976.

nothing about the quality or kind of stimulus. The signals themselves are stereotyped and virtually identical in all nerve cells. For communicating quality—the shape, pattern, or color of stimuli—different cells are called into operation. The origins of nerve fibers and their destinations within the brain— where they come from and where they are going—determine the meaning of their signals. (See Figure 1.7.)

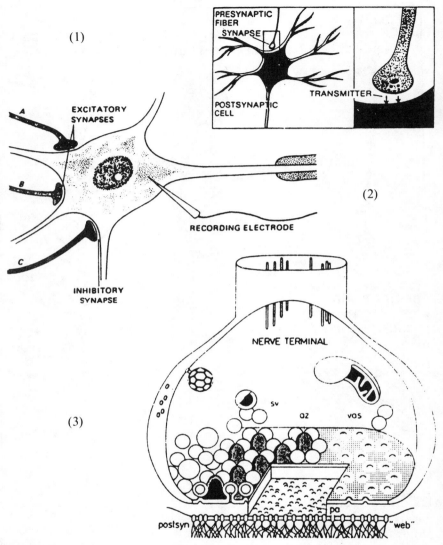

(1)

(2)

(3)

Figure 1.5. Basic features of the chemical synapse. (1) Transmitter release by the presynaptic fiber into the synaptic cleft and the postsynaptic cell. (2) Converging nerve paths with excitatory (A and B) and inhibitory (C) synapses. (3) Fine internal structure of the mammalian central synapse. Diagram shows the synaptic vesicles (sv), the active zones (az) that allow vesicle attachment sites (vas) to form on the membrane surface, and the (hypothetical) particle aggregation (pa) on the "web" of the postsynaptic membrane (postsyn). Akert, Peper, & Sandri, 1975. In Waser (Ed.), *Cholinergic Mechanisms.* Coypright © 1975 by Raven Press, New York.

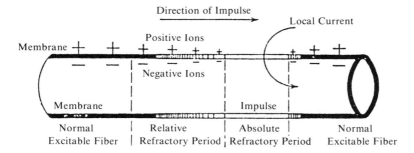

Figure 1.6. The action potential travels from left to right down the axon of the presynaptic neuron. The impulse consists of a local current as the positive and negative ions unite when the membrane becomes permeable and this current renders permeable the membrane ahead of it. The permeable membrane is shown in white and then shaded as it becomes restored after the passage of the impulse and the absolute refractory period is succeeded by a relative refractory period. Adapted from Boring, 1935.

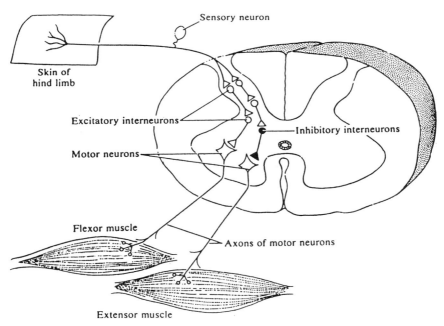

Figure 1.7. Simplified diagram of the flexion-withdrawal reflex in the cat. A tactile stimulus to the sensory neuron excites interneurons that in turn excite flexor motor cells that cause the flexor muscles to contract. The sensory neurons also activate inhibitory interneurons that inhibit the extensor motor neurons and prevent their firing. Kandel, 1976.

A small electric current applied to a nerve cell will stimulate it to activity. When physiologists began to apply electric currents to different parts of the exposed brain, they observed different bodily responses depending on the part stimulated. In 1870, Gustav Theodor Fritsch and Eduard Hitzig discovered that a mild electric current applied to the surface of the cortex of a dog produced movements on the opposite side of the dog's body. They also found that the particular region of the cortex was important—stimulation of one point of the frontal lobe led to motion of the hindlimb, another point led to motion of the trunk, and so on.

A further step was taken by the British neurologist, Sir David Ferrier (1875), who mapped several sensory regions of the cerebral cortex in this way, including an area devoted to hearing. The surprise was that when Ferrier placed an electrode on one side of a monkey's brain, the ear on the other side of the head pricked up—much as though a shrill note had been sounded in that ear.

Many experimenters have confirmed Ferrier's results and Fritsch and Hitzig's results in monkeys, dogs, cats, pigeons, even fish. At every level in the neural pathways serving each half of the brain, an input to the ear on one side will produce a "sound" in the opposite side of the head from the stimulus. Each half of the brain receives input from both ears but the crossed (contralateral) connections are stronger or faster than the uncrossed (ipsilateral) ones.

Most of the neural systems of the body run contralaterally in this way, from one side of the brain to the opposite side of the body. Our visual system is so arranged that both eyes send signals to both hemispheres, but half of the pathways cross. When our eyes are fixated on a point, all of the field to the right projects to the left half of the brain; all of the field to the left projects to the right half of the brain. (See Figure 1.8.)

At the beginning of the twentieth century there was strong evidence that the brain was divided into distinct regions to which specific functions were assigned. Yet, in spite of this evidence, most people believed that the brain contained a massive or continuous network of fibers that worked as a whole unit or aggregate field. It has taken nearly another century for neuroscientists to reject the nerve net theory and to develop the opposite position, known as the *neuron hypothesis*. This hypothesis considers discrete, autonomous nerve cells as the units of the brain and the details of their interconnections, developed by maturation and completed by learning processes, as the key to understanding how the brain works.

The twists and turnings that led to the adoption of the modern theory of localization of functions based on a marvelously orderly and precise organization of neural pathways in the brain provide an interesting chapter in the history of science, highlights of which are presented in the next section.

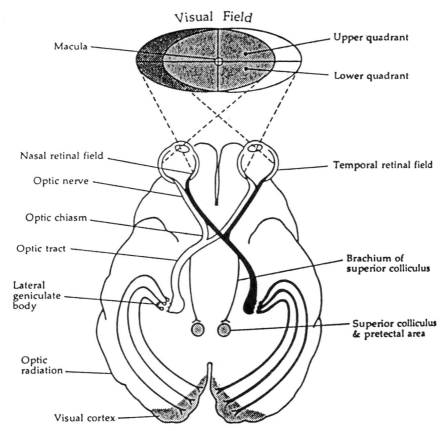

Figure 1.8. Human visual system. Both eyes send signals to both hemispheres, but half of the optic fibers cross at the optic chiasm. Angevine & Cotman, 1981.

THE PROBLEM OF BRAIN LOCALIZATION OF FUNCTION

Nothing in the history of neuropsychology has produced livelier surprises than the discoveries that cognitive, emotive, and personality traits are localizable in specific parts of the brain—enough to spin neuropsychology around one 180° turn after another. The spiral untwisting in time is not a bad image for neuropsychology. It has its parallels in both the evolutionary history and the individual development of the brain.

"Psychology," Ebbinghaus (1885) declared in a famous remark, "has had a long past but only a short history." Ideas about the mind have been proposed since antiquity, but only with the interplay between the behavioral and the brain sciences in the last century has there emerged any systematic study of the central nervous system.

Flourens: Against Localization

The study of the relations between the brain and behavior began with a series of experiments by Pierre Flourens, a nineteenth-century French neurologist. Flourens (1824) examined the effect of removing various parts of the brains of animals on their behavior. He found that no specific disturbances resulted from lesions in localized areas of the cortex. It was hard not to accept the

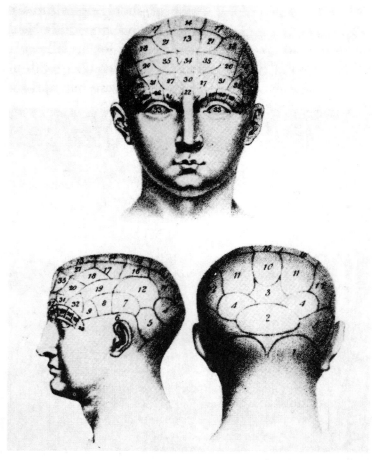

Figure 1.9A. Phrenology. Drawings from Spurzheim, 1825. Drawing reproduced by courtesy of Colin Blakemore, 1977.

conclusion that all parts of the brain were *equipotential*—injury to any one part was compensated by the activity of the remaining parts.

This came to be the accepted belief, in part as a reaction to the earlier, now discredited, notions of the phrenologists.

Phrenology: For Localization

Early in the nineteenth century, Franz Joseph Gall (1758–1828) and Johann Casper Spurzheim (1776–1832), both celebrated anatomists, claimed to be able to identify complex mental traits with localized areas of the brain. As a medical student, Gall had been good in debate and had observed that his victors had large foreheads with protruding eyes—a sign that the brain behind them was the seat of verbal intelligence. On that severely limited basis he proceeded to place other faculties, amativeness, stubbornness, avarice, pride, respect for parents, even "republicanism," in narrowly circumscribed areas of the cerebral cortex. These faculties, supposedly hereditary, were diagnosed from protuberances and depressions in the skull thought to overlie their anatomical seats in the brain. (See Figure 1.9A & B.)

Spurzheim called this practice *phrenology* and, with Gall, made charts and developed a following who promulgated the view that intellectual and personality traits, even pathological defects—e.g., love of gambling—are inherited by each person.

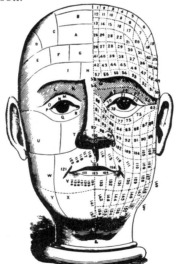

Figure 1.9B. Physiognomy was combined with a kind of "microphrenology" in 1894 by J.W. Redfield, M.D., of New York. Among the 160 numbered faculties is No. 149; "Republicanism." Drawing reproduced by courtesy of Colin Blakemore, 1977.

The ingenious attempt failed, of course. The faculties were hopelessly fanciful and undefinable, and the outer skull does not reveal the size and shape of the brain beneath. The popularity of the fad invited quackery, and then ridicule when its absurdity became obvious. This led the pendulum to swing to the opposite extreme—to the conviction that the brain had no localizable functions, but functioned as a whole.

Karl Lashley: Against Localization

The American neuropsychologist, Karl Lashley (1929), professor of psychology at the University of Chicago, later at Harvard University, argued on the basis of his long series of maze-learning experiments on rats, that the brain was *equipotential* for learning and memory. Any part could take over the duties of any other. Lashley trained the rat on a maze, then extirpated first one part of the brain, then another, and in each case was unable to demonstrate any localized impairment; no one region stored the rat's knowledge about a particular maze. Instead, all the rats had deficits proportional only to the amount of cortex that Lashley had removed. These results led Lashley to develop his theory of *mass action,* the view that the only thing of importance was not the site of damage but the amount of brain tissue left following damage. Another thetic twist of the spiral. Back to Flourens! Lashley expressed his frustration in his classic paper, "In Search of the Engram," published in 1950.

"I sometimes feel," he wrote, "in reviewing the evidence on the localization of the memory trace, that the necessary conclusion is that learning just is not possible."

Fortunately, Lashley's pessimism was short lived. The reason for his failure to find specific learning centers was his reliance on a single complex performance—maze learning—a task that can be achieved by the rat running, swimming, rolling, or tumbling head over heels toward the goal box.

Maze learning is too complex and numerous a set of functions to be localized. In common with many acquired behaviors, its properties are redundantly represented. The underlying neural processes are distributed within the brain and handled in parallel at different sites.

Contemporary Views: For Localization

New studies of the brain's neural structures combine the methods of behavioral control, electrical stimulation, precisely specified stimuli, and microelectrode recordings of single neurons in the brain. Added to these the two newest advances in brain diagnosis and research are the noninvasive tomographic techniques, computerized axial x-ray tomography (CT or CAT scan), and the even more remarkable and exciting positron emission tomography (PET scan). CT scanning measures x-ray transmission through the brain—it provides visualization of brain tissue in cross-sectional displays (brain slices). (See Figure 1.10.) These techniques can be used to diagnose tumors or lesions resulting from occlusion or hemorrhage, either of which can cause a stroke. PET scans also provide views of brain slices taken at different angles, but unlike the static pictures of CT, the new emission tomography gives us wonderfully dynamic images of the brain cells actively metabolizing. You can actually *see* different regions of the brain activated as a person engages in language or visualizes scenes.

This research reveals that the brain is elaborately specialized; neurons connect to one another in a marvelously precise fashion. Different regions of the cortex serve extraordinarily specific attentional, perceptual, and motor functions. These discoveries are bringing about a third revolution in our understanding of the cerebral basis of mental activity and complex motor behavior. And this time there will be no turning back.

Not all the scientific evidence for localization of special functions is new. The conviction that different parts of the brain play different roles was strong among many of the late nineteenth-century neurologists in Germany, France, and England. They observed the symptoms of human patients who had suffered damage to one or another part of the brain that could be diagnosed and circumscribed at post-mortem examinations. Their clinical studies convinced them that sight, hearing, and other sensations, the control of movement, even the power of speech, were strictly localized in the brain.

The brain contains distinctive regions with specific functions. Large numbers of cells doing similar tasks project to sensory regions, called sensory projection areas, where they represent the corresponding receptive surfaces of the body, the skin, the retina, the basilar membrane, the tendons and joints. Other groups of neurons, called motor projection areas, representing muscles and movements, project to motor regions in the brain and spinal cord.

These *projection areas* serve as receiving stations for sensory information and dispatching centers for motor commands. What matters in the nervous system is spatial localization. The pattern of connections between neurons— how they are linked within different parts of the brain—and where they terminate—their final address in the brain—determine the cell's role in behavior. (See Figure 1.11.)

Many examples show the importance of interconnections between nerve cells and their function in the brain. A blow to the eye produces a sensation of light. Amputees report sensations in a missing limb, even in a specific region such as the toe or knee. These phantoms arise in the nerve stump, where severed sensory fibers are irritated by scar formation that sends impulses to the region of the brain where the original nerve fibers terminate.

Most sensory neurons project to more than one region of the brain. The *thalamus* appears to be a crucial way station—all the senses (except olfaction)

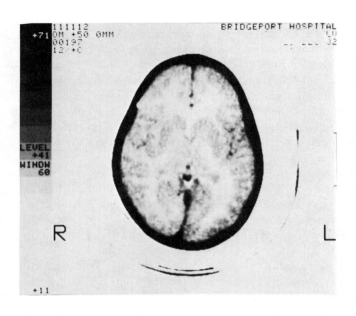

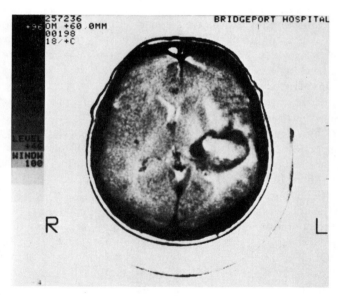

Figure 1.10. Normal (A) and abnormal (B) brain tissue is shown in CT (CAT) scans. Courtesy of Edward Wasserman, M.D., P.C., and Bridgeport Hospital, Radiology Department, Bridgeport, Connecticut.

22

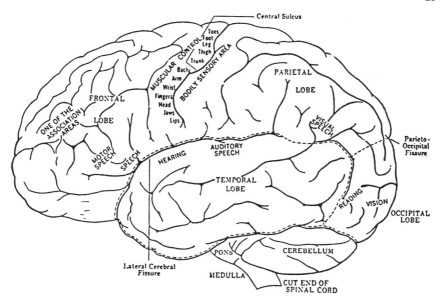

Figure 1.11. Lateral view of the human brain showing the sensory and motor projection areas and the four lobes of the cerebral cortex. Adapted from various sources.

send messages here before they enter primary sensory receiving areas of the cortex. But the thalamus is not just a relay—together with other interruptions in sensory pathways, it transforms the input and acts as an important processing center where impulses are integrated and presented to the specialized sensory projection areas in the cortex for vision, hearing, touch, and so on. The meaning of these nerve impulses depends upon the anatomical connections of the fibers conveying them—what part of the body they came from and where they are going—while the impulses themselves are all alike.

What do the primary sensory areas in the cortex do with their communications from the thalamus? They do at least two things. First, the thalamocortical projections are reciprocated—descending fibers project back to the thalamus. Thus the cortex can regulate its own incoming flow to some extent.

Second, the projection areas send fibers to other areas of the cerebral cortex. In the human brain, the largest region of the cerebral cortex is neither sensory nor motor—it is an *association area* where information from different sensory modalities is combined or associations with feelings, appetites, and motor actions formed. The evidence is fairly strong that the association cortex regulates higher mental functions: planning, thinking, language, and memory. These zones develop late in *phylogeny* (evolution) and *ontogeny* (individual development). As we go up the evolutionary series from fish to bird to

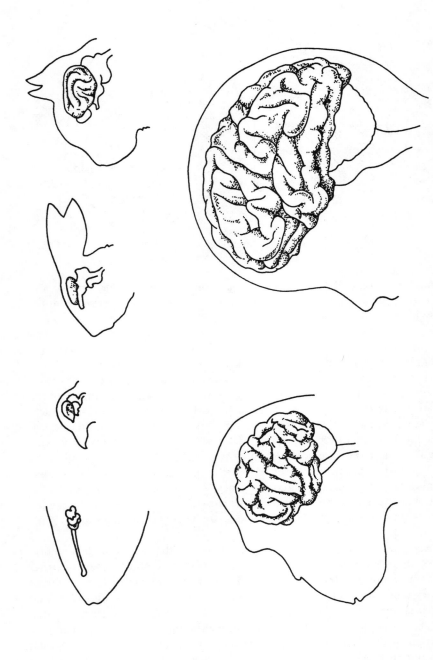

Figure 1.12. Drawings of the brain in six species: codfish, pigeon, rabbit, cat, chimpanzee, and human. Redrawn from various sources.

monkey, both the absolute amount of cortical association area and the ratio of association to projection areas increases rapidly. In the human brain, the association area is the largest part and the latest to develop in the maturation of the central nervous system. (See Figure 1.12.)

THE EVOLUTION OF BRAIN AND BEHAVIOR

The human brain in its evolution has expanded along three main lines. In a provocatively simple model, Paul MacLean (1973) of the National Institutes of Health, has characterized the three as "reptilian" (the most ancient part of the brain), "paleomammalian" (old mammalian), and "neomammalian" (the cerebral cortex). The selective staining techniques show them to be radically different in structure and chemistry. Yet the three basic formations intermesh, and despite their anatomical differences, they constitute three-brains-in-one, called a *triune* brain (MacLean, 1962, 1970, 1973). The three "brains" are nested inside one another, like Russian Easter eggs or Polish dolls. (See Figure 1.13.) The three are extensively *interconnected*. They communicate along many different lines—vertically and horizontally—and function together, forming not so much a hierarchy, as a *heterarchy,* in which control shifts from one to another in competition or cooperation at different times.

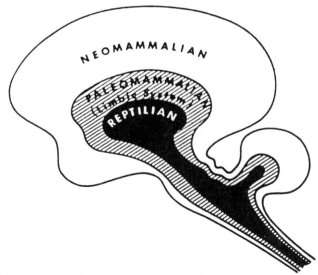

Figure 1.13. The "triune" brain as described by MacLean, 1967. In its evolution, the primate brain expands along the lines of three basic patterns: reptilian, paleomammalian, and neomammalian. Copyright © 1967 by the Rockefeller University Press.

The Ancient Reptilian Brain

Our oldest "reptilian" core forms the matrix of the upper brain stem and comprises the reticular system, lower midbrain, hypothalamus, and basal ganglia. With little or no cortex, the reptilian brain rules by routine that serves survival and procreative needs—mating, fighting, breeding, and even (nonverbal) communication (dominance, aggression, and courtship displays).

The Paleomammalian Brain (Limbic System)

The paleomammalian brain, in contrast, does possess a primitive cortex, once called the limbic lobe (limbic means "border" or "surround"), but now known as the *limbic system* to denote both the limbic cortex and the structures of the brain stem with which it has primary connections. (See Figure 1.14.) Information reaching the limbic cortex from both the inside and outside worlds with large cablelike connections with the hypothalamus make this an integrated system that uses motivational states or drives to guide behavior with respect to the basic life principle of preservation of the self and the species.

We look to the limbic system for psychotic symptoms and disturbances of emotion and mood. We can speculate that distortions of perception—

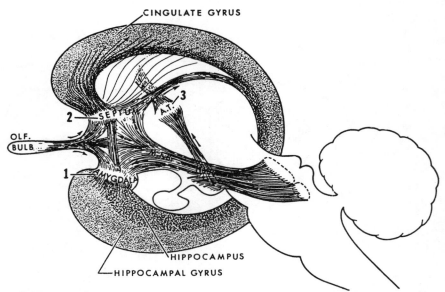

Figure 1.14. The limbic system. The diagram shows the ring of limbic cortex and structures of the brainstem with which it has primary connections. Abbreviations: AT, anterior thalamic nuclei; HYP, hypothalamus; MFB, medial forebrain bundle; OLF, olfactory. MacLean, 1958; 1967; 1970. Copyright © 1970 by the Rockefeller University Press.

hallucinations and delusions—could arise from dysfunctions within the limbic structures themselves or their receipt of chemical neurotransmitters (called *catecholamines*) from small regions of the midbrain or brainstem. *Dopamine* (like norepinephrine, a member of the family of chemically related catecholamines) neurons in the substantia nigra and the tegmentum send out widely branching fibers to the limbic forebrain, involved in emotion, and to the corpus striatum, which regulates motor activity. An excess of dopamine may be involved in schizophrenia (Sachar, 1981b); its deficiency causes Parkinson's disease (Côté, 1981). Neurons containing norepinephrine in the locus coeruleus in the brainstem also project to the forebrain and affect sleep, activity, and mood. Compelling new evidence implicates this region in behavioral depression or "learned helplessness" (Weiss et al., 1981). Clinical and experimental findings show that the lower part of the limbic ring is responsible for self-protection, eating, showing anger, screaming.

Clearly, a small brain can promote survival of the self and the species at a primitive level. The question is how the brain escapes from the domination of self-preserving drives—fighting, fleeing, feeding—to a more altruistic, futuristic concern for others and a broader expanse of space, time, and habitat.

The Neomammalian Brain (Neocortex)

Evolution superimposed new levels on the older brain not by replacing old tissue but by retaining it and covering it with new functional structures. The added layers permit new behavior patterns to emerge—language, fine manual dexterity, and the invention or discovery of tools, fire, nuclear energy, universities, team sports, and destructive warfare on a massive scale.

Newest of all, the neomammalian brain (neocortex) is evolution's most recent and sophisticated development. It appears in higher mammals and in humans, enveloping the old brain structures with massive folds of neural tissues. The neomammalian brain gives us a talking, moving picture with printed subtitles. This neocortex is a *cognitive* brain, but, as a result of its connections with the limbic system and lower subcortical levels, it is also an *emotive* brain, serving to express and comprehend rich emotional meanings. This warm emotional coloration is attributable to the ties that bind the neocortex to its roots in the older parts of the brain. The liberation of the neocortex does not sever its connections with the limbic brain or the even more primitive reptilian core. On the contrary, the limbic subdivision that comprises the pathways leading to the prefrontal cortex in the new brain connects the hypothalamus with the upper half of the limbic ring and the neocortex. This pathway bypasses the olfactory apparatus and is completely absent in the reptile. It becomes progressively larger in more highly evolved mammals, culminating its development in our brains.

Vision and audition, our prized distance receptors, freed us to some extent from the domination of the inarticulate emotive brain in the subcortical structures. The expansion of the cerebral cortex that liberated our behavior and gave us language and tools, is the key to the strategies our nervous system has evolved for our survival and perpetuation as human beings. Yet our drives and emotions remain powerful forces, arousing and directing all our activities.

The Triune Brain

The three "brains" function together in our behavior and intermesh as a *triune* brain, in which no one brain can claim consistent dominance over the others. Our conflicts, as well as the smooth integration of cognitive and emotive activities, arise from the heterarchical organization of the three brains and the numerous connections and parallel neural pathways that traverse them.

Ethologists studying the behavior of freely moving animals in their natural habitat, and clinicians concerned with patients' suffering from psychotic disorders or brain damage provide compelling reasons to bring drives and emotions to center stage if we are to understand normal and abnormal neuropsychological functioning.

THE INFLUENCE OF ETHOLOGY

A major development in the study of behavior came from outside psychology. This was the discovery that zoological and biological techniques could be applied to nonhuman animals to throw light on problems of human psychology.

An early important step in this development came from ethologists, a group of biologists interested in observational studies of insects, fish, birds, and mammals in their natural environments. Rooted in Darwin's (1860) concepts of natural selection and the doctrine of evolution, this vigorous European tradition of natural history emphasized the problems of adaptive significance of animal behavior and the nature of instinct.

This line of investigation, stressing inborn reflexes and stereotyped patterns of action based on uncontrolled observations, was anathema to the mainstream of American psychologists. During the period 1920 to 1960, the behaviorists, intent on developing an experimental analysis of behavior, concentrated exclusively on associative learning or conditioning, and three laboratory animals: the white rat, the pigeon, and the dog. Each group of research workers—the ethologists and the behaviorists—was ignorant of the work of the other or, if they knew about it, chose to ignore it.

The Cantabridgean ethologist, W.H. Thorpe, was acquainted with both lines of work and attempted to bring them together with a book (1956) on animal instinct and learning. Thorpe's attempt to synthesize the two approaches had a liberalizing influence on both sides. American behaviorists who up to that time were strongly antiphysiological and antipsychological in their rejection of species-specific differences and hereditary factors in behavior, began to appreciate the complexity of behavior, even to be a bit curious about what went on between stimuli and responses inside the "black box." Their contributions also were not lost on the ethologists who noted the objectivity of the laboratory approach. The behaviorists' ability to control variables and record data automatically compensated somewhat for the artificiality of the responses they recorded. Yet the richness and variety of behavior seen outside the experimental situation was impossible to ignore. Even the most primitive animals exhibit more than reflexes.

A particular contribution of ethologists is their discovery of a new unit of behavior, the *fixed action pattern* (Craig, 1918). Although like a reflex, the fixed action pattern is an unlearned behavioral response elicited by a specific stimulus. It differs from a reflex in two respects: it is always preceded by a phase of preparatory, appetitive, or protective activity; and its strength and other characteristics are independent of the eliciting stimulus. Instead of a relatively simple, direct response that resembles the stimulus in intensity and duration, the fixed action pattern looks no more like its trigger stimulus than the dance of the bees resembles the form, color, or site of the flowers that release the dance with which they communicate this information to the other bees in the hive.

What has this to do with human behavior? The most interesting discovery is that people and animals not only share simple reflex activity (knee jerk, scratch, and lid reflex) but many fixed action patterns as well. Eating, running, swimming, and other motor behavior consist of fixed action patterns. These are not uninfluenced by learning; indeed, animals and humans learn what, where, when, and how to eat. What stamps such consummatory acts as tasting, biting, chewing, and swallowing as fixed action patterns is the stereotyped sequence in which one follows the other.

The most remarkable application of the ethologists' new unit to human behavior is the application to *perception*. Every unitary perception is formed through individual experience. Once formed, it functions as a fixed action pattern triggered by its own releasing stimulus—the familiar face, or pet, or place.

In motor behavior, the evidence for autonomous "command cells" for complex actions is mounting. One cell can control an entire behavioral sequence to coordinate running, swimming, or mating behavior. As much as in overt behavior, the releasing mechanism for the *identification* of a biologically important object may be a *single neuron,* and the response, the act of perceptual recognition, will remain invariant, despite changes in the eliciting stimulus pattern.

For any given behavior, there must be at least one neuron that *decides,* on the basis of activity in the receptors and other neurons, whether to initiate that behavior or not. There may be as many single neural units of this sort as there are coherent behavior patterns and identifiable stimulus objects, or perception units.

This concept, astonishing to many, that an individual nerve cell can trigger organized patterns of behavior is a major theme of this book. Single nerve cells that I call *cognons* link the unit of cognition, the idea, to the unit of biology, the neuron.

Cognons are pattern or object recognition mechanisms that represent the anatomical and physiological bases for unitary perceptions and unitary motor acts. They accumulate and store the biologically significant information obtained from the external world in the brains of particular organisms. Thus they provide the mechanisms by which the adaptation of the organism is permanently changed and perfected. On the psychological side, a cognon is a mental reaction that is used in the associative processes of thought and action. On the physiological side, the cognon is a neuron, a single cell in a file or column of identical cells (clonal derivatives) in the frontal, parietal, or temporal lobes of the cerebral cortex.

The conceptual scheme attempts to deal with the neural basis of higher mental functions and to bridge the gulf between psychology and neurology—mind and brain—with a unified theory.

A BRIEF OVERVIEW OF COGNON THEORY

Any novel stimulus can lead to the formation of a cognon, or cognon file. These specialized cognitive neurons serve to integrate information from patterns of impulses leading from the receptor surface to the highest levels of the visual, auditory, or other sensory analyzer. In the formation of a cognon, three conditions are essential: (1) the arousal of the orienting reflex (sensitization); (2) the integrity of the afferent pathways (sensory neurons and synaptic transmission); and (3) the existence of cortical cognitive fields that contain available recipient cells (potential cognons).

This is an active selection theory, not unlike the revolutionary "clonal selection" theory proposed by Jerne (1967, pp. 200–205) to replace the outworn "instruction" theory of immunology. According to Jerne's new theory, which has excellent support, the lymphocytes, whose antibodies are already in existence, are continually active, searching for foreign antigens that they are preprogrammed to recognize. The action of the antigens is to select from the vast array of lymphocytes those with exactly the correct antibodies. When a lymphocyte meets its appropriate antigen, say a shot of flu vaccine, recognition follows immediately. The lymphocyte promptly enlarges and generates a group of clonal derivatives, all possessing the same receptors, prepared to shed their antibodies into the threatened bloodstream—

permanently effective immunological agents. The subject is now immune to influenza. It is not that those molecules taught naive lymphocytes what to do to make the right antibodies; they needed no instruction but were born knowing what to look for.

Similarly, an actively expectant brain cell is prepared in advance to recognize its natural target, a specific pattern of afferent impulses, a particular sensory stimulus, object, or idea. The human brain contains billions of cells preprogrammed by epigenetically determined receptors, as ready to lock on to this or that perceptual event as the frog's eye is to lock on to the movement of a fly. The new cognon promptly clones its own multiple offspring, packing a cortical column with its identical progeny, all possessing the same receptors. The result is a population of knowledgeable cells. The selected cells are now set to see or hear or touch all the things the brain experienced and to recognize them when they reappear. The number of responsive cognons in a file depends upon neuronal availability (varying with the developmental stage or sensitivity of the subject); the strength of accompanying emotional arousal; and, to a greater or lesser extent, the frequency of spaced repetitions of a particular stimulus. Sheer repetition of a stimulus without concomitant arousal results in *habituation* or depression of the response.

Once formed, the cognon cluster furnishes a relatively permanent *neural symbol* of an object, a spatial relation, a human face, a word, or other new *perception unit,* which then becomes the basis of further learning. Its retention in memory depends upon its redundancy and the extent to which it participates in higher associative processes of learning, thought, and voluntary action.

Each *cognon* may be aroused by activity in the sensory neurons that were responsible for its initial formation, or else by associative pathways in, or between, cognitive fields. When triggered by association they are *unitary images* representing absent objects or relations.

In humans, each sense can communicate with the others. We can translate what we hear into what we see and what we say. Close to the human auditory cortex is a region where the patterned sounds that form words are represented. A visual association area near the visual sensory projection zone in the occipital lobe represents nameable objects: trees, houses, colors. Cross-modal connections between the visual and auditory association areas enable the *word cognons*—patterns of sound—to be associated with the *cognons* for *visible objects.* The key to the human specialty, language, is played by this role of cross-modal associations—a sharing of symbols between modalities. Children learn that a spoon seen with the eye has the same name as the unseen spoon felt by the hand. This cross-modal transfer is difficult or absent in lower animals, and in some human patients with certain kinds of brain damage, with resulting language disorders *(aphasias)* or inability to execute certain learned movements *(apraxias).*

Language requires that certain areas of the brain be intact and also that the connections between these areas are not cut or destroyed by lesions. Some patients lack particular classes of words—for example, names of colors or names of other visible objects—but have no difficulty finding words for the same objects placed in their hands. These highly specific disorders provide the surest evidence for localization of specialized functions in the brain and will be examined in detail in later chapters of this book.

More important than the question *where,* however, is the question *how.* How is the word represented in the brain? How is an association formed? How is a group of words organized in a sentence, a paragraph, a book? These are problems that, more than others, interest the neuropsychologist and offer the thorniest challenge.

SUMMARY

Neuropsychology is a science that concentrates on the relations between the mind and the brain. It represents a new synthesis of the rapidly developing disciplines of neurophysiology, psychology, and ethology, combining cellular biochemical, cognitive, and behavioral approaches to the study of living organisms. Its main goal is to get at the facts that are universal for all nervous systems. The chief questions are what human beings know and what they do, what they want and how they learn to adapt to a varied and ever changing environment.

Although there are important differences between one person and another, in this book we will be concerned with general principles. The uniqueness of no one individual can be understood without a knowledge of its biological basis and continuity with other creatures. The neuropsychologist's special approach to mind grows out of an interest in what people and animals experience and feel, as well as what they do, and seeks to discover how these functions are controlled by the precise architecture of the brain. We begin with the problem of why we behave the way we do; the basic activities of organisms are deeply rooted in shared needs to survive and perpetuate the species.

SUGGESTED READINGS

The brain: A Scientific American book. San Francisco: W.H. Freeman, 1979. The 11 chapters in this book originally appeared as articles in the September 1979 issue of *Scientific American.* A compilation of facts about the brain and the scientists who discovered them, clearly written by the scientists themselves. Highly recommended.

Angevine, J.B., Jr., & Cotman, C.W. *Principles of neuroanatomy.* New York: Oxford University Press, 1981.

Beach, F.A., Hebb, D.O., Morgan, C.T., & Nissen, H.W. (Eds.). *The neuropsychology of Lashley.* New York: McGraw-Hill, 1969.

Blakemore, C. *Mechanics of the mind.* Cambridge: Cambridge University Press, 1977.

Bullock, T.H., Orkand, R., & Grinnell, A. *Introduction to nervous systems.* San Francisco: W.H. Freeman, 1977.

Cajal, S.R. [A new concept of the histology of the central nervous system] D.A. Rottenberg (Ed. & trans.), *Neurological classics in modern translation.* New York: Hafner, 1977.

Eccles, J.C. *The understanding of the brain.* New York: McGraw-Hill, 1973.

Gazzaniga, M.S., & Blakemore, C. *Handbook of psychobiology.* New York: Academic Press, 1975.

Kandel, E.R. *Cellular basis of behavior: An introduction to behavioral neurobiology.* San Francisco: W.H. Freeman, 1976.

Kandel, E.R., & Schwartz, J.H. *Principles of neural science.* New York: Elsevier/North-Holland, 1981. A marvelous general reference for students of biology, medicine, and behavior. Comprehensive, and handsomely written and illustrated by the faculty of the Department of Physiology and Neurology Center for Neurobiology and Behavior of the College of Physicians and Surgeons of Columbia University.

Kandel, E.R., & Schwartz, J.H. Molecular biology of learning: Modulation of transmitter release. *Science,* 1982, *218,* 433–442.

Kolb, B., & Whishaw, I.Q. *Fundamentals of human neuropsychology.* San Francisco: W.H. Freeman, 1980.

Konorski, J. *Integrative activity of the brain: An interdisciplinary approach.* Chicago: Chicago University Press, 1967; (Second Edition, 1970). A classic monograph by a brilliant, rebellious, but gentle Pavlovian student, who until his death in 1973 was Director of the Neurophysiological Laboratory at the Nencki Institute of Experimental Biology in Warsaw. The source of many ideas and inspiration for this book.

Kuffler, S.W., & Nicholls, J.G. *From neuron to brain: A cellular approach to the function of the nervous system.* Sunderland, Mass.: Sinauer Associates, 1976. A first-rate description of single-cell electrophysiological research beginning with Kuffler's own elegant series of studies through Hubel and Wiesel's unraveling of the organization of the visual system in the cortex.

Orbach, J. (Ed.) *Neuropsychology after Lashley: Fifty years since the publication of brain mechanisms and intelligence.* Hillsdale, N.J.: Erlbaum, 1982.

Schmitt, F.O. (Ed.). *The neurosciences: Second study program.* New York: Rockefeller University Press, 1970.

Schmitt, F.O., & Worden, F.G. *The neurosciences: Third study program.* Cambridge, Mass.: MIT Press, 1974.

Schmitt, F.O., & Worden, F.G. (Eds.), *The neurosciences: Fourth study program.* Cambridge, Mass.: MIT Press, 1978.

Sherrington, C. *The integrative action of the nervous system.* New York: Charles Scribner, 1906.

Sprague, J.M., & Epstein, A.N. (Eds.), *Progress in psychobiology and physiological psychology* (Vols. 1–10). New York: Academic Press, 1973–1983.

Thorpe, W.H. *Learning and instinct in animals.* London: Methuen, 1956.

Woodworth, R.S., & Schlosberg, H. *Experimental psychology* (Rev. ed.). New York: Holt, Rinehart & Winston, 1954. Unsurpassed, except perhaps for sections of the first (1938) edition of this work, written by Woodworth as sole author. A superb account of the classic research on attention, reading, perception, and learning.

Young, J.Z. *Programs of the brain.* Oxford: Oxford University Press, 1978. An admirable discussion of the specialized functions of the central nervous system by an outstanding neurophysiologist and pioneer in the study of higher invertebrates.

CHAPTER TWO

Basic Activities of Organisms

Biological facts, from genetics to neuropsychology, show that living things can properly be said to act in pursuit of particular aims. Each tries to achieve certain standards appropriate to its way of life. The result of this continual striving, choosing and deciding, through millions of years, has been a progressive accumulation of information about how best to live. Contrary to what is often said, the facts of biology show both purpose and progress in life.

(J.Z. Young, 1978)

PURPOSE AND PROGRAMS OF THE BRAIN

In his eloquent little book, *Chance and Necessity* (1972), the French biochemist and Nobel laureate, Jacques Monod asks whether a program could be drawn up enabling a computer to distinguish an artifact from a natural object—or an inanimate object from an animate one. Suppose a spacecraft is to be landed upon Venus or Mars. Could the computer determine whether strange objects found there were products of intelligent beings that, at some earlier period, perhaps, inhabited our neighboring planets? How could a computer decide, for example, that the purpose of picking up images executed by a camera belonged to some other object than the camera itself? To achieve this, the program would first have to examine the structure of the object and, second, discover its method of construction. Was the object perfectly regular—machine-stamped? Was it shaped by forces exterior to the object or by autonomous and spontaneous processes within the object itself? The computer program, said Monod, would have to recognize that the structure of a living being "owes almost nothing to the action of outside forces, but everything from its overall shape to its tiniest detail, to morphogenetic interactions within the object itself" (1972, p. 21).

Monod (I think) overstates the case. Neither humans nor animals would survive without a supporting, interacting, external environment. The human fetus requires the life support system provided by its warm, sheltered, nutritive uterine environment. Following birth, in the absence of external protective, nurturant agents, the infant would surely die. The difference between the animate and the inanimate, the living being and the artifact, is not that the organism constructs itself and the other is shaped completely from without. By this criterion, as Monod finally admits, crystals would have to be classified with living beings. In fact, the difference between the living cell and the crystal or between one species and another, from the simplest to the most complex, may be only quantitative, defined in units of information that, transmitted from one generation to the next, ensures the preservation of the specific structural standard.

This brings into focus the concept of first importance, that of *purpose*. It is only as a part of a more comprehensive purpose that any single function, such as capturing images, whether by camera or vertebrate eye, can be used as the criterion of a living organism. As tools of vision, both eye and camera are significant. Both are aspects of a larger, more comprehensive plan, or primary program, which is the preservation of the individual and the species.

"Organisms behave," J.Z. Young wrote, "...as if all their actions were directed towards an aim or goal.... Living things *do* act in a directed way... because they are not isolated systems, which would inevitably dissipate, but are influenced and regulated by the record, stored in their DNA, of an immense past sequence of events" (1978, p. 16). Young helps us understand that organisms contain standards, and also instructions to insure that actions are adjusted until each standard is met. For example, the cells of the hypothalamus regulate the amount of food and drink that the body needs to grow to its proper size and then to maintain a more or less constant weight. These hypothalamic centers regulate all the body tissues and stimulate behavior needed to supply food, sleep, warmth, or other substances to sustain life. It now seems extraordinary that many biologists and psychologists regarded the concepts of purpose and teleology as unmentionable—as if, wrote François Jacob, co–Nobel prize winner with Monod, "teleology was a woman (they) could not do without, but did not care to be seen with in public" (1976, p. 8). Indeed, Monod has argued that one of the fundamental characteristics common to all living beings without exception (is) that of being *objects endowed with a purpose or project....* Every organism achieves it with efficiency rarely approached in man-made machines, by an apparatus entirely logical, wonderfully rational and perfectly adapted to its purpose, to preserve (itself) and reproduce. (1972, p. 23)

INTERACTION WITH THE ENVIRONMENT

What do people *do?* A comprehensive answer would have to be a catalog of the hundreds of thousands of varied activities of women and men, old and young. If we were to look for one broad general answer to the question, we might find that one given by R.S. Woodworth (1940) covers the subject, not only for humans, but for all organisms. In his view, *the individual interacts with the environment.* The effective environment is both internal and external; it contains numerous things: many physical forces and conditions, gravitation, heat and cold, light and darkness, space, time, and, of course, oneself and others. Humans, being social animals, are in constant interaction with their social as well as their physical environments.

Behavior takes place in, and changes the environment. A living creature *depends* on the environment; it *resists* the environment; and, to a greater or lesser extent, it *creates* the environment.

Animals and humans depend upon the environment to supply the materials they need to sustain life: light, air, food, water, a place to sleep, a disposal for wastes, an outlet for activity, and things to manipulate in order to provide biologically important information. The *preservative* reflexes enable the organism to obtain these requirements from its environment.

The organism also *resists* the environment. The *protective* reflexes enable it to escape predators and avoid danger. Fear and pain are allies in this respect. They serve as warning signals that danger is imminent.

The individual also *creates* the environment. Human beings invent, transform, and shape the sociocultural, as well as the physical, environment. To raise food, build a bridge, teach a class, conduct an orchestra, or argue a case at law, people must talk, write, and invent agriculture, science, engineering, music, art, and justice. Women and men leave tracks of a special sort: systems of knowledge, tradition, artifacts, and an architectural landscape for future generations.

Sexuality enters here. Reproduction and the preservation of the species demand procreative activities and some cooperation between the sexes in order to reproduce and rear offspring to their own reproductive maturity. Sexual activity is a major force that changes the shape of the world.

Population growth has consequences for supplies of energy, food, and other vital resources, with deadly serious effects on entire nations.

Not only do organisms, especially human beings, change the environment, but, to a large extent, the environment changes behavior. Perhaps our activities are mainly acquired. They depend upon the conditions of the individual's past experience. Shortly after birth, human infants begin to modulate their innate responses by feedback provided by their environmental consequences. Few reflexes, in fact, preserve their original pattern throughout the development of the individual. For that reason, it is not possible in human beings to isolate and study inborn or unconditioned reflexes in their pure form. Instead, we begin our study of human neuropsychology by examining the basic activities that are common to all organisms with a highly developed nervous system. The genetic and developmental processes, which humans and other animals share, form the physiological foundation for a naturalistic science of human experience and behavior.

The rest of this chapter attempts to place human behavior in this broad framework of basic activities of organisms. The underlying theme is the purposiveness of all living creatures in their dealings with the environment. Both the internal environment, with its physiological regulation of energy balance and body temperature, and the external environment, its resources and opportunities for activity and stimulation are tools for survival.

DRIVE AND MECHANISM

The word *drive* like the words *instinct, motive,* and *purpose,* has had a checkered history, now finding itself in, now out of favor, depending upon theoretical preconceptions. Purpose, goal-directed activity, motivational states are undeniable facts of behavior. Yet the word "motive," some animal behaviorists declared, is anthropomorphic or mentalistic, tending to impute conscious purpose or intention to a rat or a worm.

Some psychologists use the two words, "motive" and "drive," interchangeably. Many prefer the word "drive" because it carries no implication of conscious experience or desire.

In this book the term "drive" will be used as a strictly physiological term denoting a specific state or condition of an organism. A *drive* is defined as a physiological system that channels energy and directs a program of activity toward the attainment of a particular goal. The subjective experiences corresponding to particular drives will be called *emotions.*

Robert S. Woodworth (1918) was the first to use the word *drive* to emphasize two characteristics of motivated behavior: its energizing (arousal) function, and its steering (directive) function. He derived the term from mechanics; a mechanism or machine must be driven if it is to do any work. The drive is not a source of energy; rather it is a need for energy. Hunger, for example, is a chemical state produced by the lack of nutritive substances in the blood—a warning that the fuel supply is getting low. Hunger, or any drive, releases energy stored in the tissues and transmits power to the effectors—the muscles and glands—that move the individual to act and to seek certain goals.

Incentives, the carrot and the stick, would lose their power without the internal processes that endow these external objects with their attractive or aversive qualities. While an incentive is outside the individual, a drive is a physiological regulator within. Animals, as well as humans, vary in their reactions to particular stimuli, at times approaching, at times avoiding, and at times ignoring the stimulus. This variability is associated with the arousal of one or another drive.

In overt behavior, drives appear as a general mobilization of activity. The observed restlessness and the increased tonus of the sympathetic nervous system, characterize what may be called a nonspecific *motivational state* that is not tied to obvious stimuli.

We cannot ask animals or infants about their experiences, but we can observe their behavior under various conditions of deprivation and satiation. Stimulation and ablation studies offer valuable data. Sweet and bitter solutions elicit specific facial expressions even in newborn infants (Pfaffman, 1982). Our own introspections provide important leads. Feelings of thirst, hunger, sleepiness, sexual tension, pleasure, and pain are useful sources of information. They are important in their own right as phenomena to be explained (Stellar, 1982). They also throw light on the relations between drives and their controlling centers in the brain.

PREPARATORY AND CONSUMMATORY ACTIVITIES

The distinction between drive and mechanism is important because it suggests that perhaps all complex behavioral sequences include two phases: one, a tonic *preparatory* goal-seeking phase consisting of variable restless searching movements; and two, a more invariant and stereotyped *consummatory* phase ending in satiation or relief. Ethologists have shown these two distinct components in every species studied: an initial arousal or drive reflex phase followed and terminated by a second consummatory phase, a more nearly *fixed action pattern*. Many forms of complex behavior fit neatly into this twofold classification. (See Figure 2.1.)

The preparatory and consummatory activities may be subdivided into two broad categories: protective reflexes and preservative reflexes. As reflexes they are programmed in the genetic blueprint of every organism. But they rapidly change their character as the result of specific experience—markedly so, in the case of human beings. No one drive can be identified as wholly genetic or unlearned; none can be said to be derived completely from experience or learning. Both inherited and acquired features characterize all

(a)

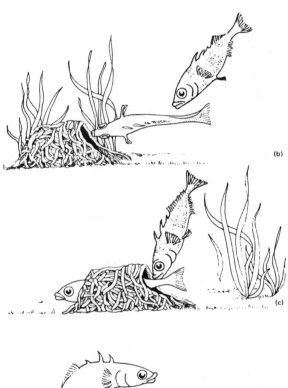

(b)

(c)

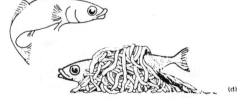

(d)

Figure 2.1. A fixed action pattern. Courtship behavior of sticklebacks. Male leads female toward nest (a), guides her into it (b), then prods the base of her tail (c). After the female lays her eggs, the male drives her from the nest, enters it himself (d) and fertilizes the eggs. Adapted from Tinbergen, 1951.

human drives. Even in nonhuman animals the drives show the influence of learning. Fernando Nottebohm (1970) found that the songs birds sing imitate those they hear, although the genetic equipment for song is laid down in the genes; just as we inherit the drive to speak, but one child grows up speaking Spanish and another Chinese. Animals learn where to find food, and what will taste good, but will poison them; and they can learn this taste aversion quickly.

The most nearly universal preparatory and consummatory drive reflexes are related to perception: the orientation reflex, attention, and habituation. We will consider them first, before turning to more specific drives.

The Orientation Reaction

When presented for the first time, many stimuli give rise to a protective drive reflex—a defensive reaction caused by the arousal of the autonomic nervous system. A sudden shadow, an unexpected noise, the sight or touch of any novel stimulus creates a complex series of physiological responses together constituting what Pavlov (1927) identified as the "orienting reflex" or *orientation reaction*. Changes occur in several systems: the pupils dilate, the head turns toward the source of stimulation, ongoing behavior is temporarily arrested, breathing and heartbeat are interrupted, general muscle tone rises, bloodflow decreases in the limbs and increases in the brain, and the electroencephalogram (EEG) shifts to a low-voltage, fast arousal pattern.

The main components of this general or nonspecific reaction to a sudden, unexpected, or unfamiliar stimulus serve as an objective index of arousal. Three elements stand out:

1. The targeting reflex, adjusting the sensory organs for the best reception of the stimulus
2. Autonomic responses of the emotive drive system
3. Desynchronization of the EEG

When an animal or human observes a familiar or biologically neutral stimulus, usually only the first of the three components is evoked. The arousal of attention, the targeting reflex, is an essential precondition for the perception of a stimulus.

Attention and the Targeting Reflex

Attention is preparatory to perception. To perceive a stimulus pattern is to discover what it is, to know its meaning and value, whether it is biologically useful or harmful, whether it can be safely ignored, or whether it invites further exploration. Before a stimulus pattern can be perceived, the observer must "pay attention" to it, psychologically speaking. On the physiological side, Konorski (1967) named attention the *targeting reflex*. He used the term "targeting reflex" as an inclusive name for the receptor and motor adjustments of the perceptual apparatus to best receive and identify the stimulus. When an unfamiliar stimulus is judged to be nonthreatening but still interesting, the defensive components of the orienting reaction drop out, and the targeting reflex, motivated by curiosity, remains in control. Visual stimuli produce a number of such attentive or inspection responses comprising the *visual targeting reflex*. The head turns toward the object, the eyes converge, the lens and pupil accommodate, and, if the object moves, the eyes follow it to hold it in clear focus.

The mechanism of the *auditory targeting reflex* is similar. The reflex consists of pricking up the ears (in animals) and, in both animals and humans, turning the head toward the source of sound and contracting the middle ear muscles in proportion to the intensity of the stimulus. These reflexes help insure the optimal reception of the sound and specify the identity of the source and its location in space.

The *gustatory targeting reflex* elicits salivation and displaces a morsel of food or liquid over the taste buds of the tongue and about the mouth. The wine taster swishes the sip of wine from side to side and front to back to best experience its flavor, texture, and body. The oenologist is concerned too with its aroma or "nose": smell and taste are closely related. The *olfactory targeting reflex* is accomplished by movements of the head and repeated sniffing.

Tactile targeting reflexes include palpating an object and running one's fingertips over its surface. These haptic responses concentrate attention on texture and shape.

The targeting reflex orients the appropriate analyzer toward the stimulus and enables it to reveal the nature of the stimulating object. By means of these receptive adjustments, the individual is able to listen more carefully, see more distinctly, touch more acutely, taste and smell more precisely, and achieve better information about the external world.

Habituation

If continued or repeated, an originally novel stimulus loses its ability to elicit the orientation reaction, and the targeting reflex is extinguished together with other components of the orientation reaction. The extinction of the targeting reflex is called "habituation." *Habituation* is the decrease or cessation of response to a continued or repeated stimulus. Psychologically speaking, we say that the individual loses interest in an unchanging stimulus and stops paying attention to it. From the biological point of view, some mechanism is needed to suppress the targeting reflex elicited by a sustained or frequently presented stimulus. Otherwise the subject would be doomed to pay permanent attention to insignificant stimuli. People do not need to be reminded all day long that they are wearing shoes, for instance. Habituation suppresses the targeting reflex to a monotonous stimulus and frees attention to focus elsewhere. If this inhibitory effect is applied exclusively to the given stimulus, then habituation will be highly selective, leaving the organism alert in all other respects. It may, however, affect the whole nervous system and produce boredom and somnolence.

The *targeting* reflex is a *drive* reflex: its goal is to reveal the nature of the stimulating object. The *habituation* reflex signals the attainment of a goal— *perception*. By freeing the individual from the bondage of a particular stimulus, habituation extends the opportunity for obtaining stimulation of different sorts. Thus we can acquire associations between different stimuli that are successively observed.

Protective Drives

Protective drives enable the organism to avoid, escape, or overcome life-threatening enemies and physical dangers. The protective drives can be further divided into defensive and offensive reflexes. The defensive (retreat or retractive) reflexes are elicited by painful stimuli or disgusting objects and are usually accompanied by fear. Confronted by a noxious or painful stimulus, a predator or an unknown threat, an animal or person may experience intense fright. One effect of fear is to mobilize the organism to action. Cannon's (1929) classic work stressed the "active" emergency reactions of "flight or fight." But it is often advantageous for a creature to keep as immobile as possible (the "sham death" or "freezing" response). This second passive defense is frequent among small animals. It seems to appear when the danger is imminent and almost inescapable.

Protective drive reflexes are elicited by potentially harmful agents. An aversive stimulus elicits a particular consummatory response directed at getting rid of that stimulus. Accordingly, the defensive reflex varies: it may be flexing a muscle, running away, stamping on or spitting out the noxious stimulus. Besides the specific defensive or aggressive act, there is a second response, either fear or anger. Offensive reflexes, fighting and aggressive attacks against predators, are accompanied by emotions of anger or rage. Although the sympathetic nervous system is aroused in both defensive and anger reflexes, there are differences in blood distribution and motor behavior. The angry face is red; the fearful one is pale. Primates use their forelimbs in anger; the hindlimbs play the dominant role in fear as in rapid running.

During contact with a noxious stimulus, the fear drive is in full operation. With escape from danger, fear subsides only gradually and is replaced by the subjective experience of relief—the mood appropriate to the successful response and termination of the emergency.

Most unconditioned fear responses are correlated with pain. But the sheer anticipation of pain is sufficient to arouse the fear reflex. Many unlearned fears are evoked by strange looking, moving objects or intense, unexpected stimuli. A sudden loud noise, a piercing scream, a mutilated body, blood—these elicit strong reactions in children at various age levels in the absence of previous experience (Jersild, 1946). Falling, loss of support, a steep cliff, may produce unconditioned fear reflexes (Watson, 1930; Walk & Gibson, 1961). But many fears are acquired by learning—a topic to be discussed in a later chapter.

Fear may also be produced by internal humoral factors and give rise to a state of prolonged anxiety without any noticeable reason. If fear operates according to the principle of positive feedback, it produces hormones that affect the chemoreceptors of the fear center. This would explain how a chronic state of defensive alertness could endure in the absence of fear-provoking stimuli.

Preservative Drives

Preservative drives seek the essentials for the survival of the individual and the survival of the species. Activity related to hunger, thirst, and reproduction has a biochemical core (Pfaff, 1980; 1982). In lower mammals, as Magoun (1958) has pointed out, these needs are "conspicuously cyclic and their periodicity is a feature characteristic of innate behavior." For example, hunger drive reflexes are stimulated by the absence of nutritive substances in the blood, arousing restless activity in search of food. When food is located, its consumption is stimulated by its taste. The response consists of salivation, mastication, and swallowing. Each bite is accompanied by an inhibition of the hunger drive, followed by a rebound excitation of the hunger drive until eventually satiation takes place and the organism stops feeding.

Within the behavioral cycle, the preservative drive reflexes are readily divided into sequential steps as preparatory or consummatory. An initial preparatory stage arouses and energizes both motor and emotional behavior. The preparatory activity may involve prolonged searching for food (or other goal) and enhanced alertness and sensitivity to relevant stimulation. It is marked by restlessness, flexibility, and extreme adaptiveness until the appropriate consummatory act takes place. This consummatory act itself is usually brief and stereotyped. It is intermittent rather than continuous: feeding, for example, results in alternating periods of partial satiation (drive inhibition) and rebound hunger (drive excitation). The cycle does not end until satiety occurs.

Mixed Nature of Many Drives

It is difficult to determine whether certain programs are preservative or protective. The individual avoids extremes of heat and cold through negative, aversive, protective means; on the positive, preservative side, the individual seeks thermal comfort. Both positive and negative aspects are associated with other drives: hunger, thirst, sleep, excretion, exercise may come under either heading. Probably for most human activities, such as home-building, both protective and preservative programs are combined. No one drive can be completely autonomous, but each can operate somewhat independently and can also be in conflict with others. In emergencies, protective drives are primary: as stated earlier, they have top priority.

Thirst is a good example of a drive that may be considered either as a protective or a preservative activity (Epstein, 1982). Thirst is an entirely subjective sensation that originates within the body when there is a need for water. The behavior that accompanies it, so-called "primary drinking," is an emergency mechanism whose function is to replace an actual deficit of fluid. When food and water are freely available, drinking is largely anticipatory of future needs. It is then governed by dietary cues and by a habitual, perhaps circadian, rhythm not a present tissue need, and is called "secondary drinking." Under the stress of dehydration, the organism will experience thirst and is driven to seek water by the mechanics that control intake of water to restore fluid deficits (Rolls, Wood, & Rolls, 1980). The amounts of water consumed vary according to diet and activity, and also from one individual to another. They probably exceed actual need under stable climatic conditions. As long as water is available, secondary drinking is far more prevalent than primary drinking and can be considered an appetitive rather than a protective drive (Fitzsimons, 1979).

LOCALIZATION OF DRIVES AND EMOTIONS IN THE BRAIN

Physiologists have known for more than a century that the brain has definite sensory and motor centers. Classical maps of the brain show specific sensory regions that receive signals from the eyes, ears, skin, and other sense receptors. Specific motor regions send signals to move the arms, legs, jaw, etc. But the idea that emotions and feelings have specific sites in the brain is new. The discovery that these motivational states or drives were localized in subcortical regions lying deep beneath the cortex came about unexpectedly as a result of a new technique. The deep structures were relatively unexplored and little was known about their functions until S.W. Ranson (1934) at Northwestern University created a revolution in brain science by developing an instrument for probing the depths of the brain with a fine needle electrode. Here was a probe that could be used to stimulate structures that lie deep in the brain without damaging the surrounding tissue. With this tool, scientists substantially overturned the persistent notion that emotional functions and motivational states were not localizable.

The discovery of the reticular arousal system in the lower part of the midbrain created a ferment of ideas about the role of the brain in emotional behavior. Moruzzi and Magoun (1949) identified an *ascending* arousing system that was responsible for activation of large parts of the central nervous system and the cerebral cortex in particular. This *reticular formation,* so called because of its netlike appearance, plays a major role in exciting the motor centers in higher levels of the brain and makes learning new motor skills possible.

While the reticular formation provides a nonspecific arousing function, investigators soon discovered a second highly *specific emotive* and *motivational* system. This new discovery brought about the realization that all drive states—sex, hunger, thirst, fear, and the like, have their own special centers in the subcortical structures of the brain. The seat of the emotions is not in the heart but in the head—specifically, in the hypothalamus and the limbic system with which the cortex is richly interconnected. Emotive or drive states are regulated by a vast number of neural pathways ascending from the depths of the brainstem up through the specialized centers in the limbic system and on to the higher regions of the cortex where the cognitive centers for consummatory acts are located.

All drives appear to have their neural centers on each of two different levels of the brain. The *lower* level is the *hypothalamus* and the *upper* level is the ring of subcortical structures known as the *limbic* system (Latin *limbus:* border or surround). The hypothalamus is located just above the pituitary complex, which hangs down from the base of the brain. The central position of the hypothalamus and its rich interconnections with the limbic system and all other parts of the brain make it a focal region in the mechanisms involved in hunger, temperature regulation, rage, and other drives. (See Figure 2.2.)

Investigations of the hypothalamic and limbic structures are made in experimental animals by destroying small foci surgically, by exciting neural pathways electrically, or by inserting chemicals into these deep recesses of the brain.

Hess's (1954) elegant experiments, for which he won the Nobel prize, showed that the autonomic responses to hypothalamic stimulation did not occur in isolation, but in *constellations* of autonomic, somatic, and motor behavior characteristic of specific emotional states or drives, depending on the region stimulated. For example, stimulation of the lateral hypothalamus of a cat caused an organized expression of anger: increased blood pressure, erection of body hair and tail, arching of the back, hissing, and other manifestations of an angry cat. The precise placement of the implanted electrode is critical. If it is implanted medial to the fornix, the attack behavior is wild; the cat growls, hisses, spits, at times urinates and defecates, and gives every appearance of furious rage. Moving the electrode just lateral to the fornix results in a quiet, well-directed attack, more like hunting than fighting

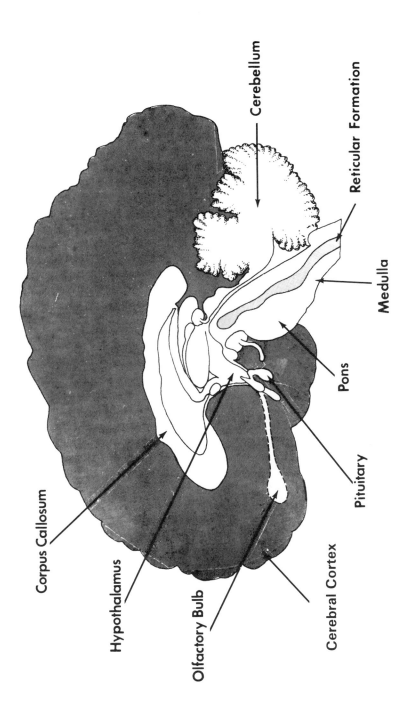

Figure 2.2. Side view of human brain showing the relation of the hypothalamus to the pituitary gland and the rest of the brain.

behavior. In both cases, the attack is stimulus bound and stops as soon as the stimulation stops.

Lesions of ventromedial hypothalamus evoke aggression and result in highly irritable animals. Similar results are produced by decortication. A decorticated cat bites, claws, lashes its tail, and gives every autonomic indication of rage. But the reaction is called "sham rage" because it appears to lack elements of directedness at an appropriate target. Sham rage is evoked by actually mild tactile stimuli and subsides quickly when the stimulus is removed. When investigators removed the hypothalamus along with the forebrain, the sham rage disappeared. Apparently, different hypothalamic structures mediate a wide range of emotional states, but their expression varies with the stimulation received by the cerebral cortex.

FUNCTIONS OF THE HYPOTHALAMUS

The hypothalamus constitutes less than one percent of the total volume of the brain, yet it controls three major systems: the endocrine system, the autonomic nervous system, and the motivational drive system. (See Figure 2.3.)

The central position of the hypothalamus enables it to link the *endocrine* and the nervous systems. Each hypothalamic cell can be stimulated by other nerve cells in higher regions of the brain. In addition to responding directly to chemical signals from adjacent neurons, the hypothalamus controls an independent system, a *peptidergic* system that contains neurosecretory cells that synthesize specific peptides. Like other neurons that have nerve processes that carry electrical impulses, these neurosecretory cells also conduct electrical impulses, but they release their signaling peptide molecules into the bloodstream where they stimulate or suppress pituitary hormones that in turn regulate the secretions of other endocrine glands.

Some of these hypothalamic hormones act early in development to influence endocrine and behavioral controls throughout life; others act during adulthood. They have surprising effects on motivation, attention, even learning and memory. What is especially surprising is the existence of peptide hormone fragments in different areas of the brain that show none of the classical endocrine effects. Within the central nervous system, endocrinologists find peptides traditionally thought to originate in the pituitary (ACTH, growth hormone, prolactin, etc.) or within the gastrointestinal system (cholecystokinin, substance P) or within the pancreas or kidneys (insulin, renin, angiotensin, neurotensin). The idea that the brain might be making insulin, for example, and using it for very different purposes than the pancreas, has led to a substantially new theory of what hormones are and how they affect the brain and behavior. Excellent reviews of this work may be found in Krieger and Hughes, 1980; McEwen et al., 1979; Snyder and Childers, 1979; and

Brain Mechanisms in Hedonic Processes

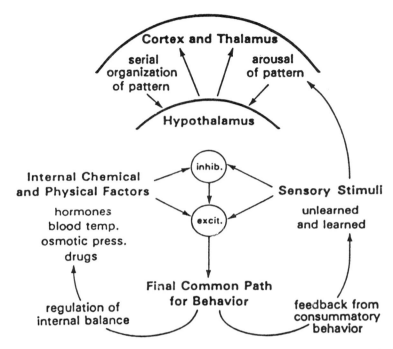

Figure 2.3. Multifactor control of motivated behavior through hypothalamus mechanisms envisaged by Stellar, 1954; 1982. Internal and external factors include stimuli arising in the mouth and gut, circulating hormones, and learning. All contribute to the final common path for motivated behavior. Stellar, 1954; 1982.

Swanson and Sawchenko, 1983. The research revealed that hormones are far more universal than anyone imagined and that they are ubiquitous in cells throughout the animal and plant kingdoms.

The most revealing evidence of peptidergic cells with neuromodulatory functions are the behavioral effects observed following intracranial administration of some of the pituitary hormones or their fragments. Experiments performed by David De Wied (1980) in Utrecht, the Netherlands, disclosed effects of ACTH, for example, on attention and motivation. Vasopressin (antidiuretic hormone) and its fragments facilitate the long-term memory process requiring the consolidation and retrieval of information. Exactly opposite effects result from the related peptide, oxytocin, which seems to be an amnesic peptide and induces forgetting.

The enhancement effects of ACTH and vasopressin on learning and memory remind us that these hormones are normally released whenever there is a threat to the body. It is tempting to think that in the course of evolution these peptides achieved a higher, more abstract function—to inform the CNS whenever something is happening that is important for survival. De Wied and his group were able to isolate fractions of these peptides and to purify them. They chose the one that was the most potent but that, unlike the cruder forms, had no effect on kidneys or cardiovascular system. The purified peptide, a vasopressin derivative, was found to have a marked effect on memory, perhaps by increasing the motivational value of environmental stimuli. This idea finds support in the fact that, after its administration, animals continued to run in order to obtain food or sex, even after the reward for this learned response was removed. There was no extinction of the learned response.

Clinical studies on humans are in agreement with the results from the animal laboratory. In healthy volunteers, ACTH increases general arousal, enhances attention, and improves short-term visual memory. In elderly subjects and in the mentally retarded, similar, though small, effects were obtained on various tests.

The discovery of these endogenous peptides is transforming neurology into the most promising of all fields in medicine. A particularly enthralling group consists of opiatelike substances, the endorphins and enkephalins. These simple peptides secreted within the brain itself possess a magical pain-killing capacity. They act at the identical sites to which morphine and heroin habitually become attached and block pain by stimulating certain neurons that in turn disrupt messages from the pain receptors (Snyder, 1977; Snyder & Childers, 1979). This finding has important implications for understanding the mechanism of drug addiction and may enable us to cope with a major social problem. By using the drug naloxone, an opiate inhibitor, investigators can now study many analgesic phenomena, powerful but unexplained placebo effects, acupuncture, even extreme stress itself, with new insight into their psychopharmacological action on brain cells. It is exciting to realize that the brain's own opioids and related peptides are present in both brain and pituitary, with possibly different and independent effects on mental functions. These new findings are creating a fever of research activity into the role of hormonal disturbances in behavior and its disorders. The potential gain for treating psychiatric and immunological diseases in new and effective ways is a powerful incentive. (See review by Krieger & Hughes, 1980).

The hypothalamus helps regulate the *autonomic nervous system* both by chemical and electrical input and output. Like other nerve cells, hypothalamic cells receive and transport signals to the viscera, and via thalamic projections provide indirect input to the cortex. In this way, we become aware of rumblings in our internal milieu and consciously experience terror, rage, or affection and joy.

Our emotional states are thus the product of the *motivational drive* system. This hedonic experience is the third remarkable function of the hypothalamus (Stellar, 1974).

Regulation of Food Intake

The role of the hypothalamus is especially interesting in the case of the drive that neuropsychologists have studied most extensively—hunger. Investigators study hunger and the regulation of food intake by making small experimental lesions in the ventromedial nucleus of the hypothalamus just above the stalk of the pituitary gland. If these lesions are made close to the midline on each side, the animal eats voraciously and gets incredibly obese, tripling its body weight in a few weeks (Stellar, 1974). (Figure 2.4 shows a rat that overate following ventromedial hypothalmic lesions compared to its sham-operated control, which did not receive a brain lesion.)

Can obesity in humans be caused by abnormalities in the same region? One such dramatic case cited by Stellar was an 18-year-old girl who became tremendously obese as a result of eating 10,000 calories a day. She was found to have a tumor that had destroyed the ventromedial nucleus of her hypothalamus. She suffered from ravenous hunger and indeed became violently angry unless she was allowed to eat. This human clinical case

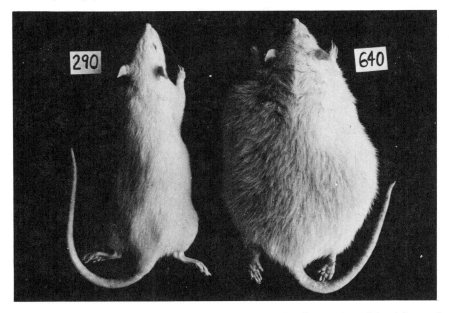

Figure 2.4. Obesity resulting from the hyperphagia produced by bilateral ventromedial lesions of the hypothalamus. Litter mate control animal is on the left. Stellar, 1974.

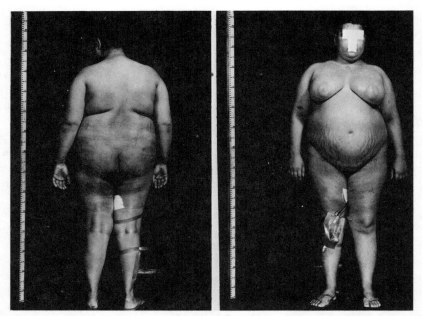

Figure 2.5.   Obesity in a young woman with a ventromedial hypothalamic tumor. Stellar, 1974.

illustrates the close connection between the subjective (hedonic or emotional) side of hunger and feeding behavior (Stellar, 1974; Stellar & Jordan, 1970). (See Figure 2.5.)

What is the specific role of the different regions of the hypothalamus in regulating hunger? To answer this question, we should look at the relation between the hunger drive and the consummatory activity it evokes. There is no doubt that hunger facilitates feeding behavior: the hungrier the subjects, the more ravenous and greedy they become. But what is the reverse relation?

The effect of feeding, the consummatory activity, on the hunger drive is curious. Does it immediately inhibit hunger? If so, that would be insufficient to trigger the satiety center in the medial hypothalamus. Yet a hungry infant, tense and excited just before nursing, immediately calms down as she begins to suck and becomes blissfully absorbed in her meal. Exactly the same thing happens to hungry animals and to all of us, in fact, when we begin to eat. The act of eating seems to suppress the hunger drive, even though satiation is far from complete and certainly insufficient to excite the satiety center in the medial hypothalamus.

Yet when food is withdrawn during a meal the hunger drive returns with rebound excitement. "L'appétit vient en mangeant." Even when we sit down at the dining table too soon after the last meal and don't feel hungry, the first taste of food arouses the hunger drive and we find ourselves eating with gusto.

For this strange paradox, Konorski (1967, p. 50) gives a plausible explanation. He suggests that the antidrive mechanism activated during ingestion of food is intimately connected with the hunger drive. The neural units involved consist of on-hunger units and off-hunger units closely intermingled in the lateral hypothalamus. These neurons form the center that controls "both the hunger drive when the animal wants food and the hunger antidrive when it receives it." Support for this theory comes from Carlson's (1916) experiment on the famous patient, Fred Vlcek, with the gastric fistula. Vlcek could chew his food normally, but this masticated food then had to be put in a syringe and introduced through the fistula into his stomach. Carlson was able to observe his patient's stomach contractions directly through the fistula and could also record them with the aid of a stomach balloon that the patient swallowed. The hunger contractions disappeared while food was in the patient's mouth, but reappeared immediately afterward and with increased intensity when the food was removed. Here is clear evidence that the taste stimulus giving rise to the consummatory response (salivating and chewing) is the chief factor inhibiting hunger. A reborn hunger excitement immediately follows the food's disappearance—at least until the subject is completely satiated. (See Figure 2.6.)

Human beings often crave a food they cannot stomach. One experiment (Stellar & Jordan, 1970) had normal college students judge their degree of hunger after a liquid milkshake was pumped directly into their stomachs. They also judged their degree of hunger following their intake by mouth of the same amount of milkshake. Comparing the two sets of judgments, the experimenters found that oral ingestion is more strongly correlated with

Figure 2.6. Templeton: proof that a rat can perceive its own satiety. From *Charlotte's Web,* p. 147, by E.B. White, © copyright 1952. Stellar, 1974. Illustration by Garth William, © copyright renewed 1980. Reprinted with permission of Harper & Row, Publishers, Inc.

subjective satisfaction than is intragastric ingestion even when the same amount of food is voluntarily ingested in the two cases. One subject tried to eat a hamburger and drink a milkshake immediately after a full intragastric meal that left him feeling unsatiated. As soon as he took one bite, he knew, as he said, "My mouth wants it, but my stomach doesn't." His behavior was controlled by the antihunger center in the hypothalamus, not by what he felt he craved when stimulated at first by the off-taste units.

This physiological mechanism expresses the principle known for sensory systems: reciprocally related units are closely intermixed. (See Chapter Four for a description of the on-units and off-units that have been detected in the visual system on every level from retina to cortex.)

Konorski's analogous hypothesis for the emotive or drive-regulating mechanisms in the hypothalamus and other parts of the brain assumes that the taste of food in the mouth stimulates on-food taste units and the absence of food after a bite is swallowed stimulates off-food taste units. These units send impulses not only to the cognitive system, but also to the emotive system of the brain—the hypothalamus and the limbic system. The on-food taste units may thus activate the antihunger units in the lateral hypothalamus to provide *short-term* cues that regulate the size of meals. These taste-activated cues are highly subject to conditioning processes.

Long-term cues have been shown to regulate body weight and are much less under cognitive control. In fact, body weight remains remarkably constant for mature animals and for most human adults without conscious effort to maintain it. Unlike body temperature, however, which is the same for everyone, body weight differs greatly from one person to another of approximately equal height and muscular build. The regulation of body weight is brought about by automatic physiological feedback systems. Several humoral signals are important in this. The glucoreceptors and other chemical receptors in the hypothalamus produce specific hungers directed to particular nutritive substances.

Gut hormones released during a meal may suppress feeding. Recent provocative evidence reveals the action of a peptide neuromodulator, *cholecystokinin* (CCK) in regulating appetite. (Della-Fera, 1979; Stellar, 1980). Not only is CCK released from the duodenum and upper intestine, it is one of the peptide neurotransmitters in neurons of the brain. When CCK is injected directly into the ventricles of their brain, animals stop feeding. Here is a remarkable hormone that has both central and peripheral effects. Like the amphetamines, it suppresses appetite, yet does not produce their disturbing side effects. The finding encourages pharmaceutical firms to search for safe, effective diet pills. It may also lead to a better theory of appetite regulation.

This promising peptide has inspired research into the possibility that other peptidergic cells act on different levels and affect different behaviors that derive from evolutionary forebears. Every week brings news of fresh discoveries involving hormones secreted by nerve cells: angiotensin in thirst and sodium appetite; steroid hormones, estradiol, and especially testosterone, in learning disabilities, stress, and autoimmune disease as well as in sexual behavior and possible critical periods for neuroendocrine programming of the developing young brain.

There is abundant evidence for the generality of the concept of common brain mechanisms for behavior and hedonic experience. Most of the time, it is correct to conclude that we eat when we're hungry and we enjoy what we eat. These various functions are closely interrelated. In order to tie them together, it is useful to consider the hypothalamic system of the brain as a cybernetic machine. Unlike any artificial machine yet developed, however, this one is endowed with a rich emotional coloration.

Homeostasis and Emotional Behavior

If a room is cold, you can maintain your body temperature by using several different mechanisms. Shivering and goose pimples (peripheral vasoconstriction) reflect an autonomic mechanism that acts on the internal environment. The hypothalamus is the agent responsible for this and other "homeostatic" processes that control temperature, heart rate, blood pressure, and water and food intake.

Walter B. Cannon (1929), who pioneered in the study of the autonomous nervous system and captured psychologists' imagination with his description of the emergency "flight or fight" reactions, used the term *homeostasis* for the process by which vital functions are maintained within a critical range. Your temperature deviates very little from 98.6°. These and other autonomic systems are controlled by homeostatic regulatory mechanisms located primarily in the hypothalamus. These controls are analogous to the servo-mechanism used to heat your home. You set your thermostat (lower now, than formerly) and when the temperature deviates from that set point, an error signal drives controlling elements to turn the furnace on or off. But the hypothalamus cannot be the sole thermostat since its removal in animals does not completely abolish all thermal control (Satinoff, 1982).

In addition to the hypothalamus, other parts of the brain, especially limbic and cortical association areas, have acquired mechanisms to regulate the external temperature and bodily comfort accordingly. Rats can learn to press a lever to turn on hot or cold air to cool or warm their skin (Corbit, 1973). Even more impressive, they can turn on a 15-second flow of cool or warm water in tubes implanted in the anterior hypothalamus to change their brain temperature. Most interestingly, the animal seems to know whether its brain or its skin is too warm or too cool. When given a choice, it would change the temperature in that area (brain or skin) that was in thermal distress (Stellar, 1982). Stellar reports analogous results for human subjects, obtained by his former student, Raymond Hawkins (1975). After immersion in hot or cold baths up to their necks, they stand up to shower, instructed to turn the dial to find the most pleasant shower temperature. Long tub exposures changed their rectal or core temperatures. As quickly as possible following such long baths, they turned the shower temperature down to very cold, or up to very hot, in the direction extremely opposite to their internal temperature change. They also rated their shower experience on a hedonic scale. The results were reported as hedonically sensational. No wonder sauna devotees adore the contrast of the icy plunge. The experiments on both rats and humans showed that skin temperature change as well as internal temperature change can be motivating as well as rewarding.

In everyday life, humans achieve thermal control by closing a window, adding a sweater, or telephoning the superintendent to turn up the heat. Obviously your cortex registers the cold (or heat) and can initiate operations on the environment to regulate the temperature.

THE LIMBIC SYSTEM

How do the higher conscious centers in the cortex communicate with the hypothalamus? In 1937, James Papez at Cornell University Medical School had an answer to this question. He suggested that the cortex is connected to the hypothalamus through the *limbic system*. Modern anatomical studies have extended Papez's ideas of the particular structures in the limbic system that connect felt emotions with hypothalamic mechanisms and coordinate the behavioral expression of emotional states.

The hypothalamus is extensively interconnected with the ring of limbic structures that surround the upper brain stem. The limbic system includes certain primitive underlying structures that I have not yet discussed, but that loom large in contemporary research: the hippocampus, the dentate gyrus, and the subiculum. The relative sizes of the hippocampus and also the subiculum have increased in phylogeny and reached their largest size in humans. This anatomical fact and much functional evidence lead to the belief that this area is critical for specialized human functions. Many studies show that, in addition, the amygdala, the septal area, and the orbitofrontal cortex—other structures also included in the limbic system—control the expression of personality and emotional behavior.

A classic and dramatic example comes from a study by Klüver and Bucy (1939) at the University of Chicago. These investigators destroyed both sides of the temporal lobe of monkeys. The resulting lesions included a number of limbic structures, in particular, the amygdala and the hippocampal formation. The results were startling.

The animals, formerly wild, became tame and enormously active sexually. They also developed remarkable oral tendencies—mouthing stones, feces, bolts, nuts, and other inedible objects. They failed to recognize familiar objects, yet attended compulsively to every visual stimulus, an apparent result of the bilateral damage to the visual association areas of the temporal cortex. The symptoms of placidity, hypersexuality, and odd oral behavior are believed to be due to the limbic lesions, particularly to the amygdalae.

The forebrain, which contains the cerebral cortex and the limbic structures, thus connects the hypothalamus and the internal milieu to the outside world.

DRIVES AND ANTIDRIVES

Both internal and external stimuli elicit drives. Although in people, sex, curiosity, sensory and motor deprivation, attention, and social needs have no well-defined physiological substrates, they are called drives because they share certain features with hunger and the homeostatic drives: arousal and satiety, internal regulation, specific appetites, and reinforcement or reward properties.

The termination of a drive is brought about by the appropriate consummatory activities. These activate neural centers that are reciprocally related to the particular drive state, as hunger is related to satiation. Since drives are excitatory, these are inhibitory mechanisms. Konorski (1967) named them "antidrives." *Antidrives* are defined as the physiological aspects of those states that arise when the given drives are satisfied. Their chief property is motor demobilization and quiet. The associated hedonic experiences Konorski called "moods." *Moods* are psychological states, such as satisfaction after a good meal or good sex or relief after escape from danger—periods of relative calm and relaxation. In contrast to the vivid emotional experiences associated with drives, moods are gentler—quiet states in which there is nothing to be done.

Satiety results in the elimination of the preparatory drive and related consummatory reflexes. This cessation of drive depends on the full arousal of the antidrive center and its concomitant, inhibition of the drive center. The distinction between the preparatory and the consummatory phase not only separates the temporal order of the two phases, but points to two different sets of neural mechanisms that underlie them.

Preparatory reflexes have two functions: they procure the agents that elicit preservative consummatory acts, and they forestall dangerous agents that evoke protective reflexes of defense or attack. The preservative drive control centers are composed of on-drive units and off-drive units that are in reciprocal relation to one another and to the corresponding antidrive centers. The hunger center consists of on-hunger units for particular nutritive substances and the reciprocally related off-hunger units with which they are closely intermixed. The off-hunger units are activated by particular taste stimuli; the on-hunger units are immediately reactivated when the tasty food is swallowed, the familiar peanuts or popcorn phenomenon. Each bite leads to the next; up to a point, you just cannot stop.

When an animal is satiated, the excitability of both the off-hunger and the on-hunger units decreases.

To some extent the different drives are antagonistic to each other. The sex drive may inhibit the hunger drive and vice versa; fear and pain normally inhibit all preservative drives. Although each drive has its own attached antidrive, the separate antidrives seem to be allied in their effects, producing relaxation. The replacement of a strong drive by its antidrive is subjectively experienced as the replacement of excitement or tension by satisfaction, relief, or pleasure, and opens the gate for other (preservative) drives to occur.

Arousal and satiation refer to the dual effects, excitatory and inhibitory, that function reciprocally in control systems such as a mechanical servo-mechanism—a thermostat or a gyroscope. All physiological systems appear to be regulated by this principle of reciprocal innervation. It is the alternation of excitatory and inhibitory activity that maintains a function within a certain range.

Internal Regulation of Drive

Internal regulation is inferred from the lack of a strict correlation between a given stimulus and a response. An animal deprived of food for some time will approach the food box eagerly and feed; an animal that has just been fed until it stops eating appears indifferent to the food box and walks right past it. This variability of response to the same stimulus is attributed to internal regulation of the hunger drive.

A particular drive like hunger can be satisfied by different foods. Yet the taste of certain foods at various times is more effective as a reward or reinforcer than the taste of other foods. Clara Davis (1928) performed a dietary experiment on institutionalized children with dramatic results. What she did was to offer children, from the time of weaning (6–11 months) to five years of age, a wide variety of nutritious foods, served cafeteria style, in small individual cups. At each mealtime the children were allowed to help themselves to as many cups of any foods they selected. A variety of fruits, vegetables, beverages, and proteins were included. No comment was made concerning a child's choice or the amount consumed. After finishing eating (20–30 minutes) the food trays were removed and portions still remaining were weighed.

The results were unexpected. Children selected one particular food at every meal; for example, one child went on a peanut butter jag, another went on a banana jag, others chose carrot sticks or orange juice and nothing else meal after meal. Then the child would switch to something else. The children were examined and weighed regularly. No ill effects appeared. They were all found to be in excellent health with normal weight gains. The experiment was continued for four and one half years with similar beneficial results.

There appears to be a "body wisdom" after all. In Davis's cafeteria feeding experiment the foods offered were all nutritious and no child was exposed to commercials for soft drinks or sugar-frosted cereals. All parents know that unless they can control this commercial pressure there is little chance of keeping "junk" foods out of their children's diet.

The reward or reinforcing aspect of drives (actually antidrives) was discovered by Thorndike (1898) in his classic puzzle box experiments on cats. The hungry cat learned by "trial and error" (or "trial and success") to pull the string attached to the trick latch and escape to a tasty bit of fish lying outside the box. Thorndike attributed his animals' accomplishment to the "satisfying state of affairs" resulting from the reward that "stamped in" the correct response. The general principle known today as the *law of effect*—a response is strengthened by its environmental consequences or reinforcement—is the key to instrumental conditioning. (See Chapter Eight.)

Contemporary behaviorists, although basing their research on the foundation established by Thorndike, reject concepts such as "satisfying" and "inner agents" as so many "psychic fictions." Is there then no objective evidence for emotional or hedonic experience in animal learning? The next section considers this problem. Up until now, the question has been: given an identifiable drive, such as hunger, where is its control mechanism in the brain located? Now the question is turned around: given stimulation of its center in the brain, what kind of drive provokes a frenzy of activity in the brain-stimulated animal?

"Pleasure" Centers in the Brain

Do animals have states of mind? Is there any objective way of telling whether an animal experiences pleasure or pain? When your dog wags his tail, or your cat purrs, it is easy to interpret these as expressions of pleasure, but how can you be sure that they are not conditioned responses, purely mechanical reflexes to feeding or stroking? Is it not anthropomorphic to attribute these responses to your pet's hedonic awareness? What about lower animals—rats, frogs, snails, ants—do they experience affective states, emotions, and moods?

We have no information as yet about how invertebrates feel. But snails, fish, and other simpler forms do exhibit specific drive states and give evidence of learning as a result of manipulations performed on these drives. There is now persuasive evidence also that pleasure and pain centers exist in the rat and in many other mammals, and that they have definite seats in the brain.

This discovery came as a surprise. Two investigators in D.O. Hebb's laboratory at McGill University, James Olds and Peter Milner (1954), were engaged in exploring the reticular system—the sleep-control area in the midbrain. In one of their early tests the stimulating needle electrode missed its target and landed not in the midbrain reticular system, but in the *septum* (at the forward end of the original neural tube) bordering on the hypothalamus, in the limbic system.

In their experiment, Olds and Milner (1954) placed a rat in a large box with corners labeled A, B, C, and D. Whenever the animal went to corner A, the experimenters gave its brain a mild electric shock. Each time the electrode in the septal area was stimulated, the animal returned to corner A. Next, Olds and Milner turned on the electric shock whenever the rat stepped in the direction of corner B. Within 5 minutes, the rat was in corner B.

"After this," Olds writes, "the animal could be directed to almost any spot in the box at the will of the experimenter. Every step in the right direction was paid with a small shock; on arrival at the appointed place, the animal received a larger series of shocks" (1956, p. 5).

In order to map the places in the brain where such an effect could be obtained, Olds put the animal in the "do-it-yourself" situation provided by B.F. Skinner's (1938) technique of lever pressing. When the rat pressed a lever, it triggered an electric stimulus to its brain, and the frequency of the response could be recorded at the same time. Left to itself, the animal then stimulated its own brain regularly about once every five seconds. When the electricity was turned off, it would try a few times and then go to sleep. (See Figure 2.7.)

The next step was to try to localize and quantify the rewarding effect of self-stimulation in various parts of the brain. When electrodes were implanted in the primary sensory and motor regions of the brain, the response rates stayed at chance level. But in most parts of the midline system, the response rates rose to 200 or more per hour. Certain areas of the hypothalamus and midbrain nuclei gave the strongest effects. Animals with electrodes in centers for control of digestive, excretory, sexual, and similar processes would stimulate themselves at incredibly high rates (2,000–3,000 per hour)—and continue for many hours. Even when hungry, they would shun food in order to self-stimulate. In some lower parts of the midbrain, however, there was an opposite effect: the rat would press the lever once and never again. This avoidance effect was found in the same areas in which Hess had found responses of rage and escape and in which Delgado had used radio-controlled stimulation to arrest a charging bull in the ring.

Clearly, emotional and motivational mechanisms have specific loci in the midbrain: certain regions of the brain control each one of the basic drives. Electrical stimulation in some areas seems to be even more rewarding than food or sex; stimulation of other areas seems to evoke pain. Electrical stimulation at many different sites in the brain is effective in strengthening the response—the hypothalamus and the medial forebrain bundle are particularly effective.

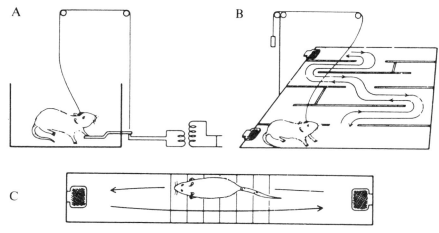

Figure 2.7 Self-stimulation experiment. (A) By pressing the pedal, the rat delivers an electric shock to its brain. Each pedal press is recorded, and the total number can reach astonishing heights as the result of mild electrical brain stimulation (EBS) applied to the medial forebrain bundle after each pedal response. (B) In the maze and the obstruction box, three responses were rewarded at one pedal and then the animal was required to shuttle to the other pedal for three more and so forth. (C) Shock through the grid floor in the obstruction box stopped hungry rats from running for food and also for mild EBS (50 mA), but increased EBS (200 mA) led to greatly increased crossings despite severe grid shock. Olds, 1976.

But how do the excited cells act upon the specific behavioral systems to intensify or reduce the self-stimulating responses?

In humans, an unquestionable factor in motivated behavior is pleasure. The pleasurable effect of intercranial electrical stimulation seems to override the tissue need for food. Food itself reinforces only a hungry animal. Brain stimulation works, perhaps, by evoking a drive state and simultaneously evoking its antidrive state—not an impossible condition if the on-units and off-units are contained within the same small area affected by the electrical stimulus.

A paradoxical finding of the self-stimulation experiments, in fact, may be related to the paradox of hunger and feeding regulation by the lateral hypothalamus. Intracranial stimulation by an electrode placed at a particular point of the lateral hypothalamus sometimes gives two contradictory effects. One effect is an increase of hunger drive, making the animal hyperexcited; in contrast, the identical stimulus may have a self-rewarding effect and serve to reinforce an instrumental conditioned response in a hungry animal (Gallistel, 1973; Gallistel, Stellar, & Bubis, 1974).

It is as though the same stimulus in the same place at one time excites the hunger drive and at another time inhibits the hunger drive, one response serving as the antagonist of the other. One way to explain this result is to consider that the electrical stimulus has two effects—it evokes a preparatory drive and it provides its consummatory or reinforcing stimulus. The dual nature of the self-stimulating electrode has increasing experimental support (Hoebel & Teitlebaum, 1962; Gallistel, 1969). Brief stimulation of the lateral hypothalamus activates fast-reacting off-hunger units; a more prolonged stimulation of the lateral hypothalamus activates on-hunger units, which have a longer latency and a higher threshold.

Olds's experiments show that changes in the hunger drive or the sex drive have different rewarding effects on particular self-stimulating points. The pleasure points, therefore, are not anonymous: they are attached to specific drives. The opposite or mixed effects in a particular small region can be explained by the assumption that on-units and off-units are closely inter-mingled in any one region of the hypothalamus, and probably in other parts of the brain as well. The remarkable frequency of the self-stimulating response does not call for a theory of a superdrive, stronger than hunger or sex. Instead it can be understood as an extension of a general principle of neuronal activity—reciprocal interaction of elements united within single receptive fields that are organized into adjacent regions of mutually antagonistic activity. In the hypothalamus and other parts of the emotive brain, such an arrangement would result in maximal excitability produced by the rebound activation of fast-acting off-hunger units or off-sex units. That hypothesis would also account for the rapid extinction of the self-stimulation response when the current was shut off and was no longer followed by reinforcement, and its rapid recovery following a single free *priming* trial (Gallistel, 1969). (The term comes from the need to "prime" a little-used pump with a bit of water to get it going again.) Gallistel showed in later experiments (1973) in which rats ran in an alley way for self-stimulation in the goal box, that rats would run faster if the priming stimulus was made more intense. But the effects of priming decayed rapidly. Increasing the intensity of the shock in the goal box also increased running speed and the effects lasted a long time. If the priming represents a drive component it is curiously transient; yet the reward stimulation in the goal box seems to involve memory.

Are these different effects related to different hedonic processes? In an attempt to analyze this problem, J.R. Stellar in Gallistel's laboratory tested rats with electrodes placed in the positively reinforcing lateral hypothalamus and rats with electrodes placed in the negative medial, periventricular system of the hypothalamus. He then compared the effects of a variety of appetitive and aversive stimuli with and without simultaneous brain stimulation. Lateral hypothalamic stimulation increased the animals' approach responses to positive stimuli and decreased their withdrawal responses to aversive stimuli.

Conversely, medial hypothalamic stimulation reduced approach responses and increased the vigor of withdrawal from aversive stimuli (Stellar, Brooks, & Mills, 1979).

Thus the brain seems to contain dual mechanisms: an approach system and a withdrawal system that can be activated by electrical stimulation that itself is either rewarding or aversive. One system seems to be responsible for arousal and the other for satiation. This evidence strengthens Konorski's hypothesis that on-drive and off-drive units are intermingled in the lateral hypothalamus to produce approach and reinforcement effects that are enhanced by electrical brain stimulation. In contrast, satiety and antisatiety units, in the ventromedial hypothalamus, together with anger- and fear-provoking centers, produce escape and avoidance effects that are facilitated by electrical brain stimulation in that region. Approach and avoidance systems thus seem to be separable, and active research now in progress (see reviews in Pfaff, 1982) seems to be leading us close to identifying the neural mechanisms involved in drive and reward functions.

Similar self-stimulation studies have been conducted on cats, monkeys, and dolphins with comparable results. All areas of the limbic system produce high rates of response, with the medial forebrain being the region most preferred.

What are the effects of subcortical electrical stimulation in humans? During such stimulation, conscious humans suffering from epilepsy, brain tumors, and mental illness generally corroborate the pattern described for other animals. Reward centers are found in humans with intense but nonspecific feelings of well being. Some individuals report pleasant sensations in particular parts of the body and sexual arousal. Punishment areas also appear in which stimulation elicits pain, terror, or anger (Delgado, 1969; Sem-Jacobsen, 1976). The impact of these self-stimulation experiments makes clear that behavior is directed toward the excitation of those centers that produce reward or reinforcement and that inhibit centers that arouse pain or punishment. Not surprisingly, many functions that are associated with pleasure or reinforcement have survival value for the organism.

Sexual Behavior

Sexual behavior shows the preparatory and consummatory (appetitive) phases characteristic of hunger, thirst, and other drives. The preparatory phase is marked by motor and emotional arousal. In our society this phase is highly flexible, and adaptive or disruptive, depending on past experiences and acquired prejudices fixating responses to specific sex objects. Sequences of human sexual responses are described (Van der Velde, 1926; Masters & Johnson, 1966) as consisting in both sexes of a four-stage cycle of response: excitement, plateau, orgasm, and resolution. The excitement stage and preceding searching behavior are preparatory; plateau and orgasm are consummatory; and the final resolution stage characterizes the antidrive, satiety of sexual drive. Variations within these stages depend on gender and age, and to a certain extent they vary also with education, religious training, and sociocultural background (Kinsey et al., 1953).

The sociobiological literature stresses the sexual aggressiveness of males, their intrasexual competition, their perpetual quest for different females, and similar insights concerning male sexuality. According to the primatologist, Sarah Blaffer Hrdy (1981), this male-focused view has blocked the understanding of female sexuality, which she defines as the readiness of a female to engage in sexual activity. This has led to two serious misconceptions. The first is that all females in a natural state—unlike males—breed at or near their reproductive capacity. The second is the view that sexual assertiveness is not adaptive for females: that copulations serve no function other than insemination. Together, these notions have led to the conclusion that natural selection would not favor the evolution of a sexually assertive woman. But studies of the reproductive careers of hundreds of women in different parts of the world show the average fertility of monogamously married women is much lower (3.7–5 births) than their theoretical capacity to conceive, although mothers differ substantially from each other in number of conceptions and in survival of their offspring.

The problem is to explain the sexual appetite of the human female. Her capacity to engage in sex on any day of the month or any time of the year, clearly, is not synonymous with ovulation.

If it will not lead to conception, Hrdy asks, then what is all this nonreproductive sexuality about? The human female is not unique in this respect: other hominoids of both sexes engage in "extrareproductive" love making. Caresses, face-to-face coupling, prolonged mutual gazing, and nonreproductive copulations are seen in both wild and captive great apes.

While bearing and raising children offer satisfactions to many, the arguments in favor of pronatalism are more often heard from husbands, parents, or in-laws than the women who have the burdens of more child care than free choice would find desirable. The implications go beyond neuropsychology and quickly become political, beyond the scope of this book.

In humans the sex drive and others are complicated by their combination with other drives. Some drives conflict with others; the antidrives are more harmonious. We learn to combine many drives in our behavior so as to optimize the satisfaction of many drives at once. We learn to satisfy hunger by eating certain foods only at certain meals. I am fond of baked potatoes and chocolate–chocolate chip ice cream, but not at breakfast. Our methods of preparation, the serving of food, the setting of the table, the company with which we dine, are important elements of our feeding behavior and the termination of hunger. It is not any one drive that must be satisfied, but the individual as a whole.

Searching Behavior and Curiosity

"Getting to know the environment" is an important basic activity of animals and human beings. Exploratory reflexes are readily observed in many animals; all rodents, for example, when moved to a new environment, explore the area before they will feed or start to build a nest (Eibl-Eibesfeldt, 1970). Curiosity, far from being "idle," seems to be as necessary for the biological adaptation of the organism to its environment as the physiological tissue needs for food or water.

Curiosity operates when no definite goals are sought; it is not the means to an end (food, sex, or power), but an end in itself. Awake and well fed, the puppy, kitten, or child is constantly in motion—actively tasting, touching, sniffing, looking, and otherwise exploring the world. The results of such exploration may be useful—as the organism learns where to go and what to do when the tissue need for food or water does arise. "Incidental" learning, unaccompanied by obvious reward or avoidance of punishment, does occur in all mammals. The rat allowed to run in a maze learns a good deal about it even when no reward has been placed in the goal box. Later, when hungry and in the same maze, but with food present, the rat shows that the blind alleys have been registered in its brain. The maze is mastered more quickly and with fewer errors than if there had been no previous learning (Blodgett, 1929). Curiosity thus connects learning with natural everyday behavior. But curiosity does more than provide useful information. The exploratory activity it evokes seems to be a biological need for stimulation.

Sensory Deprivation and "Neurohunger"

Sensory deprivation—preventing variegated stimuli from reaching the eyes, ears, and limbs of a subject—is hardly endurable for the human being. Experiments at McGill University (Heron, 1957) called for volunteers to be paid well just to lie in bed in a darkened room listening to monotonous "white noise," with cuffs on elbows and other joints to minimize tactile sensations. College students, enticed by the money and the chance to loaf and think uninterruptedly, were unable to last more than a day, two days at most, before they pushed the "panic" button. There seems to be a reaction to sensory deprivation that produces a state of restlessness, and even vivid hallucinations, amazingly similar to those produced by long-lasting hunger in a situation where food is unavailable.

A *stimulus hunger* appears to drive the organism into exploratory behavior, which thus belongs with the other preservative activities of living creatures. A striking fact: just as the general hunger for food is directed at tasting and eating particular foods, so the hunger for external stimuli is directed at particular sensory modalities; and within a sensory system— vision, for example—specific categories of visual stimuli are preferred.

Hungry to see paintings, we visit art galleries and museums. Longing to hear music, music lovers go to a concert or subscribe to an opera series. Our visual curiosity or our musical curiosity may be satiated before the end of a long series of visits to galleries or operas. They reappear, however, when the drive cycles around again.

These drives and antidrives are amazingly specific. Butler (1953), in Harlow's primate laboratory at the University of Wisconsin, showed that a monkey will repeatedly press a bar to earn, not a food reward, but simply the privilege of looking through a window at the scene outside. He will work just to see the window light up; he will work harder for a glimpse of a fellow monkey. The monkey, like the human, is a social animal and develops a genuine appetite for the society of conspecifics.

Here the neuropsychologist may ask why one certain class of stimuli evokes an attentive response while the response to other classes is relatively weak. Too little is known about the physiological mechanisms of sensation seeking and curiosity to give a satisfactory answer. It is possible that neurons of all sensory systems are, under normal conditions, in an active state because they are nourished by the external stimuli impinging upon them. If these stimuli are lacking, the neurohunger for external stimulation will activate an exploration system in the brain. If this is true, we should look for some internal (humoral) factors, perhaps in the cortex itself, which initiate exploratory behavior and direct it toward the consummatory-perceptual responses that have developed to satisfy the stimulus hungers. The *activity* drive may have its analogous source in the *motor* neurons and muscles.

The organization of the cortex into separate regions of selectively sensitive nerve cells that respond only to specific sorts of stimuli provides a possible model for this selectivity and preference. Cells that are close neighbors almost always have similar properties with regard to the features they detect in the outside world. It is not difficult to imagine that groups of cells with common feature-detecting properties are jointly activated by a given drive center and jointly inhibited by a common antidrive center.

SUMMARY

Why people behave the way they do is the problem of motivation. Physiological systems called *drives* mobilize and steer behavior. They include thirst, hunger, sex, sleep, elimination, thermal control, curiosity (stimulus-hunger), and other unlearned reflexes. These develop into specific appetites, in part resulting from internal biochemical conditions, and in part from interactions with the environment in the personal life history of the individual.

Drives arouse the motor behavioral system and initiate behavior; corresponding *antidrives* signal relief and terminate behavior. Both drives and antidrives have their hormonal centers chiefly in the hypothalamus; their higher centers are represented in the limbic system with extensive cortical interconnections. These centers comprise the "emotive" system and the integrity of "personality."

Drives and antidrives are physiological functions in reciprocal inter-action with one another, alternately exciting and inhibiting each other's activity. Their psychological counterparts are called *emotions* and *moods* respectively. Anger and fear are emotions aroused by protective drives; hunger, sexual arousal, and so on, are emotions aroused by preservative drives.

Although genetically programmed to be cyclical in humans as in lower mammals, our appetitive activities break loose from an inevitable periodicity. Notably, in contrast to the estrus cycle in other female animals, human female sexual behavior is not restricted to ovulation or reproductive period, but may be activated at any time.

In humans, the genetic programs retain their effectiveness primarily by substituting acquired controls for the biochemical clocks regulating other animals. The continuity between humans and other mammals is shown by many aspects of the protective and preservative activities in all mammalian forms.

In particular, the universality of the orientation reaction and its associated reciprocally interactive components—the targeting reflex and the habituation reflex—deserve emphasis. As the following chapters show, these processes are involved in every act of perceptual learning and play an important role in perfecting the adaptation of the individual organism to its environment.

SUGGESTED READINGS

Eibl-Eibesfeldt, I. *Ethology: The biology of behavior.* (E. Klinghammer, trans.). New York: Holt, Rinehart, & Winston, 1970.

Fitzsimons, J.T. *The physiology of thirst and sodium appetite.* Cambridge, Engl.: Cambridge University Press, 1979.

Heron, W. The pathology of boredom. *Scientific American,* 1957, *196*(1), 52–56.

Hinde, R.A. *Animal behavior: A synthesis of ethology and comparative psychology* (2nd ed.). New York: McGraw-Hill, 1970.

Hrdy, S.B. *The woman that never evolved.* Cambridge, Mass.: Harvard University Press, 1981.

Krieger, D.T., & Hughes, J.C. (Eds.). *Neuroendocrinology.* Sunderland, Mass.: Sinauer, 1980.

Morrison, A.R. Brainstem regulation of behavior during sleep and wakefulness. In J.M. Sprague & A.N. Epstein (Eds.), *Progress in psychobiology and physiological psychology* (Vol. 8). New York: Academic Press, 1979.

Morrison, A.R. Central activity states: Overview. In A.L. Beckman (Ed.), *The neural basis of behavior*. Jamaica, N.Y.: Spectrum, 1982.

Olds, J. Pleasure centers in the brain. *Scientific American*, 1956, *195*, 105–116.

Olds, J., & Milner, P. Positive reinforcement produced by electrical stimulation of septal areas and other regions of rat brains. *Journal of Comparative and Physiological Psychology*, 1954, *47*, 419–427.

Pfaff, D.W. *Estrogens and brain function*. New York: Springer-Verlag, 1980.

Pfaff, D.W. (Ed.). *The physiological mechanisms of motivation*. New York: Springer-Verlag, 1982.

Stellar, E. Brain mechanisms in hedonic processes. In D.W. Pfaff (Ed.). *The physiological mechanisms of motivation*. New York: Springer-Verlag, 1982.

CHAPTER THREE

Specialized Functions of the Human Brain

Each hemisphere seems to have its own sensations, its own perceptions, its own memories, and its own cognitive, volitional, and learning and related experiences. After the surgery, these higher mental activities seem to be out of contact with and cut off from, the corresponding mental experiences of the other hemisphere.

(Roger W. Sperry, 1968)

INTRODUCTION

The preceding chapter dealt with those basic activities found in all animals that have a well-developed nervous system and manifest motivational or emotional behavior. A main concern of this chapter is with certain functions of the brain that are, if not unique to human beings, certainly distinguishing features of human behavior. These are our more specialized abilities: language, music, art, and memory.

Most human beings can learn to speak, to read, and to write; nearly everyone can recognize simple melodies and reproduce them without formal training; there are few persons who cannot draw simple figures or construct block towers or castles in the sand; indeed, the ability to paint and sculpt realistic forms is not rare. Next consider the number of things we commit to memory: names and faces, vocabularies, multiplication tables, places, routes, and maps, a well as motor skills such as driving, dancing, swimming, opening wine bottles.

Many people complain that they have poor memories. Often the problem is that they failed to observe properly in the first place. Few people complain that they have trouble forgetting, but it is a blessing that experienced horrors and painful images tend to fade away. There may also be an advantage in forgetting unused telephone numbers and the room numbers in last year's convention hotel. It is tempting to think that forgetting makes space and synapses available for the formation of new connections.

In the preceding catalog of the unique and interesting things that people do, I said nothing about "mind." (I omit the "soul" as outside the scope of these deliberations.) But humans have minds, as the title of this book implies. Then shouldn't we be looking in the human brain for the mind, instead of just these various specialized functions?

To answer this question, modern neuropsychologists and neurobiologists reply that the entire range of functions produced by the brain is what they mean by mind. There is no "place" in the brain where mind is located. Mind is what the brain does, just as flying is what the airplane does. No one asks where in the plane flight is located, or how flight acts upon the plane to make it go. Yet certainly plane flight would cease to exist without the airplane. Mind and brain are linked in the same way. Remove the brain and mind disappears together with the organ of consciousness and volition.

True, the entire forebrain may be destroyed, and the unfortunate victim may continue to breathe unaided, and continue living—in the case of one man on record, as long as 17 years! If the subcortical centers are intact, the decerebrate animal or human maintains the functions of its vegetative systems; indeed, its responses can be modified by conditioning.

An important qualification concerns the kind and location of damage to the brain. Even the loss of the hypothalamus, the organ that regulates the autonomic and endocrine systems of the internal milieu, can have different consequences that depend on how this happened. Was it the result of a sudden insult, or a gradual degeneration of the hypothalamic nuclei, for example, by a slowly growing tumor? In the latter case, other parts of the brain have time to rearrange their functions and compensate for the loss; in contrast, the shock of a sudden lesion may be catastrophic and result in death. For this reason, neurosurgeons are particularly careful not to disturb the hypothalamus when they are operating on neighboring structures.

If the patient lives but never regains consciousness, is he "out of his mind?" Does he even have a "mind"—or "mental" functions? Consistent with the definition that mind is what the brain does—the complete set of functions produced by the brain—the answer must be yes! But it is a highly qualified yes. The remaining parts of the brain are preserving the life of that individual: they have a function—survival. But is that really what you or I mean by mind? Would we be happier with another definition of mind—one that insists on keeping conscious awareness, memory, sensory and emotional experience in mind?

Abundant evidence shows that there are levels of "minding" in the fully functional human brain. With large parts of the brain gone or inoperative, many functions are lost. Reducing the nervous system to its root core in the brainstem and spinal cord leaves out what we prize. It leaves out varied reaction and choice. It leaves out complex learning, remembering, and forgetting. It leaves out feelings, perceptions, and images. It leaves out voluntary movement and impact on the environment. It leaves out inter-actions with other individuals and reflections about them and ourselves. It leaves out joy and love and anguish and pity—the whole rich universe of experienced emotions. It leaves out the poetry.

Our central nervous system protects us from the realization that the mind is not like the individual impulses of nerve cells, its elementary units, an all-or-none activity of the brain. There are many levels and many complex and subtle variations in the activities of the human brain. Not a singular noun, but a group of verbs, the mind is a pluralistic as well as a qualitative concept, best conceived as a number of specialized functions whose limitations are, as yet, still undefined.

There is good anatomical evidence for localizing mental functions in different parts of the brain. The left and right cerebral hemispheres, long thought to be mirror images of each other, are by no means identical. This asymmetry is called *lateralization*. This chapter deals with the lateralization of the two hemispheres and their differing functions in language, spatial orientation, attention, and emotion.

HEMISPHERIC LATERALIZATION

Each hemisphere of the brain is mainly associated with one side of the body: the right hemisphere presides over the left side and the left hemisphere presides over the right side. That the human brain is not wholly symmetrical is shown by the marked dominance of the right hand, which is controlled by the left half of the brain. Yet when an area in one hemisphere is damaged the corresponding area in the other hemisphere may sometimes take over its work.

Large bundles of nerve fibers called commissures link the cerebral hemispheres. The most massive connecting cable is the corpus callosum, containing millions of nerve fibers connecting parallel centers in the two

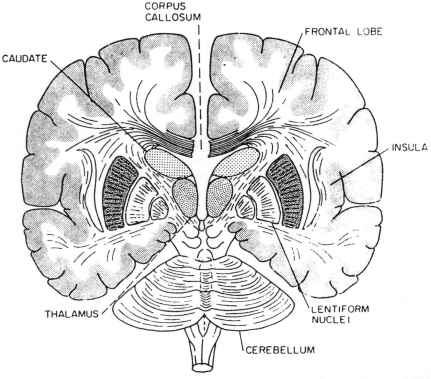

Figure 3.1. The corpus callosum cut for the relief of epilepsy. Sperry, 1974. Copyright © 1974 by MIT Press.

hemispheres. The surgical disconnection of the corpus callosum and other commissures, called commissurotomy, provides new and detailed insights into the functional architecture of the brain. (See Figure 3.1.)

BRAIN LATERALIZATION OF LANGUAGE

Speech is the specialized function that we have known about the longest. In 1836, Marc Dax, an obscure country doctor, read a short paper at a medical meeting in Montpellier, France. In it he reported that in over 40 patients with aphasia or speech disorder, all had cerebral damage on the left side, none on the right side of the brain. Dax died, his paper unpublished.

Nearly a quarter of a century elapsed before the neurologist, Pierre Paul Broca, another French investigator, announced in 1861 that autopsies on all of his asphasic patients showed lesions in a special region in the posterior portion of the frontal lobe on the left half of the brain. This post mortem evidence of speech lateralization initiated extraordinary interest in cerebral asymmetry.

Scientific observations don't become "discoveries" until the *Zeitgeist* (spirit of the time) is right. It helps if the scientist has an established reputation. Broca was a respected neurologist. His observations on the association between speech disorder and a special region on the left hemisphere was an important new finding. This area became known as "Broca's area," and the inability to speak—but with comprehension unimpaired—was called "Broca's aphasia." Similar damage to the right hemisphere did not seem to disturb language functions. Now it is generally accepted that 95 percent of all speech disorders caused by brain damage result from lesions of the left hemisphere. Certain exceptions, particularly in left-handed patients, suggest a crossed relation between handedness and cerebral dominance. This is not a firm rule. Most left-handers (about 70 percent) also have left brain dominance for language. Many others, regardless of hand preference (which varies from task to task) have bilaterally represented language centers. Among them, those with a family history of left-handedness are especially prone to bilateral presentation of language (Hécaen & Albert, 1978). (See Figure 3.2.)

Another major event equal to Broca's report on the localization of speech occurred in 1876. In that year, the 26-year-old Karl Wernicke, just four years

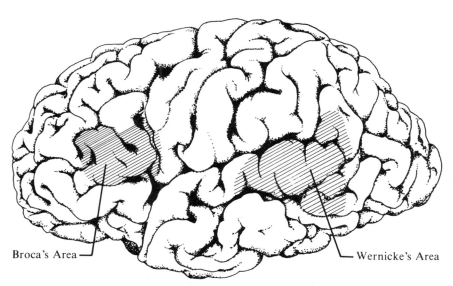

Figure 3.2. Language areas of the human brain in the left cerebral hemisphere.

out of medical school, described a new type of aphasia, a disorder of language reception. Broca had been concerned with language expression: his patient could understand, but could not speak; Wernicke's patient could speak, but could not comprehend. Wernicke's aphasia was located in the left hemisphere also; not in the front part of the brain, but in the rear, on the temporal lobe, near the sensory projection areas for sight and hearing.

THE SPLIT BRAIN EXPERIMENTS ON HUMAN PATIENTS

The most dramatic evidence for the independence of action by different parts of the brain in human beings comes from research on patients whose two cerebral hemispheres have been surgically disconnected in an attempt to prevent epileptic seizures from spreading from one hemisphere to the other.

The first human subjects studied were patients of Doctors Philip J. Vogel and Joseph E. Bogen of Los Angeles who carried out an extensive midline section of the cerebral commissures in what is considered to be the most radical surgical approach to the treatment of epilepsy. Not only was the therapeutic outcome good in these initial, apparently hopeless, cases, but following surgery, no disturbances of ordinary behavior were noticeable.

The patients became the subjects of study by the psychologist Roger W. Sperry, winner of the 1981 Nobel Prize in Physiology and Medicine for his boldly original and beautiful experiments on nerve regeneration and the effects of commissurotomy in monkeys and humans (Sperry, 1964; 1968; 1970).

Sperry had observed the behavior of dozens of monkeys following this kind of surgery and found no ill effects, leading him to expect none with these human patients. His initial impression was that the surgical disconnection had no effect whatsoever, a confirmation of work reported earlier by Akelaitus (1944) that the surgical division of the human brain leaves no behavioral deficit.

More subtle methods of testing that Sperry developed with Michael Gazzaniga and others (Gazzaniga & Ledoux, 1978; Sperry, Gazzaniga, & Bogen, 1969) who studied these patients have uncovered striking symptoms. Collectively, these are called the "syndrome of hemispheric deconnection," or, colloquially, the "split brain syndrome."

The initial studies concentrated on two of these patients who made excellent recoveries. One of the first two surgical patients, a 35-year-old woman, recovered rapidly and resumed her homemaking duties. Another split-brain patient who became a cooperative subject for the psychology experiments was a boy of 12 at the time of surgery and was talking fluently the following morning. He recited "Peter Piper picked a peck of pickled peppers" and quipped that he had "a splitting headache."

A single testing setup (see Figure 3.3) allows stimuli to be presented

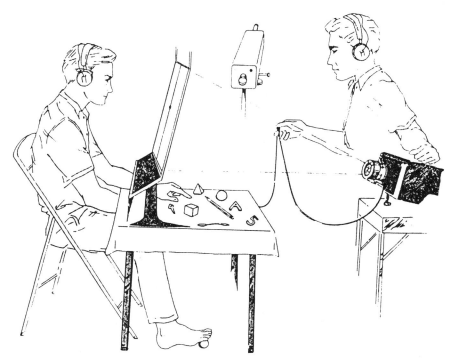

Figure 3.3.　Test setup for presenting stimuli separately to the right or left hemispheres, used by Sperry and co-workers for studying the split brain syndrome. Sperry, 1974. Copyright © 1974 by MIT Press.

separately to the right or left hemispheres and provides for separate verbal or manual responses controlled by one hemisphere only. For example, visual stimuli can be projected to the right or to the left of a designated fixation point on the center of a translucent screen and exposed for .1 second or less, too fast for eye movements to shift the material into the wrong hemisphere. If projected to the right visual field, the left hemisphere could respond verbally; if the same stimulus was projected to the left visual field, only the right hemisphere could perceive it, but being mute, could not produce a verbal response.

It needs to be stressed that the disconnected right hemisphere is not completely devoid of language functions. It can't speak because in these patients the speech centers are in the left hemisphere. But if a word, say "key," is projected on the left side of the screen, the patient, while insisting that she saw nothing, will pick out a key with her left hand from the objects on the tray.

The right hemisphere simply can't talk. But though it is mute, it is not blind, and given a chance to express itself nonverbally, shows that it can perceive, and that it can think, learn, and remember. (See Figure 3.4.)

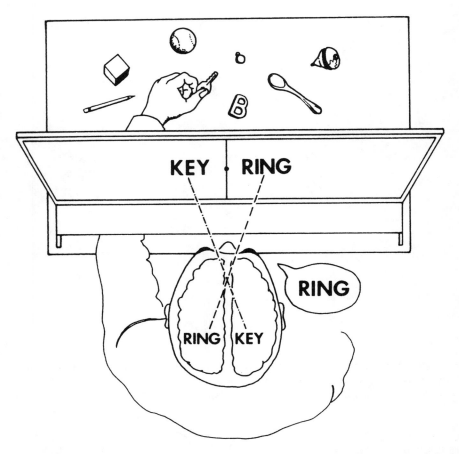

Figure 3.4. The left hemisphere reads and can say "ring"; the right hemisphere reads "key," and, although it cannot talk, it instructs the left hand to select the key. Adapted from Sperry, 1968.

When both fields are stimulated at the same time with two different words, "tea" on the left and "cup" on the right, the patient reports seeing "cup," but his left hand will point to the word "tea" on a list containing those two words among others. Never does the patient report what would appear to us as a unitary two-syllable word, "teacup."

The results for vision are not unique; tactile and stereognostic perception show much the same doubling of conscious awareness. The patients readily identify a pear or a cigarette placed in their right hand, but they can't name the same objects placed in their left hand. The problem is not one of *agnosia* (failure of recognition) in the right brain. That hemisphere demonstrates

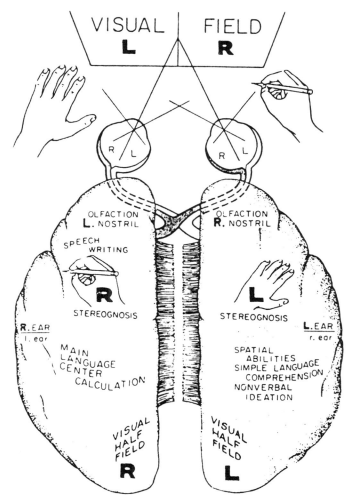

Figure 3.5. Functions separated by the surgery. Sperry, 1974. Copyright © 1974 by MIT Press.

recognition by the subject's pretending to bite the pear or smoke the cigarette. In response to a picture of a cigarette flashed to the right brain, the left hand will pick up a cigarette. If there is none on the tray, the right brain reveals its capacity for symbolic association by selecting a matchbox or an ashtray. In response to a picture of a slot machine, the right brain and left hand of one patient picked out a coin. (See Figure 3.5.)

The lateralization of emotional responses in these patients was a further indication of the independence of the disconnected hemispheres. The first hint that appropriate emotional reactions are registered by the right brain appeared when a vivid pinup shot of a nude was projected to the left visual field. The subject said she saw "nothing" but a sneaky grin and a giggle showed that the right brain gets the emotional effect but can't transfer it to its verbally expressive companion.

Five of the split brain patients were examined for lateralization of olfaction. As with the visual and tactile stimuli, the odors—lemon extract, garlic, Arpège perfume, fish oil, and others, were presented separately to each hemisphere via the ipsilateral nostril (the nerve fibers project only to the hemisphere on their own side). No odor presented to the right nostril could be named, a predictable result for the mute hemisphere, but the patient was able to point correctly to the associated object, a plastic lemon, a perfume bottle, or a garlic clove, etc. The olfactory identifications did not cross over to the left hemisphere; the subjects simply guessed at a chance level or reported that they smelled "water."

Some of the less pleasant odors gave immediate aversive reactions: wincing, facial grimaces, and exclamations, "ugh," "yuk," "phew," etc. When the examiner asked the patient to refrain from any overt expression of distaste, there was no crossover of identification. Affective, as well as cognitive, aspects of perception are apparently also divided into separate right and left realms (Gordon & Sperry, 1969).

In all of these experiments, it was necessary to prevent crossover of information from one hemisphere to the other. The right hand must be kept away from the left hand, and test objects had to be prevented from touching the face or head area. Many subtle response signals can cue in the uninformed hemisphere. For that reason, ordinary behavior in these patients was unified, and of course the two mental spheres had only one body. As Sperry and his associates noted, the two are bound to meet the same people, see and do the same things, go to sleep together and wake up together. In the absence of experimentally controlled restraints on eye movements to prevent scanning, the two brains have essentially identical experiences.

The deliberate lateralization of stimulus input by the experimenters may have exaggerated the displays of conflict by these subjects. Was there no evidence of conflict in these patients outside the laboratory? Actually, fairly frequent reports attest to the lack of cooperation between the two hemispheres. Akelaitus (cited by Geschwind, 1981) observed that one of his callosal patients used his left hand to shut a drawer forcefully on his own right hand that was reaching in to get a pair of socks. Another patient's wife complained that the patient would sometimes seem to beckon her, even embrace her with his right hand, and at the same time push her away with his left hand. Geschwind (1981) reports a similar case of a normally gentle patient who would suddenly strike his wife, but only with his left hand. The unruly or violent left hand, "la main étrangère" (the alien hand), named by the French neurologists Brion and Jedynak (Geschwind, 1981), may be a clue to the special emotional nature of the right hemisphere.

SPECIALIZED FUNCTIONS OF THE RIGHT HEMISPHERE

The powerful evidence that our left brain is specialized for language led many to call this the "dominant" hemisphere or the "major" hemisphere, implying that the right side of the brain was subordinate, minor, and inferior. Does the right hemisphere have no compensatory or superior special functions of its own? Our one-sided emphasis on language, perhaps our most distinctive human characteristic, has allowed us to overlook the extremely important spatial, attentional, emotional, and musical abilities that are possessed by the nontalking half of the human brain.

The following sections will consider the evidence for each of these right brain functions and the implications of the division of functions on the two sides of the brain. What are the advantages of cerebral lateralization—why do we have two brains? How does this division of cerebral labor arise in left handers and right handers, and what is the significance of our mental duality?

Brain Lateralization of Space Perception

Our orientation in space depends principally upon the interplay between our visual and our proprioceptive systems. In this the kinesthesis of eye movements plays a major role. The integration of visual and proprioceptive information controls our movements in two kinds of space:

1. The space of central fixation. This is the space in which we perform visual discriminations, based on the spatial features of the discrimination problem, for example, threading a needle.

2. Extrapersonal space in the region surrounding the body, outside the foveal region of central fixation and symmetrical convergence of the eyes. Orientation in this peripheral space is needed for active reach and hand manipulations and to avoid bumping into obstacles during active movements of the body.

Disorders of spatial orientation may affect either or both of these general categories. They frequently follow bilateral lesions of parietal association cortex in monkeys. But, in humans, disorders of spatial orientation appear to be particularly associated with disease or injury of the right hemisphere. Lesions in the parietal, frontal, or temporal regions of the right hemisphere may produce spatial disorientation.

There is abundant evidence that the neural representation of visual-spatial relations is localized in the right hemisphere. The right brain–damaged victim of visual-spatial agnosia cannot make or follow maps. The patient fails to make a simple diagram of a familiar room and cannot describe how to get from his home to his place of work.

Konorski (1967) reports a case of a former taxi driver, living in Warsaw, unable, following right hemispheric injury, to sketch the center of the city, drawing the streets in the wrong direction, and not knowing which streets are parallel, which ones intersect, yet unaware of his blunders. Still, he could name the streets and describe their characteristic features—verbal ability was preserved together with the undamaged left hemisphere.

The right brain outperforms the left in a number of spatial tests. In a task requiring construction of block designs to match a sample pattern, the split brain patients did better with their left hands and right brains than with their opposites. These visuospatial tasks, and especially the spatiokinesthetic problems demanding manipulation, give the nonspeech hemisphere a decided advantage.

Visual disorientation attended by errors in reaching for objects in extrapersonal space is usually more serious than errors made in reaching for an object that is centrally fixated. The suggested inference is that central fixation demands the cooperation of both halves of the brain ensuring integration. In peripheral space, only one hemisphere can be active, and if the right hemisphere is injured, orientation in the surrounding space will suffer a deficit. Why except the left hemisphere? The next section describes the syndrome of hemi-inattention or unilateral neglect, and suggests an explanation for its lateralization in the right hemisphere.

Brain Lateralization of Attention

Lesions to the right parietal area have specific effects upon attention toward objects and events in the peripheral visual fields. The chief symptom of the defect is called *hemi-inattention* or *unilateral neglect*. As early as 1896, John Hughlings Jackson described one such case of unilateral neglect or human "imperception."

> The patient began reading at the lower right corner and tried to read backward. She had difficulty dressing and finding her way about; she had developed a left hemiplegia and a left field neglect. Brain damage on the opposite or right side of the brain was found at autopsy.

Patients with hemi-inattention may fail to recognize the limbs on one side of their body as their own. They may attend to events and people only on one side; one patient with a left-sided neglect, when asked to count the people in the room, indicated only those on her right side. When asked about the others, she replied, "Oh, they don't count." The patients also deny their deficits and appear to be unaware of them, just as they ignore one side of an open book or neglect to wear one sleeve or slipper. Hemi-inattentive patients may eat from only one side of a tray or shave one-half of their face and not the other. Typically the affected side is the left side of the body or surrounding space; most reports consequently show predominant damage to the right half of the brain.

The positive features of hemi-inattention are shown dramatically in drawings. For example, one man with left-sided neglect, in drawing a daisy, placed petals only on the right side. He then rotated the page in clockwise fashion, continuing to fill in petals until a full circle was reached, revealing actually a kind of compensated attention to the affected side. The reports show many selective aspects: a patient may use the neglected left hand to put a glove on the right hand but let the left hand remain ungloved. Thus a patient may recognize an affected limb in some contexts but not others; he may show signs of startle at strangers approaching on the affected left side, but completely fail to recognize familiar persons coming from his left.

The drawings made by cases of left-sided inattention may omit or caricature the missing side. Weinstein (1977) reproduces some striking drawings of human figures made by hemi-inattentive patients. The upper left-hand drawing in Figure 3.6 was drawn by a patient with some artistic talent. He drew the right side of the body with heavy line but only lightly pencilled the other half, the mirror image of the patient's own affected side. Weinstein reports that

> actions of these hemi-attentive patients may also be 'exquisitely' selective and symbolic. (See Figure 3.6.) One woman would expose only her left breast, a man would sit only on one buttock. Another patient, when putting on his eyeglasses, placed the lens correctly in front of his good eye but over the eyebrow on his affected side. (Weinstein, 1977, pp. 5–6)

The defect is not sensory. Patients who, on testing, neglect one side of space do not collide with objects nor veer to one side when walking. When presented with the words "brake" and "clever," they read the whole words "rake" and lever," not "ake" or "ver." There is thus a sensory awareness of the affected side. Patients ignore one side not because there is a localized area of visual deficit. When they ignore one side they may refer to it verbally as "my better half," or draw a picture of a house with the window closed on the impaired side. Failure to look at or use the involved limb is not a motor deficit any more than it is strictly a sensory deficit. Subjects who do not raise both arms on command may use them both effectively at other times.

Not only are visual stimuli neglected in cases of hemi-inattention; there may be a loss of response to olfactory, taste, touch, or auditory stimuli on one side of the body only. Asked to grasp his ears, the patient may react correctly with the unaffected hand but grope in space with the other. Critchley (1966)

Figure 3.6. Figure drawings by patients with left hemi-inattention and one case of right hemi-inattention. Weinstein, 1977; 1980. With permission of Raven Press and Cambridge University Press.

reports a case of an orchestra conductor who ignored the music coming from one side of the stage; another patient was unable to go to church "because he could not stand the hymns on the affected side" and fidgeted constantly during the singing.

Hemi-inattention occurs in regard to both the motor and the perceptual sphere. The last example suggests the added involvement of emotion, mood, and consciousness. Weinstein (1977) recalls the remarkable case of an elderly lawyer who, when "examined from his good side, behaved like the courtly, Southern gentleman that he was. When approached from his left side, however, he would make remarks like, 'When are you going to get this over with, you head shrinking son of a bitch?'" These disorders also include *anosognosia* (denial of illness), disorientation for place and time, and various delusions.

The syndrome of left inattention or neglect is far more common and severe than right inattention (Heilman, 1979; Mesulam & Geschwind, 1978; Weinstein, 1980). In fact, this attentional disorder is rarely seen to affect the right side of the body or the right visual field. Here is an important difference between the consciousness of the two hemispheres.

Neglect in humans is not limited to parietal lobe lesions. It occurs following lesions of frontal, temporal, thalamic, cingulate, and other regions of the brain. Heilman and Valenstein (1972), Heilman and Watson (1977), and Weinstein (1981) stress the important contribution of the limbic-reticular system also; they point out that parietal and other lesions causing neglect are generally deep seated and rarely follow superficial cortical ablations. Both the side of the brain and cortico-limbic-brainstem interaction need to be taken into account in explaining attentional and motivational processes.

Brain Lateralization of Emotion

In studying brain laterality in human behavior, experimental psychologists have concentrated on cognitive functions related to intelligence, perception, language, verbal learning, and memory, but paid little attention to expressive and receptive aspects of emotion and motivational states in normal subjects. Despite compelling evidence for the localization of cognition, especially linguistic functions, the idea that emotions and feelings are also localizable met with disbelief.

Yet quite specific emotions can be elicited by stimulating particular regions of the brain. Now there is dramatic proof that affective aspects of language are localized in specific parts of the right hemisphere of the brain. The affective components expressed in language, such as intonation, and gesturing, and their comprehension, are represented in the right hemisphere in areas that mirror the propositional components of language, usually found in the left hemisphere. Thus damage to the right temporal lobe disturbs the comprehension of the emotional meaning of language, just as corresponding damage to the left temporal lobe, Wernicke's receptive area, disturbs comprehension of its cognitive content. Similarly, damage to the right frontal area, corresponding to Broca's expressive speech area in the left hemisphere, impairs the expression of emotional aspects of language.

These affective disorders of the right brain, called *aprosodias,* fall into the same three classes as the corresponding aphasias of the left brain—sensory, motor, and conduction disorders (Heilman, Scholes, & Watson, 1975; Ross & Mesulan, 1979; Ross, 1981). As in the cases of aphasias following injuries to the left hemisphere the aprosodias are rarely "pure." Different syndromes appear behaviorally as indifference, flattened affect, euphoria, or inappropriate affect.

Epilepsy often results in emotional disturbances that depend on which side of the brain is the focus of the seizures. Patients with temporal lobe epilepsy display chronic emotional and personality changes between seizures (Bear, 1979). These symptoms depend on lateralization in a curious way. One personality pattern appears when the epileptic focus is in the right hemisphere; a different constellation of traits is associated with epilepsy in the left hemisphere.

Bear reports that right temporal epileptics display excessive, often inappropriate, emotions. These people are notably lacking in humor and in sexual interest but manifest ardent religious fervor and tend to write voluminous notes and diaries. In contrast, left temporal epileptics express cognitive, ideational, and philosophical tendencies with little emotional content.

When the temporal lobe is removed for the relief of epilepsy, the surgery typically includes the partial or complete excision of the amygdala and the hippocampus. In consequence, the perception and expression of emotion are disturbed. But the supposed dichotomy between a rational left brain and an emotional right brain fails to be substantiated. The nature of the behavioral stimulus and the task may be as important as the side and the locus of brain damage in considering affective and personality traits.

The findings on emotional processes do not support the idea that one side of the brain is rational, intellectual, or cognitive, in contrast to an impulsive, affective, or emotional side. Instead, both hemispheres possess affective aspects, but the right and left hemispheres have different emotional response patterns. The two different patterns are frequently mixed, however, and patients with left hemispheric speech disorders are often depressed—a reaction of a normal right brain to an incapacitating deficit.

TACHISTOSCOPIC EXPERIMENTS

The tachistoscope is an instrument for presenting visual stimuli too briefly to allow eye movements to occur with its use. Visual information can be

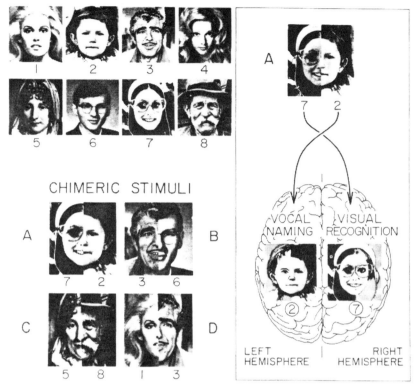

Figure 3.7. Composite face stimuli for testing hemispheric specialization for face recognition. Levy, et al., 1972. Copyright Oxford University Press. From Brain, Vol. 95, 1972. Granted by permission of Oxford University Press.

presented dichopically to each hemisphere independently without the other hemisphere having access to the information. Levy, Trevarthen, and Sperry (1972) used chimeric stimuli, consisting of pictures of faces, objects, and patterns split down the center and recombined. The right half of one face, for example, was joined to the left half of another and the subject either named or pointed to the complete picture in an array of the original pictures. (See Figure 3.7.) When the chimeric pictures were presented tachistoscopically to patients following hemispheric deconnection they described the complete picture corresponding to the face seen in the right visual field and thus by their left, talking hemisphere. Allowed to point to the picture they had seen, they chose the face seen in the left visual field and thus by their right hemisphere. Neither hemisphere was aware of the information of the other.

In later studies using the same technique, Levy (1974) tested normal subjects. Because in normals each hemisphere completed the half-image that it saw, a conflict ensued. The subjects responded either by naming or by pointing to the complete picture with either hand. Naming gave the response of the left hemisphere; pointing with either hand tended to give the response of the right hemisphere. When a verbal response is required, the left hemisphere becomes dominant, when a manual response is required the right hemisphere becomes dominant—suggesting a possible difference in the strategies used by the two hemispheres in normal persons, depending on the requirements of a task.

The superiority of the right hemisphere for monitoring space perception is highlighted by these results. Put in highly simplified form, you might say: ordinary people use their right brains for reaching and pointing to objects in space; they rely on their left brains when sitting or standing still and talking. What people "see" thus depends on what they plan to "do" about it.

DICHOTIC LISTENING EXPERIMENTS

In the normal individual, sensation is not represented purely contralaterally. Indeed there are many ipsilateral pathways. Even the total destruction of one hemisphere fails to abolish sensation on the opposite half of the body over which that hemisphere formerly presided.

An interesting technique, called dichotic listening, was developed by the British psychologist, Sir Donald Broadbent (1954), for investigating hemispheric differences in normal people. With this technique, Broadbent presents one word to the subject's right ear and a different word to the subject's left ear simultaneously. Most individuals tested dichotically in this way are able to report the words coming into both ears but the words to the left ear are reported later, because a delay is imposed by the extra synapse involved in callosal transmission. This delay is useful, but fails to prevent conflicts between ipsilateral and contralateral signals. Confusion between signals is greatest when the dichotic information belongs to the same category, both digits, for example, or both boy's names. These conflicts are caused by reciprocal interference or lateral inhibition between impulses arriving at the same centers at the same time.

Doreen Kimura, the Canadian physiological psychologist, used Broadbent's dichotic procedure for investigating hemispheric asymmetry in brain-damaged subjects. Her research (1961) with patients at the Montreal Neurological Institute involves simultaneous presentation of spoken digits to the two ears through earphones. The subjects hear three pairs of digits in rapid success to the left ear and at the same time three different pairs of digits to the right ear. At the end of the six digits the subjects' task is to report all the numbers they recall.

Patients with lesions in the left temporal area of the brain (the auditory region) report fewer digits than patients with lesions in the right hemisphere. The unexpected finding was that nearly all patients, whatever their lesions, reported the words they heard with their right ear more accurately than those they heard with their left. The right ear has better connections with the left hemisphere, where speech is analyzed, and its superiority for words is independent of the location of the brain damage. The right ear (and left hemisphere) was also found to be better at detecting nonsense syllables, unknown foreign words, and recorded speech played backwards. The explanation seems to be that, in audition, the left hemisphere is specialized for certain kinds of sounds—those generated by the human voice; other sounds—music, and even vocal, but nonspeech, sounds of coughing, laughing, and crying are picked up more strongly by the right hemisphere. Sounds expressing emotion thus show a left ear superiority (King & Kimura, 1972).

Brenda Milner (1962), also of the Montreal Neurological Institute, found further evidence of a cerebral asymmetry for comprehension of music and speech. Whereas damage to the left temporal lobe did, in her experiments, impair the perception of spoken words, damage to the right temporal lobe impaired the perception of tones. Other experimenters, using Seashore's test of pitch discrimination found a similar advantage for the normal right hemisphere. Kimura (1973) later found that melodies are also processed by the right hemisphere in both normal subjects and patients. Others (Bever & Chiarello, 1974; Spellacy & Blumstein, 1970) have similarly found a left ear superiority for nonmusicians. In the case of groups of musicians who were right handed, either no difference (Gordon, 1970) or a right ear superiority was found for the perception of melodies or rhythm. These experimenters account for the difference by supposing that musicians use an analytic strategy in listening to musical passages; those less well educated musically rely on holistic processing, and these strategic differences reflect a general functional difference between the left brain and the right. In any case, the musician's reliance on left hemisphere music perception may be the result either of inherent dominance or training and experience.

THE DEVELOPMENT OF CEREBRAL LATERALIZATION

The dichotic listening technique provides a tool for studying the development of specialized language functions. Kimura (1967) used it to determine the age at which the left hemisphere becomes lateralized for the perception of spoken words. She tested children in nursery school and the elementary grades and was surprised to find that even the four-year-old children showed a significant verbal right ear superiority (left hemispheric dominance). The finding was unexpected because the complete recovery of language function after injury to the speech area nearly always appears in children even a good deal older. These studies of recovery from aphasia led most aphasiologists to conclude that lateralization for language occurred at a much later age.

Yet even infants a few weeks old display an asymmetry in their auditory system related to human speech sounds. Entus (1977) combined the dichotic technique with observed changes in the infant's sucking rate. He presented an auditory stimulus, either voiced phonemes ("ma" or "ba") or a musical note played on the piano or viola through one or another pair of earphones to the two ears of the suckling. The infants changed their sucking rate in such a way that they received more phonemes through the right ear than the left ear and more instrumental tones through the left ear than the right. This provocative result has received support from evoked potential and EEG studies of young infants. There appears to be a lateralized preference for verbal stimuli in the left hemisphere and for music in the right hemisphere as early as three weeks of age and perhaps even earlier.

ENVIRONMENTAL FACTORS IN LATERALIZATION

A left hemisphere predominance for speech functions at an early age does not preclude plasticity of organization in the young child or even in the adult. Perhaps environmental factors begin to play a role at a very early period in the development of auditory asymmetry. Kimura (1967) decided to investigate. Her developmental studies were done first in a well-to-do residential area in the city of Montreal and replicated in California. In both regions, bright nursery age children showed strong left brain dominance for speech. She repeated the study in Hamilton in a low-to-middle-class socioeconomic area. This time the five-year-old girls (the youngest group tested) showed a significant right ear advantage for spoken words, but the five-year-old boys did not. A replication of this study among lower income children gave the same sex difference in the age of onset of lateralization. At all ages from six up, both boys and girls show higher scores for perception of speech for the right ear. Only the less advantaged five-year-old boys failed to show significant lateralization.

Thus it appears that sex and environmental factors interact to produce sex differences in the development of cerebral dominance. Lila Ghent (1961) found a parallel lag in the development of somesthetic asymmetry in boys. In a study on children, age 7 to 11, with reading disabilities, Taylor (1962) found that all the boys of his sample, but not the girls, failed to show a right ear effect. Boys with reading problems and boys from poor backgrounds lag behind girls in the development of cerebral asymmetry. Environmental handicaps and reading difficulties, however produced, seem to affect the normal development of functional asymmetry in males. There is no direct evidence that these factors affect females.

The role of experience is brought out clearly by studies of two special groups: illiterate persons, and literate, but congenitally deaf, persons. The evidence shows that aphasia is equally probable following brain damage to either the right or left hemisphere in illiterates. This suggests that experience with language may be essential for lateralization of language function to occur.

As a child develops, verbal ability can localize in either hemisphere. Albert and Obler (1978) have examined clinical records and experimental observations in several countries and find that they reveal a curious coincidence. Lateralized representation of speech seems to be associated with monolinguism. Children who grow up in bilingual or polylingual countries— Israel, for example, where everyone is required to learn Hebrew, and many learn English in addition to their native language—often lack clear lateralization. Dominance for language, when it does appear, may be either in the right or left hemisphere, and it is usually less profound. This is an advantage for those who later suffer from damage to one side of the brain. Complete aphasia is less common in Israel and bilingual parts of Canada than in the monolingual United States, France, and England, and recovery from language disorders of any degree is more sure. Albert and Obler suggest that an accident of history that led French, British, and American investigators to monopolize this branch of research accounts for the emphasis on left hemispheric dominance for language.

The frequent complete recoveries of language functions following severe brain damage to the left hemisphere emphasize the complexity of the neural pathways subserving language. The learning of a second language usually follows a different strategy than that normally used by a baby first learning to speak her native tongue. Native language learning follows a fairly uniform developmental route—babbling, then parroting and listening to one's own egocentric speech, and finally internalizing speech. Second and third language learning may follow one or more different routes, with reading and exercises in translating from one language to another a common practice that is, of course, absent in the initial development of speech.

Individuals differ widely from one another both in the innate developmental properties of their brains and in the methods with which they acquire complex skills. Verbal skills, reading, writing, and the comprehension of spoken language, even more than speech itself, provide numerous examples. Consider one example. Reading may be acquired by various routes: by learning to read written words directly as visual patterns (the whole word method), by learning to analyze words into pronounceable phonemes and say them out loud (phonics), by learning to form words from letters, by using auditory imagery, or kinesthetic word imagery, or by combination of some, or all of these methods.

Consequently, the symptoms of *alexia,* the impairment of reading following brain damage, may differ from patient to patient even when they have identical lesions. The nature of the disturbance depends upon the mechanism of reading in the particular case. Recovery from alexia may then utilize one or another of these channels that was not disturbed by the lesion.

LEFT-HANDEDNESS, SEX, AND CEREBRAL ASYMMETRY

The cerebral organization of left-handers and women has been frequently described as more nearly symmetrical than that of right-handers and men. The experimental and clinical evidence is worth examination. Important clinical and educational implications are frequently drawn from a less than robust basis of fact.

One of the first questions to be explored by the sodium amytal test was the relationship between handedness and hemispheric laterality. Wada and Rasmussen (1960) developed the sodium amytal test to determine which hemisphere controls speech, thus enabling the neurosurgeon to avoid damage to the language centers. This test asks the subject to wiggle the fingers on both hands and to count out loud as many numbers as she can, while sodium amytal, a fast-acting barbiturate is injected into either the left or right carotid artery. The drug effectively paralyzes the hemisphere on the side in which it has been injected. If the subject stops counting and fails to make any further vocal response and if also the right hand, but not the left, stops wiggling, the examiner knows that the affected left hemisphere is dominant for speech. The period of dysfunction is brief, but sufficient to make a reliable positive determination.

The sodium amytal test reveals that a significant number of left-handers, in contrast to 95 percent of all right-handers, have speech lateralized in their right hemisphere. Curiously, a sizable proportion of left-handers have speech in both hemispheres, suggesting that for them lateralization is weak or absent.

As the term "sinister" (Latin: "left") connotes wickedness or evil, this group, many of whom were found to have a family history of left-handedness, seems to have a peculiar or anomalous cerebral organization. Do familial left-handers lack the adaptive advantages of cerebral asymmetry? Kolb and Whishaw (1980) report that their study, using a neuropsychological test battery administered to college students, found no differences in intellectual ability between left-handed and right-handed subjects. Other investigators have confirmed these results.

An important consideration is that many people who write with their left hands are right-handed in other respects. Handedness is not absolute; indeed, many people are ambidextrous. The figure usually cited for the number of left-handers in the total population is an estimated 10 percent—but the actual number of totally left-handed persons is probably much smaller.

Although a majority of the total population is female, little attention has been focused on women and the question of differences in cerebral organization based on sex. Recently, however, behavioral and neural scientists have begun to investigate female behavior and its underlying biology. The swing of the pendulum has led to an explosion of interest in sex differences.

Are brains organized differently in women than in men? The clearest evidence for a sex difference in hemispheric lateralization comes from studies of the effects of brain damage. Herbert Lansdell (1962) at the National Institutes of Health noted that males more often than females suffered deficits in visuospatial tasks following right temporal lobe operations for the relief of epilepsy. He also showed that males, far more frequently than females, suffered deficits in verbal functions following surgery of the left hemisphere. Lansdell had predicted that these specialized deficits would be related to the side of the lesion. What surprised him was that his predictions were correct for males only, not for females.

Additional studies supported this finding. Jeanette McGlone (1978) reports data based on a battery of psychological tests on 85 right-handed adults with brain damage. Some had lesions of the right hemisphere; some had lesions of the left hemisphere. The incidence of aphasia following left brain injury was three times as frequent in males as in females. These aphasics were excluded from the study sample for whom verbal and performance test scores on the Wechsler Adult Intelligence Scale (WAIS) were compared. For the group with left brain lesions, the results showed striking impairment on the verbal tests in males, but not in females. No significant deficit on the nonverbal tests appeared for either sex, regardless of the side of the damage. But where scores on the nonverbal items and scores on the verbal items were compared, a difference due to the side of the lesion was again found for men, but not for women. Right brain damage affected spatial performance, and left brain damage affected verbal intelligence in these male, but not female, subjects.

These combined studies indicate that verbal and spatial abilities are represented more bilaterally in left-handers than in right-handers and more bilaterally, also, in women than in men.

But why should this be so? In humans, differences between the sexes in behavior, homosexuality, and gonadotropin regulation are often seen. The origin of these differences and the degree of genetic and hormonal influence compared to a lifetime of social influence is unknown. Ehrhardt and Meyer-Bahlburg (1981) review the available data and conclude that prenatal hormones have limited effects on human psychosexual dimorphism. They do not determine sexual orientation, and their effects on general intelligence and specialized cognitive abilities are negligible.

The inference from the outcome studies that left-handers and women are genetically at a disadvantage is debatable. Differences in cerebral laterality associated with hand preference and gender may reflect not genes so much as the differential influences of early experience and social handicaps imposed upon deviant or less powerful groups.

The world and its tools are built to fit the needs of the "normal" majority. Left-handers constantly find themselves out of synchrony with an environment devoid of any but right-handed scissors, right-handed writing surfaces on classroom seats, right-handed pencil sharpeners, and so on. The left-handers among my students nearly invariably express their sense of disadvantage as a result of this right-handed bias that our culture imposes. Of course, left-handedness may be the result of early damage to the left brain (during a difficult birth, for example, and attendant forceps injury). Any resulting motor or sensory deficits on the right side of the body would lead to the development of compensating right hemispheric functions. If so, they may mask a genetically predisposed cerebral asymmetry.

The observed sex differences in cerebral functional asymmetry need to be interpreted with extreme caution. There is no direct anatomical evidence for greater symmetry in female brains. Of course, not all investigations of sex differences find them; and negative results are far less likely to enter the literature than positive results.

Critics note the tremendous variability in every trait, including lateralization, within each sex and the need for larger groups than the 10 or 15 subjects often used as the basis for broad generalizations. Careful writers report measures of variability together with mean differences. When these reports are examined, one generalization repeatedly and firmly does emerge. There are larger differences between one woman and another, and also between one man and another, than the differences between the "average" woman and the "average" man.

Differences in early stimulation may offer a plausible explanation for the reported differences in lateralization associated with left-handedness and gender. The greater bilateral symmetry found for left-handers and women may be the result of early strong bonds between the two hemispheres. A recent finding of sexual dimorphism in human fetal *corpora callosa* suggests an anatomical basis for greater interhemispheric integration in females than in males (Baack, Lacoste-Utamsing, & Woodward, 1982). The relatively larger size and shape of the female splenium provides a genetic or hormonal basis for the complementary training of both sides of the brain. Girls more than boys, and sinistrals more than dextrals, are socialized to control emotional and antisocial tendencies of the right hemisphere (recall the "unruly" left hand). I hypothesize that young females, especially, are trained to be responsive to affective stimuli, and unlike males, freely to express their feelings in emotional inflection, gesturing, and body language. At the same time as these environmental factors encourage the development of right hemispheric functions, they also encourage female social dependence and attendant verbal abilities presided over by the left hemisphere. These combined factors may strengthen early specialized maturation of both halves of the brain and continued utilization of the growth of larger interconnecting commissures between the two. (Lacoste-Utamsing & Holloway, 1982). Bilateral symmetry of function may be the normal result of these combined morphological and social-learning factors in the definition of gender roles in contemporary society.

Anatomical Asymmetry

Consider again the simple fact that aphasia following damage to the left hemisphere is far more frequent than it is following damage to the right hemisphere. In normal human subjects with no brain damage, the experimental evidence from a variety of sources—dichotic listening techniques, tachistoscopically presented words and other stimuli, EEG and evoked potential recordings, and the sodium amytal test—agrees in showing dominance for verbal functions in the left half of the brain.

The apparent anatomical symmetry of the two halves of the brain seems to be inconsistent with their obvious functional asymmetry. This paradox remained curiously unexplained until 1968.

In that year, Norman Geschwind and Walter Levitsky decided to look into the matter. With the aid of no more sophisticated tools than a camera and a ruler, Geschwind and Levitsky (1968) measured 100 human brains, paying particular attention to the *planum temporale,* a posterior region on the surface of the temporal lobe that forms part of Wernicke's area. The results were clear cut. They showed that this region is generally larger on the left side than on the right; indeed, the difference between the corresponding regions on the two sides is visible to the naked eye—once attention has been drawn to it. (See Figure 3.8.) Geschwind's and Levitsky's data showed the left planum to be larger in 65 percent of the brains; the right planum was larger in only 11 percent of the brains, and the rest were approximately equal in size.

Marjorie LeMay (1977) subsequently confirmed these results using computerized X-ray tomography (CT scanning) a technique in which an image of the brain is reconstructed from a set of x-ray projections of successive cross sections. Using the CT scan and several other methods, such as carotid arteriography, which LeMay developed for diagnosing tumors and vascular disorders of the brain, LeMay and Culebras (1972) observed this and other cerebral asymmetries even in the human fetus.

TWO BRAINS: TWO MINDS?

Nowhere is the idea of mental duality more compelling than in the split brain experiments. From the striking unawareness in each hemisphere of the mental activities going on in the other, it is hard not to believe that these callosal patients have two separate brains, each with a mind of its own. After four years of intensive studies of these split brain patients, Sperry writes: "In the split brain syndrome we deal with two separate spheres of conscious awareness, i.e., two separate conscious entities or minds running in parallel in the same cranium, each with its own sensations, perceptions, cognitive processes, learning processes, memories and so on" (1968, p. 318).

Further observations reveal that these disconnection symptoms may be partially compensated by reeducation, particularly in the young patient. How

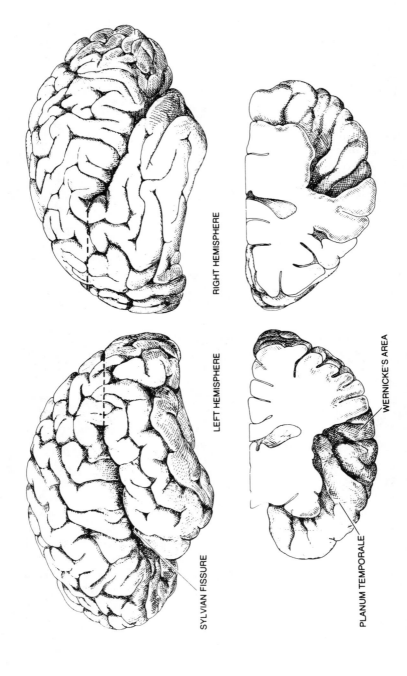

RIGHT HEMISPHERE

LEFT HEMISPHERE

SYLVIAN FISSURE

PLANUM TEMPORALE

WERNICKE'S AREA

Figure 3.8 Anatomical asymmetry of the cortex. The cut left hemisphere shows a larger planum (shaded area) than the right (lower) illustration. From N. Geschwind, "Specializations of the Human Brain," *Scientific American*, September, 1979. Copyright © 1979 by Scientific American, Inc. All rights reserved.

far such compensation can go must await future evidence as these commissurotomized patients continue to live and to learn. As yet we do not know whether a new cross integration can take place in the absence of the commissures that link the two hemispheres in our ordinary brains.

Thinking about our ordinary cerebral hemispheres leads some people to ponder the possible benefits of having two brains—each playing a different role. Does it make room for an expanded consciousness?

Roland Puccetti, professor of philosophy at Dalhousie University in Nova Scotia, asks us to consider this question: Since we have two normally functioning cerebral hemispheres, do we have two minds? Puccetti's (1981) target article, "The Case for Mental Duality: Evidence from Split-Brain Data and Other Considerations," has engaged 17 spirited peer commentaries in the debate. Most commentators stress the unity of the normal mind; others are sympathetic to mental numerosity, suggesting that it may be even greater in the intact brain than in the disconnected hemispheres of the commissurotomy patients. The idea of a multiplicity of mental entities in one body is not new; psychoanalytic theory and the frequent reports of cases of "multiple personality" have familiarized the public with many-in-one speculative models that float free of neurological substrates.

What is different and subtly disorienting about this controversy is that it appears in a learned professional journal, *The Behavioral and Brain Sciences,* and is argued by eminent, highly respected research neuroscientists. The key to their involvement is that they now have an organic model, one solidly grounded on the hard facts of anatomy and physiology. There is abundant evidence for parallel wiring in the central nervous system. The brain has a spatial organization that allows different neural pathways to deal with the same incoming information in different ways and to send their transformations out in many directions.

Certainly many examples could be cited for independence of action by various parts of the brain in all of us. No one is wholly free from conflicts of feelings: we harbor incompatible beliefs to which we cling even when we become aware of their inconsistency. We believe strongly in peace, yet thrill to a military parade; we believe it's wrong to kill deer for meat we don't need, but love to eat venison steak; we believe in equality for all, yet resent the intrusion of blacks, Jews, women, hispanics into our club; we believe that the government should levy income taxes to support public welfare, yet groan at tax collection time.

There are certainly splits between our feelings and our convictions—yet we find ourselves rationalizing when this is pointed out to us. The emotions thrust up into consciousness by our limbic system are often antithetical to our cognitive beliefs and desires. The cognitive cortex seems to be impotent, for example, to control penile erection and orgasm in the absence of the affective cooperation of lower sexual centers in the emotive brain.

Geschwind (1981) reminds us of the impossibility of producing even a normal smile in command. The photographer instructs us to smile or laugh, but, since we attempt to comply with our cortex, the smile in the picture looks glazed and unnatural. The results are different when the photographer tells us a funny joke; then the smile is a normal response to a limbic stimulus reaching us from a subcortical pathway that controls emotional expression.

Sperry wrote: "I have often thought that a computer with a sense of pain and pleasure, not to mention color perception, hearing, and other feelings in the conscious introspective sense might well be a much more proficient computer than a similar machine without the conscious properties (1965, pp. 454–455).

I agree, but I would emphasize the affective aspect. The critical property is not cognitive; the sensors on our modern space shuttles are already far superior to our human analyzers. No, not sensory perception, and not speed or motor power, but feelings, emotions, and moods are what make the difference between the organism and inanimate objects. The key to human learning and creative thought—to science, music, literature, and art, may lie in our emotive brain systems, in the amygdala, the hippocampus, and the hypothalamus, and the rich emotional coloration they give to our cognitive cerebral cortices, left and right.

How, then, does this book answer Pucetti's question? With a normally intact set of interconnected hemispheres, how many minds does its owner possess—one, two, or many? Before I answer this question, let me remind you of the neuropsychologist's definition of mind—not a noun but a set of verbs denoting many different activities. The mind represents the functions of the brain—a set of processes carried out by the brain. As I pointed out earlier, mind is what the brain does, just as flight is what the plane does. Let me carry the analogy one step further.

The plane may have two engines. Does it have two transportations? Of course not. But having two engines may offer a flexibility that is decidedly advantageous. Not only does the redundancy provide a fail-safe measure, a hedge against engine trouble, but the two engines working together can deliver twice as much power as one alone.

Since the two brains have only one common source of energy and one body between them, the sole advantage of the double brain appears to lie in the fact that one can replace the other in an emergency. But, as Sperry (1964) pointed out, intracranial space is tight. Do we really need the right-left duplication that normally prevails? How essential is it to have two brain centers to tell us that we are too hot, or too cold, or that what we hear are voices, what we smell is coffee, or that we are sad, or hungry, or sleepy?

A single set of controls could do the job nicely. People and animals have indeed shown that the early loss of one hemisphere caused no major deficit in their mental functions. Brain damage in children under age five will not provoke aphasia at all, while between ages five and ten, if aphasia appears, it is transient and clears rapidly (Lenneberg, 1967). When the dominant hemisphere is removed in adults, however, in order to excise large infiltrating tumors, or to treat uncontrollable epileptic seizures, usually speech is disrupted, and the aphasia may be permanent. We are thus dealing with an anatomical and a functional asymmetry of the brain that develops during ontogeny. By eliminating duplication, each hemisphere can play a different role. This makes space available for increasing specialization of functions. Duplication is probably most useful early in life when injuries are more likely to influence ontogenic development. Once past critical periods of maturation and the assignment of functions to specific addresses in the brain, specialization and differentiation accelerate. Biological growth follows an exponential function.

In this connection, Kupfermann (1981) writes:

> Lateralization may reflect the ultimate extension of a principle that serves to organize neurons into progressively larger functional units because of an evolutionary adaptation that minimizes the amount of "wiring" and maximizes the speed of communication between neurons that are likely to act in concert.

Denenberg (1981) has reviewed the research in animals and finds that functional asymmetry, when present, is similar across species. According to this view, communicative functions will be lateralized in the left side of the brain, and spatial and affective functions will be on the right side of the brain. Notably, songbirds have their vocal control nuclei on the left side (Nottebohm, 1980).

The supporting data for other species are slender, but Denenberg's review has the merit of calling attention to functions that human studies with their focus on language and handedness tend to ignore, especially the lateralization of space perception and spatial orientation.

An evolutionary perspective led Webster (1977) to suggest that brain asymmetry was biologically adaptive for problems of spatial position and territoriality. An asymmetrical brain might better enable its owner to identify and remember its homesite and other significant spatial locations.

Have you ever emerged from the subway and been totally lost as to which direction to go—what was east, what was west, which way uptown, which way downtown? The environment offers no natural clues to aid the organism in determining what is right and what is left. The bilateral symmetry of the body also makes it difficult to discriminate right and left. We often need a marker—a wristwatch, or a ring on the left hand—to tell ourselves which direction to take. A functional asymmetry of the brain is a surer guide.

THE NATURE OF HEMISPHERIC SPECIALIZATION: AN OVERALL VIEW

The attempt to summarize the voluminous body of research into human cerebral asymmetry has led to numerous proposals for a unitary divisional principle, none of which is on all fours.

It is clear that lateralization exists. The left hemisphere of the human brain is lateralized for speech and handedness, features that are very noticeable in humans, and the first to be stressed in research. Lateralization exists also in functions that are important for the survival of all species. The lateralization of spatial, attentive, affective, and motivational behavior in the right hemisphere of the human brain may be in part shared by some other species. There is no question that these functions play a significant role in human life, and, no less than verbal functions, they are considerably influenced by environmental factors and early experience.

Many have sought to find a single overriding principle of specialization to characterize the distinction between the left and the right hemispheres. The traditional verbal/nonverbal dichotomy is obviously inadequate. Both hemispheres possess considerable power of linguistic comprehension and inter-modal association. The capacity for cross-modal association may, in fact, be the key to the role of words as symbols, so that "pen," for example, stands for the object you see, feel, write with, put in your pocket, and look for—when you need to sign your name.

While the left hemisphere plays a dominant role in the expression of the content of speech, the right hemisphere mediates the expression of tone, accent, emotional gesturing, and other affective components of language. On the receptive side, the left and the right halves of the brain both comprehend the substantive and the affective aspects of language. The left hemisphere is superior (faster, more accurate) at reporting or reacting to verbal stimuli; the right hemisphere is superior in reacting to nonverbal stimuli and dominates in spatial perception and orientation.

There is strong evidence from behavioral, electrophysiological, and clinical studies that the right hemisphere is primarily involved in attentional processes. Unilateral neglect of the left side of space is a frequent result of damage to the right hemisphere but rarely affects the right side of space.

Since in the intact brain each half of the afferent cortex perceives only its own half of space, how do the two halves get joined together to produce a fused image? It must be that fusion takes place at the midline; that would allow a complete picture to be formed of the scene on which the foveae of our eyes are converged. Here is the explanation of the functional significance of the corpus callosum. Fibers in this commissure knit the two hemifields together. Cells with receptive fields that straddle the midline combine inputs from both eyes, and the fibers in the callosum extend the receptive field across the midline (Berlucchi, 1974).

The discovery of lateralized affective disorders such as *aprosodia* as a result of damage to the right hemisphere of the human brain has led to the proposal that, although the left verbal hemisphere is our "cognitive brain," the right hemisphere is our "emotive brain." Some writers describe the left brain as "logical, cold, rational, sequential, analytical" and the right brain as "synthetic, warm, intuitive, time-independent, and holistic." These terms are not well defined, and they build on slight evidence that is constantly changing as new data emerge.

SUMMARY

The search for a single overarching principle of cerebral asymmetry has failed. The co-existence of dependence and independence of action both within and between the two hemispheres makes it unlikely that there is any one fundamental distinction or dichotomy of function. What we find is more complex and more interesting. The questions for future research are to discover the principles of integration and the causes of psychological conflicts and disturbances.

SUGGESTED READINGS

Denenberg, V.H. Hemispheric laterality in animals and the effects of early experience. *The Behavioral and Brain Sciences,* 1981, *4,* 1–49.

Gazzaniga, M.S., & Ledoux, J.E. *The integrated mind.* New York: Plenum Press, 1978.

Geschwind, N. Disconnexion syndromes in animals and man. II. *Brain,* 1965, *88,* 585–644.

Geschwind, N. Specializations of the human brain. In *The brain: A Scientific American book.* San Francisco: W.H. Freeman, 1979.

Harnad, S., Doty, R.W., Goldstein, L., Jaynes, J., & Krauthamer, G. *Lateralization in the nervous system.* New York: Academic Press, 1977.

Hécaen, H., & Albert, M.L. *Human neuropsychology.* New York: Wiley, 1978.

Heilman, K.M. Neglect and related disorders. In K.M. Heilman & E. Valenstein (Eds.), *Clinical neuropsychology.* New York: Oxford University Press, 1979.

Milner, B. Hemispheric specialization: Scope and limits. In F.O. Schmitt & F.G. Worden (Eds.), *The neurosciences: Third study program* (75–89). Cambridge: MIT Press, 1974.

Mountcastle, V.B., & Mountcastle, M.D. (Eds.). *Interhemispheric relations and cerebral dominance.* Baltimore: Johns Hopkins Press, 1962.

Nottebohm, F. Brain pathways for vocal learning in birds: A review of the first 10 years. In J.M. Sprague & A.N. Epstein (Eds.), *Progress in psychology and physiological psychology* (Vol. 9). New York: Academic Press, 1980.

Nottebohm, F. A brain for all seasons: Cyclical anatomical changes in song control nuclei of the canary brain. *Science,* 1981, *214,* 1368–1370.

Sperry, R.W. Problems outstanding in the evolution of brain function. *James Arthur lecture on the evolution of the human of the human brain.* New York: The American Museum of Natural History, 1964.

Sperry, R.W. Mental unity following surgical disconnection of the cerebral hemispheres. *The Harvey Lectures,* Series 62. New York: Academic Press, 1968.

Sperry, R.W., Gazzaniga, M.S., & Bogen, J.E. Interhemispheric relationships; the neocortical commissures; syndromes of hemisphere disconnection. In P.J. Vinkin and G.W. Bruyen (Eds.), *Handbook of clinical neurology* (Vol. 4). Amsterdam: North Holland, 1969.

PART TWO

Afferent Systems: The Neuropsychology of Perception

CHAPTER FOUR

Functional Architecture of the Cerebral Cortex

Afferent nerve fibers are not high fidelity recorders, for they accentuate certain stimulus features, neglect others. The central neuron is a story-teller with regard to the nerve fibers, and it is never completely trustworthy, allowing distortions of quality and measure.... Sensation is an abstraction, not a replication of the real world.

(Mountcastle, 1975)

AFFERENT, EFFERENT, AND ASSOCIATIVE SYSTEMS

The brain contains three main functional systems: (1) afferent or sensory systems, (2) efferent or motor systems, and (3) associative systems linking particular parts of the afferent systems to each other and to the executive organs controlling the muscles and glands.

The analysis of sensation, the control of movement, and the integration of movement with sensory experience are the three major functions of the nervous systems of all animals that have a well-developed cerebral cortex. Comparatively elementary sensory and motor functions are located in their own specialized regions of the cortex. Every part of the body has its own

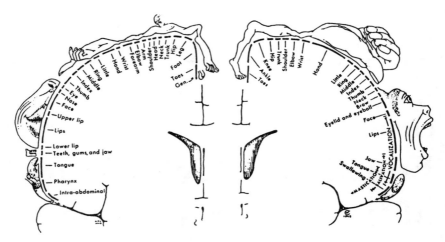

Figure 4.1. Classical sensory and motor maps of the body projected on the cerebral cortex. The left homunculus is the cortical projection of major somatosensory body parts; the right is the cortical projection of the motor system. Penfield & Rasmussen, 1950. Copyright © 1950 by Macmillan.

topographic representation in a particular cortical region as shown in the map of the somatic sensory and motor regions of the human cerebral cortex. (See Figure 4.1.)

The areas representing the face and the hands seem disproportionately large; it is not the size of the part of the body that counts, but its ability to discriminate and the precision with which it must be controlled.

The primary somatic sensory area receives information from the skin, the joints, the bones, and the muscles. The motor area, right ahead of it, is a mirror image that sends signals to control the movement of those body parts. A similar pair of somatic sensory and motor regions is mapped in both hemispheres. The left motor cortex controls movements of the right half of the body, and the left somatic sensory area receives sensations from the right side of the body. The right hemisphere performs these functions for the left half of the body.

The other senses send information to their primary projection areas in different lobes of the brain. The occipital lobe at the rear of the brain receives visual input; the temporal lobe contains the primary auditory cortex; the parietal lobe contains the somatic sensory projection area, and the motor cortex is located in the frontal lobes. These primary motor and sensory areas occupy only a relatively small area of the extensive human cortex. (See Figures 4.2 and 4.3.)

In fact, the traditional primary somatosensory cortex S1 of higher primates contains as many as four separate, complete, and parallel representations of the body, rather than one. Each of the representations differs from

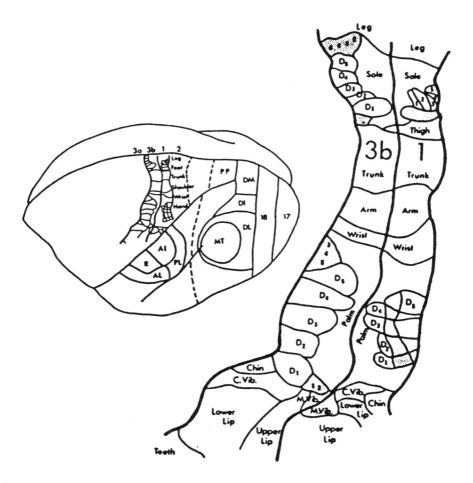

Figure 4.2. New conceptions of the organization of post central parietal somatosensory cortex show that the primary region contains multiple representations of given body parts. Left: dorsolateral view of monkey brain. Right: detail with representations of the digits in area 1 and area 2 of a macaque monkey. Data for digits 1–3 are shown. Note that these digits are represented separately in each architectonic field, and that the two representations are joined at the finger tips so that the representations are roughly mirror images of each other. Kaas et al. Copyright © 1979 by the AAAS.

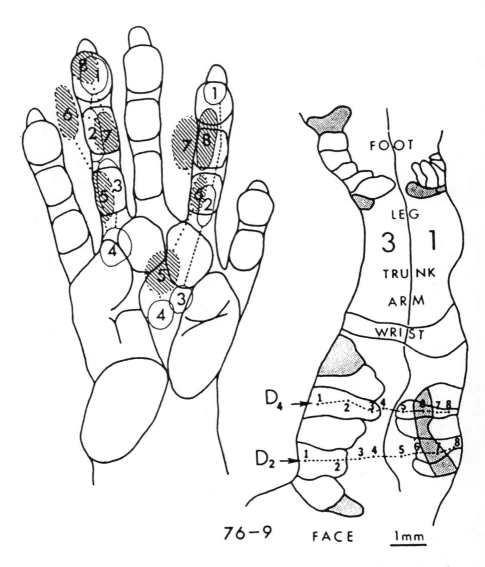

Figure 4.3. Receptive fields for two rows of recording sites across the separate hand representations in areas 3b and 1 of an owl monkey. Both anterior to posterior rows produced similar progressions of receptive fields from digit tip to palm and back again to digit tip. Thus the digits are systematically represented once in area 3b and again in area 1 in mirror image fashion, although the dorsal hairy surfaces of the digits have representations (shaded) that are displaced from the recording sites of the glabrous digits. Kaas, et al., 1981. Copyright © 1981 by MIT Press.

the others in the details of its organization and functional role. Instead of simple, continuous homunculi, the multiple representations have a micro-organization consisting of repeating "minicolumns" and "macrocolumns" that differ from individual to individual and from species to species (Kaas et al., 1981).

Most of the cortex in humans was formed in the latest stages of evolution and is given over to complex functions outside the primary sensory and motor areas. It is known as an "association" area because it connects signals of different origin into coordinated patterns. Specialized functions are located in circumscribed regions of association cortex as the result of individual experience.

As we saw in the last chapter, the localization of speech and other language functions, space perception, and the emotions have their special areas of association cortex in which they are represented. In this part of the book, we will examine the afferent systems, which provide information about the environment and feedback from our own activities. This is the neuro-physiological basis of sensation and perception.

THE FUNCTIONS OF THE AFFERENT SYSTEMS: SENSATION AND PERCEPTION

What do we perceive—sensations, features, or objects? In the early experimental psychological laboratory, the human observer was trained to intro-spect carefully and to report on the specific sensations aroused by various stimulus presentations. Given a weight to lift, if the observer reported something about the object and not the pressure on the skin of his hand or the tension in the muscle of the wrist, he was rebuked for committing a "stimulus error." The early structuralist view was that our sense organs receive stimuli, and that stimuli produce sensations. These are then combined by associative processes into the perceived qualities of objects. The structuralist approach met strong opposition from rebellious new schools of psychology.

Gestalt psychology countered that perceptions are not syntheses of sensory elements but exist at the outset as organized wholes. Even before the advent of Gestalt psychology, Ehrenfels (1890) had established the reality of "form qualities." We respond not to absolute properties of stimuli, but to the relations between them. A melody may be transposed from one key to another, and, although every single note is different than before, we may not even be aware of the change. The relations between the notes are the form qualities.

The influential founder of the functionalist school, William James, had lashed out also against the structuralist doctrine. "To introspection, our feeling of pink is surely not a portion of our feeling of scarlet; nor does the light of an electric arc seem to contain that of a tallow-candle in itself. Our perceptions," he argued, "are of definite and probable things" (1890, Vol. II, p. 546).

In fact, the elementary sensations are unconscious. We do not hear the sound wave harmonics tht make up our auditory experience; we do not perceive the spatial frequencies that comprise our visual experience. There is a good physiological reason why these sensory components or features are not attended by consciousness. The sensory centers cover only a relatively small portion of the cortex of the brain. Most of the cortex is nonmotor and nonsensory. Its function is to perceive, to imagine, to remember, to think, to invent—these are verbs that denote mental activity: the construction of patterns and relations between ourselves and the environment, the life of the mind.

The perception of an object through sight depends not only on the visual projection areas but on the activity of a special cerebral region, the function of which is simply to perceive a certain sort of object. We can, it is true, analyze a visual object into component features, contours and angles, but the analysis takes place, not on an elementary sensory level, but on an even higher level of sophistication and abstraction.

The situation is even more clear in other afferent systems where the isolation of perceptual elements is often impossible. The taste of a given dish is recognized as such. So also is an odor or the sound of a voice of a given person.

James's view correctly anticipated the direction of current research. Although stimulation begins at the sensory surface, we experience neither elementary stimuli nor compounds of associated sensations. The light you see, the sounds you hear, the heat you feel—these reveal more than elementary sensations—what you get are objects: human faces, familiar voices, music, sunshine. You are generally not aware of the components from which these perceptions are derived.

The clearest evidence we have that perception is different from sensation, and depends on the brain, comes from the observation of ambiguous figures.

The equivocal staircase figure is a classical example. (See Figure 4.4.) You perceive first the upper side of the stairs, then the lower side of the stairs, and the two percepts continue to alternate—each one a distinctly different, even *antagonistic,* perception of the same stimulus input. The stimulus pattern does not change, but the perception changes. Something inside the organism must change to shift the perception from one quality to another. The alternation does not require eye movement. Although such movements may influence the fluctuations of perception, they are more likely to follow than to initiate them (Woodworth, 1938). The change from one perception to the other can occur in examining the after-image of the figure. The fact that the alternation appears even in the after-image, fixed on the retina, proves that the identical sensory stimulation need not produce the identical perception.

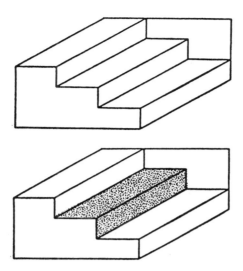

Figure 4.4. The Schröder staircase. The three-dimensional appearance of the line drawing reverses as the staircase is seen now from above, now from its underside. (Note that the shaded step and rise going up to the left splits into two parts when seen from below.)

AFFERENT (SENSORY) SYSTEMS ARE ANALYZERS

For the human being, it is probably true that everything we perceive—each object, person, sound, or scene, even our own feelings—is known to us through learning. A particular type of perceptual learning process provides our brains with information concerning the external world in which we find ourselves, and also with feedback generated by our own activity. This is the function of the *afferent systems*.

The different afferent systems—vision, hearing, and other senses—are called *analyzers* because they possess powerful sorting mechanisms for separating complex wholes into their parts (Konorski, 1967; Luria, 1966a; Pavlov, 1927; Sokolov, 1963). We can speak of the visual analyzer, the auditory analyzer, the somatosensory analyzer, and so on, covering for each sense organ the entire afferent system from the receptor surface to its highest centers in the brain. Each analyzer is exquisitely tuned to its own unique set of adequate stimuli: the eye to light waves in the visible spectrum; the ear to sound waves in the audible range; the skin and muscles to mechanical pressures; the nose to odiferous molecules, and so on.

The analyzer is a multichanneled receiving apparatus or tuner selectively responding to its own adequate channels and separating signals from noise. The analyzer acts not only as the receiver, but also as the interpreter of sensory information from the environment and the feedback from the activities of the organism. From the multitude of diverse stimuli impinging on the organism, each analyzer extracts those particular stimuli for which it is selectively sensitive.

Each analyzer, according to Konorski (1967), is built on the principle of a multilevel construction. The bottom or surface level is the receptor; the highest level is the cortex.

According to Pavlov and his followers' theory of sensation as an *active* reflex process, every analyzer contains *efferent* (motor) neurons and *inter-neurons,* as well as *afferent* (sensory) neurons so that impulses are sent to muscles and glands as well as to sensory receiving centers in the cortex. Each new or potentially significant object elicits an *orienting* (or investigatory) reaction in the organism. The orienting response consists of the generalized arousal of the organism, and selective adjustments or *targeting reflexes* of the sensory and motor apparatus for the optimal observation of the stimulus object. (See Chapter Two.)

Until recently, the process of perception was usually considered to start passively with the physical stimulus exciting a receptor and initiating activity in silent nerve fibers that went directly to the higher centers of the central nervous system. This concept of perception now appears oversimplified.

Instead we find that afferent neurons are continuously active. An external stimulus modulates that activity, increasing or decreasing it, and sets up patterns of excitation in many parts of the nervous system. No mere passive receiver of stimuli delivered by the environment, each analyzer actively seeks stimulation adequate for its excitation and sorts out those to which it is selectively sensitive. The ear responds to sounds of the external world and in humans is especially tuned to comprehend speech. The eye is sensitive to light stimuli and responds to objects and to space by means of the light reflected from the physical world to the remarkably sensitive receptors, the rods and cones at the back of the retina. But the excitation of the sensitive receptors of the eye, the ear, and the skin provides only the first stage in a sequential series of *reaction stages.*

THE CONCEPT OF REACTION STAGES

The brain controls behavior by means of its ability to integrate the activities of the nervous system. J. Hughlings Jackson (1896) first showed that perception depends upon centers in the brain as much as upon the peripheral sense organs from which messages are received by these centers. Robert S. Woodworth (1927) developed this idea into the concept of *reaction stages.* Before the cortical regions are reached and before interpretation takes place, the input from the periphery is transformed by convergent and divergent pathways in a series of reaction stages. Each reaction stage is a progressive transformation and integration of the preceding stage, representing successively newer, more precise levels of neural processing. Only the cortical association levels are represented in conscious experience.

Stimuli striking the receptive surfaces (eye, ear, or other sense organ) initiate a series of events that result in action by the brain to make (or suppress) a motor response. Intervening between the initial stimuli and the final behavioral act, there may be an extraordinarily complex and varied sequence of reactions, including mental and emotional reactions: percepts, feelings, images, and intentions. "Now the relation of each stage in the total process to that which just precedes it is the relation of response to stimulus.... Each stage is aroused by the preceding stage, and in turn arouses the stage which follows" (Woodworth, 1927, p. 62). In addition to the responses directly traceable to the environmental stimuli, Woodworth suggested that other responses are synchronously excited by intraorganic stimuli from various parts of the nervous system. These reactions follow each other, not as a chain and not in a continuous flow of energy throughout the organism, but in a heterarchical succession of stages. Each stage is a fresh reaction to the preceding stage and concomitant neural events, and each stage in turn provokes new reactions involving fresh neural mechanisms in the stages that follow.

Each reaction takes time: each stage has its own latency and duration. The total response may be compared to a succession of overlapping waves of activity—the successive awakening to activity of different parts of the organism. Converging impulses of different origin are combined at each stage into an entirely new message that takes account of all the inputs. This process is called *integration* (Kuffler & Nicholls, 1976, p. 20).

The sense of excitement in the brain sciences today began about 30 years ago with the experimental verification that different sensory systems of the brain actually do work in this way. The key to the mind is in terms of its elementary units—individual nerve cells. By studying nerve cells with analytical techniques, we have learned about the functioning of the nervous system as a whole.

THE NEURAL CODES

Different afferent fibers convey information that gives rise to different sensory experiences, but all use the same types of action potentials. All follow the general rule: they encode the *intensity* of stimuli by the frequency of discharge of their action potentials—a *frequency code*. According to the frequency code, the stronger the stimulus, the greater the frequency of firing of any single responsive fiber. A stronger stimulus also activates a greater number of receptors and increases the size of the population of active neurons—a *population code.* The same principles apply to the motor systems; an increase in the population of active efferent fibers, and in the frequency of their individual action potentials, increases the strength of the muscle contraction.

Afferent fibers generally communicate *quality,* not by any temporal pattern of activity, but by their place or location in the system. Somatic sensory fibers use a *place code* for specifying the kind of stimulus—light touch or deep pressure, for example—that evokes their response. A similar pressure on the eyeball also arouses a sensation of light; a blow in this region may cause you to "see" stars. The place code depends on where the nerve fibers come from and where they are going, their point of origin and their terminal address in the brain. These sites (and the various stations on the way) specify *what,* apart from its strength, the stimulus is, and *where* it is located in the body or surrounding space. An excellent illustration is the phenomenon of *paradoxical cold.* The temperature receptors are punctate: they can be mapped on a grid stamped on the back of the hand or wrist by successively applying warm and cold stimuli to the separate spots. If now you apply a heat stimulus of 45° centigrade to a single cold spot, what the subject will experience is not heat or pain but cold. The otherwise painful heat stimulus excites cold receptors so that they increase their firing rate. Regardless of the actual stimulus, the cold fiber population of neurons delivers only its own specific sensation—cold.

This specificity is the basis for what we now call a *labeled line code.* Fast pain is an abrupt and sharp sensation carried by large, myelinated, fast-conducting "A" fibers; slow pain is a sickening sensation carried by unmyelinated, small, slow "C" fibers. The distinction is important. Delayed information that a stimulus is noxious may result in damage to tissue long before the sensation reaches the brain. Fast-acting fibers allow the subject to act promptly to escape from a possibly injurious stimulus. Mechanical nociceptors (*nocere:* to injure) are activated by strong, sharp, or pointed things. Sometimes more deeply embedded chemoreceptors are also activated and serve to prolong the effects of the quickly adapting mechanoreceptors. The labeled line code conveys a remarkable specificity. It tells us that the pain we feel is sharp, an emergency signal, or that the fruit is sweet, or the soup salty. In these cases, the sensory pathways lead directly from specific receptors to their terminals in the brain.

Curiously, there is one respect in which the *temporal pattern of activity* in a somatic sensory receptor makes a difference. Rapidly acting mechanoreceptors are particularly sensitive to high frequency sinusoidal mechanical stimuli. These produce a sensation of *vibration* deep in the tissues. Slow frequency sinusoidal mechanical stimuli evoke a light *flutter* in the skin surface, the brush of a feather or a butterfly's wing across the tiny hairs of the arm. Anesthesia of the skin raises the threshold of the flutter sense but has no effect on vibration sensitivity. Here, then, is a somatosensory pattern code, analogous to the coding systems used by the pattern frequency analyzers for sensory quality—audition (sound wave frequency) and vision (spatial frequency).

In these last two, our most important distance receptors, the pattern of activity is critical. The auditory system, a temporal frequency analyzer, depends in large part on *pattern coding.* We can hear tones as high as 15,000 to 20,000 hertz (cycles per second) and discriminate the pitch of slightly different frequencies—faster by far than the capacity of any nerve fiber to put out spikes. Nerve fibers have a refractory period that limits their maximum rate of firing to about 1,000 impulses per second. The problem has been to find the code that this analyzer uses to represent pitch with the fidelity that appears so strikingly in our ability to tune musical instruments and to discriminate vocal intonation. The problem is compounded when we recall that frequency of discharge is an intensity code and cannot be monopolized to convey pitch or other qualitative dimensions of the stimulus.

Hermann von Helmholtz (1877), famous sensory physiologist of the nineteenth century, proposed that the basilar membrane, the receptor organ of the inner ear, which is narrow at its base and widens toward the apex of the cochlea, acts like many independently tuned resonators, much like piano strings, each activated by a different frequency. His idea was that the independent resonators would cause a small place on the basilar membrane to vibrate. A century later, George von Békésy (1960) showed that a traveling wave moves along the membrane causing not a small, but a large, area to vibrate. However, the peak motion of the basilar membrane in response to sounds of different frequencies does occur at the points predicted by Helmholtz. Auditory (eighth-nerve) fibers that project from the spiral ganglion cells of the cochlea are only a single hair cell in width. Although an individual fiber will respond to a range of frequencies, each fiber is most responsive to a particular frequency called its *characteristic frequency.* As the frequency of the stimulus increases, the peak motion progresses toward the base (the narrow end) of the cochlea.

Interestingly, fibers with tuning curves centered on very low frequencies may fire on only some presentations of their characteristic frequency and not on others. Their responses are probabilistic and may phase lock, that is, occur only at a particular time during each cycle of their characteristic frequency. Such fibers utilize two different codes: a *place code,* since they innervate the apex (wide end) of the cochlea, and a *volley principle,* since they respond in a predictable way to a recurrent temporal aspect of the stimulating wave form. This generosity on the part of nature may be the reason that we can not only hear the pitch of bass or very low tones, but also perceive the vibrations they produce.

The special features of neurons, their distinctive shape and outer membrane capable of generating nerve impulses, and especially their terminal buttons, at *synapses* or junctions between neurons, enable them to transmit information from one cell to another largely by chemical messages. The discharge of a neuron reflects the activation of hundreds of synapses by converging neurons. The neural impulse travels from the dendrites or cell membrane itself through the axon to the synapse. At the synapse the terminal ends or synaptic knobs at the ends of the axon release a package of chemical substance called a *neurotransmitter*. The arrival of a nerve impulse by any of the impinging neurons at the dendrites of the neuron next in line may have one of two effects, excitatory or inhibitory, on the postsynaptic neuron. The dendritic system of this neuron sums the activity of many other neurons by producing *graded potentials* that will determine whether or not the neuron fires. Eccles and his associates first showed how postsynaptic graded potentials follow each volley of presynaptic stimulation. They depend on the nature of the presynaptic stimulation and consist either of depolarization or hyperpolarization of the postsynaptic membrane. If they depolarize, they increase the probability of the neuron firing and are called excitatory postsynaptic potentials or EPSPs; if they hyperpolarize, they decrease the probability of the neuron firing and are called inhibitory postsynaptic potentials or IPSPs.

The algebraic summation of these excitatory and inhibitory impulses will determine the response of the neuron receiving them. The firing of the neuron is an all-or-none response, unlike the dendritic graded potential; the action potential either occurs or it does not—there is no in-between. Many neurons converge their signals on any single cell, and each neuron sends divergent signals to many other cells.

The use of very fine wires enables neuroscientists to penetrate a tiny column of brain cells without injury to surrounding tissue. By connecting the microelectrode to a recording device, they can monitor the activity of a single cell at a time. (See Figure 4.5.) This research has provided the most elegant and sophisticated analyses of the localization of higher functions of the brain. One such microelectrode is carefully placed next to a nerve cell in a specific area of the brain and linked to an oscilloscope. The researcher can then watch the tiny voltage changes which occur in the cell, called "action potentials" or "spikes." The rate at which the spikes occur represents a code for the neuron's activity. This rate depends upon the nature of the visual or auditory stimulus that is responsible for exciting that particular cell. For example, if a researcher records the spikes from a given brain cell in the visual cortex of a cat and presents a visual pattern of vertical stripes on the screen facing the cat's eye, the cell may burst into an excited frenzy of spikes. Turning the stimulus pattern on its side to expose the same stripes in horizontal orientation returns the cell to its original cruising rate of firing. This happens because the cell responds preferentially to vertical stripes and is indifferent to other orientations. Like the sensory hearing cell with its characteristic *temporal frequency,*

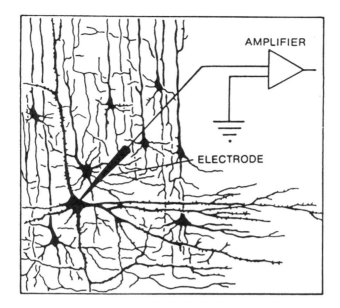

Figure 4.5. Extracellular recording with a fine wire microelectrode placed close to the nerve cell. Kuffler & Nicholls, 1976.

the cortical visual cell has a characteristic *orientation,* and, as we shall discover, it also has a characteristic *spatial frequency,* responding maximally to certain patterns of spatial information and not at all to others. These microelectrode studies of the visual system in animals reveal the highly specialized functions of single brain cells and give new insight into the startling precision of their sensitivity and their local connectivity.

THE ORGANIZATION OF THE VISUAL ANALYZER

Light striking the retina of the eye initiates an intricate process that results in vision. The transformation of physical light waves or quanta of energy into a meaningful representation of the external world occurs partly in the eye but mostly in the brain.

Think of what is involved in seeing a moving object, for example, a baby watching its mother's face, one of the first objects the baby learns to recognize. The face is now close by, now far away, now leaning down, now frowning, now smiling. The ever-changing pattern of stimulation must be integrated into a coherent, unitary object.

Now neuropsychologists think they have begun to understand how this task is achieved.

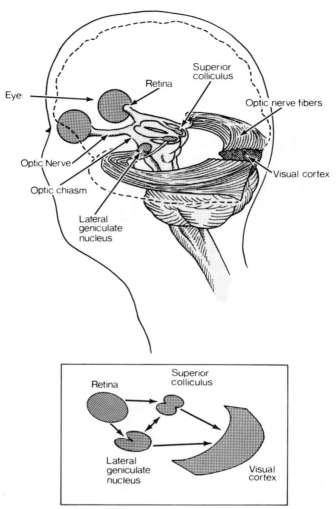

Figure 4.6.   The visual analyzer. The optic pathways radiate from the retina to the visual cortex via the lateral geniculate nucleus and the superior colliculus. Redrawn from various sources.

The process begins with the photochemical responses of 130 million light-sensitive receptor cells, the *rods* and *cones,* in each *retina.* These receptors *transduce* light energy into electrochemical signals to other cells in the retina (bipolar cells) and these in turn excite or inhibit ganglion cells, so called because many messages converge on each one. The ganglion cells summate and funnel the information they receive into the optic nerve, a bundle of one million nerve fibers that leaves the retina and leads, via the lateral geniculate body, a way station in the thalamus, to the primary visual

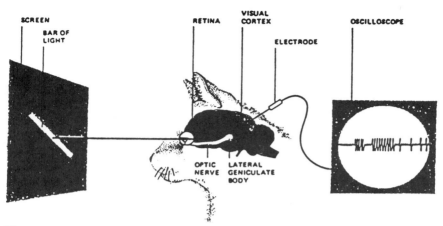

Figure 4.7.   Mapping the receptive fields of the activity of single cells in various regions of the visual analyzer. Kimball, J.W. *Biology* (4th Edition) 1978. Copyright Addison-Wesley Publishing Company, Inc., Reading, Ma. Reprinted with permission.

cortex (striate cortex) of the brain. The reduction from 130 million to 1 million signals means that a good deal of selectivity has already taken place in the retina. (See Figure 4.6.)

Receptive Field Studies

Stephen J. Kuffler, working with cats at Johns Hopkins Hospital in 1952, discovered that patterning takes place at the early stages of the process, in the ganglion cells of the retina (Kuffler & Nicholls, 1976). These ganglion cells are spontaneously active even in the dark. Kuffler found that some of the cells would increase the frequency of their firing if he shone a small spot of light in a circular area of the retina; others would decrease the frequency of their firing. An increase above baseline firing was called an "on-response"; a decrease was called an "off-response." A given cell produced an on-response or an off-response depending on where in the retina the light fell. That region of the retina that influences the firing rate of a cell is called the *receptive field* of the cell. (See Figure 4.7.) Stimulation outside the receptive field produces no effect at all. The field itself can be subdivided into two distinct regions, one of which acts to increase impulses, and the other to suppress impulses in the cell. A spot of light has *opposite* effects depending on its exact position within the receptive field. In one area, for example, the light excites a given cell, but, if Kuffler simply shifted the spot by one millimeter across the retina, the firing decreased. The tiny shift converted the "on" response to an inhibitory "off" response. Lighting up the entire area even with a very bright flash does not have the marked effect of a spot of light placed on the exact center of the receptive field of a given ganglion cell. (See Figure 4.8.)

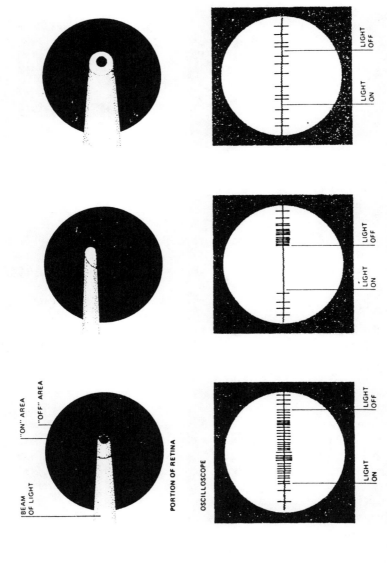

Figure 4.8. Receptive fields of retinal ganglion cells. Left: light falling on a small circular field of the retina increases the activity of an "on-center" ganglion cell. Center: light directed around the perimeter of the "on" area suppresses that ganglion cell. Right: light shining on both areas produces no new effect. Other ganglion cells have a central "off" area ringed by an "on" surround. Kimball, 1978.

A simplifying principle emerges. All the receptive fields of the ganglion cells are concentric circles, but there are only two basic receptive field types: the "on-center" with "off-surround," and the "off-center" with "on-surround." In the "on-center" type, turning on the light produces a vigorous response if it completely fills the center of the receptive field. Turning off the light stimulates the center of an "off-center" cell. The spotlike center and its surround are antagonistic; therefore, if they are illuminated simultaneously, they tend to cancel each other and there is only a weak response (or none) from the ganglion cell. The size of receptive fields depends on their location in the retina. They are smallest in the center of the eye where acuity is highest.

The cells next in line in the lateral geniculate body (geniculate means "kneeling," and here the layers of visual cells are bent like a knee) have the same characteristics as those found in retinal ganglion cells: circular receptive fields with on-centers and off-surrounds, or, conversely, off-centers and on-surrounds. An intense, diffuse light over the entire retina does not affect a geniculate cell as strongly as a small spot that precisely covers the center of the cell's receptive field.

The critical point emerges. These cells are essentially *contrast* detectors. It is the difference in illumination between the center and the surround of the cell's receptive field that determines the cell's response. Even at the earliest stages of the visual processing, the retina and the geniculate cells extract relevant information about the outside world. Because these cells have circular symmetry, they respond well to a dark line or a bar of light in any orientation; what matters is that the stimulus covers a large part of the center region and only a small part, or none, of the surround. These cells thus respond to the relation between the light level in one small area of the scene and the surrounding illumination—an early stage of segregation between figure and ground.

Beyond the lateral geniculate bodies, new fibers course back through the brain to the visual area of the cerebral cortex. In an elegant series of studies, David Hubel and Torsten Wiesel (1962; 1968; 1969) of Harvard University Medical School have mapped further stages of the visual process in the cortex of the cat and the monkey. They were recognized for this research by the award in 1981 of the Nobel Prize in Physiology and Medicine.

Single Cells in Visual Cortex

Hubel and Wiesel's technique was to anesthetize a cat or monkey and have the animal face a screen on which patterns of light were shone that could be focused on the retinal surfaces. A fine microelectrode recorded the responses from a single cell in the visual pathway. By mapping the areas on the screen that increased or decreased the impulse frequency above or below baseline (spontaneous discharge) level, these investigators were able to determine the location and shape of the receptive fields of individual cells. Note that no matter how far along the visual pathway any visual cell might be, it requires an image on the retina to evoke a meaningful response in that particular cell. Every cell is linked, however indirect and complex the route, to the receptive surface of the retina and thus depends ultimately on this proximal stimulation.

The key to the success of Hubel and Wiesel's approach was that they asked one question repeatedly for each single neuron into which they penetrated with a microelectrode. They asked, not simply, "What does it see?" but "What is the most effective stimulus for evoking a response in this particular cell?" Since all the impulses appear alike, they had to find out what stimulus evokes the greatest frequency of discharge in the cell. To answer this question, many different stimuli had to be presented. Instead of shining bright flashes without any form, Hubel and Wiesel presented lines, bars, and slits, patterns of light and dark with different shapes, sizes, and orientations.

Simple Cell, Complex Cells, and Hypercomplex Cells

Hubel and Wiesel found that the best stimuli for the cells in the visual cortex were not circular spots or rings, but straight lines. A large group of cells they called "simple" responded to slits on a dark background, or dark bars on a light background, or edges, contours, or boundaries between light and dark areas. Whether or not a simple cell responds depends on the orientation of the stimulus and its position on the receptive field of the cell. "Each cell may seem to have its specific duties; it takes care of one restricted part of the retina, responds best to one particular shape of stimulus and to one particular orientation" (Hubel, 1979, p. 8).

A second group of cortical cells called "complex" also respond best to bars, slits, or edges provided they are properly oriented. Unlike simple cells, however, they respond to moving lines or gratings swept across the receptive field and thus are not particular about the exact position of the stimulus. Rather it seems as though one complex cell performs a primitive sort of generalization over a wide area—"that's a vertical set of lines"—and another cell—"horizontal bars moving up"—in the visual field.

At still higher levels, Hubel and Wiesel found that cells require stimuli that are even more precisely defined than those accessing the complex cells. "Hypercomplex" cells respond only to appropriately oriented lines, slits, bars, or lines with stopped ends and that move in only one direction, left to right, or up and down. Still further on, "hypercomplex cells of higher order" demand stimuli that are stopped at both ends with corners or angles that shape their receptive fields into rods and rectangles. A narrow bar will cause the higher order hypercomplex cell to discharge. But the bar must not exceed a certain width, nor can a grating exceed a certain spatial frequency, or it will decrease the activity of the cell because it encroaches on the inhibitory areas. (See Figure 4.9.)

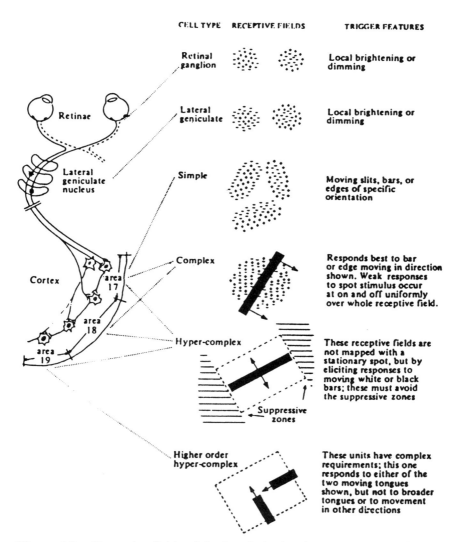

CELL TYPE	RECEPTIVE FIELDS	TRIGGER FEATURES

Retinal ganglion — Local brightening or dimming

Lateral geniculate — Local brightening or dimming

Simple — Moving slits, bars, or edges of specific orientation

Complex — Responds best to bar or edge moving in direction shown. Weak responses to spot stimulus occur at on and off uniformly over whole receptive field.

Hyper-complex — These receptive fields are not mapped with a stationary spot, but by eliciting responses to moving white or black bars; these must avoid the suppressive zones

Suppressive zones

Higher order hyper-complex — These units have complex requirements; this one responds to either of the two moving tongues shown, but not to broader tongues or to movement in other directions

Retinae

Lateral geniculate nucleus

Cortex — area 17

area 18

area 19

Figure 4.9. Receptive fields of single cells in the visual cortex. The diagram shows cell types and trigger features at various stages in the visual system of the cat. The primate brain is similarly organized. Barlow & Mollon, 1982. By permission of copyright holder © 1982 Cambridge University Press.

The higher the order of the cell, the more refined the cell's requirements for stimulation. In addition to orientational specificity, higher order cells demand some *discontinuity,* such as a line that stops and forms an angle or a corner. Thus an extra inhibitory area seems to be added to the two on either side; the stimulus must not extend into any of the three forbidden areas. *Lateral inhibition* has increased the specificity of the cell.

As the successive levels of the visual analyzer are traversed from retina to upper layers of the cortex, the demands made on a stimulus for activation of a neuron become increasingly precise, not for position in the visual field, but for shape, orientation, and size.

Now we can begin to understand why the infant can recognize her mother's face whatever its position in the visual field. In the transformation from simple cells to complex cells, the visual information will generalize from an exact position to a more abstract perspective in which field position is no longer critical. Knowing the organization of the receptive fields in the retina, we can determine how they are transformed at each reaction stage. At each stage, the ability to abstract is increased, the cells becoming both more specialized and more organized in their requirements for activation. Certain elementary requirements, such as retinal position, drop out; other more sophisticated stimulus attributes, such as orientation and directionality of movement, come into play. As the cells increase in the complexity of their requirements for optical stimulation, they also disregard alterations in minor aspects. It is as though absolute values lose their importance; the critical feature for the hypercomplex cells' response is, instead, the *relation between selected elements.*

COLUMNS OF THE STRIATE CORTEX

Orientation Columns

Instead of haphazard arrangement, the cells are lined up in a way that makes it easy for them to interconnect and perform their exacting analyses. Repeated cortical penetrations gave a clear picture. With the electrode moving at right angles to the surface through the thickness of the gray matter, the series of single cells—simple, complex, and hypercomplex—encountered one after the other have the identical field axis orientation. Cells with similar receptive field position, similar eye preference, or similar orientation, reveal an interesting regularity. If they share a common property, they are grouped together. But when the electrode was driven obliquely from the surface, a different picture emerged: the field axis changed in steps of 10 to 20 degrees repeatedly as though a series of columns with slightly different field

orientations was transversed. Separate columns exist for each field orientation, and they are arranged in parallel series corresponding to the *successive*
positions of the second hand on the face of a clock. (See Figure 4.10.)

Eye Dominance Columns

In any single vertical electrode penetration, Hubel and Wiesel found that
neighboring cells proved almost invariably to favor the same eye. When they
shifted the microelectrode across the cortex, the eye preference shifted about
every half millimeter, switching abruptly from left eye to right eye. The cortex
thus proved to be partitioned for ocular dominance in a very precise and fairly
equitable way.

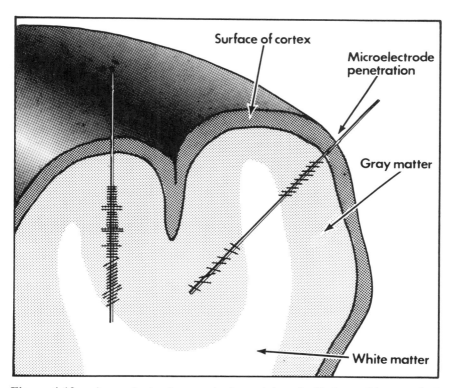

Figure 4.10.   As an electrode records the activity of cell after cell in a vertical
penetration from surface to white matter, the axis orientation of receptive
fields remains the same. Successive penetrations in an oblique direction show
that the axis orientations change progressively and often abruptly. Redrawn
from Hubel & Wiesel, 1962; 1963.

The existence of small steplike changes in orientation and abrupt alternations of eye preference in horizontal or oblique penetrations, together with the absence of any change either in orientation or eye preference in vertical penetrations, strongly hinted at a vertical partitioning of the cortex. Narrow columns of cells with identical or nearly identical properties seemed to run from the surface of the cortex down to the white matter of the brain. Except for occasional abrupt reversals in orientation preference, neighboring columns seemed to serve neighboring orientations around the clock face. Adjacent columns also seemed to convey input from one eye or the other in alternation. How were these two functions—orientation and eye dominance—organized? What was needed was some anatomical method of verifying the electrophysiological results.

Anatomical Confirmation

At about this time, Louis Sokoloff and his group at the National Institutes of Mental Health invented the 2-deoxyglucose technique for selectively staining the most active neurons in the brain. With this procedure, the experimenter injects an animal with the chemical that has been labeled with a radioactive isotope and stimulates one eye so as to activate particular neurons responsive to selected input from that eye. (See Figure 4.11.) For example, the experimenter may move a pattern of black and white vertical stripes back and forth in front of the animal's right eye. This pattern will stimulate particular neurons that respond to vertical gratings moving both to the left and to the right via the right eye. Slices of brain tissue are then removed and pressed against a treated photographic plate that is sensitive to the radioactive particles. This will reveal the location of those cells most activated by the preceding stimulation.

The results delighted Hubel and Wiesel. The autoradiographs confirmed the existence of narrow columns (roughly half a millimeter wide) extending through the full thickness of the cortex and running from the surface to the white matter below. The investigators were even more impressed by the results obtained using complementary methods based on axonal transport. (See Figure 4.12.) These showed the functional architecture of the visual cortex in all three dimensions (Gilbert & Wiesel, 1981; LeVay, Hubel, & Wiesel, 1975).

Rather like a zebra's, the stripes are irregular, especially near the center of gaze and along the line that maps the horizon. Yet the width of a set of two adjacent stripes (about .8 millimeter) is constant. The columns are grouped into blocks of tissue (about one millimeter square and two millimeters deep) with interdigitated orientation columns and ocular dominance columns. Hubel and Wiesel call the block containing the whole set of columns for analyzing lines of all orientations by both eyes a *hypercolumn*.

The hypercolumn is a module. Hubel and Wiesel (1979, p. 95) write: "To know the organization of this chunk of tissue is to know the organization for

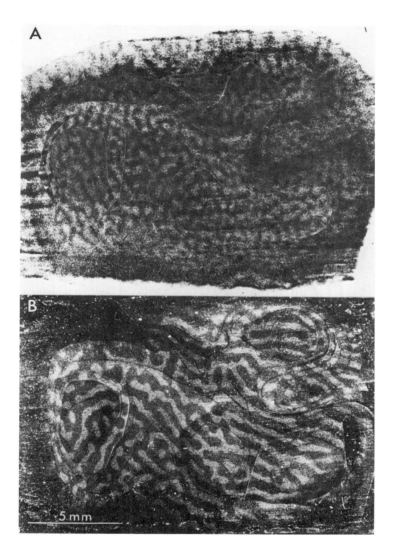

Figure 4.11. Orientation and ocular dominance columns are revealed by autoradiographic labeling as patterns of alternating dark and light bands in sections of monkey visual cortex. The radioactive label accumulates in the metabolically active neurons following the prolonged presentation of a stimulus in a given orientation and to a given eye. (A) Orientation columns appear as curved bands of uniform width. (B) Ocular dominance columns demonstrate the preference of columns of single units for stimulation via either the left or the right eye. Hubel, Wiesel, & Stryker, 1978. Courtesy of David H. Hubel. By permission of Alan R. Liss, Inc. Publisher.

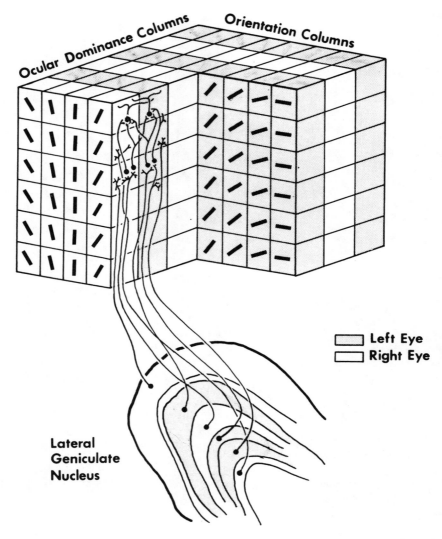

Left Eye
Right Eye

Figure 4.12. A cubic module or *hypercolumn*. Columns of the visual cortex receive input from the lateral geniculate nucleus (LGN). Alternate layers of the LGN each send input from only the left eye or the right eye. These projected afferents are segregated in ocular dominance columns that are orthogonal to the vertical orientational columns. In any single column, the cells respond optimally to their preferred orientation and either the left or the right eye. Adapted from Hubel & Wiesel, 1972; 1974.

all of area 17 (the striate cortex); the whole must be mainly an iterated version of this elementary unit."

Beyond area 17, what happens?

Area 17 sends not just one, but several, projections to areas 18 and 19 (secondary and tertiary visual projection cortex). This suggests that the higher order cells in these regions have different functional properties from area 17. For example, S.M. Zeki (1980) at University College, London, finds several regions in area 18 that code for color, while others code for movement.

Spatial Frequency Columns

Recent evidence adds a new basic minicolumn to join orientation and eye dominance in processing visual stimulation: *spatial frequency.* A grating pattern consists of alternate light stripes and dark stripes: spatial frequency refers to the number of such stripes, defined in terms of cycles per degree of visual angle. The finer the spacing, the higher the number of cycles per degree; the wider the spacing, the lower the number of cycles per degree. Russell DeValois and his group (Albrecht, DeValois, & Thorell, 1980; Tootel, Silverman, & DeValois, 1981) at the University of California at Berkeley found that the optimal spatial frequency varies from neuron to neuron and demonstrated with both single-cell recordings and the Sokoloff staining technique that spatial frequency is indeed organized in narrow columns of cells with identical spatial frequency (size-detecting) sensitivity. (See Figure 4.13.)

Cells sensitive to higher spatial frequencies (finely spaced patterns) are confined to the area centralis in the striate cortex; lower frequency units are more widely distributed, as would be expected for very large or close objects. We use central fixation where acuity is highest for reading fine print; large objects can be observed even in dim illumination from the corners of the eye. Here then is another major example of columnar organization in the primary visual cortex. The strategy allows signals from the receptors to reach the cortex by several parallel pathways, each carrying similar but not identical information. This arrangement avoids needless duplication, but allows a specialized division of labor by different groups of cells.

Each region not only handles different sorts of information, but the opportunities for interconnections between inputs serve to provide the richness, color, and detail that create a visual world.

COLUMNS IN THE SOMATIC SENSORY SYSTEM

The arrangement of columns into three-dimensional blocks in the primary visual cortex is not limited to the visual system. Similar columnar architecture was found by Vernon B. Mountcastle (1978) of Johns Hopkins University

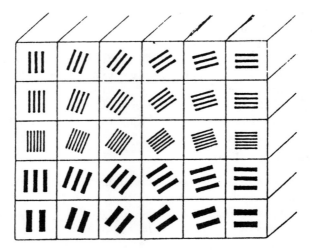

Figure 4.13. Cubic module of the cat striate cortex showing the possible arrangement of receptive fields according to their spatial frequency and orientation. The gratings in each row have the same spatial frequency and those in each column have the same orientation. Maffei, 1978.

School of Medicine in the *somatic* sensory area of the cortex. (See Figure 4.14.) There the basic topography is a map of the opposite half of the body on which two sets of columns are superimposed, one for pressure stimuli from the skin or joint receptors and another for light touch. Still other columns of cells respond only to movement of hairs on the skin.

Perhaps the columnar subdivisions found for vision and somesthesis will be generalized to audition and other sensory areas. If this turns out to be the case, a remarkable and simplifying principle emerges. The cortical neurons processing related information are packed together in an orderly, functional arrangement of fine periodic subdivisions. Groups of neurons do indeed perform similar jobs—an economical arrangement that saves long lines of communication and speeds up connections.

THE ORGANIZATION OF THE CEREBRAL CORTEX

The human cerebral cortex has six horizontal cell layers. These layers vary in the size, shape, and density of their cells. They may be distinguished also by their thickness and the ramification of their dendrites.

In the late nineteenth century, Brodmann used the distinctive properties of the six cell layers to divide the cortex into 50 different *cytoarchitectonic* regions. These are known as *Brodmann's areas,* and his numbered map

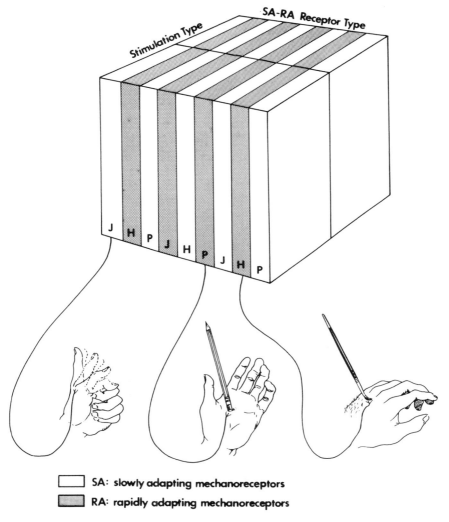

SA: slowly adapting mechanoreceptors
RA: rapidly adapting mechanoreceptors

Figure 4.14. The somatosensory cortex is also arranged in cubic modules. Here each vertical column from surface to white matter responds selectively either to joint (J), pressure (P), or hair (H) receptors. Horizontally, the cortex is organized in layers that receive alternately from slowly adapting and rapidly adapting mechanoreceptors. Modified and redrawn from Mountcastle, 1957.

(Brodmann, 1909) is in active use today to specify the location of different functions as they are revealed by new electrophysiological or staining techniques. (See Figure 4.15.)

The six layers are functionally important in two different ways. First, they project back to different regions of the brain where the signals regulate different aspects of behavior. Secondly, the layers represent a ladder of complexity or increasing specificity of cellular reactivity. For example, in vision, cells of similar complexity tend to be located in the same layer. Cells with circularly symmetrical receptive fields and thus no preferred orientation

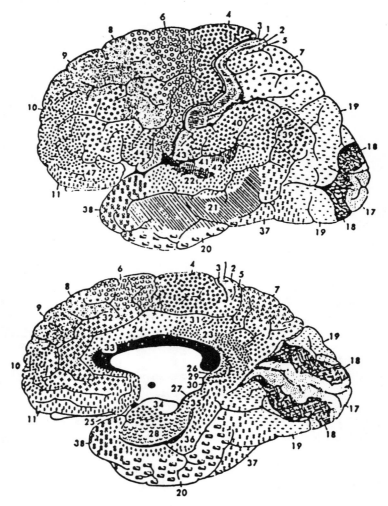

Figure 4.15. Brodmann's cytoarchitectonic maps. Brodmann, 1909.

are found low in layer IV, the single cells just above them in the upper part of layer IV; the complex cells begin in layer III, and the higher order hypercomplex cells are in layer II.

The laminar organization of the visual cortex has important consequences for the distribution and further processing of visual information. Layer VI projects back to the lateral geniculate nucleus, and this exerts feedback control on the input coming from that region to the cortex and elsewhere; the pyramidal cells of layer V project to the superior colliculus where they aid in tracking movements of the eyes; the stellate cells of layer IV integrate the local input, and layers II and III feed forward to still higher centers in the association cortex where they participate in consciously experienced visual perception and form associations with other sensory and motor units.

In the somatosensory cortex, the six horizontal cell layers are cleaved by narrow vertical columns that run from surface to white matter. Each column is specific for a submodality, joint, pressure, and hair stimulation. The columns are further partitioned into two types of mechanoreceptors: rapidly adapting and slowly adapting cells. The different layers project to different parts of the brain.

Powerful new methods are now beginning to reveal the location of specific functions in the largest part of Brodmann's map—the association areas of the cortex beyond the primary and secondary projective regions.

But only the primary sensory and motor areas have fairly distinct boundaries; the boundaries of the secondary areas are less distinct, and the tertiary, and even more central association areas are still less clearly circumscribed. That does not mean, however, that their functions are less specific or specialized. The general rule seems to be widespread: increasing selectivity and complexity together with greater abstractness or symbolic function as we move in from the receptive surfaces of the body toward the centers of association and integration in the most newly evolved parts of the brain.

FEATURE-EXTRACTING NEURONS

In a well-known paper with the unforgettable title, "What the Frog's Eye Tells the Frog's Brain," Lettvin et al. (1959) reported their discovery that the frog's retina contains neurons that respond selectively only to certain specific stimulus features: moving edges, a light turned on or off, convex boundaries, dimming of illumination, and changes in contrast. One particular type of retinal cell is of especial interest because it does not respond to changes in light intensity but gives a vigorous discharge to a small dark circular spot moved rapidly across the unit's receptive field.

What role could such feature-signaling neurons in the nervous system play in a psychological theory of perception and cognition? Colin Blakemore (1974), professor of physiology at Oxford University, divides them into two general classes: *species-specific* and *universal feature detectors.* Species-specific feature detectors are neurons that are found only in some species and not others. Some elements of the environment may be critical for the survival of a particular species of animal, and the process of natural selection has targeted certain classes of neurons for their specific concern. They do not seem to require prior experience on the part of the animal to become effective but may be fully functional at the time of hatching or birth.

Such feature-detecting neurons might evoke stereotyped reactions in the triggerlike fashion described by ethologists for inborn "fixed action patterns" in birds and fish. (See Chapter Two.) The frog lives on flies, and evolution has provided the frog's eye with retinal cells that function exclusively, as the brilliant psychophysiologist Horace Barlow (1953) of Cambridge University suggested earlier, as "bug detectors." These cells provoke orienting and snapping responses of the frog directed at prey. The evocative stimuli for these ganglion cells must be moving—a frog surrounded by motionless, or dead but still edible, flies will starve to death. Here, in the language of the ethologist, is an "innate releasing mechanism" that responds selectively to "sign" or "key" stimuli that fit the lock of each member of a class of neurons at the biologically appropriate moment. Key stimuli are usually simple. They can be discovered by experiments with models of different stimulus patterns or "dummies." For a herring gull to roll an egg into its nest, the egg must be spotted; the butterfly and hummingbird react to colors when visiting blossoms; crickets and grasshoppers react to their own specific song; chicks will follow their own mother's call, but not others'.

In the stickleback fish, the red belly releases fighting; a wax model, even a wooden pencil, with a red underside, but otherwise unfishlike, is attacked at once. (See Figure 4.16.) If the model is turned upside down, no fighting is released. The "red belly below" is the critical feature for the female also, but unlike the aggressive male, she will be attracted by the red-bellied male stickleback (Tinbergen, 1951). Yet several key stimuli may summate in their effectiveness for a particular response. Add to the red belly, the head-down threat position of stickleback rivals, and the combined strength of these cues will release much more intensive male fighting behavior than either feature alone. Tinbergen suggested that in the nervous system of each animal there is a pooling station that integrates the different features (red color, below; head-down threat position) and, by summation, in this instance of the male stickleback, evokes an aggressive attack. Theoretically, all of the stickleback's behavior, whether male or female, could be accounted for by the activity of one central neuron for each fixed action pattern: attack, defense, courtship, mating, feeding, and so on, through the list of drives. (See Figure 4.17.)

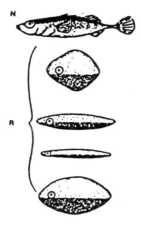

Figure 4.16. Stickleback models. Only the top form (N) without red belly escapes attack. Odd-shaped, red-bellied dummies (R) release attack responses. After Tinbergen, 1951.

Barlow and Hill (1963) described ganglion cells in rabbit retina that are selective for direction and orientation. In higher mammals, not the retina, but the cortex, contains feature detectors. Single cells in the visual cortex of cats and monkeys are highly specific in their responses to spatial frequency or size orientation, and also sensitive to the binocular disparity or stereoscopic distance of the stimulus (Hubel & Wiesel, 1979; Barlow, Blakemore, & Pettigrew, 1967). In fact, Blakemore concludes: "Every species whose visual system has been probed by microelectrodes has been found to possess a limited number of classes of neurons, each sensitive to a particular combination of elementary sensory events, which one could call a feature" (1974, p. 105).

Some feature-detecting neurons are found in all visual systems that have been investigated and are perhaps universal in all sighted creatures. Examples of *universal feature detectors* in all *visual* nervous systems that have been probed by microelectrodes include the following classes of neurons, each sensitive to a particular combination of sensory stimuli:

Universal Visual Feature Detectors

1. Contrast or edge detectors—respond to local contrast between a light area and a dark area. (On, off, and on-off cells discharge briefly at the beginning or end of a period of illumination or at both the onset and offset of a light.)
2. Movement detectors—respond to changing contrast or drifting dark-light boundaries.

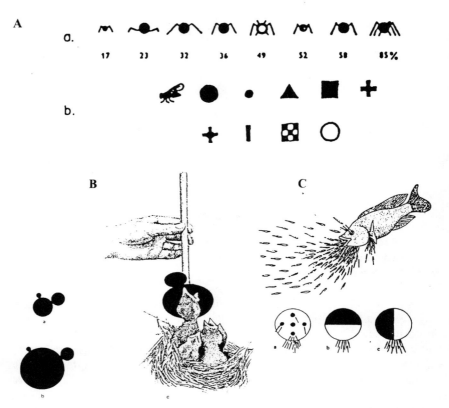

Figure 4.17. Key stimuli or releasers of fixed action patterns. (A) (a) Dummy stimuli that release mating display in spiders. (b) Releasers of predatory stalking behavior in spiders. (B) Two-headed models that release gaping in birds. Eibl-Eibesfeldt, 1970. (C) Young cichlids, when startled, move toward their mother's mouth. They also respond to dark and light disks. Eibl-Eibesfeldt, 1970.

3. Direction of movement detectors—respond to edges moved in one direction across the receptive field.
4. Size or spatial frequency grating detectors—respond to specific bar widths or number of cycles per degree of visual angle in a grating of dark and light stripes.
5. Orientation of edge detectors—respond to horizontal, vertical, or oblique position of lines, stripes, or gratings.
6. Overall luminance detectors—respond to dimming or brightening of illumination.

Many purely spatial features of visual stimuli are encoded by a *single* population of cells. For vision, the mathematically simplest spatial signal is not a line or an edge but a grating whose luminance varies sinusoidally along one axis. This sine wave grating, the homologue of a pure tone in the auditory system, has been found to be the most effective stimulus for exciting cortical neurons in the primary visual projective areas in cat and monkey, (Tootell, Silverman, & DeValois, 1981). These cells respond selectively to the main parameters of sine wave gratings: spatial frequency, orientation, contrast, and phase. Anatomical evidence by selective staining produces direct confirmation. These spatial frequency-selective cells are organized in narrow vertical columns in the striate cortex, perpendicular to, and extending across, all layers.

The most dramatic evidence for spatial frequency selective mechanisms has been obtained with electrophysiological and behavioral techniques in human adults and infants, even as young as six weeks (Fiorentini, Pirchio, & Spinelli, 1983).

Accordingly, the approach for investigating the transmission of spatial information through the visual system has been borrowed from electrical engineering. Spatial signals, like temporal signals, are selectively amplified, and noise is filtered out by means of processes considered to be in cascade from external source to receptors, and proceeding through successive levels in the thalamus and sensory cortex. But what happens next?

The fundamental characteristic of perception is that it enables us to recognize behaviorally important objects and events. The critical problem has been to find how the brain uses neural signals elicited by isolated stimulus features to put together a recognizable human face or city street. In short, we need to move from feature descriptions to object descriptions (Crick, 1979).

In order to do so, we need first to recognize that features may not be innate properties of hard-wired anatomy as first thought by extrapolating from the work on the frog retina, but may be the result in our brain cells of a process of active selection and learning from experience.

In mammals and especially in humans, the final organization of feature-detecting neurons into pattern or object recognition units is fundamentally determined by the individual's early experience. In short, we are dealing here with a learning process—one that is different for everyone and results in the construction of a unique reality for each individual. To universal feature detectors and species-specific feature detectors, we need to add a new category: *creature-* or *person-specific object detectors.* But to get from *features* to *objects,* we have to solve the critical problem of how the brain uses specialized feature detectors, however broadly shared by other creatures, to construct its unique universe of recognizable objects, persons, and places. The next chapter addresses this difficult question.

SUMMARY

The afferent systems—vision, hearing, and so on—are called *analyzers* because they contain powerful sorting mechanisms for selecting and distributing information coming into the receptors from the environment and feedback from the organism's own activities. Afferent fibers project both convergent and divergent impulses upon successive levels of the analyzer.

Different afferent fibers convey information by means of different neural codes. *Frequency codes* convey the *intensity* of stimulation; *place codes* and *pattern codes* convey the *quality* or kind of stimulation coming into the system. Many neurons are highly specific: their shape, size, and location in the analyzer determine their speed of conduction and the kind of experience they produce. These are called *labeled lines*. Fast, sharp pain and slow, aching pain, for example, are carried by different labeled lines. *Pattern* codes are important in the auditory analyzer for communicating the pitch of musical tones, and to some extent are used by the other analyzers as well.

The visual cortex and the somatic sensory cortex are highly organized in a modular arrangement. Each module is made up of narrow vertical columns containing cells that respond to identical or nearly identical specific patterns of stimulation or receptive fields. In the visual cortex, the cells in any one column all respond to the same orientation, with the same eye preference. Neighboring columns are influenced by neighboring orientations around the clock and alternate eye preference. A comparable segregation into columns is found for spatial frequency or its reciprocal, stripe width. An analogous columnar organization appears in the somatic sensory cortex also. There, separate columns serve the submodalities of light touch, deep pressure, and joint position. The modality-specific columns run from the surface of the cortex to the white matter of the brain. They are organized into three dimensional blocks of tissue that are iterated over and over again to form topographic maps of the receptive surfaces of the body—the skin, and the retina. These blocks of fine periodic subdivisions, called *hypercolumns* or *macrocolumns,* are the modular units of the working brain; they form the "functional architecture of the cerebral cortex." Cortical columns serve as anatomical devices to bring cells together so as to generate new levels of abstraction at successive tiers. Cells that are close neighbors appear to have identical functions: they are stacked in slender, vertical columns that extend from the white matter of the brain up through the gray bark of the cortical surface. Cells in the striate cortex in distant columns "scrutinize" in exquisite detail different parts of the field to yield a topographic mapping of retina onto cortex. Cells in somatosensory cortex similarly map the surface of the entire body onto the brain.

The single most important recent advance in brain research is the anatomical confirmation of these modular units partitioned into narrow columns by selective staining and autoradiographic techniques. This anatomical evidence is paralleled by the physiological discovery of an important general principle of functional integration: the antagonistic organization of receptive fields into excitatory and inhibitory regions. This functional organization reveals a key strategy of the central nervous system—the creation of *contrast detectors*. Contrasts of brightness, color, size, and form are the mechanisms that make possible our ability to perceive, not the absolute properties of stimuli, but the *relations* between them.

SUGGESTED READINGS

Blakemore, C., & Campbell, F.W. On the existence in the human visual system of neurons selectively sensitive to the orientation and size of retinal images. *Journal of Physiology,* 1969, *203,* 237–260.

Brown, J.L. Sensory systems. In *Best & Taylor's physiological basis of medical practice* (9th Ed.). Baltimore: Williams & Wilkins, 1973.

Campbell, F.W., & Robson, J.G. Application of Fourier analysis to the visibility of gratings. *Journal of Physiology* (London), 1968, *197,* 551–566.

Held, R., Leibowitz, H.W., & Teuber, H.-L. (Eds.). *Handbook of sensory physiology: Perception* (Vol. VIII). Berlin: Springer-Verlag, 1978.

Hubel, D.H. The visual cortex of the brain. *Scientific American,* November, 1963.

Hubel, D.H., & Wiesel, T.N. Receptive fields, binocular interaction and functional architecture in the cat's visual cortex. *Journal of Physiology* (London), 1962, *160,* 106–154.

Hubel, D.H., & Wiesel, T.N. Receptive fields and functional architecture of monkey striate cortex. *Journal of Physiology* (London), 1968, *195,* 215–243.

Hubel, D.H., & Wiesel, T.N. Brain mechanisms of vision. *Scientific American,* September, 1979.

Kandel, E.R. Somatic sensory system III. In E.R. Kandel & J.H. Schwartz (Eds.), *Principles of neural science.* New York: Elsevier/North Holland, 1981.

Kelly, D.D. Somatic sensory system IV. In E.R. Kandel & J.H. Schwartz (Eds.), *Principles of neural science.* New York: Elsevier/North Holland, 1981.

Kuffler, S.W., & Nicholls, J.G. *From neuron to brain: A cellular approach to the functions of the nervous system.* Sunderland, Mass.: Sinauer, 1976.

LeVay, S., Wiesel, T.N., & Hubel, D.H. The pattern of ocular dominance columns in macaque visual cortex revealed by a reduced silver stain. *Journal of Comparative Neurology,* 1975, *159,* 559–576.

Merzenich, M.M., & Kaas, J.H. Principles of organization of sensory-perceptual systems in mammals. In J.M. Sprague & A.N. Epstein (Eds.), Progress in psychobiology and physiological psychology (Vol. 9). New York: Academic Press, 1980.

Mountcastle, V.B. Modality and topographic properties of single neurons of cat's somatic sensory cortex. *Journal of Neurophysiology,* 1957, *20,* 408–434.

Schmitt, F.O., Worden, F.G., Adelman, G., & Dennis, S.G. (Eds.), *The organization of the cerebral cortex.* Cambridge: MIT Press, 1981.

CHAPTER FIVE

The Neuropsychology of Object Perception and Pattern Recognition

The possession of mental images could well confer an important adaptive advantage on an animal by providing a reference pattern against which stimulus patterns can be compared; and it may well be an efficient form of pattern recognition. It is characteristic of much animal, as well as human, behavior that patterns are recognized not as templates so rigid that slight deviations cause the pattern to be rejected, but as multidimensional entities that can be matched by new and slightly different stimulus patterns, as when a familiar object is recognized from a novel point of view.

(Griffin, 1976, p. 84)

Words are not the labels of concepts completed earlier and stored away; they are the labels of a categorization process or family of such processes. Because of the dynamic nature of the underlying process, the referents of words can so easily change, meanings can be extended, and categories are always open. Words tag the processes by which the species deals cognitively with its environment.

(Lenneberg, 1967)

INTRODUCTION

The last chapter traced some of the steps along the path from eye to brain that make it possible to recognize patterns and objects. Even abstract concepts can be built up from simple stimulus features. In fact, seeing is a process of abstraction. Many different patterns of features enter the retina yet are identified as the same thing—a triangle, a human face, the question mark. (See Figure 5.1.)

Figure 5.1.   Different patterns of features are recognized as being the same thing: variations on the question mark.

What a person sees depends on learning. No two people looking at the same scene will take away the same image. Seeing is believing, but the beliefs are created by the brain. They depend upon the viewer's past history of experience and the categories that have been shaped by this experience in order to interpret the world and give it meaning. Subjective category systems act as selective filters, determining what features are regarded as important.

This chapter is concerned with the process by which particular features are put together into categories of nameable objects and events, and into the categories of relations between them. Indeed, physical stimuli never recur exactly. What we call the "same" object or event is different in some respect on a later occasion from what it was on an earlier one. When we "recognize" something as familiar, our perceptual system ignores or reconciles the disparity, and we respond as we did before. This is the phenomenon of stimulus *generalization*. The baby's spontaneous extension of names to new objects reveals the ease of generalization—calling the strange man "daddy" comes first. Only later does the child learn that this word applies to one particular individual. Adults also fail to make distinctions between objects whose features are similar. Consider the common failure of monolingual speakers to hear the different and separate words of a foreign language. Westerners say that all Chinese faces look alike because Westerners do not observe their distinctive features. It seems to be natural to organize the world around us into categories, categories in which each instance shows some similarity to other instances.

Conversely, many people learn to make exquisitely precise distinctions between similar objects or events. The Eskimos, for instance, are able to discriminate between thirteen kinds of snow, and the trained eye of the radiologist can discern the locus and extent of a carcinoma from a brief inspection of an x-ray slide that appears a chaotic blur to us. It is with such questions of generalization and discrimination, of sameness and difference, that inform our perceptual categories, that this chapter deals.

THE HUBEL AND WIESEL MODEL

We have seen that the receptive field of a visual nerve cell at an early stage of the sensory process is organized in such a way that its central portion is excited by light and its periphery inhibited, or conversely. By the simple device of taking a number of such roughly circular on-center fields in a row and interconnecting them, Hubel and Wiesel (1962) proposed that the visual system builds a line detector. A series of these fields located vertically one above the other may converge upon a single cortical neuron whose combined receptive field has an elongated shape with vertical orientation. For such a unit the appropriate releasing stimulus is not a diffuse spot of light but a luminous vertical line flanked on both sides by dark inhibitory areas. These cells are thought to combine their output in turn to build up increasingly complex and selective feature detectors. (See Figure 5.2.)

SPATIAL FREQUENCY CHANNELS

An alternative model to Hubel and Wiesel's has been proposed by Campbell and Robson (1968) based on evidence that the visual system in monkey and human has channels selectively sensitive to spatial frequency. (See Figure 5.3.) Campbell and Robson describe their model as follows:

> The visual system behaves not as a *single* detector mechanism preceded by a *single* broad-band spatial filter but as a number of independent detector mechanisms each preceded by a relatively narrow-band filter "tuned" to a different frequency.

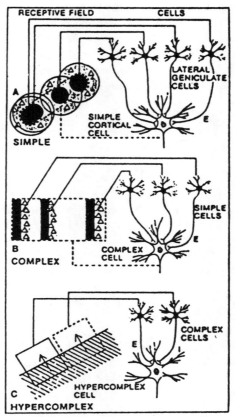

Figure 5.2. Hubel and Wiesel's model: The visual system builds up complex objects and patterns by successive integration of inputs selected by highly specific feature detectors. Redrawn from Hubel & Wiesel, 1962, 1965, by Kuffler & Nicholls, 1976.

> Each filter and detector would constitute a separate "channel" and each channel would have its own contrast-sensitivity function. On this basis the envelope of the contrast-sensitivity functions of all the channels would be the contrast-sensitivity function of the overall visual system. (1968, p. 564)

Campbell and Robson bring together psychophysical and neurophysiological evidence of separate channels within the visual system having band-pass characteristics with different optimum spatial frequencies. Their findings show that the maximum selectivity that could be achieved is limited by the area over which integrative processes could operate. (See Figure 5.4.)

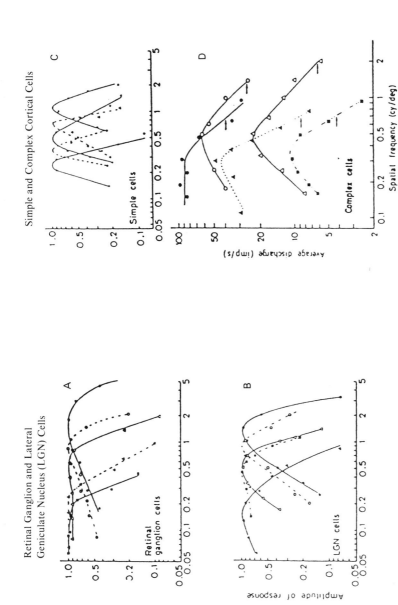

Figure 5.3. Responses of (A) retinal ganglion cells, (B) lateral geniculate nucleus (LGN) cells, (C) simple cells, and (D) complex cells to a sinusoidal grating as functions of spatial frequency. Each curve represents a different cell in a monkey brain. From the retina to the simple cells of the cortex, there is a progressive tuning of the single cells to a given spatial frequency; complex cells are more widely responsive. Adapted from Maffei & Fiorentini, 1973. Reprinted with permission of *Vision Research, 13,* 1255–1267. Copyright © 1974 by Pergamon Press.

Thus a picture emerges of functionally separate mechanisms in the visual nervous system each responding maximally at some particular spatial frequency and hardly at all at spatial frequencies differing by a factor of two. The frequency selectivity of these mechanisms must be determined by integrative processes in the nervous system, and they appear, to a first approximation at least, to operate linearly. (p. 565)

The resultant psychophysical function, called a "contrast sensitivity function," affords a useful measure of visual acuity over the entire range of visual patterns of all sizes. The concept of spatial frequency channels in vision offers a striking analogy to audition, for the ear can analyze a compound

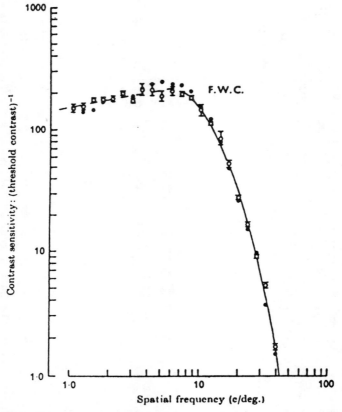

Figure 5.4. Human contrast sensitivity as a function of spatial frequency. Overall, the human visual system is most sensitive to contrast with sine wave gratings that have spatial frequencies of about 2–3 cycles per degree. Contrast sensitivity drops off at higher and lower spatial frequencies. Blakemore & Campbell, 1969.

sound into its component vibrations. Pursuing the analogy, many visual scientists attempt to apply the Fourier theory to vision, as well as to audition where acoustical engineers have been using it with great success. The central idea is that lines and bars, the stimuli that Hubel and Wiesel used in their experiments, and gratings of various spatial frequencies, or indeed any spatial pattern, can be filtered in terms of linear Fourier theory into their sinusoidal wave components and then resynthesized. (See Figure 5.5A.) The combined neurophysiological and psychological findings clearly suggest that information about the orientation, spatial frequency, and phase content of the visual image has been coded by the visual system. Decoding, then, may provide the neural mechanism by which we perceive and actually recognize objects. (See Figure 5.5B.)

The Campbell and Robson model offers the attractive possibility that the eye, like the ear, does have harmony, but in the domain of space rather than time. (See Figure 5.6.) The two models are not really inconsistent with each other nor with the data: both assume a clear progression of neural levels in which information about the properties of visual stimuli are integrated in a cascade of increasing specificity and abstraction.

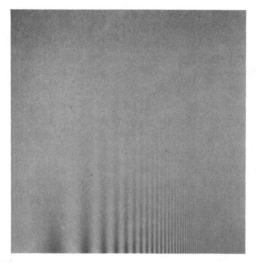

Figure 5.5A. Sinusoidal grating with a logarithmic variation in function of spatial frequency and in contrast demonstrates the loss of contrast sensitivity at low and high spatial frequencies. The contrast decreases from the bottom to the top but at one height is the same for all spatial frequencies. Intermediate spatial frequencies are visible at much lower contrast than either the high or low spatial frequencies. Variable frequency grating courtesy of J.G. Robson and F.W. Campbell.

Figure 5.5B. This computer-plotted stimulus produces Fourier components of a square wave (odd harmonics from the 1st to the 59th). Anstis, 1976.

FROM FEATURES TO OBJECTS

A neuropsychological theory of pattern recognition must accomplish three things. First, it must explain in terms of synaptic transmission how a suitable abstract description or a neural symbol of an input image is built up. Second, it must tell us how such a description is stored. And third, it must account for the swift and confident recognition of a familiar object—a human face, or voice, or word, or the letters of the alphabet. How, in short, does the brain retrieve, out of all the descriptions stored in it, just the right match for the stimulus out there in the environment?

These neural symbols might be regarded as high level units derived from the activation of low level transit units that represent features. Look around you. What you seem to "see," effortlessly and immediately, is a book, a desk, or a telephone—clusters of features that in each case must have been mediated originally by activity in various levels of your visual analyzer.

There remains a large gap between orientationally sensitive or spatial frequency sensitive neurons and the patterns and objects of our everyday experience. The series of reaction stages of increasing complexity clearly depends on the experience of the individual observer. But given the essential interaction with the environment, we can assume that all members of the species having the same apparatus construct their orientational and spatial frequency detectors in much the same way. The heart of our problem is to explain the leap from neural feature detectors, or channels, to object recognizers. This demands something more—perhaps qualitatively different. To the normally sighted adult, everything seen has a certain significance—a central meaning.

Squirrel.

When I say, "I see a squirrel," the words convey, not a sensory account, but a conceptual one. (See figure.) In a purely visual sense I have an image, perhaps fleeting, of the side view of a small animal with a bushy tail, but I know that it has another side, that there is space around it, and that it has eyes and whiskers and other features that I do not literally see. What is the bridge between the sensory and the conceptual account?

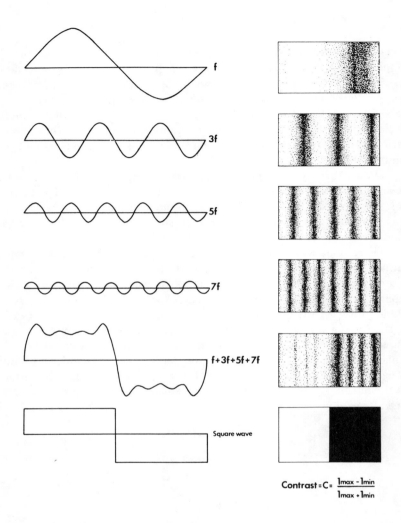

$$\text{Contrast} = C = \frac{\text{Imax} - \text{Imin}}{\text{Imax} + \text{Imin}}$$

Figure 5.6. Campbell and Robson's model is based on spatial frequency channels that enable the visual system to analyze and synthesize spatial information. The figure shows a Fourier series of component sine waves that add to synthesize a square wave (bottom row). A cross-section of the luminance along each sine wave is shown at the right. The coefficients are odd multiples of the fundamental frequency (1f, 3f, 5f, 7f); the corresponding amplitudes are 1, 1/3, 1/5, 1/7. The amplitude of modulation is expressed as *contrast* given by (1max − 1min)/(1max + 1min). By adding all higher harmonics the square wave synthesized by the full series has an amplitude 0.785 (π/4) times that of the fundamental sine wave.

We need to proceed from cells representing specific features (whether line or spatial frequency detectors) to physiological mechanisms representing objects. This process most probably requires a step-by-step activation of neural symbols at many levels of integration so that earlier ones can help in the construction of later ones. The problem is to find which features go together to form a unit with the integrity and constancy of a recognizable object. This is the fundamental problem of organization or grouping that the Gestalt psychologists brought forcibly to our attention as phenomena important for understanding of perceptual mechanisms. The German word *Gestalt* means *form* or *configuration*. The key idea is that the parts of a perceptual organization are not separate and independent; rather, the parts interact to form a whole that is different from their mere collection or sum. (See Figure 5.7.)

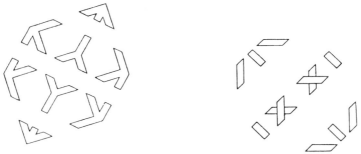

Figure 5.7A. Fragments do not organize themselves in the absence of information for occlusion.

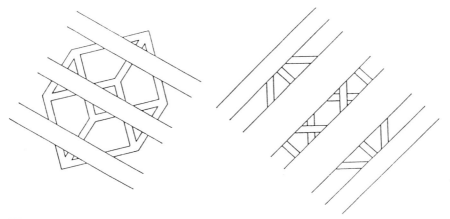

Figure 5.7B. The same fragments as shown in Figure 5.7A. Added line segments provide information for occlusion, revealing organized forms. Kanizsa, 1974.

In studies of perception and imagery no accepted configurational unit comparable to the Hubel and Wiesel cell has emerged. Yet a cognitive or perceptive unit would have great utility if it could be shown to obey general laws of nervous activity and to take part in the higher mental processes of learning and thought. Horace Barlow (1972) proposed a single-neuron doctrine for perception, but he stopped short of the notion that our unitary perceptions could be unique events, each corresponding to the firing of a single neuron.

Indeed, the concept of a "gnostic unit" (from the Greek *gnosis*—to know) was introduced earlier by Konorski (1967) as the neural substrate for a unitary perception. Konorski's idea was to extrapolate from the model developed by Hubel and Wiesel and to explain the origin of perceptions experienced by humans and animals, "not by assemblies of units but by single units in the highest levels of particular analyzers" (1967, p. 75). Even very complex patterns could be represented by single neurons in the cerebral cortex by means of successive coding and integrating of stimulus features that were the adequate stimuli for single cells—transit units—on lower levels of the visual system. These features furnish the sensory elements for simple and complex cells in the striate and peristriate areas and constitute the raw material in Konorski's model for the biologically meaningful stimulus patterns that project to neurons in the higher visual areas. There they are finally perfected for use in the associative processes and in the behavior of the organism.

In the hierarchical schema developed by Hubel and Wiesel, the units of the higher levels of the visual system are formed by the convergence of appropriate presynaptic sensory neurons at lower levels. A new unit of the highest level, accordingly, may represent the top of a pyramid, but an inverted pyramid in which the number of units exceeds those of the lower levels, because the same nerve cells take part in the formation of many divergent combinations. From the one million fibers leaving the retina in the optic nerve, many of which diverge to the midbrain, there is an ever-increasing number of synaptic connections made within the visual cortex by incoming fibers. Both the excitatory fibers (on-units) and the inhibitory fibers (off-units) converge upon synapses at successive stages. Thus the recipient neurons are composed of both the presence of certain components and the absence of others.

Once the transit units have transmitted their input to a neural unit of the higher order—"these stimulus-patterns no longer participate as separate items in the further information processing, since they are amalgamated into the whole and thus completely lose their individuality" (Konorski, 1967, p. 76). This unit cannot be subdivided, but, like other single cells, it obeys the laws of the nervous impulse: its activity is an all-or-none affair.

As the Gestalt psychologists showed, our perceptions are not analyzable into compounds of associated sensations. But, then, neither are they always "good" Gestalten, well-organized wholes. As a result, we experience neither raw sensations, nor platonic universals. What we get are objects—apples, sparrows, human faces—to which we attach names, labels, meanings.

COGNONS: THE UNITS OF PERCEPTION AND COGNITION

Konorski (1967) believed that our unitary perceptions are represented by single neurons ("gnostic units") in the highest levels of particular analyzers— gnostic or cognitive fields representing the various senses: touch, sight, hearing, taste, and so on. I call these neural units responsible for particular perceptions "cognons." The word *cognon* is easy to pronounce; it replaces two words with one; and the name ties the unit of the psychology of cognition to the unit of biology, the neuron, the single cell in the cognitive field that furnishes the perception unit its anatomical and functional substrate. To "cognize" is to know, to perceive, or to recognize.

A cognon is the unit of perception or the unit of cognition that represents a known, biologically meaningful stimulus pattern. On the physiological side, a cognon is a single cell in the cortical center of an afferent system; on the psychological side, a cognon is the unit of mental reaction (unitary percept or image) that is used in the associative processes and in the symbol manipulations of organisms.

Although we have no direct evidence that our conscious experience consists of the activity of cognons, there is abundant indirect psychological and neurological evidence to support the hypotheses developed in this chapter. The concept of the cognon as an elementary unit of thought, derived from perceptual learning, but constrained by the prewired cellular structure of the brain, seems to be what we have been looking for, as a start toward a systematic physiological theory of intelligent behavior.

THE MONKEY'S PAW CELL

A beautiful example of a cognon is described by Gross, Rocha-Miranda, and Bender (1972). These investigators at Princeton University were studying the inferotemporal cortex in macaque monkeys when they encounterd a particularly stubborn neuron from which they were unable to elicit any response, no matter what stimulus they tried. Finally, one of the experimenters began to wave his hand in front of one monkey's eyes. Immediately the reluctant neuron sprang into an excited burst of activity. What was the cell responding to? For the next 12 hours the experimenters tirelessly tested the cell's response to one silhouette after the other—symmetrical patterns, five-pointed stars, leaf patterns, cutouts of the human hand, and, finally, a cardboard model of

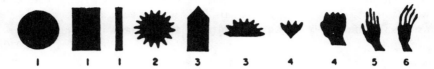

Figure 5.8.　　The cut-out silhouettes ranked in order of increasing effectiveness. Gross et al., 1972.

the monkey's own paw. That stimulus evoked the most vigorous response. Perhaps it should not be surprising that such a biologically meaningful and natural stimulus object is importantly represented in the cognitive field of the monkey's brain. (See Figure 5.8.)

VISUAL CONSTRUCTION OF OBJECT PERCEPTIONS

We now come to grips with the question with which this chapter began. Granted that a perception unit can be represented by a neural symbol, a cognon, how is a suitable abstract description of the novel stimulus pattern built up? We have seen that the visual system, for example, is endowed with neurons that respond selectively to such stimulus features as orientation, edge, and spatial frequency or stripe width. But how do we get from edges and orientation to the perception of a table or a human face?

Initially, every new object or scene presents a complex configuration of stimulus features to the perceiver. Is there a coding process by which the complex object "out there" instructs its neural representative inside the brain as to what it is? The best evidence we have on the encoding process comes from studies of eye movements during the visual perception of complex objects.

How does the human eye examine new or complex objects? When we first perceive an object, do we trace out the outlines and contours with our eye as the hand of a blind person palpates an object in order to identify it? In looking at a picture, do we scan the whole surface uniformly? It's been known for a long time that, when we read, the eyes do not move smoothly along the line of print, but jump from one fixation point to the next in a series of saccades. Are there similar patterns of eye movements in exploring complex objects or pictures?

By means of an ingenious experimental device, an ocular "cap" that can be attached by suction to the human eye, Yarbus (1967) achieved a continuous record of the position of the eye as it observed various photographs of objects and scenes. With the use of a mirror and a lever attached to the "cap," Yarbus recorded eye position on the moving film of a photokymograph. In one series of experiments, the optical device moves with the eye and confronts the observer with a stationary visual field. The interesting consequence is that contours, colors, and other features rapidly fade and disappear. The eyes move, but their effects are eliminated: objects stationary relative to the retina quickly bring visual perception to an end.

An unchanging retinal image causes the eye to stop working. Here is a general principle of broad application. Our sense organs rapidly habituate to a continuing input; a fresh stimulus is necessary to evoke a response. Moving things, sudden changes, attract attention and excite neural activity because they tell us something new.

Under normal conditions, during perception of complex objects and scenes, how does the eye obtain the information necessary to perceive them accurately?

The records of eye movements (see Figure 5.9) show two striking characteristics. First of all, when freely examining complex objects, the human eye fixates mainly on certain elements or features and ignores or neglects others. Second, the features that attract attention are determined by the observer's interest or mental set. Only certain elements attract the responsive eye.

 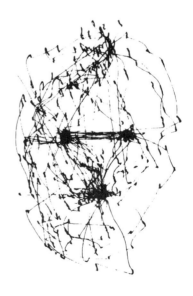

Figure 5.9. Records of eye movements during free inspection of a girl's face. Yarbus, 1967.

The eye rests much longer on these selected features and returns to them again and again. What determines the eye's choice? Is it the outlines or contours, the degree of detail, or the extreme lightness or darkness of a particular element that attracts attention?

To this multiple-choice question, analysis of the records gives a clear answer. None of the above! The elements of the picture that hold attention are not outlines or contours. Although borders may be important initially to separate figure from ground, they are quickly passed over in favor of other features of interest. These are elements that, in the observer's opinion, contain the useful and essential information for perception.

As Yarbus points out, features that fail to draw the observer's attention do not contain such information. Many details tell the observer nothing new or useful: fine details, color, extremes of contrast are not necessarily carriers of significant information. What does attract attention are faces, particularly expressive eyes and smiling lips. Eyes and lips are mobile and expressive elements that communicate emotion and attitude, usually the most telling elements in a representation of the human face.

It is interesting to note that the observer returns repeatedly to the important elements as though to reexamine them. "The impression is created that the perception of a picture is usually composed of a number of 'cycles', each of which has much in common" (Yarbus, 1967, p. 193). On the face of the little girl (Figure 5.9), note the repeated fixations on first one and then the other of the girl's eyes. The cycle lasts longer the more complex an object and the more associations it arouses.

A striking finding was that different cyclical patterns result when the same picture is examined under different instructions given the observer by the experimenter. (See Figure 5.10.) For example, the record made following the instruction, "Estimate the ages of the people shown in the picture," shows few reiterated movements, but the problem, "Estimate how long the unexpected visitor has been away from the family," shows many more reiterated movements. The problem facing the observer determines the order of the fixations, their duration, and these distinctive cyclic patterns of examination.

The striking aspect of these eye-movement records is that, except for the initial important segregation of figure and ground where contours are important, perception ignores the physical details of construction that provide the adequate stimuli for cells at lower visual projective levels. Instead, it concentrates on answering more sophisticated questions: What are those expressive eyes saying to me? What are the ages of the people in the picture? How long has the visitor been away? Even under free examination with no specific question in mind, the observer scans the picture in a way that insures ready recognition when it is again presented. The eye movements are not simply elicited by the stimulation—they are performed in order to obtain

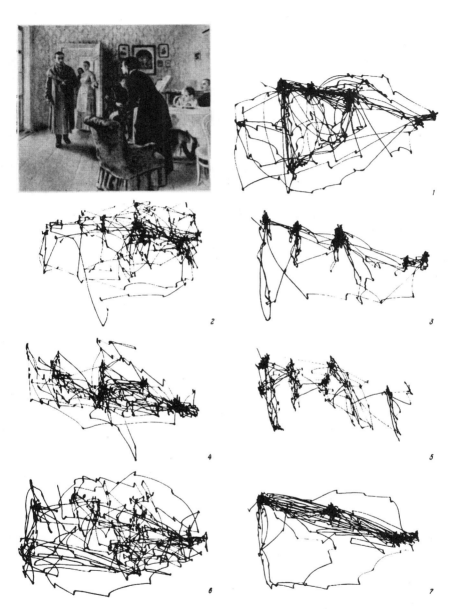

Figure 5.10. Distinctive cyclical patterns of eye movements result from different instructions to the observer. Yarbus, 1967.

stimulation. The process emphasizes motivation and the intelligent analysis of the picture into meaningful categories—categories that are already present as cognitive fields in the brain of the perceiver.

The problem arises—where do these cognitive fields come from? Do they depend wholly on the individual experience of the organism, or are they prearranged according to the evolutionary development of the species?

HEREDITY AND ENVIRONMENT AS FACTORS IN PERCEPTUAL LEARNING

The formation of cognons in the human brain is based both on heredity and interaction with the environment. Heredity provides the genetic instructions for the maturation of the essential apparatus—nerve cells and potential connections between them—in the pathways of the various analyzers.

Perceptual learning as a result of exposure to particular stimulus patterns in the environment transforms these potential connections into actual active connections. In order for this transformation to take place, two prerequisites are critical:

1. a state of arousal at the moment of exposure to the stimulus pattern, and
2. available recipient neurons for integrating and storing the information transmitted from the receptors to the higher levels of the given afferent system.

The process begins with attention, motivated by a preparatory drive that Pavlov called the "orientation reflex," and described as the "investigatory" or "what is it" reaction to a novel stimulus (see Chapter Two). Under the facilitating influence of the orientation reflex with its generalized arousal of autonomic and behavioral components, and the modality-specific targeting reflex, a potentially active, but dormant, recipient cell is aroused by an unfamiliar object or event, and the formation of a new cognon occurs.

Clearly, neurons must be available for transmitting, selecting, integrating, and preserving messages presented by the environment. Both transmittent and recipient neurons are essential, and they must be unoccupied except by the "specific" impulses delivered at the moment of exposure to the stimulus configuration to be grasped by perception. Still, perceptual learning fails to take place unless "nonspecific" impulses from the drive centers are simultaneously delivered by the emotive system.

The resulting state of arousal is known as "sensitization." The critical point is that recipient cells in the brain must be under the joint influence of "specific" impulses impinging from the environmental stimulus pattern, and "nonspecific" impulses from the emotive centers in the limbic system if they are to become engaged as true perception units or cognons.

Once engaged, the cognons may serve as more or less permanent symbols of the object or event that gave rise to them initially. From then on, that object or event need only catch the attention (evoke the targeting reflex) of the individual in order to reactivate the cognons that represent it. The familiar object will be recognized immediately (unless it is so obscured or degraded that it fails to activate the corresponding cognon).

Perception units are thus the product of a particular type of learning process, dependent on inherited, potentially available neural structures. They are unique in the individual's experience, both with regard to the particular constellation of stimulus elements they represent, and the feeling, tone, or emotional quality that accompanies their formation.

In the absence of visual experience during a critical period of development, the individual may never be able to use the sense of sight to perceive objects or visual space.

Marius von Senden (1960) compiled a number of reports of cases of persons born blind who were later operated upon, usually for the removal of cataracts. Designed to open their eyes, the operation failed in most cases to restore their sight for many months or years, if ever. As von Senden shows, these postoperative patients do not immediately begin to "see," but instead undergo a long, gradual, painful, and sometimes impossible transition period from a predominantly tactile to a visual mode of perception.

While many patients recognize colors fairly soon after getting habituated to what at first appears to be dazzling light, they fail to be able to use color to identify objects. They do not then turn to other visual features (contours, for example, receive not the slightest attention) but call upon all their other senses to aid them—touch, hearing, smell, and even taste.

The fundamental problem for the congenitally blind, despite successful surgery, is the absence of any visual targeting reflex and the consequent inability to make any distinction between figure and ground. As von Senden describes his typical findings:

> Once the patient has overcome his post-operative intolerance to light, and his eyes are opened to the world of colours, he immediately finds that in whatever direction he happens to be looking, he is confronted with a visual space, the depth and breadth of which are severely restricted in comparison with that of the normally sighted. The depth of this visual space is bounded by the nearest coloured surfaces.... These patches of colour still appear blurred and hardly stand out from one another. He sees them all at a certain distance from him...[with] no awareness of the existence of anything beyond or to either side...because of his inability to put a voluntary stop to the spasm in both eyes. His eyes continue to jerk this way and that around the central point he is looking at.... In this initial stage, vision is a purely sensory

awareness of colour-impressions, simultaneously presented at right angles to the line of vision, and still devoid of shape.... The subject cannot say anything about them, nor can he initiate motor reactions toward them. He merely finds them located somehow and somewhere at an indeterminate distance in space, and does not initially take them for things at all.... The rolling of his own eyeballs leads him to notice the occurrence of a movement, and he then mistakenly describes an object as moving when it is not in fact doing so. (von Senden, 1960, p. 294)

Von Senden's patients give striking testimony of the crucial importance of experience, of learning to see, without which no visual images can exist. One unusually sensitive psychological report was of an 18-year-old American named Joan who did recover her sight, although slowly. Her report reads:

As Joan learned to use her eyes she found that almost nothing was really the way her hands had told it was when she was blind. She was confounded by the discovery that each new person who was brought in to see her had an entirely different face. She had thought that all faces were much alike except that some were rounder than others. (von Senden, 1960, p. 63)

The blind may use the same word as the sighted but with a vastly different imagery. This is brought out in another passage from the same case:

While Joan is now able to tell us of the curious notions the blind entertain of the world about them, she can't enlighten her blind friends much about the new world that she has just graduated into. "You can't tell a person how anything looks unless he has once had eyes that saw," she says. "The words don't mean a thing to him."

When she saw that a tree was ten times as tall as her father and mother she thought her eyes were playing a trick on her. Of course she had been told and knew perfectly well that trees grow to great heights but descriptions of anything taller than a blind person can reach with a stick are just empty words. (p. 65)

The main impact of these observations is to throw the strongest possible doubt on the primacy of contours or the primitive unity of figure and ground in visual perception. The patient has no visual awareness of shape, and as von Senden points out, he fails to "conjoin the perception of two colours in the relation of figure and ground" (p. 302). The bright reflection on a silver spoon in one instance and on the moon in another are taken to be holes. Even after a patient has begun to see objects and to identify visual patterns, he is unable to recognize shape in pictures. Von Senden cites a typical example:

The first time she was handed photographs and paintings she asked: "Why do they put those dark marks all over them?" "Those aren't marks," her mother explained, "those are shadows. That is one of the ways the eye knows that

things have shape. If it were not for shadows many things would look flat."
"Well, that's how things do look," Joan answered. "Everything looks flat
with dark patches." (von Senden, 1960, p. 211) (See Figure 5.11.)

PERCEPTUAL LEARNING: THE FORMATION OF COGNONS

The development of normal perception requires exposure to stimulus patterns
and objects early in infancy and the process of forming new cognons continues
throughout life as the result of individual experience. How is this achieved?

Perceptual learning is a nonassociative, elementary form of learning,
simpler than associative learning such as the conditioned reflex, formerly
thought to be the primitive unit of learning. All associative learning involves
the formation of a connection between two stimuli, or between a stimulus and
a response. Nonassociative learning requires no pairing. It is based on two
primitive and universal processes: habituation and sensitization. Habituation
was described in Chapter Two as the decrease in response to a continued or
repeated stimulus. The ability to stop responding to a monotonous stimulus is
adaptive: it allows the individual to pay attention to a new or more critical
target.

Sensitization is another important type of nonassociative learning. It
consists of an increased reflex response to a stimulus that follows the arousal
of the orientation reflex. Whereas habituation is an inhibitory process,
sensitization is an excitatory or facilitative process.

When any creature is confronted by a novel stimulus, its first response is
the orienting reflex, combining nonspecific alerted attention, autonomic
arousal, and the modality-specific targeting reflex. This "what is it?" reaction
prepares the organism to identify the stimulus and to take whatever action
may be necessary to deal with it. Sensitization is defined as the prolonged
enhancement of an animal's investigatory response to a stimulus as the result
of the arousal of the orientation reflex by the stimulus itself or by another
stimulus. With repeated stimulation by the same innocuous stimulus, the
orienting reflex decreases, and eventually the animal ceases to respond
(habituates) to the particular stimulus.

However, recovery from habituation takes place if the stimulus reappears
at a later time or resumes some particular meaning for the individual and
evokes the targeting reflex. Although you have heard your own name called
thousands of times, its unexpected sight or sound elicits the targeting reflex.
Most of the objects that surround us vary in significance, depending on what
we are doing and what we need. If we need to know the time, or to get a
drink—then we notice the clock, or the water glass, that have gone unnoticed
until that moment.

What is the physiological mechanism of this learning and forgetting, this
sensitization and habituation? Although the intimate mechanisms of these

A

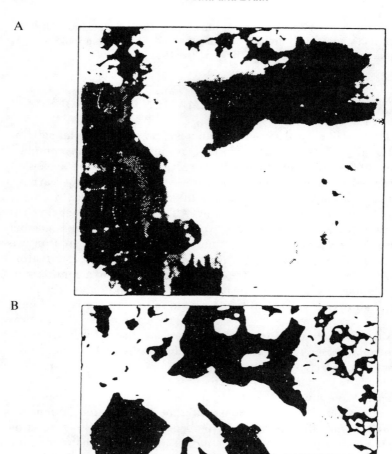

B

Figure 5.11. Can you see a distinctive object? Or does everything look "flat with black patches?" (A) Cow face; (B) bearded man with shawl. (C) Sketch of cow face hidden in Figure 5.11(A). (D) Sketch of bearded man hidden in Figure 5.11(B).

elementary learning processes have long been sought, the remarkable experiments by Kandel and his associates on simple animals have only recently begun to reveal their nature.

THE NEURAL MECHANISM OF PERCEPTUAL LEARNING

Are all neurons alike? Within any one nervous system, certainly, neurons are unique. This was shown as early as 1907 by the German biologist, Richard

C

D

Goldschmidt, who examined the ganglia in the brain of a primitive worm. He found that each ganglion contained exactly 162 cells, without any variation in number. Not only that, but each cell also always occupied the same characteristic position in every single worm he examined.

Goldschmidt's work went unheeded until Kandel, Kupfermann, and their associates at Harvard Medical School began to study the large marine snail, *Aplysia*. Here was another simple organism in which these scientists found it possible to identify specific cells and study their firing patterns. Most interestingly, these cells always make the same kinds of connections to other cells. Some connections are always excitatory; others are always inhibitory.

In the abdominal ganglia of *Aplysia* the cells are few in number and very large, making it possible to study them in a way that immensely complex neural systems, like ours, or other mammals, discourage.

Kandel and his associates discovered that habituation involved a change in the strength of the connection made by sensory cells on their central target cells, the interneurons and the motor neurons (Kandel & Schwartz, 1981; 1982). The critical change was found in the terminals of the presynaptic sensory neuron. These release a neurotransmitter consisting of uniform packets or quanta of chemical molecules. Each quantum contains the identical amount of transmitter substance and the number of quanta released determines the excitatory postsynaptic effect on the recipient cell. The application of a weak stimulus to the siphon of the snail, *Aplysia,* causes its gill to contract and withdraw into the mantle cavity. (See Figure 5.12.) Repeating the same stimulation decreases the response, and it soon disappears altogether for a short period of time. Then it may reappear in response to renewed

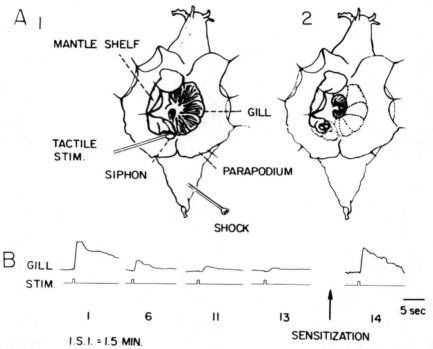

Figure 5.12. (A) Experimental arrangement for behavioral studies in *Aplysia* showing the gill in a relaxed position. (1) A gill-withdrawal reflex is elicited by a water jet (tactile) stimulus to the siphon. (2) Gill after withdrawal. The dotted lines indicate the former relaxed position. (B) Photocell recordings showing sensitization and habituation of the gill-withdrawal reflex. After 13 stimuli, the reflex response was reduced to less than 30% of its initial value. Arrow: noxious sensitizing shock applied to the tail reinstates the reflex response. Kandel & Schwartz, 1982. Copyright © 1982 by AAAS.

stimulation, showing spontaneous recovery. The decrease in response is habituation, a simple form of learning. Its recovery is a form of forgetting. Castelluci and Kandel (1976) have shown that the sensitization mechanism entails the same locus of synaptic transmission as habituation. But habituation depresses activity; sensitization enhances activity. The neurons that mediate sensitization end near the synaptic terminals of the sensory neurons and enhance their release of neurotransmitter. They do this by increasing the number of quanta turned loose by each action potential in the sensory neuron—a process called "presynaptic facilitation." (See Figures 5.13 and 5.14.)

Sensitization and habituation can thus be seen as opposing forms of learning mediated at the same locus—the presynaptic terminals of the sensory

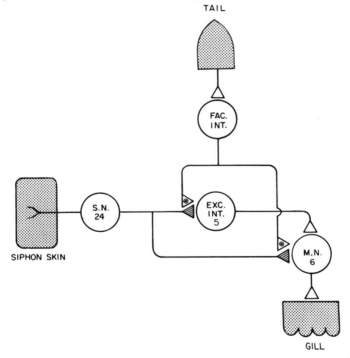

Figure 5.13. Depression and facilitation underlie behavioral habituation and sensitization at the synapse. Sensitizing stimuli to the tail activate neurons that excite facilitative interneurons (FAC.INT.). The facilitatory cells, in turn, end on the synaptic terminals of the sensory neurons (S.N.) where they modulate transmitter release. EXC.INT. denotes excitatory interneurons, and M.N. denotes motor neurons. After a single shock to the tail the experimental animals had significantly longer gill withdrawals than control animals. Adapted from Kandel, 1979; 1982. Copyright © 1982 by AAAS. Courtesy of Eric R. Kandel.

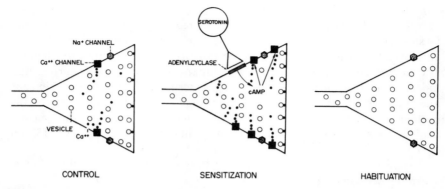

Figure 5.14. Model of short-term sensitization and habituation as envisioned by Kandel, 1979; 1982. The control cell (left) fires before either sensitization or habituation has set in. A nerve impulse in the terminal membrane of the neuron opens up channels for calcium ions (Ca^{++}) in parallel with the sodium channels (Na^+). Sensitization (center) releases the transmitter serotonin. It acts on an enzyme, adenylcyclase, that catalyzes the synthesis of cAMP, which increases the influx of calcium ions. The calcium causes a greater binding of transmitter vesicles to release sites and enhances the release of transmitter into the synaptic cleft. Habituation (right) produced by repeated impulses in the terminals depresses the calcium influx and inactivates the synapse. The critical change underlying short-term habituation occurs at the same chemical synapse as that underlying sensitization. Thus the same locus can be regulated in opposite ways by opposing forms of learning. Courtesy of Eric R. Kandel, M.D.

neurons. The one enhances the release of neurotransmitter; the other reduces it. Both processes are reversible. Sensitization actually reverses depressed behavior by arousing the orientation response to a habituated stimulus that has become newly important. For example, the satiated animal shows habituation to the food box and passes it by without a glance. But, some time later, hungry once more, the sight of the food box arouses excited attention and, thus sensitized, the animal approaches it eagerly.

Most of the familiar objects that surround us in daily life have this twofold nature; that is, they are alternately insignificant or neutral and then significant, depending on the condition of need or drive. It is attractive to speculate that the strength of drive at the time a cognon is formed might well have a powerful effect on its excitability. Perhaps the strength of the drive could even be proportional to the number of cognons representing the given stimulus. The next section describes the way in which these multiple cognons might be organized.

THE ORGANIZATION OF COGNONS IN COGNITIVE FIELDS

Each unitary perception is thought to be represented in a cognitive field, not by a single neuron, but by a number of equivalent units, probably one or more columns of cognons. This iteration of cognons occurs because the arousal of a cognitive field by a new stimulus pattern excites all unengaged units of sufficient sensitivity within that local area. These may divide into multiple identical progeny by cloning receptors. Thus we have to imagine myriad pattern recognition units, at least one narrow file or minicolumn of redundant units for each particular type of object or pattern that we can recognize. Each such column is flanked on one or both sides by columns of antagonistic units, representing "negative spaces," the holes between things, the ground of figure-ground organization. (See Figure 5.15.) The spaces between and within forms are as important as the forms themselves for seeing shape. Artists' teaching manuals help students to "really see" familar things by stressing the need to look at the space around the object—for example, to draw the image upside down or to work with negative spaces (Edwards, 1979; Kim, 1981). By looking at things in this new way, the students begin to improve immediately. They eliminate the too-familiar cognons that trigger their old stereotyped responses (see Figure 5.16) and strengthen fresh new ones. Drawing with the unaccustomed left hand sometimes has the same liberating effect, either by activating previously inhibited cognons in the right hemisphere or strengthening new connections. In well-known ambiguous figures, like the vase and profiles, the

Figure 5.15. Hypothetical interhemispheric columnar organization of a cortical module representing men, women, and children. Adjacent columns contain on-units (positive spaces) and off-units (negative spaces) often visible as complementary afterimages.

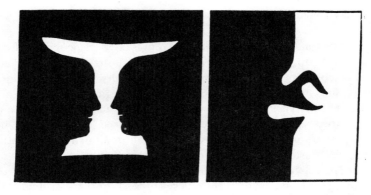

Figure 5.16. Negative spaces are formed by reversing contour directions. (A) Figure and ground reversals from Rubin, 1915. (B) *Swans,* by M.C. Escher. By permission of the National Gallery of Art, Washington: Gift of Mr. C.V.S. Roosevelt.

negative spaces have the advantage of familiarity, resulting in spontaneous alternation.

The impingement of both inhibitory and excitatory impulses produces columns of on-units flanked by columns of off-units for every unitary perception. Strong lateral or pericolumnar inhibition insures mutual exclusivity of the rival percepts.

A picture of the cortical association areas composed of millions of minicolumns representing all the things you have experienced and, potentially, their negative spaces, may strike you as unbelievable. Does this seem to require an impossibly large number of units and columns? Not any more.

A ferment of constructive excitement in the neurosciences has been caused by the unexpected discovery, in one region of the cortex after another, of just such minicolumns (narrow vertical cylinders) in sufficient number and arrangement in local circuits to provide the anatomical building blocks this conceptual scheme requires. Schmitt and Worden (1978) bring together impressive evidence that the cortical cells are arranged in radially oriented cords or minicolumns extending across the cortex. The cells in each minicolumn may constitute a single clonal derivative (each cell a clone of the others in that column) and thus have identical response properties, but their thresholds may vary (Meller & Teztlaff, 1975; Rakic, 1977; Mountcastle, 1978).

Very recently, Patricia Goldman-Rakic and Michael Schwartz (1981) reported the first evidence that callosal (contralateral) terminals alternate with association (ipsilateral) units in side-by-side minicolumns. Here in the monkey prefrontal association cortex are cerebral mechanisms underlying hemispheric integration. The major news is that right hemisphere axons alternate in short but regular sequences with left hemisphere axons, much as right eye dominance columns alternate with left eye dominance columns in the primary visual cortex of the same species. The whole set of columns constitutes a building block for integrating spatial and temporal information in the frontal lobes. (See Figure 5.17.)

The dimensions and the number of the neurons contained within each minicolumn have been specified with amazing precision by Rockel, Hiorns, and Powell (1974). By these counts, each column contains about 110 cells in all species of mammals studied, except for 260 cells in the striate cortex of primates. The column diameter (about 30 millimicrons) also appears remarkably constant throughout the cortex. As a result, the human cortex contains an estimated 5 million minicolumns. These, in turn, are composed of about 60 billion nerve cells (Mountcastle, 1978), about one-half of the estimated total number of cells in the entire brain.

> The autoradiographic technique also reveals a similar modular organization in cortico-subcortical connections. The principle of segregation of afferent information applies as much to subcortical as it does to cortical targets—and is remarkably constant from species to species, suggesting that evolutionary gains reflect an increase in number, rather than in the kind, of afferent module. (Goldman-Rakic, 1982)

THE CATEGORICAL NATURE OF PERCEPTION

Konorski (1967) emphasized the discontinuity between the hierarchical model of Hubel and Wiesel and the categorical nature of experienced perception. Neither animals nor humans normally pay attention to the "lines," "edges,"

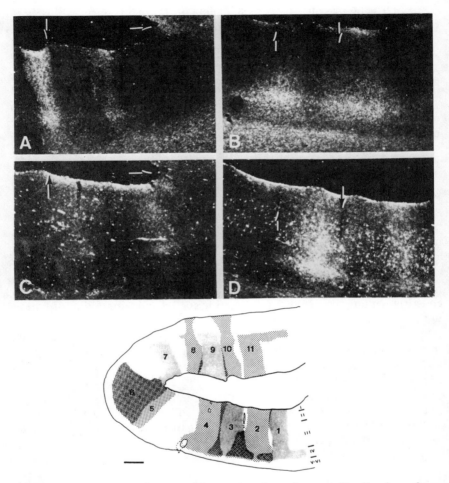

Figure 5.17. Autoradiograms illustrating the columnar distribution of two classes of cortico-cortical projections in the principal sulcus of the primate brain: (A) and (C) callosal (interhemispheric) fiber columns from the right hemisphere alternate with (B) and (D) associational (ipsilateral) terminals in the left hemisphere. (E) The lower figure is a composite diagram of two adjacent sections cut through the convergence zone in the principal sulcus. Autographically labeled callosal fiber columns (1, 3, 6, 7, and 9) are indicated by fine stipple; associational fiber columns (2, 4, 5, 8, 10, and 11) originating in the parietal cortex are shown in coarse stipple. The interdigitated pattern suggests a modular "hypercolumn" in the prefrontal association cortex for interhemispheric integration. Goldman-Rakic & Schwartz, 1982. Photographs courtesy of Dr. Patricia S. Goldman-Rakic. Copyright © 1982 by AAAS.

"gratings," or "angles" that were the adequate stimuli for simple, complex, and hypercomplex cortical cells. Konorski realized that selective attention was an indispensable condition for the excitation of a cell, and yet the very cells that provided the building blocks for conscious unitary perceptions had their peak responses to stimuli that were apparently meaningless and neglected by the perceiving subject.

Here is an impasse that recurs over and over again in psychology—the use by the brain of cues for different perceptual functions that are ignored by the observer or unavailable to conscious introspection. Binocular disparity is one such; in fact, movement parallax, binaural time differences, and all the remaining depth, distance, and other spatial cues upon which our spatial perception depends, are inaccessible, except as the result of sophisticated ad hoc analyses.

Normally, no one pays attention to afterimages although they certainly exist in our visual reception and can be separated from the whole patterns we actually perceive and react to. Certain elements completely resist analysis. Which eye receives a given image? What acoustic elements account for the spectrum of a child's familiar voice? What is in that dish whose taste we instantly recognize? The objects are what interest us—not their elements.

Once these elements are integrated into the unitary perceptions represented by cognons, they no longer retain their individuality. As Konorski put it, "A unit of the higher order representing some integrated stimulus pattern does not 'know' from which components it is synthesized" (1967, p. 76).

The organization of the cortex into separate regions of selectively sensitive nerve cells, responding only to specific sorts of stimuli, provides a promising model for this selectivity and categorical preference. Cells that are close neighbors almost always have similar properties with regard to the features they detect in the outside world. It is not difficult to imagine that columns of cells with common feature-detecting properties are jointly activated by a given drive center and inhibited jointly by a common antidrive center.

Note especially that the same receptors and the same units of lower levels take part in different combinations in various cortical zones. Overlap and economy are the two key words in nature. The more developed the brain of a given species, the more levels that brain contains. While the primary projective areas remain relatively constant in various animals, our brains developed by superimposing on them new layers of cortical integration. This makes possible the gradual discovery of ever smaller units of analysis—multiple new cognons are formed while the earlier ones are retained.

MULTIPLE REPRESENTATION OF OBJECTS AND PATTERNS

Most stimulus objects that we deal with in life are represented not by one set of cognons but by two or more different sets. Concrete nouns—*chair, dog,*

Figure 5.18.   Chairs belonging to the same category are readily classified by the human perceiver—a difficult task for the computer.

fork—all seem to have double, perhaps multiple, representation. When you shut your eyes and call up the image of chair, what do you see? Probably something to sit on with a wooden seat and back and four legs. But you use the word *chair* for metal, upholstered, leather, swivel, pedestal, and many other kinds of chairs. (See Figure 5.18.) Your prototypical chair is a stereotype that is probably no more typical of the class than any other particular specimen. Yet Eleanor Rosch, Carolyn Mervis, and their colleagues have produced impressive evidence that prototypes play a major role in our mental imagery. (Mervis & Rosch, 1981; Mervis & Pani, 1980; Rosch, 1973a, 1973b, 1975; Rosch & Mervis, 1975; Rosch, Mervis, Gray, Johnson, & Boyes-Braem, 1976.) (See Figure 5.19.)

Consider the word "grandfather." A grandfather is simply the father of a parent. Yet, he must be old, bent, bespectacled, bearded, of beaming wrinkles and gentle ways. So it comes as a shock to you to learn that your car-racing friend with his smooth young face is a grandfather. Does your image of grandfather change? Not at all. What is most likely to happen is that your grandfather stereotype remains in one set of cognons just as before, but now you make room for a new set of cognons representing youthful, daring grandfathers. The new set does not replace the old set; instead, you now have two sets of related but independent cognons in place of one. Certainly some such process is currently changing our notions of "feminine" and "masculine" behavior even as we cling to old sex stereotypes.

In other categories, one set of cognons may represent the general properties of a given class of objects; other sets represent particular examples or even a single unique item. So you have cognons for automobiles in general, those that represent cars of different makes and those for your own car. Similarly, you have cognons for birds in general, and those representing robins, pigeons, and other species. You have units representing human faces in general, faces belonging to different groups (women, men, children, various ethnic groups) and faces of your particular acquaintances, family members and significant others. (See Figure 5.20 and Chapter Six.)

Figure 5.19. Some categorical exemplars: A prototypical apple, doctor, cake, bathtub. Each familiar object is recognized immediately as a unitary perception—a *cognon*.

This double or multiple representation of stimulus objects of a given category has interesting neuropathological consequences.

A lesion in one cognitive field may abolish the ability to perceive a particular stimulus object, whereas the ability to perceive the category to which it belongs may be preserved. Since the relations between consecutive levels of each analyzer are based on the convergence-divergence principle, and the principle that each level possesses more units than the preceding one, divergent connections outnumber convergent ones. As a result, the units of the highest level, the higher-order cognons, are more numerous than the units at any lower level. A patient with brain damage may be unable to recognize familiar landmarks, but knows that they are buildings. Another may fail to identify the faces of his own wife and children, but knows that they are faces. The specificity of these agnosias seems incredible until one realizes that significant objects are represented by many cognons, some of which may be destroyed when others are spared by injury or disease.

SUMMARY

Perceptual learning or the formation of cognons (perception units) is a primitive nonassociative kind of learning process—belonging with habituation and sensitization. In fact, by sustaining the orienting reflex to a neutral stimulus, sensitization may be equated with the state of arousal prerequisite for the formation of a cognon.

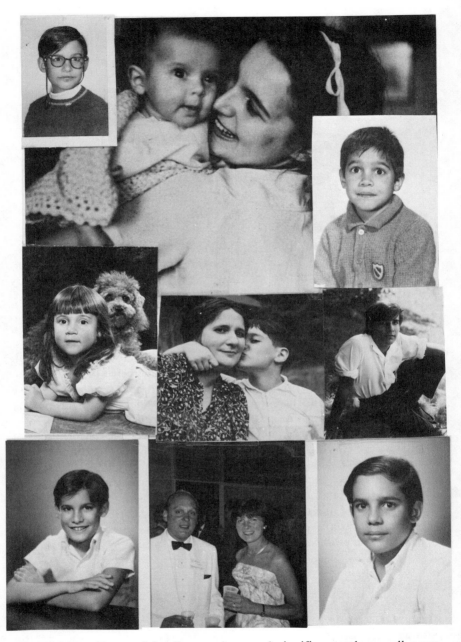

Figure 5.20. Faces of family members and significant others—all correspond to their respective cognons.

Habituation and the extinction of the orientation reflex are a kind of confirmation that perceptual learning has actually occurred. Indeed, a stimulus pattern must be recognized as the same thing the organism has previously experienced or no habituation would be manifest. The simple fact of decrement of response to a repeated stimulus is proof of recognition memory. Something must change; something new either in the stimulus or in the organism must be added or subtracted in order for dishabituation to take place. Then the familiar stimulus once again evokes the targeting reflex, and, if not too distorted, it will be recognized.

The ability to recognize a human face at a glance is a feat whose analysis is as yet beyond scientific description. As Yarbus's research on eye movements shows, during free examination of photographs of faces and scenes, the observers' eyes do not trace out contours or edges, but repetitively fixate selected features. Introspection is unable to specify which aspects of a pattern are thus singled out, but these components must form the deep structures underlying cognition.

In higher mammals, and human beings especially, cognons are not inborn, but they resemble fixed action patterns in two respects. They are relatively invariant in their response. Once initiated, the activity of a cognon is independent of the strength and duration of the eliciting stimulus. The cognon response, like the fixed action pattern, seems to be generated by a central nervous system mechanism (a central program) that does not require feedback from the receptors. This property of cognons has a remarkably interesting consequence. The cognon can be activated in the absence of any eliciting stimulus. In fact, the cognon, once formed, is free of its formative stimulus and begins to function as an internal representation, a mental symbol, that is, as a unitary *image* in imagination and recall.

The question arises: how can a mental representation be triggered without an external stimulus? This is the problem of imagination, memory, and thought. The three chapters on association attempt to answer this question. But first, I would like to present to you the key psychological and neurological evidence for the existence of cognons in the human brain.

As yet, we lack direct electrophysiological or anatomical evidence that unitary perceptions are represented by cognons in the human brain. We do have, however, a vast amount of indirect evidence from the experimental laboratory and from clinical neuropathology, including electrical brain stimulation in conscious human epileptic patients. I shall survey these sources of evidence beginning with the analysis of the psychological properties of cognons for which there is robust experimental support.

SUGGESTED READINGS

Barlow, H.B. Single units and sensation: A neuron doctrine for perceptual psychology? *Perception,* 1972, *1,* 371–394.

Barlow, H.B., Narasimhan, R., & Rosenfield, A. Visual pattern analysis in machines and animals. *Science,* 1972, *177,* 567–575.

Boring, E.G. *Sensation and perception in the history of experimental psychology.* New York: Appleton-Century-Crofts, 1942.

Braddick, O., Campbell, F.W., & Atkinson, J. Channels in vision: Basic aspects. In R. Held, H.W. Leibowitz, & H.-L. Teuber (Eds.), *Handbook of sensory physiology: Perception* (Vol. VIII). New York: Springer-Verlag, 1978.

Bregman, A.S. Asking the "what for" question in auditory perception. In M. Kubovy & J.R. Pomerantz (Eds.), *Perceptual organization.* Hillsdale, N.J.: Erlbaum, 1981.

Bruner, J.S., Goodnow, J.J., & Austin, J.G. *A study of thinking.* New York: Wiley, 1956.

Campbell, F.W. The transmission of spatial information through the visual system. In F.O. Schmitt & F.G. Worden (Eds.), *The neurosciences: Third study program.* Cambridge: MIT Press, 1974.

Campbell, F.W., & Robson, J.G. Application of Fourier analysis to the visibility of gratings. *Journal of Physiology,* 1968, *197,* 551–566.

Kandel, E.R. *Cellular basis of behavior: An introduction to behavioral neurobiology.* San Francisco: W.H. Freeman, 1976.

Kandel, E.R., & Schwartz, J.H. Molecular biology of learning: Modulation of transmitter release. *Science,* 1982, *218,* 433–442.

Koffka, K. *Principles of Gestalt psychology.* New York: Harcourt Brace, 1935.

Köhler, W. *Gestalt psychology.* New York: Liveright, 1947.

Konorski, J. *Integrative activity of the brain: An interdisciplinary approach.* Chicago: University of Chicago Press, 1967.

Rosch, E. Principles of categorization. In E. Rosch & B.B. Lloyd (Eds.), *Cognition and categorization.* Hillsdale, N.J.: Erlbaum, 1978.

Rosch, E., & Lloyd, B. *Cognition and categorization.* Hillsdale, N.J.: Erlbaum, 1978.

Senden, M. von. *[Space and sight]* (P. Heath, trans.). Glencoe, Ill.: Free Press, 1960.

Thompson, R.F., & Spencer, W.A. Habituation: A model phenomenon for the study of neuronal substrates of behavior. *Psychological Review,* 1966, *73,* 16–43.

Wittgenstein, L. *Philosophical investigations.* New York: Macmillan, 1953.

Yarbus, A.L. *Eye movements and vision.* New York: Plenum, 1967.

CHAPTER SIX

Categories of Perception in Particular Analyzers of the Human Brain

Perception involves an act of categorization.... We stimulate an organism with some appropriate input and he responds by referring the input to some class of things or events.

(Bruner, 1957, p. 123)

Adequate perceptual representation involves the learning of appropriate categories, the learning of cues useful in placing objects appropriately in such systems of categories, and the learning of what objects are likely to occur in the environment.

(Bruner, 1957, p. 127)

All human perception consists of categorized rather than isolated perceptions.... I mean that I do not see the world simply in color and shape but also as a world with sense and meaning. I do not merely see something round and black with two hands; I see a clock and I can distinguish one hand from the other. Some brain-injured patients say, when they see a clock, that they are seeing something round and white with two thin steel strips, but they do not know it is a clock; such people have lost their real relationships with objects.

(Vygotsky, 1967, p. 33)

INTRODUCTION

This chapter will present the psychological evidence for the cognon theory of brain functions in perception and in cognition. The specifically neurophysiological evidence for the theory will be considered in a later chapter. All the data undergirding the premise that the human brain structures experience into discrete categories of cognons cannot be contained even in two chapters. That is the burden of the entire book.

The following sections deal with the results of two major sources of support for cognon functions in human behavior. These are, first, the accumulated evidence of a century of widely diverse psychological experiments on human perception and memory. Here is an immense body of solid research to show that subjective experience is represented in separate categories of unitary perceptions. The second source of support is based on recent laboratory investigations of selective perceptual adaptation and selective modification of behavior in human subjects. The curious aftereffects of exposure to specific categories of stimulation offer a noninvasive psychological probe into neural channels in the human cortex analogous to the microelectrode studies of highly specific properties of single neurons in cat and monkey cortex. This work is beginning to provide answers to such questions as: How modifiable is human perception and action? Is the individual changed as a whole, or are specific categories of perception and action changed by experience? What is the process by which neural connections can be transformed by individual experience? Can there be recovery from brain damage, and if so, how?

Myriad experiments conducted over years of psychological research demonstrate that mental representations correspond with remarkable accuracy to objects and events in the physical world. These mental representations called *cognons* are the means by which we try to comprehend reality. Six psychological properties of cognons have central importance. Let us look at them briefly.

THE PROPERTIES OF COGNONS

1. The first property of cognons is that they are pattern or object recognition devices. A cognon can recognize a face and tell an old one from a young one; it can recognize a voice and tell a male from a female; it can recognize a printed letter in a variety of type fonts; it can recognize handwriting even though the words written are illegible; it can recognize a hidden figure in a puzzle, a military target buried in camouflage. (See Figure 6.1.)

Figure 6.1. Hidden figures. (A) Dog (Street, 1931). (B) Horse and rider (Street, 1931). (C) "My Wife and My Mother-in-Law" by W.E. Hill. Originally published in *Puck*, 1915, and reproduced by Edwin G. Boring, 1930. (D) How many faces do you see? Drawing by Gerald H. Fisher.

Figure 6.2. (A) Photograph of a scene with normal perspective relations. (B) Identical photograph as in Figure 6.2A except that duplicates of distant lamp and fence posts have been inserted in foreground. From Evans, 1948. Copyright © 1948 by John Wiley & Sons.

The cognon represents a standard or model for a given stimulus object, bending the actual stimulus input to this standard without regard for photographic accuracy. This rectifying character of the cognon—its ability to correct a retinal projection to accord with its model—is what accounts for the constancies of perception (Gregory, 1966, 1968; 1970; Koffka, 1935; Woodworth, 1938). We see the roundness of a coin as we turn it this way or that, in spite of its varying elliptical projection (Stavrianos, 1945). We see the man walking away from us as constant in size despite his shrinking visual angle at the eye (Gilinsky, 1951; 1955; 1980). Even the photograph (Figure 6.2) shows this tendency to size constancy.

The cognon can extract the basic forms of an object from a background of irrelevant objects despite large changes in stimulation at the receptors; that is, it can "read out" the meaning and essence of real objects. Except at a crude level, this is something that cannot as yet be done by machines. Computers can discriminate fingerprints and block print, but the absolute identification of human faces and signatures is subtler and more sophisticated (Selfridge & Neisser, 1960). What the computer fails to "see" is what you "know" from past experience to be there.

2. A related property of cognons is their categorization. Studies of stimulus generalization and discrimination find the sense of sight, hearing, touch, smell, and so on, each contain separate categories of unitary perceptions based on differences between their elements (Gleitman & Jonides, 1976; 1978; Rosch, et al., 1975; 1976; Jonides & Gleitman, 1972). Files of related cognons are localized in different small areas of the brain. For instance, the visual pattern system contains categories representing human beings, animals, small manipulable objects, keys, pencils, cups; large movable objects, chairs, bicycles, cars; immobile objects, buildings, roads, trees; and far-off scenes, mountains, rivers, landscapes (Konorski, 1967). The visual space system categorizes spatial relations into such polarities as near and far, above and below, left and right, inside and outside (Graham, 1965; Noton & Stark, 1971a.b.). The auditory system divides heard sounds into categories also—music, voices, spoken words, whistles, bells, and noises of the external world (Broadbent, 1958; Kimura, 1967; Studdert-Kennedy & Shankweiler, 1970).

3. An important property of a cognon is its integrity—its activation as a single, unitary, indivisible event. When there is more than one way of perceiving a pattern, we perceive first in one way, then another. The alternatives do not mix but succeed one another in mutually exclusive fashion (Rubin, 1915; 1921; Woodworth, 1938). The separation allows comparison; thus we can appreciate the meaning of a pun, auditory or visual. (See Figure 6.3.)

Comprehending a word is an all-or-none affair; either it is recognized as a whole or it is not recognized at all. Since a word is a unitary perception, the change of one vowel modifies the whole word and makes it unrecognizable. So

Figure 6.3. *Day and Night.* Woodcut by M.C. Escher, 1938. Gift of George Hopper Fitch. By permission of Yale University Art Gallery.

my French acquaintances often do not understand a French word spoken by me. Although I think I pronounce it exactly as they do, they hear something I do not. Sometimes we do not understand a familiar word, not because it is mispronounced, but because its sound is muffled by a noisy background.

We may fail to recognize a figure that is embedded in a picture puzzle even though we have seen the isolated figure hundreds of times before (Gottschaldt, 1926). In Figure 6.4 we struggle to see the pattern as a thing. If we are successful in penetrating the camouflage, the recognition occurs as a unitary experience and the pattern is grasped as a whole. How do we manage to impose organization on such fragmentary information as this? Once you have extracted the hidden form, you can readily reconstruct it every time you meet it again. What is the basis for this remarkable stability? (See Figure 6.4.)

The significant information must have been stored in a more or less permanent file from which it is retrievable, given the same or sufficiently similar cues on subsequent occasions.

4. The cognons are higher-order feature detectors—they are acutely selective integrators that extract the essential elements and ignore or actively suppress the nonessential elements in complex stimulus patterns. They are the

Figure 6.4. Ronald James's photograph demonstrates the organization imposed on visual perception by the brain. Blakemore, 1977.

Figure 6.5. A caricature. Missing contours are supplied by your Charlie Chaplin cognon.

mechanisms that finally analyze the converging coded signals and compare them with criteria previously laid down by genes or learning for initiating complex motor action. So they provide for animals the built-in trigger units or "releasers" of the ethologists (Hess, 1958; 1964; Lorenz, 1950; Tinbergen, 1951), and they accentuate for us the significant outlines and contours of objects known from past experience. It is easy to see that not all elements of a projected stimulus pattern are necessary for its recognition. A caricature made by only a few lines may represent the original so well that everyone recognizes it without hesitation. (See Figure 6.5.)

The principle of selectivity of relevant elements for high-level feature detection parallels the selectivity of receptive fields of the single-cell studies by Hubel and Wiesel (1962; 1968) in the visual pathways from eye to brain.

This selective process has a remarkable obverse side. Elements that are not there physically are supplied or created by the brain and form the basis for some intriguing illusions. Indeed, even when physical contours are missing, the visual system supplies subjective or illusory contours (Kanizsa, 1976; 1979). This is brought out especially well by figures (such as Figure 6.6) in which a contour is subjectively completed across a homogeneous portion of

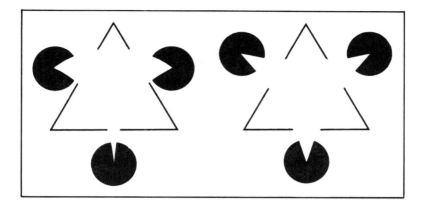

Figure 6.6. Illusory contours. Kanizsa, 1979. *Organization in Vision.* Copyright © 1979 by Gaetano Kanizsa. Reprinted by permission of Praeger Publishers.

the field. The cognon has a creative function—it has invented a figure that seems to have no stimulus counterparts, no physical reality. Even children experience the illusion, yet know that it is subjective. So Fiona, age 9, remarked, "I see a triangle that isn't really there!"

5. Another important property of cognons is the complementary, yet opponent, character of their elements. Among the units of the lower level converging upon a given perceptive unit, both on-units and off-units play an equal role—the pattern of adequate stimuli for a given cognon contains paired complements. The interesting result for perception is that the elements disappear. You never see a reddish-green or a yellowish-blue. These comple-

mentary colors form disappearing color-pairs, and what you see is gray (Ladd-Franklin, 1929; Woodworth, 1938).

If one element of a given stimulus pattern is missing or replaced by a different one, either the change will not even be noticed and the presented pattern will excite the cognon to respond—or the change in the pattern will prevent its recognition. Then the pattern will not be accepted as belonging to our perceptive file, but will be considered a completely new pattern.

It sometimes happens that an object is recognized but that something seems to be changed in it. What has changed may not be immediately apparent. The failure to identify what is amiss shows that the particular elements do not participate as such in our perception. Errors in reading mutilated words show that the mutilations are usually not seen as such. In a pioneer study Pillsbury (1897) exposed words with a letter omitted, a false letter substituted or a letter blurred by typing x over it. The subject was asked to report what letters were seen. Some of the reports are shown below:

Letters Exposed	Word Read	Subject's comments
kommonly	commonly	"But I can't make out the first letter."
fashxon	fashion	"Didn't see the i."
duplably	culpably	"The c was not clear."
foyever	forever	"There is a hair across the r."
disal	deal	"There may be something between e and a."
uvermore	evermore	"Seems to be an m before it."
danxe	danger	"The r seemed faint."
verbati	verbatim	"The last two letters seemed a little dim."

These results are still some of the best evidence we have that the elements that converge on a cognon are complementary. Woodworth writes: "An important fact stands out in the comments: O sees details which he cannot use in reading the word.... He reads 'foyever' as 'forever,' but thinks there must be a hair across the r; or he reads 'danxe' as 'danger' but admits that the r seemed faint" (1938, p. 740).

The observer's failure to realize precisely what is wrong with the word shows that the particular elements do not enter as such in his perception. Another important fact emerges in the reports. The misreadings are of probable real words—they are not nonsense. The influence of context, of familiarity—and of unit activation—is unmistakable. As a high-level decision unit, the cognon has the capacity to decide whether a threshold signal of a predetermined criterion has been met and to make an either-or, go–no-go reaction.

It is this property of mutual exclusivity that shifts perception from one alternative figure to another in reversible perspective drawings. As we have seen, the integrity principle prevents the merger of the two percepts—if one is seen as figure, the other is seen as ground. (See Figure 6.7.)

The problem remains: why is it that once a given organization has been achieved, the advantage shifts, and figure and ground reverse roles? The principle of complementarity provides a physiological basis for this multi-stabilty of perception (Attneave, 1971). The fine balance of sensitivities within the visual pathways leading to the activation of a given cognon is followed by the habituation response, and the disappearance of the corresponding percept. Immediately the visual system adjusts the balance to compensate for the lost response and activates the paired complementary cognon. Figure and ground shift places. The principle of complementarity is related to the physiological contrast mechanism that excites the seesaw interplay between the successively activated cognons.

6. An important property of unitary perceptions is the reciprocal interference between cognons of the same category. Try to remember the names of seven or more persons at a party after a single introduction (Miller, 1956a; 1956b). You can hardly do so. Even though the names are pronounced distinctly and you pay particular attention to each one, you cannot grasp them all. All-digit dialing of telephone numbers brings out this difficulty also; the numbers belong to the same category. We do better with a combination of words and numbers: (212) Butterfield 8-0306 is easier to recall than its all-digit equivalent (212) 288-0306. A number like (914) 941-1914 is hardest of all to remember. The transposed identical numbers compound the antagonism. Not only do we have to identify the digits, but must keep them in order as well (Estes, 1973; 1975).

Perceptions from different sensory systems show no such antagonism. We can read and listen to music, or eat and converse at the same time because the respective perceptions belong to different categories. Only when one activity arouses a strong emotion such as anger or fear, then a person—for example, a driver caught in a difficult situation—stops listening to a conversation and becomes totally absorbed in, say, avoiding traffic. Here the interference is not between rival perceptions, but between the emotions produced by these perceptions. The stronger emotion—fear of an accident, in this case—absorbs the driver's attention and inhibits other activity.

The mechanism of opposition between cognons of the same category arises from the powerful lateral and pericolumnar inhibition within any one region of the cerebral cortex. Good examples, besides figure-ground reversals, or perceptual rivalry, are the shifts in perception illustrated by simultaneous contrast and the negative aftereffects (see Figure 6.8) of brightness, color, tilt, size, and curvature (Breese, 1899; Campbell et al., 1973; Cohen, Bill, & Gilinsky, 1968; Favreau & Corballis, 1976; McCollough, 1965).

A

"All is Vanity"

B

C

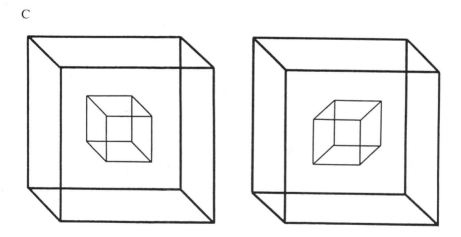

Figure 6.7. Ambiguous figures. (A) "All Is Vanity." Gilbert, 1892. (B) Rabbit-duck from Joseph Jastrow, 1900. (C) Double Necker cube: a cube within a cube. Both cubes appear to reverse in depth. When parallel (1) they reverse together; otherwise (2) the inner cube reverses more quickly than the outer cube. The effect is the same with one eye closed—a form of monocular rivalry. After Adams & Haire, 1959.

Figure 6.8. Figural aftereffects. (A) Redundant line pattern generates shimmering multicolored complementary afterimages. From MacKay, 1957. (B) Combination spiral appears both to expand and to contract when rotated. The aftereffects are the exact reverse of those that produced them.

In addition to these general properties of cognons, we hope to understand what features make cognons unique. First, we can try to specify what categories there are in the various analyzers. We will begin with vision.

CATEGORIES OF UNITARY PERCEPTION IN THE VISUAL ANALYZER

Vision offers a favorable system for detailed study of the organization of cognons in the cerebral cortex. Because of its importance for human perception, the visual system is the most thoroughly investigated. It is, therefore, the best known of all the analyzers and may serve as a paradigm for the others.

Many of the electrophysiological and anatomical staining techniques that are helping to unravel the organization of the visual system are also used to investigate the auditory and the somatic sensory system. Thus we shall have an opportunity to compare these three sensory systems. From their similarities, a general picture of cortical organization emerges—one that is wonderfully precise in anatomical design, yet sufficiently flexible to allow us to learn to recognize instantly millions of objects and events perceived during the course of a lifetime, and to name them—making language possible.

A striking characteristic of the visual system is that it seems to be not one, but several, light-sensitive systems. This multiplicity is not unique to vision: every analyzer—somatosensory, auditory, and so on—contains multiple pathways, each with its own specialized function. The information coming into the eye is sorted into particular subsystems, or modalities, conducted in parallel pathways or mechanisms of vision.

Our visual system contains five major subsystems:

1. Light and darkness—illumination.
2. Spatial relations and places—*where* is it?
3. Movement, direction, velocity—*what* is it *doing?*
4. Colors—surface and expanse hues, brilliance and saturation.
5. Patterns, objects, and people—*what* or *who* is it?

These subsystems are matters of everyday adaptation and survival for all normally sighted humans and many other species. Each subsystem is further divided into particular *categories* of visual perception.

Let us examine the categories of unitary perception mediated by vision, then turn to the categories of unitary perceptions belonging to the other analyzers.

LIGHT AND DARKNESS: GENERAL ILLUMINATION

Numerous experiments support the primary distinction between light-sensitive pathways for general illumination (light and darkness) and visual pathways for the perception of objects and visual space. The most common biological rhythms are circadian—those with a period of 24 hours. Under natural conditions, all known mammalian circadian rhythms are entrained by the light-dark cycle of day and night. According to current ideas, many of these rhythms manifest self-sustained oscillators (biologic clocks) endogenous to the brain. (von Holst, 1973; Wilson, 1966).

Perception of Changes in Brightness

The visual system plays a significant role in sleep-vigilance activity and protective activity. Darkness may produce sleep in diurnal animals like us, and wakefulness in nocturnal animals. The sudden shadowing that occurs with the approach of a predator may elicit fear, freezing, or flight in small mammals, in frogs, and in fish.

"Perhaps the most striking feature of the vertebrate retina," Ratliff (1965) suggested, "is a pronounced specialized sensitivity to temporal changes of illumination" (p. 169). The visual system exhibits marked transient responses to sudden changes in stimulus intensity. My dissertation (Steinman, 1944) was based on human experiments designed to examine human reaction time to sudden changes in illumination. The next section gives the results.

Reaction Time to Sudden Change in Brightness

Reaction time affords a means of studying perception as being dependent on the kind and intensity of a stimulus. In the *simple* reaction time experiment there is only one stimulus and one response at every trial. At the ready signal, the subject prepares to react as quickly as possible when the anticipated stimulus arrives. An electric timer measures the interval between the presentation of the stimulus and the response. Results of such studies show that for light, sound, and other stimuli, the strength of the stimulus is an important determinant of the speed of reaction. The stronger the stimulus, the faster the reaction.

The simple reaction time experiment serves as a tool for the study of intensity *discrimination* by requiring the subject to react to a sudden change in intensity. A change in luminance or brightness may be barely perceptible, or it may be large and clear; it may start from an absolute level of low or high intensity; and it may represent a step up or a step down in intensity. Reaction time may be shown to depend on all three factors: the initial intensity level, the size of the step, and the direction of change—whether it is an increase or a decrease in brightness.

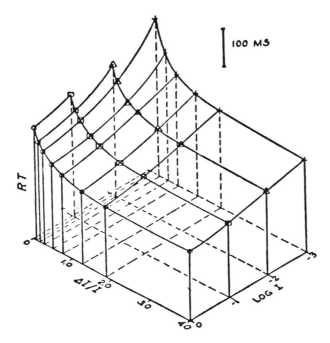

Figure 6.9. Reaction time to changes in brightness. The height of the lines represents reaction time, which is jointly determined by intensity level (Log I) and relative size of change in intensity ($\Delta I/I$). Faster reactions (shorter lines) result from larger stimulus changes. Steinman, 1944.

I found that each one of these factors significantly determines reaction time. Seated in front of a lighted disk, the subject prepared to react as soon as the lighted disk was perceived to brighten or to darken. The results showed that reaction time was markedly affected both by the absolute level of intensity and by the size of the brightness change. The higher the initial level and the larger the change, the shorter were the reaction times. (See Figure 6.9.)

This is a *simple* reaction because there is only one stimulus and one response and the subject could be highly prepared in advance to respond. Yet the method is a reliable measure of discriminatory ability because it measures the reaction to a change from one level of stimulation to another. The larger the step up or down, the faster the reaction; the smaller the step up or down, the slower the reaction. Since the threshold varied from moment to moment, there were some failures to respond to the very small brightness changes. What is of interest is that even beyond the 100 percent point of correct responding (no missed reactions), there was a consistent decrease of reaction time as the change in brightness grew more noticeable.

Surprisingly, the *direction* of change as well as the amount of change was a factor influencing reaction time. Reactions to decrements (apparent darkening) were always faster than reactions to increments (apparent brightening) of light intensity. Even when the subject was unable to discern the direction of change—but simply saw a flicker—the result was the same. Decrements gave shorter reaction times than equally small or equally large increments of brightness change.

In further studies (Steinman, 1944), the subjects *rated* the *perceived magnitude* of various amounts of brightness change by using a seven-step scale—the greater the apparent change the higher the number the subject was told to report. The results were consistent—subjective magnitude agreed with reaction time. Ratings were higher for larger changes and for decrements, as compared with smaller changes and increments, just as response latencies were shorter for these conditions.

The systematic nature of these findings reflects a basic difference in the underlying physiology of responses to increments and decrements. The use of reaction time gives a prompt and reliable measure that mirrors subjective experience and throws light on the mechanisms involved. The results suggest that two different populations of nerve cells, different categories of *cognons,* regulate response to illumination—one for lightness and the other for darkness.

Babies Scan Differently in Darkness and in Light

Eye movement studies, even in very young babies, provide supporting evidence for dynamic visual activity in darkness different from that in light. How do newborn infants react in the absence of light? Apparently, sleeping babies open their eyes abruptly to a rapid offset of light. Thus newborns are capable of responding to small brightness shifts through their eyelids. Even more impressive, newborns as young as eight hours of age open their eyes in darkness and scan actively (Haith, 1973). In his stimulating monograph, *Rules that Babies Look By,* Haith (1980) shows that the newborn actively constructs a visual world by controlled scanning in darkness, and also in light, but then only when contours are available. The strong differential effects of light and of dark, even in the very young infant, suggest that light and dark are qualitatively different conditions, not simply two levels of a simple quantitative dimension.

Most persuasive are Haith's attempts to explain how the newborn "gets going" and "keeps going"—a way of thinking about visual behavior, not as a series of static responses to external stimuli, but as ongoing activity in which the baby pursues a biologically given agenda. Newborns move their eyes virtually every one-half second. One overriding principle seems to govern visual activity in the early weeks—"to maximize cortical firing rate" (Haith,

1980). Two scanning routines serve the function of keeping the firing rate at a high level—an *ambient* search routine and an *inspection* or *focal* scan routine. The ambient search routine serves to find targets for inspection. It governs the continuous eye-movement activity and operates in darkness when the cortical firing rate is low. The focal scan routine comes into play when a target is detected and it produces contours, crossing back and forth over edges. Since cortical cells appear to be tuned to fire to contours, this process perfects a stable convergence mechanism. As the eyes converge on an edge, a higher firing rate results; the system seeks convergence and this perhaps accomplishes the formation of more complex binocularly driven cells in the cortex. The activity that produces a high firing rate, fixating and scanning near areas of multiple spatial frequencies, also keeps babies looking at the most informative parts of their visual field.

AMBIENT AND FOCAL VISION

Babies cannot tell the investigator what they see, what their internal representation of the world looks like. But they behave as if their voluntary motor acts were continuously being guided by some sort of perception that is not too different from our own. In the process, vision must be closely attuned to physical events in the sense that action must conform to the physical world. From this point of view, a seen object is biologically important if it is accurately located and identified.

There are two questions here: Where is it in space? What size (shape or texture) would it have if it were close enough to be seized or touched in some way? The answers to these questions depend upon two kinds of visual perception—the location of objects in visual space and their visual identification as unique objects.

The two visual functions, locating and identifying, are now believed to be subserved by anatomically distinct brain mechanisms (Held et al., 1967–1968). The main idea is that vision involves two parallel processes—one *ambient*, determining space-at-large around the body, the other *focal*, examining detail in small areas of space in central vision. But each one of these processes, in turn, contains several subdivisions. We turn next to ambient space perception and its subdivisions.

VISUAL PERCEPTION OF SPATIAL RELATIONS

The visual system concerned with the spatial relations between the observer and the environment, and between various parts of the environment, plays a significant role in human and in nonhuman behavior. Specific types of spatial unitary perceptions include the following three sets of categories:

1. *Egocentric Space Perception:* The relations between objects and ourselves. For example, the distance of an object and its position in the vertical and horizontal planes relative to our own position in space. (See Figure 6.10A.)

2. *Allocentric Space Perception:* The distances and relations between objects—near-far, left-right, above-below, inside-outside, contiguous-separate. Many pairs are reciprocally related. (See Figure 6.10B.)

3. *Visual Movement Perception:* The seen movement of a part of ourselves or an object through space—its direction, velocity, acceleration, type of movement (smooth, jerky, etc.). This category may also be subdivided into egocentric and allocentric motion in relation to the self and to other objects, respectively.

VISUAL MOVEMENT: REAL AND APPARENT MOTION

Driving an automobile in traffic confronts the human eye with a series of complex visual problems. The driver has to be able to discern and to anticipate many swiftly changing scenes.

Photographic records of eye movements made with one television camera to record the scene and another to record a magnified reflection of a spot of light reflected from the cornea by a special optical device worn by the driver, tells us what the eyes are looking at. The records reveal what features attract notice and also much that is overlooked (Thomas, 1968).

The driver's eyes flick rapidly about the scene in a series of saccades, or jumps, from one fixation to the next. Nothing, of course, is seen during the saccade that may reach a speed of more than 500 degrees per second. What the eye does fixate are the edge of the road, passing vehicles, the outlines of tall buildings, a crossing pedestrian. But the most powerful visual stimulus is *movement*.

The eyes are strongly drawn to flashing lights, such as those of a turn indicator on the car ahead, or a neon sign at the side of the road. When the image of an object strikes the periphery of the retina, the eyes swing involuntarily so that the object is focused on two foveas and can be perceived in detail. Although the periphery of the retina is poorly equipped to resolve detail, it is exquisitely sensitive to movement in the corner of the eye. This motion sensitivity at the edge of the visual field demonstrates that the retina functions as an effective wide-angle early warning system.

An object does not actually have to move to exert a strong attraction. *Apparent visual movement* is a familiar phenomenon on the motion picture

B

Figure 6.10. (A) Egocentric space perception. (B) Allocentric space perception. Drawings by Susan McGoey.

screen. The motions that you see on the screen are illusory in that you actually get a series of still snapshots separated by brief intervals of time, and the projector casts these fixed images and blank intervals at a rate adjusted to give natural, lifelike, rapid, or slow motion effects for your entertainment.

The psychological study of these effects led to the founding of Gestalt psychology when Wertheimer (1912) demonstrated the *phi* phenomenon. He showed that two short vertical lines, one centimeter apart, could be exposed one after the other to give different effects, depending primarily on the time-interval between the exposures. If the blank interval is greater than 200 milliseconds, the two lines are seen to be really successive and stationary; if the interval is shortened to less than 30 milliseconds, the appearance of succession is lost. At intermediate interstimulus intervals, the observer sees one line or even an indeterminate *something* moving from the first position to the second. The Gestalt psychologists attached theoretical importance to the phenomenon because it presented to the brain of the perceiver a powerful visual illusion that cried out for explanation.

People do not need to be able to identify an object in order to locate its position, its direction, or its velocity of movement. In fact, we can be completely unfamiliar with certain objects and still determine precisely how they are spatially and temporally related to each other and to us. These highly specialized perceptions are unitary; that is, the evaluation of their spatial relations is immediate and does not require the transfer of gaze from one point to another.

We now know that the visual system contains independent mechanisms for the detection of motion (Enroth-Cugell & Robson, 1966; Kulikowski & Tolhurst, 1973) that are separate from the feature detectors for contours and colors. If the neurons representing unitary perceptions of motion are activated, the same cognons are affected, regardless of whether the motion is physically real or only apparent.

COLOR VISION

The artist trains her eye to analyze the total reflected light and to distinguish the component colors of illumination and object. For this to be possible, the stimulus characteristics must be separately perceivable. The experienced observer can separate the impressions received from two subsystems, one for perceiving the brightness or lightness of the illumination, the other for perceiving the brightness or lightness of the object. This analytical ability requires training. The artist learns to discriminate the sensory stimuli coming from the external illumination from those reflected by the object. This is possible only because independent categories of *cognons* exist in parallel to permit comparisons.

In every case, experiments show that, when the field of view is narrowed to a single object, constancy of any of its stimulus attributes disappears. As Woodworth and Schlosberg (1954) point out in the case of object color, in order to know the object color we must be able to see the illumination. Yet, in order to use the reflected light as an index of object color, we must be able to see the color of the object—a circular tangle until we realize that:

1. Normally we see more than one object simultaneously in the field of view, and
2. Indirect vision affords a total impression of illumination; indeed, we perceive regions of different illumination revealed by highlights and by shadows.

Katz (1935) made an interesting distinction between two or more modes of color perception. We are most familiar with object or surface color because it is an important cue for identifying objects. But we readily see other color, such as the cloudless sky viewed from an open field or from a mountain top. It then appears as a blue expanse of color at no definite distance. We look through a tube at a uniform surface and the surface color vanishes. What we see instead is an expanse, or aperture color, that appears to be three-dimensional and self-luminous. A surface color is two-dimensional and opaque, and reflects the illumination impinging upon it.

Other modes of color appearance have been identified (sparkle, transparency, luster, etc.) and the illuminating engineer, artist, or anyone concerned with light and lighting, needs to recognize how best to produce a given mode of color perception. The existence of separate mechanisms, *cognons,* for these various modes is supported by the finding that perception can take place in one or more modes simultaneously (Beck, 1972; Evans, 1948). On the basis of both human and monkey experiments, the conclusion is compelling that, in general, we register the general level and color of illumination as well as the differences in illumination by one set of cognons, and the colors of objects by parallel processes involving different sets of cognons (Land, 1959; 1964; Zeki, 1980). It is the integration of these two modes of visual information that maintains the invariance of visible things, or object constancy, in an ever-changing environment.

VISUAL PERCEPTION OF PATTERNS, PEOPLE, AND OBJECTS

Perhaps the most intriguing visual specialization is that concerned with the perception of patterns, people, and objects.

The capacity for processing detailed visual information by means of saccadic eye movements is highly developed in human beings. Focal vision enables our eyes to explore a frontal area that subtends about 45 degrees while the head is kept in constant orientation (Held et al., 1967–1968). The saccadic eye movements provide a succession of spatially discrete samples. At each fixation, the observer experiences a heightened resolution of a particular part of the field in the center of clear vision. The intake of this information gives rise to a unitary perception—the activity of a cognon.

The main categories of cognons that represent particular things and persons in visual perception, based on psychological data and clinical neuropathology, are distinguished from each other on psychological and neurological grounds. They can be divided into two major groups: animate objects and inanimate objects.

1. Inanimate Objects

(a) *Small, manipulable objects.* Everyday objects that we handle and move about in various positions so that we see them in different orientations and at various distances against different backgrounds, include pens, paper clips, cups, utensils, keys, watches, coins, eyeglasses, and similar objects. Their neural units form strong bidirectional associations with the corresponding units of the somatic sensory analyzer, provided by holding or touching the specific objects.

(b) *Large, mobile objects.* Closely related to the first category, there is a group of larger movable objects—bicycles, automobiles, and other things on wheels, and pieces of furniture that can be moved. Those can be seen as a whole only from some distance too far to allow the whole object to be scrutinized by touch. Probably they are represented in vision by different sets of cognons, those representing the object seen as a whole, and those representing parts of the object seen closely—for example, the hood, or dashboard and steering wheel of the car, the top of the desk, or the wing of the plane.

(c) *Nonmanipulable objects.* Large, stationary objects, buildings, trees, airports, and so on, are too large to be moved. They are seen only in relation to their background. They are often unrecognizable in a new setting or a changed orientation. For example, when the object is inverted, it can only be recognized by an act of mental inversion.

(d) *Signs* (alphanumeric symbols, printed words, musical notes). The category containing letters of the alphabet, short words, digits, and other signs is directly involved in intermodal and symbolic processes. Printed letters are typically oriented in both vertical and horizontal dimensions—some are asymmetrical—and are all composed of specific combinations of straight and curved line elements. Each letter and number is associated with a particular articulate sound, a phoneme or a word, with a kinesthetic pattern used in writing it.

(e) *Handwriting*. Familiar handwriting can be recognized even when the individual letters or words cannot be identified. This fact shows that handwriting belongs to a separate category of perceptions distinct from that of printed signs or symbols.

2. Animate Objects

(a) *Human faces* (individual women, men, children, friends, self, significant or famous persons)

(b) *Facial expressions* (smiling, hostile, sad, unpleasant, etc.)

(c) *People* (familiar persons, moving bodies, social interactions, etc.)

(d) *Animals* (domestic, wild, pets, birds, fish, insects, etc.)

(e) *Postures and actions* (hands, fingers, limbs, head, trunk, body
     language)

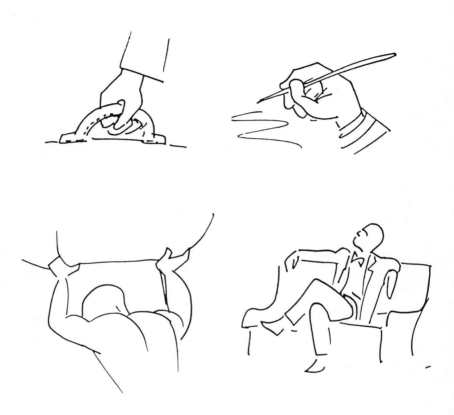

Psychological experiments reveal robust evidence for these categories of
animate objects as distinct, separable, and unique entities of experience.
Chapter Nine presents the findings based on clinical observations of patients
with brain damage. This evidence reveals that circumscribed lesions of
different parts of the brain lead to the loss of highly specific perceptual and
cognitive capacities. For instance, one area of the brain is specialized for
recognizing human faces and, if injured by disease or injury, may lead to the
total inability to recognize familiar faces *(prosopagnosia)* while all other
categories of visual perception are spared. Separate regions of the brain are
specialized for other unique categories of perception. This principle of
categorization is increasingly evident in normal human subjects also and, as
the next section shows, can be demonstrated strikingly in noninvasive
experiments on perceptual adaptation.

SELECTIVE ADAPTATION EXPERIMENTS ON HUMAN SUBJECTS

Your lack of constant awareness that you are receiving stimulation from the seat of your chair arises from a rapid decline in the frequency of afferent impulses from the region of contact. This mechanism of peripheral habituation, or *adaptation,* as it is often called, also applies to central neurons, or cognons, that respond initially to specific patterns of sensory input.

In the visual cortex of the cat and monkey, these adaptation effects are highly specific for orientation and for spatial frequency, the key features governing the response of nerve cells in this region of the brain. The evidence is based on microelectrode records of the responses of single cells to repeated or prolonged stimulation.

Similar direct electrophysiological evidence, of course, is not available for the human brain, but there are strong inferential grounds for assuming the existence of orientation- and frequency-specific neurons in our brains. This indirect evidence is based on experiments demonstrating selective adaptation and other aftereffects in human subjects.

A series of experiments on adaptation to visual patterns in human subjects was conducted in our laboratory at the University of Bridgeport (Gilinsky, 1967; 1968; Gilinsky & Mayo, 1971).

Our initial excitement came from the discovery of highly specific aftereffects of adaptation to visual patterns. (See Figure 6.11.) Following the inspection of a high contrast grating of light and dark *vertical* stripes, the observer was *unable* for some time to detect a similar low contrast grating of vertical stripes. However, *horizontal* and *diagonal* gratings of equally low contrast were not affected by adaptation to vertical stripes, but were immediately perceptible. The analogous result followed the inspection of either a horizontal grating or a diagonal grating. In other words, there is a selective rise in threshold for the detection of gratings with the *same orientation* as the inspection grating. This elevation in contrast thresholds occurs only for gratings with greatly similar orientation and spatial frequency.

These experiments provide a noninvasive probe into neural mechanisms in the human visual system. The mechanisms here described appear to be remarkably similar in their response characteristics to the single cells found by Hubel and Wiesel's microelectrode experiments in the visual cortex of cat and monkey. The full extent of this similarity was brought home by further quantitative experiments (Gilinsky & Mayo, 1971). We found that narrow channels in the human visual system are selectively sensitive to the orientation of contours in much the same way as shown by single cells in the anatomically similar visual cortex of the monkey.

But critics suggested that our results may not have been reflections of the narrow orientational selectivity of different channels of neurons in the cortex of the brain so much as purely peripheral effects in the retina of the eye.

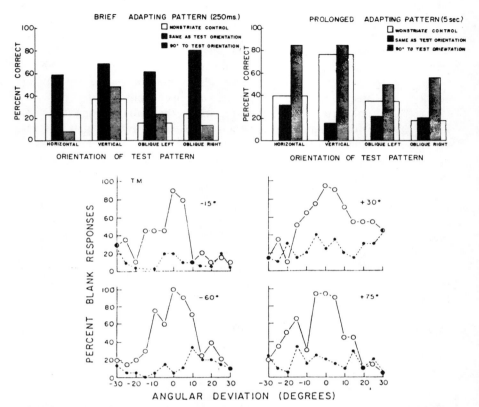

Figure 6.11. (A) Gratings of dark and light lines produce masking effects on successively presented gratings with the same orientation. The amount of masking depends on the duration of prolonged exposure to the initial display. Gilinsky, 1967. (B) The amount of masking depends on the degree of similarity of orientation of the inspection and test. Masking peaks after adaptation to the identical orientation as the test pattern. Thus adaptation is selective for specific categories. Gilinsky & Mayo, 1971.

Interocular Transfer of Selective Adaptation

To test this possibility, our group conducted an experiment (Gilinsky & Doherty, 1969) on interocular transfer, to determine whether adaptation to a grating exposed to only one eye, would transfer and decrease the sensitivity of the *nonexposed* eye. If so, the adaptation effect could be attributed to a *central* locus in the visual system beyond the points at which the impulses from the two eyes interact.

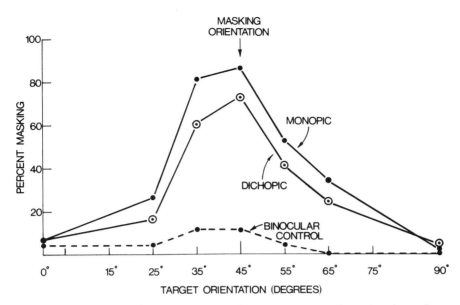

Figure 6.12. Masking produced by interocular transfer of orientation specific adaptation. The graph shows the percentage of masking as a function of the orientation of the test pattern for monopic, dichopic, and binocular control conditions. Masking peaks at 45°, the orientation of the adapting grating. Gilinsky & Doherty, 1969. Copyright © 1969 by AAAS.

The results show a significant masking effect of the adaptation grating on the *unadapted* eye. The masking effect decreases markedly as the angle of orientation of the target grating deviates from the orientation of the adaptation grating in the unadapted eye, just as it does in the adapted eye. The masking effect (see Figure 6.12), predictably, is smaller because in normal visual cortex fewer cells are monocularly driven than binocularly driven.

The significant masking effect found with dichopic viewing is proof that *interocular transfer* does occur. Hence the adaptation is *cortical.*

These results are confirmed and extended by further interocular experiments. (Blakemore & Campbell, 1969; Blakemore & Sutton, 1969; Blakemore, Nachmias, & Sutton, 1970; Campbell & Maffei, 1970.)

Here is robust evidence that the visual cortex of humans, like that of the cat and the monkey, contains neurons selectively sensitive to the orientation and spatial frequency dimensions of visual images. One must conclude that these adaptable cells are located in the cortex because they show interocular transfer and because they are exquisitely sensitive to orientation. In stark contrast, all the cells examined in the visual pathways at lower levels (ganglion cells and geniculate cells) have round, symmetrically organized receptive fields, making them insensitive to orientation. It is reasonable to conclude that cognons in the human cortex are narrowly selective for orientation and spatial frequency.

Sensory adaptation, seen as a progressive decline in sensitivity to prolonged stimulation, provides a moving baseline of neural activity from which small deviations above and below, can be discriminated. Its biological usefulness is that it permits a distance receptor, like the eye, to broaden its "receptive range," Sherrington's (1906) trenchant term for the slice of the external world to which a sense organ will respond. By reducing the reactivity to absolute properties, adaptation (or habituation) emphasizes relations and contrasts, especially abrupt changes in stimulation. An unchanging stimulus tells us nothing, and is rejected by the nervous system; a new stimulus is an event, and evokes a brisk response. One of the most interesting and provocative implications of the selective adaptation experiments is their ability to show how much information is required and just what information is important for the recognition of complex patterns.

Consider the question: How can a computer be made to recognize a human face? Our brains can readily tell one face from another and pick out a familiar face from a crowd, but the problem of translating faces into formal descriptions or objective instructions for machine recognition is still unsolved. Yet some progress has been made toward its solution by using computer-generated block portraits.

In Leon D. Harmon and Julesz's (1973) experiments, a beam of light is used to scan a filmed portrait and divide the picture into squares whose brightness values are the average of all the points within the square. The final result may resemble the block portrait of Figure 6.13 whose 560 squares, each of which is uniform in brightness, can be stored as digital information on magnetic tape. Viewed from close up, one sees an assemblage of squares or gray levels. Viewed from a distance, however, or by squinting or jiggling, the picture can be recognized as a familiar face.

The effect of distance, squinting, or jiggling the picture, is to blur the already degraded image. Why should blurring improve recognition? The explanation lies in the "noise" that tends to obscure the image. In everyday life we try to listen to sounds that are often masked by various types of noise. The noise that most interferes with our ability to detect acoustic signals consists of tones whose frequencies are close to those of the target signal. This is known as "critical-band masking" (Fletcher, 1953).

The mechanism of selective adaptation that causes the dramatic rise in the detection threshold of a visual signal is analogous to the critical-band—masking noise in hearing. A picture, like a sound, can be described as the sum of simple component frequencies. Optical signals consists of spatial frequencies whose combination makes up their spatial spectrum. The spatial spectrum of pictures consists of two dimensions of various densities of dark and light areas and the component spatial frequencies can be removed by

Figure 6.13. A computer-processed photograph. The stimulus is both test and mask. Harmon & Julesz, 1973.

filtering. The enhancement of block portraits by blurring is caused by the removal of masking frequencies, especially the noisy higher frequencies that represent fine detail. Low-pass filtering, therefore, enhances perception by blurring the sharp edges of the block squares.

Julesz and Harmon's experiments show that those components of the noise that fall within about two octaves of the critical frequency for recognition are primarily responsible for masking the original picture. Removal of only the frequencies adjacent to the signal on both sides improved recognition of the blurred portraits. Harmon concludes that *critical-band masking,* not the very high frequencies alone, is the key to the suppression of recognition.

The experimental investigations of selective adaptation reviewed here can be used to determine the width of the critical bands for various dimensions of stimulation and categories of perception on which recognition of subtle patterns depend. Here is additional confirmation that it is not specific features as such—the eyes, ears, or nose—that produce recognition of a face, but subtle relational patterns, represented by key spatial frequencies of various orientations that are stored as *cognons* and filed for later retrieval.

Psychological research on intact human beings demonstrates the existence in human vision of neural channels similar to those found by electrophysiologists using microelectrode probes into the visual cortex of cats and monkeys. These human experiments reveal parallel results—*selective adaptation* and *negative aftereffects.* The significant rises found in contrast thresholds and the remarkable perceptual shifts are precisely tied to particular categories of perceptual experience, while leaving others intact.

These selective aftereffects of stimulation are not confined to the visual system. Every analyzer can be shown to involve related threshold adaptation effects and contrast aftereffects contingent on specific categories of stimulation and of perception. But to what extent can perceptual and behavioral adaptation in human subjects be reorganized by distorting goggles or prisms that invert or reverse the familiar world of ordinary experience?

Prism Rearrangement Experiments

Up to now, we have considered the effects of short-term perceptual adaptation—the clear-cut alterations that occur in the perception of tilted lines and spatial frequencies that result from recent, brief exposures to particular stimulus patterns. There is little doubt that prolonged fixation of one pattern can affect the subsequent reaction to similar patterns. We are led to conclude that continued excitation of one set of cognons has a depressing effect on them and also on related cognons belonging to the same category of perception.

But how modifiable is perceptual organization as a whole? Are firmly established associations between cognons in different analyzers capable of disruption by new experiences? One question concerns the relation between different aspects of the perceptual world, such as vision and bodily orientation. Can a person learn to overcome the distorting effects of an inverting prism or a reversing mirror that turns the world on its head? George Stratton (1897) was one of the first psychologists to try to answer this question. He wore an optical device for two weeks that inverted the visual scene and reversed right and left. He was able gradually to adjust his movements to the optical rearrangement, but his report left some doubt as to whether he actually learned to *see* the inverted world as being correct. That question was left for later investigators, notably the Austrian psychologist, Ivo Kohler.

Ivo Kohler's (1962; 1964) ingenious experiments gave a dramatic answer. Kohler and the subjects of his Innsbruck experiments survived long periods of wearing prism goggles that reverse right and left, or up and down, and uncovered an adaptive process that overcame established habits of a lifetime. An important consideration is that these modifications of behavior do not imply that cognons have permanently, or even temporarily, reorganized their connections. The changes that occur after wearing reversing or inverting goggles are functional or plastic changes and are reversible. Once the goggles have been removed, the formerly established visual and motor habits quickly return.

The value of these experiments is that of a probe to discover the genesis of correct perception as well as the formation and transformation of conditioned instrumental reactions. For the clinician whose interest is in the application of neuropsychological principles to the rehabilitation of patients with brain damage, they possess a special appeal.

The subjects wearing the reversing goggles had, at first, insuperable difficulties in their locomotor behavior, if it was guided by vision. For example, going down the street, turning the corner—whether on foot, bicycle, or skis—is generally controlled by the alternation of visual and kinesthetic images—especially eye movements of motor acts. These images contradict the required new patterns, and Kohler found that it was much easier for his subjects (including himself) to move in a well-known space with his eyes closed. Yet, after practice guided by certain rules, they were able to perform with their eyes open, and eventually to *see* correctly in the strange environment (Gilinsky, 1981).

Kohler's subjects had to reverse a lifetime of experience with specific associations between kinesthetic, somesthetic, and labyrinthine-spatial centers and vision. What was truly amazing was that the sensory aftereffects of tilt, curvature, size, and color, following prolonged wearing of the distorting spectacles, were contingent upon specific eye movements—looking left or right, up or down—and also on the specific kinds of objects being observed. "Again and again," Kohler wrote, "standards of size, angulation, and movement within a single retinal area were found to vary, even though the stimulus remained the same" (1964, p. 122). The crucial question arises, why should this be so?

With the help of *cognon theory,* we are able to understand how the visual system is organized so as to bring about these different situational aftereffects. Observations that seemed at first to be bewildering—the apparently paradoxical split between rapidly transformed, small objects that normally appear in any position, and inverted printed letters and numerals that show a greater resistance to rehabituation—are no longer surprising.

These objects and printed symbols are represented by particular categories of cognons in the different perceptual systems. As we have seen, the visual pattern system contains categories representing small manipulable objects, large movable objects, human faces, animals, and far-off scenes—mountains and landscapes. The visual-space system categorizes spatial relations, giving us near, far, above, below, left, right, in front, behind. The auditory system divides heard sounds into categories also—music, voices, words, and noises of the external world. Imagine hearing the sound of the water rushing down the cascading falls on your left, but sighting the precipice of these falls on your right. Such was the experience of the prism-wearing subjects in this strange world.

In the day-to-day world of familiar experience, the subjective standards of the cognons are formed under consistent conditions of eye and body position and of movement. For each object—the hand, the face of a friend, a house, a fly—there is a certain *normal viewing distance;* its size at this distance becomes the standard size for this particular object. Not only size, but shape and orientation conform to the *normal viewing angle* and to the direction of gaze. When attention is directed to a familiar object, its neural symbol, or cognon, bends the immediate perception to this standard without regard for photographic accuracy. This integrity of the cognon, its ability to distort a pattern to its standard, is what accounts for the constancies of perception.

Under abnormal conditions of stimulation, the old models no longer fit. All asymmetrical objects: the letter *B,* all printed words and sentences, faces, feet, shoes, and gloves—are firmly associated with the subjective left-right and normal viewing angle. Their changed positions confuse and disorient the subject in the prism experiment (like *Alice Through the Looking Glass,* Carroll, 1872). But small manipulable objects that ordinarily occur in any position—the key, the cup, the chess piece, *etc.*—have no unique location or orientation. As long as it is manipulable, it is movable, and can appear in its normal way.

As the subject adapts, accordingly, his visual perception changes in a *piecemeal* fashion. Some parts of the visual field are perceived correctly; others remain reversed. "Vehicles driving on the 'right' (and the noise of the motor agreed) carried license numbers in mirror writing. A strange world, indeed!" (Kohler, 1964, p. 155).

> Yet, subject Grill went beyond this stage and eventually achieved almost completely correct impressions, even where letters and numbers were involved. Mirror reading became well established. Following removal of the spectacles, the mirror world (temporarily) returned; p's were seen as q's, b's as d's, and in a clock face, 10:30 was read as 1:30. (p. 160)

Words failed to play a helpful role in rehabituation to inverted visual space. The separate cerebral lateralization of verbal and nonverbal functions explains why. The visual-spatial system is in the right brain, the language system is in the left hemisphere. Hundreds of times a day, false movements had to be overcome by the subject saying to himself, "Always do the opposite, head into danger, walk in the direction that you want to turn away from...."

Behavior, no more than vision, is not corrected in one simple step, but in stages. The process of rehabituation teaches us that neither behavior nor perception is unitary.

Kohler's (1964) remarkable experiments showed how different aspects of the perceptual world such as vision, audition, and bodily orientation can be realigned by adaptation, based on adjustments to a looking-glass world. When Kohler and his subjects first wore their distorting spectacles, they were severely handicapped. But, as time went on, there was selective adaptation, and eventually actions and perception became adapted to the strange world— so completely that, wearing their inverted lenses, these subjects could ski in the Alps and ride their bicycles through the streets of Innsbruck.

When they finally removed the reversing goggles, there was a marked contrast effect. Colors were abnormal and everything looked strange. But readjustments to the old familiar world followed quickly, as the habits and coordinations of a lifetime reasserted themselves. Following removal of inverting prism spectacles, the expected negative aftereffect occurs: the world is now distorted in a direction opposite to that of the adaptation prisms. Normal correct vision returns as long as the appropriate neural units, the necessary cognons, have been established by early visual experience. Here is an adaptive process of great significance, and compelling support for our categorization principle of cognon activity.

CATEGORIES OF UNITARY PERCEPTION IN THE VARIOUS ANALYZERS

The experiments showing modification of perceptual organization in vision revealed how highly specific to particular categories these adaptations really are. Similar specificity exists in the nonvisual analyzers. The optical rearrangement experiments imposed more than visual effects; the subjects needed to realign sounds heard on the left with sights perceived on the right, and with movements of the body, head, limbs, hands, and eyes, involving readjustments of coordination in the kinesthetic, auditory, somatosensory, and other systems. New cross-modal associations between earlier established cognons were required.

A detailed examination of the categories of perception in the various analyzers is beyond the scope of this book, but I will present a brief outline of the probable divisions based on the available evidence. The next section considers each one of the analyzers in turn and lists their known categories of unitary perceptions or cognons.

The Auditory Analyzer

The auditory analyzer, like the visual, is a distance receptor, and contains a number of relatively independent subsystems of hearing. Distinct subdivisions serve the identifying function and the localizing function, just as two visual mechanisms serve to inform the sense of sight both *what* an object is, and *where* it is located in space. The list of auditory subsystems follows:

1. Sounds of the natural external world (wind, thunder, sea, hail)
2. Sounds of artifactural objects (bells, sirens, horns, motors)
3. Music (melodies, musical instruments)
4. Human voices (speech sounds)
5. Cries, laughter, groans, animal vocalizations
6. Auditory space and spatial relations

These submodalities are carried by parallel pathways believed to represent different stages of evolutionary development. The more recently evolved pathways overlay, and perhaps suppress, more ancient and primitive pathways. With the expansion of the human neocortex, both audition and vision have added new and more sophisticated levels of analysis to their activities—language being preeminent, but music and art also serving time-binding and space-binding functions.

The Kinesthetic Analyzer

The kinesthetic system gives us information about the active movements of our body and its parts. It informs the central nervous system about events produced by the central nervous system itself—its own activity, or sensory feedback. Sensory feedback is needed for the performance of motor acts, particularly when they are new and complex. But even well-practiced activities, like speech, require normal feedback. Experiments on delayed auditory feedback show how disruptive the effect can be, producing stammering, slurring, even complete inhibition of speech.

The kinesthetic receptors, called *proprioceptors,* signal *tensions* of muscles to the brain, where they are translated in a series of two steps: first, messages from muscular and tendon stretch receptors are encoded into the language of muscular *contractions:* second, these elementary contractions are recoded into the proprioception of complex *movements.* This translation machinery is believed to reside in the *cerebellar* cortex—in other words, signals enter the cerebellum to tell it about muscle tensions, and signals about contractions leave the cerebellum to enter the cerebral premotor cortex where they are integrated to represent bodily movements. The most important categories of *unitary kinesthetic perception* are:

1. Hand movements (particular, skillful hand and finger movements are involved routinely in washing, dressing, eating, manipulating keys and cigarettes, writing, etc.)
2. Body movements (axial movements of head, trunk, face)
3. Oral movements (speech)
4. Mouth and throat movements (eating, singing, coughing, blowing into wind instruments)
5. Locomotor behavior (walking, running, climbing, swimming)
6. Spatial skills (movements associated with acrobatics, mazes, sports, ballet)

The kinesthetic analyzer plays a central role in Konorski's (1967) model of the integrative activity of the brain. Konorski's ideas about the kinesthetic analyzer are of particular interest in two respects: first, he believed that the kinesthetic system differed significantly from other afferent systems in having a feedback role in motor activity; second, within the kinesthetic analyzer, the neural units play the role of programming devices for skilled motor acts.

The kinesthetic units thus play two different functional roles. They provide information about the active movements of the body, face, and limbs, and they make possible the performance of these voluntary or instrumental movements.

The ability to execute integrated movements consisting of unitary behavioral acts is called *praxis*. Normal praxis demands the close cooperation of the kinesthetic and the visual space system. One extracts movement information produced by the body's own activity, and the other provides position information about the body and the objects in the environment with which it interacts. The integration of the two systems must be nicely adjusted to continually changing conditions of the body, as it reaches for, and manipulates, things and events in the immediately surrounding space.

The Somatic Sensory Analyzer

The somatic sensory analyzer allows us to recognize objects through touch, to perceive changes in bodily position, and to experience warmth, or cold, or pain. Their receptors respond selectively to damaging stimuli and are spread over the body, giving them the name of *somatic* or *skin* senses. The skin senses comprising the somatic analyzer are divided into numerous subsystems; these mediate both simple and compound sensations (Kandel, 1981, pp. 184–198). The important categories of the somatic analyzer are:

Simple Sensations	*Compound Sensations*
1. Pain (fast & slow)	1. Vibration—flutter
2. Touch	2. Itch—tickle
3. Pressure	3. Position (limb, body, mouth)
4. Taste (salty, sweet, bitter, acid)	4. Sexual excitement, stroking, orgasm
5. Temperature (warm, cold)	5. Shapes and textures of objects (stereognosis)
6. Movement and direction on skin	6. Food tastes (texture, temperature, and odor, combined with gustatory elements)

The Olfactory Analyzer

Olfaction, like the joint and muscle sense, has relatively few subdivisions. The olfactory sense, highly developed in insects and some mammals, such as dogs, fails to permit humans to make fine distinctions and to compare odors in any orderly way, without specialized training. We have no comprehensive smell vocabulary, but we simply identify different odors by naming their natural source in particular objects, such as jasmine, ether, mint, coffee, etc. (See Figure 6.14.)

In olfaction there is a direct pathway from the sensory receptors in the olfactory bulb to the limbic system. Perhaps this is the result of an evolutionary development that made the olfactory system the earliest distance sense. The sensing of distant objects by smell is phylogenetically the most primitive system for tracking far-off sources of food and other animals.

Types of Noses

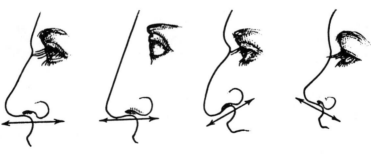

Straight nose	Greek nose	Arched nose	Upturned nose
(Augustus)	(Venus de Milo)	(Dante)	(Socrates)
Horizontal base	Horizontal base	Aryan type	Base inclined upward
		Base inclined downward	

Figure 6.14. Various types of noses contain receptors for the olfactory analyzer. Bossy, 1970.

Unlike other distance receptors (seeing and hearing), the olfactory system has few levels and no abstract neural processing of constituent features other than intensity. "A rose is a rose is a rose" because of geraniol, a 10-carbon compound, and it is the geometric conformation of atoms within the molecule that determines the unique fragrance.

Odors provide important cognons not only for aesthetic pleasure or appetitive drive reflexes; they warn us of dangers—the smell of gas, spoiled or putrid food—or they provoke fear in a predator as in the protective reflex of the skunk. The intimate connection between olfaction, gustation, and the limbic system helps to explain their powerful role in memory, recognized by Proust (1924) in his well-known tea-dipped madeleine that recalled the lost past. There is little doubt that the integration, storage, and remembrance of these events demand the participation of unique neural units or cognons.

The Emotive Analyzer

How do you know when you are happy, or sleepy, or in need of a drink? How do you know when you are feeling angry, guilty, anxious, depressed, or interested in someone? Our vivid hedonic experiences corresponding to our drives and antidrives—our emotions and moods—are the product of the emotive analyzer. Poignant messages from the internal milieu reach the hypothalamus and the limbic system to interact with the higher cortical centers. These parts of the brain tell us that we are hungry, or in pain, or in love; they constitute the emotive system, and the afferent or receptive side forms the *emotive analyzer.*

Patients whose prefrontal cortex has been removed are no longer bothered by chronic pain. They may report that they perceive pain, but the associated strong emotional experience is lacking. Apparently, forebrain mechanisms or cognons are necessary for vivid emotional reactions. Like other unitary perceptions, emotive cognons belong in separate categories that do not mix. Either we love or we hate our father; although these powerful emotions directed at a particular person frequently alternate, their unity and integrity remain, and ambivalence is a common experience. Each emotion or drive is qualitatively different from all the others because each is satisfiable by a unique goal and arouses a different antidrive.

SUMMARY

The principle of categorization of unitary perceptions of cognons is supported by many psychological experiments on human subjects. This chapter has shown that particular categories of cognons in the visual analyzer are selectively adapted by specific exposures to visual stimulation ranging from brief inspections of tilted lines to weeks of wearing distorting goggles that invert and reverse the familiar world. The results are clear evidence of perceptual modification and alterations in behavior that are highly specific in their effects. Not only visual perception, but every analyzer, is served by multiple parallel pathways that divide up their corresponding mental representations, or cognons, into unique categories of experience.

The data from psychological experiments are beautifully supported by parallel observations in the animal laboratory and in the clinic. Human neuropathology and neurosurgical ablation studies on animals provide important sources of information for the multiplicity and specificity of categories of cognons, in every aspect of cognition and behavior. We will turn to a discussion of what these neurological investigations can contribute to our understanding of cognition following an examination of associative learning.

SUGGESTED READINGS

Anstis, S.M. Apparent movement. In R. Held, H.W. Leibowitz, & H.-L. Teuber (Eds.), *Handbook of sensory physiology* (Vol. 8) *Perception.* New York: Springer-Verlag, 1978.

Attneave, F. Multistability in perception. *Scientific American,* 1971, *225,* 62–71.

Fisher, G.H. Ambiguity of form: Old and new. *Perception and Psychophysics,* 1968, *4,* 189–192.

Gilinsky, A.S. The effect of attitude upon the perception of size. *American Journal of Psychology,* 1955, *68,* 173–192.

Gilinsky, A.S. Orientation-specific effects of patterns of adapting light on visual acuity. *Journal of the Optical Society of America,* 1968, *58,* 13–18.

Gilinsky, A.S. Reorganization of perception: A Konorskian interpretation of the Innsbruck experiments. *Acta Neurobiologiae Experamentalis,* 1981, *41,* 491–508.

Gilinsky, A.S., & Doherty, R.S. Interocular transfer of orientational effects. *Science,* 1969, *164,* 454–455.

Gilinsky, A.S., & Mayo, T.H. Inhibitory effects of orientational adaptation. *Journal of the Optical Society of America,* 1971, *61,* 1710–1714.

Haith, M.M. *Rules that babies look by: The organization of newborn visual activity.* Hillsdale, N.J.: Erlbaum, 1980.

Harmon, L.D., & Julesz, B. Masking in visual recognition: Effects of two-dimensional filtered noise. *Science,* 1973, *180,* 1194–1197.

Held, R., Ingle, D., Schneider, G.E., & Trevarthen, C.B. Locating and identifying: Two modes of visual processing. *Psychologishe Forschung,* 1967–1968, *31,* 44–62, 299–348.

Kanizsa, G. *Organization in vision: Essays in Gestalt perception.* New York: Praeger, 1979.

Kohler, I. Experiments with goggles. *Scientific American,* 1962, *206,* 62–72.

Rosenblith, W. (Ed.). *Sensory communication.* Cambridge: MIT Press, 1961.

Spillman, L., & Wooten, B.R. (Eds.). *Sensory experience, adaptation, and perception:*

Festschrift for Ivo Kohler. Hillsdale, N.J.: Erlbaum, 1984.

Stromeyer, C.F. Form-color aftereffects in human vision. In R. Held, H.W. Leibowitz, & H.-L. Teuber (Eds.), *Handbook of sensory physiology VIII, Perception,* New York: Springer-Verlag, 1978.

Sutherland, N.S. Outlines of a theory of visual pattern recognition in animals and man. *Proceedings of the Royal Society;* Series B: Biological Sciences, (London), 1968, *171,* 297–317.

Teuber, H.-L. Perception. In J. Field (Ed.), *Handbook of physiology, Section I: Neurophysiology* (Vol. 3). Washington, D.C.: American Physiological Society, 1960.

PART THREE

Associative Systems: The Neuropsychology of Learning and Cognition

The preceding three chapters discussed the role of the analyzers in providing perceptual input to the brain. The forming of perceptual units in the cognitive fields of the afferent systems is only the first step in the integrative activity of the brain. The next stage is the association of unitary percepts or cognons caused by their synchronous excitation. Associative learning is followed by the utilization of these associations for behavioral acts. The rest of this book will deal with these more complex forms of learning, memory, and the utilization of learned movements for voluntary action.

Until very recently, associations, learning, and mental functions were treated as though they took place inside a black box. Neurobiologists have now opened up the black box and begun to explore its anatomical contents in very simple animals in the context of their behavior. The tradition has been to regard these creatures with very few nerve cells as possessing no more than the most elementary forms of behavior—reflexes and instincts. The human brain has trillions of cells, and human behavior is complex. The crucial question at this point is: what does the human brain and human behavior have in common with simpler animals? Where there are points of similarity there may be general principles of organization that can illuminate our understanding of ourselves.

About 10 years ago evidence began to accumulate that the same learning processes, including classical conditioning, occur in similar forms in both vertebrates and invertebrates and can be investigated in a leech, a snail, or a rabbit. We share many behavioral patterns with other species, and these can be effectively studied in simple animal models that would be impossible in us. New discoveries emerging from these studies are causing ripples of excitement and optimism that neuroscientists are solving the mysteries of brain and behavior.

On the basis of these up-to-date and sophisticated cell-biological and neurophysiological underpinnings, I would like to offer a theoretical conceptualization oriented toward psychological issues and classical concerns of interest to experimental psychologists, psychiatrists, and students of human personality and development. What follows is necessarily quite speculative, but it is as good a fit to data on simple animal models as can be found at present. I will try to be as concrete and specific as possible to permit these ideas to be tested and thrown out; or, more hopefully, to be refined by further research.

CHAPTER SEVEN

Images, Hallucinations, Dreams, and Cross-Modal Associations

Sensations, once experienced, modify the nervous organism, so that copies of them arise again in the mind after the original outward stimulus is gone. *No mental copy, however, can arise in the mind, of any kind of sensation which has never been directly excited from without.*

(William James, 1890, Vol II, p. 44)

One day in April...Jack Hawthorne ran over and killed his brother, David. Even at the last moment he could have prevented his brother's death by slamming on the tractor brakes, easily in reach for all the shortness of his legs; but he was unable to think, or rather, thought unclearly, and so—watched it happen, as he would again and again watch it happen in his mind, with nearly undiminished intensity and clarity, all his life.

(John Gardner, 1981, p. 31)

GENERAL PHYSIOLOGY OF ASSOCIATIONS

Associations between perceptions and images belonging to different cognitive fields are based on the formation of synaptic connections between the corresponding cognons. The term "association" refers to the relation between stimuli or percepts from the viewpoint of the experiencing individual; it is a psychological concept. The term "connection" denotes the anatomical substrate of the association; physiologically speaking, a "connection" is the actual chemical (or electrical) transmission across a synapse between pre- and postsynaptic neurons.

In order to form *perception units,* the first-order cognons, as Chapter Five explained, the prerequisite is the existence of ontogenetically developed potential connections in the pathways leading from the transmittent to the recipient neurons. In the formation of a cognon, the potential connections become actual connections when a state of arousal, produced by impulses arriving from the unspecific emotive system, exists at the moment of exposure to the stimulus pattern. Then synapses become effective for transmission of impulses between corresponding cells. Only when the sensory neurons are in a state of arousal can they release neurotransmitters to the potential perceptive units of the cognitive fields to establish new cognons.

In the development of new *associative* processes, the situation is slightly different. Here both the transmittent and the recipient cognons must be synchronously excited through the already-established connections leading to them from the lower afferent pathways. The critical condition for actual connections to be established between cognons is the arousal of all participant neurons by the emotive system. Two (or more) sets of cognons taking part in the association, and their excitatory stimuli from receptive neurons in the periphery, must now be under the facilitatory influence of the unspecific arousing system. This condition for associative pairing is indispensable for providing the proper *address* for messages coming from disparate transmittent units. In order to form a perception unit initially, no special addressing device is needed, since the formation of actual connections is ensured by the convergence of impulses on preformed recipient units, the ontogenetically designated cognons.

WHAT ACTIVATES A COGNON?

Cognons not only are activated by direct stimulus input from the receptors, but may be excited intracortically by association. Whereas stimulation from the periphery gives rise to unitary perceptions, excitation of these units by associative pathways produces *images.*

The most obvious fact about images is that they are mental experiences. All conscious organisms have them. Obviously they vary widely in the fidelity with which they represent the actual surrounding universe, but then, so do perceptions.

How are images related to perceptions? Though similar in many ways, our images and our perceptions seem very different from each other.

Introspectively we say that our images are "in our minds"—what we perceive is "out there." This subjective distinction is not a mere quantitative thing: it's not that our images are always weak or faint, our perceptions vivid and strong. In fact, we may perceive an object in a haze or fog very dimly, scarcely there, but still outside in the external world; yet we see in our "mind's eye" a strong and lively image of a scene from a play we have witnessed, a coveted jewel, or an absent lover.

THE PHYSIOLOGICAL BASIS OF IMAGES

Our psychological conviction internalizes the image but externalizes the percept. This distinction between a percept and an image must have an underlying physiological counterpart. What could it be? What is the physiological basis for the psychological distinction between percept and image?

The answer to the question comes from the indispensable condition that accompanies perception—the presence of the *targeting reflex*. When we perceive a stimulus, our receptive apparatus adjusts for the optimal reception of that stimulus. Both afferent and efferent impulses in the stimulated transit pathways of the projective area of the appropriate analyzer are activated, causing us, if only momentarily, to look closely, to listen sharply, to pay attention. In contrast, when we create an image, we activate the same single unit, the identical cognon, via intracortical associations. The targeting reflex is absent. Thus we get no feedback from the sensory apparatus, and the image appears to be spontaneous.

PSYCHOLOGICAL PROPERTIES OF IMAGES

Once established, images are retained and can be recalled as long as associative pathways are intact. Yet no targeting reflex, no scanning, no scrutiny of an imaginary object is possible. In all other respects, images are like unitary perceptions. They obey the same laws and have the same properties—integrity, constancy, and rivalry.

Indeed, the *integrity* of an image is even clearer than that of a percept. Most visual and auditory perceptions are complex, being made up of a number of associated cognons acting together. Reading a letter in longhand, it is nearly impossible to separate what is written from how it is written. In the absence of the physical letter, an image can evoke the familiar handwriting without also evoking any images of particular words.

A second striking characteristic of images is their *constancy*. Since images are looked at in the absence of the object that they represent, they maintain a stability that a changing presented pattern might destroy. This constant property emerges vividly following a traumatic event. After witnessing a tragic accident, the picture of the victim's mangled body remains as stable as a photograph in our mind. We hear the same cry of horror as if fixed on a tape.

> And now, from nowhere, the black memory of his brother's death rushed over him again, mindless and inexorable as a wind or wave, the huge cultipacker lifting—only an inch or so—as it climbed toward the shoulders, then sank in the cheek, flattening the skull—and he heard more real than the morning, his sister's scream. (Gardner, 1981, p. 39)

This *flashback* property gives certain images a strength that many perceptions lack. Formed under the influence of a powerful emotion, a clear and vivid image stays with us obsessively for a long time. Eventually, the emotion lessens and the cognons involved are less often activated, but true forgetting may never take place.

A third important property of images is their *rivalry*. The mutual antagonism between images belongs to the same physiological mechanism that underlies unitary perceptions. Perception usually suppresses all images antagonistic to it because a strongly activated cognon inhibits competing cognons.

Images are free from the binding power of the stimulus input. Yet a persistent image often prevents competing and wanted images to emerge in consciousness. Sometimes you try to recall a particular name—but it eludes you. It seems to be on the *tip of the tongue,* but the name that appears is not the one you seek. Many false names occur; you recognize that they are wrong although they resemble in some way—word shape, phonemes, or ethnicity— the one you want. Only by deliberately avoiding the attempt to recall will the correct name eventually come to mind.

There is no better description of this experience than that by William James.

> Suppose we try to recall a forgotten name. The state of our consciousness is peculiar. There is a gap therein; but it is not a mere gap. It is a gap that is intensively active. A sort of wraith of the name is in it, beckoning us in a given direction, making us at moments tingle with the sense of our closeness, and then letting us sink back without the longed-for term. If wrong names are proposed to us, this singularly definite gap acts immediately so as to negate them. They do not fit into its mold. And the gap of one word does not feel like the gap of another, all empty of content as both might seem necessarily to be when described as gaps. (James, 1890, Vol. I, p. 251)

Brown and McNeil (1966) devised an experiment to study the tip-of-the-tongue phenomenon by presenting subjects with the definition of an uncommon English word and asking them to supply the word. They found that when recall is imminent there is likely to be accurate *generic* recall. Other words than the wanted one are brought back: they resemble the target word in sound or form, but not in meaning; or they are similar in meaning, but differ in sound or form.

The accuracy of generic recall supports the *categorical* hypothesis. Retrieval is accessed via categories of meaning or categories of abstract form, presumably because the relevant cognons are stored in categories on the basis of these similarities. The subjects appear to know the correct number of syllables or letters in the word sought, or they know the semantic class to which it belongs. To take a single example—for the word *sextant* the subjects heard this definition, "A navigational instrument used in measuring angular distances, especially the altitude of sun, moon, and stars at sea." Subjects gave words with similar sounds—*secant, sextet,* and *sexton.* Words with similar meanings included *compass, dividers,* and *protractor*—words linked with navigation, instruments, or geometry.

The similarities between the competing words reveal their intracategorical origins. The resultant rivalry is predictable from the categorical principle of cognon theory that cognons within the same category are mutually antagonistic.

It is essential to grasp the fundamental concept of a unitary percept or a unitary image, represented by a cognon. Critics have ridiculed the concept of single cells as mediators of our perceptions and images, labeling them "grandmother cells." They object that there would have to be one unit for grandmother in her rocking chair, another unit for grandmother leaning down to pick up her knitting needles, and so on to an infinity of cells for all possible combinations. The answer to that objection is that it confuses complex perceptions with "pure" unitary perceptions and images. The cognon represents the pure unitary perception or unitary image, free from all particular associations.

When we visualize those objects that are not tied to any one place because their location is changeable, we strip them of those accidents of place. When I imagine the face of a particular friend I "see" the face isolated before my eyes without any externalization. "Grandmother" is a pure image, a unit of thought, not a sensory quality. Although I can certainly visualize her in many different aspects, these aspects are attached via the activity of associated cognons arising from connected images or complex perceptions.

Of course, some familiar objects have a permanent definite location. When I close my eyes and imagine my library, I see my desk in front of the book shelves. I visualize it always in its own place, but the realization of its location occurs in my mind, and I can move it, in imagination, to somewhere else.

Visual perceptions, in contrast to images, are always projected to those places in which the stimulus pattern seems to operate. Because of this, sometimes we are fooled. Not realizing that they are within our eye, we try to brush away the *muscae volitantes* (flying motes) that we see before us. But to no avail; the shapes continue to drift in front of us.

In a classical experiment, C.W. Perky (1910) told her subjects to imagine a banana on the blank screen in front of them. Then, without informing them, she projected a faint picture of bananas on the screen. The subjects reported "images" that were faithful copies of the actual projection. Perky deceived her subjects into believing that they were imagining the perceptions (to which she exposed them) they really were receiving. Apparently her suggestion to them relaxed their targeting reflexes to the extent that they were unaware of receiving stimulus input from the outside.

Based on this explanation, we might suppose that if a person has lost his sensory input by damage to the receptive surface or afferent pathways up to the projective area, after his cognons have been formed, his images would remain intact, although perceptions would no longer be possible.

For example, patients who have developed cataracts long after they had formed extensive repertoires of cognons, continue to have visual images of their previous experiences, but they can no longer see. When these cataracts are removed, the patients who lived through a sighted period in early life recover their vision and are able to recognize familiar objects and persons by sight. Others, less fortunate, who had not formed the actual associations during critical periods of development (as von Senden's cases showed) are unable to learn to see even though their eyes and receptive pathways are now intact. (See Chapter Five.)

These facts illustrate the importance of the period of life during which lesions are sustained by particular afferent systems. Damage to the brain at or soon after birth can have a far more devastating effect than damage to the adult. As William James said, "The blind may dream of sights, the deaf of sounds, for years after they have lost their vision or hearing; but the man *born* deaf can never be made to imagine what sound is like, nor can the blind *born* blind ever have a mental vision" (James, 1890, Vol. II, p. 44).

Even more striking is the fact that the *site of damage* can make a crucial difference in the resulting defect. Lesions sustained in all the transit levels including the projective area of a particular afferent system abolish all sensory input but leave the images of that system unaffected. Beethoven wrote his magnificent *Ninth Symphony* after he was totally deaf. In contrast, lesions sustained in the cognitive area of a given analyzer do not affect the sensory input, but make impossible the integration of that input into perceptions and their recall as images. A patient of Charcot, cited by Critchley (1966), suddenly lost all power of visual memory of shapes and colors. He tried with all his might to imagine the features of his children, his wife, but was completely unable to do so. Even his dreams were affected; in place of visual images, formerly vividly represented, only sounds remained. "Furthermore, he had even forgotten his own appearance. Visiting a gallery on one occasion, he found his passage obstructed by a stranger of whom he begged pardon; only to discover that he was confronting his own reflection in a pier-glass" (Critchley, 1966, p. 313).

INTERRELATIONS BETWEEN PERCEPTIONS AND ASSOCIATIONS

Normally, when cognons are excited by a fully adequate stimulus arriving from the receptors, no associations get through. If, however, the stimuli are not adequate, then messages coming from association areas may *summate* with those coming from the stimulus-object to produce or facilitate recognition of the object.

Examples abound. If we expect the arrival of a particular friend, we may even at a great distance recognize her immediately. If we hear a lecture in a noisy hall, we easily recognize the words we expect to hear and lose the others. Finding typographical mistakes in reading proofs is difficult because the context masks spelling errors and transposed letters.

The general principle of summation is that the more abundant and precise the associative messages reaching the cognon, the more vague, slight, and meager the perceptual messages can be; yet recognition can occur. Note that as long as messages are arriving from the receptive surface, the experience will nearly always take the form of perception and not of image. This is because the actual stimulus pattern, however indistinct, elicits the targeting reflex—the sufficient condition for perception.

Not all stimulus objects disclose themselves accurately upon eliciting the targeting reflex. If the stimulus pattern is hazy, incomplete, or strange, but subliminally activates a number of cognons, the given association may select a set of units that represent, not the actual object, but another one. These false perceptions are "illusions." Which associations will be selected depends on our mental set or drive state. Alone on a dark night in a place that is strange, or known to be dangerous, we may easily mistake a bit of crumpled paper for an assailant or hear something suspicious stirring in the wind blowing through the trees. The same stimuli that evoke frightening illusions in a state of anxiety may evoke shouts of laughter in convivial company. Even the same emotion may be ambiguous, so that social cues or previous instructions may dominate and shift the interpretation of internal cues, produced by adrenaline, from anger to elation (Schacter & Singer, 1962).

THE PHYSIOLOGICAL BASIS OF HALLUCINATIONS

When cognons are activated, but no stimulus objects are actually presented, the experiences sometimes are projected to the external world. These experiences have all the properties of perceptions, but, since there is no external stimulus, we call them *hallucinations*. Hallucinations may be defined as false perceptions experienced in the absence of external stimuli.

The puzzling phenomena of hallucinations raise the problem of their physiological mechanism. Do dreams and hallucinations have the same cause? What makes them so lively and often terrifyingly real?

Konorski (1967) explained the mechanism of hallucinations by assuming that the units of the cognitive fields—the cognons—not only receive fibers from projective areas but also send fibers to these areas. This assumption is based on definite neurological evidence, although different names have been used to refer to it. Hans-Lukas Teuber (1960) of MIT spoke of a "corollary discharge" self-produced by active movements sending feedback to sensory areas.

The corollary discharge reverses the usual idea of brain function proceeding from the sensory to the motor side and proposes instead that a discharge proceeds from motor to sensory structures. This "feed forward" prepares the sensory structures for an anticipated change. A good example is the control of voluntary eye movement. During a voluntary shift of gaze, the world stands still because the oculomotor system prepares vision for the predicted change in the relative position of objects. Passive motion of the eyeball by pushing against the eye makes the world move, because the counterbalancing corollary discharge is missing.

This mechanism has important implications for many forms of brain pathology in which impulses from eye movements are abnormal or lacking completely.

In hallucinations and, as we shall see, in dreams, rapid eye movements send afferent impulses to the visual projection areas, which are at the time unoccupied by incoming visual stimulation from the receptors in the retina.

Under these conditions, if a given set of cognons is activated by association, the impulses from these units can run to the projective area and excite the units ordinarily stimulated by a particular stimulus object. Since activation of the receptive units of this area gives rise to the corresponding targeting reflexes, the conditions for the appearance of perceptionlike experiences—hallucinations—are fulfilled.

But why, if impulses run down to receptive units as well as up from these units to the cognons, don't we in our associative processes experience hallucinations all the time? Why are they exceptional?

A tentative answer may be that backward connections leading from the cognitive to the receptive units are poorly developed and only thrown into activity under certain conditions. What are these conditions?

To begin, during the main part of our waking life we are constantly being bombarded by stimuli from the outside world. Our receptors are constantly working, and in the projective areas in the cortex the lines are busy.

Incomplete messages coming down from the cortex are simply *kept away*. Even when we close our eyes, we "see," not nothing, but something. We see darkness because the off-units of the projective areas are activated and they exert a strong reciprocal inhibition in those areas that should be excited by the messages arriving from the active units of the visual cognitive field.

If, however, the units of the projective areas are really idle, the conditions that favor hallucinations appear. Thus, in the perceptual isolation studies at McGill University in Montreal, college students were deprived of pattern vision for hours. They were continuously stimulated by "white" noise and wore cardboard gauntlets on their arms and hands to preclude changes in proprioceptive stimulation. During the deprivation period many subjects experienced hallucinations, suggesting that the lack of normal stimulation is a precipitating condition of hallucinatory effects. This explanation is strengthened by the further reports of illusory motion of objects the subjects saw upon release from confinement. It is possible that disturbances in the perception of patterns and motion result from a temporary inability of the subject to discriminate movements of his own eyes from those of the environment. Similarly, after cataract removals, the eyes of patients show continual irregular and dissociated movements (see Chapter Five)—a peculiar *ataxia* (loss of muscle coordination) of gaze as noted by Riesen (1958) in chimpanzees reared in darkness or under patternless (uniform) light.

Konorski's distinction between hallucinations and perceptions applies only to those analyzers that separate the cognitive from the projective areas. In phylogenetically older analyzers such as the "smell" brain, no such separation exists. A hay fever sufferer, allergic to cut grass and plants, started to sneeze when exposed to plastic turf. Confronted with an artificial bunch of realistic-looking roses, another person, allergic to roses, broke out with the symptoms of his allergy. Again, both the projective and the cognitive nerves play exactly the same roles in the exteroceptive skin senses, and the same units are excited whether the impulses originate in the receptive surface or in the association areas of the cortex. Since the units concerned cannot tell where the excitation comes from, the images that arise via association pathways act as full-blown hallucinations. That is why, Konorski thought, when we see a dirty person scratching himself, we have a real, and not an imaginary, itching ourselves, as if being invaded by fleas, and experience a somesthetic hallucination. Ribot (1911) vividly describes this sort of hallucination. To take just one example, "A butcher remained hanging by one arm from a hook, he uttered frightful cries, and complained that he was suffering cruelly, while all the time the hook had only penetrated his clothes, and the arm was uninjured" (p. 143).

An important conclusion follows. A hallucination should be considered as a phylogenetically earlier associative phenomenon than an image. Although we can only speculate about the mental experience of subhuman animals, objective evidence for dream states in dogs, cats, and other mammals is mounting. Finally, the accounts of extraordinarily vivid dreams and images in children, especially eidetic images, suggest that hallucinations, which play a large role in ontogeny, decrease in importance as the individual matures.

DREAMING AND THE FUNCTION OF SLEEP

In sleep, the sensory input from receptors is cut off. Neither on-, nor off-messages from the sensory pathways reach the cerebral cortex. Therefore, the images produced by associations find the way clear and take the form of hallucinations. We call this *dreaming*.

Dreams are a vivid and intense experience for most people. Although some find it difficult to believe, nearly everyone does dream regularly at periodic intervals during sleep (Aserinski & Kleitman, 1955).

Can dreams be studied objectively? Here, as in the studies of arousal level, the electroencephalogram (EEG) has proved to be a valuable tool (Dement & Kleitman, 1957). The EEG reflects the activity of the brain by means of scalp electrodes and shows rhythmic fluctuations in electrical waves that range from very slow waves of 8–12 hertz (cycles per second) to faster waves of 20–50 hertz. The frequency is closely correlated with the state of arousal of the subject.

The alpha rhythm, characterized by a regular rhythm of 8–12 hertz, occurs during relaxed wakefulness only if the eyes are closed. Any mental effort, or even simply opening the eyes, interrupts the alpha rhythm and replaces it with faster waves. (See Figure 7.1.)

The transition from wakefulness to sleep occurs in stages marked by a series of EEG patterns. The EEG pattern is *desynchronized* in dreaming, although the subject remains asleep. This cortical activation is called *paradoxical sleep*. During paradoxical sleep, sleeping subjects make many rapid eye movements (REMs) under closed lids, and this activity occurs periodically throughout the night. During these REM periods, the middle ear muscles are also phasically active, but there is profound loss of general muscle tonus. It is difficult to arouse the REM sleeper, although the human sleeper is more likely to awake spontaneously from REM sleep than from nonREM sleep. Awakened during the REM period, the subjects usually reported a dream. Awakened during other stages of sleep, subjects reported few, if any, dreams.

The occurrence of the REM state during a night's sleep appears to follow a general sequence alternating between periods of deep sleep. The long duration of REM periods, 10–40 minutes, suggests that, contrary to popular belief, a dream occurs in real time. Dement (1976) correlated the length of dream reports with REM sleep duration and showed that the episodes matched closely.

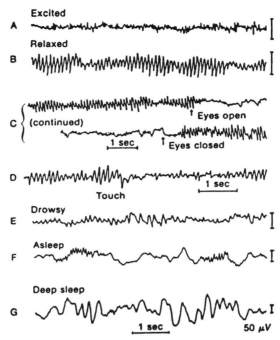

Figure 7.1. The electroencephalogram (EEG) or "brain waves" recorded from the scalp of a human subject. (A) In the alert subject, the EEG has a low amplitude, fast wave pattern. (B) In the relaxed state, alpha waves appear. (C) Opening the eyes (arrow) blocks the alpha rhythm, but it returns soon after the eyes are closed. (D) Touching the subject also blocks alpha. (E) In drowsiness, a transition to the next stage is seen. (F) During sleep, runs of 14-Hz rhythms are superimposed on the slow waves; these are called "sleep spindles." (G) In deep sleep, large amplitude slow waves replace all fast activity. This figure does not show the last stage—fast wave rapid eye movement (REM) or D (desynchronous, dream) sleep. EEG records of H.H. Jasper, 1941. From W. Penfield & T.C. Erickson (Eds.), *Epilepsy and Cerebral Localization,* 1941. Courtesy of Charles C. Thomas, Publisher, Springfield, Illinois.

Within the REM period the most interesting physiological indicators are the curious PGO (pontine-geniculo-occipital) spikes, first described by the neurophysiologist, Michel Jouvet (1974). The PGO spikes are high amplitude sharp waves that occur in intermittent phasic bursts throughout the REM period at a rate of 60–100 per minute. (See Figure 7.2.)

PGO spokes are of interest, first, because they are consistently associated with surges of activity in other physiological systems—eye movements, muscle twitches, heart rate changes in different species—and secondly

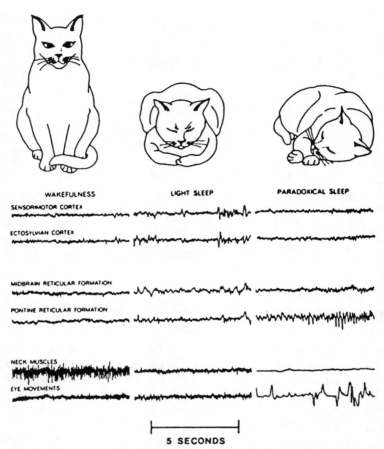

| WAKEFULNESS | LIGHT SLEEP | PARADOXICAL SLEEP |

SENSORIMOTOR CORTEX

ECTOSYLVIAN CORTEX

MIDBRAIN RETICULAR FORMATION

PONTINE RETICULAR FORMATION

NECK MUSCLES

EYE MOVEMENTS

5 SECONDS

Figure 7.2. Polygraphic recordings of the adult cat showing activity in various regions of the brain, neck, and eyes during wakefulness, light sleep, and paradoxical (REM or dream) sleep. Note the disappearance of all but pontine (PGO) spikes and eye movements during paradoxical sleep. Blakemore, 1977. Modified from Jouvet by permission. *Mechanisms of the Mind.* Cambridge University Press. Copyright © 1977 Cambridge University Press.

because, as pressure for REM sleep increases as a function of prior REM deprivation, the phasic PGO activity becomes more frequent.

PGO activity also occurs during nonREM periods and during wakefulness. The relation between PGO spikes and eye movements during wakefulness makes PGO spikes appear to be neural signs that are elicited by novel stimuli. They appear to signal a process of reticular activation and thus alertness in general.

This idea gains support from observations that cats can be made to exhibit paradoxical sleep without atonia. Morrison (1979) created paradoxical sleep in cats by making small pontine lesions that caused them to raise their heads with their eyes open and to attempt to stand and walk, yet with all the other characteristic signs of paradoxical sleep. Throughout these episodes the cats appear to be constantly orienting and searching. This activity seems to be the result of spontaneous brainstem neural activity identical with that normally produced during wakefulness by external stimulation. The absence of atonia in Morrison's cats leads him to conclude that a pontine mechanism ordinarily inhibits activity during paradoxical sleep, a dampening system that allows the organism to sleep without overreacting to possibly startling stimuli. The advantage of this mechanism reminds us of Freud's idea that we dream in order to preserve our sleep from inadvisable desires (or actions) but leaves open the question, why do we dream? In fact, dreams and hallucinations are so prevalent in all mammals that they must have some biological significance. Many studies confirm the near universality of dreaming in all homeothermic (warm-blooded) animals, as well as the compensatory activity caused by dream deprivation (Dement, 1970).

Jouvet (1975) makes this claim explicit by emphasizing the danger of sleep to the organism. Would evolution have produced a state during which an animal cannot react adaptively to threatening stimuli unless it fulfills some important function, he asks. Jouvet says the function of dream or paradoxical sleep is to "organize or program genetically constituted or instinctive behavior." Sleep is essential to prime dreaming, to insure that the body of the sleeper does not move, however active her dream life, running or flying. The sleeper must be in a safe environment. The first night or so in the dream laboratory, sleep fails to guard dreaming, and so no records are possible. The brain acts to stop any input or output during sleep, so that oneiric (dream) activity can run off, undisturbed. Jouvet's theory is well supported by the biochemical events that prime or block sleep and by the vast amounts of paradoxical sleep that occur prior to birth and in the newborn mammal. The relative amount of dream sleep increases with the level of complexity of the developing brain. In ontogeny, the amount of paradoxical sleep is closely related to the degree of development of the central nervous system, reaching adult levels only when the maturational process is almost complete. Less sleep is needed as we grow older; why we continue to dream is still an unsolved puzzle.

Might not the vivid visual hallucinations produced by emotional states lead to an arousal of the visual cognitive area? The messages produced in the visual cognons flow downward to the visual projective area and activate the units controlling the targeting reflexes. This is what gives the pseudoperceptual, hallucinatory character to our dreams. Dreaming and rapid eye movements are closely correlated because the targeting reflexes find no definite external stimulus on which to focus.

HALLUCINATIONS CAUSED BY PATHOLOGY OR DRUGS

A somewhat different mechanism of hallucinations is in operation in pathological states involving strong emotional excitement. Associations between the emotional system and particular sets of cognons are so strongly excited that the impulses fired by them can break through to the projective area to override the incoming impulses from the periphery. This is what happens in states of delirium—the patient who is fully concentrated on his delusions projects them to the external world.

One group of consciousness-altering substances—mescaline, LSD, or psilocybin—are called *hallucinogenic* drugs because they can produce dramatic changes in perception, not unlike hallucinations. They do not produce true hallucinations, however, in that the perceiver does not usually mistake them for reality (Barron, Jarvik, & Bunnell, Jr., 1964). The subjective effects commonly reported are visual displays of extraordinary vividness and glowing color, or, when the eyes are closed, the appearance of a striking, constantly changing display. Auditory experiences, such as conversations between imaginary persons, or music, are sometimes reported, and there are also a variety of hallucinatory odors, tastes, and bodily sensations.

But the most remarkable thing about hallucinations is that they are very similar in different persons. Ronald K. Siegel (1980) at the Neuropsychiatric Institute at the University of California at Los Angeles reports experiments with mescaline, LSD, psilocybin, and other drugs in which certain forms appear with amazing constancy. Earlier, Heinrich Klüver (1966) found four constant types of mescaline-induced hallucinations. The first—a grating, lattice, honeycomb, or chessboard—is highly similar to the often highly colored geometric patterns found universally in archetypal forms, for example, in the weaving and art of the Huichol Indians of Mexico. A second type resembled cobwebs. A third was a tunnel or funnel, and the fourth, a rotating spiral coming closer or going away. All four forms are found in delirium, sensory deprivation, direct electrical brain stimulation (as we shall see in the next section) and in migraine headaches. Those associated with migraine resemble the grids, lattices, and concentric circles of the first type. Especially noteworthy in this group is the "fortification illusion" (see Figure 7.3)—a horseshoe consisting of bright zigzag lines appearing at an expanding outer edge (Richards, 1971).

In later stages of drug-induced hallucinations, complex images appear. These are thought to be an activation of images already stored in memory and expected to be almost infinitely diverse. But no. What is particularly intriguing about them is that they are actually represented in very few categories: religious symbols (72 percent); images of small animals and human beings (49 percent), which are mostly friendly cartoon characters. Of course, subjects differ widely in their use of words.

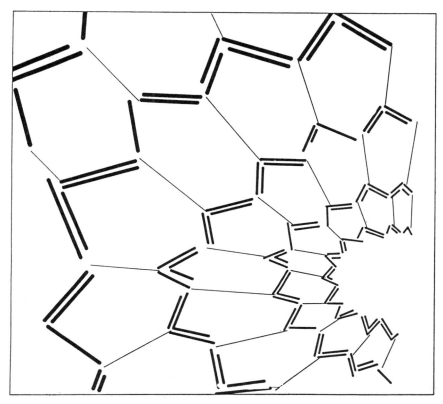

Figure 7.3. Serrated arcs and a honeycomb pattern suggest the hexagonal organization of the fortification illusions. From W. Richards, "The Fortification Illusions of Migraines," *Scientific American,* 1971, *224,* 84–96. Copyright © 1971 by Scientific American, Inc. All rights reserved.

Siegel decided to train subjects to use a standard descriptive code based on the previous frequently reported forms, colors, and movements. Hundreds of different slides illustrating the different categories were each projected for eight milliseconds with a one-second pause between displays to teach subjects a code with which they could rapidly classify their flow of images after taking either a hallucinogen or a placebo. No subject knew what or how large a dose he was taking. Untrained subjects were also tested to see if their reports of visual experiences were similar. The results were fascinating. Tested in the dark with their eyes open, the trained subjects could readily classify most of the images into the categories of the reporting code. The hallucinogens produced lattice-tunnels, while colors shifted from blue to red, orange, and yellow. Pulsating movements became more organized with explosive and rotational patterns. Still later complex images included childhood memories and scenes with strong emotional associations, often elaborated with fantastic embellishments. Brought into a botanical garden, but wearing goggles through which they could not see, the subjects "saw" birds, airplanes, or trees, but these were also superimposed on lattice-tunnel and explosive configurations. At the peak of the hallucinatory experience, they asserted that the images were real—they became true hallucinations. (See Figure 7.4.)

Physiological and behavioral effects are often observable following the ingestion of the hallucinogens. There may be sympathetic effects—dilated pupils, increased blood pressure, and EEG desynchronization, as in cortical arousal. Both the subjective and the objective effects depend on the properties and potency of the dose, the situation, and the basic personality traits of the person taking the drug. As in the case of alcohol, it is never the hallucinogen alone that is at work (Barron, Jarvik, & Bunnell, 1964).

Hallucinations can also be evoked by direct electrical stimulation of the brain. Here is a dramatic source of support for cognon theory.

NEUROLOGICAL EVIDENCE OF COGNONS BASED ON HALLUCINATIONS

As a result of his astonishing ability to evoke hallucinations, Wilder Penfield, a Canadian brain surgeon, gave us the best evidence we have on the localization of consciousness. Operating on epileptic patients, he hoped to remove the area that was the focus of the epileptic attacks. In seeking the precise spot in the brain that would arouse the curious mental aura that preceded the seizure, he made a remarkable series of discoveries. His method was to use a gentle electric current to stimulate the exposed surface of the cortex of a conscious patient lying on the operating table. The patient felt no pain, but reported a variety of sensations, depending on what cells and fibers were under the stimulating electrode. Stimulation of the visual cortex in the sensory projection area in the occipital lobe made the patient see flashes of light, stars, or swirling colors; stimulation of the touch area produced "numbness" or "tingling" sensations on the skin. But the most interesting effects occurred when Penfield moved the stimulating electrode to the temporal lobe region between the visual and other sensory receiving areas.

Human subjects who have had epileptic discharges in the temporal region are remarkably susceptible to hallucinations produced by direct electrical stimulation of the temporal lobes. Penfield and his associates (1950; 1954; 1959; 1963) describe dramatic examples in which electrical stimulation of specific points causes the patient to relive a past experience, e.g., hear voices or music, or experience vivid emotions. Penfield and Rasmussen (1950) report an illustrative case.

Figure 7.4. The spiral form and lattice tunnel are characteristic of visual hallucinations. Hallucinogenic drugs produce geometric patterns and rotating spirals with marked universality in different individuals and in artifacts from a wide variety of cultures. From R.K. Siegel & L.J. West, *Hallucinations: Behavior, Experience and Theory,* John Wiley, 1975. By permission of John Wiley & Sons. Reproduced from original artist proof by courtesy of R.K. Siegel, Ph.D.

The patient, a girl of 14 years, injured in infancy, suffered frequent attacks characterized by sudden fright and screaming, followed by falling and occasionally a major convulsion. On questioning, she recalled a scene in which she saw herself at the age of 7 years, walking through a field when a man came up from behind her and said: "How would you like to get into this bag with the snakes?" She was terrified and screamed to her brothers, and they all ran home. Under local anesthesia for an osteoplastic craniotomy, stimulation of points on the lateral aspect of the temporal lobe produced in the patient a cry of terror: "Oh, I can see something come at me! Don't let them come at me!" She remained staring and fearful for 30 seconds, although the stimulation was much shorter in duration.

Apparently, as a result of the pathological change in her cortex caused by the early injury, the epileptic discharge followed the well-worn synaptic pattern that was capable of evoking the childhood memory. When the cortex was stimulated directly, this neuron pattern could be reactivated by associative pathways. When the electrodes were held in place, the hallucination unfolded along with the dread in a reenactment of the original scene of her fright.

Penfield concludes from this and many additional cases that the temporal cortex provides access to a "storehouse of potential recollections." Stimulations of the same cortical regions in nonepileptic patients, however, did not produce hallucinations. The explanation must be that the irritation foci in the impaired regions of epileptics produce a state of increased excitability resulting in strong discharges into the corresponding projective area, suppressing incoming messages and causing hallucinatory effects.

When the exposed hemisphere was the dominant (usually left) side, the electrode seemed to produce an interference with the speech mechanism. For example, the assistant showed one patient a picture of a butterfly, which he knew he was expected to name. Penfield reports:

> He remained silent though he made a gesture that suggested exasperation. After withdrawal of the electrode, he exclaimed as though with relief: "Now I can talk, butterfly." Then he added, "I couldn't get that word *butterfly* and then I tried to get the word *moth....*" The speech mechanism had failed when called upon. To his surprise he found himself aphasic. The electrode's current had inactivated the speech mechanism without interfering with the man's capacity to perceive and to reason. (1966, p. 231)

When Penfield applied the electrode to the corresponding area on the other side of the brain (the right hemisphere) there was no aphasia, but the patient might report an amazing alteration of thought. One of two types of response was produced. In some instances, the patient interpreted the present experience as something uncannily familiar or strange and frightening, looming closer or going away. Even more curious, in other instances, the patient might experience a sudden flashback, an awareness of a previous episode deeply rooted in memory. One woman reported, as soon as Penfield applied his stimulating electrode to her right temporal lobe that she heard the choir sing in her church in Amsterdam. It was Christmas Eve, and she felt again how beautiful it was even as she lay on the table in the Montreal operating room. Another patient, a young South African cried out in astonishment when similarly stimulated, "Yes, Doctor; Yes, Doctor! Now I hear people laughing—my friends—in South Africa!" After Penfield had withdrawn the electrode the patient described his experience. He had seemed to be with two young women, his cousins, on their family farm. Still, he knew he really was in Montreal and he could speak to the doctor.

Most of these reports were of visual experiences, although many were auditory or some combination of visual and auditory scenes. Stimulation of the first temporal convolution on the right caused one patient to say, "I just heard one of my children speaking...and I looked out of my kitchen window and saw Frankie there in the yard."

Penfield concludes:

> The uncommitted cortex which remains after speech has taken its position may be called, for convenience, the interpretive cortex. Electrical stimulation sometimes produces a sudden change in automatic interpretation of those things of which the individual is at the moment aware. Or, stimulation activates a neuron sequence that constitutes the record of the stream of consciousness. That record is not in the interpretive cortex, but at a distance from the point of stimulation. It is activated by axonal conduction. The record may be located in the diencephalon, but I suspect that the hippocampus and the amygdaloid nucleus on the two sides may also have something to do with the process of recording experience. (Penfield, 1966, p. 233)

What light does this material cast on the nature of perception? When the sudden interpretive signaling is examined, it carries the conviction that comes to all of us when we recognize something that we have perceived before—"Hello, there's thingamabob again!" Small changes may bring about a sense of change in the object or event experienced as familiar—the lines in a friend's face or the gray in his hair. The feeling of "seen before" or "experienced before" is hardly separable from the feeling of "repeat performance—with a difference." All of this, Penfield concludes, is involved in perception, but it is automatic perception rather than reasoned analysis.

The results of electrical stimulation of the brain also show clearly that neuron connections are established for two separate mechanisms, one for the projection or sensory areas and one for the interpretive or association areas.

Anatomically these areas have quite different interconnections within the brain. The projection areas send axons only to adjacent areas belonging to the given analyzer; for example, the visual projection area in the occipital lobe sends axons only to the visual cortex. But the association areas send their axons to various parts of the brain through long associative pathways. It is reasonable to assume that these association areas contain the cognons that are located in the highest levels of the cognitive brain and that integrate the activity of the nervous system.

An important fact emerges from these more than 1,000 craniotomies under local anesthesia, about 500 of them in the temporal area. Only in that area has the neuronal record of consciousness been activated. Penfield's own conclusion is that the "sensory areas in the cortex are not end stations, as so many physiologists have considered them to be. They are way stations, or interruptions, each on a cortical detour that leads back to a subcortical target" (Penfield, 1966, p. 231).

Although precise localization, whether cortical or subcortical, remains for future research to discover, there is clearly a nonsensory place in the brain where past experiences are stored. When the electrode is applied repeatedly to the same point on the exposed temporal cortex, the patient would report the identical experience: being in a hall listening to the music of an orchestra, or watching an entertainer in a cafe—the patient may even hum the recalled music. These hallucinations provide vivid evidence that the brain has stored an anatomical record of a stream of consciousness. A strip of time seems to have run forward again at time's normal pace as though pathways of excitation were formed and made permanent by neuronal facilitation.

Hallucinations only appear under extraordinary conditions of emotion, disease, or altered states of consciousness. Under the normal conditions of everyday life, what factors produce associations? What factors strengthen them and lead to permanent memories? These questions point to the problem central to both neurobiology and psychology—the mechanisms of associative learning and memory. Later chapters will attempt to answer these questions. As a preliminary, it may be helpful to consider the formation of cross-modal associations and their role in the acquisition of language.

CROSS-MODAL ASSOCIATIONS

The formation of associations is most effective when the paired stimuli are not only contiguous in time but also contiguous in space. Associations between the various features of the same object are readily formed by primates and other higher animals. An orange is seen and felt to be round, thick skinned, and juicy when cut. It is more difficult to associate aspects of separated stimuli. It is particularly difficult to form associations between events that are

Pairs of stimuli

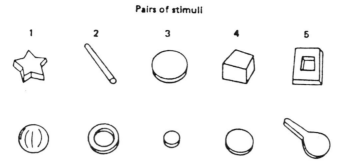

Figure 7.5. Pairs of stimulus cookies used to test cross-modal transfer. Cowey & Weiskrantz, 1975. Reprinted with permission of *Neuropsychologia, 13,* 117–120. Copyright © 1975 by Pergamon Press.

widely separated in space or time, although human beings can bridge the gap and link remote stimuli by mediated or verbal symbols.

Cross-modal matching means that the subject is allowed to feel, but not to see, an object and then is presented with objects that can be seen but not touched. For example, a human subject can readily select a wooden cube by sight as the same object previously felt but not seen. Complex objects are less readily cross-matched. Still, very young children and chimpanzees can certainly perform touch-to-vision matching even if the objects are shown only in photographs or line drawings (Weiskrantz, 1977). Cowey and Weiskrantz (1975) also tested rhesus monkeys on the cross-modal problem by feeding them in total darkness with chow molded into distinctive geometric shapes. Some shapes had good-tasting chow, others tasted awful. When the monkeys were allowed to choose shaped chow by sight alone, they carefully avoided the bad-tasting shapes. Following removal of the neocortex, they lost this ability for cross-modal matching. (See Figure 7.5.)

ACQUISITION OF LANGUAGE

Language learning is generally thought to be a special case of cross-modal matching. Language also requires a temporal patterning that preserves the serial order of sounds over time. Both cross-modal matching and temporal integration involve the manipulation of central representations, or images, and the evidence points to the neocortex—in most people, the neocortex of the left hemisphere—as specialized for these abilities.

The well-known linguist, Noam Chomsky (1966; 1975) of MIT, has argued forcefully that, although words must be learned, the syntax of language is genetically given and uniquely human.

Language acquisition certainly goes well beyond *imitation*. No child hears all the sentences he is ever going to use. Nor is differential social reinforcement the explanation for the achievement of grammar. The rules are rarely articulated. In most native speakers the rules of grammar are largely unconscious, and the child receives little or no correction for grammatical errors or praise for being correct. Semantic, as well as grammatical, development proceeds without explicit tutoring.

Eve V. Clark (1973) of Stanford has examined children's speech and noted several interesting developments in their use of words. The first time children use a word, she found, they generalize it immediately to refer to many objects, based on some feature of the original object. For example, one little girl called her father's watch a "tick tock," then proceeded to extend the word to include all watches, clocks, a gas meter, and a bathroom scale with a round dial. The meaning of words gradually narrows down to coincide with adult usage. Since a word is a cognon, the child's rampant overgeneralization, based on similarity of shape, size, or configuration, exemplifies the categorical property of cognons.

Donald R. Griffin (1976) of Rockefeller University, the discoverer of bat echo location, claims in a provocative little book, against Chomsky, that animals exhibit communicative behavior of surprising sophistication and effectiveness. He reviews the work of Lindauer (1971) and von Frisch (1967) showing that the bee dance communication system is not tightly linked to food or any one simple requirement. The same dances, with variations, are used for different things—food, water, the location and suitability of a potential hive to be constructed. Different dancelike motions have diverse communicative functions. To take one good example, the buzzing run performed on the surface of the swarm, unlike the waggle dance, is followed by a mass exodus that seems to obey the dancer's command, "Okay, let's go."

The genetic instructions that allow the waggle dance of the bee, or her buzzing run, to communicate to her mates the exact location of a rich source of food or the desirable site for a new hive, involve the ability to learn a coded pattern of communication. Chomsky, while insisting on the genetic basis of human language, fails to recognize the evolutionary continuity between species that has revolutionized our view of ourselves. As Griffin (1976) eloquently shows, the conclusion is inescapable even on the criterion of language—there is no rigid dichotomy between human and animal behavior.

Griffin (1976) disagrees forcefully with claims, such as Chomsky's, that "language is the essence of humanness" and that animals, therefore, are "mere beasts" devoid of the ability to reason. On the contrary, Griffin describes animal communicative behavior in bee, bird, and chimpanzee as flexible and effective, differing only in form and degree, but not in kind, from human language.

The chimpanzee is capable of relatively complex communication, although it is expressed more readily by manual gestures than by vocalization. Goodall (1975) observed that chimpanzees, in the wild, use gestures and facial expressions that are effective. Menzel (1973) showed that captive chimpanzees combine gestures in complex patterns, not yet deciphered by human investigators, but apparently capable of conveying, or even *intentionally* withholding, information from their conspecific companions.

Following their lead, Gardner and Gardner (1969) decided to train a wild-born young female chimpanzee, Washoe, to use well over 100 different words from the American Sign Language (Ameslan). Washoe proceeded to invent some of her own and to use them all in conversation with her human teachers. She combined signs in meaningful ways to make comprehensible sentences and to transfer them appropriately to new situations. She used the sign for *open* to request the opening of boxes, on which, in controlled blind experiments, she was able to name pictures not visible to the experimenter.

Others have successfully trained chimpanzees in languagelike communication, using plastic tokens as words (Premack, 1971) and even a computer keyboard. In these experiments, vocabularies are limited to symbols or keys, but they yield surprising communicative skills. Chimpanzees can communicate far more complex concepts than had been previously thought possible below the human level.

Griffin (1976) finds in animal communication no basis for the assumption that animals lack any conscious intent to communicate. "This belief that mental experiences are a unique attribute of a single species is not only unparsimonious," he concludes, "it is conceited.... Awareness probably confers a significant adaptive advantage by enabling animals to react appropriately to physical, biological, and social events and signals from the surrounding world with which their behavior interacts" (Griffin, 1976, p. 104).

In the perception of speech, as in reading, we hear (or see) words, not phonemes, because we have a code based on our familiarity with the language. The key to the code is an ordering principle based on the stored representation of familiar sound sequences in the brain cells or *cognons* for the corresponding stimulus patterns.

Speech perception and production are evidently processed by configurations, not by segments. We hear individual segments, but they are immediately assigned to classes or categories. In the parlance of linguists, "tokens are converted into types." It is in the realm of syntax, however, that the emergence of rules appears most clearly.

Short trains of sequences in language seem to be stored in packages or quanta. These are cognons and, once acquired, can be applied in many different situations and levels of complexity. The organizing principle appears to be a temporal ordering of sound sequences in language and auditory or visual scans in perception. The general principle is analogous in all analyzers, except that in visual perception, whether in reading or in identifying objects, the patterns have spatial as well as temporal dimensions so that questions about the curvature of lines, and their symmetry or asymmetry, may assume critical importance.

As we have seen, the basis for perception, language, and action is the stored representation of familiar patterns in the cells of the cortex. These *cognons* permit their possessors to function adaptively, even though they confront completely new elements never before encountered, by assigning them to an appropriate ordering category.

BIOLOGICAL CONSTRAINTS ON ASSOCIATIVE LEARNING

Konorski (1967) repeatedly stresses the importance of biological constraints in associative learning and response differentiation. In no species are associations formed that are completely arbitrary.

In human learning, to be sure, the names of things, with a few onomatopoeic exceptions, like *hiss, sizzle,* or *pop,* do seem to be arbitrary. We learn to pair names with faces, and telephone numbers with places, by an associative process that makes us seem to be able to relate anything with anything else. Although we can learn arbitrary relations, however, we form associations very much more readily between things that *belong* together.

Thorndike (1931) showed that subjects can associate two words when they occur in the same sentence more easily than when they occur in two different, although adjacent, sentences.

William is a plumber. Tom is a doctor. Alice is a psychologist. Linda is an actress.

When those sentences are read out loud to a class, and then the question is asked, the students easily recall that William is a plumber, and Tom is a doctor, but not that the word Tom followed plumber, or that the word Alice followed doctor, despite their closer contiguity. Thorndike called this *belongingness.*

Human beings readily pair nonsense patterns consisting of curved lines with other curved lines and also with cool colors and waltz music; they pair jagged lines with hot colors and jazz (writer's Vassar College unpublished experiments) because they belong together. People's names also seem to fit some persons better than others. Schoenfeld (1942) found that college students assign trait stereotypes to names: *Richard, good-looking; Bertha, fat; Adrian, artistic; Barbara, charming;* and *Linda, sophisticated;* perhaps revealing a "kernel of truth" based on the tendency for behavior to conform to expectations (and movies, or novels). It might be interesting to repeat his experiment today. Would *Charles* be *princely; Carl, sagacious;* and *Diana, gracious?*

In animals as in humans, the belongingness relation is built-in or species-specific, making certain *potential* connections available for the formation of new actual connections, others not.

WORD ASSOCIATIONS REVEAL RESPONSE CATEGORIES

That humans, often unknowingly, do make certain paired associations much more readily than others is brought out by the extensive evidence on word associations. In a classic study, Kent and Rosanoff (1910) listed 100 familiar words and gave each one orally to 3,000 human children and adults of both sexes with various educational and vocational backgrounds. The subject, seated with his or her back to the experimenter, was requested to respond to each stimulus word with "the first word that occurs to you other than the stimulus word." The author assembled the results and tabulated the frequency of each response. The most frequent responses for various groups are shown for some of the stimulus words in Table 7.1.

TABLE 7.1
The Most Frequent Responses Given by Various Groups
in a Word Association Test (Kent-Rosanoff, 1910).

Stimulus	*Response*	*1,000 Children*	*1,000 Men and Women*	*1,000 Men in Industry*
TABLE	eat	358	63	40
	chair	24	274	333
DARK	night	421	221	162
	light	38	427	626
MAN	work	168	17	8
	woman	8	394	561
DEEP	hole	257	32	20
	shallow	6	180	296
SOFT	pillow	138	53	42
	hard	27	365	548

(Woodworth & Schlosberg, 1954, p. 54)

When the various frequency tabulations are compared, striking group differences come to light.

Adults frequently give opposites *(dark-light)* while children rarely give opposites but tend to "stay by" the thing described by the stimulus word. That is, they tell something about it: a *table* is to *eat;* a *man,* to *work; soft* is a *pillow.*

How can one tell precisely what meaning a child has constructed for a word? Some of the most fascinating observations concern the meanings of the pairs of words that function as opposites for adults. Breyne Arlene Moskowitz (1978, p. 196) reports that when children three to five years old are asked in individual tests which one of two cardboard trees has "more" apples on it, they will point correctly. But they will readily point to that same tree when asked which one has "less" apples. They act as though they know the meaning of "less" and that "less" means "more."

Further studies revealed similar systematic errors in which opposites, "same" and "different," "big" and "little," "tall" and "short," "wide" and "narrow," were confused. In learning a pair of word opposites, one word is learned first and its meaning is overextended to apply to the other member of the pair. The word that is learned first represents the common dimension of meaning of the word pair—the general category. Only later do children acquire the parts of the meaning, the ends of the pole, that distinguish the two. Here is striking confirmation of the role of complementary units—on-units and off-units—in the initial formation of a cognon, responsible for primitive generalization, and the acquisition of discrimination between antagonists when later conditions demand it. Only then do new cognons develop to permit the utilization of new words for different responses. In this way, *discrimination,* a purely perceptive process allowing the formation of new cognons, enables *differentiation* to take place. Discrimination precedes differentiation.

An important point is that discrimination of two patterns ("more" and "less") does not occur by transforming the cognons concerned, but through developing new units in addition to the old ones. Thus the child retains the general concept of *quantity,* but can use two different responses to denote the two comparatives. Later she will acquire still finer degrees of quantitative analysis—as the scale becomes increasingly refined and precise in conformity with physical features of the outside world. The strong link between the polar opposites that emerges in adult word associations must be the result of their initial identification in the mind of the child.

The word association task tells us interesting facts about language and its development. And it reveals the complex intermingling of constraints of various sorts in speech. Multiple choice forms of the association test are used for the purpose of distinguishing people of different backgrounds and attitudes—for example, tests of vocational interests or masculinity-femininity. Such applications are of limited value for they are based on population norms that lean heavily on stereotyped responses.

But this very limitation is significant from the point of view of this discussion of the constraints on associative learning. The main point of interest for us is that human verbal associations are not arbitrary. They are lawful. The simple fact that most adults give the same response to a given stimulus word tells us that language has become so firmly established with use that free associations are not really free. Actually they are highly dependable indications of, perhaps not species-specific responses, but certainly verbal community–specific responses. Children are more idiosyncratic—their responses are slower, more thoughtful, and more often unique—because they are not yet fully socialized in the grooves of language clichés. Those habits are still in the process of becoming.

SUMMARY

Cognons are high-level neural units in the cognitive fields of various analyzers that integrate the converging afferent impulses and take part in the associations that form the basis for thought, memory, and voluntary action. Excitation of cognons by messages coming from the periphery (sensory receptors) produces perceptions; excitation of these units by association within the brain produces images.

Unitary perceptions are accompanied by the targeting reflex adjusting the sense organs to the optimal reception of a stimulus. This reflex gives perception its mark of external reality and is absent in the image. The image may be sharp and vivid, but it allows no scrutiny for the discovery of further details and is localized internally.

Hallucinations arise when sensory input is cut off by sleep or strong emotional states. The sensory inhibition allows messages to flow downstream from cognitive areas to projective areas. This neural activity in the projective areas gives the hallucination and the dream the psychological quality of a perception. In the alert waking state these areas are busily occupied with incoming messages from the outside world. The increase in importance of dream (REM and PGO) sleep with the development of the central nervous system suggests its evolutionary role in programming potential connections for later use.

The formation of new associations requires, first, the existence of potential or prefunctional paths in the nervous system developed in ontogeny in both humans and animals. Second, the subject must be aroused by a drive. Third, the cognons that are the actors in the associative process must be stimulated concurrently. The temporal contiguity between the members of the pair is essential.

These principles of associative learning are well brought out by experiments on the conditioned reflex, the subject of the next chapter.

SUGGESTED READINGS

Brown, R. *Psycholinguistics: Selected papers.* New York: Free Press, 1970.
Brown, R. *A first language: The early stages.* Cambridge: Harvard University Press, 1973.

Clark, E.V. On the child's acquisition of antonyms in two semantic fields. *Journal of Verbal Learning and Verbal Behavior,* 1972, *11,* 750–758.

Clark, E.V. What's in a word? On the child's acquisition of semantics in his first language. In T.E. Moore (Ed.), *Cognitive development and the acquisition of language.* New York: Academic Press, 1973.

Cowey, A., & Weiskrantz, L. Demonstration of cross-modal matching in rhesus monkeys, Macaca mulatta. *Neuropsychologia,* 1975, *13,* 117–120.

Gardner, B.T., & Gardner, R.A. Teaching sign language to a chimpanzee. *Science,* 1969, *165,* 664–674.

Griffin, D.R. *The question of animal awareness.* New York: Rockefeller University Press, 1976.

Huxley, A. *The doors of perception and heaven and hell.* New York: Penguin, 1959.

Jouvet, M. The function of dreaming: A neurophysiologist's point of view. In M.S. Gazzaniga & C. Blakemore (Eds.), *Handbook of psychobiology.* New York: Academic Press, 1975, (pp. 499–527).

Kupfermann, I., & Weiss, K.R. The command neuron concept. *The behavioral and brain sciences,* 1978, *1,* 3–39.

Lenneberg, E.H. *Biological foundations of language.* New York: Wiley, 1967.

Lenneberg, E.H., Nichols, I.A., & Rosenberger, E.F. Primitive stages of language development in mongolism. In D. Rioch & E.A. Weinstein (Eds.), *Disorders of communication* (Vol. XLII). New York: Hafner, 1969.

Lynch, J.C. The command function concept in studies of the primate nervous system. *The Behavioral and Brain Sciences,* 1978, *1,* 31–32.

Maruszewski, M. *[Language communication and the brain: A neuropsychological study]* (G.W. Shugar, trans.). Hawthorne, NY: Mouton, 1975.

Moore, T.E. (Ed.). *Cognitive development and the acquisition of language.* New York: Academic Press, 1973.

Penfield, W., & Rasmussen, T. *The cerebral cortex of man: A clinical study of localization of function.* New York: Macmillan, 1950.

Penfield, W., & Roberts, L. *Speech and brain mechanisms.* Princeton, NJ: Princeton University Press, 1959.

Premack, D. Language in chimpanzee? *Science,* 1971, *172,* 808–822.

Premack, D. *Intelligence in ape and man.* Hillsdale, N.J.: Erlbaum, 1976.

Rumbaugh, D.M. (Ed.). *Language learning by a chimpanzee: The Lana project.* New York: Academic Press, 1977.

Siegel, R.K. Hallucinations. *Scientific American,* 1977, *237,* 132–140.

CHAPTER EIGHT

Associative Learning, Conditioning, and Insight

The next day therefore I had the picture, and on the following Mrs. Bridgeworth, whom I had notified, arrived. I had placed it, framed and on an easel, well in evidence, and I have never forgotten the look and the cry that, as she became aware of it, leaped into her face and from her lips.... She had recognized on the instant the subject; that came first and was irrepressibly vivid in her. Her recognition had, for the length of a flash, lighted for her the possibility that the stroke had been directed. That came second, and she flushed with it as with a blow in the face. What came third—and it was really most wondrous—was the quick instinct of getting both her strange recognition and her blind suspicion well in hand. She couldn't control, however, poor woman, the strong colour in her face and the quick tears in her eyes. She could only glare at the canvas, gasping, grimacing, and try to gain time.
                    (Henry James, The Tone of Time. *Originally published in 1900)*

ASSOCIATIVE LEARNING AND THE CONDITIONED REFLEX

Previous chapters dealt with the nonassociative elementary forms of learning. Habituation, sensitization, and perceptual learning are nonassociative because they involve a single stimulus and an increase or a decrease in a single response. Yet they belong under the heading of *learning* because all are changes in behavior as a result of interaction with the environment, that is to say, by experience.

Since sensitization and perceptual learning involve the attachment of a response to a previously ineffective stimulus, they are precursors of *associative learning*—the subject of this chapter.

The key factors in the transition from nonassociative to associative learning are the requirements for pairing two stimuli or pairing a stimulus with a response. The main forms of associative learning and the rules for pairing have been worked out in the experiments on the *conditioned reflex*. The earliest conditioning experiments were introduced by Pavlov at the beginning of the century.

CLASSICAL CONDITIONING

The prototype, called *classical conditioning,* is based on Pavlov's (1927) discovery that an inborn reflex, such as salivation in response to food in the mouth, could be acquired by a previously neutral stimulus, say a bell tone. By repeated pairing of the bell sound, the *conditioned stimulus* (CS) with the food as the *unconditioned stimulus* (US) served to a hungry dog, the bell sound alone will give rise to the salivary response, the *conditioned reflex* (CR).

Pavlov regarded the conditioned reflex as the basic building block of all learning since it seemed to represent the formation of an actual connection in the brain as the result of experience. It is clear that in classical conditioning the animal learns something about the relation between two stimuli. The formation of the association requires the pairing in close temporal contiguity of activity in two specific pathways. One pathway is activated by a drive-related stimulus, the other by a neutral stimulus. (See Figure 8.1.)

Pavlov used the term *reinforcement* to denote the strengthening of the tendency of the CS to elicit the CR by repeatedly pairing the CS and the US. When the CS appears and is not followed by the US, the nonreinforced trial leads to the undoing of the CR; in Pavlov's terms, the CR undergoes *experimental extinction.*

Conditioning is a form of associative learning that depends on the temporal pattern of stimulation. The laboratory analysis of conditioning in animals is made possible by using a response that is overt and measurable, such as salivation, or limb withdrawal to an electric shock. Thus the conditioning experiment offers a privileged case of associative learning. As a result of the paired presentations of the conditioned and the unconditioned stimuli, actual connections are established between their corresponding perceptive units. These are made manifest by presenting the conditioned stimulus and omitting the unconditioned stimulus on a test trial; if the conditioned stimulus elicits the response characteristic of that elicited by the unconditioned stimulus, conditioning is said to have taken place. Human

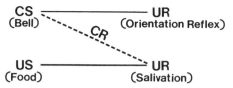

Figure 8.1. Diagram of a classical (Pavlovian) conditioning experiment.

beings experience these connections introspectively because the perception of one of these stimuli evokes the image of the other.

Rules of Formation of Classical Conditioned Reflexes

The synapses are the gaps or junctions between neurons that transmit impulses. The increase of transmissibility at synapses linking the presynaptic and postsynaptic neurons accounts for the modification of behavior called associative learning or conditioning. In order for the classical conditioning procedure to effect this synaptic transmission, four conditions are necessary:

1. *Drive.* Aroused by the appropriate drive state, the subject must *pay attention* to the presented pair of stimuli. This insures the physical arousal of perceptive fields to which the cognons representing the conditioned and unconditioned stimuli belong. Speaking physiologically, the *targeting reflexes* directed at both the CS and the US permit their optimal reception and bridge the interval between them.

2. *Paired* presentation of the CS and US. Their close *temporal contiguity,* with the CS preceding the US, is an essential prerequisite. The best procedure for the formation of the CR occurs when the CS precedes the US in *overlapping* sequence. You always see lightning first, then hear the thunder: within limits, the shorter the interstimulus interval, the more strongly the association will be established. If the thunder follows on the heels of the flash of lightning, the electrical disturbance must be close by, and it will be experienced as exceedingly intense.

3. *Stimulus intensity.* The brighter the flash and the louder the sound, the greater the strength of sensory and emotive arousal. These factors of magnitude—both in the component stimuli and the evoked reaction—are also important determinants of associative strength.

4. *Repetition.* The more frequently the sequence is repeated, the more firmly its neural connectivity is established in the brain. The establishment of a classical CR in the experimental laboratory generally takes place gradually and requires repeated trials. Note that repetition of the CS without presenting the US is the absence of reinforcement and results in *extinction* of the CR.

The procedure for studying conditioning in animals has been successfully used to reveal the laws governing the formation of interperceptive associations. According to this associative concept of the mechanism of conditioning, the effects of the CS should consist only of those effects included in the unconditioned reflex or UR. Indeed, the experiment is designed to produce the original CR (salivation, leg withdrawal, cardiovascular effects, etc.) in response to a new stimulus, the CS. Typically, this is the case. The CR is usually the same as the UR. But are they always *identical?*

Preparatory and Consummatory Conditioned Reflexes

Often the classical CR seems not at all the same thing as the UR. Take the food CR, for example. The usual Pavlovian method pairs the CS with presentation of food in a bowl moving into position. The UR consists of salivating, seizing, chewing, and swallowing the food, while the only effect during the CS-US interval is salivation. The other elements are absent from the CR. How can the CR be said to be identical with the UR? As Konorski points out, the CS is not followed directly by the US (food in the mouth), but by the *sight* of a bowl with food. This visual stimulus elicits a natural motor act, that is, taking the food before eating it. In the absence of the opportunity to seize the food, one would not expect feeding to occur. This argument finds support in experiments in which the CS is immediately followed by the proper US. Acid placed directly in the mouth following the CS elicits as a CR, vigorous mouthing movements, identical with those occurring in response to the US.

Where other differences exist between the effects of the CS and the US, they can be explained by the realization that two forms of classical conditioning can occur in response to the same stimulus. The two forms of conditioning correspond to the two stages of drive-related behavior described in Chapter Two—preparatory drives and consummatory reflexes.

The *hunger CR* is mainly produced by the experimental situation connected with feeding: it consists of motor excitement, sensitivity to external stimuli, especially taste, and also to hunger contractions of the stomach. The *food CR* is produced by the CS (bell or light) immediately preceding the presentation of food and consists of salivation and inhibition of the hunger contractions of the stomach. The food CR is established as a secondary stage of alimentary conditioning, since initially it requires the hunger drive to be present. As Chapter Two showed, the hunger drive is usually a *tonic* and prolonged process, manifested by restlessness and searching behavior, while food intake is a *phasic* consummatory process, beginning and terminating abruptly.

A well-established food CS, similar to the food US, calls forth the partial suppression of the hunger drive. When the CS appears, the animal becomes quite calm. Like the UR, the CS also elicits a state of hunger antidrive, suppressing the motor excitement characteristic of the hunger drive. The animal calms down because the CS is a guarantee that food will soon follow.

In general, all classical CRs are composed of two relatively independent CRs, the drive CR and the consummatory CR. This is true of defensive CRs as well as preservative CRs. The fear drive CR is established by linking the CS units with the fear units of the limbic system; the consummatory CR (shock CR, acid CR, etc.) is established by linking the CS units with the US units specific to the reinforcement. The subject calms down because the shock (or its termination) now becomes a fear antidrive CS, since it is regularly followed by a period of total security.

In observing the behavior of dogs in food conditioning, experimenters find that various animals behave very differently during the interval between the CS and the US. Some dogs become immobile while others display strong motor excitement. The reason for the difference is that immobility is the posture taken during the consummatory *food* UR, while excitement reflects the *hunger* drive. The important point is that the same stimulus, the appearance of food, has two different effects. The sight and smell of food initially arouses hunger and the restlessness characteristic of the *hunger* CR; only later, after appropriate training, does it transform gradually into a *food* CR, consisting of salivation and inhibition of the hunger contractions of the stomach.

We tend to overlook the situational stimuli by undue emphasis on the sporadic CS and the US. Yet the hunger CR is typically conditioned to the experimental situation; the food CR is conditioned to the presentation of food. This distinction may be clear in your own experience. Human beings become conditioned to experience hunger (the hunger CR) when they sit down at the table, even when they have eaten shortly before and are actually satiated. Yet they start to eat and find themselves actually hungry in the process. They develop food CSs, which are stimuli associated with the taste of foods they like. Listening to the gourmet describe the delicious meal served at a famous restaurant, or reading about food and seeing pictures of beautifully prepared dishes, we salivate—we don't seize the pictures and lick them.

Neural Mechanisms in Conditioning: The Search for the Engram

The distinction between drive CRs and consummatory CRs suggests that different neural structures may be involved in the two forms. Do different neural mechanisms underlie different classes of learned responses? This question, first articulated by Lashley (1950) as the search for the engram (the locus of specific memory traces) has proved to be one of the most baffling in science.

Early in the history of conditioning it became clear that, despite Pavlov's insistence on the cerebral cortex as *the* organ of conditioning, decorticated animals are capable of forming CRs (Culler & Mettler, 1934; Oakley & Russell, 1977; Konorski, 1967). There is good evidence that some perceptions are preserved after cortical lesions occur and may serve as the basis for subcortical conditioning. Animals from whom the neocortex has been removed fail to discriminate complex visual or auditory patterns in the stimuli presented. Removal of the lower brain structures produces a more fundamental deficit because these lesioned animals often fail to react to the very occurrence of these stimuli. Although previously established CRs disappear, there is evidence that these neodecorticated animals can still acquire and preserve new CRs. The key question is: where is the essential neuronal plasticity that codes the memory?

In the search for the engram—the neural substrate of learning and memory in the brain—Richard Thompson and co-workers have made a new and provocative series of discoveries (Thompson et al., 1983). They have focused on a model that provides a simple and clearcut form of associative learning: classical conditioning of the rabbit nictitating membrane (NM) response. (See Figures 8.2 and 8.3.) First developed by Gormezano and his associates (1962), the rabbit NM response to an air puff US involves both NM extension (eyeball retraction) and eyelid closure simultaneously. The conditioned NM response (CNMR) to an acoustic stimulus ties into a large behavioral literature on animal and human eyelid conditioning.

The question these investigators set themselves was: What is the circuitry that codes the essential plasticity of learning and memory for the conditioned response (CR)? Of course there might be any number of memory traces widely and diffusely distributed in the brain. But for this standard delay CR, there might be just one—the essential "primary engram." If so, the challenge was to find it—to discover where in the brain this circuit could be localized and characterized.

Using electrophysiological recording of neural unit activity over a wide range of conditions, Thompson's group identified certain brain structures as centrally involved in the learning of this conditioned response. Two structures of particular interest emerge. The first is the hippocampus. The second is the cerebellum.

Consider the hippocampus first. Pyramidal neurons in the hippocampus rapidly develop a very clear model of the behavioral conditioned response. Thompson et al. put it succinctly:

> In brief, over a wide range of conditions that impair or alter acquisition, maintenance, or extinction of the learned response, *the learning-induced increase in hippocampal unit activity invariably precedes and accurately predicts subsequent behavioral learning performance.* The hippocampal response has all the properties of a direct measure of the inferred processes of learning and memory in the brain. (1983, p. 173)

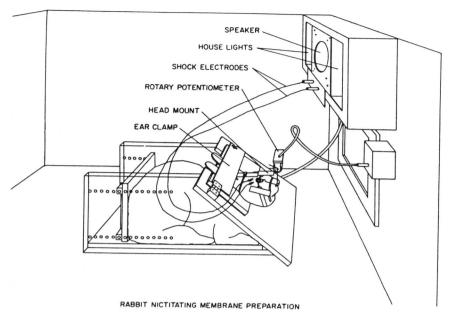

SPEAKER

HOUSE LIGHTS

SHOCK ELECTRODES

ROTARY POTENTIOMETER

HEAD MOUNT

EAR CLAMP

RABBIT NICTITATING MEMBRANE PREPARATION

Figure 8.2. Classical conditioning experiment with the rabbit. The rabbit is placed in the restraining box with the headset arranged for electrical recording from the eyelid nictitating membrane response (NMR). The CS is a tone. The US is either an airpuff or an electric shock to the paraorbital region. Gormezano, Kehoe, & Marshall, 1983.

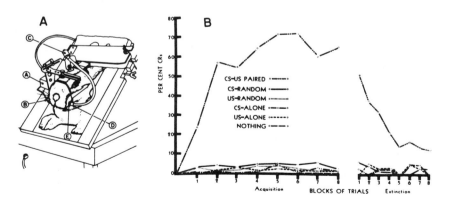

A

B

PER CENT CRs

CS-US PAIRED
CS-RANDOM
US-RANDOM
CS-ALONE
US-ALONE
NOTHING

Acquisition   BLOCKS OF TRIALS   Extinction

Figure 8.3. Examples of acquisition and extinction of conditioned eyelid (NMR) responses plotted against blocks of trials. Gormezano et al., 1983.

257

Yet following prior bilateral ablation of the hippocampus and, indeed, following the removal of all brain tissue above the level of the thalamus, the rabbit *can learn* the standard delay eyeblink CR (in which the US overlaps the termination of the CS). Is it correct to infer that higher brain structures are not *normally* involved in classical conditioning? Clearly not. The hippocampus is essential for the formation of a *trace* CR in which a period of no stimulation intervenes between CS offset and US onset. The term "trace" conforms to the obvious fact that the animal must be responding to a trace left by the acoustic CS in the nervous system, since it is no longer sounding when the CS appears. The hippocampus thus plays an indispensable role in trace conditioning, providing a bridge across the empty interval between the CS and the US. Moreover if conditioning involves the recognition of a complex or abstract pattern as the CS, then the higher brain structures are needed. But early in the history of conditioning it became apparent, as we have seen, that a CR could be established in the absence of the forebrain. A decerebrated animal could be readily conditioned. The essential circuitry, at least for the standard delay CR (not the trace CR) must exist in the midbrain-brainstem.

In order to locate this circuit, one must independently vary the CR and the UR; that is, it is necessary to show that the unconditioned reflex pathways are not a critical part of the essential plasticity coding the learned response. Mauk, Warren, and Thompson (1982) succeeded in doing this by using morphine after training and observing the behavioral performance of the NMR components of the learned response (CR) and the UR separately during five 8-trial blocks and then injecting the animals with naloxone, a morphine antagonist. The results were striking. The CR was immediately abolished by morphine and reactivated just as quickly by naloxone. But neither drug had *any* effect at all on the UR, the reflex response to the corneal air puff. Thompson writes: "The highly specific naloxone-reversible action of morphine on the CR appears to provide a powerful tool for the study of the learning circuitry in the brain. It must somehow inactivate some portion of the essential neuronal plasticity coding the learned response" (1983, p. 183). (See Figure 8.4.)

What is the mechanism of this powerful reversal effect? Based on the large body of evidence that both morphine and the endogenous opioids act more on learned fear or anxiety than on pain *per se,* Thompson concludes that the aversive component of the conditioned eyelid response is conditioned fear.

The search for the engram of this conditioned fear response next underwent a mapping study. For this purpose, Thompson and his group developed a chronic micromanipulator system to permit mapping of learning-related increases in unit activity. These were prominent in certain regions of the cerebellum, the reticular formation, and the cranial motor nuclei. The most interesting result was the appearance in the *cerebellum* of a temporal neuronal model of the *learned* behavior response. This growth of unit activity (see Figures 8.5 and 8.6) began on day 2 of the training and reflected the amplitude

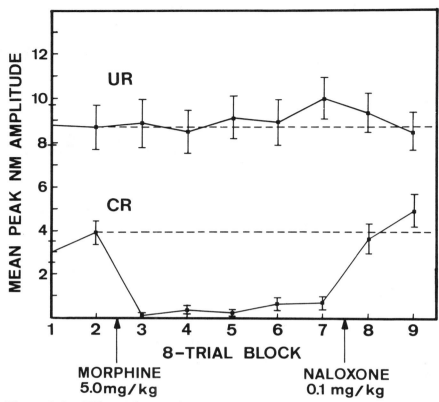

Figure 8.4. Effects of morphine and naloxone on behavioral performance of the learned response (CR) and reflex (UR) components of the NMR. Mauk et al., 1982. Copyright © 1982 by AAAS.

and time course of the learned behavioral response. But at no time did the unconditioned reflex NM response appear in the cerebellar model. The contrast between learning-induced response in cerebellum and that in the hippocampus is remarkable. The hippocampus models the entire behavioral response; the cerebellum shows only the *learned* response. Additional lesion studies confirmed the electrophysiological evidence. Ablation of the cerebellum on the side of the learned response completely and permanently abolished the CR: it had no effect on the UR reflex. This means that the deficit is not due to motor impairment. The animal could respond to the air puff—it could *perform* the response—it lost its *memory* for the learning-induced response. The engram had been scooped out by the operation on the lateral cerebellum. The conclusion has an immense body of solid support: the lateral cerebellum ipsilateral to the eye being trained is essential for the learned eyelid and NM responses.

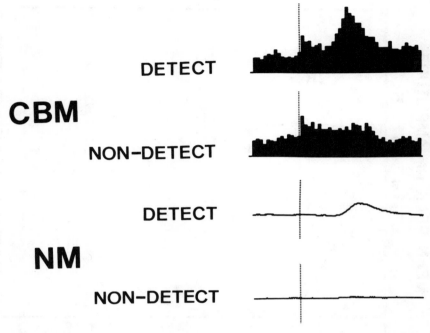

Figure 8.5. Histograms of neuronal activity recorded from the cerebellum on detection and nondetection trials to stimulus onset (vertical line) of threshold level noise. Thompson et al., 1983.

Does this beautiful demonstration imply that all learned responses involving discrete striated muscle movements have their locus in the cerebellum? It is too soon to tell. At least three qualifications may be noted:

1. The NMR is a ballistic response and like other rapid, repetitive or discontinuous movements (e.g., saccadic eye movements) is too fast for continuous sensory feedback. The temporal coordination of these rapid movements must be designed prior to their initiation, and this preprogramming ostensibly takes place in the cerebellum. In contrast to such step movements generated by the cerebellum, slow smooth movements, called ramp movements, are radically different. We can move our hands or legs voluntarily at almost any speed (within limits). The programs for these ramp movements, once they are automatized as learned skills, may have their locus, not in the cerebellum, but, as Konorski (1967) assumed, in the *basal ganglia*. Although the functions of this group of nuclei are still largely unknown, evidence for a ramp generator in the striatum of the basal ganglia comes from human pathology (Kornhuber, 1974). Lesions of the basal ganglia produce signs of release such as tremor, chorea, and ballism. These are common

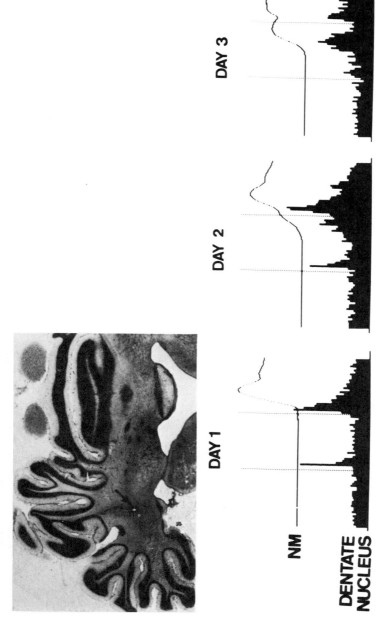

DAY 1

DAY 2

DAY 3

NM

DENTATE
NUCLEUS

Figure 8.6. Growth of unit activity in the ipsilateral cerebellum over the course of learning. The recording site is indicated by the arrow in the photograph of the cerebellar slice. The first vertical line indicates the onset of the tone; the second vertical line indicates the onset of the airpuff. Unilateral ablation of the left cerebellum completely abolished the CR but had absolutely no effect on the UCR. McCormick et al. *Proc. Natl. Acad. Sci. (USA)* 79(1982), p. 2733. Reprinted by permission.

symptoms of Parkinson's disease. One deficiency symptom, *akinesia*, affects the initiation of movements or changes of movement, making it difficult for the unfortunate victim to lie down, or sit up, turn, or stop walking. The patient attempts to compensate for the defect in the basal ganglia by replacing large ramp movements by small rapid saccades regulated by the cerebellum, an often impossible feat. The convergence of cortical input from many areas onto striatal cells puts the striatum in a strategic position to be importantly involved in the selection and learning of motor behavior.

The prefrontal cortex, whose loss destroys the ability to delay response in a spatial test, sends projections to the neostriatum, particularly to the caudate nucleus—an important region of the basal ganglia. For some, indeed, perhaps many learned movements, further search for the engram might look to the basal ganglia.

2. The rabbit NMR is a response to an aversive stimulus. It may be premature to generalize these results to appetitive unconditioned stimuli. Moreover, in the special case of taste aversion conditioning, the separation between the CS and the US may extend to several hours. According to Garcia and Ervin (1966) the neural mechanisms underlying food-related stimuli are anatomically distinct from those associated with exteroceptive stimuli. If, after testing a distinctively flavored food, an animal suffers gastrointestinal distress, it will avoid future ingestion of that food. The efficacy of the sickness-inducing US is strongly linked to taste as the CS; other CS cues (as in the "bright-noisy-water" experiment of Garcia & Koelling, 1966) are not effective. The nature of the US is also important. Pairing gustatory stimuli with noxious electrical stimulation of the paws does not lead to a learned taste aversion. The nature and the locus of this specialized memory trace with its long time span pose a mystery. What and where is the engram?

3. Many investigators concur that conditioning may occur as two processes or phases. In Chapter Two you may recall that drives or preparatory reflexes (both protective and preservative) have characteristics radically different from those of consummatory reflexes. As analogous division separates conditioned responses into two groups.

Thompson suggests that the latter group involves mechanisms that underlie the learning of the specific adaptive motor response, that is, the consummatory CR. It is this adaptive defensive response, in this case, the NMR, for which he has found the engram. This is an important advance. The first group of drive-conditioned responses includes conditioned fear and may involve, beyond brainstem-hypothalamic mechanisms, hormonal actions within and outside the central nervous system. There are excellent reasons, also, to suppose that some of the essential plasticity in primates and other animals is stored in the limbic system and the cerebral cortex. The cortex increases in importance in higher animals. The differences are not in kind, but in degree of complexity, and the extent of the time span and the space span that the conditioned associations can bridge.

Adaptive Advantage of Classical Conditioning

In terms of *cognon* theory, classical conditioning occurs when two cognons are activated synchronously. One of the units gives rise to the perception of a current external stimulus (the CS); after conditioning, it evokes the image of the second biologically important (reinforcing) stimulus (the US) as a result of the linkage pairing the two cognons.

The ability of one cognon to arouse a second cognon to activity from within the brain confers an adaptive advantage, particularly when it enables the animal to anticipate the future food (or shock) and then to compare its image with the sensory input given by the physical arrival of the US and its actual perception. In the words of Carew, Hawkins, and Kandel: "Conditioning is thus thought to represent a prototypical example of the learning of causal relationships by animals and humans" (1983, p. 397).

Is Classical Conditioning Related to Nonassociative Learning?

In Chapter Five we saw that elementary nonassociative forms of learning share common properties and may be governed by similar properties in many different species. Habituation, sensitization, and perceptual learning are universal features of behavior, and the same underlying neurophysiological and molecular mechanisms may be at work in the human infant, the active rat, and the marine gastropod mollusc. In fact, the study of the snail, *Aplysia,* with its very few and very large identifiable nerve cells, has proved to have great utility for examining the mechanisms of habituation and sensitization.

We saw that both habituation and sensitization share the same locus, the presynaptic terminal of the sensory neuron and that the two processes appear to be mirror images of each other. Habituation decreases the response to a repeated innocuous stimulus by reducing the amount of transmitter released by the sensory neuron at the presynaptic terminal where it connects with the motor (or interneuron). Sensitization reverses habituation. Exposing an animal to a new or noxious stimulus strengthens its responses to a variety of sporadic stimuli.

The ability of a sensitizing stimulus to enhance the response to a previously ineffective stimulus or one to which the animal has become habituated offers an interesting parallel to classical conditioning. Both processes enhance the response to an initially weak stimulus. But sensitization does not teach the animal anything about the relationship between the sensitizing stimulus and other stimuli. There is no consistent contingency. Classical conditioning is fascinating because, through it, we learn about relations between events—*if A then B*. It enables us to make predictions about our environment.

The crucial procedural difference between sensitization and classical conditioning is that in the one there is no consistent temporal contiguity; in the other, classical conditioning, temporal pairing is essential. The time relations are critical; the CS must precede the US and the intervening stimulus interval (ISI) is strictly determined by the nature of the subject and the task. For the rabbit NM eyelid response optimal conditioning requires that the ISI not be shorter than 50 milliseconds nor longer than 200–300 milliseconds.

Still, the points of similarity between conditioning and sensitization raise the intriguing possibility that they may share common principles of neural organization. Can the marine snail, *Aplysia,* be successfully conditioned? Recently, Carew, Walters, and Kandel found that, in addition to being enhanced by sensitization, the siphon-and-gill withdrawal reflexes can also be modified by classical conditioning. What they did was to apply a mild tactile stimulus to the siphon (the CS) with a moderate shock to the tail (the US) that produced a reliable withdrawal reflex (the UR).

After 5 to 15 pairing trials, the conditioned animals showed greater siphon-and-gill withdrawal to the weak CS than did control animals who had received no shocks or received merely unpaired (sensitizing) shocks.

An interesting aspect of the conditioning experiment is its utility for studying perceptual discrimination and the differentiation of response. The two phenomena are related; both result from generalization, the natural tendency for an animal to respond in the same way to similar stimuli. But discrimination and differentiation are not identical. A young child may be quite able to see that two birds, a chicken and a goose, for example, are different, but she calls them both "chickie." She can discriminate, yet she cannot use the discrimination to make two different responses.

The conditioning experiment is a useful tool for examining the discriminative capacity of different organisms and their ability to respond differentially.

The CR, especially when newly established, is likely to generalize to any stimulus that resembles the one used in conditioning. If a tone is used as the CS, then any other tone, higher or lower, will also give the response. In the snail, if a touch on the siphon has been paired with a shock to the tail, as in the experiment just described, then a touch on either the siphon or the mantle shelf will elicit the withdrawal defense reflex. Can the response be restricted to the stimulus to the siphon and withdrawn from the stimulus to the mantle shelf? (See Figure 8.7.) Carew, Hawkins, and Kandel (1983) reported that, indeed, the siphon withdrawal component of this reflex can be differentially conditioned by pairing the tail shock (US) with a tactile CS to *either* the siphon or the mantle shelf. Each of these areas is innervated by its own population of sensory

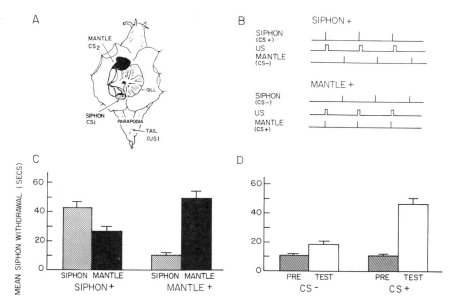

Figure 8.7. Demonstration of differential classical conditioning of a defensive withdrawal response in *Aplysia*. (A) Dorsal view of *Aplysia* showing the siphon and the mantle shelf—two sites used to deliver conditioned stimuli. The unconditioned stimulus (US) was an electric shock. (B) Paradigm for differential conditioning: one group (Siphon+) received the siphon CS (CS+) paired with the US and the mantle CS (CS−) specifically unpaired with the US; the other group (Mantle+) received the mantle stimulus as CS+ and the siphon stimulus as CS−. (C) Results of experiment using the paradigm of (B). The Siphon+ group showed significantly greater responses to the siphon CS than to the mantle CS, whereas the Mantle+ group showed significantly greater responses to the mantle CS than to the siphon CS. (D) Pooled data from (C). Test scores from the paired (CS+) and the unpaired (CS−) pathways are compared to their respective pretest scores. This comparison shows that the paired pathway exhibits significant differential conditioning. Carew, Hawkins, & Kandel, 1983. Copyright © 1983 by AAAS.

neurons and each pathway can be activated independently to serve as a CS. The differential conditioning can be acquired in a single trial and can be retained for more than 24 hours. Moreover, it increases in strength with repeated trials. In further studies, these investigators found that two separate sites on the siphon skin (within the same cluster of sensory neurons) can also serve as discriminative stimuli. This result is of particular interest for cognon theory because it restricts the possible cellular loci to the particular sensory neurons involved in this associative learning.

The Role of Classical Conditioning in Human Life

In much human behavior an overt CR is absent or difficult to specify. Probably this is also true in animal learning, but human associative learning is accessible through introspection. There is excellent reason to believe that the same principles that govern conditioning in the experimental laboratory also govern conditioning in everyday life. The scientific information suggests some interesting applications to human affairs.

Conditioning in human behavior goes well beyond the salivary reaction, the eyeblink, and the knee jerk. It is attractive to think that it includes such diverse responses as appetitive and aversive emotional reactions to objects, situations, and people. Conditioned fears, or *phobias,* as well as conditioned likes and specific appetites, in life and in literature, illustrate the wide applicability of Pavlov's discovery. Conditioning plays a large role in human behavior. Four areas, in particular, show robust evidence of CRs in *every* person. These are: feeding, sleep, social behavior, and language.

Feeding habits in people are strongly conditioned by time and place. Hunger CRs are developed in every society according to the regularity with which meals are eaten. The consistency with which crowds gather at midday for lunch is amazing and, within a given social group, almost sanctified. The consistency not only of mealtimes, but type of food and amount eaten at a particular hour of the day seems natural and irreversible. But one can easily imagine that it is based primarily on classical conditioning. If so, these habits can be extinguished or modified.

The relations between the hunger CR and the food CR in human behavior follow the rules described for animals. Hungry and learning that dinner is about to be served, we immediately calm down, our strong hunger drive appeased until the moment when we actually place food in our mouths, swallow, and the food CR takes over. The first morsels of tasty food cause the hunger drive to reappear. Due to conditioning, even the overfed, who are rarely truly hungry, are able to consume the entire meal with great satisfaction.

Sleep activity also has a dual aspect: a *sleep drive* (the *somnolence* or *drowsiness* UR), psychologically the *desire* to fall asleep, and the *actual sleep reflex* (the *sleep* UR). *Somnolence* due to sleep deprivation, like hunger, is mainly conditioned by the clock; we tend to fall asleep at the same time every night, or take an afternoon nap at the same hour every day. That the drowsiness is conditioned is manifest by finding that if we stay up past the usual time or are unusually preoccupied during the accustomed nap time, we find that the desire for sleep has dissipated—until the next day. The *sleep* CR is generally established by habitual activities prior to falling asleep at night. Lying down, the position taken, turning off the light, the feeling of the bedclothes, are CSs that act rapidly to induce actual sleep. In traveling, the changed situation may make it uncommonly difficult to fall asleep until, following prolonged deprivation, the sleep drive takes over, compelling sleep.

Perhaps the most significant, and also the most neglected, area of conditioning in human beings is in their social behavior. The social environment constitutes center stage for human action from birth to death, and social stimuli shape every aspect of our behavior. Thus it should not surprise us to find that our reactions are closely associated with our emotional give and take with other persons and their communications to us.

As just one example, consider how we react to significant others in our lives. Every person that we know intimately elicits an emotional reaction in us, love, hate, disgust, fear, or some alternation of these feelings and attitudes. These emotional CRs are most likely formed as a consequence of their behavior toward us in accordance with the principles of classical conditioning. Thus the sight, or sound, or image of a particular person becomes a conditioned stimulus and elicits a corresponding drive CR—a fear reflex, or sexual reflex, or other emotive reaction.

Closely related to our emotive reactions to other persons are those evoked by the words they speak or write. Language or verbal conditioning is the key to advertising, the art of the hypnotist, the playwright, and the novelist. Whatever we denote as *suggestion* is due to conditioned associations.

Nabokov painted one unforgettable image after another. Here is an excerpt from an appreciative commentary:

> Watching Ada painting early in the novel, Van proceeds at length to let his parched lips travel down her "warm hair and hot nape" until he experiences a "despair of desire." And this situation touches off a persistent theme in Nabokov:
>
> "Silently he would slink away to his room, lock the door, grasp a towel, uncover himself, and call forth the image he had just left behind, an image still as safe and bright as a hand-cupped flame—carried into the dark, only to be got rid of there with savage zeal; after which, drained for a while, with shaky loins and weak calves, Van would return...."
>
> Narration subtly stresses the episode as habitual: "would slink away... would return." "Himself" is a typical Nabokovian sexual synecdoche. Less obvious is the fact that the image left behind, when called forth, becomes both a mental and physical one in the all-revealing darkness: "an image still as safe and bright as a hand-cupped flame." Considering the close cooperation here between mind and matter, such double symbolism seems most appropriate. And the word *safe,* as a semi-pun, consistently supplements both images. (Rowe, 1971, pp. 114–115)

An Overall View of Classical Conditioning

Classical conditioning consists of the formation of associations between neutral stimuli and biologically important stimuli—those that give rise to unconditioned reflexes. Since the basic activities of organisms consist of two classes—preparatory (drive) reflexes and consummatory reflexes (fixed action patterns)—the same duality is true of the corresponding conditioned reflexes: hunger and food, fear and pain, somnolence and sleep. Classical conditioned reflexes are mainly identical with unconditioned reflexes. They differ only in that the conditioned reflexes come to be elicited by any of a wide variety of previously ineffective stimuli as a result of the conditioning process. The key to the process is the pairing of the neutral (CS) and the biologically important (US) stimuli in close spatiotemporal contiguity. The laws of conditioning with respect to reinforcement schedules, timing, discrimination, and the like, appear to be the same for all organisms from fish and birds to higher mammals including human beings.

Classical conditioning plays an important role in human behavior, especially in four areas of everyday life—feeding, sleeping, socializing, and verbal or symbolic behavior. (See Figure 8.8.)

INSTRUMENTAL OR OPERANT CONDITIONING

In 1933, Jerzy Konorski, Pavlov's student, with Stefan Miller discovered a new form of conditioning that he called *Type II* to distinguish it from Pavlovian or *Type I* conditioning. Later, in 1938, the well-known behaviorist, B.F. Skinner, now emeritus professor of psychology at Harvard University, independently extended Pavlov's concept of the classical conditioned reflex by showing how a new type of conditioned reflex could be acquired by the organism as the basis for complex voluntary or *instrumental* movements. Skinner called it *operant* conditioning because the response *operated* on the environment to produce a stimulus. The critical point was the discovery that the reaction itself was instrumental in producing a biologically important or unconditioned stimulus. Motor behavior was thus shown to be conditioned by its environmental consequences.

What about mental or symbolic activity? The classical Pavlovian conditioned reflex was dismissed by other investigators as relevant only to *autonomic* reactions with *no* cognitive significance. The instrumental or operant conditioned reflex was an overt *motor* response. Indeed, the experiment on operant conditioning as developed by Skinner and other American behaviorists emphasized the invisibility of any eliciting stimulus, and the topic of ideational behavior was largely neglected in conditioning theory.

But a good deal of evidence can be brought to show that instrumental conditioning is based on associative learning and is understandable as *cognon* activity.

We learned in Chapter Two that the excitation of drive centers arouses

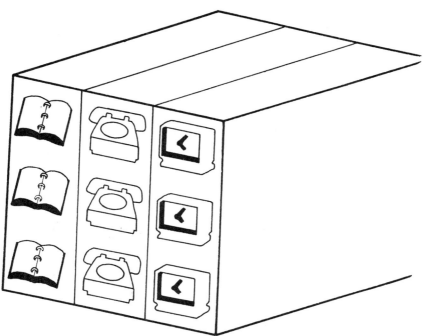

Figure 8.8. Three powerful conditioning stimuli in human behavior—the calendar, the clock, and the telephone.

the central motor behavioral system to activity and increases the sensitivity of the afferent systems for processing input. Any movement that the individual makes in this state of drive arousal may or may not produce the stimulus object (goal or reinforcement) required for consummatory action. If the given movement has the instrumental effect (inhibits or reduces the drive) and leads to the state of antidrive, one may say that the response has been reinforced and is more likely to recur under the same conditions.

A trained seal who has learned to turn a somersault to get a fish from its keeper has made an instrumental response. Unlike Pavlov's dog who gets his meal whether or not the bell has evoked salivation, the seal must make the correct response or get no fish. (See Figure 8.9.)

At first, instrumental and classical conditioning appear to be totally dissimilar processes involving different paradigms of stimuli and responses. In classical conditioning, the experimenter maintains control of the stimuli, and the presentation of the US is not dependent on whether or not the subject makes a particular response. In developing a salivary CR to a tone, the food follows the tone whether fifty, five, or zero drops of saliva were given to the tone. The reinforcement is not a reward for a correct response.

Figure 8.9. Instrumental (operant) conditioning. A trained dolphin leaps for a fish.

As it turns out, reinforcement is not synonymous with reward in the instrumental conditioning procedure either. The escape from an aversive stimulus—say, an electric shock—is said to be negatively reinforcing. A response that enables the subject to avoid or escape punishment is certainly rewarding, but many avoidance responses are learned in one trial as the result of punishment. Again, a certain stimulus may be a reward in one situation, but may have the opposite effect in another situation. Premack (1962) showed that a child who will work a pinball machine for a candy reward may come to offer the candy to the experimenter for the privilege of being allowed to play the machine—the Tom Sawyer effect. Indeed the only way to tell whether a given consequence is reinforcing is to see whether the subject repeats the response that produces the alleged reinforcement. The argument that an animal likes a food if he comes back for more and then that he comes back for more because he likes it, of course, is circular and explains nothing. The principle of reinforcement is operational only: it describes what the experimenter does but does not explain the mechanism underlying conditioning.

Neuropsychologists are coming to realize that the two forms of conditioning are basically similar. The same laws govern classical and instrumental conditioning, and they now appear to have common neural mechanisms (Konorski & Miller, 1933; Miller & Konorski, 1928; 1969). Both show generalization, extinction, discrimination, similar effects of timing and various reinforcement schedules, and higher-order conditioning. (See Figure 8.10.)

Extinction and Spontaneous Recovery

A CR can be weakened or *extinguished*. The classical CR will gradually disappear if the CS is repeatedly presented without being reinforced by the US. In consequence, the CS becomes a signal that *no* US will follow. Similarly, the instrumental CR will undergo experimental extinction as a result of repeated nonreinforced trials. What accounts for extinction? Pavlov attributed it to a process of inhibition directly opposed to the excitation that produced the CR. But the facts speak otherwise.

Extinction may be explained most simply by assuming that a connection is formed between the cognon representing the CS and a cognon representing the *lack of the CS*—an off-food unit, for example. Thus the extinction procedure establishes a negative CR to CS, antagonistic to the positive CR. But it leaves the old, previously established connection unaffected. A CR that has been extinguished can be reinstated by presenting further reinforced trials, that is, by reconditioning.

The extinction and reconditioning of a conditioned response is thus the decrement of a response followed by its enhancement. In the same way that a new stimulus, when repeatedly presented alone, becomes a signal that no biologically important change will follow, so the original conditioned

CLASSICAL CONDITIONING

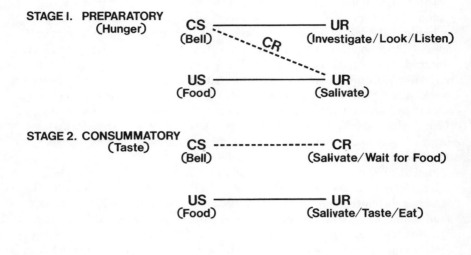

STAGE I. PREPARATORY
(Hunger)

CS ————————— UR
(Bell)   Investigate/Look/Listen)

CR

US ————————— UR
(Food)   (Salivate)

STAGE 2. CONSUMMATORY
(Taste)

CS ---------------- CR
(Bell)   (Salivate/Wait for Food)

US ————————— UR
(Food)   (Salivate/Taste/Eat)

INSTRUMENTAL CONDITIONING

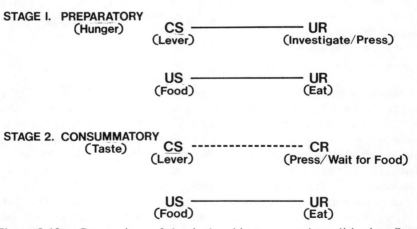

STAGE I. PREPARATORY
(Hunger)

CS ————————— UR
(Lever)   (Investigate/Press)

US ————————— UR
(Food)   (Eat)

STAGE 2. CONSUMMATORY
(Taste)

CS ---------------- CR
(Lever)   (Press/Wait for Food)

US ————————— UR
(Food)   (Eat)

Figure 8.10. Comparison of classical and instrumental conditioning. Stage 1 represents behavior in the early trials; Stage 2 after conditioning has occurred, i.e., after the original investigatory behavior. Tasting and eating cannot be consummated in the absence of food. The main differences between the two types of conditioning arise from the different investigatory acts in the two cases—looking and listening in classical conditioning; pressing the lever in the other. Pressing the lever brings reward but looking and listening to the bell can cease without stopping the food supply (or the airpuff or shock in the aversive conditioning experiments). After Woodworth & Schlosberg, 1954.

stimulus, when not followed by the unconditioned stimulus, leads to habituation. Extinction, then, is equivalent to habituation.

Spontaneous recovery, like dishabituation, occurs after a period of rest or renewed arousal of drive. An extinguished CR reappears—evidence that it is not really abolished. Eventually, as extinction trials continue and the new negative CR is strengthened, the old positive CR disappears. Typically, it can be reestablished in fewer trials than were required for its initial formation.

The transformation of conditioned responses from positive to negative, and their readiness to undergo reversal, has interesting implications for human behavior. The next section offers some thoughts as to how this may become manifest in our interpersonal relations.

Ambivalence in Human Life

The interrelations between human beings are never static. Persons develop and change, situations change, and the conditioned social responses change also.

As commonly portrayed in soap operas, not without a basis in reality, the feelings of a woman for a man may be entirely positive—adoring, sexual, trusting—when a disturbing event intrudes. The man proves to be less than perfect, deceitful, alcoholic, abusive, or unfaithful. The jarring behavior produces a new attitude of fear, bitterness, or revulsion, and suppresses the old conditioned connections. But, though suppressed, they are not lost. Suppose the man dies. The old feelings revive; her thoughts are full of tender memories of him and completely block out all the unpleasant ones. Or he lives and peace is restored. Then relations may return to their previous form—but should the episode of abuse or infidelity recur, then memories of the old episode return.

In most of our dealings with the significant people in our lives, there is some ambivalence with many nuances and shades of feelings. The conditioned stimulus—a lover, a parent, or a child—acquires a dual role eliciting alternately now the attractive, now the aversive, conditioned response, sometimes with amazing rhythmicity.

What is interesting is that these two attitudes are quite separate and do not mix. A striking point is that under the influence of one CR, the emotion may be very strong and we not only experience intense annoyance or intense affection, but also all images associated with that attitude emerge. We now recall all the earlier situations in which we felt the same way. It is as if we mobilize supporting data to strengthen the CR of the moment. The basis for this phenomenon lies in the connections between the drive units and the cognons with which the CR was concurrently excited.

Since the old and the new drive units are in reciprocal relations, the CR that is stronger in the given situation becomes predominant, but leaves the old, previously established connections unaffected. Their restoration is a much easier process than their initial formation and the reversal shift needs only establish their relative dominance over the antagonistic units.

Drive and Arousal in Instrumental Conditioning

A major effect of the excitation of drives is both the arousal of afferent systems and the arousal of the central motor behavioral system. The coincident excitation of a particular drive with a given movement is the essential condition for the formation of an association between the two.

Bring a hungry dog to a certain situation and give him food there. The hunger CR is quickly established in this situation. When again you bring the dog to the same place, he will display motor agitation and signs of hunger. If now the dog performs a series of movements, either spontaneously or in response to external stimuli, and immediately following one of those movements you give him food, you will not be surprised to find that same movement made the next time the procedure is repeated. The important point is that one of a number of possible movements is selected and stabilized because it produces the desired food, or speaking operationally and physiologically, because the instrumental response coincides with the reduction or inhibition of drive.

The essential prerequisites for the formation of an instrumental conditioned response are: *drive*, a *movement* followed by *drive reduction*, (or *antidrive*), and the temporary *cessation* of trained movement.

The objection sometimes given to the drive reduction theory of instrumental behavior demands consideration. Critics argue that in both humans and animals instrumental responses are established in the absence of a consummatory response. Male rats learn to go to a compartment containing a receptive female without being allowed to copulate. I would answer that sexual consummatory responses are not restricted to the final ejaculatory component. Drive reflexes, as we saw in Chapter Two, are not limited to observable elementary tissue needs, but include curiosity, social stimulation, and, in higher animals, love and affection. In human relations, drives are often directed to meeting persons to whom we are attached, especially when we have not seen them for a long time. Merely caressing and hugging, and being caressed and hugged, are powerful consummatory (drive satisfying) responses not only in human beings but in many primates (Hrdy, 1981). Who will deny that contact without coitus may be drive reducing (reinforcing) to rats also?

The Motivational Basis of Instrumental Movement

The last section emphasized that drives are essential for the formation and elicitation of a given instrumental response. Two types of connections are involved: (1) those providing impulses that release this movement, and (2) those that select which movement has to be released. Drives thus play a dual role—energizing and selecting.

In Konorski's view, energizing connections run from the emotive brain (drive centers in the hypothalamus and limbic system) to the central motor behavioral system. Response-selecting connections run from the cognons of the sensory analyzers (including the emotive analyzer) to the cognons of the kinesthetic analyzer that send their orders to the executive centers.

Konorski's notion of the *central motor behavioral system* includes the whole set of behavioral acts, innate and acquired, that the animal has at its disposal. Any of these acts can become instrumentalized. The important distinction is between *active* movements—those performed by the animal voluntarily—as opposed to those *passive* movements forced upon it by an external agent, such as the electrical stimulation of an efferent nerve.

A second important concept that Konorski introduced is that unitary motor acts, programmed by kinesthetic (afferent) cognons require no peripheral feedback for their instrumentalization. They are ready to go, the efferent side of the circuit having only the executive role.

In normal life, instrumental responses are performed under changing external circumstances. Accordingly, different acts are thrown into operation on different occasions. A commonplace example is our way of bringing various kinds of food to our mouths: we perform different instrumental acts when the dish in front of us contains a sandwich, a cup of soup, a steak, or a bunch of grapes.

Thus the instrumental response is determined by a situation (or stimulus) that releases a certain motor act and the drive that is terminated by it (and leads to the corresponding antidrive).

Theories of Instrumental Conditioning

To account for the selection and stabilization of the successful instrumental response, various principles have been proposed. In the history of American psychology, Edward Thorndike's (1898) early work on the puzzle box is often cited for revealing the *Law of Effect* in animal learning. As stated in 1911, Thorndike's *Law of Effect* pointed out that "satisfying consequences" (food rewards, escape from the puzzle box) strengthened a stimulus-response connection, while "annoying consequences" (punishment) weakened them. (See Figure 8.11.)

By stressing the consequences of the instrumental CR in producing the (reinforcing) US, the effect theory is appealing, but unsatisfyingly circular. How do we know that the consequences are satisfying or not, until the response has been learned (or not learned)? The same problem has plagued the concept of reinforcement.

To break this circularity, a number of psychologists (Hull, 1943;

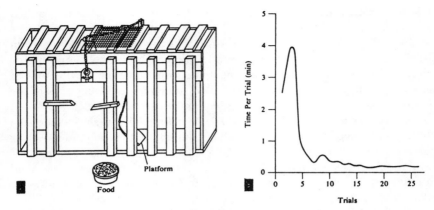

Figure 8.11. A problem box used by Thorndike for experiments on learning. The cat must depress the platform to raise a bolt and then pull one of two latches to open the door. A typical learning curve is shown on the right. Kandel, 1976.

Konorski, 1967; Miller & Dollard, 1941; Spence, 1951) kept the convenient term "reinforcement" as an operational concept only and replaced the reward-punishment theory with the physiological mechanism of *drive reduction*.

In terms of the drive reduction hypothesis, any given movement that is followed by a reduction in drive relieves tension and will be strengthened. Maladaptive and unsuccessful responses will drop out in the competition with the final successful response.

Although there are problems with it, reduction or inhibition of drive is the better construct in many ways. Since *drive* and *antidrive* covary with need, control can be exercised experimentally over hunger or thirst by increasing the period of deprivation and regulating the quantity of food or water intake. Our increased knowledge of the physiology of drives and antidrives and their centers in the brain enables the experimenter to take advantage of this approach. Specific physiological processes can be studied for their effects on reward and escape learning. A logical progression from such thinking has been the use of behavior as a measure of brain manipulation. When both physiological and behavioral measures agree in such experiments, we can open windows on the mind.

Instrumental Conditioning Motivated by an Acquired Drive

Starting from the conviction that many drives, such as the desire for money, approval, and status, are acquired by learning during the socialization period, Neal Miller (1948) showed in a neat experiment how a drive may be acquired and then used to promote the learning of new voluntary movements. Miller worked with pain and fear in rats using a simple apparatus, consisting of two compartments separated by a door. One compartment (a box, actually) was white with a grid on the floor; the other was black without a grid. Placed in the white box, the animals received an electric shock from which they escaped through the open door into the black box. Their reaction to the pain of the shock did not have to be learned. But even on nonshock trials the rats persisted in running from the white box into the black one. They had acquired a *drive*—a *fear* of the white compartment. Miller then investigated a second stage of learning. The door (previously open) was closed. The only way it could be opened was by rotating a little wheel just above the door. The animals learned to escape without further shocks from the white box by turning the wheel. The acquired fear drive was able to motivate the learning and performance of a completely new habit. The connection between the cues in the white box and the fear was learned. The acquired fear drive could motivate new learning of an instrumental response that produced a reduction in the strength of the fear drive and the intense stimuli accompanying it.

When the first trial on which turning the wheel no longer opened the door, the animals stopped performing this response and began to exhibit various other responses. One of the responses, pressing a bar, did cause the door to open and allow the animal to remove itself from the fear-producing cues in the white box. In a series of trials during which the wheel-turning response was progressively crowded out, the rats acquired the new bar-pressing habit.

The flexibility with which the animals tried various, possibly adaptive, responses to a changed environment (turning the wheel, pressing the bar, and other means of escape from the white box) and the selection of the successful instrumental response demonstrates that animals (and humans) will learn not a single set of muscle twitches but *what to do* to get to a safe place.

In this experiment, and confirmed by subsequent ones, the animal learns two associations. First it acquires a fear response to the painful stimuli in the white box, presumably by classical conditioning. Second, it learns to turn the wheel to open the door. This is instrumental learning, reinforced by fear reduction by getting away from the fear-producing situation. What appears to be avoidance learning, difficult to explain because there is no aversive stimulus, may be better understood as an escape from a pain-induced acquired fear.

The drive-antidrive theory (or drive reduction theory) applies to the instrumental conditioning of both preparatory and consummatory reflexes. Pain as a preparatory drive leads to the acquisition of fear, itself a preparatory drive, now connected with conditioned stimuli and capable of energizing and directing new instrumental habits utilized to produce the consummatory reflexes.

On the psychological side, the drive is the *emotion* of fear as experienced by the animal and is the motivational factor in these experiments.

Also, from the animal's point of view, the proper movement is the one that will remove or reduce the fear and avoid the pain of shock. Safely through the open door into the black box, the animal can breathe with relief—the antidrive replaces the drive.

When an animal cannot control the pain—when there is no way to escape or avoid the shock—then depression of active behavior occurs. The depression generalizes to other movements. Being exposed to an uncontrollable series of electric shocks is said to teach an individual that "nothing he does matters—he becomes helpless" (Seligman & Maier, 1967; Seligman, 1972).

Such "learned helplessness" or behavioral depression induced by an uncontrollable stressor seems to be brought about by noradrenergic changes in the brain. Specifically, Weiss, Goodman, and their group at Rockefeller University have shown a decrease in norepinephrine (NE) in the locus coeruleus region of the brainstem to be a primary cause of such behavioral depression (Weiss et al., 1981). Following intense uncontrollable tail shocks, their animals showed depressed motor activity (immobility in a swim test) and NE deficits 90 minutes, even 48 hours later, but not 72–96 hours later. Thus, besides the immediate or short-term effect, there is a conditioned emotional response to the situation that reinstates NE depletion for some time after stress. After three days following stress, however, NE-synthesizing enzymes emerge to protect the subjects from continuing depression. (See Figure 8.12.)

The control animals, provided with an avoidance-escape apparatus, a wheel that could be rotated to terminate or postpone the tail shocks, showed no behavioral depression on any postshock test and less severe NE depletion than their yoked, unavoidably shocked partners. The results point to the importance of the protective consummatory reflex and its probable role as an instrumental CR in coping with stress. (See Figure 8.13.)

The important point is that conditioned fear responses have strikingly different behavioral and neurochemical effects according to whether they represent preparatory drive reflexes associated with failure to cope or consummatory acts that terminate fear and lead to its relief.

By means of this explanation, I think we can retain the advantages of the hardheaded neurophysiological theory without losing the cognitive understanding that brings adaptive significance and practical implications to this line of research.

COGNITIVE VERSUS BEHAVIORIST EXPLANATIONS

The choice confronting the student of neuropsychology presents a dilemma. Should one adopt a physiological (reductionist or molecular) theory of conditioning and learning or a holistic, cognitive one? We now realize that animals and humans do not learn as blindly as stressed by Thorndike and Skinner, but that their responses are constrained by previous learning and

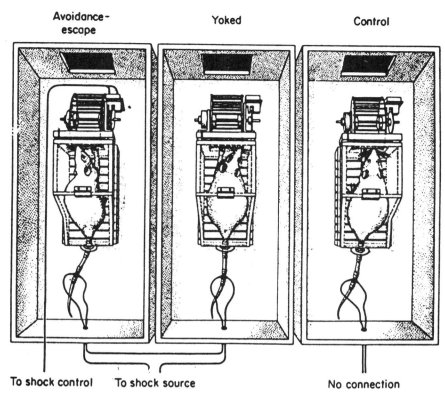

Avoidance-escape   Yoked   Control

To shock control   To shock source   No connection

Figure 8.12. Apparatus for studying the effects of uncontrollable shock. The avoidance-escape rat (left) can control the shock by turning a wheel. Electrodes fixed to the tails are wired in series so that the yoked rat (center) receives exactly the same shocks but his wheel is not connected to the source. The control rat (right) is not connected at all to the source and receives no shocks. Animals in all groups receive the same subsequent tests of behavior and measurements of brain monoamines. Weiss et al., 1981.

physiological structures. Mental associations are built on neural connections, much as neural connections are built on experienced associations. They are two sides of the same coin.

The old dichotomy between stimulus-response and cognitive theories becomes particularly acute in many psychology textbooks when the discussion of conditioning ends and the chapter on insightful learning and creative problem solving begins.

The differences between the approach taken by Wolfgang Köhler (1887–1968), the influential Gestalt psychologist, and the behaviorists loomed large in the early debates on whether animals and humans act stupidly and mechanically or intelligently and productively.

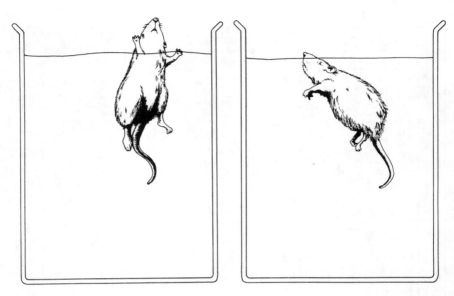

Figure 8.13. Behavioral activity tests show the avoidance-escape rat (left) struggling to escape from the swim tank, front paws breaking through the suface of the water. At the right, the uncontrollable shock rat does not swim but floats to the surface only to inhale and then sinks back into the tank. Behavioral depression after uncontrollable shock (e.g., 90 min. post stress) derives from noradrenergic changes in the locus coeruleus; later deficits (48 hr. post stress) derive the same neurochemical (NE) depletion amplified by conditioned fear response. After Weiss et al., 1981.

LEARNING BY INSIGHT

Köhler worked with chimpanzees, a far more intelligent animal than rat or cat, but Köhler also believed that Thorndike had biased his results by using trick puzzle boxes with hidden latch strings. In this and other experiments using mazes with blind alleys, trial and error was necessary; the animal was given no opportunity to display an intellectual solution.

Köhler (1924) demonstrated insight in the chimpanzee by a simple procedure. He placed a banana (a favored fruit) beyond reach, just outside the cage. The ape quickly saw that a long stick inside the cage could be used to haul in the banana. When the stick proved too short, the ape joined two sticks together, clumsily; they fell apart frequently, but the animal managed to make a tool long enough to get the fruit. In other experiments, chimpanzees learned

Figure 8.14. A chimpanzee insightfully uses a human tool. After Köhler, 1924.

to use boxes as footstools, dragging them under the banana and, when necessary, piling boxes on top of one another to reach the prize. One gifted chimpanzee, Sultan, even pulled Köhler himself by the arm to stand under the banana and then climbed upon his new human tool. (See Figure 8.14.)

Köhler concluded that his animal subjects demonstrated *insight* into the important relations of the situation that organized their solutions to the problems. His criteria for insight were:

1. The solution appeared suddenly, perhaps even after a period of inactivity.
2. Once a solution was found, it was used again without delay or preliminary trial and error.

3. Transfer—the solution was applied to new problems when the situation was changed.

The suddenly perceptual reorganization of the elements of the situation —experienced introspectively by humans as the AHA!, flash, or Eureka experience, seemed to Köhler unmistakable. Yet the apes were prone to act without examining the situation fully each time. In attempting to stack boxes they made many mistakes before they achieved a stable step ladder. Even bright Sultan tugged and thrashed at a rope hung by its loop over a hook. The behavior is not as stupid as it looks; many things—stability, friction, joints, and so on—are not immediately obvious. Even human beings with superior IQs have to discover them by manipulating things and checking their movements. Ruger's nail puzzles (Woodworth & Schlosberg, 1954) and, more recently popular, Rubik's cubes, are good examples of the need to discover constructional properties by active manipulation. Human social behavior poses analogous difficulties. Direct inspection is necessary but insufficient.

A COMPARISON OF THREE TYPES OF LEARNING

No hard and fast line can be drawn between instrumental conditioning and insightful learning of the sort stressed by Köhler and the Gestaltists. Given the opportunity to perceive the various elements of the situation and the requisite prior experience and development of a response repertoire, problems can be solved rapidly and with apparent insight. When the situation is unclear and the key to solution hidden, then trial-and-error behavior in even the experienced subject results.

There seems actually to be a continuum between the three kinds of learning discussed in this book—perceptual learning, associative learning, and insightful learning. It is not necessarily that one form is higher or more complex and cognitively superior to another. Although perceptual learning (sensory integration) occurs early in ontogeny, it continues into adult life, barring brain damage, until death. Moreover, the development of cognons based on *learning sets* becomes more and more abstract and sophisticated. Learning by *insight* may therefore reflect, not a new, totally different neuropsychological mechanism but, actually, the formation of *higher-order cognons*. Although of higher order, Sultan's ability to stack boxes also required him to adjust their positions to make them sufficiently stable to provide a foothold. Not insight alone but some trial and error, too, or as Woodworth (1947) puts it, all conditioning involves a "trial-and-check" process. The *checking* aspect reintroduces classical conditioning as a vital component in problem solution and higher or cognitive learning. Animals and humans need to compare the results of their movements with their intended goals. In both insightful and instrumental learning, the perceived result of the movement is a CS and the attainment of the desired stimulus object (reinforcer) is the US.

My analysis is not meant to deny any differences between the three kinds of learning—certainly, there are differences in procedure and in demands on the subject's intelligence. But they fit together and their dynamic role in ongoing behavior is continuous and proceeds in a dialectic manner. No one form is simpler or more elementary than another; each form—thesis, antithesis, and synthesis—helps to advance the individual's continuously spiraling reaches to grasp the prize.

The neurophysiological mechanisms on which the three forms of learning build may, in turn, share a common basis. The results obtained so far with simpler organisms suggest that there is only one form of neural connectivity— one unitary principle of association in the central nervous system. The amazing uniformity of synaptic transmission in every species studied and the discovery of a chemical basis for transmissibility leads me to believe that this approach rests on a solid basis of fact.

I draw your attention to my conviction in order to convey to you some sense of the optimism and excitement felt today by investigators in brain science. But I do not for a minute want to obscure or deny the advantage of studying and analyzing separate segments, successive thetic twists, of the three-dimensional behavior spiral I have described.

To conclude, I would like to summarize the main points of each form of learning. Perhaps we can identify three different principles of learning from the psychological point of view of what is learned and how, in each case, even though the physiological mechanisms are common to all three. Though one physiochemical basis of connecting runs through the various forms, neuro-psychologists must continue to insist on examining phenomena on their own level and in their own special vocabulary, to avoid the genuine fallacy of reductionism to an indistinguishable and unprofitable homogeneity.

THREE PRINCIPLES OF LEARNING

1. Sensory integration and the formation of perception units (cognons)—a mental consummatory reaction.

   Based on the principle of sensitization (orientation reflex) and nonassociative learning, especially during critical periods of maturational development, yet continuing throughout life.

   Results in unitary perceptions, images, and hallucinations; learning sets, concepts, higher order cognons, insight.

   Knowing *what* is out there, to be used in later recognition and recall.

2. Associative learning of classical conditioning.

    Based on the principle of drive arousal and contiguity of two (cognon-arousing) stimuli, a neutral (previously ineffective) conditioned stimulus and an unconditioned (ethological releaser or trigger) stimulus.

    Results in acquired drives—fears, appetites, aversions, and fixed action patterns—cross-modal associations, language.

    Knowing *what goes with,* or *follows, what.*

3. Instrumental conditioning

    Based on drive arousal and contiguity of a voluntary active response (spontaneous or evoked kinesthetic cognon) and a cognon aroused by an unconditioned stimulus (reinforcer) that reduces drive and initiates the reciprocal antidrive state.

    Results in a self-produced new stimulus object (arousal of cognon or receptive unit) to be used in consummatory response.

    Knowing *how* or *what to do, given drive and situation.*

The interweaving of the three kinds of knowing outlined above appears in complex voluntary action. The problem of *insight* or learning via the sudden perceptual (Gestalt) reorganization of the entire field, or parts of it, may appear at various levels of complexity in all three forms, because all of them involve perceptual learning and mentation.

SUMMARY

Conditioning is an experimentally privileged form of associative learning because it opens a window for observing the attachments of new stimuli to overt unlearned reflexes and the transformations of these reflexes into instrumental or voluntary motor acts. By observing both nerve cells and the animal's behavior as it learns, we are beginning to understand how learning occurs.

The distinction in classical conditioning between preparatory drive-conditioned reflexes and consummatory conditioned reflexes helps make clear that the conditioned reflex is the same as the original unconditioned reflex. Thus the conditioned stimulus serves as a substitute for the unconditioned stimulus, but with different effects in the two cases that are often confounded in the laboratory. Hunger, as a preparatory drive, becomes conditioned to time and place of feeding, mediated by subcortical centers in the emotive brain; salivation is a consummatory act, conditioned to the sporadic stimuli preceding the activation of tasty food recognition units or cognons in the cerebral cortex. Both classically and instrumentally conditioned reflexes provide strong evidence to support a cognon theory of associative learning. The key principles in both forms emphasize potential connections between cognons—drive, arousal, temporal contiguity, and the necessity for repeated, although periodic, reinforcement to prevent extinction of the conditioned reflex. In classical conditioning, the experimenter controls the occurrence of the reinforcing stimulus. The instrumentally conditioned reflex itself produces the reinforcing stimulus.

The distinctions between the various procedures used in conditioning are to a certain extent arbitrary and conceal the continuity between associative learning, trial and error, and insightful learning. The underlying physiological mechanisms are shared by the three forms of learning and are the basis for abstract symbolic processes as well as simpler mental functions.

There is reason to believe that associations formed by conditioning procedures are never forgotten or lost by disuse, but are reversible in the sense that they are permanently available as synaptic connections and can be reestablished following extinction. The process of extinction is thought to substitute the off-unit for the on-unit—that is, the conditioned stimulus becomes a signal that "*no* unconditioned stimulus will follow" the conditioned stimulus.

The next chapter provides neurological support from clinical psychopathology for these ideas of associative learning. We will examine the increasing physiological evidence in human patients with brain damage that connections between cognons are precisely organized in categories belonging to particular analyzers.

SUGGESTED READINGS

Gormezano, I., & Kehoe, E.J. Classical conditioning: Some methodological-conceptual issues. In W.K. Estes (Ed.), *Handbook of learning and cognitive processes* (Vol. 2). *Conditioning and behavior theory.* Hillsdale, N.J.: Erlbaum, 1975.

Gormezano, I., Kehoe, E.J., & Marshall, B.S. Twenty years of classical conditioning research with the rabbit. In J.M. Sprague & A.N. Epstein (Eds.), *Progress in psychobiology and physiological psychology* (Vol. 10). New York: Academic Press, 1983.

Köhler, W. *The mentality of apes.* London: Kegan Paul, 1924.

Konorski, J. *Conditioned reflexes and neuron organization.* Cambridge: Cambridge University Press, 1968. (Originally published, 1948.)

Konorski, J. Classical and instrumental conditioning: The general laws of connections between "centers." *Acta Neurobiologiae Experimentalis,* 1974, *34,* 5–13.

Maier, S.F., & Seligman, M.E.P. Learned helplessness: Theory and evidence. *Journal of Experimental Psychology,* 1976, *105,* 3–46.

Miller, N.E. Motivation and psychological stress. In D.W. Pfaff (Ed.), *The physiological mechanisms of motivation.* New York: Springer-Verlag, 1982.

Pavlov, I.P. *[Conditioned reflexes: An investigation of the physiological activity of the cerebral cortex]* (G.V. Anrep, Ed. and trans.). New York: Dover, 1960. (Originally published, 1927.)

Skinner, B.F. *The behavior of organisms: An experimental analysis.* New York: D. Appleton-Century Co., 1938.

Skinner, B.F. *Science and human behavior.* New York: Macmillan, 1953.

Thompson, R.F. In collaboration with McCormick, D.A., Lavond, D.G., Clark, G.A., Kettner, R.E., & Mauk, M.D. The engram found? Initial localization of the memory trace for a basic form of associative learning. In J.M. Sprague & A.N. Epstein (Eds.), *Progress in psychobiology and physiological psychology* (Vol. 10). New York: Academic Press, 1983, 167–196.

Thompson, R.F., Berger, T.W., Berry, S.D., Hoehler, F.K., Kettner, R.E., & Weisz, D.J. Hippocampal substrate of classical conditioning. *Physiological Psychology,* 1980, *8,* 262–279.

Thompson, R.F., Berger, T.W., Cegavske, C.F., Patterson, M.M., Roemer, R.A., Teyler, T.J., & Young, R.A. The search for the engram. *American Psychologist,* 1976, *31,* 209–227.

Thorndike, E.L. *Animal intelligence, experimental studies.* New York: Macmillan, 1911.

Weiss, J.M., Goodman, P.A., Losito, B.G., Corrigan, S., Charry, J.M., & Bailey, W.H. Behavioral depression produced by an uncontrollable stressor. Relationship to norepinephrine, dopamine, and serotonin levels in various regions of rat brain. *Brain Research Reviews,* 1981, *3,* 167–205.

Woodworth, R.S. Reënforcement of perception. *American Journal of Psychology,* 1947, *60,* 119–124.

CHAPTER NINE

Disorders of Cognition and Behavior Following Brain Damage

INTRODUCTION

This chapter offers incisive neurophysiological evidence for the principle of categorization of cognons in human perception and in cognition. This evidence is based on facts derived from clinical pathology of the association cortex in human patients. The specific disturbances following brain damage offer strong support for the theory of discretely localized unitary perceptions and images in different parts of the brain. In human psychopathology the disorders of perception and of behavior that result from lesions of the cerebral cortex—the *agnosias, aphasias,* and *apraxias*—reveal multiple dissociations between selected categories of deficits that depend on the locus of the disease or injury to the brain.

BRAIN DAMAGE

The human brain is unique among mammals because of the greatly increased volume of cerebral cortex that covers it. Unlike the cortex of the rat, which, except for a tiny central area, is completely sensory or motor, most of the human cortex is neither sensory nor motor. Instead we have a large mass of cortical tissue on both sides of the central gyrus that divides the motor and the somatic sensory areas and pushes the visual projection area back to the rear.

The term, *association cortex* provides a unifying label for the largest mass of cortical tissue in the human brain—one that suggests its integrative activity in coordinating complex functions, such as reading, and talking, and playing tennis.

We know that lesions in the projective area produce deficits different from those produced by lesions in the associative areas. Lesions in the projective areas produce specific and well-defined sensory deficits—for example, after lesions sustained in the somatic projective area, tactile and joint sensitivity of a particular bodily part contralateral to the lesion is impaired. Damage to the occipital lobe on one side of the brain produces blindness on one side of the visual field (hemianopia) with the result that messages from the corresponding receptive surface cannot reach the brain.

Unlike the primary sensory defects caused by injuries of the sensory pathways or their cortical projection zones, the lesions of the *association cortex* may produce severe disturbances in the integration of sensory information and prevent its utilization in guiding motor behavior.

The association cortex is not a geographical representation in the sense that it offers a point-for-point mapping of *receptive fields*. Recall that the *receptive field* of a nerve cell is that area on any receptive surface (e.g., the skin or the retina) that can influence the activity of that cell. Instead, the association cortex seems to provide a *categorical* representation of the movements of its possessor and the space and things contained in the surrounding environment.

The association cortex, in fact, consists of the highest, most abstract levels of particular analyzers. If neural symbols representing nameable objects—apples, beds, helicopters, car keys, friends, and TV stars—are stored anywhere as anatomical mechanisms, they are most likely to be here in the association cortex. According to the theory advanced in this book, here will be found cell groups clustered in *categories* that represent similar sorts of things. Their common biological origin or psychological significance binds them into *unified categories* distinct from other categories. Within each such category, moreover, there must be individual symbols, perhaps single cognons, or files of cognons, to represent each unique object, *my desk,* or *Jane's picture,* as a unitary perception, distinct from others.

Lesions of particular fields of the association cortex produce cognitive disorders called *agnosias* from *a* (loss) and *gnosis* (to know). *Prosopagnosia* (*prosopon*—face) is the loss of the ability to recognize faces, a highly specific form of visual agnosia following injury to the underside of the occipital lobe extending forward to the inner side of the temporal lobes of *either* or *both* cerebral hemispheres (Geschwind, 1979). (See Figure 9.1.) Essentially the disorder consists of an inability to recognize previously well-known people by visual perception of their faces. Close friends as well as new acquaintances and pictures of famous people can't be identified, although the patient shows no impairment of recognition of other objects, forms, or colors. The human face is one of the first meaningful patterns to appear repeatedly before the eyes of an infant, and face recognition quickly becomes associated with other perceptions, visual, auditory, olfactory, tactual, and emotional. A powerful set of face cognons must develop in early experience to represent faces in general, and then discriminations form between particular faces—mother, father, sister, doctor, playmates, and teachers. Hécaen (1962) describes a patient who was completely unable to recognize the faces of familiar persons, even his own

INFERIOR ASPECT OF THE HEMISPHERES

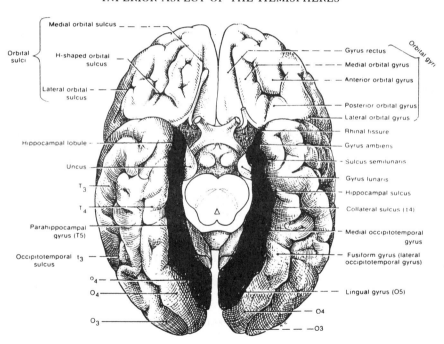

Figure 9.1. *Prosopagnosia,* the inability to recognize faces, is caused by damage to the underside (heavily shaded areas) of the occipitotemporal lobes of either or both cerebral hemispheres. Bossy, 1970.

wife, but he immediately recognized them when he heard their voices. He could also recognize a famous person from his photograph when he saw the entire figure, or when some evocative detail gave a clue, such as the wig of Louis XIV or some special facial feature. He described his deficit by saying, "I clearly see the details of your face, your mouth, your nose, but it is like a blur.... I am no longer able to see the faces as a whole."

Another patient was similarly disturbed. He looked at the chin and the mouth, then carefully inspected the sides of the face, nose, eyes, and forehead and, according to his own statement, "could not put it all together." When he looked in the mirror, he stated that his own face appeared blurred and strange to him. But he was able to recognize facial expressions—anger, surprise, joy, fear—and he had no difficulty in identifying objects pictured or named, and even his dreams he reported as unchanged. Evidently, he had lost the cognons for faces, but not for facial expressions, and his cognons for inanimate objects were unimpaired.

AGNOSIAS AND DISCONNECTION SYNDROMES

We can distinguish disorders of perception or speech caused by injuries to *particular cognitive fields,* clustered around the projective zones of each analyzer, from disorders caused by lesions severing connections between them. Powerful connections exist between each sensory analyzer and the limbic system; these pathways are indispensable for emotional and autonomic responses to external stimulation. The cognitive fields of various analyzers are connected by long pathways that penetrate into the white matter beneath the cortex, forming narrow funnels. They are even more vulnerable than cortical areas, since damage that penetrates the white matter can produce extremely serious disorders. Accordingly, we can discern two forms of clinical syndromes: (1) those resulting from damage to particular cognitive fields and (2) those resulting from injuries to the long pathways that interconnect them.

Lesions of cognitive fields result in *agnosias*; lesions that sever the pathways connecting these fields result in the *disconnection syndromes,* named by Geschwind (1965). To be sure, the agnosias are accompanied by disconnections, but the reverse is not necessarily true. Since neurons of a particular cognitive field send their axons to many different cognitive fields, when one pathway or fasciculus is broken, the others need not be affected, and the field itself, though partially disconnected, is preserved.

The distinction between the agnosias and other disorders depends on two criteria: (1) the lack of a primary sensory disturbance, and (2) the demonstration that the failure of recognition is not simply a failure of naming. The fundamental concept in the agnosias is the failure of recognition within a particular analyzer (vision, audition, etc.) and a particular class of objects belonging to that analyzer. Thus a visual agnosia may affect only small manipulable objects, while large inanimate things, and all animate objects—persons, animals, limbs, and their representations—are named correctly. This selectivity demonstrates the absence of a single general faculty of recognition—instead, "there are multiple parallel processes of appropriate responses to a stimulus. To describe the behavior correctly, we must describe the pattern of loss and preservation of responses to each particular type of stimulus" (Geschwind, 1965, p. 167).

DISORDERS OF OBJECT PERCEPTION: THE AGNOSIAS

Derek Denny-Brown (1962) of the Harvard University Medical School held that true agnosia was absolute in two respects: first, the perception units for one class of objects are not formed; and second, such objects cannot even be imagined. Thus agnosia does not relate to a perception arrived at with difficulty or in some distorted form, or even reached by some other sense. If, owing to agnosia, patients cannot recognize an object except by touch, or a face except by the sound of its owner's voice, they lack the visual concept of that object or face. In short, they have lost not only the ability to form a particular category of perception, but also its memory image.

The separation between categories of inanimate objects and categories of animate objects is based on strong neurological evidence. The selectivity of visual *agnosia* is an essential clinical fact.

> Visual object agnosia refers to a specific variety of perceptual defect: a brain-damaged patient can see an object shown to him, but cannot appreciate its character or meaning. Not only is he unable to name the object or to demonstrate its use, but he also cannot remember ever having seen it before. (Hécaen & Albert, 1978, p. 194)

This is no sensory defect; it is a perceptual defect of the visual cognitive cortex, and it is selective for inanimate objects.

Hécaen and Albert report many clinical cases in which the visual perception of inanimate objects was selectively impaired, whereas other visual perceptions remained intact. These subjects are able to describe the shape, outline, and interior parts of an object without being able to name it or show how it is used. If the object has a characteristic odor, taste, or sound, or if allowed to palpate the object, the subject can immediately name it. The name is not lost, and the meaning or use of the object is not lost—except to visual perception. The patient readily appreciates spatial information and can recognize familiar faces immediately, even from small photographs. The defect is specific for visual objects of a particular category.

The patient misidentifies the most common objects of everyday life. He calls a hat a "little pot," a ball is "a round block of wood," a pen is a "cylindrical stick," and a bicycle is called "a pole with two wheels, one in front, one in back" (Hécaen & Albert, 1978).

Thus the patient is perfectly able to recognize the outlines and the shape of the object, but contours and dimensions do not yield visual identification. Features of the syndrome that seem to be common to all the reported cases are useful in determining what categories of perception are impaired and which are spared. The patients have no difficulty in visually locating objects, and they immediately recognize visitors before they begin to speak. They recognize pictures of animals and can describe the appearance of persons and animals in fairly concrete detail. These subjects have no speech disturbances; objects placed in their hands, an ashtray for example, can be immediately named. Their visual-spatial orientation and depth perception are normal, and they can read and name signs and symbols—letters, numbers, and words—fluently and accurately. But they fail completely to recognize inanimate objects presented to them or displayed in pictures. Shown a picture of an airplane, a patient says, "That's a design, but I can't remember what it is"; a picture of a table, "that represents . . . only what could it represent?"; a car, "I can't name it; I don't know what it could be."

There are other cases, however, in which patients with visual agnosia are unable to identify letters or colors, but are nonetheless able to recognize large objects, faces of family members, and meaningful designs. In cases of visual object agnosia in which elements of detail can be described out loud, a patient may ultimately succeed in deducing the nature of the whole by adding the pieces together. One patient shown the six-pointed Star of David said: "It is made up of two sets of closed, three-sided figures which interlock." Asked whether he recognized it as a Star of David, he replied, "Not exactly. But it is the most logical conclusion" (Hécaen & Albert, 1978, p. 194). Sometimes one single element of the object, a critical feature, may be sufficiently meaningful to the patient to permit identification of the entire object. One patient thus identified a boat by the presence of its mast.

Other aspects of meaningfulness that aid recognition are movements of the object (taking matches from a box, pulling a dollar from a wallet), or placing the object in an appropriate context (bedroom slippers placed under the patient's bed). But these features may also give rise to false recognition. For example, Hécaen and Ajuriaguerra (1956) describe a patient who, seeing the examiner bring a spoon to his lips, declared, "There, that thing must be a cigar or a cigarette, something you bring to your mouth like that."

Certain common factors may underlie the failures of recognition of different categories making their diagnosis uncertain or difficult. For example, spatial orientation is a feature of signs, so that inverted and rotated letters are extremely difficult to read; a familiar problem to one seated on the inside of a window on which a word is printed to be read by those outside; upright spatial orientation is also important for the recognition of faces. Yin (1969) showed how difficult it is for subjects to recognize faces presented upside-down that had previously been seen in a normal position. The critical problem may involve facial expression as well as the general impression of the normally oriented face, stressed by Yin. When particular features, the eyes and the mouth, are presented upside-down in a normally oriented face, the distortion is painfully exaggerated. (See Figure 9.2.)

Injuries to the occipital region of the cortex may cause a selective deficit of letter and word recognition, but preserve other forms of visual perception. This syndrome, known as *alexic agnosia,* may take various forms. For example, only certain letters may be confused or may fail to be recognized, depending on their similarity, frequency of use, or position in the alphabet. Such patients could write to dictation, but could not copy printed text. Writing was preserved when words were heard, because the corresponding kinesthetic cognons were available. Copying was not possible because the visual perception of letter patterns was abolished.

Of particular interest is the preservation of the ability to recognize familiar handwriting, even when the individual letters could not be identified. This fact shows that unitary perceptions of familiar handwriting belong to a separate category of perceptions, represented in a different cognitive field from that of printed letter symbols.

In such a disorder as visual object agnosia, the patient cannot name a pencil or suggest a use for it when it is presented by the examiner. Yet, a moment later, given some paper on which to write her name, the patient will pick up the pencil from any other objects and begin to write. The patient is unable to light her cigarette or wave goodbye when requested to do so, but another time will correctly light her cigarette and spontaneously wave goodbye to bid a genuine farewell.

The contrast between the patient's inability to name an object shown to her or to show its use in response to a request and her evident ability to use it in a natural context shows the lability of the disorder. This has important clinical implications. The patient's manifest symptoms depend upon her degree of motivation, how well she feels on a given day, whether the examination is just beginning or coming to an end, with attendant fatigue and perseverative errors. Naming errors also depend on how common the object is, how strong its emotional taint, and how early in life its name was learned. These variable factors make the results of an examination uncertain and the diagnosis extremely difficult.

Despite these obstacles, the clinical pathological data reveal remarkably consistent categorical defects. The specificity of these disorders seems incredible, but is completely consistent with the *cognon* hypothesis of discretely localized categories of perception and imagery.

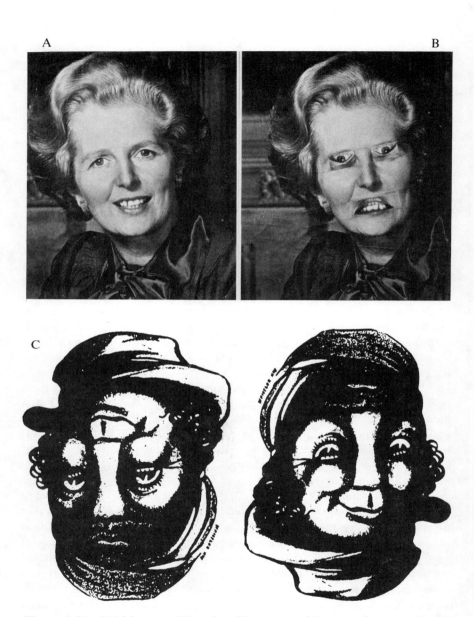

Figure 9.2. (A) Margaret Thatcher: The two upside-down faces are similar. (B) Turn the page upside-down. The inverted eyes and mouth create a dramatic difference in Mrs. Thatcher's expression. Courtesy Peter Thompson, 1980, with apologies to Mrs. Thatcher. Reproduced by permission of Pion Ltd. (C) Another reversible face.

DISORDERS OF LANGUAGE: THE APHASIAS

Both Broca's aphasia and Wernicke's aphasia result in an impairment in speech, not necessarily its total loss. The patterns of disordered speech are different in the two forms of aphasia. (See Figure 9.3.)

Lesions to Broca's area result in a variety of language disorders; the classical syndrome called *motor aphasia* or *expressive aphasia* is an isolated disorder of articulation in which comprehension, reading, and writing are intact. It is not a muscular failure; eating and other oral functions of mouth and tongue function normally. In the early stages of *pure* motor aphasia, when speech appears, it is often labored and slow; the patient may be able to produce a limited range of meaningless phonemes or syllables and to string them together in a rhythmic pattern representing normal intonation. Singing of melodies is often preserved, as well as prosody (expressive intonation); a fact that has given rise to a new approach to aphasia therapy, melodic intonation therapy.

Geschwind (1979) calls attention to the particular difficulty these patients

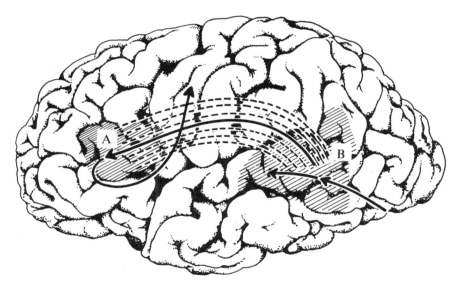

Figure 9.3. Broca's area (A) is connected by the arcuate fasciculus to Wernicke's area (B) in the language dominant (usually the left) hemisphere. In Wernicke's model of *aphasia* the angular gyrus converts visual language (written words) into auditory speech (heard or spoken words) and vice-versa. Damage to the angular gyrus disrupts cross-modal associations and causes loss of memory for words and grammar. Adapted from Geschwind, 1972; 1979.

have in forming sentences. Complex grammatical constructions, pronouns, and connective words disappear; instead, the speech has a telegraphic style. Geschwind's patient, when asked about a dental appointment said hesitantly: "Yes... Monday... Dad and Dick... Wednesday... nine o'clock... 10 o'clock ...doctors...and...teeth" (Geschwind, 1979, p. 111).

Geschwind finds Wernicke's model still applicable to these defects, and writes:

> In this model the underlying structure of an utterance arises in Wernicke's area. It is then transferred to Broca's area, where it evokes a detailed and coordinated program for vocalization. The program is passed on to the adjacent face area of the motor cortex, which activates the appropriate muscles of the mouth, the lips, the tongue, the larynx, and so on. (1979, p. 111)

The model explains the loss of comprehension, reading, and writing. When a word is heard or said, the sensory signals must pass directly or indirectly through Wernicke's area. The auditory signal goes from the primary auditory cortex to Wernicke's area.

There is good evidence that the *angular gyrus,* located just above Wernicke's area in the left hemisphere, is involved in *visual word memory.* This region, unique in the human brain, turns written language into spoken language and vice versa. Not only are cross-modal associations—visual to auditory and auditory to visual—carried on here, this region also stores the memory of the rules of grammar and of spelling.

When a word is seen, the visual signal first goes to the *angular gyrus,* to be translated to the auditory form; writing a word from dictation elicits the auditory form of the word in Wernicke's area and passes the information back to the angular gyrus from where it is sent to the muscles in the hand and in the fingers that control writing.

Damage to Wernicke's area, accordingly, disrupts all aspects of language; damage to Broca's area impairs speech, but leaves comprehension undisturbed. Another important area, the *arcuate fasciculus* connects Wernicke's and Broca's area. When this connection is destroyed by a lesion, the *disconnection* "leaves speech fluent and well articulated but semantically aberrant; Broca's area is operating but it is not receiving information from Wernicke's area" (Geschwind, 1979; Geschwind & Kaplan, 1962).

A lesion in the *angular gyrus* disconnects the visual and the auditory word images, causing a disturbance in reading, but not in speaking, as long as both Broca's and Wernicke's areas remain functional. The ensuing deficit may be called auditory-visual aphasia, to indicate the connections affected.

An excellent description of this syndrome, taken from a Russian paper by Stolyarova-Kabelyanskaya (1961), appears in Konorski's (1967) book. If coherent enough to explain, the patient may say that the names of the objects have lost all their meaning for him: they are recognizably words, but they appear to be in a foreign language that he does not know.

Asked to point to the floor, the patient may point to a window; another says, "Floor, floor, floor. This is the wall; no it is after all the floor (indicating the wall). Is it not?"

A patient who had suffered a thrombosis and developed a pure auditory-visual aphasia could not comprehend words heard that indicated everyday objects. When the examiner said, "spoon," the patient selected a pencil. "This is in some sense spoon—a spoon for writing." "Watch"—"Let us say that this is watch" (Correct). "Comb"—"Comb, comb, this is in some sense a comb" (takes a bunch of keys) "one comb, second, third, many combs." This man could read the name of the object and he could write it on request. The failure was due to the disconnection between the sight of the object and the sound of its name. Postmortem findings showed that the pathways leading to the occipital region from the second temporal convolution in the left hemisphere were totally destroyed.

Another important verbal category is that of *motor actions.* Here belong verbs, verbal nouns, and adverbs. The strength of the connections linking the kinesthetic cognons representing motor acts and the word-kinesthetic field is vividly revealed by the fact that when we name a given act, we tend to perform it, at least in a rudimentary form. The speech of patients suffering from amnesic aphasia due to injuries of the posterior speech area is composed of verbs rather than nouns. By contrast, patients with anterior speech area damage have a telegraphic style, using only nouns. Either the Broca aphasic has lost the ability to structure sentences, or the connections required for naming motor actions have been injured.

DISORDERS OF READING AND WRITING: THE ALEXIAS AND AGRAPHIAS

The thesis that reading and writing are based on quite different cognitive fields finds support from alexic patients in whom reading is impaired, but writing remains normal. Patients with primary alexia are unable to identify letters and numbers, yet able readily to identify other visual patterns, faces, animals, and so on. Secondary alexia is diagnosed when the subject can discriminate signs, but cannot name them because the connections between the visual-sign field and the word-auditory field are injured. The test for this is to ask the patient to copy a text, a function severely impaired in primary alexia, but preserved in secondary alexia. Unlike primary alexia, which is an *agnosic* defect, secondary alexia is a form of *disconnection* disorder.

The loss of visual-word memory produces a functional illiterate; the patient can no longer read, write, spell, or comprehend spelled words. The disturbance of spelling is a clue to the nature of the disturbance of the angular gyrus. Dejerine (1891) first described a case with a right hemianopia in which the sudden loss of the ability to read and to write was due to a lesion of the inferior three-quarters of the angular gyrus. Another of his patients was unable to read letters, words, or music, but could write correctly, either spontaneously or to dictation. Curiously, he could not read what he had just written, although he could recognize letters by tracing their outlines with his hand. Dejerine took the preserved ability to mean that the "visual word center" was intact. The first case (called "pure alexia with agraphia" was the result of a lesion of a "memory center"; the second patient, a case of "pure alexia without agraphia") could read kinesthetically, but suffered from a disconnection between this memory center and the anterior speech area. Thus, although he could not use sight alone to read, he could still name pictured instruments, and he continued to operate an intellectually demanding business successfully. (See Figure 9.4.)

Subsequent cases have confirmed the diagnosis of a lesion involving the left occipital cortex and the splenium of the corpus callosum. When this connection is destroyed by a lesion, there are one or more disruptions of paths between the right visual cortex and the angular gyrus. The patient can still recognize and can name objects, but not written words or letters. Why should recognition of objects be preserved, but not words? When you consider that objects have rich associations in several modalities—we can recognize an apple by sight, smell, touch, or taste—it follows that the arousal of such associations permits us to find alternative pathways across the corpus callosum if one is disconnected. Word blindness, together with lost color naming, are purely visual-auditory disturbances. Words and colors cannot be smelled, felt, or bitten, and naming them must rely on a connection between the visual-word memory center and the speech center. Interesting support for this hypothesis comes from the finding that the reading of numbers is frequently preserved in alexic patients. Perhaps the strong associations of numbers with counting on the fingers and repeated or rhythmic motor acts in childhood provide alternative pathways to the visual-auditory ones. Thus, even when their visual cognons are lost, numbers can be read, via kinesthetic cognons, but not letters or words.

DISORDERS OF SYMBOLIC THOUGHT: THE ASYMBOLIAS

The principal evidence for specific disorders of thinking *(asymbolia)* consists of disturbances in reading and in calculating. A focal lesion around the left angular gyrus may be followed by a clear-cut alexic type of aphasia in which speech is intact but the patient is unable to read words, or can read words, perhaps, but cannot read letters or identify numerals or operational symbols

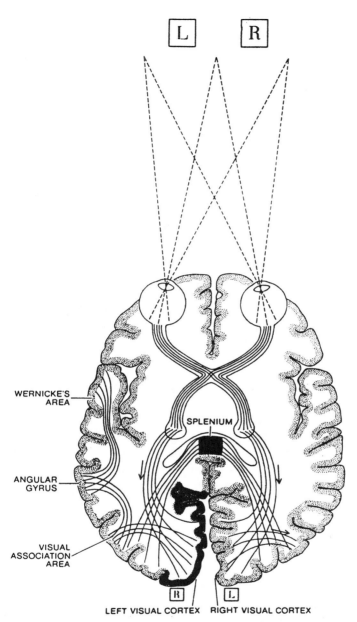

Figure 9.4. An injury to both the left occipital cortex and the splenium of the corpus callosum disconnects pathways between the right visual cortex and the angular gyrus causing *alexia,* loss of ability to read words, while sparing visual recognition of objects. From "Language and the Brain," N. Geschwind (Vol. 226, pp. 76–83). Copyright © 1972 by Scientific American, Inc. All rights reserved.

(acalculia). The patient may show an even more specific form of reading disability, being able to read words in one typeface but not in another. More usual, Critchley (1966) reports, is a dissociation between graphic symbols written by hand and those appearing in print. Here is definite evidence of a category distinction between handwritten and printed signs.

Dementia refers to a deterioration in intellectual capacity, by definition irreversible. It is usually a demonstrable organic condition to be separated from a deterioration of personality and other disorders of a psychotic disease. Some of the fundamental defects that comprise dementia are listed by Critchley (1966): difficulties in retention, attention, lack (or ocassionally an excess) of spontaneity, poverty of ideas, undue tidiness or slovenliness, and disturbed consciousness. Critchley stresses also the incongruency or inappropriateness, the antisocial character, especially, of the conduct underlying psychiatric global dementia. He writes:

> Particularly suggestive of dementia as opposed to agnosia (or aphasia) is the occurrence of incontinence by a patient who is not at all drowsy, in circumstances which make the act blatantly offensive or improper. The patient who exposes his person and urinates in the dining room, for example, is not for a moment behaving like a victim of a lesion in the after part of the brain. Similarly, sexual offences, indecencies, financial extravagance or miserliness are not usually encountered in patients with agnosia. (Critchley, 1966, p. 380)

Affective states inappropriate to the occasion, as well as disorientation involving time, place, and person are also suggestive of dementia. A study of the patient's language may give important clues to the mental state. Speech may be progressively impoverished or change qualitatively toward increasing repetitions and stereotypy. Finally, the demented patient is essentially unable to deal with new problems and unfamiliar situations. Routine work may be carried out satisfactorily, but as soon as the patient is confronted by unexpected demands, he fails to cope.

DISORDERS OF SPACE PERCEPTION

Loss of orientation, loss of sense of place, loss of memory for place were described even before the beginning of the century, but their isolation as separate syndromes only appeared later on.

Hécaen and Albert (1978) classify the various disorders of perception and manipulation of spatial information as follows:

1. Disorders of *spatial perception* (absolute and relative localization)
2. Defective *manipulation* of spatial information (loss of spatio-temporal concepts, unilateral spatial agnosia, or hemi-inattention)

3. Loss of visual *topographical imagery*
4. Balint's syndrome (paralysis of *gaze*)

1. Disorders of Spatial Perception

Bender and Teuber (1974) distinguished disorders of *perception of spatial relations* from impaired general level of mental functioning. They found that perceptual disorders of spatial localization occurred in three dimensions of visual space, often accompanied by changes in the appearance of the size, shape, and color objects.

Many spatial perceptual disorders are not obvious to the patient. They include loss of stereoscopic vision; although the surrounding scene may appear as flat as a colored picture, the defect is not noticed until it is demonstrated with a stereoscope. In exceptional cases the patient is well aware that depth perception is lost. Critchley reports a case of a woman with a right parieto-occipital lesion who

> realized that she was unable to visualize the location of objects at home; as she ordinarily possessed an exceptional and "photographic" type of visual imagery and memory, her present disability was all the more striking. At the same time, she discovered that she had lost stereoscopic vision and that everything she looked at would appear flat and uninteresting. As she gazed out of her window, she could see a wall, and beyond that, the street. Now it would seem to her that people strolling along the pavement were actually walking on top of the wall. (1966, p. 329)

2. Defects of Manipulation and Place Memory

A patient suffering from a disease of the *right* hemisphere of his brain may be completely unable to draw any kind of map. Given a contour map of his country, he is unable to indicate the principle cities, or rivers, or bordering oceans, even though these were all well known to him before the disease. He cannot draw a sketch of his apartment, or show the location and relative position of the windows and doors.

These and similar tests are used to diagnose *visuospatial agnosia*. They tend to show the loss of images rather than the names of spatial relations. Lesions in the rostral part of the occipital region of the right hemisphere give rise to the syndrome of visuospatial agnosia. The independence of this right brain area from the verbal association areas in the left brain suggests that our perception of spatial relations generally requires no verbalization. Our visual orientation in space is usually accomplished by imagery and only rarely associated with words. Verbal directions, in fact, are frequently confusing— we need to translate directions, "Take the next left turn, then at the traffic signal make a right, and then another right..." into kinesthetic or visual images. The most useful directions call attention to landmarks, especially if their name or their visual appearance is a bit odd, e.g., "The White Elephant Gift Shoppe," the "sign pointing to the Enchanted Hunter Hotel, just before the right turn," and "Turn left at Joe's Pretty Good Grocery," (John W. Senders, personal communication). A map is a fine aid, but difficult to consult while driving.

In patients with right parietal disease, the symptom of losing oneself is a conspicuous feature that often brings the illness to the attention of relatives, although the patient may be strangely disinterested. One woman was found in the wrong end of the village looking for the butcher; another was almost lost because she could not find the gates of a familiar plot. Another patient, a 49-year-old male, went far past his proper destination in a bus, and, walking back, found great difficulty in finding his house.... "Indeed, he will often pass his home without knowing that it is his.... [Eventually] he would ask his wife to leave a light on so that he could recognize his house more easily"(Critchley, 1966, p. 337). The patient had a verified occlusion of the right middle cerebral artery.

Other patients with parietal disease have been described as "muddled" over the correct spatial orientation of verbal or numerical symbols. Comprehension of the meaning of such adverbs as *right, left, up, down, out, back, below, behind,* is frequently defective in patients with disorders of spatial imagery; often this confusion is accompanied by the inability to read the time. Mirror reversals are common.

Hécaen reports the case of a woman who was unable to tell the time by looking at the position of the hands on a clock—yet she could identify the object itself as a clock. Such defects of spatial perception may be related to a disruption of the spatial coordinate system. Paterson and Zangwill (1944) describe a patient who was able to recognize and solve segments of a spatial problem, but could not integrate the elementary spatial relations into a coherent pattern. Their patient was uncertain whether he had ever been in a particular room. Although he recognized individual pieces of furniture, he could not grasp the overall arrangement of the furniture, doors, and windows in order to recognize the room as a whole—a defect characterized as a piecemeal approach to problems of drawing and of constructing block patterns. These and similar disorders of spatial perception often appear after lesions of the posterior parietal cortex.

In human pathology, the variety of disturbances following parietal injuries makes us wonder whether this area has a unitary specialized function. We have noted disorders of speech, spatial orientation, attention (to one-half of space especially), and impairment of higher-order categorization. Taken together, the findings clearly reveal the parietal cortex as centrally involved in symbolic information processing. Specific defects are lateralized, with verbal disturbances resulting from left hemispheric lesions and spatial disturbances resulting from right hemispheric lesions.

Experiments on monkeys provide excellent physiological and behavioral evidence for the role of cognons in the parietal cortex in *ambient spatial* vision. Findings from single-unit recordings, experimental ablation, and clinical studies of this cortical region show a striking consistency. Motter and Mountcastle (1981) report a remarkable series of studies of the parietal lobe combining the methods of behavioral control, visual stimulation, and single-neuron analysis in 10 macaque monkeys. These experiments identified hundreds of light-sensitive neurons that responded to stimulus movement and direction over a wide range of velocities. Visual fixation and the angle of gaze had a powerful effect upon the excitability of these parietal light-sensitive neurons. Evidently these neurons are neither simply "sensory" nor simply "motor" in function, but are involved in complex functions comprising both perception and the visuokinesthetic guidance of action (See Figure 9.5.)

In an excellent review of both the clinical and the experimental literature on the posterior parietal cortex, James C. Lynch (1980) finds that this area, together with many other parts of the brain, contains many different cell classes. Are we forced to admit that the concept of localization of higher nervous processes in the brain must once more be abandoned? Not at all. These various mechanisms are distinct, but they are not necessarily independent. Indeed, a strong argument can be made for the functional unity of these different cell types.

Thus Motter and Mountcastle (1981) stress their findings on the anatomical side of projections received from the retinocollicular system and its upward thalamocortical projections—signals though to provide information about the spatial location of objects, not their contours, orientation, or color. The inferior parietal lobule is thus a higher processing area of the visual-spatial system concerned with the representation of objects and events in the immediately surrounding visual space. But it is not simply visual. The region also contains many neurons (possibly 70 percent of the total) that are not sensitive to light and were therefore eliminated from further investigation by Motter and Mountcastle. These include tactile, kinesthetic, and other cell groups that contribute to the total integrated behavior of the whole organism as it reaches for and manipulates objects in space. The general hypothesis put forth by Motter and Mountcastle is attractive and sufficiently flexible to admit the contribution of several sensory modalities and of action initiatives to the unified behavioral goal. They conclude that the region contributes to "a continuing updating of a central neural image of immediately surrounding space and to the perceptual constancy of that space during bodily movement... properties suitable for the attraction of gaze and attention to objects in the peripheral visual fields" (Motter & Mountcastle, 1981, p. 3).

The central importance of this parietal system for attracting visual, and

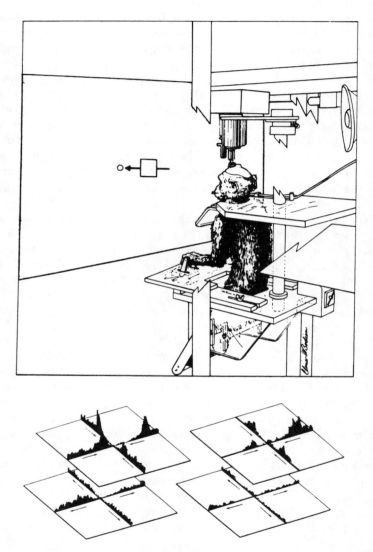

Figure 9.5. Monkey experiment showed the importance of neuronal activity for directed attention or mental set. The histogram displays summarize the responses of a neuron during the movement of the light stimulus across the visual field. Motter & Mountcastle, *Journal of Neuroscience, 1,* 13–26. Copyright © 1981 by Society for Neuroscience.

even supramodal, attention to moving objects and to coordinating perceptual and manual operations with events in space is a major discovery.

It is this system that is responsible for coordinating the action of hand and eye in behavioral space and for the impairment that results in clinically observed defects, such as hemi-inattention (See Chapter Three) associated with lesions of the parietal lobe. But one needs to take into account that hemi-inattention in human (and monkey) pathology is not limited to damage of the parietal lobe. It occurs as the result of lesions in the frontal and temporal lobes and in various subcortical regions (Weinstein, Kahn, & Slote, 1955; Heilman & Valenstein, 1972). These neuropsychologists also call attention to the role of hemisphere specialization and corticolimbic-reticular interactions in the syndrome of hemi-inattention. The joint collaboration of the emotive and the cognitive systems is essential for effective coordination of hand and eye in behavioral space.

3. Loss of Topographical Imagery

Tests to reveal visuospatial agnosias usually do not deal with perceptions as much as they do with *images* of spatial relations and their loss. Places with which the patient was well acquainted before brain injury cannot be visualized. This category thus involves *recall memory.*

A frequent consequence of parietal damage is the loss of ability to call up visual images of a geographical sort. The loss of visual images may entail places, but not persons or particular objects. Critchley (1966) reports several cases in which a patient finds it difficult to conjure up a mental picture of a familiar environment—his home, bedroom, office, streets in his neighborhood, and so on. The impairment is highly selective; other visual images are undisturbed.

With the loss of topographical memory or spatial orientation, the brain-damaged patient is unable to orient himself in space. Hécaen and Albert believe that the disorder consists essentially of an inability to recognize the significance of topographical cues. The category and even the style of buildings in the city can be readily identified, but a church or hospital no longer serve as landmarks for place. Similarly, the patient can identify articles of furniture—a table, a bed, or a door—but cannot use them as topographical cues. However well the patient may have learned to locate these objects before his illness, they are no longer useful spatial cues. In milder cases the cues are still usable because they have been so well learned, but in a new environment (such as the clinic), the patient gets hopelessly lost.

4. Balint's Syndrome

Balint's syndrome refers to a disorder described by Balint in 1909 as a *psychic paralysis of gaze,* manifested by the subject's inability to direct his eyes at will toward a point in his peripheral field of vision.

Spontaneous attention for any visual stimulus is markedly reduced. Instead, visual attention is centered on whatever passes directly into the axis of fixation; when the gaze has not been fixed, the patient's eyes wander until they fall upon an object by chance, and then fixate on that object. So a patient pours water from a bottle he is holding onto the table, next to the glass. He cannot see more than one object at a time, because he cannot shift his gaze from one to the other, and if shown several identical items, he cannot count them, being confused as to whether or not an object has already been counted.

Balint's syndrome is a set of eye movement defects and may seem to belong under the heading of kinesthetic apraxia rather than spatial vision. But it is a failure of response to a visual target—no peripheral stimulus is sufficient to capture visual attention. One of Hécaen's patients, for example, was offered a lit match to help him light his cigarette. The match was brought within two inches from the end of the cigarette, but the patient, looking at the tip of the cigarette held between his lips, was unable to respond visually to the flame. This is a good example of the close inter-relation between vision and attention. The paralysis of gaze causes gross errors to occur when a subject wishes to grasp an object in the surrounding visual field.

DISORDERS OF MEMORY: THE AMNESIAS

Disorders of memory may result from factors that interfere with the acquisition of new material, its retention, or its retrieval from storage. The immediate registration of new information may take place normally, but the material may be rapidly forgotten and impossible to recover. There is abundant proof that unilateral temporal lobectomy results in specialized memory deficits, depending on which hemisphere, left or right, has been invaded. Patients with temporal lesions in the speech-dominant hemisphere (usually the left) have measurable defects in verbal memory; a corresponding removal from the nondominant right hemisphere leaves verbal memory intact but impairs visual, spatial, and auditory memory. In both groups the deficits are greater, the larger the invasion of the hippocampal structures attached to the temporal lobectomy. The hippocampus must serve a vital function in the retention of simple information in the face of distraction.

Corsi (1972) has systematically shown the importance of the hippocampal damage in memory disorders for specific materials and also the differential effects of left and of right hippocampal removals. The greater the extent of hippocampus destroyed by the surgeon's knife, the more profound the memory loss. Following temporal lobectomy, those patients with hippocampus spared performed as well as normal control subjects. Those with the most radical hippocampal excision showed the most rapid forgetting. These experiments clearly confirmed the earlier evidence that the nature of the memory loss depends on the side of the temporal lobectomy. The spatial memory task (recall of a visual location) was severely impaired after right temporal lobectomy, but not after left. By contrast, the left temporals performed poorly on the verbal memory task (recall of consonant trigrams) following various time intervals filled with distracting activity to prevent rehearsal. The inability to retain new information beyond a brief period, corresponding to the span of immediate memory (so-called *anterograde amnesia*), is seen after *bilateral* lesions in the medial temporal lobe structures that include the hippocampus and the parahippocampal gyrus. Patients with these lesions show a severe, lasting, and global memory disorder.

Brenda Milner (1970) described the details of the amnesic syndrome produced by bilateral medial-temporal lesions. The radical excisions were performed by Dr. William Scoville as a treatment for psychotic and for epileptic illness. (It was he who reported the drastic memory loss, in 1954, in all cases in which the hippocampus had been invaded bilaterally.) Subsequently Scoville and Milner (1957) and Milner (1962, 1966, 1968) followed the one nonpsychotic patient intensively. The patient, Henry M., failed to remember anything that had happened since the operation, *(anterograde amnesia)* and showed some loss of memory *(retrograde amnesia)* for the period covering one or two years just before the operation. The forgetfulness applied to all ongoing events including the recognition of neighbors and even such simple perceptual material as colors or sounds.

A remarkable case of the loss of the power to remember nearly *anything* for more than a few moments, Henry M. lived in a terribly constricted world of his own ever since an operation on his brain, in 1953, that removed both of his temporal lobes as well as the underlying hippocampus inside each of them. The drastic procedure created "a child of the moment"—Henry M. worked at a state rehabilitation center and could learn new skills of *movement,* but he was unable to give any account of his job or place of work, and he could not form any new stable, conscious, perceptual, or verbal memories. Although Milner spent many hours with Henry, she was an utter stranger to him on each new occasion that they met. Henry preserved his old memories, formed before the awful insult to his brain, but events and experiences since then either did not establish cognons, or, if they did, they could not be retrieved as conscious experiences. His uncle died after Henry's operation, and whenever Henry was reminded of his uncle's death, he mourned as though he was learning it for the first time.

Curiously, Henry M. did recognize numbers and could retain them, at least for a short time, and he could repeat them to his examiner (Wickelgren, 1968). His short-term or recent memory thus seemed to be preserved, but it had some peculiar features. Brenda Milner asked him if he could repeat this number, "584." He did, and then explained: "It's easy. You just remember 8. You see, 5, 8, and 4 add to 17. You remember 8; subtract it from 17 and it

leaves 9. Divide 9 in half and you get 5 and 4, and there you are: 584. Easy"
(Milner, 1970, p. 37).

A minute later Henry M. was unable to recall either the number, 584, or
any of the associated complex train of thought. Indeed, he could not know
that he had been given a number to remember.

In order to determine whether Henry M. might be capable of some sort of
learning with intensive practice, Milner trained him on a stylus maze learning
task, in which the subject must discover the correct path leading from one
metal bolt to another, guided by a clicking error signal, informing him of his
mistakes. Henry M. failed to show any progress on this task over a period of 3
days and 215 trials. When Milner shortened the maze from 28 to 9 bolts, he
eventually succeeded in making 3 successive errorless runs, but only after 155
trials and 256 errors.

He was, however, unable to succeed on a maze just two choice points
longer than this short path—a powerful reminder of the amnesic's inability
to retain a sequence even slightly longer than his immediate memory span.

In marked contrast to paired comparison and to maze test results, Henry
M. had a normal learning curve on a motor-learning task—mirror drawing.
Using a star pattern hidden from direct view, but visible as reflected from a
mirror, the subject must learn to trace the outline with a pencil, keeping
between the double contour lines. Although Henry M. improved on this task
over a 3-day period, beginning each new session at the highest level previously
attained. Henry M. had no recollection that he had done the task before; it was
completely unfamiliar.

His amnesic problem was not in immediate perception, nor in retrieval
from memory, but in acquisition of new information for long-term memory.

Why could Henry not learn anything new? Consider that his ability to
form new conscious experiences, new perceptions, and new images was
abolished—but new motor learning was spared. How can the global nature of
Henry's memory deficit and this one curious exception be explained?

It would seem that the ability to form new cognons, or associations
between them, in the sensory modalities of vision, hearing, or somathesis,
requires the integrity of the medial temporal hippocampal system.

The hippocampus functions significantly in the orienting reflex associated
with the identification of a novel stimulus. As the mechanism for evoking the
specific targeting reflexes involved in vision and audition, the integrity of the
pathways linking the hippocampal system to the temporal cortex, the
association areas for these particular analyzers, must be maintained. The
destruction of this system selectively impairs new perceptual learning,
preventing the formation of cognons, while allowing new motor associations
to be formed in the prefrontal regions of the cortex. As long as connections
between the limbic system and the premotor areas of the frontal cortex are
spared, the subject can update or program new motor skills by means of the
undamaged kinesthetic association cortex.

It seems clear that the hippocampus is essential to the formation of both verbal and nonverbal *perceptual* memories, although it is not itself the site of *cognons* representing long-term memory. Nor is the hippocampus involved in the formation of new motor skills. Lesions of the bilateral medial temporal region including the hippocampus interfere with the ability to hold information in the face of an interfering activity that competes for the individual's attention. It is not that the hippocampal patients are abnormally distractible. The critical cause of the memory defect seems to be the loss of the *sensitization* mechanism that sustains attention to a new stimulus sufficiently long to form a new *cognon*. That is why recognition memory, as well as recall of new information, is permanently lost. The reason why motor skills can still be acquired is that the corresponding kinesthetic cognons are formed, not in the posterior or medial sensory regions of the association cortex, but in the region anterior to the motor cortex—the prefrontal area. In terms of Ryle's (1949) distinction between "knowing how" and "knowing that," the amnesic patient still knows *how* and can still learn *how*—but no longer can learn *that* an event occurred or *that* two things, *A* and *B*, are the same or are different from each other.

DISORDERS OF EMOTION: THE APROSODIAS

Elliot D. Ross at the University of Texas Southwestern Medical School in Dallis, describes the unusual case of a 34-year-old schoolteacher who suffered a stroke in the right hemisphere (Ross & Mesulam, 1979). As expected, her entire left side was affected; both sensation and movement on that side was impaired. But the striking feature of her complaint was the absence of the slightest expression of feeling. She recited the sad news of the breakup of her marriage in a peculiarly empty and expressionless voice. Although she claimed that she *experienced* emotions, she was unable to convey any feelings.

One month later, although she had recovered from the paralysis of her left leg and was able to return to work, she faced a new and serious dilemma. Unable to communicate any emotions through her voice or behavior, she could not discipline her students or her own children at home. Even when she insisted, "I am furious," no one paid any attention to her, because her voice was so flat and expressionless.

Marcel Mesulam of Harvard Medical School had a similar patient, an engineer with right brain damage, who was unable to express emotion. Both the engineer and the schoolteacher spoke in a monotone that failed to convince others of their sincerity. Although they experienced emotions inwardly, they lacked normal prosody—the ability to impart emotions through expressive intonation and gesturing. These right brain–injured patients can identify the emotions expressed by others' speech, but they cannot mimic the appropriate tone of voice.

Recently, Kenneth H. Heilman (1979) at the University of Florida College of Medicine, reported cases of patients with right brain injuries, who had preserved normal articulation and grammar in speech, but could not identify the emotional signals communicated by the language of others. Whereas Ross's schoolteacher had a problem analogous to Broca's aphasics— she could speak, but could not express the emotions that render speech vivid and convincing, Heilman's patients, like Wernicke's aphasics (who could not comprehend propositional speech) failed to comprehend the emotional components of speech. Ross calls these syndromes the *aprosodias*. Thus both halves of the brain have responsibilities for language. The division of language functions between the two halves of the brain is impressive. Ross concludes that "the left hemisphere is responsible for what we say, and the right hemisphere for how we say it."

Put this simply, Ross's statement may lead us to infer incorrectly that the right hemisphere regulates all emotions and that the left hemisphere is cold and unfeeling. We can dismiss the idea that the two hemispheres are polar opposites emotionally. Damage to either brain often produces depression, but that is a reaction of a normal hemisphere to the experience of deficit. The indifferent, even euphoric reaction, often noted in right brain pathology, is sometimes just as dramatic following injury to the left hemisphere. A euphoric reaction frequently results from a left brain lesion in Wernicke's area. But some distinction remains. Geschwind writes: "While the Wernicke's aphasic often laughs and shows unconcern *about his speech disorder,* he does not manifest the more widespread unconcern often observed in the right hemisphere patient—e.g., loss of personal modesty, incontinence of urine, and social inappropriateness" (1981, p. 26).

DISORDERS OF LEARNED MOVEMENTS: THE APRAXIAS

Apraxia (inability to act) is a disorder of voluntary action caused by damage to the motor cortex. The disturbance is not a paralysis or impairment of the muscles or motor pathways. Apraxic disorders are disorders of the execution of learned movements that cannot be accounted for by weakness, sensory loss, or noncomprehension of verbal commands.

Liepmann (1905) first introduced the concept of apraxia as the "inability to perform purposeful movement," a psychological rather than a muscular or motor disorder. For Liepmann, the voluntary motor act is the result of a mental idea of the movement and the motor effect that this idea evokes. This included the ideas of the purpose of the action and the possible ways of performing the action—including visual and kinesthetic memory images stored in the corresponding regions of the cortex. The retrieval of these associations may be so firmly established by previous experience as to be automatic. The corresponding ideas or images will be stripped of complex associations and will function as unitary kinesthetic programs, analogous to unitary visual or auditory percepts. Liepmann thus anticipated the concept developed in this book of *kinesthetic cognons.*

Circumscribed lesions of the premotor cortex may make the plan of the movement impossible because the patient cannot create an image of the required movement—that is, the necessary kinesthetic cognon has been destroyed. In other cases, the image of the required movement is present, but the connections between the image and the motor neural apparatus are interrupted. The patient knows what to do, but cannot put the action into effect. The distinction is that between a kinesthetic agnosia and a kinesthetic disconnection syndrome.

Liepmann's theory of apraxia is surprisingly modern. It gives higher motor functions the same organization as higher sensory functions and finds support in evidence that the cortical apparatus of voluntary movements is localized in the motor area of the cerebral cortex, and the corresponding subcortical motor centers are located in the cerebellum and the basal ganglia (see Chapter Twelve).

Apraxic agnosia is thus a defect of the ability to create a kinesthetic action program, what Bernstein (1967) called the "motor task." Such disturbances of voluntary movements, also known as *kinesthetic apraxias,* affect the ability to select the required kinesthetic impulses for bringing about a movement. A patient with kinesthetic apraxia can control the direction of his movements; he can hold a knife or spoon in the correct position. Yet, when he attempts to grasp an object, to fasten a button, or tie a shoe lace, he cannot select the right movements with the affected hand. The disorder is caused by lesions, usually in the motor cortex of the left hemisphere and thus incapacitates the right hand (although it may develop into an apraxia of both hands, because the motor program or kinesthetic cognon is in the left hemisphere only).

Visual input helps compensate for the disturbances of voluntary movements. For example, the patient is helpless when asked to show how tea is poured into an imaginary cup because the necessary objects are not present visually. Given a pot and a cup, however, the patient performs the act correctly. To give you an impression of the experience, try to snap the fingers of your left (or nondominant hand). Most people can snap the fingers of their right hand smartly. but may be unable to make any snapping noise with their left hand, unless and until they watch carefully and, by visual means, initiate the inexperienced with the experienced fingers.

Movements in response to commands, without the benefit of visual guidance, are difficult for the apraxic patient. Geschwind (1975) points out that apraxic patients may readily carry out one class of movements in response to certain commands, but, given other commands, may completely fail to respond. For example, the patient will respond correctly and without hesitation when asked to "Look up," "Bend the head," "Kneel," "Walk backwards," yet be unable to respond to other commands, involving seemingly simple gestures: "Make a fist," "Salute," "Wave."

Why does the apraxic patient execute one set of learned movements but fail the other? The mechanism of "axial" movements belongs to the first category—movements involving midline structures, the eyes, the trunk, the neck, even the eyelids—bilateral structures that are preserved following commissurotomy (the split brain patients had no difficulty in carrying out axial movements). By contrast, movements involving individual limbs belong to a different category of kinesthetic action. Underlying these two dissociated categories of praxis are different sets of neural mechanisms—two different sets of cognons.

Facial movements give a striking illustration. After bilateral damage to the face area of the precentral motor cortex, patients are unable to move their mouth and lips to simulate various emotions in response to verbal commands. Commands for facial movements are carried out by the pyramidal system; emotional expressions are transmitted from the limbic system to the nonpyramidal mechanisms for execution. We normals also need a genuinely amusing stimulus to activate the nonpyramidal system to produce a natural smile.

The categorical nature of kinesthesis finds strong support in these clinical observations. The existence of separate motor systems explains why apraxic patients fail certain tasks and not others. Here are alternative routes by which patients attempt to respond in spite of disconnecting lesions.

Additional clinical findings lend further support to the theory. A surprising phenomenon was shown by a patient of Geschwind with classical Wernicke's aphasia. He completely lacked comprehension of speech and made no response to simple questions. In remarkable contrast to these failures, he responded promptly to the three-part axial command: "Roll over, stand up, and turn around" (Geschwind, 1975, p. 194). Geschwind accounts for this unexpected demonstration of comprehension by suggesting that the human right hemisphere has a special capacity—although in this patient it is grossly word deaf, and lacks comprehension of all other aspects of speech, it can respond correctly to axial commands.

It is tempting to speculate on the origin of the capacity to carry out axial commands. Dogs who "sit," "roll over," and "beg" on command suggest that, in common with emotional expression, this is a phylogenetically older function than other aspects of language.

DISORDERS OF PERSONALITY: SOCIAL MISBEHAVIOR

At about half past four in the afternoon of September 14, 1848, a 25-year-old man named Phineas Gage, foreman of a construction gang near the small town of Cavendish, Vermont, put some gunpowder in a prepared opening in the roadbed and tamped it down with his crowbar. The powder ignited and the crowbar flew back and drove a hole through Gage's forehead and ripped through the frontal lobes of his brain and out the top of his head. His men were astonished when, a few minutes later, their admired foreman, whom they had believed was killed instantly, sat up and spoke. Gage not only survived the explosion, but lived for 12 years with the hole in his head, and the bilateral loss of his frontal lobes from the medial orbital region upward to the precentral region made by the one-inch-wide, three-and-one-half-foot-long iron rod. (See Figure 9.6.)

His personality and social behavior changed completely after the accident. Whereas he had been amiable and well liked, a persistent, energetic, and cheerful leader, he became fitful, irreverent, profane, impatient, obstinate— according to his doctor, "a child in his intellectual capacity and manifestations; he has the animal passions of a strong man" (Benson & Blumer, 1975). He was so much unlike his former self that he could no longer be tolerated by his fellow workers: he supported himself by traveling around the country, exhibiting his crowbar and his scarred forehead. His skull and iron rod are now on permanent exhibit at the Warren Anatomical Museum of Harvard University Medical School.

Many other case histories have confirmed the effects of frontal lobe damage on social behavior and personality. Benson and Blumer report excellent psychiatric studies of patients showing outward apathy, flattened affect, little verbal output, and reduced sexual interest following brain damage—a syndrome they term *pseudodepression.* By contrast, the *pseudopsychopathic* syndrome characterizes patients like Gage who lack tact and restraint, who are coarse and abusive, sexually promiscuous, and generally restless and emotionally reactive.

These changes in emotional and social behavior reflect dramatic involvement of the frontal lobes in human personality, but are difficult to correlate with specific lesions in known structures. Human brain injuries are rarely localizable in circumscribed regions, and opposite effects in different patients may seem to arise from identical injuries in the brain parts affected. Patients with damage to other areas, particularly temporal lobe lesions, often show similar changes in affect and personality. For these and other reasons that prevent objective clinical assessment of human emotional and social behavior, investigators have turned to animals for controlled observation. Rats, cats, monkeys, and other animals all show symptoms of abnormal social, sexual, and motivational behavior following lesions of the frontal lobes. Still, the entire cortex, not just the frontal area, is extensively interconnected with the deeper-lying structures of the emotive brain. And lesions sustained anywhere in the brain, caused by tumors, penetrating missile wounds, epilepsy, or other disease, can produce striking deficits in emotional, social, and motivational behavior.

Figure 9.6. Bust and skull of Phineas Gage and the tamping bar that drove the hole through his frontal lobe. He survived but with so changed a personality that he seemed a different man. By permission of the Warren Anatomical Museum, Harvard University Medical School, Boston.

SUMMARY

The existence of cognons is supported by strong neurological as well as psychological evidence. Anatomical localization of particular categories of cognons in different analyzers is shown by the selective defects of functions. There is abundant proof that *unilateral* temporal lobectomy results in specialized memory deficits, depending on which hemisphere, left or right, has been invaded. Patients with temporal lesions in the speech-dominant hemisphere (usually the left) have measurable defects in verbal memory; a corresponding removal from the nondominant right hemisphere leaves verbal memory intact but impairs visual, spatial, and auditory memory. In both groups, the deficits are greater, the larger the invasion of the hippocampal structures attached to the temporal lobectomy. The hippocampus must serve a vital function in the retention of simple information in the fact of distraction.

SUGGESTED READINGS

Bender, M.B. *Disorders in perception.* Springfield, Ill.: Thomas, 1952.

Benson, D.F., & Blumer, D. *Psychiatric aspects of neurologic disease.* New York: Grune & Stratton, 1975.

Critchley, M. *The parietal lobes.* New York: Hafner, 1966. (Originally published, 1953).

Geschwind, N. Disconnexion syndromes in animals and man. II. *Brain,* 1965, *88,* 585–644.

Geschwind, N. *Selected papers on language and the brain.* Boston: D. Reidel, 1974.

Hamburg, D.A., Pribram, K.H., & Stunkard, A.J. (Eds.). *Perception and its disorders.* Baltimore: Williams & Wilkins, 1970.

Hécaen, H. Clinical symptomatology in right and left hemisphere lesions. In V.B. Mountcastle (Ed.), *Interhemisphere relations and cerebral dominance.* Baltimore: Johns Hopkins Press, 1962.

Hécaen, H., & Albert, M.L. Disorders of mental functioning related to frontal lobe pathology. In D.F. Benson & D. Blumer, *Psychiatric aspects of neurologic disease.* New York: Grune & Stratton, 1975.

Hécaen, H., & Albert, M.L. *Human neuropsychology.* New York: Wiley, 1978.

Konorski, J. Pathophysiological mechanisms of speech on the basis of studies of aphasia. *Acta Neurobiologie Experimentalis,* 1970, *30,* 189–210.

Luria, A.R. *Higher cortical functions in man.* New York: Basic Books, 1966.

Luria, A.R. *Human brain and psychological processes.* New York: Harper & Row, 1966.

Nicholi, A.M., Jr. *The Harvard guide to modern psychiatry.* Cambridge: The Belknap Press of Harvard University Press, 1978.

Pribram, K.H., & Broadbent, D.E. (Eds.). *Biology of memory.* New York: Academic Press, 1970.

Rioch, D. McK., & Weinstein, E.A. (Eds.). *Disorders of communication.* (Research publications: Association for research in nervous and mental disease, Vol. 42.) New York: Hafner, 1969.

Talland, G.A., & Waugh, N.C. (Eds.), *The pathology of memory.* New York: Academic Press, 1969.

Weinstein, E.A. Behavioral disorders associated with hemi-inattention. In E.A. Weinstein & R.P. Friedland (Eds.), *Hemi-inattention and hemispheric specialization.* New York: Raven Press, 1977.

Weiskrantz, L. Experimental studies of amnesia. In C.W.M. Whitty & O.L. Zangwill (Eds.), *Amnesia.* London: Butterworths, 1966.

CHAPTER TEN

Thinking, Attention Span, and Judgment

How many several objects can the mind simultaneously survey, not with vivacity, but without absolute confusion? I find this problem stated and differently answered, by different philosophers, and apparently without a knowledge of each other. By Charles Bonnet the mind is allowed to have a distinct notion of six objects at once; by Abraham Tucker the number is limited to four; while Destutt-Tracy again amplifies it to six. The opinion of the first and last of these philosophers, appears to me correct. You can easily make the experiment for yourselves, but you must beware of grouping the objects into classes. If you throw a handful of marbles on the floor, you will find it difficult to view at once more than six, or seven at most, without confusion; but if you group them into twos, or threes, or fives, you can comprehend as many groups as you can units; because the mind considers these groups only as units.

Sir William Hamilton, 1859

The number of items that can be perceived at any moment is extremely small.... Such limitation of perception cannot be separated from similar limitations in memory and, in fact, perceptual span and memory span are not distinguished in psychological experiments. One can hold in immediate memory and manipulate, as in mental arithmetic, only a certain number of items, whether these are derived by perception or by recall. Experience

consists of a succession of such groups of items. It is as if the brain produces
"quanta" of activity and experience consists of a sequence of such groups or
"quanta."

Lashley, 1954

INTRODUCTION

In this chapter we focus on the problem of thought—a problem many believe
to be the most important and the most challenging to confront the
neuropsychologist. Donald O. Hebb, brilliant author of the first book to
allude in its title to neuropsychology, *The Organization of Behavior: A
Neuropsychological Theory,* published in 1949, considered the problem of
thought central to psychology. Hebb saw it as "some sort of process that is not
fully controlled by environmental stimulation yet cooperates closely with that
stimulation. From another point of view, physiology, the problem is that of
the transmission of excitation from sensory to motor cortex" (p. xvi). Hebb
continues: "The failure to handle thought adequately or how to conceive of
cortical transmission has been the essential weakness of modern psychological
theory" (Hebb, 1949, p. xvi).

That failure persists. Humans take pride in their capacity for thought—
especially for productive, creative thinking. Yet neuropsychologists become
tongue-tied when the topic of our most treasured mental activity arises.
Thought, if effective, expresses itself in action. Sometimes, however, the goal
of thought is to *delay action.* You decide to wait until conditions are more
propitious, or you try to arrange optimal conditions. Thinking is a way of
discovering obstacles and devising a way to overcome them—to make plans
and anticipate possible consequences before taking action. In what follows, I
would like to present a set of behavioral considerations that neuroscientists
need to take into account if they wish to address complex behavior.

RECENT OR TRANSIENT MEMORY

Consider the important constructive role in thought of transient memory
processes—the short-term planning for future behavior. You may decide in
the morning while getting dressed what must be done that day: letters to write,
a trip to the cleaners, a lecture to be prepared, library books to return,
shopping needed. The list may be kept entirely in mind, directing behavior,
and as the items are accomplished, they are crossed off to make room for other
images. The delay may be much longer than a few minutes; it lasts overnight
when you put your keys in a certain dresser and know exactly where to find

Figure 10.1. Alice and the White Queen. In Lewis Carroll's (1896) *Looking Glass* world, the White Queen lived in reverse. "There's one great advantage in it," she said, "that one's memory works both ways."

them in the morning. The ability to keep a mental list is important. It is important also to keep track of the priorities and the order in which things must be done. Konorski (1967) calls this role of transient memory its *prospective* role. It is your mental agenda or action program. (See Figure 10.1.)

Another side of this process is its *retrospective* aspect—that is, the recent memory of the acts that you have actually performed. One must remember that one has locked the back door, turned off the radio, the lights, and the stove before leaving the house; otherwise one must return in order to check. One must remember that one has taken one's medicine and notified the post office of one's forwarding address. Both prospective and retrospective memory play significant roles in our ongoing behavior.

The sensitization theory of transient memory implies that the recurrently activated cognons are in a state of facilitation because there is an after-discharge of enhanced neurotransmitter at the presynaptic terminals. The sensitized cognons are grasped by the new stimulus patterns, and images appear obsessively, not on the basis of association, but on the basis of sensitization of the appropriate units and their arousal both by specific and nonspecific facilitating impulses. Lying in bed after the day's work and play, we call to mind the events of our day and experience the corresponding images much as we experience the actual events as they occur.

The prospective use of transient memory is its ability to help us program our activities for the immediate future. Images of all these future tasks recur until they are done; then we make use of retrospective transient memory to check off the list.

THE DELAYED REACTION EXPERIMENT

Precisely this type of behavior in experiments on animals and children was introduced by Walter Hunter (1913) and called the "delayed response" or "delayed reaction" experiment. This important research was the first evidence of rudimentary symbolic processes in nonverbal organisms. The subject receives a cue signaling the location of the food or a toy but is not free to go there until after a delay.

These investigations typically sought answers to the following questions: (1) What is the maximal delay period between cue and response for various species of animals? (2) What cues does the subject use? (3) If bodily orientation toward the correct goal is prevented, or if the animal is distracted during the delay, in what way is the delay period "bridged" by the subject? The subject's behavior during the interval may throw light on the nature of the symbolic process.

The results of these studies clearly suggest that when bodily orientation is not maintained during the interval of delay, the cue for "locating" the food tray in space during the action of the preparatory stimulus must necessarily furnish the cue that the animal actually uses in the postdelay run. The memory of this cue must then be based purely on intracentral neural processes going on in the brain during the delay period. These are the processes of recent or transient memory.

Where in the Brain Are the Cues?

Where are these transient memory traces localized? According to the cognon theory, we may assume that the recent memory of particular stimuli depends on the cognitive fields involved in their perceptions and images. Thus damage to a particular cognitive field will destroy the particular cognons representing certain objects. For instance, a lesion of the audioverbal field will produce a loss of transient memory for words and damage of the face-cognitive field will abolish transient memory of familiar faces.

Evidence that this is so is brought out dramatically by experiments following surgical ablation of different parts of the brain (See Chapter Nine).

The delayed response test concerns a particular kind of recent memory— the recent memory of directions in space. Jacobsen (1935) showed that delayed responses are dramatically impaired or abolished by prefrontal lesions in monkeys and apes. Presumably the recent memory for the spatial itinerary to the goal is located in the prefrontal cortex.

The special significance of lesions of the prefrontal area is the impairment of the ability to plan (or delay) motor behaviors because their images are destroyed. The lack of kinesthetic imagery of particular types of behavioral acts explains why it is that patients who are able to recall an instruction and can even repeat it verbatim are yet unable to fulfill it. Their knowledge is preserved in the cognitive fields of their auditory or visual analyzers, but it is disconnected by the prefrontal lesion from their motor cortex, and the performance fails.

One cannot conclude, however, that all recent memory depends upon the intact functioning of the frontal lobes. Konorski and Lawicka (1964) developed a diagnostic test to study the recent memory of various modalities. Using tones of various pitch, lights of various intensity, and tactile stimuli applied to various places on the body, their test consisted of the following simple schedule. The experimenter presented a compound consisting of two stimuli in which (1) the same stimulus, whatever it was, when repeated twice (SxSx) was reinforced; (2) two different stimuli (SxSy) were not followed by reinforcement. When the first component in either case is applied, the subject does not know whether reinforcement will follow, because this depends on the comparison with the second component that is presented several seconds after the first one. Thus the subject cannot prepare in advance or use proprioceptive cues as in the delayed response test.

The results are clear-cut. When the stimuli both belong to the same modality—visual, auditory, or tactile—ablation of the prefrontal area does not impair performance on this test. Yet ablation of the anterior parts of the temporal gyri affected the test of auditory memory, and ablation of the posterior parts of the inferotemporal area led to a similar impairment of visual memory. Each part of the brain thus assumes responsibility for its own modality of recent memory. The division of categories of perception between cortical areas of the brain thus has its counterpart in recall—as much for recent events as for stable or permanent long-term memories.

THE PROBLEM OF SERIAL ORDER IN THOUGHT AND ACTION

In a remarkably persuasive paper, entitled "The Problem of Serial Order in Behavior," Karl Lashley, the influential neuropsychologist, pointed to what seemed to him to be "the most important and also the most neglected problem of cerebral physiology" (1951, p. 114). He called attention to temporal integration as an aspect of the most complex functions of the brain that reach their highest development in human thought processes—especially language. Not only language, but the logical and orderly arrangement of many types of behavior, in animals as well as humans, is their most striking feature. As Lashley wrote: "Temporal integration is not found exclusively in language; the coordination of leg movements in insects, the song of birds, the control of trotting and pacing in a gaited horse, the rat running the maze, the architect designing the house, and the carpenter sawing a board present a problem of sequences of action which cannot be explained in terms of successions of external stimuli" (1951, p. 144).

In midcentury, the only explicitly physiological theory that attempted to account for the temporal coordination of serial activity postulated chains of reflexes in which the performance of each element of the chain provides excitation of the next.

Donald O. Hebb (1949) formulated the first "neuropsychological" theory of thought to account for the performance of complex, temporally integrated activity. He postulated chains of sensory neurons in which the activation of each element of the series led to the excitation of its neighbor across the adjoining synapse. Repeated stimulation of specific receptors would then lead to the formation of a "cell assembly" that could act briefly after stimulation has ceased and prolong the time available for stabilizing the pattern of activity into a structural growth. The theory claimed to account for expectancy, attention, and interest. Implicit in it is the view that perceiving is a simple chain of central processes in which each element serves to arouse the next by direct association. Hebb was thinking in terms of simple associative chains, built up by experience and maintained by reverberating loops of excitation. Although not attacking Hebb's view directly, Karl Lashley (1951) raised a number of critical objections to the associative chain theory, and subsequent evidence on perceptual and motor organization shows clearly that the cell assembly account is untenable. Instead, we find a multiplicity of integrative processes, largely autonomous and separably reactive to influences from both above and below. The chain association theory, whether of cell assemblies in perception or motor sequences in action, does not work.

Lashley (1951) argued that the order of vocal movements in pronouncing a word, the order of words in a sentence, the order of sentences in a paragraph, and the order of ideas in thought have no intrinsic dependence on temporally adjacent elements. Instead each element takes its position from associations with remote as well as with near meanings. He gave a particularly good example with the sentence, "The mill-wright on my right thinks it right that some conventional rite should symbolize the right of every man to write as he pleases" (p. 116). Here the word "right" (with its homophones) is noun, adjective, adverb, and verb, with at least 10 meanings that are determined not by any direct associations with other words but by broader relations. The meanings (and the spelling) of the word "right" in the sentence are not inherent in the words themselves. The order is imposed by some other agent.

The Schema of Order

If order is not inherent either in the motor units themselves or the ideas to be expressed, then what imposes the serial order on behavior? All psychologists

Figure 10.2. Continuing set.

assume some factor of *set* or *determining tendency* to account for the persistent steering force that orders and directs adaptive behavior over its time course.

Set as a genuine fact of behavior is illustrated by the alert posture of runners on the starting line of a race and later, in the way they take the curves of the race track, leaning inward. (See Figure 10.2.) Some generalized pattern obviously initiates and continues to regulate and coordinate specific acts as they occur.

This is evident also in the ease with which a new structure can be imposed upon motor activity. Speech and written language present striking examples. Consider the facility with which a translator provides an instantaneous replay into English or a foreign language with a radically different syntax, or the quickness with which children can invert words or restructure them into pig Latin. The frequent transposition errors in typing, writing "thses" for "these" or "adaption" for "adaptation" are anticipatory in nature. Contaminations in speech ("Time heals all wounds" becomes "time wounds all heels") are added evidence that remote letters or words are readied in advance of their proper place in a sentence and expressed too early.

These common examples suggest a preprogramming of expressive units prior to their actual activation. But the mechanism is subject to interference.

Just now I wrote "infer..." before I checked myself and changed to "interference." Distraction or haste trips the holding device that keeps these units in check until they are called for. There is an over-readiness to react, and, without some warning device, a catch test or "Vexirversuche" as in a reaction time experiment, the anticipatory set overrides the effectiveness of the checking mechanism and an error results.

Stimulus factors, direct sensory factors, direct sensory stimuli play a minor part in regulating either the intensity or duration of physiological events serving well-practiced or anticipated perceptual or motor activity. A unitary perception or motor act can be preset or primed by preparatory activity independently of any sensory controls.

The rapidity with which successive acts in sequence can occur is far greater than can be accounted for by summating reaction times to the individual segments of the coordinated sequence. In successive finger movements, the pianist may strike as many as 16 keys in definite and changing order far more rapidly than could be achieved in the time required to read the notes or to obtain sensory feedback for the muscles involved in playing. Some preliminary process of excitation plays a decisive role in temporal integration.

Such patterns of coordinated movement may be transferred directly to other systems than the one practiced. The pianist can transpose the pattern of finger movements to another key or transfer playing from the right to the left hand. In such transfer, as from the right to the left side of the body, an analysis of the movements shows, not a reduplication of the muscular patterns on the two sides but a reproduction of movements in relation to the space coordinates of the body. Not specific movements, but trajectories of the movements, are retained in the transformation. The amplitude, speed, and directions of movement relative to body position are invariant. Thus, if the right arm is rotated forward and swung to the right, the left arm will rotate forward and swing to the left. Systems of space coordinates influence the motor system so that every movement of body or limbs is made with reference to the space system. Sight and hearing, the distance receptors, are also constantly modified and referred to the same space coordinates. Memories of objects also position them in the space system. In fact, as the research on mnemonics shows, images of spatial position or *loci* are among the most helpful cues to recall the identity of objects.

Curiously, the role of spatial position may be interchangeable with that of temporal position. In order to develop a viable theory of thought it may be helpful to look at the close interconnections between memory for spatial position, memory for temporal position or serial order, and attention. Perhaps a unifying concept underlying these seemingly diverse functions may be found in a simple idea—the concept of span, and the associated limitations on our ability to process information.

THE CONCEPT OF SPAN

The unifying concept is the *span*—the span of attention, the span of immediate memory, the span or scale of absolute judgment. The span of attention points to the limitation of stimuli to exert control over responses. The fundamental fact of attention is that only some of the potential stimulus flux acts as *input* to the organism. Attention is selective. The memory span stresses the parallel fact of limitation on the *output* of the system. Memory is selective. There is a third, less well-recognized span, *intermediate* between, but also overlapping and controlling the other two. Noting the increasingly longer sentences spoken by children as they grew older, Brown and Fraser (1963) referred to the *programming* span and the corresponding limitations on the creative constructions of language.

The concept of span, derived from the span of the hand, conveys two ideas. One is the distance between two limits. How wide is the extent or space between the tip of the thumb and the tip of the little finger in the outspread hand? Here is a handy portable *scale,* a standard of comparison that can be applied repeatedly anywhere—to a height, to a width, to a circumference. The second idea stresses the act of grasping and the associated strategy of comprehension. How much can be encompassed at one time by opposing thumb and fingers, by focusing and converging the eyes, by a selective operation of the mind?

In the literature of psychology we find references to a variety of spans: the span of apprehension or attention, the span of immediate memory, the span of absolute judgment, the eye-voice span in reading, the eye-hand span in telegraphy and typing, and, as noted here, the programming span in creating new sentences, or in reciting digits backwards in intelligence tests. Although the relevant experiments are widely separated under different headings and appear to answer different questions about diverse materials and sense modalities, certain common characteristics are striking. I would like to draw your attention to a remarkable uniformity in these diverse span functions and to suggest a single underlying mechanism in the central nervous system. This is a hypothesis—to be accepted or rejected on the basis of the evidence. The next section examines the evidence.

THE SPAN OF ATTENTION, MEMORY, AND JUDGMENT

If an individual can recite six digits after one reading lasting one-tenth of a second, how many readings (or how much time) will she require for 12 digits? Clearly, the problem cannot be solved by simple proportion, but demands an experiment. Many experiments show clearly that the time jumps disproportionately beyond six.

Woodworth noted several challenging facts demonstrated by the simple test for digit span: "The fact that the memory span is limited presents something of an enigma; for if you can recite six digits immediately after hearing them, why can you not hold these, take on six more and recite the whole twelve? If you run over the list a few times, then you can recite it in its entirety. This effect of repetition is (another) fact to be explained..." (1938, p. 17).

We do not know why the span is limited, or why it expands with mental age (from two digits at age 2½, to six digits at age 10 and up to eight digits at "Superior Adult" levels) (Terman & Merrill, 1972), or how repetition achieves its effects over shorter periods of time.

Hunter and Sigler (1940) viewed the span of apprehension as a problem in visually controlled discriminative behavior and studied the effects of known stimulus factors, exposure time, intensity, and the number of objects presented on the *ability to discriminate this number*. They varied the conditions over a wide range, and by including the important initial portions (small number and brief exposures) revealed a basic discontinuity in the function relating the span to total stimulus energy.

Hunter and Sigler found that the number span depended on both light intensity and duration of exposure in conformity with the Bunsen-Roscoe law when the number of dots ranged from 1–7 dots. For larger numbers, above 7–8 dots, the compensation of intensity for the short exposure time did not work; more time was then necessary to enable the subject to count or to group the dots.

They interpreted their results as follows: "The span of discrimination from 1–7 dots, which is a single discriminatory event, is determined by the photochemical processes in the eye up to that duration at which the sensory contribution is complete..."(p. 177). Beyond that critical duration, increasing the exposure time had no influence on the span; the event in question was over. For reports of larger numbers of dots, longer durations are necessary because we are dealing with more than one event—even eight dots involves counting and takes us over the boundary of a single discriminative event.

Subsequent investigators (Hurvich, 1940; Kaufman, Lord, Reese, & Volkmann, 1949) have argued that the limitation is central, not sensory, and have obtained reaction time data that support the inference that there is one primary process mediating the discrimination of small numbers of dots and that additional processes are required to mediate the discrimination of large numbers.

A series of experimenters (Von Szeliski, 1924; Saltzman & Garner, 1948; Kaufman et al., 1949) found an increase of reaction time as the number of dots increased from 1–6 dots. In every case, there was a discontinuity in the curve at about six dots. Kaufman (1949) presented randomly arranged fields of dots from 1–210, and found two functions, one holding up to six dots and then changing abruptly to a different function between report time or confidence and the number of stimuli presented.

The traditional test for the span of attention or apprehension requires the subject to identify what he has seen or heard following a single presentation of the stimuli. He has only one trial with any one group of items. The present experiments extend the usual procedure by exposing the same items repeatedly and requiring the subject to attempt to reproduce them after each exposure. The repetitions are continued until the reproduction is perfect, and the number of repetitions required gives a measure of the difficulty of the task in each case.

By this simple extension, the experiment on the span of attention becomes an experiment on learning or memorizing and provides a bridge between processes ordinarily treated under separate headings.

This coupling of perception and memory in a single experiment also reveals some unsuspected links between the different spans: the span of attention, the span of absolute judgment, and the span of immediate memory, and helps unify and explain these previously unrelated phenomena.

LIMITS ON THE IMMEDIATE MEMORY SPAN

There is compelling psychological evidence that more than one process is involved in normal memory. Consider verbal memory. In the serial retention of well-defined verbal items such as digits, letters, or words, each item enters a temporary storage system from which it can be retrieved as long as attention to it can be sustained. This temporary store is called *immediate memory span, primary memory, transient, or short term memory,* interchangeably. Two limitations on immediate memory span are well established. They are the number of items in the series and the rate or duration of exposure at which they are presented. (Hunter & Sigler, 1940; Waugh & Norman 1965). The physiological traces do not decay autonomously in time, but are disrupted by shifts of attention—that is, by competing processes—as the targeting reflex (attention) is diverted to new stimuli.

The traditional experiment on the span of immediate memory requires the subject to identify the items exposed after a single hearing or a visual display that is too brief to permit a shift of fixation.

Experiments on the immediate memory span all agree in showing a definite upper limit at about the same small number of responses. The exact value of this limit varies from one subject to another, with stimulus conditions and with the variety of things experimenters have counted.

Even so, the range has been surprisingly narrow. As George Miller (1956) showed in his famous paper with the intriguing title, "The Magical Number Seven, Plus or Minus Two: Some Limits on Our Capacity for Processing Information," there is abundant evidence of a small, definite upper limit to the span of immediate memory.

For the average human subject, under given conditions, the limit, in terms of responses, whether they are the spoken names of letters, words, or numbers, shows a remarkable constancy, the constancy of a single *cognon* or *perception* unit.

From one type of span to the next, for college students, under a variety of laboratory conditions, the limiting *number* found by one experimenter after the other, has turned out to be *six*. (Hunter & Sigler, 1940; Kaufman et al., 1949; Pollack & Ficks, 1954; Saltzman & Garner, 1948; Taves, 1941; Waugh, 1960; Simon, 1974). Whatever the stimulus materials, whether visually or orally presented; whatever the method of measurement, direct recall or reaction time, there is clear evidence of two processes, one process below *six* items, and another process above that magic number. In every case, the results show a dramatic *discontinuity*—and inevitably in the same place—at *six*.

Thus the span of attention can encompass no more than *six* items, or *six* well-organized groups of items. The span of short-term memory shows that *six* items can be identified in the order in which they were presented after one reading.

THE SCALE OF ABSOLUTE JUDGMENT

The span or *scale of absolute judgment* (the rating scale) can distinguish no more than *six* categories for many different sensory attributes and dimensions of judgment. Although this method, sometimes called the method of *single stimuli*, is usually considered under the head of psychophysics, it provides a measurement not only of sensory magnitude but also of short-term memory. The experiment confronts the observer with one member of a series of stimuli to be judged against the background of the assemblage of preceding stimuli. (See discussion in Woodworth & Schlosberg, 1954, p. 97ff.) Each stimulus as it comes is to be judged in absolute categories—as *high, medium, low*—or ordinal numbers—*one* to *seven*, or *nine*, or *twelve*—or as many as the subject wants to use to rate the subjective magnitude of the stimuli along the dimension specified.

The first few stimuli are judged pretty much at random, but the subject soon adjusts to the range of stimuli encountered and uses the categories consistently, corresponding closely to the physical stimuli. If the experimenter then shifts the range of stimuli, as by removing the lowest and adding higher ones, the subject shifts the subjective scale and readjusts the categories to suit (Volkmann, 1936; Rogers, 1941; McGarvy, 1943).

The important point is that the judgments, although absolute in form and made one at a time, are actually relative to the presented group of stimuli; that is, they are stimulus-anchored by the upper and lower bounds of the stimulus range that must be kept in the memory store during successive judgments.

The results of these experiments clearly demonstrate that subjects can use no more than *six* categories of response, regardless of the physical range or density of the stimuli presented. If the subject uses more than six categories, the scale breaks into two or more segments, no one of which contains more than six subjective categories of judgment (Taves, 1941; Kaufman et al., 1949).

THE NUMBER SPAN

Nowhere is this limitation more clearly illustrated than in the traditional experiment on the *span of attention,* actually the *number span* in which the subject reports "how many" items were presented, too briefly to be counted, to each one of a display of dots containing anywhere from one to one hundred dots. Or the stimuli may be successively presented too rapidly to be counted, either visually in a series of flashes or auditorily in a series of beeps. In all of these diverse experiments on judged numerousness, one result stands out. It is that the judged number matches the presented stimulus number when *six* or fewer items are presented. The judged number continues to increase as the number of stimuli increase, but beyond six the typical result increasingly underestimates the presented number. Here is about as good evidence as one could wish that there is a natural process with a clearly determinable upper limit that does not exceed *six*. This process, called *subitizing* (from the Latin *subito,* suddenly) is to be distinguished from *counting* and also from *estimating.* It is an immediate or unitary perception and thus represents the activity of one *cognon.*

THE MAGIC NUMBER *SIX*

The result is amazing. It is not tied to any single procedure. The span of attention, the span of absolute judgment, the subitizing span, the immediate memory span for digits or other verbal materials all exhibit a uniform and dependable invariance. The invariant feature appears to lie in the behavior of the organism who is responding and not in the stimuli or manipulations of the experimenter.

I wish to emphasize the amazing constancy with which the number *six* designates, not a stimulus set, but a *response set,* the set of ordered categories of verbal response. For a wide variety of methods and experiments, the limit of immediate memory, in terms of responses, whether they are the spoken names of letters, words, or numbers, shows a remarkable constancy from one type of memory span to the next.

Herbert A. Simon (1974), Nobel Prize winner and professor of computer science and psychology at Carnegie-Mellon University, gives a striking example. He cites evidence about the formation of higher-order cognons ("chunks") from experiments on chess perception. Adriaan de Groot (1965) put chess positions taken from actual games in front of subjects; then, after about five seconds he removed the 20 to 25 pieces and asked the subjects to reconstruct the positions. Chess grandmasters and masters could do this without error; amateurs could locate only about a half-dozen pieces correctly. But the remarkable difference vanished when the pieces were arranged on the board at random. Then the grand masters and masters performed no better than the amateurs. Their performance in the first situation cannot be explained by attributing to them some extraordinary perceptual capability.

What the chess expert can do is based upon the wealth of associations he has formed from experience with actual games. These associations relate every square, every piece and its permissible moves, and every position to one another into the same number of cognons as in the random pattern. The chess master has preorganized mental structures—the standardized language of chess—that enable him to recode the chess position composed of 24 pieces into six higher-order cognons. This familiar vocabulary enables the chess master to duplicate the position of every piece rapidly and accurately without even looking at the board. From this and further studies, Simon concludes that "the psychological reality of the chunk has been fairly well demonstrated, and the chunk capacity of short term memory has been shown to be in the range of five to seven" (Simon, 1974, p. 487).

What is a "chunk?" In our view, it's a *higher-order cognon*—that is, a perception unit formed through experience that integrates the distinctive features of a given position and can readily be stored in memory until needed for later recall.

Other examples can be added. Consider the six primary colors, including black and white (three opponent color pairs); six odors in Henning's smell prism (Woodworth & Schlosberg, 1954); observers can make absolute identifications of six tactual points in Braille; six absolute pitches in tones (Pollack & Ficks, 1954); six visual areas (Reese, Reese, Volkmann & Corbin, 1946–1952); six lengths of lines (Reese et al., 1953); six words in speech uttered between pauses or hesitations (Goldman-Eisler, 1954); and six days to create the universe (Genesis).

But, you will object, the span is not truly invariant. "Superior adults" as already noted, achieve a digit memory span of eight or more items, the average six-year-old no more than four; Newton identified seven colors, and our week contains seven days. Miller (1956b.) also recognized this slippage in the title of his paper when he added "plus or minus two." Within mental age groups there is a good deal of variation also.

Fair enough. But the discovery of a precise numerical constant (nearly invariant) is so rare in psychology that we cannot afford to dismiss it as mere coincidence or magic without further searching and examination. Is there some way to account for these observed variations?

There are two problems. First, can we determine what causes the span in our experiments to vary? Second, can we discover whether there is a neurological constant that we can fine-tune at its core?

With regard to the first problem, we need to find systematic variations in the span that are correlated with particular experimental conditions.

SYSTEMATIC CONSTRAINTS ON THE SPAN

There is, in fact, abundant evidence for such systematic constraints. Upon investigating, we find that the precise numerical value of the span is systematically controlled by three sets of conditions.

1. The mental age of the subject
2. The conditions of stimulation, i.e., the amount, rate, duration, intensity, and past frequency of use of the stimulus items
3. The amount of information demanded in the report, i.e., whether the report requires an answer to one or more of these questions about the input data:
    How many? (how much?)—quantity
    Of what sort? (what is it?)—quality
    In what order? (where?)—position

The traditional experiment (Woodworth, 1938, p. 686) on the span of attention (the number span) gives the answer to the first question under condition 3—How many?—the discrimination of quantity. The span thus measured is a special case of the absolute judgment scale and a pure example of the "natural number" of categories. (See Figure 10.3.)

ORDER AND ITEM EXPERIMENTS

In the typical experiment on the immediate memory span, the subject's task is more complicated, although it seems merely to ask for the items that can be

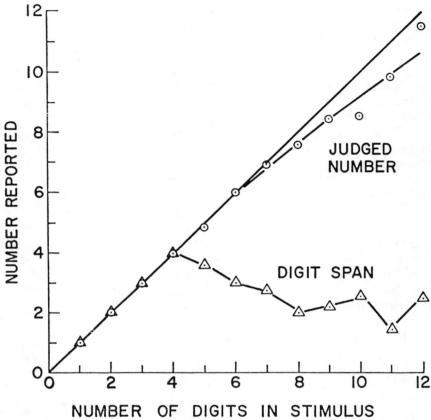

Figure 10.3. "Subitizing." When the subject is instructed to report the *number* of digits presented, the judged number is correctly reported ("subitized") up to six items. Beyond *six,* judged number continues to increase with presented number but at a declining rate and the number is underestimated. The same subject under identical conditions but instructed to repeat the digits in order gave the function plotted here (triangles).

reproduced correctly after a single reading. In reciting the list, the subject has actually two tasks: she must *identify* the digits (or other items), tell *what* they are, and *order* them by placing each item in its correct *location* in the sequence.

Experiments are needed to determine whether the two tasks thus confounded can be separated, and whether each one independently gives rise to the same numerical span. To separate the *order* from the *item* information, I undertook such experiments (Gilinsky, 1964) using digit strings flashed on a screen for .010 second. Each string was repeated until the subject could recall it correctly. The number of repetitions or exposure duration was the dependent variable. There were three sets of instructions:

1. *Serial order* instructions
    Forward: "Name the digits from left to right in the usual order."
    Backward: "Reverse the order and name the digits backward, from right to left."
2. *Free recall—any order* instructions
    "Just name the digits that you see in any order you wish. Pay no regard to the position in which they appear or to their repetitions within the string. You need only identify what digits there are."
3. *Identity given—order required*
    The subject is told in advance of the stimulus exposure what the digits are and how many there are. For example, "You will see six digits; they will consist of the numerals 1,2,3,4,5, and 6, but they will be in some other order than the natural number sequence. Just tell me what that order is in which you see them."

Experimental Results

The length of exposure required for correct recall *(duration threshold)* was used to measure immediate memory span. It is an inverse measure because the longer the time, the smaller the momentary span. The data (see Figure 10.4) for both the forward order and the backward order fall on the same lines and are fitted by one function—with two branches. The lower branch extends from 1 to 5 digits, and it shows that duration thresholds increase regularly with an increase in the number presented, even within the immediate memory span, below six digits. At this point there is a *discontinuity* in the slope of the function. The upper branch starts at six digits and rises steeply as the number increases to nine digits, the limiting number for this subject at this stage of practice.

The lowest line shows the results for free recall. A single straight line with no discontinuity at all is the remarkable finding. When the subject is free to report the digits in *any order,* thresholds are lower, the discontinuity disappears, and a single continuous function relates performance to the number of items presented.

What happens when ordering, but not identifying is required, the subject having been told what digits to expect?

The results (see Figure 10.5) give two surprises. First, there is a sharp break in the functions. *Ordering* alone is sufficient to produce the characteristic discontinuity. Second, the break appears, not between five and six, but at

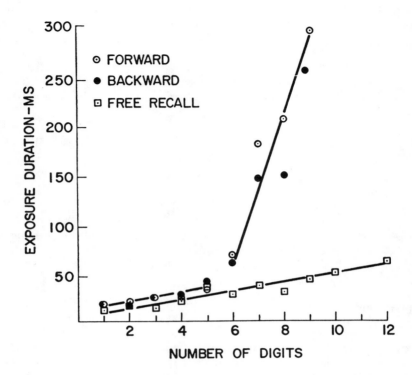

Figure 10.4. Strings of 1–12 digits were flashed briefly on the screen. The number of repetitions required for correct recall is plotted against the number of digits in the string. The total duration of exposure affords a measure of the digit memory span and increases regularly as the presented number of digits increase from one to five digits. Note the sharp discontinuity at *six* digits for *ordered* recall, both forward and backward.

four digits. From one to four, a horizontal straight line is a good fit for the date points; beyond four, the curve rises steeply as the number of digits increases.

This new lower bound on the digit span was puzzling. Why only four? A plausible hypothesis suggested that brevity of exposure, by increasing the difficulty of the task, reduced the span.

To test this idea, a second traditional experiment was run, requiring identifying and ordering of digits. The new feature was to add six different durations of exposure from 10 to 100 milliseconds. Figure 10.6 shows the results. Each function has two branches, but the break between the two comes at different points, increasing with increasing exposure duration to *six*. The digit span is systematically influenced by the difficulty of the task.

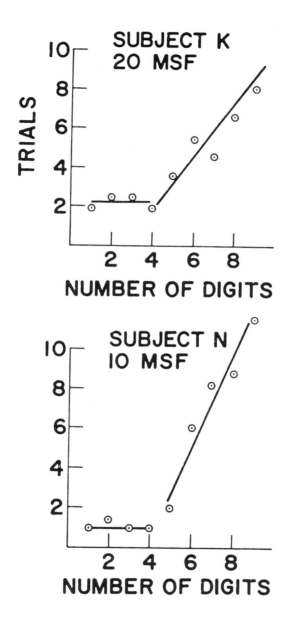

Figure 10.5. Recognition thresholds in terms of frequency of exposure required for correct arrangement in forward order of digits whose identity is already known.

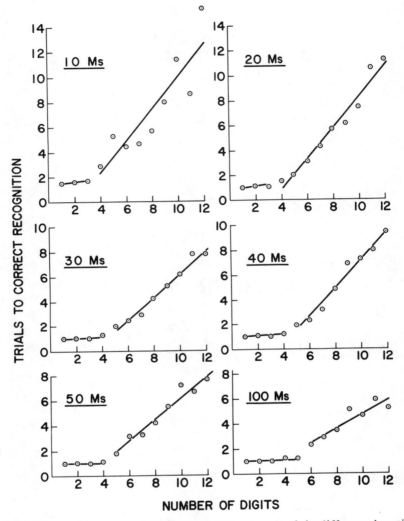

Figure 10.6. Mean recognition thresholds at each of six different durations of exposure shown at the upper left of each plot. Every function shows two branches: (1) a primary branch that grows from three to five digits as the duration of exposure is increased from 10 to 100 ms. and (2) a secondary branch fitted to a least squaresline. The slopes of these computed functions decrease fairly regularly as duration of exposure increases, as follows: 1.29, 1.25, 0.94, 1.14, 0.85, 0.57, corresponding to 10, 20, 30, 40, 50, and 100 ms., respectively. Beyond the span of immediate memory, the task gets easier with more exposure time. Given more time to look, the span itself expands in size but the upper limit is clearly fixed below six digits. Gilinsky, 1964.

THE ORDERING FUNCTION IN BEHAVIOR

The significant discovery is that the critical determinant of the discontinuity in the memory span is the requirement to preserve the order of position of each item in the series. Where the subject is free to report the digits in any order, the discontinuity disappears and is replaced by a single continuous function. Where the task demands that the subject report the digits in their correct order, forward or backward, the typical break is seen at three to six digits. The precise location of the break, the upper limit of the span depends on conditions—the time allowed for perception and the ability of the subject.

Since the discontinuity appears when ordering is required, but disappears when ordering is not required, we are compelled to conclude that order preservation is the critical determinant of the span. The ability to process information is limited by the quantity of data the subject can take in (exposure duration) and the number of responses to be placed in serial order in the report. What then determines the observed uniformity in these diverse experiments? The hypothesis I would propose is that these different spans are, indeed, all manifestations of a single underlying process. The unifying concept is an operation—the *ordering* function in behavior. A string of spatially extended numerals is not a mere juxtaposition of elements. The numerals are arranged in a certain order, and if that order is subtle or random and the subject has no familiar schemas available, he must improvise and find some satisfactory method of mapping the stimulus order. A mathematical demonstration, a train of logical reasoning, also demands a correct ordering of the elements. Isolated, unconnected, the contents mean nothing. It is the placing of them in order that is the heart of the feat.

The importance of serial ordering in behavior was emphasized by Lashley (1951), who suggested that every action is controlled not only by incoming stimuli, but also by an anticipatory plan possessing a specific order or structure. The anticipatory nature of the process shows itself in motor behavior, getting ready to run or strike; in common errors, transposition errors in typing; preplacement of items in speaking, or of turns in a maze.

Lashley (1951) argued persuasively that language, particularly the grammar or syntax of language, must be explained in terms of an anticipatory structure, not contained in the elements or the words themselves, but imposed upon the elements as they are received by a listener or produced by a speaker. Experiments (Brown, 1970; Braine, 1963; Lenneberg, 1967) on language learning by children show clearly that what is learned in addition to vocabulary is the grammatical order or structure of the language. The child must learn what goes next to what and how what comes *later*—sometimes several words removed in the sentence—changes the meaning and the inflection of what comes *earlier* in an utterance. Obviously, no simple associative, or left-right, one-dimensional, unidirectional device could accomplish this.

What is the range of action of this integrating mechanism? Certain obvious limits are suggested by the facts of the *time span* and the *space span* of behavior, by the limits of selective attention and short-term memory, and by the shifts and displacements of the subjective scale.

The number of categories a subject can organize into a single scale of judgment is definitely limited, and, further, if he has to use more categories, he will organize them into two or more single scales. The use of a second scale does not imply a second discriminatory mechanism, but rather a second application of the first one. The finding concerns the "natural" number of categories that a subject selects and uses after being shown the stimulus material. It is supported by evidence given by the discrimination of a number of different visual aspects, area, position, and number. The data show that no single scale contains more than *six* categories.

The present experiments on the digit span show that the critical determinant of the discontinuity in the span is the requirement to preserve the order or location of each item in the series. When the task demands that the subject report the digits in their correct order, forward or backward, the typical break is seen at 3–6 digits, depending on conditions. When the subject is free to report the digits in any order, the discontinuity disappears and a single continuous function is found to relate the performance to the number of digits presented.

What has ordering to do with the span of absolute judgment? Just this: to assign a category number to an object of judgment is to *order* it in a scale of subjective magnitudes. To call an object a *three* is to say something very specific not only about the object so assigned, but also about its relation to other objects above it and below it in the scale—to order them all in relation to *three,* the category on the number scale, and to each other. These other objects need not be represented in consciousness at the time. To take an example from Woodworth, "A 'heavy' baby is heavy in comparison with the general run of babies, but those other babies are not thought of while you are lifting the particular baby" (1938, p. 440).

In a subjective scale of judgment that is well anchored at both ends to the ends of the stimulus range, the responses are accurate, rapid, confident, and stable. The absolute scale shows its elasticity when one of the anchors is displaced upwards away from one end of the scale. But the scale is not indefinitely elastic, and under the stress of increasing displacement of the anchoring agent, eventually breaks down.

The same general principle applies to the memory span. Like the absolute scale, the memory span has a top and bottom, a lower and an upper bound. The initial items and the most recent ones are best retained. The serial position effects are evidence that the span, as well as the scale, is suppored by anchorages. When these anchorages are pulled too far apart, too many data to encompass and handle, the memory span reveals the upper limit of its elasticity and the performance breaks down.

THE COGWHEEL IN THE THINKING MACHINE

The key to the universality and flexibility of thought may be contained in the fundamental discontinuity and related shifting of the span or the scale. I like to think of it as revolving—a *cogwheel*. The function of the organic cogwheel is to transform physical processes by mapping cognons to objects and events. The hypothesis evolves from Kenneth Craik's (1943) idea that thought provides a small-scale model, a cognitive map, in which neural symbols represent physical things and relations in the external world. The power of the symbolic model to predict external events and to create new combinations may be attained at the expense of two features of physical models. (1) The symbolic model has no permanent or lasting existence; instead there are possibilities of repeated re-creations. Thought can leap from one order of magnitude to another—from the structure of the single cell to the structure of the universe—and back again. (2) The symbolic model contains no large quantity of data or detail. Instead, there is a small number of distinctive features, anchors, or symbolic markers in any single map. The capability is that of a miniature, highly versatile scale model that permits rapid shifts from one map to another of the same or different terrains.

Within the finite time span of a single behavioral event, the average adult can form well-ordered sets of exactly *six* categories, no more. The average three-year-old child can form well-ordered sets of *three* categories or elements. The small span of the child reflects a cognitive limitation of the immature central nervous system. Certainly it cuts across single sensory modalities; what data are available for children are uniform. The three-year-old counts to three, responds to commands at the count of three, has both a visual memory span and an auditory span of three, and finally composes sentences of three words, whereas last year he was limited to two.

Under some conditions (e.g., 10 millisecond exposures), the average adult is reduced to the level of a three-year-old. The diminutions of the span observed in adults results partly from sensory constraint, partly from changes in grouping strategy. The normal adult can respond in less than six, but no more than *six ordered categories* to stimuli presented to any modality. In other words, the span seems to be a joint function of central cerebral development and stimulus conditions that may be more or less optimal. The developmental stage of the central nervous system sets the upper limit of the span functions; within the limit thus imposed, the differential sensitivity of the receptors and the controlling stimulus variables exert their further constraints on the behavior we call "thinking."

The conclusion is compelling that the number *six* is the precise numerical constant we are seeking in psychology, but that it designates not a stimulus set, but a response set—the set of ordered categories that controls a unitary response or cognon.

IS MIND A GROUP?

Our cogwheel is a hexagon. At any one moment it contains, in the mature human brain, six cogs or one group of six unitary cognons. The six cogs are not present from birth but develop in an orderly progression (like teeth) during the early years. The span depends on mental age (the Stanford-Binet gives 2 digits at age 2½; 3 digits at age 3, and so on up to 6 digits at age 10). This suggests a process of physiological growth in the central nervous system. The small span of the child reflects a central rather than a sensory limitation.

The versatility of thought depends on the group of transformations that leave the diverse spans invariant. Cognitive functions, like breathing, digestion, and other functions of the organism are not continuous, but periodic or cyclical. The cogwheel revolves and discharges its characteristic spanning function. For a given organism at a given developmental level, perhaps the system forms a symmetry group.

The theory of groups is a powerful branch of mathematics that has revealed underlying relations between parts of algebra and geometry that were long considered to be entirely distinct and unrelated (Eddington, 1956). The term *group* has many meanings in *mathematics*. I use the term here in the sense that Keyser did: "Some definite class of thing together with some definite rule, or way in which any member of the class can be combined with any member of it (either with itself or any other member)" (1956, p. 1538).

A simple example of such a class is the set of whole numbers including zero, and the rule of combination, ordinary addition. This class forms a *group* because it obeys the following four conditions:

1. If *a* and *b* are members of *C*, and *o* is the rule of combination, then aob is a member of *C*; that is, *aob* = *c*, where *c* is some member of *C*. Thus 3+4 = 7, and 7 is a whole number.
2. If *a, b, c,* are members of *C*, then *(aob)oc* = *ao(boc)*; that is, the rule of combination is associative. (2+3)+5 = (5+5) = 10
3. The class *C* contains a member *i* (called the *identity* member) such that *aoi* = *ioa* = *a*.   6+0 = 0+6 = 6
4. If *a* is a member of *C*, then there is another member *á* (called the *reciprocal* member) such that *aoá* = 0.   2+(−2) = 0.

Figure 10.7. Some symmetry groups: Snowflakes and beehives form hexagons. Why *six*?

The members of the class may be arithmetic numbers, geometrical points, atoms, or undefined; they may be finite or infinite; the rule of combination may be an arithmetic operation, (e.g., addition, multiplication), geometrical (rotation), or undefined; it may be commutative or noncommutative (2+3=3+2, but $\frac{2}{3} \neq \frac{3}{2}$.

Two important concepts arise in group theory—*transformation*, the idea of change in motion; and *invariance*, the properties of a structure, object, or expression that remain the same under transformations. Any object in physical space may be moved by sliding it from one end of the desk to the other; it retains its shape and dimensions; these metric properties are therefore invariants. But its visual angle changes continuously—the fact that it remains constant in visual perception has therefore seemed paradoxical. In contrast, the full moon on the horizon appears much larger than it does at the zenith. Since photographs of the moon show that it remains invariant under this transformation of orientation across the sky, its lack of apparent constancy is considered to be an astronomical visual illusion (Gilinsky, 1980).

Group theory thus has to do with the changes and the constancies of the phenomenal world. Keyser tells us to look at the domain of sight and sounds and motions for evidence of groups. Consider *color* perception. Let C be the class of all sensations of color including white and black, and the rule of combination, the *mixing* of such sensations. The mixture of any two, according to the rules, produces a third, intermediate between the two. In the case of complementaries, red and green, or yellow and blue, we get gray, the disappearance of color. Evidently condition 4 is satisfied. Are conditions 2 and 3 also satisfied?

Next consider *emotions* and *moods, drives* and *antidrives;* do they have the group property? We have spoken throughout this work of *association;* in the realm of ideas and in the realm of motor skills the question of combination is fundamental. Has every individual mind the general group property?

I am not going to lead you into the mystifications of supermathematics nor pretend that I am competent to do so. It is sufficient to raise the question and to suggest that in neuropsychology as in the older sciences, we may study the *structure of a set of operations* without specifying the materials used or the nature of the operations that ultimately give us knowledge or truth. The mode of interlocking of the operations may be expressed while their nature remains unknown and perhaps unknowable. Yet characterization of the structure may be essentially what we are after in seeking to know the physical world as it manifests itself in our experience.

Mind appears to be a group of interlocking operations. The weight of the evidence suggests that the precise number, the order of the group of cognitive functions, varies with the maturity of the organism and the conditions of stimulation and response. There is a definite upper limit—at *six ordered categories of response*. Verbal responses, words and numbers, are the countable linguistic correlates of the span and the scale. Where the number appears to exceed *six,* one suspects that the subject has taken more than one look—the cogwheel has revolved more than once. Where the number falls below *six,* within the limiting span, it has been jointly determined by the competence of the organism and the adequacy of stimulation.

My experiments (Gilinsky, 1964) left a question not unlike the one that puzzled Kepler in 1611, why do snowflakes always fall in the shape of a six-cornered starlet? What biological, chemical, or physical mechanisms fix this upper limit on thought and memory? If, indeed, it does not exceed six, why *six*?

SUMMARY

The converging evidence from a variety of experiments on the span of attention, the span of immediate memory, and the scale of absolute judgment points to a unifying theory of a *central ordering group (COG)* whose function is to provide the serial order in thought and action.

The elements of the theory are as follows:

1. Three spans—the span of attention, the immediate memory span, and the category scale of absolute judgment—show a definite upper limit at the same small number of responses.

2. The precise number varies with the quantity of material presented, with the duration and frequency of exposures, and with the mental age of the subject. Thus both the span and the scale appear to be elastic—but the range of variation is narrow.

For most college students or keen adults, under most laboratory conditions, the number of categories that can be organized into a *single scale* is *six.* When there are more categories to use, then the subject will organize them into two or more single scales. The parallel phenomenon appears in the memory span when there are more than six digits or other unitary responses to be reported in sequence. Then the span has to be applied more than once; the time required to master the ordered series takes a sudden jump. These multiple spans and scales appear as discontinuities in the functions relating the variables of response to the variables of stimulation.

3. Within the limits imposed by the mental age and the momentary alertness of the organism, the length of the span is systematically controlled by the adequacy of stimulation. The less adequate it is, the smaller the obtained span, and the fewer categories it contains.

4. Within the span, the serial position curve shows the classical bowed shape. The first and last items in the string are learned first; the middle items are learned last. The top and bottom of the stimulus range, similarly, are judged most consistently and confidently.

5. When the subjects are not constrained to *match the order* of the

elements in the stimulus, but are free to report them in *any order,* then the break in performance does not occur at the usual upper limit. However, when the identity of the stimuli is known to the subjects in advance, and their *only* task is to order the stimuli, then the typical break does occur at or below six responses.

6. The *ordering* operation appears to be the critical determinant of the limiting span. The limit of both the span and the scale is the fixed number of unitary responses that can be kept in order by memory until they are released.

What determines this upper bound? Here is a challenging problem for the future neuropsychologist.

SUGGESTED READINGS

Beach, F.A., Hebb, D.O., Morgan, C.T., & Nissen, H.W. (Eds.). *The neuropsychology of Lashley.* New York: McGraw-Hill, 1960.

Craik, K.J.W. *The nature of explanation.* Cambridge: The Cambridge University Press, 1943.

Eddington, A.S. The theory of groups. In J.R. Newman (Ed.), *The world of mathematics* Vol. 3. New York: Simon & Schuster, 1956.

Keyser, C.J. The group concept. In J.R. Newman (Ed.), *The world of mathematics* (Vol. 3). New York: Simon & Schuster, 1956.

Konorski, J. The physiological approach to the problem of recent memory. In J.F. Delafresnaye (Ed.), *Brain mechanisms and learning: A symposium.* Oxford: Blackwell Science Publication, 1962, 115–132.

Lashley, K.S. The problem of serial order in behavior. In L.A. Jeffress (Ed.), *Cerebral mechanisms in behavior: The Hixon symposium.* New York: John Wiley, 1951.

Miller, G.A. Information and memory. *Scientific American,* 1956a, **195,** 42–46.

Miller, G.A. The magical number seven, plus or minus two: Some limits on our capacity for processing information. *Psychological Review,* 1956b, *63,* 81–96.

Russell, I.S. Brain size and intelligence: A comparative perspective. In D.A. Oakley and H.C. Plotkin (Eds.), *Brain, behavior and evolution.* London: Methuen, 1979.

Simon, H.A. How big is a chunk? *Science,* 1974, **183,** 482–488.

Simon, H.A. *The science of the artificial.* Cambridge, MN: MIT Press, 1969.

CHAPTER ELEVEN

Remembering and Forgetting

We search in our memory for a forgotten idea, just as we rummage our house for a lost object. In both cases we visit what seems to us the probable neighborhood *of that which we miss. We turn over things under which, or within which, or alongside of which, it may possibly be; and if it lies near them, it soon comes to view. But these matters, in the case of a mental object sought, are nothing but its* associates. *The machinery of recall is thus the same as the machinery of association, and the machinery of association, as we know, is nothing but the elementary law of habit in the nerve-centres.*

(William James, 1890, Vol. 1, p. 654)

We know that animals retain traces of their previous experience arising during reflex activity. Only man, however, can make deliberate changes in his environment in order to create methods of influencing his own memory. Tying a knot in his handkerchief, cutting a notch, or marking the item to be memorized by a certain sign, he lifts his memory to the level of controllable processes.

(A.R. Luria, 1966, p. 22)

INTRODUCTION

Our discussions in previous chapters could come under the general heading of *Memory* because they dealt with its various stages—attention, sensory integration, association, thinking, recognition, and recall.

We saw that perceptual learning focused on the organization of sensory information resulting in the formation of unitary perceptions that make *recognition* possible. Associative learning produces images that recur in *recall.*

The reality of recognition and recall prove that earlier *learning* took place and is *retained* over some period of time. It left some enduring record in the brain, presumably in the form of *cognons,* that can be *retrieved* (reactivated) by the various afferent and interneural pathways.

STAGES IN MEMORY

Three stages are involved in the memory process:

1. *Acquisition or learning*
2. *Retention*
3. *Retrieval*

Each of these stages affects memory. *Acquisition* or *learning* comes first. In order to remember anything, it must have been experienced before. *Memory* depends primarily upon the strength and stability of cognons serving as recognition units and secondarily upon the connections established by the coincident activity of two or more participant cognons. The effectiveness of these cognons and their connections (the degree of *retention*) depends upon the extent of synchronous arousal of the participant units at the time of learning. This in turn depends upon factors operating on the formation of the original cognons and then on the establishment of associations between them.

Fully established associations are never completely forgotten. However, they are susceptible to suppression by fresh associations that are antagonistic to the earlier associations. The weakening of antagonistic new associations permits the restoration of the original associations. In other words, remembering is greatly affected by what happens during the interval of *retention.*

Retention can be studied only indirectly by use of a retrieval test, whether of recognition, recall, or relearning.

In *recognition* the object is given, whereas in *recall* the object must be found. Recognition seems to be a simpler process; often a name or a fact that cannot be recalled is recognized as something we have or have not encountered before. The "no" response to an unfamiliar stimulus is as emphatic as the "yes" response to the familiar one. The multiple choice or true-false type of examination seems to be a *recognition* test; the essay examination demands *recall* and is often less preferred by students for that reason. But the advantage of recognition depends on the exact form of the test. A recognition test may be made very difficult by using items that are very similar to each other. Perhaps the most sensitive test of retention is *relearning.*

A subject may be unable to recall a test of words or a poem, or even to recognize it as something familiar, but the relearning of the identical material can be achieved with some *savings* of time and effort, proving its retention over the interval.

Conditions affecting each one of the three stages can strengthen memory or cause forgetting to occur. Let us look first at the conditions affecting the earliest stage of the memory process.

THE STRENGTH AND STABILITY OF COGNONS

If cognons serve as more or less permanent symbols of stimulus patterns, the question arises: why are some stimulus patterns more readily recognized than others? Why are we more confident and quicker to identify certain stimuli as familiar while with others we hesitate, unsure whether we ever did see them or hear them before? Sometimes perception or our cognons even seem to play tricks on us when we feel that someone or some place that we never before experienced seems uncannily familiar—the déjà vu experience. Why is that?

In order to answer these questions, it must be understood that more than one neural unit or cognon for every recognizable object is established by the process of perceptual learning. A weak stimulus that normally would excite a single cell only on a small fraction of its presentations will be detected more frequently by an observer having a large number of responsive cognons. The larger the number of cognons representing a particular fact, and the more extensive their connecting pathways, the greater its retentiveness in memory.

THE REPLICATION OF COGNONS

The number of cognons or neural units that represent a particular object or pattern may vary as a consequence of variation in the cells' sensitivity. In the course of initial formation, what determines the number of activated cognons that represent a given stimulus pattern?

Five factors are abundantly evident. These are:

1. Repetition of the stimulus pattern
2. The strength of the facilitative arousal accompanying the stimulus presentation
3. The age of the subject
4. Whether the subject is in a critical period of development
5. The existence of competitive interaction by other stimulating events.

1. Repetition is one factor that fixes the size of a set of cognons. It may be that the greater the frequency of presentation of a stimulus the greater the

probability of reaching the threshold of a population of cognons that potentially represent that pattern, but were not initially engaged by it. This factor invokes the concept of cognons having different, and perhaps variable, thresholds. Spacing of repetitions is necessary in order to prevent habituation to the same stimulus. Even though different units may be activated on successive presentations of the given stimulus, some generalization of habituation will occur.

2. The second factor, strength of arousal, is also related to threshold variability. If the perception takes place against a background of strong arousal, then it may be assumed to affect the sensitization mechanism and thereby enhance the release of neurotransmitter turned loose by the sensory neurons that converge on the target cells. Thus a larger number of cognons will be influenced and increase the size of the memory store for that percept.

3. Third, age is important. A young subject has a large number of potential units available to provide actual cognons. As the individual matures and acquires more experience, fewer unoccupied units remain available for forming new cognons. Probably some cognitive fields are depleted faster than others; my category for people's names seems uncommonly crowded, and my memory for new names correspondingly fleeting and uncertain.

In young subjects whose cognitive fields are partially formed, the number of potential units in a set will be larger than in older subjects whose free cognons diminish with age or may even atrophy beyond a critical period. The result is the frequently greater retention of earlier than later memories, and their better preservation after damage to particular neurons. Infarcts (dead or dying tissue) following cerebral vascular accidents (strokes) are apt to increase with age also and result in loss of cognons.

4. The age of the organism is linked to its maturational stage of development. Particular sorts of perceptual learning occur most readily, if at all, during a so-called *critical period,* a period in the development of an organism when it is maximally sensitive to certain environmental stimuli. Outside of this critical period the same environmental stimuli may have little effect. An example is the attachment of the infant to its parent; this is illustrated in many species by the phenomenon of *imprinting.* In birds, imprinting is a kind of early learning that provides the basis for attachment. When a newly hatched duckling is ready to walk and first exposed to a moving stimulus—usually the mother duck, it will approach and follow the stimulus. But if it is exposed to a wooden duck on wheels or the legs of the experimenter at the critical moment, from then on it will follow the model on which it was imprinted (Hess, 1958). Imprinting not only cements the attachment, but enables the bird to recognize its own species and may direct its future choice of

a mate. According to the present theory, imprinting is the establishment of a *cognon,* one that is extraordinarily stable and usually irreversible.

Another line of evidence comes from studies at the University of Wisconsin of socially deprived monkeys (Harlow, 1962). A few hours after the monkeys' birth, Harlow separated them from their parents and their peers. Monkeys reared in isolation from all other monkeys, although fed daily (by remote control), became socially and psychologically deviant. When returned to the monkey colony, an isolate did not play with the other monkeys and did not defend itself when attacked, but simply crouched in a corner chewing on its fingers and toes, or rocking back and forth—much like an autistic child.

In human children also there is good evidence for a critical period of perceptual and social learning. In the learning of a language there are probably several critical periods (Lenneberg, 1967). As a child approaches puberty it becomes more and more difficult to learn a language, and, after 14, it may be impossible to acquire the native accent of a second tongue. Social as well as sensory influences make themselves felt in the learning of verbal and other social behavior at critical periods. Like Harlow's monkeys, children suffer severely from early social deprivation (Spitz, 1945; 1946).

More recent studies (Hubel & Wiesel, 1963; 1970; Hirsch & Spinelli, 1971; Blakemore, 1974; Mitchell, 1980) provide direct physiological evidence that sensory deprivation early in life can not only alter behavior radically, but reveal a biological basis for these environmental influences—changes in the anatomical structure of the cerebral cortex. We are growing to realize that experience or its absence can have effects on brain tissue as profound as organic disease or injury.

A brief early experience during a critical period of development may cause extraordinarily specific and irreversible aftereffects. The closure of one eye in a newborn kitten results in permanent damage (Wiesel & Hubel, 1963). By alternately obstructing first one and then the other eye, kittens are prevented from using both eyes together; as a result, they fail to develop the binocular disparity connections they need for depth perception, even though their cortical neurons respond normally to each eye separately. (See Figure 11.1.) The same defect can be produced by squint, whether genetically, as in some children, or artificially in experimental animals.

Moreover, the specific response selectivity of cortical neurons can be shown to depend on what an infant kitten has seen. If during their early visual experience, kittens are exposed to vertical stripes, but deprived of exposure to horizontal and other orientations—a kind of environmental surgery—the cat fails to develop horizontal stripe detectors in the visual cortex. Similarly, if kittens are exposed to horizontal, but not vertical stripes, they have no vertical stripe detectors. (See Figure 11.2.)

The timing of the sensitive period is extraordinarily specific. As few as four hours of visual stimulus deprivation at the height of the critical period, (the fourth week in the life of the cat) may result in a permanent structural

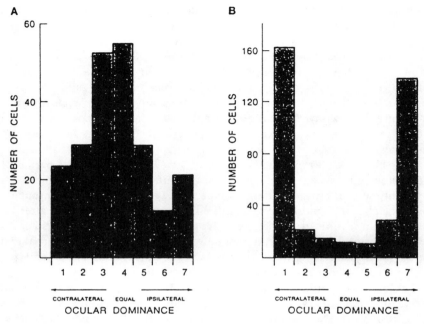

Figure 11.1. Kittens prevented from using both eyes together during early development fail to form binocular disparity connections needed for depth perception. (A) Ocular dominance distribution of 223 cells recorded from striate cortex of normal adult cats in a series of 45 penetrations. Hubel & Wiesel, 1962. By permission of The Physiological Society (London). (B) Ocular dominance distribution of 384 cells recorded from four kittens with strabismus. Hubel & Wiesel, 1965. By permission of the American Physiological Society.

change (Blakemore & Cooper, 1970; Van Sluyters & Blakemore, 1973; Muir & Mitchell, 1973).

The critical period in humans may last considerably longer than in cats and other animals. The best evidence comes from humans with amblyopia and other ocular abnormalities—strabismus, astigmatism, cataracts, or other refractive errors. People, like cats and monkeys, form cognons on the basis of their individual past experience. There is a sensitive time in the life of every organism when particular kinds of cognons are readily formed; once past that critical period, it is too late for particular kinds of perception units to become established.

5. Competitive interaction, the fifth factor, is strongly supported by experiments on the effects of monocular deprivation on cells in the visual cortex of cat and monkey. LeVay, Wiesel, and Hubel (1981) showed that

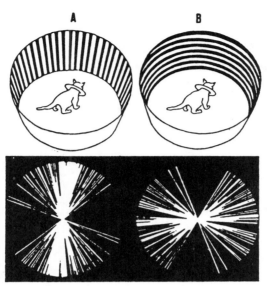

Figure 11.2. "Environmental surgery." Deprivation of early visual experience with either vertical or horizontal stripes causes loss of stripe detector neurons for the selectively missed orientation. The kitten wears a ruff around its neck to confine visual experience to the specific striped environment. In the lower part of the figure each line represents the optimal orientation for one cortical neuron. Left: vertically striped environment (72 cells tested). Right: horizontally striped environment (52 cells tested). Blakemore & Cooper, 1970. Reprinted by permission from *Nature,* Vol. 228, pp. 477–478. Copyright © 1970 Macmillan Journals Limited.

ocular dominance columns are only partially formed in the newborn macaque monkey. Their further development is completed by three to six weeks of postnatal age. Monocular lid suture at birth distorts the normal sorting process and results in cortical columns of unequal width (LeVay et al., 1981). (See Figure 11.3A–D.) The columns for the open eye are about three times wider than those for the closed eye. Monocular deprivation can also cause a reexpansion of afferents; that is, they can be shown to reinvade territory that has already become the possession of the other eye if the suturing occurs at a later stage. Most interestingly, the reverse suture experiment, in which the deprived eye is opened and the original seeing eye closed, allows the initially deprived eye to regain its influence and in fact to become the physiologically dominant eye, a result found previously for the cat (Blakemore & Van Sluyters, 1975) and the monkey (Blakemore, Garey, & Vital-Durand, 1978). (See Figure 11.3E.) The striking feature of these experiments is the physiological plasticity of the developing nervous system. The competitive interaction between the two eyes has marked anatomical as well as functional

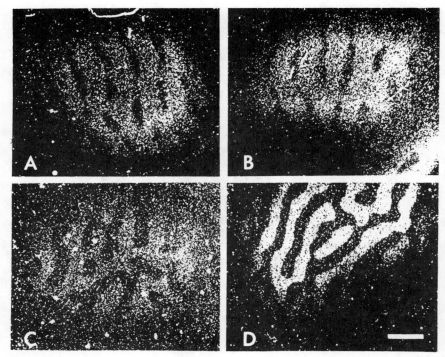

Figure 11.3. Monocular deprivation in the newborn macaque monkey at any age up to about six weeks distorts the normal sorting process and causes the bands of afferents for the open eye to become about three times wider than the bands for the closed eye. Later eye closures and, in animals deprived monocularly from birth, reverse sutures can cause a re-expansion of afferents that have already segregated out into columns. The anatomical effects of long-term monocular deprivation begun at 2 weeks (A), 5½ weeks (B), 10 weeks (C), and adult (D). In each case the nondeprived eye was injected. The main decline in susceptibility to the anatomical effects of deprivation was between 5½ and 10 weeks. The picture in D is indistinguishable from normal. Bar = 1 mm. LeVay, Wiesel, & Hubel, 1981. Right. (E) Reconstruction of an electrode track in a monkey whose right eye was closed at 5½ weeks of age (see autoradiograph in Figure 11.3B). The contralateral eye dominated completely (ocular dominance group 1) except for two short stretches matching the gaps in the autoradiograph in which the deprived eye dominated. (F) This reconstruction of an electrode pass through the visual cortex in a monkey that was reverse sutured at 6 weeks of age agrees with the autoradiography in showing a restoration of approximately even balance between the eyes. The string of numbers shows the alternation of eye dominance in agreement with the bands shown by autoradiographs. LeVay, Wiesel, & Hubel, 1981. Copyright © 1981 by the Massachusetts Institute of Technology.

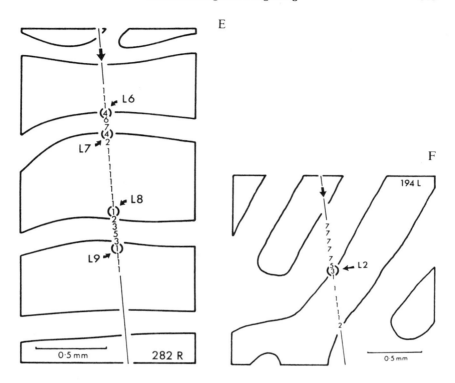

effects that change the structural organization of the visual cortex. Whether similar competitive effects occur between cognons or categories of cognons in humans remains to be shown by future research. The possibility is suggestive of a form of immunization of actual cognons against being entered by other stimulus patterns.

MNEMONICS AND THE ASSOCIATIVE PROCESS

The factors influencing perceptual learning make it seem as if the learner was receiving impressions quite passively. Nothing could be further from the truth. The learner is intensely active during the reception of the stimuli and in the associative process. Even in the act of *retrieval*, we often re-create the past in the effort to make sense of it.

Psychologists have in fact begun to reconsider ancient Greek and Roman techniques for improving memory—the classical devices called *mnemonics*—and find that they can be surprisingly effective. As we shall see, mnemonics make demands for the active participation of the mnemonist in both the process of acquisition and retrieval from memory.

Frances A. Yates, the English historian, describes the classical mnemonic techniques in *The Art of Memory* (1966).

The key to mnemonics is the establishment of *loci* or places, and time to develop *images* to connect them with the material to be remembered. Yates's (1966) description of the classical art of memory shows that the art belonged to the orator to enable him to deliver long speeches from memory. His first step was to imprint on memory a series of places, usually a house, or an intercolumnar space, a corner, or square. The ancient orator moved through his memory building or series of places whilst making his speech, drawing from the memorized places the images he has placed on them.

The most effective mnemonics use certain kinds of images rather than others. Some images are strong and sharp and stay long in mind. Others are banal and easily slip from memory. The images to seek are those that are striking, novel, exceptionally ugly, frightful, or ridiculous; those we are likely to remember for a long time. The things we cannot forget when they are real, we will also retain when they are images of our own invention. The very act of inventing the images to memorize is a further aid to recall because it arouses our active participation.

Active observation, then, attention to the items to be remembered, and the effort to create vivid images and relate them to an ordered series of places, a spatial schema, are the keys to remembering isolated or unrelated elements.

The general principles underlying the method of loci and rules for selecting images are similar to those used in advertising. The creation of memorable images and the arousal of drives by using limbic stimuli, fear, sex, and status strengthen the associations. Commercials utilize rhyming and jingles because they enforce a unique ordering and transform time into space. Thus both verbal and nonverbal associations are formed, involving the participation of both hemispheres of the brain and furthering hemispheric integration.

AN ASTONISHING MEMORY

Luria (1968) describes the extraordinary feats of a mnemonist, a man endowed with virtually limitless powers of memory for particulars, but a crippling inability to generalize the particulars into concepts. The man's memory for concrete objects and words from his earliest childhood haunted him; it seemed as if he could not forget! Luria began to study S., a 30-year-old newspaper reporter, at the suggestion of the paper's editor. Each morning the editor handed out assignments to his staff, long lists of names and addresses, information to be covered that day. The reporter never took any notes, but when the editor was about to reproach him, S. repeated the entire assignment, word for word, surprised that there was anything unusual about his memory.

Luria proceeded to test S. with a series of words, then numbers or letters, reading them slowly or presenting them in written form. He was able to repeat the entire list of 50 or even 70 items without any mistakes. Not only that; S. could reproduce a series in reverse order just as simply as from beginning to end. All that he required was a three-to-four–second pause between items. Later sessions revealed that he could reproduce any length series whatever, even though these had been presented to him several months before; he merely required a little time to revive the situation in which the original list had been read to him, to "see" the room in which he had been sitting, and to "hear" the doctor's voice reading to him. Otherwise S. reproduced the list with the same ease he had demonstrated earlier. His memory capacity was uncanny.

How did he manage to do this? The only way to find out was to question S. himself. His explanation seemed simple. He said he continued "to see" the written list imprinted in his memory. But there were additional elements at work. He had an especially vivid form of synesthesia: every sound he heard immediately produced an experience of light and color, a sense of touch and taste as well. Lines, blurs, and splashes would emerge, some with distinct textures and forms, when he heard tones or voices speaking. The visual quality of his recall was a fundamental factor in his ability to remember words. As he described it:

> When I hear the word *green,* a green flowerpot appears; with the word *red,* I see a man in a red shirt coming toward me; as for *blue,* this means an image of someone waving a small blue flag from a window.... Even numbers remind me of images. Take the number *1.* This is a proud, well-built man; *2* is a high-spirited woman; *3* is a gloomy person (why, I don't know); *6* a man with a swollen foot; *7* a man with a mustache; *8* a very stout woman—a sack within a sack. As for the number *87,* what I see is a fat woman and a man twirling his mustache. (Luria, 1968, p. 31)

S's mnemonic technique was to convert a series of words into a series of graphic images. Luria explains: "When S. read through a long series of words, each word would elicit a graphic image. And since the series was fairly long, he had to find some way of distributing these images of his in a mental row or sequence. Most often (and this habit persisted throughout his life), he would 'distribute' them along some roadway or street he visualized in his mind" (1968, p. 32).

To recall a series, "He would simply begin his walk, either from the beginning or from the end of the street, find the image of the object I had named, and 'take a look at' whatever happened to be situated on either side of it" (Luria, 1968, p. 33).

The capacity of this memory to store and retain images seemed unlimited. S. could reproduce long series, even 10 or 16 years after the original presentation. The question then became: was it possible for him to forget?

The answer to the question was that S. frequently *omitted* a word from a series, but scarcely ever reproduced material inaccurately. When S. omitted an item it seemed that he did not "forget" it; he had placed it in a spot that was poorly lit or in which the item blended into the background and was not readily noticeable. For example, when he omitted the word *pencil,* he explained:

> I put the image of the *pencil* near a fence...the one down the street, you know. But what happened was that the image fused with that of the fence and I walked right on past without noticing it. The same thing happened with the word *egg.* I had put it up against a white wall and it blended in with the background. How could I possibly spot a white egg against a white wall? Sometimes if there is noise, or another person's voice suddenly intrudes, I see blurs which block off my images. It's these blurs which interfere with my recall. (Luria, 1968, p. 36–7)

The key to the mnemonist's technique was his ability to convert each word into a vivid image and then, most importantly, to place each image in turn on a particular doorway, storefront, or fence post in a Moscow square—forming a cognitive map of ordered spatial images. By mentally moving through the locations of the spatial representation of the square, S. could find the images of the items he had stored and recall them. The *method of loci,* as Yates showed, can be used repeatedly for an indefinite number of memory tasks.

The mnemonist's problem was that he could not forget. More usual is the problem of the individual who cannot remember.

LOSS OF MEMORY: FORGETTING

First described in 1887 by Sergei Korsakoff, loss of memory has diverse pathological causes, including alcoholism, nutritional disease, meningitis, encephalitis, Alzheimer's disease, electroshock therapy, and other head trauma. Korsakoff's syndrome is characterized by four symptoms: an amnesia for recent events; a spatial, or more commonly a temporal disorientation; confabulation; and false recognition (Brion, 1969). Both *retrograde amnesia* (loss of memory for events prior to brain damage) and *anterograde amnesia* (inability to retain new information following the injury) are involved. The fact of retrograde amnesia suggests that there is more than a simple defect of storage, since the deficit affects memories whose initial fixation may have been normal. If recovery occurs, the retrograde amnesia disappears first for remote events and gradually for events up to the time preceding the cerebral

insult. Probably retrograde amnesia is a retrieval disorder, whereas anterograde amnesia is really a learning deficit.

Disorders of memory are frequently associated with advancing age,
although the remarkably wide range in memory test scores among the elderly
points to qualitatively different types of memory impairment (Kral, 1969). In
one form in which certain data (a name or a place or other parts of an
experience) are temporarily unavailable, what is forgotten typically belongs to
the distant rather than the recent past; in another, the subjects are unable to
recall events of the recent past.

The existence of a general or global memory loss is actually rare. Elliott
Ross (1982) has shown that disorders of recent memory do not affect all
sensory systems equally. Newly described clinical syndromes reveal sensory-
specific deficits that depend on the location of the brain damage. This is
precisely what *cognon theory* would predict. To take just one striking
example, Ross reports the case of a patient with a profound and absolute loss
of recent visual memory but no loss of remote visual memory, and no loss of
either recent or remote auditory, tactile, or other sensory memories. The
man had recently moved into a new three-room apartment and had great
difficulty in finding his way around, making frequent wrong turns and
confusing rooms. He was unable to draft an accurate floor plan of his
apartment, yet could draw the plan of his parent's house with perfect accuracy
since he had complete access to his remote visual memories. His permanent
spatial disorientation in new environments was due to a disconnection
between the uninjured visual areas and the medial-temporal lobes, the result
of a lesion of the inferior longitudinal fasciculus that carries visual information
from occipital to the temporal lobes. Recent visual memory was disrupted
because visual information could no longer be processed by the medial
temporal lobes.

EVIDENCE FOR TWO KINDS OF FORGETTING (AMNESIA)

Anterograde Amnesia

Anterograde amnesia—an inability to learn new information—reveals the
role of the temporal cortex and underlying limbic structures in memory. The
dramatic case presented in Chapter Nine is a striking example. Henry M.
submitted to deliberate bilateral insult to his brain in order to overcome an
epileptic disorder. The radical surgical procedure destroyed the hippocampus
and associated structures inside the temporal lobes on both sides of the brain.
Brenda Milner (1970) who has followed this case for over a quarter of a
century, found that although the patient retained skills and knowledge

acquired up to the time of his operation, he was unable to store any new memories in his present file. He was attentive and seemed to be able to register limited amounts of new information but, without constant rehearsal, it quickly disappeared. He was aware of his disorder, saying:

> Every day is alone in itself, whatever enjoyment I've had, and whatever sorrow I've had.... Right now, I'm wondering. Have I done or said anything amiss? You see, at this moment everything looks clear to me, but what happened just before? That's what worries me. It's like waking from a dream; I just don't remember. (Milner, 1970, p. 37).

Milner concluded from this and similar cases she studied that the hippocampus plays a vital role in long-term memory for new information. Because older memories can be retrieved and the patient can carry on a conversation, the retrieval mechanism and immediate memory are still functioning. What has been disrupted is the ability to transfer material from short-term to long-term memory, and, for this function, the integrity of the amygdala and hippocampus seems to be necessary (Zola-Morgan, Squire, & Mishkin, 1982).

Retrograde Amnesia

Electroconvulsive shock therapy throws a patient into a brief convulsion and material memorized just before the shock cannot be recalled a few hours later. Such a *retrograde amnesia* (loss of memory of the recent past) is commonly observed after a severe blow to the head, causing a concussion after an accident. The memory gap for the few minutes or hours immediately preceding the accident is often explained as due to lack of time for "consolidation of the traces" before the brain is subjected to an abnormal physiochemical condition. As the patient recovers, the memories come back, the most recent ones last.

Experiments on animals show similar effects. By passing an electric current through the head of a rat, soon after every trial in a learning experiment, Duncan (1949) slowed down the learning to avoid a shock by leaving a preferred dark box and going to a safe and bright box. The sooner the shock was administered after each trial, the slower was the learning. Was poor learning due to fear? A control experiment administered shocks to the hind legs that induced even more fear but scarcely disturbed the learning process. Duncan concluded that the cause of the difficulty was not fear but cerebral shock immediately following the training trial.

These results suggest that memory traces need time to stabilize. But do they support the consolidation hypothesis? Recent memory traces are vulnerable to disruption much more than older ones. But it is difficult to explain the recovery of lost memories by human subjects. If they were prevented from consolidating, how and why do they return?

THEORIES OF FORGETTING OR RETENTION

The failure of memory may have several causes, any of which are called *forgetting*. But neuropsychologists have asked whether forgetting is produced by conditions at the moment of attempting to recall or recognize (*i.e.,* a *retrieval* failure) or by events during the *retention interval* following learning. Of course, memory failure may be due to faulty observation at the time of original learning, but that is a problem of selective attention and concerns immediate, transient, or short-term memory.

In this section I will consider forgetting from long-term memory.

Atrophy from Disuse

Contrary to common belief, there is no evidence that memory traces simply decay from *disuse*. The mere lapse of time is a negative factor. Something going on in the organism during that time must be the cause of a failure to remember. A striking fact is the retention from one year to the next of skills that have not had any review or opportunity for practice. The best examples are motor skills—you remember how to swim, how to ride a bicycle, how to drive a car, even though you have not practiced any of these things, sometimes for years. Some atrophy from disuse occurs simply because the muscles are in poor shape from lack of exercise. The neural mechanisms also may lose their prime condition unless actively maintained.

Proactive Interference

Forgetting may be caused by the interference of an earlier activity on the retention of later learning. The persistence of excitation in highly aroused cognons after initial stimulation may prevail over new stimulation. Examples are presented in the following discussion of perseveration.

Perseveration

Perseveration, the repetition of responses although incorrect, is a common symptom following lesions of any part of the cortex. Patients with temporal lobe lesions find tremendous difficulty with the problem of switching from sorting cards on the basis of one criterion, say, color, to another, such as shape. Their responses, quickly acquired on the first sorting task, tend to perseverate. Perseveration is frequent also in parietal patients and is believed to be especially characteristic of patients with frontal lobe damage. It is related to forgetting, an amnesic disorder.

Perseveration is a common symptom in anterograde amnesia. The patient still has access to his earlier past. Brenda Milner (1966, pp. 115–116) describes this persistent recall in Henry M. who brought up such memories endlessly:

> He is also apt to tell long anecdotes from his school days, repeating them to the same person on different occasions, since he does not realize that he has told them before. These stereotyped stories, which resemble the reminiscences of an elderly person, are presumably all he has with which to occupy his thoughts when he is not actively engaged in some task.

Aphasic speech produces many examples of perseveration—the patients says "boy, boy, boy" or, having correctly named the *coin* presented to him, gives the same response to a watch, a purse, spectacles, and so on.

When the test is resumed after a rest, the first one or two responses the patient gives are correct, followed by the obsessive tendency to name different objects shown by one definite name. Why is this so?

Note that the patient commonly utters the name of an object *belonging to the same category* as the object shown to him. Presented with a picture of a pig, he may correctly respond *pig,* a picture of a cart is correctly named *cart,* but a picture of a mouse presented next is called a *little pig* (Konorski, 1967, p. 203).

These erroneous responses are instances of perseveration that can be explained by the facilitatory aftereffect produced in particular cognons following their arousal by the first stimulus objects shown to the patient and named correctly by him. This is a forward interference effect or *proactive inhibition* that persists until an intermission allows some competing activity to interfere. Errors that are perseverative may be names of similar objects that possess some emotional significance for the patient—for example, coin or cigarette. Better-known words or simply a word with greater common frequency may replace the perseverative response. Word frequency plays an important role in normal word choices, as the free word association tests show, and it is not surprising in amnesic aphasics also.

Emotional factors are important in normal conditions also, as when you call a person by someone else's name or confuse responses in talking about significant content. Sigmund Freud made these erroneous responses conspicuous in his *Psychopathology of Everyday Life* (1901), although he overemphasized as the sole cause forbidden suppressed desires slipping past the censor of the superego.

Retroaction

Reader, if you have to prepare to take two course examinations on the same day, will studying for the second test drive the first one out of your mind? What is the best way to study for both exams? The underlying question is whether rest between studying for the two courses prevents *retroaction*—that is, the back-action of the second study process upon the first. If the retroaction is negative, as you might suppose, it would be *retroactive inhibition* or *retroactive interference*. You might think of rest as a way of clearing the slate before tackling the task ahead. But retroactive inhibition might not allow time for the first learned material to soak in and be retained for the future.

FACTORS IN RETROACTIVE INHIBITION

Müller and Pilzecker (1900), who discovered retroactive inhibition, proposed a *consolidation* theory. They recognized that newly learned items *perseverated* for a time after exposure and needed that period to soak in. Their observation that some degree of *after-excitation* (sensitization) follows learning is a genuine fact, and consolidation may require rest or relaxation or some nonconflicting activity.

Many questions arise. Can retroactive inhibition be reduced by a short rest immediately after learning? If not, what activities following learning are most likely to aid the consolidation process? What activities are apt to interfere?

Several variables are important—the difficulty of the activity undertaken during the retention interval, its timing, and its similarity to the original learning task. The last has been tried in many experiments.

Similarity of Tasks

When a list of items is learned—for example, words—a second list of similar words will cause retroactive inhibition. If the first list contains digits, then a second list also of digits produces more retroactive inhibition than words or other materials.

The amount of retroactive inhibition clearly increases with the *degree of similarity* between lessons. The interference effect is obtained when both tasks require the same methods of responding—both recognition tasks, or both recall—or when both consist of a similar operation, for instance, canceling numbers. Retroactive inhibition is greatest when there is threefold similarity: in materials to be learned, operations, and drives.

Sleep Following Learning

Sleep following learning favors retention considerably (Jenkins & Dallenbach, 1924). When student learners of nonsense syllables go to sleep soon after the memorization task, their recall is better than if they had remained awake. If the hour between learning and the retention test is spent in sleep rather than daytime activities, *some* forgetting occurs. If the time spent in sleeping is lengthened beyond two hours, even up to eight hours, however, there is no further memory loss.

The conclusion of various experiments on sleep versus activity following learning is that forgetting does not result from mere lapse of time or decay of old impressions. Instead it is a matter of the interference or inhibition of some process by antagonistic activity. The research on similarity shows that some activities produce more inhibition and intrusions than others. The greatest interference comes when old and new stimuli require conflicting responses. Then there is competition between them, resulting in retroactive inhibition.

Here is compelling evidence for the *categorization* principle of cognon theory. Similar stimulus materials are registered within particular categories of perceptive units and there is intracategory antagonism. Again, similar unitary motor acts, reaching, locomotor, or expressive speech acts within single categories of the kinesthetic analyzer are mutually antagonistic. Under the influence of a particular drive, antagonistic responses inhibit one other. This factor is clearly brought out by the experiments on instrumental conditioning. Nonreinforced responses—motor acts preceding the correct drive-reducing, or reinforced, response—are inhibited. The successful instrumental act retroactively inhibits all the unsuccessful ones that precede it. The greater inhibitory effect on similar responses sharpens differentiation and speeds learning, obviously an adaptive advantage.

We must still explain the peculiar, rapid initial decline of the forgetting curve. Why is sleep directly after learning beneficial? And why should nonsense syllables and other meaningless material show greater retroactive inhibition than meaningful sentences that are more similar to everyday life activities?

The odd shape of the forgetting curve—its rapid initial decline and later leveling off—suggests that retroactive inhibition must affect the after-excitation or sensitization process rather than any later activity of consolidation. Long-term retention seems to require the absence of interference with some process immediately following learning. What is this process? We know that rehearsal or repetition helps retention. And we know that transient memory or the immediate memory span is limited, not by time, but by the number of items put into the serial memory store.

THE PROBLEM OF SHORT-TERM AND LONG-TERM MEMORY

The most controversial problem in the neuropsychology of behavior concerns the *mechanisms* of learning and memory. The anatomical structure of the nervous system in both vertebrates and invertebrates is known to develop according to a predetermined genetic plan; neurons are linked in precise ways so that a given set of cells invariably connects only to certain other cells. If these pathways are "hardwired," how is it possible for behavior to be changed by experience? We are faced with a paradox. The modifiability of behavior is an obvious fact. Many different sorts of learning take place, and learning produces changes, not only for short periods lasting a few seconds, but also for long durations, weeks and even years. Even in organisms as simple as the snail, the cockroach, and the flatworm, structurally invariant neurons and synapses are evidently capable of functional changes as the result of the animal's experience.

How does this come about? What types of changes does learning actually produce in the nervous system? How and where is memory stored?

One appealing approach to this problem is based on the distinction between *short-term memory* (also called immediate, recent, or transient memory) and *long-term memory*. The influential neuropsychologist, Donald O. Hebb (1949), emphasized this distinction, and Konorski (1967), Neisser (1967), and many other investigators have pursued this lead.

On the psychological side, there is clear evidence of extremely short time effects, effects that last for a fraction of a second and then disappear. Somewhat longer retention of new information is common also. We can remember many newly acquired facts for a few seconds, minutes, even hours or days before we forget them. Although recently acquired material is rapidly lost, one might ask how so much can be remembered for a short time?

> Someone sounds a note for you to sing: a second or two later you can strike the exact note but if you wait half a minute you get it only approximately. At first the note seemed to "ring in your ears"... really in your brain... and you seem not to recall it but only to hold on to it. In many cases you have the feeling that the just past sensation or experience is still "echoing" or continuing in weaker intensity. This feeling may not prove anything but it suggests the hypothesis that a brain activity started by a stimulus does not cease abruptly when the stimulus ceases, but rather continues for a short time. (Woodworth & Marquis, 1947, p. 566)

Such continuing activity would explain many aftereffects that persist for a time following stimulation, then die out.

Such very brief short-term memory occurs after exposure to visual stimuli and is called *iconic* memory. A person can retain a few letters or digits flashed on a screen, but the accuracy of recall decreases rapidly. The time course of decay, like that of the visual afterimage, depends on the brightness of the display and is due in part to photochemical processes in the retina.

The more interesting question is: what determines more stable remembering? How can the brain, as a physiochemical system, *know* anything—or develop the delusion that it does?

NEUROPSYCHOLOGICAL THEORIES OF MEMORY

Two theories of the neuropsychology of memory are especially worthy of examination: the theory of *dynamic change* and the theory of *plastic change.* The first theory, the theory of *dynamic change,* emphasizes the persistence of cycles of activity in interconnected neurons following their stimulation. The basic assumption that learning sets up cycles of activity in the brain is sometimes attributed to Alexander Forbes (1922), the Harvard physiologist, sometimes to Lorente de Nó (Eccles, 1952, p. 218).

Hebb (1949) elaborated the concept of self–re-exciting circuits as an explanation for immediate or short-term memory. In the short term, Hebb held that neural activity can be sustained by reverberation of impulses within a closed chain of interconnected neurons. This "cell-assembly" of reverberatory activity led, as Hebb put it, to

> lasting cellular changes that add to its stability. The assumption can be precisely stated as follows: When an axon of A is near enough to excite cell B and repeatedly or persistently takes part in firing it, some growth process or metabolic change takes place in one or both cells so that A's efficiency as one of the cells firing B, is increased. (Hebb, 1949, p. 62)

Hebb did not specify the nature of the supposed growth process or metabolic change that he believed to underlie the more stable long-term memory. Indeed, persistent reverberation of impulses often failed to materialize, and Hebb (1961) later rejected his former theory on the basis of new data that showed, despite interference with supposed reverbatory activity, continuous improvement in retention.

The conditions that supposedly limit or restrict memory to a brief duration are events immediately preceding or immediately following the learning period—a traumatic blow, electroconvulsive shock, or severe stress. Yet, even after a convulsive seizure or a concussion that appears to interrupt the activity of an assumed reverberatory circuit, the memory for the immediately preceding events may return. If the memory had been completely destroyed, its recovery would be impossible.

In addition to these problems for Hebb's earlier theory, the simple fact of habituation requires that any afterdischarge be self-limiting. Otherwise the bombardment of impulses in a closed chain would be perpetuated, perhaps forever.

Further physiological studies of neural networks showed that neurons mediate inhibition as well as excitation. A closed chain of neurons might contain an inhibitory connection that could prevent re-excitation. Konorski (1967) took this idea to explain habituation, a feature he believed to be an essential aspect of the activity of every neuron taking part in any active circuit. The reciprocal innervation of a reverberatory circuit by a constant stream of excitatory impulses to sustain the targeting reflex and the inhibitory habituation reflex that damped the local circuit could account for a restricted transient or short-term memory. Although the hypothesis is appealing, there are few experiments to support it.

Lorente de Nó, in fact, disclaimed authorship. Reportedly, he pointed out in a footnote to his chapter on the anatomy of the cortex in Fulton's book

> that the distribution of recurrent fibers is such that the probabilities of reverberating activity are vanishingly small. There are so few connections from any one cell to any given cell, that the only chance of getting reverberation is by complete organization. The "feed-back" effects are to modify rather than to stimulate—otherwise we would be in convulsions all the time. (See Rioch, 1954, p. 236.)

The second theory, the theory of *plastic change,* states that each remembered sensation results in some permanent, physical alteration in the brain. Both influential theorists—Hebb (1949) and Konorski (1967)—assumed that some form of consolidation involving *plastic change* was necessary to explain long-term memory. The general hypothesis is that stable learning involves a functional change in neurons themselves or in their interconnections, perhaps a change in the resistance of certain synapses. Konorski (1967) believed that potential connections (those developed by ontogeny) could become actual connections as the result of experience. Presumably, certain synapses at the junctures of anatomical pathways are capable of changing their properties and mediating persistent alterations in behavior.

William James (1890) anticipated our modern conception of plastic change. For James, the "law of habit" (or associative learning) was a physical fact, like creases or folds in a garment. He believed that native tenacity or physiological retentiveness differed enormously from infancy to old age, and from one person to another. For the majority of persons, sheer *frequency of repetition* is the essential condition for the persistence or permanence of the neural paths.

Not only repetition but the *number* of such paths is the major distinguishing feature of a good, as opposed to a poor, memory. The more numerous they are, the prompter and the surer the memory of a particular fact will be.

> In mental terms, *the more other facts a fact is associated with in the mind, the better possession of it our memory retains.* Each of its associates becomes a hook to which it hangs, a means by which to fish it up when sunk beneath the surface. Together, they form a network of attachments by which it is woven into the entire tissue of our thought. The secret of a good memory is thus the secret of forming diverse and multiple associations with every fact we care to retain. (James, 1890, Vol. 1, p. 161)

Most of us have a relatively good memory for facts connected with our own pursuits. The jocks who fail to retain textbook facts may astonish you with their detailed and accurate knowledge of individual athelete's records and game scores. They may be a walking dictionary of sports statistics. Investment bankers remember Wall Street figures, interest rates, and stock prices; politicians remember constituents' names and other politicians' speeches; scientists remember data that support their theories, and so do we all.

In every case, the things we like to think about stick because we do think about them in numerous ways and weave them into a system. In a system, every fact and every relation is connected with every other—thus related items are well retained, while unrelated or nonassociated facts are forgotten.

THE NEUROPHYSIOLOGICAL MECHANISM OF MEMORY

Learning and memory, especially the profound and long-term changes in behavior that result from experience, are mysterious. Until recently all attempts to understand their mechanisms of action were thwarted. Now neurobiologists working with small systems of neurons in simple animals are providing new ideas about memory and learning and the way they work that have significant implications for human behavior.

Eric Kandel and his collaborators have shown in elegant experiments on the large marine snail *Aplysia,* which presents a simple model system for studying various forms of learning, that long-term as well as short-term memory can be identified by plastic changes that take place in the structure and functioning of particular nerve cells and their interconnections.

These studies have examined the defensive withdrawal reflex of the gill in this invertebrate. A mild tactile stimulus to the siphon causes the gill to contract and withdraw into the mantle cavity. As we saw in Chapter Five, with repetition of the innocuous stimulus, the animal decreases its response to it and may cease responding altogether, a form of nonassociative learning called habituation. The immediate memory for habituation is stored as a temporary decrease in the effectiveness of the synaptic connections between the sensory neurons and their target interneurons and motor neurons. The reason these synapses become less effective is that the sensory neurons release progressively less transmitter substance. This transient decrease in transmitter release is in turn controlled by a decrease in the free calcium current in the presynaptic terminal.

How long can this plastic change last? Can it give rise to long-term memory? The *Aplysia* gives a clear answer. Long-term habituation may be brought about by simply repeating the stimulus-training sessions. With sufficient repetition there is a complete and prolonged inactivation of the previously functioning synapse. Four or more repeated training sessions of the siphon-gill withdrawal reflex produce long-term habituation in *Aplysia* that lasts for weeks.

The disrupted connection can be promptly reinstated, however, by stimulating the pathway with a sensitizing stimulus. Sensitization, you will recall, is the animal's reflex response to a nasty experience. (See Figure 11.4.) Reactivation occurs quickly and is localized to exactly the same site as that found in habituation—the presynaptic terminals of specific neurons. Sensitization facilitates action by increasing the calcium current that regulates the number of quanta of chemical transmitter released in the presynaptic terminals.

Thus sensitization and habituation are opposite effects. One increases the influx of calcium that allows the transmitter vesicles to bind to discharge sites—a critical step needed to liberate transmitter into the synaptic cleft. The other decreases the concentration of calcium in the presynaptic terminals and reduces the amount of transmitter released by the impulse.

These opposite changes in the efficacy of the synapse take place at the same locus—the synapses made by the sensory neurons onto motor neurons and interneurons. The critical changes result from the reversal of the same regulatory agent, an increase or a decrease in the calcium current controlling transmitter release at that common locus, the same set of sensory synapses. Thus short-term memory is not reverberating activity in closed chains of neurons, as former investigators had supposed, but is actually a functional (plastic) change in the strength of a previously existing set of connections. (See Figure 5.13.)

With the recognition that certain forms of learning can alter the strength of synaptic connections for several hours or days, the question arises whether

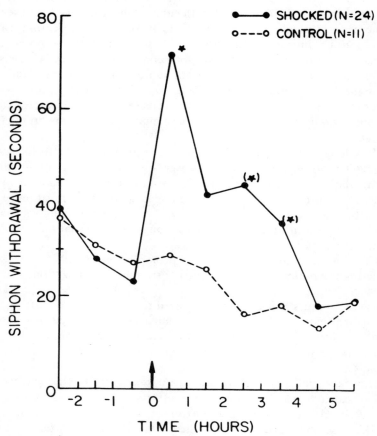

Figure 11.4. (A) Left: time course of sensitization after a single strong electrical shock to the tail (arrow). After this sensitizing stimulus the experimental animals had significantly longer withdrawals than controls for up to 4 hours. (B) Right: neural circuit of the gill component of the defensive withdrawal reflex to siphon stimulation. The sensory neuron (S.N. 24), excitatory interneuron (EXC. INT. 5), and the motor neuron (M.N. 6) are all unique, identified cells. Stimulating one of the facilitating interneurons (FAC. INT.) causes presynaptic facilitation of the connections between the sensory and the motor neurons. Kandel & Schwartz, 1982. Courtesy of Eric R. Kandel. Copyright © 1982 American Association for the Advancement of Science.

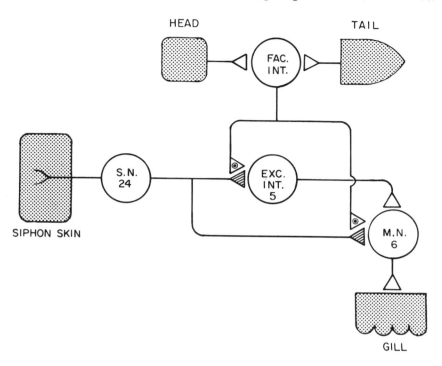

similar biochemical mechanisms could account for learning that persists for months or even years. Is long-term memory continuous with short-term memory? Does the long-term process have a different locus and require a different mechanism than immediate memory?

Both behavioral and cell biological studies show that short-term sensitization grades into long-term sensitization. A single painful shock produces sensitization in the sea snail that lasts for hours. Sixteen consecutive sensitizing stimuli prolong the memory for several days; sixteen spaced stimuli (four per day for four days) prolong it for several weeks. Two independent experiments show that short- and long-term sensitization also have a common cellular locus.

These findings suggest that the structural changes at the synapse that underlie short-term memory may be shared by simple forms of long-term memory.

LEARNING INVOLVES MORPHOLOGICAL CHANGES

Very recently, this suggestion has received morphological support. Craig H. Bailey and Mary Chen (1983) examined the fine structure of sensory neuron

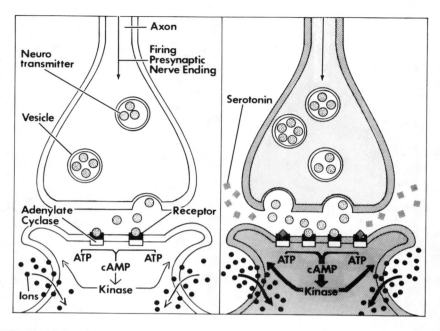

Figure 11.5. (A) Animals trained for long-term habituation (left) have smaller active zones and a decreased number of vesicles than their controls. (B) Animals trained for long-term sensitization (right) have larger active zones, many more vesicles, and release significantly more neurotransmitter into the synaptic cleft than their controls. Presynaptic facilitation is mediated by serotonin that is believed to increase the amount of the enzyme adenylate cyclase and stimulate formation of cAMP which increases ion flux and amplifies the efficacy of the synapse. After Bailey & Chen, 1983. Redrawn from various sources.

presynaptic terminals. They compared the active zones of these terminals, the critical site of plasticity for both the short- and the long-term forms of sensitization, in animals whose behavior had been modified by training and in control animals. The comparison showed dramatic morphological differences between the trained and the control groups. Two effects were striking: the size of the active zones was greatly enlarged in the experimental group, and the number of vesicles associated with each active zone had also increased in relation to the controls. Conversely, animals trained for long-term habituation were found to have smaller active zones and a decreased number of vesicles associated with each active zone than their controls. (See Figure 11.5.)

Since the total number of vesicles associated with active zones per sensory neuron is directly tied to the transmissive capabilities of sensory neurons, the investigators conclude that these structural changes are clearly involved in learning. In a highly trained neuron, the amount of transmitter released by a single action potential depends critically on the nature of the training and its effect on the fine structure of the release sites. Active zones thus appear to be plastic rather than immutable components of the synapse. The normal set of release sites serves as a scaffolding for behavior—a set of potential connections that can be enhanced or depressed for shorter or longer periods of time. Their observed alterations by training represent an anatomical substrate for memory consolidation.

An important implication of these findings is the obliteration of the classical sharp line between short-term memory and long-term memory. The concept of an absolute distinction has in any case been hard to maintain. When does a recently acquired bit of information disappear? For how long a time do certain memories persist? We do not know. What we do know is that, at least in simple forms, short-term learning grades into long-term learning at a common cellular locus—an appealing and enormously simplifying result.

A MOLECULAR MODEL OF LEARNING AND MEMORY

With the realization that stable and profound morphological and functional changes at the synapse result from training, the crucial question becomes: what are the molecular mechanisms that underlie them? If we can show that general principles of molecular biology that apply to the nervous systems of all animals account for these plastic changes in simple organisms, then it might be possible to explain human learning and memory.

Kandel and his associates propose an attractive model that pieces together the biochemical sequence of steps that underlie elementary learning and memory. Since the activity of a chemical agent is essential to transmission at a chemical synapse, the main structures involved are the presynaptic vesicles, the synaptic cleft, and the receptor sites. The synaptic vesicles are small globules that store uniform packets or quanta of the chemical transmitter used at the particular synapse. At the axon terminal of any one presynaptic neuron, it is generally thought that only one neurotransmitter substance is produced and stored in the vesicles for release into the synaptic cleft. A number of substances have been identified as neurotransmitters in the vertebrate brain. They fall into two major groups: One group consists of acetylcholine and certain monoamines—dopamine, norepinephrine, and serotonin—as well as the amino acids—GABA, glutamate, and glycine; the second group consists of a variety of neuropeptides discussed in Chapter Two.

The same neurotransmitter can have different effects, depending on the postsynaptic receptor proteins to which it binds. Acetylcholine, for example, acts in opposite ways on skeletal muscle cells and on heart muscle cells, exciting the former and inhibiting the latter. Thus synapses can be classified as excitatory or inhibitory because the receptors are decisive.

Kandel and Schwartz (1982) describe a specific sequence of molecular steps that mediate synaptic transmissions in *Aplysia.* (See Figure 11.6.)

1. The action potential of the presynaptic terminal causes an influx of free calcium current (Ca^{2+}) that leads vesicles to fuse with release sites.

2. The release sites liberate serotonin (in this animal, the likely transmitter for presynaptic facilitation) into the synaptic cleft.

3. The transmitter molecules diffuse across the cleft to be taken up by the receptors on the postsynaptic membrane that determine whether the target cell should fire an action potential or not.

4. The transmitter, when released, also acts on the membrane of the presynaptic sensory neuron and *leads to the formation of a new reaction inside the cell.* This reaction increases the concentration of a small molecule— cyclic adenosine monophosphate (cyclic AMP or cAMP). If we think of the chemical transmitter as the first messenger, then cAMP is a second messenger that amplifies and prolongs the signal. The process requires that the neurons mediating sensitization end near the synaptic terminals of the sensory neurons that synapse with the motor neurons for the gill withdrawal reflex. This process, called *presynaptic facilitation,* is interesting because it shows that neurons have receptors at two quite different sites. One site contains receptors (on the cell body and dendrites) that determine whether a cell should fire an action potential or not. The other site contains receptors (at the synaptic terminals) on the axon. These determine how much transmitter each action potential will release. The cellular activities regulated by cAMP and Ca^{2+} overlap to a large extent; both are second messengers that provide a mechanism for greatly amplifying the initial signal.

5. The stimulated synthesis of cAMP in turn causes the phosphorylation of a protein kinase inside the cell that inactivates the potassium ($K+$) channel and allows more Ca^{2+} to flow into the terminals.

6. An influx of calcium allows transmitter in the vesicles to bind to discharge sites and amplifies the efficacy of the synapse.

The biochemical cascade that increases cAMP and Ca^{2+} levels is commonly used in chemical signaling by all cells. In animal cells, cAMP exerts its effects by activating specific enzymes called *cAMP-dependent protein*

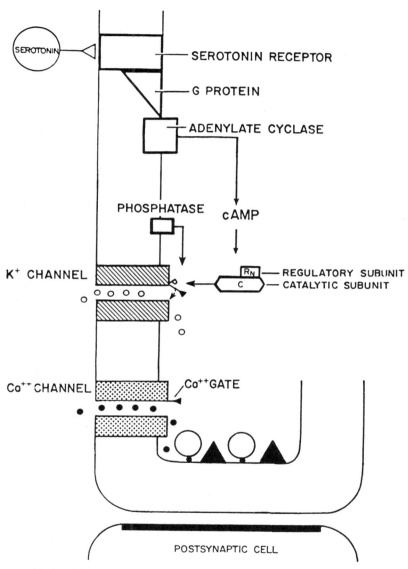

Figure 11.6. Molecular model of presynaptic facilitation underlying sensitization. Kandel & Schwartz, 1982. Courtesy of Eric R. Kandel. Copyright © 1982 American Association for the Advancement of Science.

kinases. A protein kinase is an enzyme that catalyzes the activities of proteins by phosphorylation; that is, it links a phosphoryl group to a side chain of amino acids in the protein, changing their configuration and their function. The protein kinase activated by cAMP has been shown to consist of two types of subunit—a regulatory subunit to which cAMP binds and a catalytic subunit that catalyzes the phosphorylation of the substrate protein molecules. In the absence of cAMP, the two subunits form an inactive complex. The binding of cAMP alters the conformation of the regulatory subunit, causing it to release the catalytic subunit, which is thereby activated.

In consequence, the cAMP-dependent kinase will bind to the presynaptic membrane, causing the closing of potassium channels and thereby slowing the repolarization of the action potential. The important net effect would allow more synaptic vesicles to bind to release sites and release more transmitter, thereby amplifying the response.

THE MECHANISM OF ASSOCIATIVE LEARNING AND MEMORY

Associative learning goes beyond the elementary forms of nonassociative perceptual learning (habituation and sensitization). While the elementary forms teach the learner to recognize or identify the stimulus object, associative learning applies to the relations between objects or events as well as to the occurrence of the events themselves. Classical conditioning is an obvious example. In classical conditioning, an initially weak or ineffective stimulus becomes conditioned (a CS) and produces a behavioral response after being paired with a strong unconditioned stimulus (a US). What we learn about causal relations through classical conditioning enables us to make predictions such as *if CS then US*. The CS thus becomes a signal that the US will follow.

Although sensitization is a simple nonassociative form of learning, it is of special interest because it is the enhancement of a reflex response to one stimulus as the result of exposure to a drive-related stimulus. Now that we know that sensitization results from the increased effectiveness of a previously existing synapse, we are tempted to ask whether a similar mechanism could explain classical conditioning. If sensitization is a precursor of classical conditioning, we could thus link associative learning to nonassociative learning.

Perhaps the components that account for nonassociative sensitization could serve as the basic mechanism for classical conditioning. Something else is needed, however. For classical conditioning to take place, two stimuli must be temporally paired. A temporal specificity mechanism is necessary.

In order to obtain classical conditioning with the mechanisms for sensitization, further amplification is essential to give a larger, longer-lasting response. In addition, the activity caused by the CS and the US must be contiguous. Like the process of fertilization by egg cell and sperm cell, their activities must converge at a common point in time. How and where do the two critical events—the CS and the US, or their neural symbols, the cognons—become linked in a contingent relation to one another?

The pairing in associative learning demands that the extra amplification occur when and only when the US follows the CS. The interstimulus interval must obey the laws of classical conditioning demonstrated by behavioral evidence. Thus, in addition to the mechanisms for sensitization, the sequence of steps must enable the US impulse activity to enhance that in the CS neurons—a presynaptic facilitatory effect that persists and is augmented on each pairing trial.

This effect could be achieved by the general theory developed by Kandel and Schwartz (1982) for the formation of nonassociative long-term memory. The model posits an alteration in gene expression leading to the synthesis of a new kinase, an enzyme that catalyzes the activation of an enzyme. In contrast to the agent sufficient for the formation of a short-term memory, this new kinase has the power to prolong the memory and insure its preservation over a long period. The new kinase is brought about by the activation of adenylate cyclase to increase cAMP by modifying the calcium influx. (See Figure 11.7.)

The strength of this theory lies in its ability to account for classical conditioning by the same biochemical cascade that increases cAMP and Ca^{2+} as intracellular mediators of extracellular signals that are commonly used as second messengers for chemical signaling. If CS-stimulated activity in the sensory neurons precedes the input from the US neurons, as it must since, unlike sensitization, conditioning does not work in reverse, then the pairing must enable the US impulse activity to enhance that in the sensory neurons responding to the CS. The US activates the facilitating neurons and the facilitating neurons then cause presynaptic facilitation of the CS sensory neurons. What happens is that the facilitation persists so that the next time you test the CS it still shows the effect of the enhanced facilitation.

The theory has two novel features: (1) a hypothesized new regulatory subunit with a greater sensitivity to cAMP and (2) a specific site for this subunit, allowing the kinase to be bound to the presynaptic membrane near the synaptic action mediating the memory.

Where does this cAMP-facilitated action take place? The answer has appeared and is beautifully simple. Hawkins et al. (1983) tested various possibilities and provide direct support for the terminals of the CS sensory neurons as *the sites* for the associative learning. The mechanism for temporal specificity in classical conditioning takes place *within the sensory neuron itself*.

Translated into the language of cognon theory, this means that the cognon representing the unitary perception of the neutral CS (bell tone, weak touch, or visual signal) stores the memory for its temporally paired US and

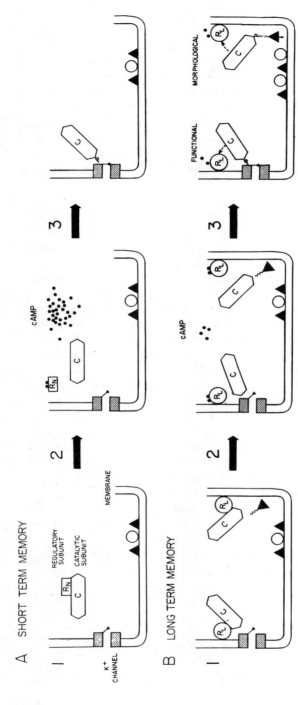

Figure 11.7. A model for the biochemical basis of long-term memory. (A1) In short-term memory a normal regulatory subunit (R_N) has no particular orientation with respect to a substrate membrane protein associated with the K + channel. Relatively high levels of cAMP are needed to activate (C) the catalytic subunit (A2) to phosphorylate the membrane protein (A3) and thus enhance release of transmitter. cAMP diminishes quickly and the memory fades. (B1) In long-term memory a new class of regulatory subunit (R_L) produces a site-specific protein kinase that is advantageously oriented with respect to both the channel and the mechanism that lines up transmitter vesicles. (B2) Since this new kinase has higher affinity for cAMP, less cAMP is needed for (B3), which leads to the stable enlargement of the synapse morphologically, and greater persistence of memory because it is embodied in R_L, a protein molecule. Kandel & Schwartz, 1982. Courtesy of Eric R. Kandel. Copyright © 1982 by the American Association for the Advancement of Science.

acquires the ability to "call up its image" in anticipation of the expected event. At the level of consciousness, this is the mechanism of hallucination; at subcortical levels, it insures the activation of the anticipatory behavior. In this way, the adaptability of the animal to its environment is strengthened.

The molecular hypothesis emphasizes the basic interrelatedness of all forms of learning. Associative learning and nonassociative learning both involve the modulation of cell transmission and do so by regulating ion channels. Habituation is depression of release by inaction of the calcium ion channel. Both sensitization and classical conditioning lead to enhancement by increasing the calcium influx.

The mechanism could be very general. Indeed Walters and Byrne (1983) report independent and similar results in another group of neurons in *Aplysia*. The possible application of a similar mechanism to the vertebrate nervous system is causing ripples of optimism and excitement among neuroscientists. It could well be that some such mechanism operates in human learning as a facilitatory system of neurons that project very diffusely. The contingency factor demands differential activity in neurons that are sensitive to the facilitating transmitter. A likely candidate for the facilitating mechanism in complex nervous systems is one of the diffusely projecting aminergic systems, known to play a role in arousal and depression. There may be many facilitating neuromodulators specifically localized in different regions of the brain. What we now have is an important lead to show us what to look for.

This work offers an enormously powerful and simplifying general principle to explain the importance of environmental factors and learning in the expression of new patterns of behavior.

Experimental analyses of learning and memory at behavioral, neurological, biochemical, and molecular levels provide direct evidence to support the model outlined in this book. In this model, many factors share in the cascade of events that result in learning and memory: at the psychological level, emotional arousal and attention; at the neurophysiological level, drive and antidrive; at the cellular level, presynaptic facilitation and depression; at the molecular level, within the neuron, cAMP-dependent kinase and possibly new gene products.

The various levels are related by a common locus of functional and morphological plasticity and, in associative learning, by a common temporal specificity. No single level is more valid or important than another. Each level represents a different manifestation of the same fundamental processes—how behavior is modified by experience and how this change is retained to produce more or less stable memory.

Learning and memory take place, not in a complex network of neurons but in change of efficacy at a single locus, a monosynaptic connection between a sensory neuron and other neurons. The key is synaptic plasticity mediated from below by cAMP and transmitter release, from above by drive or emotion and the need of the organism to learn what events cause things to happen in the world outside.

AN OVERALL VIEW

One is compelled to believe that learning, once thought to be a purely psychological process, vastly different from organic growth or tissue change, can produce equivalent or even more profound impact on behavior. A cognitive or neural activity can operate upon the organic substrate to modify its nature, and it can do so permanently and irreversibly.

The question is *where* in the brain are these memory "traces" (associations or conditioned responses) stored? Previous chapters have shown that neural symbols representing unitary perceptions or images belonging to the different sensory modalities are stored as *cognons* in their respective cognitive fields in the association cortex. Associative memories representing the connections between various cognons must necessarily be stored as modifications of those long intracortical connecting pathways, presumably as persistent facilitatory effects on transmitter release at presynaptic terminals leading to the appropriate cells.

It is not likely that these memory traces are localized in just one small region. In even a simple learning task, many channels are activated and form separate associations—actual connections between intramodal and intermodal cognons. The greater the number of such associative channels, the longer the period of retention will be, and the more readily retrievable a memory. There is ample opportunity for the distribution, if not exact reduplication, of activity throughout extensive cerebral areas. Such wide distribution of memory traces could explain Karl Lashley's failure to destroy particular learned discriminations by cutting away more and more extensive regions of the brain.

The paradox of the brain as a precisely wired device, like a computer, yet capable of permanently changing its structure by interacting with the environment, can be understood as the ability of a myriad of integrated circuit chips to effect widespread programs of activity.

The evidence is mounting that the persistence of memory depends on changes in functional effectiveness of previously existing chemical synaptic connections. The greater the number of such connections involved in the formation of associations between units, and the larger the number of such units, the greater the probability that newly learned items and events will be retained. Day-to-day behavioral experiences, calling forth conditioned images, verbal and motor rehearsals leading to still other conditioned images, strengthens these connections and adds new ones to reinforce earlier learning.

The stability of long-term memory is thus a function of the number of associations that feed into it. It is important also to consider the strength of the individual associations. The chief factors here are determined by the ontogenetic stages that formed the synapses initially. Here belong the genetic influences and critical early periods of development in which previously existing connections became effective (or were lost). Here too we must recognize the crucial impact of drive arousal under which the associations are established and maintained.

Whether other forms of memory depend on more profound structural changes than those outlined in this chapter remains for future research to discover. As far as is known now, all learning and memory processes can be seen as occurring at the same sites and resulting from the same general principles of functional modulation of synaptic terminals of appropriate cells.

SUMMARY

The ability to remember both specific events and general rules is basic to every other higher mental process—perception, thought, language, and creative imagination. Every expression of science and art depends upon highly selective acquisition, retention, and retrieval processes. The important questions are how we can remember and why, in both ordinary affairs and in certain cases of brain damage, we forget.

Mnemonic techniques use loci and imagery to improve retention. They are effective because they force the learner to take an active role in creating associations and organizing material into larger spatiotemporal units—higher-order cognons—for retention and subsequent retrieval.

Theories of forgetting attempt to account for the rapid loss of newly learned items. Proactive and retroactive inhibition stress the interfering effect of activity directly preceding or following acquisition of new material. Competition between similar stimuli for the control of different behavioral acts is a major cause of such interference. The disorders of memory encountered by the clinician are characterized by a striking dissociation between various aspects of memory. The facts of abnormal forgetting provide useful evidence for the localization of sensory-specific units—cognons—within categories belonging to particular analysers.

Investigations of learning in small systems of neurons support a unified theory of plastic change in which short- and long-term memory are stages of a single memory process. Tests of the plasticity theory of learning reveal that chemical synapses can undergo more or less persistent alterations in functional effectiveness (enhancement or depression) as the result of activity. Plastic anatomical and functional changes in the presynaptic terminals of active cognons may be regarded as a general form of information storage over shorter or longer periods. Genetic and developmental processes provide the scaffolding. Experience provides the contents of cognition and behavior.

Experience works through three processes: learning, the acquisition of knowledge about the environment; memory, the more or less persistent retention of new knowledge; and retrieval, the ability to use cues furnished by the environment to recognize, recall, or relearn previously acquired knowledge. Learning from experience is no less biological, no less uniquely determinative, no less powerful than heredity in shaping cognition and behavior over a lifetime.

SUGGESTED READINGS

Eccles, J.C., Ito, M., & Szentagothai, J. *The cerebellum as a neuronal machine.* Berlin: Springer-Verlag, 1967.

James, W. *Psychology: The briefer course* (G.W. Allport, Ed.). New York: Harper Torchbooks, The Academy Library, 1961.

Kandel, E.R. *Behavioral biology of aplysia.* San Francisco: W.H. Freeman, 1979.

Luria, A.R. *The mind of a mnemonist.* New York: Basic Books, 1968.

Milner, B. Brain mechanisms suggested by studies of temporal lobes. In F.L. Darley (Ed.), *Brain mechanisms underlying speech and language.* New York: Grune & Stratton, 1967.

Rosenzweig, M.R., & Bennett, E.L. (Eds.). *Neural mechanisms of learning and memory.* Cambridge: MIT Press, 1976.

Warrington, E.K., & Weiskrantz, L. Amnesic syndrome: Consolidation or retrieval? *Nature.* (London), 1970, **228,** 628–630.

Yates, F.A. *The art of memory.* Chicago: University of Chicago Press, 1966.

PART FOUR

Efferent Systems: The Neuropsychology of Motor Behavior

CHAPTER TWELVE

Efferent (Motor) Systems: Action Programs

The motor activity of organisms is of enormous biological significance—it is practically the only way in which the organism not only interacts with the surrounding environment, but also actively operates on this environment, altering it with respect to particular results. The theoretical lag observed in this area in comparison with the physiology of receptors or of internal processes is therefore very puzzling.

(Bernstein, 1967, p. 114–5)

INTRODUCTION

How can we explain voluntary action? Analysis in terms of stimulus-response units is extremely schematic and fails to convey behavior as a continuous process. For example, how shall we break up the horse's walking into a series of steps? The foreleg and the hindleg steps overlap in time and this overlap shows that there is some unity persisting for longer than a single step.

The eye-voice span in reading aloud affords a well-recorded example of overlapping processes in a behavioral sequence (Woodworth, 1938). The eyes keep several words ahead of the voice. While one word is being pronounced another word is being seen, and intervening words are in the neural processor. The interval between seeing a particular word and saying it aloud is about one or two seconds. The time span of this behavior greatly exceeds that of a single reaction to a word (i.e., about four-tenths of a second) and enables the reader to secure more continuity, phrasing, and expression than if she were to read each word separately with her normal reaction time.

Many simpler acts—running, swimming, washing, and hammering— show a smoothness that is very different from a sequence of separate movements. There is a consistent and persistent steering force at work throughout each such performance. Woodworth (1937) called this inner steer a "goal set" as a conceptual means of taking care of the time span of a unitary

Figure 12.1. Persisting "goal set." Courtesy of Andrew Emery Garson.

Figure 12.2. "Situation-and-goal set."

act. "Goal seeking in its lowest terms is the following of a consistent temporal pattern under the control of a persisting set" (Woodworth, 1937, p. 152). (See Figure 12.1.)

A behavior segment never terminates in a movement but always in sensory impulses resulting from the movement. Introspectively it is clear that muscular contraction in itself is almost never our goal. What interests us are the consequences of our movement.

Did our stone hit the mark? Did our high jump clear the bar? Did our search down the aisle of the supermarket reveal the brand of coffee called for by our shopping list? Any one of these goals can be achieved by a variety of different movements. What distinguishes a set of voluntary movements as a unitary act is the attainment of the intended goal.

The challenge to the neuropsychologist is to discover the physiological mechanism that underlies the representation of both intention and goal and fuses them into an integrated action.

Woodworth's (1937) concept of "situation-and-goal" set, while nicely descriptive of voluntary behavior that is at once responsive both to current stimulation and oriented toward the future, needs a solid neurophysiological substrate. (See Figure 12.2.)

WHAT IS VOLITIONAL IN VOLUNTARY ACTION?

The ability to preprogram a movement, to do what one wants to do, and not to do what one does not want to do, is the enigma of the *will*. Are we forced to conclude that "the will" is an illusion on the part of some befuddled metaphysicians? Most neurophysiologists today would agree with Sherrington (1906) that voluntary movements are built on a base of reflex processes. A self-delivered instruction puts the nervous system in a specific state or *voluntary set.*

In sum, two classes of inputs impinge on the motor cortex of the brain and generate the impulses directed to the motor neurons in the spinal cord and influence the local motor apparatus—body, arms, legs, head, and so on. One channel operates according to the laws of reflex action—the transcortical servo-loop (Evarts, 1973a; 1973b). The other channel used in voluntary movement originates in the basal ganglia and cerebellum and passes to the motor cortex by way of the thalamus. The first channel seems simplest. The second is more difficult to understand. How is it that the phylogenetically older subcortical structures are required for volition when simple reflexes are produced within the neocortex?

If volitional movement does not exclude reflexes and is largely outside consciousness, then what does "volitional" signify? Ragnar Granit (1977) the Swedish neurophysiologist, expressed it admirably: "What is volitional in voluntary movement is its purpose."

IDEOMOTOR ACTION: THE ACTION PROGRAM

William James's concept of *ideomotor* action has not been replaced by any more cogent or viable idea of the process of volition. In 1890, he wrote:

> Whenever a movement *unhesitatingly* and *immediately* follows upon the idea of it, we have ideomotor action. We are then aware of nothing between the conception and the execution. All sorts of neuro-muscular processes come between, of course, but we know absolutely nothing of them. We think the act and it is done; and that is all that introspection tells us of the matter. (Vol. 2, p. 522)

James's view aroused heated debate about the necessity of images, ideas of the amount of innervation or strain necessary for muscular contraction, and kinesthetic feelings and sensations. But James himself was quite clear that mental *imagery,* or the "idea of the *movement*" was *not* required to precede a movement in order that it be voluntary. He left no doubt that it is "*the anticipation of the movement's sensible effects,...*sometimes very remote... that is its *sufficient motor-cue*" or, as modern neuroscientists call it, its "*action program.*"

Volitional action, programmed action, is, above all, purposive action. "The marksman ends by thinking only of the exact position of the goal, the

Figure 12.3. The highly trained sensorimotor coordination of a skilled ballerina.

singer only of the perfect sound, the balancer only of the point of the pole whose oscillations he must counteract"(William James, 1890, Vol. 2, p. 497).

Often, of course, we think of an act for a long time without the action taking place. This is because the ideas of opposing ends inhibit the original ideas. The moment these inhibitory ideas cease, the block is released and the original intent springs forward into action.

We are now in a position to attempt an explanation of the mechanisms underlying voluntary motor behavior. The intent to perform a movement does not inhere in the muscles or the motor nerves or in thinking out what movements to make; it involves, first, the activation of motor association areas of the cerebral cortex in the kinesthetic programming centers of the brain. How does this system work?

Consider the problem of the gymnast poised for a complicated somersault on the tight rope, or the precise control of a surgeon looking through a dissecting microscope to move a scalpel with an accuracy of a fraction of a millimeter. How does the brain direct those muscles that enable human beings to perform these incredibly delicate and exacting feats of muscular balance and control? (See Figure 12.3.)

THE CONCEPT OF CENTRAL CONTROL

In the field of motor behavior, a remarkable fact is emerging repeatedly in studies of locomotion, alimentation, respiration, and other rhythmic behavior in a wide diversity of animals. The fact is that "the central nervous system does not require feedback from the sense organs in order to generate properly sequenced, rhythmic movement during repetitive behavior" (Delcomyn, 1980). Studies of walking in grasshoppers, flying in crickets, and swimming in gastropods all show compellingly that the commands for the activation of these spatially and temporally coordinated patterns of movement originate from the central nervous system. They are influenced by sensory events and elicited by stimuli; they depend on drive or motivation and thus reflect internal hormonal states. But the general principle of a "central pattern generator"—the concept of central control—is revolutionizing our ideas of motor behavior and the efficacy of single neurons in the brain. Here is the basis for the idea that human voluntary actions are preprogrammed by *cognons* in the cerebral cortex of the brain.

Individual cells exert a control over behavior that is specific and sometimes surprisingly powerful. Working with sea snails, crayfish, and goldfish, C.A.G. Wiersma (1938) discovered the "command cells" that coordinate an entire behavioral sequence. These include the neural control of the heartbeat (accomplished by only four cells in Aplysia); blood circulation (a dual-action neuron here); and a single command cell whose one impulse causes the goldfish to flee from threatened danger. (See Figure 12.4.)

Motor coordination depends on the integration of muscular movements by a central action program. The action program generates complex sequences that are organized within the central nervous system. They do not rely on external stimuli or their signals sent from the receptors in the periphery. The program comes, not from without, but from within. The question arises: what governs the apparently intelligent variations in movements that are beautifully adapted to abrupt and often radical changes in conditions of the environment and the state of the organism?

The insect scurries across continuously changing terrain, up and down blades of grass, sand, stones, and mud, and corresponding sensory signals must induce variations in locomotor behavior. After amputation of its middle legs, the postoperative roach immediately runs off with an entirely new gait without special practice or experience. On the one hand, the behavior is exquisitely responsive to minute changes in external environmental circumstances; on the other hand, the behavior is well organized to make optimally effective use of the available motor apparatus at any moment.

THREE DIVISIONS OF THE CENTRAL
MOTOR BEHAVIORAL SYSTEM

Voluntary motor acts are represented in a central motor behavioral system. In higher mammals this system has three major divisions: the *cerebrum,* the

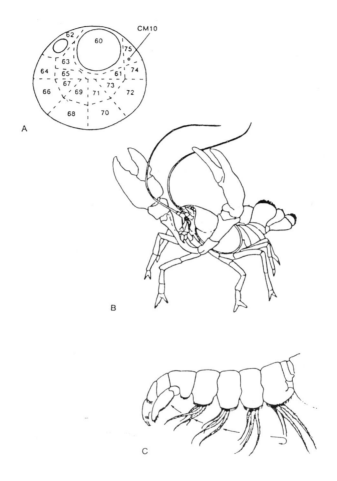

Figure 12.4. A single "command cell." (A) When stimulated, releases the defensive posture shown in (B). Another specific command neuron releases dynamic, rhythmic movements, such as swimmeret beating (C). Wiersma, 1958. Courtesy of the Society of Experimental Biology and Medicine.

Mind and Brain

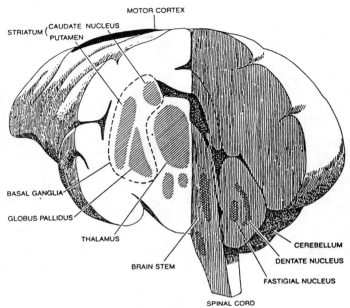

Figure 12.5. Brain of macaque monkey seen from rear. The drawing reveals subcortical structures that control movement. *Basal ganglia:* the caudate and putamen segments of the striatum and the globus pallidus are surrounded by a broken line. Near the center line is the *cerebellum* sectioned to expose its interior dentate and fastigial nuclei. At top left, the *motor cortex* of the cerebral cortex is activated via the thalamus (center). From E.V. Evarts, "Brain Mechanisms of Movement," *Scientific American*, 1979, *241*, 164–179. Copyright © 1979 by Scientific American, Inc. All rights reserved.

cerebellum, and the *basal ganglia.* (See Figure 12.5.) Each great nuclear system is essential for voluntary motor control. Each plays a separate role, but all work in concert to bring about complex serial actions and skilled movement patterns, especially those serving verbal communication and fine manual dexterity. The two main routes carrying impulse traffic to and from the cerebral cortex to the brainstem are called the *corticobulbar* and *corticospinal* tracts. (See Figure 12.6.)

The simple reflexes of the two phylogenetically earlier divisions are "voluntary" in the sense that they have become functionally connected to conditioned stimuli to form instrumental conditioned responses. Their programming centers are located in the *cerebellum* and *basal ganglia* and send signals to the motor cortex by way of the thalamus.

In contrast to simple unconditioned and conditioned reflexes, complexly organized movement patterns have their programming centers in the *cerebral cortex.* That a specific location actually exists in the brain to serve as a *motor*

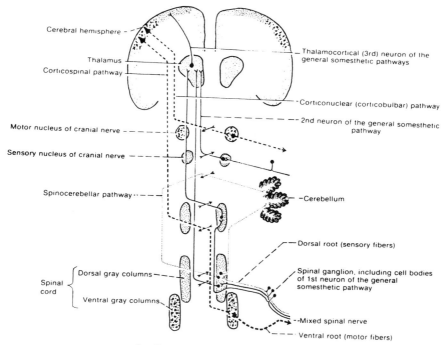

Small arrows indicate decussations.

Figure 12.6. Central motor behavioral system showing the main cortico-spinal and corticobulbar pathways. Bossy, 1970.

cortex was unknown before its discovery by Fritsch and Hitzig in 1870. Before that time, the cerebral cortex was widely believed to contain only thoughts, certainly not movements.

The next step was the detection of a special set of giant *pyramidal* neurons that sent axons down from the motor cortex to make direct connections with spinal cord neurons. These are *Betz* cells, named for their Russian discoverer, Vladimir Betz (1881). Their centers in the association cortex encode instructions for action. Many smaller pyramidal cells come from area 6 in front of the motor cortex and also from somatic sensory areas 3, 2, and 1, in the parietal lobe (see Fig. 12.2). They send off many collaterals to other parts of the brain called a *corollary discharge* to keep them informed in a kind of neural update of the commands sent to the musculature. The descending pyramidal tract neurons innervating muscles *code* for the intended force required to produce movements. An *extrapyramidal* system, including the cerebellum and the basal ganglia is now known to be inseparable from the pyramidal system.

Compelling evidence expressed by scalp potentials localizes the *cognons* of the kinesthetic system serving human speech and complex manipulation skills in the premotor area of the frontal lobes of the neocortex. About 30 percent of all movements requiring somatosensory regulation fibers originate there. Another 30 percent of movement fibers arrive from area 6, in the prefrontal lobe anterior to the motor cortex, and the remaining 40 percent arise in the parietal and temporal lobes.

The cerebral cortex analyzes and synthesizes patterns of movement and stores them in memory. But voluntary movement is impossible without the cerebellum and the basal ganglia. These subcortical structures contain the function generators that convert the highly focused programs of the cerebral cortex into spatiotemporal motor patterns. Rapid movements are pre-programmed by the cerebellum with regard to both their timing or rate and their duration. Saccadic eye movements, for instance, are not under voluntary control. Nothing you can do will make them faster—or slower. Slow smooth movement, following a moving target with the eyes, in contrast, requires a ramp generator that is relatively more dependent on voluntary control but is also controlled by the external stimulus—the moving target. The basal ganglia serve as ramp generators for slow, voluntary movements of different speeds and durations.

The motor cortex of the cerebrum takes the output of the cerebellum and the basal ganglia and processes them still further. This cerebral processing is needed to regulate sophisticated motor actions, the visual scrutiny of complex patterns and objects, or the coordinated movements of all parts of the body in playing tennis.

These highly developed structures are widely linked to cognons of the emotive system and to cognons of particular analyzers, sight, hearing, touch, and so on, by means of synaptic connections established during the life history of the individual. These connections enable the individual to select and release programs of action in a flexible and dynamic coordination. Behavior is thus adapted to changing states of the organism and to momentary shifts in the conditions of the environment. Loops playing through the basal ganglia are essential to initiate movement. At the same time, the open loop of the cerebellum provides preprogrammed information to the motor cortex.

The direct cortical control of the distal limb muscles by lateral corticospinal pathways is a relatively late evolutionary development. This enables higher primates, including the human actor, to move individual muscles independently from one another. This capacity, known as *fraction-ation of movement,* is lost completely after lesions either of the pyramidal tract or the cerebellum. The victim is unable to grasp an object by opposing fingers; the hand becomes a shovel and can be used only by contracting all the digits around the object. (See Figure 12.7.)

Kornhuber (1974) draws an interesting distinction between two sets of

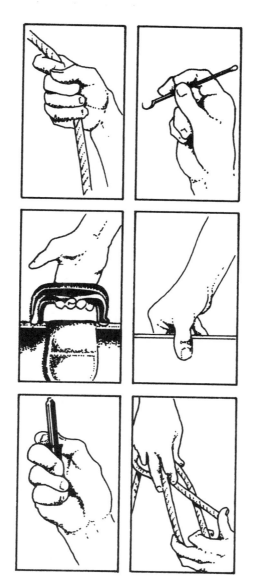

Figure 12.7. Some manipulative functions of the human hand.

mechanisms that regulate motoric interaction between cerebrum, cerebellum, and the basal ganglia. He calls them *strategy,* and *tactics. Strategy* is under the control of drive. Hunger arouses the central motor behavioral system to search for food. The resulting movements are under the control of factors (blood sugar, etc.) sensed centrally in the hypothalamus. *Tactics* of search depend on factors in the environment and their central representation in the various analyzers—specific visual and somatosensory units in the association cortex conditioned to particular instrumental acts. Motor learning in complex human skills takes place in the forebrain.

Evidence for the involvement in movement of these different parts of the brain derives from studies of the *praxic* (movement) disorders. Parkinson's disease, Huntington's chorea, and tardive dyskinesia are diseases of the *basal ganglia*. Diseases of the *cerebellum* affect synergy, the coordinated contractions of agonistic and antagonistic muscles that make possible smoothly controlled movements. *Ataxia* of gait (the "drunken sailor's" walk) results from lack of synergy. Abnormal muscle tone, tremor, and speech articulatory disorder *(dysarthria)* are due to *cerebellar* lesions.

The control of both the strategy and tactics of movement becomes voluntary at a higher level when the *cerebral cortex* enters to program the intended motor activity. Luria (1966) describes a patient who exemplifies the distinction between intention and ability to act.

The patient with severe brain damage caused by a tumor of the left frontal lobe is instructed to *lift his hand.* If his hand is lying on top of the bedclothes the verbal instruction readily triggers the movement. If, however, his hand is under the bedclothes and he has first to take it out, he cannot obey. The action becomes impossible and the patient exclaims helplessly, "yes, of course, lift my hand"—yet he makes no movement to do so. The deficit is not in the executive organs; obviously the arm and hand muscles are capable of the movement. The inability to perform the act lies in the absence of its program due to the lesion of the left frontal lobe.

In contrast, the patient with Parkinson's disease, a disease of the basal ganglia, suffers from a rhythmical tremor at rest, rigidity of muscle tone, slowness in getting up from a chair—symptoms resulting from a loss of dopamine in the corpus striatum and related degeneration of nigrostriatal fibers. The Parkinsonian patient wants to initiate movement; he intends to button his jacket or put on his shoes, but cannot execute his program. He can "get set" but cannot "go."

In patients with Huntington's chorea, another form of basal ganglia disease, unwanted movements occur that resemble the movements aimed at by healthy subjects, but the goals seemingly aimed at by the patient are never attained. The victim of Huntington's chorea finds himself making movements that he does not intend.

RHYTHMIC ACTION (VON HOLST'S OSCILLATORS)

A pacemaker generates rhythmic signals all by itself. The frog's heart continues to beat hours after it has been removed from the frog. As Gallistel (1980) vividly tells us, many components of the nervous system, like the heart, are pacemakers or oscillators—little neural clocks that go tick-tock, tick-tock, without any input from outside the body. Each tick goes to one set of muscles; each tock sends a signal to the antagonistic set of muscles. The rhythmic back and forth movements of the legs, wings, or fins in the locomotion of their owners are controlled by these endogenously active oscillators.

Not only locomotor behavior, but eating, drinking, grooming, waking, and sleeping also depend upon neural oscillators. In fact, these neural oscillators enter into every sort of behavior. They are the basis for *central programs* that run off without the help of descending signals from the brain. Eric von Holst (1973) discovered the principles of nervous coordination (that enable a handful of oscillators to generate many different patterns of behavior) in place of the old chain-reflex theory of the nervous coordination of movement.

Von Holst arrived at a new theory of coordination in the nervous system that emphasized two special principles that apply to oscillators—the *magnet effect* and *superimposition*. The simplest oscillation is sinusoidal; a swinging pendulum describes a sine wave; the traces made by a vibrating tuning fork, a point on the rim of a running wheel, and a pacemaker neuron in the animal or human nervous system all approximate sine curves also. Every complex movement can be obtained by the combination of the inputs of two oscillators. Whether the movement is made by an insect's leg, a bird's wing, or a person's arm, the trajectory (tracing) of the movement can be obtained by *superimposing* two sinusoidal curves with different frequencies. (See Figure 12.8.) In superimposing two sinusoids, one adds the value of one curve at a given instant to the value of the other at the same instant; the compound curve is determined by the values of three parameters of each one of the component curves—amplitude, frequency, and phase. If the two component curves are 180 degrees out of phase, one will cancel the other and the result will be no movement at all. If the curves are completely in phase, their superimposition will result in additional and mutual facilitation. Intermediate phase differences add to corresponding patterns of superimposed wave motions or functional patterns. Usually one rhythm attempts to impose itself on the other. This battle for dominance is what von Holst called the *magnet effect*. We can easily rotate our two arms with the same rhythm. When we try to move our two arms with different rhythms, we experience difficulty. The battle between the arms may be won after some practice, especially if we beat twice as fast with one arm as with the other. If we lie on our backs and try to move

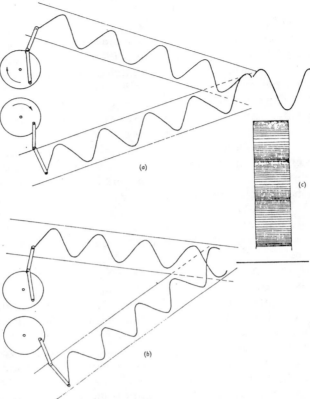

Figure 12.8. Superimposition of two sinusoids: (A) waves meet in phase; (B) waves meet 180° out of phase; (C) mapping the interference pattern.

our legs with different rhythms we usually fail; the magnet effect of the leg rhythm is stronger than that of our arms.

Thus the magnet effect is the form in which one automatism fights for control of the other. Its biological usefulness occurs when it continually stabilizes two rhythms with a reciprocal relationship in which one augments the action of the other. It is only then that superimposition permits harmonious coordinated action. Superimposition combines the outputs of the oscillators; the magnet effect coordinates the oscillators themselves in order to maintain a common tempo and fixed phase difference. The coxswain exerts a magnet effect on her crew by repeatedly calling, "Stroke!—stroke!"; the conductor exerts a magnet effect by marking the tempo with a baton; any momentary difference in rhythm is compensated for by speeding up or slowing down to the leader's tempo. The child can keep pace with her father's footsteps only by taking several small steps to his longer stride; she keeps in phase by repeatedly double stepping; a little hop (ball-change), with the same foot leading, keeps father and daughter in synchronous phase.

Aspects of this struggle appear in the attentional and perceptual side of behavior as well as in motor action. This analogous sort of rivalry may be the result of higher cortical oscillators responsible for the alternations of ambiguous figures, reversible figure and ground, and similar familiar, but puzzling, fluctuations of perception (see Chapter Five).

The all-pervasiveness of rhythmic discharge in the nervous system is paralleled by oscillations in physical materials. One falls in step with a band; and a thousand feet stepping in time with a slow rhythm, Ellington's "Satin Doll," resulted in a tragic accident in a new Hyatt Hotel in Kansas City when the suspended walkway collapsed under the impact of the temporally spaced vibrations of dancing feet which were transmitted to the steel structure. The aerodynamic stability of a suspension bridge depends on the engineer's knowledge and ability to build into it a robust resistance to the magnet effect of winds on its supporting cables. "Galloping Gertie" (the Tacoma bridge that collapsed) is an object lesson given to every engineering student before being licensed to practice. (See Figure 12.9.)

Figure 12.9. "Galloping Gertie." The Tacoma-Narrows bridge shortly before it broke up in a 42 mph wind on November 7, 1940. The roadway can be seen twisting around its long axis in dynamic oscillation. Photograph courtesy of Dr. D.B. Steinman.

THE ORIGIN OF VOLUNTARY MOVEMENTS

How do action programs develop and become perfected as higher order skills? The infant pulling herself up to stand, taking her first tentative steps, is just learning to walk. Both maturation and exercise are necessary to achieve the graceful skill and exquisite balance and control of the champion athlete or prima ballerina. What brain mechanisms are required to form these complex functions?

Movements performed by animals and humans originate in three different ways:

1. They may originate as unconditioned reflexes to various noxious or other trigger stimuli (kicking, crying, sneezing, scratching, swallowing, etc.).
2. They may be produced as the result of an external force (manipulation of an arm or limb, pressure on the body, passive flexion of the leg, and the like).
3. They may be induced by electrical stimulation of the central nervous system, particularly the motor cortex of the brain.

Can all these movements be instrumentalized? In other words, can they be uncoupled from external control and transformed from reflex or passive movements into active, voluntary self-produced movements? Let us examine each of the three categories, one by one.

Instrumentalization of Unconditioned Reflexes

There is extensive evidence that, in animals, most unconditioned reflexes can be used for instrumental conditioning. Such motor acts as scratching, flexing the hind leg, and licking the anus that were never before used by the organism for securing food may be rapidly transformed into food-securing reactions (Konorski, 1967). We can teach a dog or a cat to sit, flex a leg, press a pedal, draw in some object from outside the cage, and to perform various locomotive responses for food or other reward.

Still, some motor acts are more easily conditioned than others. The manipulative movements of the forelimbs are most readily established as instrumental food responses. The pigeon pecks naturally at food as an unconditioned reflex. Conditioning the pigeon to peck at a disk in order to receive a food reinforcement is thus a simple matter. These responses already possess the food reward character, and training merely transfers the response to the experimental situation.

The ability to establish functional connections between small groups of cells when they are simultaneously or sequentially activated is a general property of all organisms that possess a central nervous system. Such connections, of course, can only occur between those cell groups that are linked by prefunctional (potential) connections formed during ontogeny. Thus some movements produced by passive displacement of the limbs or other parts of the body cannot be instrumentalized—that is, they are incapable of being integrated into a program of active, self-produced movements. For example, the flexion of the hind leg in dogs in response to an electric shock to the paw appeared to Miller and Konorski (1928) as a perfectly adequate method for the formation of a conditioned food response. Although with dogs they were occasionally successful, they were unable to apply the same technique to cats. Every attempt to instrumentalize the flexion of the hindleg in cats resulted in a total failure, possibly because, unlike the dog, the cat's shorter limbs enabled her to preserve her balance without *actively* opposing the experimenter's lifting of her hindleg.

The essential special difference is the length of the limbs. In long-limbed animals, such as dogs and goats, the passive raising of the leg endangers the preservation of the body's balance and is actively opposed. Such active muscular opposition is as important as active muscular conformity in transforming a reflex into a volitional motor act.

Turning to human experience, we can hardly cancel a sneeze at will or swallow when the mouth is completely dry. The nearly ubiquitous human complaint of constipation attests to our frequent inability to regulate the excretory response by instrumental training. It seems that the more firmly a given reflex action is yoked to a stimulus eliciting it, the more difficult its emancipation from that stimulus becomes.

Instrumentalization of Passive Movements Impossible

What about passive movements of the body or limbs? If a passive movement is followed by reinforcement or drive reduction, will it become instrumentalized? Will its reinforcement lead to the formation of a conditioned instrumental response? There is good reason to believe that the answer to this question is *no*. Only active *self-produced* movements can be utilized as conditioned instrumental responses.

Experiments on visually inexperienced newborn kittens by Held and Hein (1963) provided a dramatic demonstration of the importance of active versus passive displacements of the body for the visual guidance of behavior. (See Figure 12.10.)

Some kittens were allowed freely to explore the experimental compartment by moving actively about. Each one was tied to a small carriage in which a litter-mate rode. Wherever the lead cat went, the vehicle with its passenger followed. Thus both animals traversed the same space and both had access to the same visual stimulation. Yet subsequent tests showed that only the kittens in the first group were able to use vision to guide their movements. The passive kittens completely failed to solve visual-motor problems—for example, they

Figure 12.10.   The lead cat sees and walks actively; the passenger in the cart
is passively exposed to the same visual stimulation but prevented from using
her legs. Later tests show that only the active kitten develops depth discrimination.
Held & Hein, 1963. Copyright 1963 by the American Psychological Association. Adapted by permission of the authors.

could not place their paws on supporting planks, but were just as likely to claw
the air between the planks. Unable to see what they were doing, they behaved
like blind animals.

But what is it about active or self-produced movement that makes it so
different from passive movement in its effects? A possible interpretation of
these findings is that attention to visual space stimuli must be aroused in order
for the necessary cognons to be established for visual motor coordination.

An interesting experiment by Walk, Shepherd, and Miller (1978)
supports this hypothesis. They gave confined kittens their only visual
experience by allowing them to view some mouse-sized cars speeding up,
down, and around a toy track repeatedly. The kittens watched intently. Later,
although they had not been able to see and use their legs under visual
guidance, they showed good discrimination of visual space. The experimenters concluded that attention, not self-induced locomotion, was the key to
perceptual development of visually guided behavior. Unlike the passive
passenger kitten of Held and Hein, these animals had been visually exposed to
stimuli that had significance for them, that aroused the visual targeting
reflexes and kinesthetic feedback from active eye movements. Under the
influence of drive, perception is reinforced.

Held (1965) also carried out experiments on humans in which one group
of subjects with prismatic (distorting) goggles on their eyes were allowed to
observe only passive movements of their arms. A second group of subjects
performed active movements to point at targets in their visual field, which was

also prismatically displaced by the goggles. The active group readily learned to compensate for the prismatic displacement of the target; the passive group showed no improvement. Thus the conclusion is compelling: the subject must perform the given movement by herself in order to reproduce it in instrumental conditioning.

Neal Miller (1969) of Rockefeller University has impressively demonstrated in rats the behavioral modification, or instrumental conditioning of autonomic responses, traditionally confined to classical conditioning experiments. Miller successfully conditioned heart rate, blood pressure, even temperature regulation, supposed *involuntary* reactions.

The clinical application of these results to human patients has met with mixed success. Some individuals have been able to modify their blood pressure or other autonomic reactions by monitoring their visible effects as pointer readings on a scale, but there is little evidence as yet of direct, positive transfer or benefits outside the laboratory.

The important question arises as to whether *all* the motor and glandular effects of unconditioned reflexes can be made instrumental (voluntary) by the appropriate procedure. The answer is uncertain, of course, since it is always possible that some appropriate conditioning procedure exists for every response, but has not yet been tried.

Yet is is clear that some unconditioned reflexes are very difficult to condition as instrumental responses. Take yawning, for example. The dog's yawning reflex may be reinforced by food, but instead of true instrumental yawning, the animal simply opens its mouth. Humans also experience difficulty in producing certain unconditioned reflexes voluntarily. Even an experienced actress can't weep realistically on command. She can make real tears flow only by recalling and re-experiencing sorrow or grief, thus evoking a limbic stimulus.

Direct Brain Stimulation Elicited by Passive Movements

The evidence from the clinic and the experimental laboratory strongly supports our subjectively experienced distinction between active and passive, or voluntary and involuntary activity. Raising your hand to ask a question is self-initiated and voluntary; the feeling is quite different when your hand is passively lifted by an external agent.

In Wilder Penfield's craniotomy patients, mild electrical stimulation applied to the exposed motor cortex during surgery produced various movements. "The patient may be astonished to discover that he is moving his arm or leg...or to hear himself vocalizing, but he never has the impression that he has willed himself to do those things"(Penfield & Roberts, 1959, p. 35). The *drive* to act is absent.

Stimulation of a sensory area also interferes invariably with the normal, active, motor control of that area. Applied to the postcentral gyrus, Penfield's electrode caused a sensation of tingling in the contralateral thumb. The patient was unable to use that thumb to explore the texture of an object as long as the stimulation continued.

In some areas the electrical stimulus produces inhibition of specific movements, and the arm or leg lies motionless, even though the patient tries voluntarily to move it. Whether the effect of electrical stimulation is to activate or to inhibit a movement, the patient is powerless to resist the interference by any exercise of will.

Penfield and his associates found the effect of applying electrical currents to the cortex was first an electrical *interference* with the normal function of the local area under stimulation and second an electrical *activation* of some more or less distant ganglionic mechanism that had a normal functional connection with the local area of cortex.

HOW ARE VOLUNTARY MOVEMENTS RELATED TO REFLEXES?

The neuroscientists who specialize in the study of motor behavior tell us that reflexes and voluntary movements are *not* opposites. The pioneer investigator Hughlings Jackson (1931) insisted that volitional movements are subject to the laws of reflex action. If that is so, what happens when a person wants to carry out a muscular response that is exactly opposite to a normal reflex response? To paraphrase an illustration from Evarts (1979), a ballet dancer who trains herself to fall forward when she is pushed from behind must train herself to overcome the normal reflex response to preserve her equilibrium that would make her lean backward. Her centrally programmed movement requires that she now shift out of the closed loop (reflex) mode of response that preserves equilibrium into an open loop (voluntary) mode of response that will result in her pitching forward (into the arms of someone waiting to catch her). Ingenious techniques that enable experimenters to place microelectrodes in the brain of an animal and record from them while it is executing skilled movements show how the cortex exerts this control.

Evarts and Tanji (1976) studied the activity of motor cortex neurons in monkeys that had been first trained to react to the involuntary movement of their arms by holding a handle immobile for a few seconds. The reflex reaction is under continuous closed loop control by negative feedback to the Betz cells from the sensory area of the cortex. How would the motor cortex neurons react to new instructions to push a handle forward in response to a green light cue and pull a handle back to a red light cue? They examined the relation between voluntary and reflex responses by training monkeys to stabilize a handle (much as a marksman must stabilize his gun). The immediate reflex response (to stabilize the handle) thus had to be replaced by a voluntary, differentiated push or pull of the handle in response to the color cue. (See Figure 12.11.)

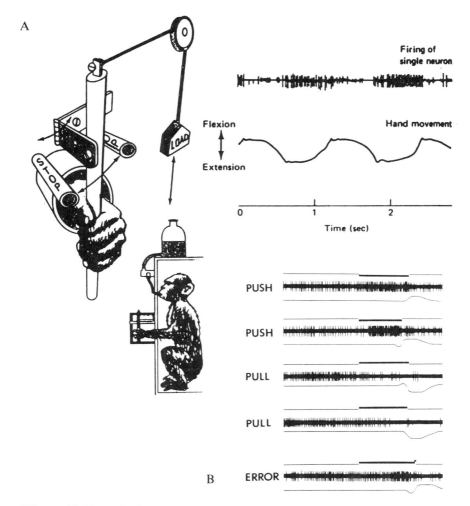

Figure 12.11. (A) By moving the handle, the monkey changed a potentiometer output that controlled the position of the track lamp. The monkey was required to maintain alignment between track lamp and target lamp. Evarts, 1980. (B) Relationship between the neuronal response to an instruction and the occurrence of an error of performance (bottom trace marked "error"). The instruction was pull but the activity of the neuron increased instead of decreasing. The response of the monkey to the perturbation on this trial was pushing (see top two traces) rather than pulling (third and fourth traces), which had been called for by the pull instruction. Evarts & Tanji, 1976; Evarts, 1981. By permission of the American Physiological Society.

403

The signals that control the open loop preprogrammed movements do not come from the same sensory area of the brain that controls reflexes. Sensory feedback is critical for stabilizing the position of the hand in space despite movements of many parts of the body. The control of reflexes is thus transcortical.

The control of centrally programmed, open loop preprogrammed movements is an ascending one; that is, the pathway runs from cerebellum to thalamus to cortex. Cells in the cerebellum fire well in advance of the muscular reaction to a learned visual cue. Another set of cell groups sends signals to the thalamus in addition to the input from the cerebellum. The cerebellum converts messages about the stretching of muscles and tendons into messages about movements; somesthetic proprioceptors inform the brain about the positions of the limbs (Konorski, 1970b).

The relations between higher centers and lower centers are thus not fixed, not one of master and servants, but the more flexible commutability of subordinate and executive roles, expressed in the interpretation of biological systems as heterarchies rather than rigid hierarchical trees.

KINESTHETIC COGNONS: PROGRAMMING UNITS FOR COMPLEX VOLUNTARY MOVEMENTS

The *kinesthetic centers* in the premotor association areas of the cerebral cortex store the action programs that select and release complex skilled voluntary movements. These high-level programmers are cognons in the highest centers of the kinesthetic analyzer. They are targets for sensory input as well as a source of motor output. In many ways they are similar to cognons in the association areas of the perceptual analyzers related to vision, audition, and the other senses.

Like other cognons, the kinesthetic cognons are neither primarily sensory nor primarily motor neurons: they are both. They serve as acquired releasers of other interneurons that send orders to the executive muscle centers. Thus they represent the integration of elements that have been linked by experience. The strength of the connection between a particular kinesthetic programming unit and a given stimulus depends on the recency and the frequency of the linkage pairing them under the influence of a particular drive. Drive plays an essential role by providing arousal in the corresponding cognons or neural centers. The subjective side of this neural activity involves paying attention to the limb to be moved and the accomplishment of the goal of the movement.

In other words, a voluntary act is formed and executed according to the laws of instrumental conditioning. The conditioned instrumental reflex (CR) is established between the representative of the "reinforcing"(unconditioned) stimulus (US) and the kinesthetic center (cognon) involved in the performance of that movement. This CR quickly becomes linked to a set of conditioned stimuli (CSs), a situation, or context that sets the occasion for the response to occur. Instrumental conditioning thus depends on two types of connections, those linking the cognon of the CS with the cognon of movement, the unconditioned response, and those connecting the cognon of movement, the kinesthetic center programming the instrumental movement with the US— the intended goal.

A motor program requires the organism to be active in three-dimensional space and engaged in behavior having a time span greater than that of a simple reaction to a single stimulus. The cognition implied in a program is not separated from doing, and goal seeking in animals is an obvious fact of their behavior.

In well-known experiments on delayed reaction, goal set is often visible in the persistent posture of the animal during the period of delay (Chapter Ten). When the animal is not permitted to remain pointed toward the goal, but is taken briefly into another room and then returned, the response when released will be prompt and sure. Some implicit program or intention to go to a specific place has bridged the interval. We need not suppose that this program is consciously planned. Yet certainly it incorporates past experience and the goal being sought. The results of past exploration and stimulation are stored, if only briefly, and this memory is retrieved when the actual situation is presented again. But the delayed response is dramatically impaired by bilateral frontal lesions, as Jacobsen (1935) first showed in chimpanzees. Subsequent studies of human research on patients confirmed Jacobsen's results and sought to discover where in the prefrontal area the trouble arose.

An even more pertinent question is: what is the cue that guides the individual in making the correct delayed response? Konorski and Lawicka (1964) proposed the hypothesis that the essential cue is provided by the *spatiokinesthetic image* of the itinerary to a given goal. Thus, in the animal experiment when one of the food cups is signaled by a preparatory cue, this cue evokes the associated set of spatiokinesthetic units or cognons that program the appropriate response. That program is then fulfilled when the subject is released.

The hypothesis gains support from several observations: Performance of the delayed response is best when the stimulus cue is contiguous to the food cup. A buzzer sounded right next to the correct food cup is a much clearer and more direct signal than a remote one. The role of contiguity is common to all conditioned experiments.

The placement of food cups, one of which the subject must choose, is critical also. If the alternatives are at right angles to one another, the spatiokinesthetic discrimination is easy. If they are closer together, making an acute angle with the starting point, the discrimination is difficult, and delayed response performance falters.

These observations strengthen the hypothesis that the prefrontal area is the site of spatiokinesthetic cognons for motor programs.

Monkeys, dogs, cats, and rats with frontal lesions of both hemispheres are severely disturbed in delayed response tests, not because their short-term memory is impaired, but because they are unable to program the spatio-kinesthetic performance in the frontal control centers. They have lost the capacity to plan ahead. They cannot recall what movements are necessary, and in what order they are necessary, to reach the intended goal.

Feuchtwanger (1923) conducted one of the few systematic studies of large numbers of patients with brain damage. The injuries to these patients were caused, not by lobotomies, but by gunshot wounds sustained in World War I. Feuchtwanger's comparison of 200 frontal and 200 nonfrontal patients led him to conclude that the specific changes following frontal lesions were not intellectual or memory defects, but emotional (ranging from euphoria to depression), and, most strikingly, an *incapacity for making plans or programs of action.*

In keeping with the asymmetry found in other parts of the cortex, the left frontal lobe is concerned with the programs for movements related to language (speech and writing), and the right frontal lobe controls movements related to nonverbal abilities, such as gestures and emotional expressions. Both frontal lobes, however, play an important role in nearly all behavior, and bilateral lesions have far greater effects than do unilateral frontal lesions.

MATCHING PROGRAM AND PERFORMANCE

What tells a pitcher just when to release the ball? How does a player know exactly when to swing the bat? Even in the absence of sensory feedback from the periphery, a person must *feel* that a movement has been ordered because of the very fact that the appropriate kinesthetic units have been centrally activated. But the crucial test of appropriate execution is the comparison between the intended goal and the achieved result. That requires some place and some mechanism for checking whether there has been a match or a mismatch between program and performance. The prepared action program or behavioral plan has targeted a particular consummatory aim.

The preparatory stage of goal-directed behavior, the targeting of the task, is not, however, limited to the elaboration of a suitable action program. It must also provide potential opportunities for comparing the action performed with the initial program and for assessing its success or failure.

Most neuropsychologists agree that an essential role in this drive-associated behavior is played by the frontal lobes. Patients with lesions of the frontal lobes lose this ability of critical appraisal because they no longer receive information concerning internal bodily states. Frontal lobe lesions are characterized in clinical psychiatry by two main symptoms: incapacity for making plans or programs of action and absence of critical appraisal. Luria (1966) described patients with severe frontal lobe lesions as impulsive but unable to connect with objectives, perseverating in maladjustive responses, unaware of their own defects, and even satisfied with their actions, however defective they may be. Here are some examples given by Luria: A patient with a frontal lobe tumor poked the fire with a broom and boiled a piece of cloth in a pot instead of the food she intended to cook; another severely injured frontal case, asked by the doctor to light a cigarette, continued to strike the burning match on the box for a long time after having lit the match.

A less severely affected man could do this correctly, but if the task was made more complicated and he was asked to light a candle, this less familiar action easily disintegrated into simpler fragments: the patient lit the match, then blew it out; or took the candle, put it in his mouth and attempted to smoke it as if it were a cigarette. The verbal instruction thus appears to trigger the required action but cannot inhibit irrelevant associations that arise as the result of the patient's previous experience. Some previous stereotype replaces the adequate performance of the required program.

In all these cases we are dealing not so much with the forgetting of the instruction by the subject as with a disturbance of the mechanism of comparison between performance and initial task. Behavior ceases to be regulated by a particular program and is not corrected by comparison between the original plan and its actual performance.

These disturbances resemble some of the reactions observed in very young children. Luria (1966) describes experiments with a child aged two to two-and-a-half years not yet able to carry out a conditional motor reaction in response to a verbal instruction: "When the light shines, squeeze the balloon." The child heard the words, "When the light shines" and immediately began to look for the light, forgetting to give the requested reaction; on hearing the words, "press the balloon", he started to press the balloon without waiting for the cue. The same difficulty was observed in the adult patient with a massive lesion of the frontal lobes. Like the child, he could not create the preliminary connections corresponding to the instruction and could not respond to the correct signal. After several signals the patient replied each time; "Yes, I must press," but did nothing and later simply gave up responding. Interestingly, the patient was able to repeat the verbal instruction, but when asked why he did not squeeze the balloon, he began to assert that he had done so, although in fact he had made no movement.

In the child, however, the instructional response could be conditioned by having her say "squeeze" each time the light went on. The adult patient could say "squeeze," but this combination of verbal and motor response did not, in his case, have the desired effect. The regulating effect of the patient's speech, distinctly effective in the normal child, was profoundly disturbed in these pathological cases. What stands out as an essential manifestation of the frontal syndrome is the dissociation between speech and action.

The critical importance of the frontal lobes in mediating the regulating influence of speech is strikingly shown by Luria's experiments with conflicting instructions. For example, the patient was told: "In response to one signal you must press twice; in response to two signals you must press once." In another task the patient was instructed to respond to a prolonged signal with a short pressure and to a short signal with a long pressure. Luria reports that patients with brain damage outside the frontal lobes could usually carry out this test, but, for patients with frontal lobe lesions, it was almost impossible.

The same experiments in children led to success when they were combined with the children's own verbal repetition of the instruction. The regulatory influence of self-produced verbal instructon, so striking in the child, was ineffective in the frontal patient.

SUMMARY

Voluntary movements enable the organism to change its relation to the external world, either by changing its own position or by manipulating objects in space. The coordination and regulation of motor acts is thus a problem of fundamental importance for neuropsychology.

Well-established and rapidly performed rhythmic actions are relatively independent of sensory feedback that is necessary for slower, less well-practiced movements. Individual cells, called *command* cells, or at cortical levels, *cognons,* integrate, revise, store, and direct the action programs for coordinated joint and muscle activity. These motor centers are localized in two divisions of the central nervous system. At the subcortical level, the command cells for rapid, saccadic movements originate in the cerebellum and for slow, smooth, ramp movements in the basal ganglia, and reach the motor cortex by way of the thalamus. At the higher cortical level, the motor centers are cognons located in the kinesthetic programming units of the frontal lobes and other association areas in the neocortex. The kinesthetic cognons play a dual role: on the one hand, they have an afferent function, receiving feedback for self-evaluation via the thalamus from the proprioceptors in the somato-sensory and sensory muscular apparatus; on the other hand, they serve as high-level programming mechanisms for the execution of complex motor skills. With practice and consequent motor learning, a greater amount of the movement can be preprogrammed in the basal ganglia and the cerebellum. The behavior can then be executed rapidly and smoothly without thinking about it. Exploratory movements, in contrast, are provisional and subject to continuous revision until preprogramming can be perfected.

SUGGESTED READINGS

Bernstein, N. *The co-ordination and regulation of movements.* London: Pergamon, 1967.

Côté, L. Basal ganglia, the extrapyramidal motor system, and diseases of transmitter metabolism. In E.R. Kandel & J.H .Schwartz (Eds.), *Principles of neural sciences.* New York: Elsevier/North Holland, 1981.

Delcomyn, F. Neural basis of rhythmic behavior in animals. *Science,* 1980, *210,* 492–498.

Evarts, E.V. Brain mechanisms in movement. *Scientific American,* 1973, *229,* 96–103. (a)

Evarts, E.V. Brain mechanisms of movement. *Scientific American,* September, 1979, 241. Reprinted in *The brain: A Scientific American book.* San Francisco: W.H. Freeman, 1979.

Gallistel, C.R. *The organization of action: A new synthesis.* Hillsdale, N.J.: Erlbaum, 1980.

Holst, E. von. Relative coordination as a phenomenon and as a method of analysis of central nervous function. In E. von Holst, *The behavioral physiology of animals and man: Selected papers.* Coral Gables, Fla.: University of Miami Press, 1973.

Kennedy, D., Evoy, W.H., & Hanawalt, J.T. Release of coordinated behavior in crayfish by single central neurons. *Science,* 1966, *154*(3750), 917–920.

Konorski, J. The problem of the peripheral control of skilled movements. *International Journal of Neuroscience,* 1970b, *1,* 39–50.

Kornhuber, H.H. Cerebral cortex, cerebellum, and basal ganglia: An introduction to their motor functions. In F.O. Schmitt & F.G. Worden (Eds.), *The neurosciences: Third study program.* Cambridge: MIT Press, 1974.

McGeer, P.L., Eccles, J.C., & McGeer, E.G. *Molecular neurobiology of the mammalian brain.* New York: Plenum, 1978.

Shepherd, G.M. *Neurobiology.* New York: Oxford University Press, 1983.

Wilson, D.M. Insect walking. *Annual review of entomology,* 1966, *11,* 103–122.

CHAPTER THIRTEEN

A Unified Grammar of Perception and Action

The course of rhythmical live movements may be represented in the form of rapidly converging trigonometric series. I have been able to demonstrate that a diversity of rhythmical human movements (walking, striking with a hammer, filing, piano-playing, etc.) may be interpreted to an accuracy of within a few millimeters in the form of a sum of three or four harmonic oscillations, the so-called Fourier trigonometric sums.

(Bernstein, 1967, p. 23)

THE ACTION CODE

The code for skilled movement must specify the movement itself, not the neuromuscular activity required to realize that movement. The problem is to explain how the brain represents the skilled movement in memory. But if the code specifies the form of a movement, what sort of a code can do this? This is much the same sort of problem that the Gestalt psychologists worried about in their attempts to explain the perception of organized wholes and complex patterns. We recognize faces, handwriting, voices, and melodies despite vast differences in expression, medium, and context. The corresponding sensory events in each case yield a bewildering variety of neural impulses and synaptic

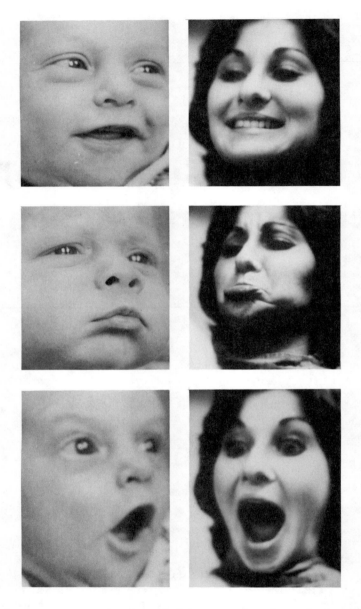

Figure 13.1. Photographs of a model's happy, sad, and surprised expressions and an infant's corresponding expressions. Field et al. Copyright © 1982 by the AAAS. Photographs courtesy of Tiffany M. Field.

connections. How does invariant recognition emerge from these ever-changing, confusing data? The problem of the perceived constancies of objects and events, despite variations in stimulation, is analogous to the problem of the constancy of skilled movements and action patterns.

An economical and attractive hypothesis emerges from the analogy. The brain may use the same code in reverse for both types of constancy; perceptual and action constancy share a common biological purpose. Why not a common language and a common alphabet?

The idea that the last stage of the perceptual process and the first stage of the motor process are one and the same would solve the problem of imitation. A two-week-old infant mimics her daddy—he sticks his tongue out, she sticks her tongue out; he puckers his mouth as if to whistle, and she follows (Meltzoff & Moore, 1977). Even a 36-hour old neonate can imitate facial expressions (Field, Woodson, Greenberg & Cohen, 1982). (See Figure 13.1.) The process of imitation in young children, monkeys, and birdsong is uncanny. The mystery disappears if, in perceiving a movement, the brain formulates the commands that produce the corresponding voluntary movement. Konorski (1967) conceived the idea that the kinesthetic analyzer translates the language of muscle tensions into the language of perceived movements—that is, into voluntary action programs. Echoing Jackson's statement that "the brain 'thinks' in movements and not in muscular contractions," Konorski wrote, "the brain 'thinks' in objects perceived and not in their elements" (1967, p. 106). The problem is to discover how our brains manage to correlate mental and motor functions—thought and action—in a unified code. It is attractive to think that perception and voluntary movement share a common alphabet and a common grammar. What neural mechanisms might underlie such integrative activity?

TOPOLOGY OF GROWTH AND FORM

In his marvelous book, *On Growth and Form* (1961), the natural historian, classicist, and mathematician, D'Arcy Thompson asks us to examine the forms of living things—the shell of a nautilus, the shape of a fish. He shows how topological, not metric, principles govern evolution. Homologous structures in different species will be qualitatively similar though they will, in fact, differ in a multitude of particular little ways. Two organisms of related genera may look entirely different—yet their shapes will be homeomorphic. (See Figure 13.2.)

In comparing feature by feature, the anatomist finds hundreds of little differences of angle, length, curvature, and so on, but D'Arcy Thompson saw that they were all simply the topological expressions of a comprehensive change of shape. Consider the change of a shape produced by drawing it on a sheet of rubber. Distorting or stretching the rubber changes the shape in every

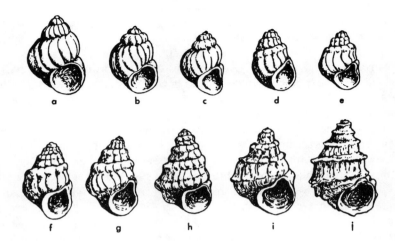

Figure 13.2.   Evolution of one species of snail into another. Thompson, 1961.

single particular—but the transformation can be grasped *as a whole* by a simple formula that describes the way the rubber has been stretched. D'Arcy Thompson simply took the ordinary Cartesian grid of graph paper and showed how, by changing its direction and tilt, one might sense the pervasive transformation that expresses the relationship between *Diodon* and *Orthagoriscus* living in a single Euclidian sea. (See Figure 13.3.)

The lesson for us is that we do not have to seek 100 different explanations for the child's ability to recognize any canine as a *dog* or any feline as a *cat,* although her experience has been limited to one or two members of each species. Similarly, one can grasp the transformation between very differently worded sentences of the language (even different languages) as an expression of their topological structure. Finally, we can express the relationship between the movements of entirely different sets of muscles engaged under various circumstances at different times in a common task by a topological transformation that gives us, instantly, the same end goal of the motor behavior.

D'Arcy Thompson shows how pervasive are certain elementary forms—the sphere and the cylinder, the logarithmic spirals of the horns and the shells that grow by accretion while remaining unchanged in shape, the geometric packing adopted by cellular aggregates. The physicist and the engineer see and use the sophisticated relatives of these simpler forms. The graceful curve of the undulating cable that supports every suspension bridge is a *catenary;* wondrously, its mathematical formula also describes the form of the logarithmic function that relates experienced sensation to stimulus intensity, Fechner's psychological law, according to the famous engineer and bridge builder, David B. Steinman (personal communication). (See Figure 13.4.)

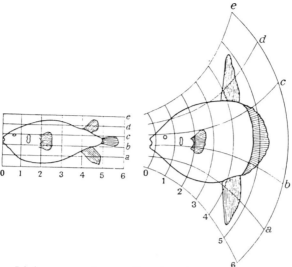

Figure 13.3. Living organisms of today have gradually evolved from simpler shapes by small variations in their coordinates. Thompson, 1961.

Figure 13.4. The beautiful curve formed by the cable of a suspension bridge forms a hyperbolic cosine function called a *catenary*. Photograph of the St. Johns Bridge at Portland, Oregon, designed and constructed in 1929–31 by D.B. Steinman, C.E., Ph.D., the writer's father.

415

Figure 13.5.   A single topological class: the letter *A*.

TOPOLOGICAL INVARIANCE

N.A. Bernstein, (1967) the Russian physiologist and influential theorist of movement, draws an important distinction between the *topology* and the *metrics* of any geometrical representation. In the analysis of an act of movement in time, or a linear figure, a graphic design in space, its *topology* refers to the totality of its *qualitative* peculiarities, whereas its *metrics* denote magnitude or its *quantitative* properties. For example, the topological properties of a linear figure include whether it is open or closed; whether its lines intersect with one another; and also their number: whether it is a three-, four-, or twelve-sided polygon, or a five- or six-pointed star, or a member of still some other topological class. Topological properties of a geometrical figure remain unchanged when the figure is distorted, bent, or when it undergoes a size change. (See Figure 13.5.) Every printed letter is a separate topological class of the first order while the single class of letter *A* contains all styles and forms of *A,* regardless of dimension, outline, or calligraphic embellishments. Bernstein calls attention in this respect to the chalk figures for the game of hopscotch that appear on concrete pavements every spring— all representative of the same topological class of the first order. The habitual scheme with which a child also draws a house, or a man, is also a determinate topological class and shows remarkable universality among children of the same age everywhere (Gardner, 1980). According to the hypothesis put forth here, these topological classes are categories of unitary cognons.

The child draws a face, even in side view, with two eyes, two legs, two arms. (See Figure 13.6.) Topological concepts—"between," "next to," "above," "below," "open," "enclosed," and "enclosing"—are discriminated very early, long before Euclidean properties of space are learned (Piaget & Inhelder, 1956).

Figure 13.6. A collection of children's drawings. Children draw "tadpoles" all over the world. Gardner, 1980. (A) Reproduced by permission of N.H. Freeman & S. Hargreaves. Directed movements and body proportion effect in pre-school children's human figure drawings. *Quarterly Journal of Experimental Psychology*, 1977, *29*, 227–235. (B) Figure 30 from J. Goodnow. *Children drawing*, 1977. Reprinted by permission of Harvard University Press.

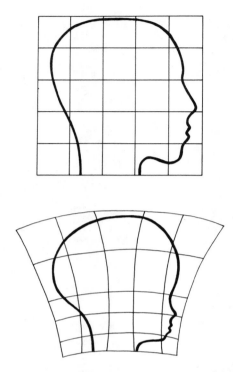

Figure 13.7. Changes in proportion of the human head from baby to adult.

THE CONSTANCY OF OBJECT PERCEPTION BASED ON TOPOLOGY

We are able to recognize objects despite radical changes in their shape. We can identify a familiar face at a glance whether we view it from near or far, from above or below, or even whether years have passed since we saw it last. If the face has radically altered, grown older, fatter or skinnier, or has lost or grown hair, moustache, or beard, recognition may be hesitant or may fail, but remarkably often, the change in shape does not destroy the individual's identity. Indeed, it may furnish an important cue to age (Pittenger & Shaw, 1975; Pittenger, Shaw, & Mark, 1979). (See Figure 13.7.)

When an artist caricatures a face, she applies nonrigid transformations to it. (See Figure 13.8.) Such transformations not only fail to destroy the perceived identity of a face, but, on the contrary, they frequently serve to enhance it. Caricatures of objects are often more easily recognized than either photographs or line drawings accurately scaled to the original objects. The

Figure 13.8. Groucho. Drawing by David Levine. Reprinted with permission from *The New York Review of Books.* Copyright © 1979, Nyrev, Inc.

question arises: how is it that nonrigid transformations preserve and accentuate accurate recognition?

Ethologists have noted that highly caricatured representations of natural prey or predators are more likely to release innate fixed-action patterns in animals than the real object. In insects, frogs, fish, and birds, a single trigger stimulus may mean a mate, food, or a threat. The newly hatched herring gull chick pecks at its parent's bill for food. Hinde (1970) reports that the most effective model to elicit pecking has a contrasting red patch near the tip of the bill.

A whole series of biologically significant features are unqestionably topological properties of physiological space. We recognize objects on the basis of their topology, not their metrics, as when we identify a leaf as belonging to a maple tree, although this particular leaf is different in size, color, and markings from every other maple leaf. Still, even to a pigeon it is unmistakeably a maple, not an oak, birch, or locust leaf, because all maple leaves belong to one and the same topological class (Cerella, 1979). (See Figure 13.9.)

Figure 13.9. Effective stimulus releasers have topological properties. The "baby schema" (left) is considered to be "cute"; adult forms (right) do not activate the drive to care for the young. Eibl-Eibesfeldt, 1970.

THE CONSTANCY OF ACTION BASED ON TOPOLOGY

Bernstein made two striking observations. First he demonstrated that complex movements were extraordinarily mobile, plastic, or variable. Any one task is performed with a vast number of *degrees of freedom*. Secondly, movements can be represented by their component *sinusoidal oscillations*. Let me try to explain: Different methods based on different combinations of active brain units will serve an intended motor scheme or plan. Hammering a nail, for example, is performed by one group of muscles if the initial position of the elbow is flexed, and by a completely different group if it is extended. The act of writing or drawing changes radically if the writer is standing or sitting down. The same action transfers readily from one motor system or muscle group to another. Handwriting shows the generality of the action; a person can write his signature on paper, on the blackboard, or with a stick in the sand; the result is much the same. There is thus a *constancy* of action. Bernstein concludes that the movements of live organisms, no less than their perceptions, are determined by topological categories (Bernstein, 1967, p. 45).

This result is important for understanding the recovery following injury of an impaired motor function. The retraining of a patient after amputation of a limb necessarily makes use of remaining muscles. Brain damage may leave all the muscles intact, but specific higher mental functions may be selectively disturbed. Speech loss or writing difficulties found in cases of stroke or cerebral tumors affecting the language areas, usually in the left cerebral hemisphere, are frequently temporary. The restoration of lost functions following lesions depends upon the principle stressed by Bernstein—the "degrees of freedom" principle. Compensation, not regeneration of function, is the rule.

Luria (1966) describes a particularly interesting illustrative case. A prominent designer, recovering from a wound in the left temporal area, found that, although he still retained his ability to design, he was completely unable to write. For six months he was given exercises in copying passages from texts, which he could do, but he made no progress in spontaneous writing or writing from dictation. The writing disturbance was caused by a defect arising from a lesion in the acoustic region just outside Wernicke's area.

> Being deprived of his intact articulatory analysis, such a patient is unable to identify accurately the sound to be written down. His writing is severely disturbed, but in these cases the rational substitution of intact links for the defective elements (this time by changing to the use of acoustic methods or visual analysis of the shape of the mouth) will help to restore the disturbed function. (Luria, 1966, 67–68)

There was little use having the patient practice the direct copying of words he was able to see. Appropriate retraining had to replace the disturbed function—the direct acoustic analysis of the phonetic structure of speech by other methods available to the patient.

The principal method used to help this patient made use of the visual analysis of articulation. Watching carefully in a mirror, the patient pronounces the word to be written down. Together with kinesthetic aids to analyze the articulatory composition of words, the patient, three months later, was able to write again. Not vicarious functioning (in the sense that another part of the brain takes over the specific methods of analysis and integration of the damaged regions), but instead, "complex functional systems acquired during postnatal development can be transferred to new, intact mechanisms in the service of a common task."

PERSONAL STYLE BASED ON TOPOLOGY

Movements that leave no trace are just as certainly topologically invariant as handwriting. There exist topological classes to which we may assign gait, touch in music, accent of voice, carriage, footsteps—the myriad of personal characteristics of movement by which we identify familiar persons instantly and unmistakeably. This is what we mean when we speak of *style*—the realm of live actions that retain their topological properties of the first, and also of higher orders.

What is of immediate interest is the marked analogy between perceptual and motor organization. Both visual perception and movement are equally indifferent to metric dimension. Both are exquisitely sensitive to orientation in space. It is difficult to recognize words rotated 180°, or even 90°, just as it is difficult to draw figures upside-down or on their sides. The problem of serial order, as Lashley stressed, is also a serious concern in both receptive and expressive functions.

In this connection it is striking that dyslexic children draw the mirror images of individual letters, ꓭ instead of B, but will not write or read entire words from right to left. Transposition errors in writing and speech are also partial and selective, affecting only particular letters or syllables and not entire sentences. There must be separate mechanisms or programs that are to some extent independent of each other.

Certain differences between the visual field of perception and the motor field of active movements are also characteristic. The first is bilateral symmetry, important in the psychology of perception but absent in the motor field. Another distinction, and one that is especially relevant to its topology, is that in the motor field, but not in the visual field, straight lines need not be distinguished from curved ones. Successive movements also are rarely repeated exactly, particularly those of a cyclical nature. Bernstein refers to these characteristics of a movement cycle as being (1) *nonrectilinear* and (2) *oscillating* "like a cobweb in the wind."

The indifference of the motor control center to metric variation, each of which demands a different muscular formula, and even a completely different set of muscles, is of the greatest interest for *cognon* theory. The equal facility with which each variation of movement can be made—for example, drawing a circle large or small, on the ground, or on a vertical surface—is evidence that all of these variants are determined by a single higher-order directional mechanism. One and the same cognon must possess the geometrical or topological representation, the very abstract motor image of spatial form. Bernstein's hypothesis (and my preceding analysis leads me to share his view) asserts that these higher-order motor "engrams" (here *cognons*) have the same topological regulation as is found in external space, or the motor field, far removed from the joint-muscle schemata. In short, the localization pattern of

Figure 13.10. Any trajectory—the curve formed by a point moving through space—can be analyzed into its component oscillations or sine waves. These are multiple exposures of a subject walking while wearing a black suit with white tape along the arm and leg. White dots mark the head and main joints of the limbs. Shutter is opened 20 times per second. Reprinted with permission from N. Bernstein, *The Coordination and Regulation of Movements,* 1967, Pergamon Press, Ltd.

the movement stored in the cognon is its projection of external space in the form, not of its metric, but of its topological properties.

Bernstein, a mathematician as well as biologist, had an interesting hunch that our central nervous systems contain exact formulae of skilled movements. A movement formula embodies the exact course of a movement in space and time. Such a description gives the trajectory of the movement. Now any trajectory—the curve traced by a point moving through space—can be analyzed into its component oscillations or sine waves.

Bernstein (1967) discovered that the skilled movements of craft operators and athletes could be analyzed into planar trajectories traced out by points on the limbs, trunk, and head. He recorded the trajectories by mounting tiny light bulbs at critical points all over the body and photographing the paths traced by the lights with a high speed cine camera. (See Figure 13.10.)

APPLYING FOURIER SYNTHESIS TO MOVEMENT

On examining these records, Bernstein came to a remarkable conclusion. Every trajectory of a skilled repetitive movement could be synthesized using three, and only three, suitably chosen fundamental sinusoids, one for each plane, and the first three harmonics of each fundamental. Every complex wave is built from its component sinusoids, and a straight line (AB, point A to point B in any spatial plane) consists of the superimposition of such component harmonics, the sum of Fourier's trigonometric series.

The startling revelation is that the brain represents learned movements by extracting the sinusoids as an action alphabet from which they may be synthesized. Movements are composed of their elementary or component oscillations.

A Fourier theory of movement coding parallels the Fourier theory of hearing and also that of visual sensory coding, developed by Campbell and Robson (1968) to explain spatial vision. Light, like sound, consists of waves in motion. But, whereas the frequency of sound waves denotes their temporal parameter, the frequency distribution of light and dark luminance cycles in a plane denotes the transmission of visual spatial information. In movement, spatial information consists of the frequency distribution of trajectories in geometric space.

Gallistel (1980) cites Pew's sine wave-tracking experiment to illustrate the idea. In the experiment, the subject tries to keep his pointer on top of a target that moves back and forth in a sinusoidal undulation. The experimenter varies the frequency of undulation and records the movements made by the subject to correct his errors in aligning pointer and target. At low frequencies, error-correcting movements result from the perceived discrepancies between the position of the pointer and the position of the target. At higher frequencies, subjects switched to a different mode of control. They generated their own sinusoidal movements and adjusted the parameters of their movements so as to match the trajectory of the pointer to the trajectory of the target. In this higher-level mode of control, the error signal no longer adjusts position; rather, it adjusts the phase, period, and amplitude of the movement to agree with the phase, period, and amplitude of the target.

If the subject's tracking performance was accurate—right on target—then the movement he generated could be described by the same *six* numbers as the movement of the target. A sine wave can be specified by its *period (frequency)*, its *amplitude*, and its *phase*. In addition to those three values, we need to know three more to identify the plane in which the oscillation occurs. "Is the target undulating up and down, back and forth, or from side to side? *Mathematically speaking, the formula of the target's trajectory is a six dimensional vector*" (Gallistel, 1980, p. 338).

A neural oscillator putting out a sinusoidal signal represented by a string of six numbers is a movement formula. The first number specifies period (spatial frequency); the second, amplitude; and the third, the phase relation between concurrent or overlapping oscillations. The remaining three numbers specify action in each of three spatial planes. The formula can be stored in memory, combined with other information and sent to instruct motor neurons to generate muscular action. The *cognon,* the neural embodiment of a memory, records the values and the order of *six* signals. Is it mere *coincidence* that the span of immediate memory or attention shows an invariant upper limit of *six* items? (See Chapter Ten).

Of course, highly skilled actions generate much more than sinusoidal movements. The power of this idea stems from the generalizability of the theorem of Joseph Fourier (1768–1830), the French mathematician, for this special case to the reproduction of any movement whatsoever.

The Fourier theorem enables us to represent any trajectory as the sum (superimposition) of sinusoidal components of the trajectory. Thus the program for a skilled movement need specify only the appropriate set of sinusoidal components necessary to construct a certain trajectory which is the aim of the movement. The details of neuromuscular activity required to realize the movement under different circumstances is left to lower units.

Now the question arises: where are the higher neural units (cognons) that represent the Fourier syntheses of skilled movement trajectories located in the brain? We have no direct evidence that such action cognons actually exist. But there is strong indirect support from clinical and behavioral investigations that the kinesthetic analyzer in the premotor area of the neocortex is a device for programming movement. The kinesthetic analyzer, like visual and auditory analyzers has an afferent function: it gives us information about our self-produced movements. But unlike other analyzers, the movement analyzer has a second very important job: it sends orders through lower centers to the muscles in the absence of any sensory feedback from them. The cognons in the kinesthetic centers are independent and autonomous programming units for organizing and executing instrumental acts.

This theory of kinesthetic cognons is supported by the unitary and integrated nature of particular motor acts and by strong antagonism between different acts. Patting your head and rubbing your stomach is a classic example. Once the kinesthetic cognons are established for particular acts, the role of these units changes radically. Now they begin to function independently of the sensory input to which they owe their function, and they can mediate higher-order habits without feedback from the proprioceptors in the muscles, tendons, and joints. The important result is that after a given motor skill has been established, the corresponding cognons that embody its formulae can become connected through associative fibers coming from other cognitive fields and can transmit the orders for its performance to the executive centers. The kinesthetic cognons then play three different functionally significant roles: (1) they encode information that is produced by the central nervous system itself, that is, by self-produced active movements; (2)

they handle information about movements in the external world performed by moving targets, persons, animals, video games, animated cartoons; (3) they play the role of programming devices for skilled motor acts.

A COMMON CODE FOR PERCEPTION AND ACTION

The term *topological properties* is used to identify the high-order invariants in behavior and the environment that specify objects or objectives and their possible transformations. The properties of the action plan interlace with the properties of the optic array in systematic fashion. It is tempting to speculate that the mapping of one is projected onto the mapping of the other in an arrangement that preserves their order. This would provide the basis for the close connection between perceptual and motor behavior: the guidance of movements by vision and other senses.

Visual information is processed through the establishment of progressively more abstract representations, from the specification of relations of contrast, orientation, movement, and phase, to the identification of patterns and objects.

Information enters action in the motor system in reverse progression. The action plan unfolds as an orderly succession of progressively less abstract, more detailed, and highly specified instructions to the muscles involved in movement. Complex acts are built through the fitting together of relatively autonomous units. The initial instructions are necessarily precise.

Gallistel (1977) quotes Turvey as saying: "Perceiving and acting are dual representations of common neural events." Insofar as one perceives a given object, one is prepared to respond to it. Perception and the plans for voluntary action are thus bound together and intimately interwoven by the central nervous system. Perceiving is necesssary for action (one could hardly act if one could not perceive). The converse is also true. To see clearly one must look; to hear distinctly, one must listen. Looking and listening require active movements of the observer.

By employing now one, now another, set of motor impulses, the constancy of the final behavioral effect is preserved. Note that the constancy of action parallels the constancy of perception.

The plasticity of the locomotor system was shown by experiments in which completely new sets of muscles led to a previously learned goal. Rats can swim through a maze previously run and reach the goal box with the aid of a completely new set of muscular impulses. In Lashley's experiments, a rat originally skilled in running a particular maze, could, after bilateral hemisection of the spinal cord at different levels, or even total extirpation of the cerebellum, perform amazingly well by rolling head over heels toward the intended goal.

The perception and the production of speech are good examples of interdependency in human behavior. Speech perception and speech production are interlocked.

Both aspects of speech, the receptive or perceptual and the expressive or motor, present in a striking form the integrative functions of the brain that reach their highest development in human thought processes. The study of language reveals a particularly abstract feature of behavior: its *temporal* integration. The perception of complex visual scenes and subtle patterns calls for a theory of *spatial* integration.

Here is a unifying theory applicable to both the perception and the expression of behavior—one that unites temporal and spatial integration into a single, general principle. Perception and action are controlled by central programs that consist of invariant topological functions.

SUMMARY

The concept of topological invariance gives rise to the tantalizing hypothesis that the representation of an action and the representation of an object use the same coordinate structures. Bernstein's (1967) cinematographic records of adult workers and children in action performing repetitive movements offer striking support for this idea, enabling him to compute the invariant components of motor patterns in time and space. Electrophysiological data from single cells in the motor cortex of active monkeys add confirming evidence that such computations are, in fact, performed by the motor system (Evarts, 1979).

The idea of movement is not necessarily a conscious representation of the muscular activity to be undertaken, but an unconscious synthesis of the (sinusoidal) components to be ordered by the action program. The motor image or the idea of a movement is thus simply the programmed trajectory in space and time that is encoded in the kinesthetic cognon that initiates the program.

Characteristic properties of the *motor field,* like those in the *visual* field (the analogous concept in perceptual behavior), reflect topological, not metric, relations. The constancy of action has its counterpart in the constancy of object recognition with similar adaptive significance for behavior. In addition, this shared *topological invariance* suggests a unifying general principle of broad subsumptive power. The action code and the perception code may possess precisely the same underlying alphabet and syntax. One is the mirror image of the other. Sensory integration is thought to process incoming information by means of Fourier analysis and synthesis; voluntary movements are directed and coordinated by reversing the receptive process in the expression of the motor activity. The application of spatial frequency information-processing both to the visual field and to the kinetic processing of rhythmic movements in the motor field, show that both reception and expression obey the same mathematical formulae. Both psychological and neurological evidence support the concept of cognons as embodying these formulae in the form of perception and action codes. It thus begins to appear that we can define the phenomena of behavior, including voluntary actions and mental representations, in terms of the mathematical and physical sciences. Higher mental functions, perceptual and motor images, are characterized not by photographic, but by topological, schemata. These schemata lend themselves to analysis by mathematical equations. A picture emerges of the brain and behavior, voluntary motor skills, and neural images as closely coupled systems conforming to the identical mathematical and physical laws that govern all natural phenomena.

SUGGESTED READINGS

Arnheim, R. *Art and visual perception.* Berkeley: University of California Press, 1975.

Cerella, J. Visual classes and natural categories in the pigeon. *Journal of Experimental Psychology: Human Perception and Performance,* 1979, *5,* 68–77.

Courant, R., & Robbins, H. Topology. In J.R. Newman (Ed.), *The world of mathematics.* New York: Simon & Schuster, 1956.

Gardner, H. *Artful scribbles: The significance of children's drawings.* New York: Basic Books, 1980.

Gombrich, E.H. *Art and illusion: A study in the psychology of pictorial representation.* Princeton: Bollingen Series, Princeton University Press, 1972.

Pittenger, J.B., Shaw, R.E., & Mark, L.S. Perceptual information for the age level of faces as a higher order invariant of growth. *Journal of Experimental Psychology: Human Perception and Performance,* 1979, *5,* 478–493.

Thom, R. *Structural stability and morphogenesis.* (D.H. Fowler, trans.) Reading, Mass.: W.A. Benjamin, 1975.

Thompson, D'Arcy W. *On growth and form.* (J.T. Bonner, Ed., abridged edition). Cambridge, Engl.: Cambridge University Press, 1961.

PART FIVE

Integrative Activity of the Brain

> *The spiral is a spiritualized circle. In the spiral form, the circle, uncoiled, unwound, has ceased to be vicious; it has been set free. I thought this up when I was a schoolboy, and I also discovered that Hegel's triadic series expressed merely the essential spirality of all things in their relation to time. Twirl follows twirl, and every synthesis is the thesis of the next series. If we consider the simplest spiral, three stages may be distinguished in it, corresponding to those of the triad: We call "thetic" the small curve or arc that initiates the convolution centrally; "antithetic" the larger arc that faced the first in the process of continuing it; and "synthetic" the still ampler arc that continues the second while following the first along the outer side.*
>
> *A colored spiral in a small ball of glass, this is how I see my own life.*
>
> V. Nabokov, 1947, Speak Memory, *p. 204*

In this final part, I try to apply cognon theory to some of the most controversial questions in biology and psychology—the nature-nurture debate; the relations between the emotive and cognitive brain functions and their role in psychiatric disorders; the problem of "free will"; and the significance of consciousness, particularly self-consciousness.

At the present state of our knowledge, it is obvious that many of my ideas concerning the activity of the brain will prove to be inconsistent with new data and will need revision. Yet I have tried to state these ideas as clearly as possible, hoping that they will stimulate research either to find further support or to be decisively contradicted. I see as my chief contribution an attempt to offer a broad systematic framework of ideas even though some of them will be shown to be wrong.

The discussion that follows recapitulates many of the key points made in earlier chapters. The two final chapters will thus serve as a general summary of the principles of neuropsychology that appear in my subtitle to describe the aim of the book.

CHAPTER FOURTEEN

Heredity and Environment in the Development of Complex Skills

*All the milk consumed by the baby fails to make him more and more milky,
for he changes it chemically into human muscle, bone and brain. The
hereditary factor carried by the ever multiplying chromosomes is present in
every cell of the body and is just as influential in the later stages of
development as at the very beginning.*

(Woodworth, 1940, p. 203)

INTRODUCTION

No one would argue that individuals are all alike. Variability in characteristics
provides the raw materials on which natural selection works. But this raises at
once the question why individuals differ from one another. To what extent do
they differ because of different heredity? To what extent do they differ because
of different environment?

When we say that a person has a certain ability, can sing a D above high C, for example, our clearest evidence is that we have heard her do it. The ability to sing is doubtless dependent on structure: mouth, throat, and larynx, and also on brain structure. Acquiring skill must modify structure in some respect. The central question, then, is whether the individual can learn to do something, whether she has the *capacity* to do it. Capacity cannot be directly observed; the only direct evidence is performance and that depends on both heredity and environment. A child's capacity, for the time being, is limited by her immature stage of development. With further development, her capacity for both muscular and cognitive performances will increase.

Studies of normal behavioral development show that it follows an orderly progression. Babies creep before they can walk, and they walk before they run or skip. Yet if the newborn infant is supported and held so that his feet can touch the ground, he will engage in stepping movements—perhaps as many as 10 to 15 steps (McGraw, 1963). Although these rhythmical steps are fairly well organized, they are not initiated by the baby. The action is localized in the muscles of the hips and legs, uninfluenced by the upper part of the body. The infant could step as well even if he had no brain, and, indeed, the newborn baby is without a cortex. The simple fact is that even at birth, and for several months thereafter, the cerebral cortex is not functioning in the human infant.

THE PARADOX OF NEURAL ORGANIZATION

The most striking feature of the nervous system is the extreme orderliness of the connections made during development. It is as if each neuron had built into it an awareness of its proper place in the system. A small population of stem cells originate in germinal zones, and, by a sequence of cell divisions, they generate daughter cells, called *young neurons,* that migrate to their final positions in various parts of the nervous system. "From each region of the brain the newly formed cells migrate outward, passing by previously formed young neurons, so that the nervous system is formed in an 'inside-out' fashion" (Hirsch & Jacobson, 1975). (See Figures 14.1, 14.2, an 14.3.)

Given this invariant structure—extensive systems of large nerve cells, with long axons linking the various parts of the nervous system, laid down by developmental programs under strict genetic control—the remarkable thing is the capacity of sensory stimulation by the environment to change the functions of the interconnections and to produce learning and memory. The question before us throughout this book has been: what provides the necessary flexibility, indeed *instability,* to make possible such adaptive advantages? If the structure of the nervous system is innately determined and "hard-wired," how is learning possible?

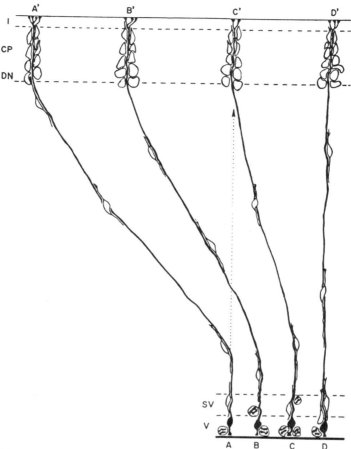

Figure 14.1. Young neurons migrate outward in vinelike spiral growth around their slender supporting cells—the radial glia. All neurons in the ventricular (V) and subventricular (SV) zones migrate from A–D to the cortical plate (CP) where they establish ontogenetic radial columns A–D. Rakic, 1981. Copyright © 1981 by the Massachusetts Institute of Technology.

William James recognized this paradox. He wrote:

The dilemma in regard to the nervous system seems, in short, to be of the following kind. We may construct one which will react infallibly and certainly, but it will then be capable of reacting to very few changes in the environment—it will fail to be adapted to all the rest. We may on the other hand, construct a nervous system potentially adapted to respond to an infinite variety of minute features in the situation; but its fallibility will then

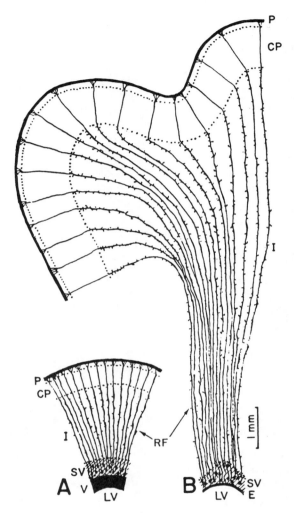

Figure 14.2. Drawing shows the radial glial cells in a Golgi-stained preparation through the wall of the cerebral hemisphere of (A) an 81-day-old fetal monkey (E81). (B) Section from the corresponding region of the cerebrum in an E131 fetus. Abbreviations: CP, cortical plate; E, ependyma; I, intermediate zone; LV, lateral ventrical; P, pial membrane; RF, radial fiber; SV, subventricular zone; V, ventricular zone. Schmechel & Rakic, 1979. Reprinted by permission from *Nature,* Vol. 377, pp. 303–305. Copyright © 1979 Macmillan Journals Limited.

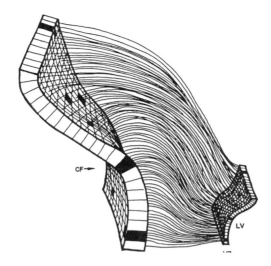

Figure 14.3. Schematic 3-dimensional reconstruction of a portion of the occipitoparietal junction on the medial cerebral wall of an 80-day-old monkey fetus. Radial glial fibers stretch and curve to span the full thickness of the cerebral wall from the lateral ventricle (LV) to the cortical plate (CP). These elongated cords are thought to provide lateral constraints during cell migration and enable precise reproduction of the mosaic of the ventricular zone (VZ) on the enlarged and distorted cerebral surface. Reproduced from P. Rakic, Neuronal migration and contact guidance in the primate telencephalon. *Postgraduate Medical Journal,* 1978, Supplement (1), Vol. 54, 25–40, by kind permission of the editor.

> be as great as its elaboration.... its hair-trigger organization makes of it a happy-go-lucky, hit-or-miss affair. It is as likely to do the crazy as the sane thing at any given moment. (1890, Vol. 1, Chap. 5, p. 140)

Evolution has found a solution for this dilemma by constructing a brain governed by a *selecting* agency. The key to selection is *survival.* In the interest of the protection and the preservation of the self and the species, many particular drives have evolved. These bring pressure to bear in favor of the behavior that serves the chief goals of the brain's owner. The termination of hunger, thirst, fear, pain, and other drives, and their replacement by antidrives are powerful mechanisms for exerting selective pressure to perform certain acts and to inhibit others. For the sake of steering a complex nervous system, these energizing and directing forces require a constant flow of information from the external as well as the internal environment. All biologically useful information depends on these two sources. Behavior builds a foundation created in part by heredity and in part by environment. External environmental influences become of prime importance at, and even before, birth. For example, androgens in the uterine environment may exert masculinizing effects on the female as well as the male embryo even before birth. During early critical periods following birth, also, insufficient or excessive sensory, hormonal, or social stimulation can have devastating and irreversible effects on later development. An outstanding example appears in the link between left-handedness and autoimmune disease.

LEFT-HANDEDNESS AND AUTOIMMUNITY

The pervasive dominance of handedness, especially right-handedness, in human activity, is surely not without functional significance. Indeed, the renewed emphasis on cerebral asymmetry has called attention to the possibility of a link between left-handedness and autoimmune disease. Geschwind and Behan tell us "there is very strong evidence that left handers have a very high risk of developing certain diseases, some of which are very serious" (1982, p. 141). The common difficulty in learning to read called *dyslexia* has long been linked with left-handedness in relatives of those afflicted with the learning disorder. In a well-controlled study, Geschwind and Behan (1982) compared the frequency of left-handedness in patients with migraine or immune disorders in the neurological clinics in Glasgow and in 1,142 general population control subjects free of these disorders. They found a significantly higher frequency of left-handedness among the patients. (See Figure 14.4.) These investigators propose that a genetic susceptibility to disease may manifest itself in different forms in different people. Thus it is a mistake to look only for a particular disturbance in a family. *Myasthenia gravis,* for example, an autoimmune disease, in one family member may be related to different autoimmune conditions, or even language disorders or migraine headaches in other family members. Geschwind and Behan suggest that both the autoimmunity and the neurological effects may result from excess production of, or sensitivity to, testosterone in the fetus, affecting the development of brain structures.

The effect of an oversupply or reaction to testosterone may be to *slow the growth of the left hemisphere.* As a result, males more often than females are left-handed, and they are also more prone to language disorders, such as stuttering and dyslexia, as well as to many autoimmune diseases. In contrast, a profoundly devastating autoimmune disease, *lupus erythematosis,* affects females far more severely than males and develops in them at an earlier age. Certain hormones may protect females from the development of this and other disorders as well.

Our increasing understanding and consequent ability to suppress inherited diseases—insulin for diabetes or diet for phenylketonuria (PKU)—

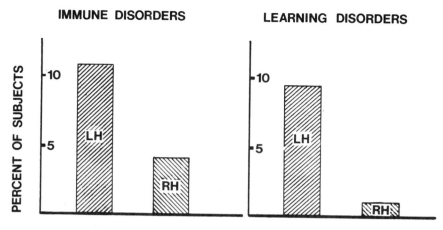

IMMUNE DISORDERS   **LEARNING DISORDERS**

**FREQUENCY OF DISORDERS AMONG
LEFT HANDERS (LH) AND RIGHT HANDERS (RH)**

Figure 14.4. The frequency of immune disorders and learning disorders among strongly left-handed individuals is significantly high. Data from Geschwind & Behan, 1982.

emphasizes the fact that genes do not operate in a vacuum. PKU is interesting because it is a severe form of mental retardation caused by a single gene. About one baby in every 15,000 is born with the deficiency in an enzyme that allows the body to transform phenylalinine into another amino acid for building the nervous system. The absence of this enzyme causes PKU, but it can be treated, if detected early enough, by a special diet containing a very little phenylalinine.

This fact highlights the common fallacy of regarding heredity as unchangeable, and only environmental factors as capable of modification. Modern neuropsychology provides a new perspective on human nature. We are as much the natural expression of our environmental shaping as of our genes. We need to understand both sets of commands, the genetic and the environmental, in order to find ways of treating illness and injury and of educating all persons to achieve their potential to grasp the fullest enjoyment of life.

EARLY EXPERIENCE AND LEARNING

Many studies demonstrate the crucial role of early experience in the development of our precise neuronal architecture (see Chapter Five). Cell differentiation appears to depend on the immediate neighborhood of surrounding cells—the internal environment. But it depends also on the external environment and on the stimulation it affords to the sensory receptors (Chapter Eleven). The visual system is a striking example. An absence of normal visual stimulation during an early critical period in the life of an animal leads to altered development of the visual cortex. In the set of experiments in which one eye is closed at successively later ages, there is clear evidence that anatomical change can and does take place postnatally. Here is a kind of plasticity that is more than a mere misrouting of normal development. It is more akin to axon sprouting involving an actual reexpansion of the shrunken bands of the fourth layer in the visual cortex. (See Figure 11.3.) The next step will be to study the events underlying the recovery of visual function and to determine how long the period of anatomical plasticity can last.

CRITICAL PERIODS IN HUMAN DEVELOPMENT

There is considerable evidence for the existence of critical periods for acquiring skills during human development. The timing of these optimal periods for various kinds of learning depends on the biological processes of neural growth and differentiation called *maturation*. In this process, both hereditary programs and stimulation from the environment are critically involved. Maturation is not precisely correlated with age, since there is considerable age variation among human children with respect to stages of development. But the maturational mechanism does produce an invariant sequence of stages divided into several natural periods, marked by important changes in behavior.

The critical importance of early visual experience is shown in humans by the failure of patients with congenital cataracts to develop normal sight following later removal of the cataracts (von Senden, 1960). A dramatic parallel is shown by the incapacity for normal neuromuscular and social development as a result of early social deprivation. In humans, the resulting deficit is particularly marked in the area of language development. In speaking, reading, and writing, as in vision and other sensory analyzers, there are critical periods of development that are linked to chronological age and maturation of the central nervous system (Lenneberg, 1967).

An experience that lasts only a moment may produce memories that last a lifetime. Such enduring changes, called memory traces or engrams, must be stored as functional or structural processes in the central nervous system.

We now have evidence that experience can produce long-term plastic alterations in many different species of animals. Exposure to behavioral and sensorial experience of an organism, particularly during development, can induce anatomical, biochemical, and electrophysiological changes in synapses that form the associative links in neural tissue.

Research on the effects of environmental variables have shown that substantial modifications can be affected by two classes of manipulation: environmental enrichment and environmental deprivation. Previous chapters have described the powerful effects of selective sensory deprivation, particularly during critical periods of development.

Exposure to an enriched environment also results in dramatic changes. Rosenzweig, Krech, and Bennett (1961) housed three groups of rats in different environments that provided different opportunities for activity and experience. In the enriched condition (EC) animals were placed in large cages with many cage mates and toys and things to do. A second group was isolated in small single animal cages called the impoverished or isolated condition (IC). The third group was placed in the standard colony environment with three rats per cage and little opportunity for informal learning.

The experimenters found changes in the brains of the EC animals that were truly extraordinary. The EC group had brain weights that were much greater than the others. These differences in weight were found to be related to differences in cortical thickness. More refined neuroanatomical measures then showed that these brains had greater numbers of dendritic spines, more dendritic branching, and larger synaptic contacts than the controls. Differential experience also causes changes in brain chemistry, including increased synthesis of proteins and changes in levels of activity of the enzyme acetylcholinesterase (AChE).

Could these differential effects of experience be attributed to actual learning? Perhaps the fact that the EC rats were handled more often and moved about more than their littermate controls could account for the effects? Or perhaps the IC animals lost in brain development as a result of their relative inactivity. The effects could not be explained as the negative results of sensory deprivation because they were not restricted to critical periods of maturation, but could be observed throughout the life span of the animals. Also sensory deprivation experiments make no requirement for active participation of the subjects but show changes in receptive fields in immobilized animals.

The investigators have performed innumerable control experiments to rule out suggested factors other than learning-induced structural and chemical changes. We now have strong evidence that the varied training procedures produced differential learning and memories resulting from enhanced storage of protein in the brains of the experimental animals. These changes in protein synthesis could take place at synapses or even within single neurons shown by investigators with isolated nerve cells taken from snails. It is clear that elementary aspects of mind, or mentation, as it is sometimes called, can be found within the activity of just a very few neurons. Perhaps these elementary cell molecular events can be combined to yield the secret of much more complex processes of creative thought and achievement.

Potential or prefunctional connections are required to arrive at a certain stage of motor and cognitive readiness. Then, and only then, given the requisite stimulation by environmental input, can normal *functional specification* and *validation* take place. The child shows this readiness in the eagerness with which she repeats the same activity (standing up, walking, emptying and refilling her pail, digging roads and tunnels, etc.), each at its particular time (McGraw, 1963).

NEUROMUSCULAR MATURATION AND MOTOR LEARNING

Myrtle McGraw (1963) reminds us that conditioning experiments suffer from a major limitation. From their inception in Pavlov's laboratory, they have relied on results obtained from the reactions of animals whose nervous systems were presumably mature, regardless of the species investigated. Educational programs based on the application of the reactions of mature animals to growing infants and children are, she found, worse than futile—they handicap learning.

A certain amount of neural maturation must take place before any function can be modified by specific stimulation. In famous experiments with identical twins, Myrtle McGraw (1963) deliberately attempted to modify behavioral development by giving one of the pair special early training. The result depended on the activity involved. Bladder control, for example, was not achieved any earlier despite weeks of diligent hourly practice and training. Other activities, notably tricycling, were actually made worse by premature training. One must conclude that there are critical periods for the learning of skills. Before neuromuscular maturation has reached a state of readiness, training may be counterproductive. However, opportunities for practice at the critical stage must be provided, or many forms of learning may be difficult or impossible. Earlier chapters have shown the importance of critical periods for the optimal development of social and language skills as well as for motor skills.

Training in any particular activity before the neural mechanisms have reached a certain state of readiness is counterproductive. But given ample opportunity at the critical period of maturation, specific achievements can greatly exceed ordinary expectations.

There are critical periods in the development of neuromotor functions analogous to those discussed earlier for perceptual functions. The advancement of any particular skill in any particular child can be accomplished with economy and success at those periods, not before. We don't know whether the critical period for a particular function in humans has a finite duration beyond which further delay would deny its development. That has to be determined by further research.

What is of particular interest is that, if an opportunity is provided at the right time, the skills of infants can be brought to very high levels of performance. It is certain that whether a function does emerge, the child exhibits an extraordinary urge to exercise it. When the baby has just learned to pull herself up by grasping the bars of her crib, she does so repeatedly, even though she needs help to get down again and cries until she gets it. The urge for repetition and exercise of a particular aspect of behavior shows that it has just reached the threshold of performance.

Regressions or declines in proficiency are an inherent part of the process of growth. McGraw suggests that these declines appear concurrently with the emergence of some new function or a new aspect of a particular activity. Even mere anatomical change, bodily growth, may be a major factor in altering the learning situation for a child. "For the six-year-old roller skating and slide climbing are different problems than they are for the toddler because the bodily proportions differ; the legs are relatively longer in the older child, and static equilibrium is reduced" (McGraw, 1963).

Learning capacities seem to change during development in a stepwise manner—thus animals and humans learn things that facilitate further learning—a kind of exponential growth. They may also learn not to learn—a negative learning set that brings a critical period to a close. Nowhere is this more unhappily evident than in the phenomenon of "learned helplessness"— an affliction that Maier and Seligman (1976) stressed as an acquired sense that one can no longer control one's environment. The victims of such depression simply give up trying. Nothing they do "matters" or leads to drive reduction. The concept of drive reduction was discussed earlier as indispensable for conditioning consummatory responses. Excellent evidence implicates a neurochemical basis for the behavioral depression resulting from uncontrollable stress (see Chapter Eight; Weiss et al., 1981). This chapter re-emphasizes the role of reinforcement in the development of complex behavioral skills.

The "tide of natural growth" does not flow steadily or in one direction— rather, it manifests a *spiral* course, as Gesell, Ilg and their collaborators (1943) have so beautifully demonstrated, weaving back and forth, but continually moving toward maturity, first in one direction, and then in another.

SPIRALITY OF GROWTH AND FORM

The essential quality of spiral growth, here clockwise, there counterclockwise, has its counterpart in the asymmetry of the right and left cerebral hemispheres and their diverse specialized functions. In its migration, the neuron must take a particular direction, and it grows by turning and twisting to the left or to the right around its slender supporting stem, the glial cell, toward a certain destination. (See Figures 14.1–14.3.)

As Medawar tells us:

Figure 14.5. Spirality of growth and change: The shell of *Nautilus pompilius* forms a continuous logarithmic spiral—a potentially infinite sequence of chambers.

> The central characteristic of biological growth is that that which is formed by growth is itself capable of growing: the interest earned by growth becomes capital and thereupon earns interest on its own behalf. We must therefore plot the growth of organisms not against an ordinary arithmetic scale, equal subdivisions of which represent equal additions of size, but against a logarithmic scale, of which equal subdivisions represent equal *multiples* of size. (Medawar, 1967, p. 31)

Why has the human brain in its evolutionary development assumed a particular form? Clearly, on this basis, the brain's most familiar visible appearance, its richly folded surface, must have enabled it to compress the greatest volume into the smallest cranial space. The process is not yet, and may never be, complete. Helen Fisher (1982) suggests that human babies are being born prematurely at an increasing rate. The period of helpless dependency is progressively lengthening in order to accommodate the demands of a grossly immature nervous system. Stephen J. Gould (1977) expresses the same idea when he tells us that *neoteny*—not recapitulation of the phylogenetic adult form in the process of ontogeny—is the process of evolutionary advance. We are becoming more, not less, childlike, as we are born increasingly prematurely and require longer and longer periods of maturation and learning. Thus the role of the external environment and the neonatal intensive care unit become correspondingly more important in human evolution.

These observations fall neatly in line with Konorski's ideas about the need for *potential* connections as an essential prerequisite for associations to be manifest in behavior. No potential connections exist before the neuro-muscular and neuroperceptual maturation occur. This means that maturation and learning are closely intertwined in the formation of associations between cognons. Attempts to draw a distinction between them, like attempts to measure the separate contributions of heredity and environment to the establishment of cognons, are doomed to fail.

These are not different processes but different facets of the same fundamental process of behavioral and cognitive development, of growth and change. Kandel and Schwartz (1982) provide an excellent review of the recent exciting work exploring the molecular mechanisms underlying learning and memory. Most important, the authors relate information at different levels of analysis: behavioral, cell-physiological, molecular, and genetic. Their analysis of the problem central to both neurobiology and psychology, the distinctive event that converts short-term to long-term memory, leads them to posit a new regulatory subunit, able to synthesize new proteins and initiate striking morphological changes in the terminals of the trigger neurons, essential for long-term memory. Because maturation and learning are intimately related, it is attractive to think that the same regulatory subunit operates in both forms of behavioral modification. Perhaps both processes involve expressions of specific genes. If so, it may soon be possible to discover how genetic expression, critical periods, and environmental influences underlie the development of complex skills.

THE DEVELOPMENT OF COMPLEX SKILLS

Jean-Pierre Rampal plays the flute with a melodic line, a delicacy, and a sureness that never fail to delight his appreciative listeners. What is it that distinguishes a virtuoso like Rampal from run-of-the-mill flutists, or, indeed, what distinguishes any master of a complex skill from the mediocre performer? Both natural aptitude and intensive practice are necessary. No one can say which is more important or resolve genetic potential in its constituents. We can, however, examine the learning of complex activities with the object of discovering what these experts really learn, and by what process they reach this high level of mastery. Such studies have been made of simpler skills, telegraphy, typing, and reading (Bryan & Harter, 1897; Cooper, 1983; Woodworth, 1938).

QUALITATIVE IMPROVEMENT IN PERFORMANCE

A student of telegraphy learns rapidly during the first few weeks. Tests on successive weeks show that the number of letters sent or received each minute increases markedly in the first few weeks and then more and more slowly. A landmark study shows the typical learning curves (Bryan & Harter, 1897). (See Figure 14.6.)

The curve for sending rises in a broad sweep and then flattens out in an

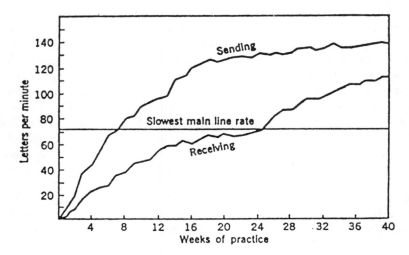

Figure 14.6. Learning curves of a student of telegraphy. The height of a curve above the baseline shows the number of letters sent or received per minute. A rise of the curve denotes improvement. Note the plateau in the receiving curve followed by improvement. Bryan & Harter, 1897.

asymptote, suggesting a "physiological limit" for the given student. The receiving curve rises more slowly than the sending curve and flattens out after four months' practice with little further improvement. The student may become discouraged at this apparent limit, well below the minimum standard for commercial employment. The student who does not drop out, but persists, however, will find his curve making a fresh sweep upward before flattening out again at a higher level, well above the standard.

The flat stretch or plateau in the learning curve, followed by a subsequent rise, marks a change in the student's method of attack. The new period of rapid progress is the result, not of simply speeding up the movements of fingers on the telegraph key, but of improved methods.

At first, students learn each letter as a little pattern of dots and dashes. In sending, they spell out each word and then transmit the letters, one by one, in terms of their separate patterns. As these letter patterns become more and more familiar through practice in sending and receiving, the student can speed up and become adept at letter habits.

But an expert telegrapher must graduate from letter habits to word habits. These emerge with further practice. The rhythmical pattern of a whole word becomes a familiar unit. A few short, much-used words first become units, then longer and longer words, and eventually, the telegrapher acquires control over entire phrases.

Much the same thing happens in learning to type (Woodworth, 1938). First, beginners learn where each letter is located on the keyboard and which finger is used to strike it. With practice, letter habits become fixed. Further practice integrates these finger movements into familiar word units, then into phrase units, and these *higher units* give speed and smoothness. Typists at this stage perform without attention to the individual letters; indeed, they may not be able to fill in the correct letter on a blank map of the keyboard. They have graduated to larger and different units in which their eyes on the copy are well ahead of their hands. These qualitative improvements in performance form *higher-order cognons.*

HIGHER-ORDER COGNONS

New higher-order cognons are created when the cognons already formed constitute elements of more complex stimulus patterns. Then new complex units are formed according to the same principles found for the formation of unitary perceptions of objects and patterns—feature-detecting afferent cells.

The process of forming higher-order cognons is shown by one process of learning how to read—an analytical process. At first, the child learns to identify single letters. Each letter forms a cognon in the corresponding cognitive field of either the visual or the auditory analyzer. Later he can put them together to form words. Familiar words can be read as units. Each word is then a cognon. J. McKeen Cattell (1886a; 1886b) found by experiment that the time required to read a familiar word like "cat" was as short as the time required for a single letter. A reaction that can take place in a given period of time can be called a *perception unit—*or *cognon.* Using a tachistoscope with an exposure duration of 10 milliseconds, Cattell found that his subjects could read three to four unconnected letters, two unconnected short words, but four connected short words. What is perceived, Cattell concluded, is not the individual letters or elements, but the "total word picture." And, one must add, the meaning of the stimulus pattern. That is why familiar words or connected words could be read as whole units. As we have seen, an important property of the cognon is its ability to encode meaning. On the basis of these experiments, schools turned to the "whole word method" of teaching children to read.

The more advanced you are as a reader, the greater your span of apprehension, the more you can take in in a single brief flash of the tachistoscope. Speed-reading techniques are based on the ability of readers to increase their span, that is, to compress more and more information into a single targeting act of fixated attention—to pack in more letters, more words, longer and longer phrases—by using contextual cues and fragmentary features of the text to provide meaning. But that is not the whole story. The speed and accuracy of reading are not determined by eye movements or even the stimulus data that enable you to recognize a word or phrase. What matters is the "central meaning-getting" process (Woodworth, 1938). The slow reader is helped by learning to eliminate excessive fixations and regressive eye movements. But this inefficient motor behavior is probably not the cause, but the effect, of poor reading (or writing). What makes reading difficult and slow is the inability to understand the material (often this is less the reader's fault than the writer's for failing to make the ideas clear).

The landmark study of Bryan and Harter (1897) showed how practice affects both perceptual and motor skills. The transition is from the letter to the word habit, and eventually the learner can "take in several words at a mouthful, a phrase, or even a short sentence." In sending, he anticipates, but in receiving, he learns to "copy behind," letting two or three words come in before he starts to copy. This can be observed in other perceptual skills—the "simultaneous" translator of a language learns to beware of anticipation, but allows time to get the sense of the message. She then provides the interpretation, usually in bursts of five or six words at a time.

In telegraphy, typing, reading, and interpreting, we can discern certain common patterns (Book, 1908; Cooper, 1983). In every case, the learning curve shows an interesting shape. Following an initial rise, the curve flattens to a plateau; then, after remaining flat for a few weeks, the curve goes up again. The plateaus are periods of transition—from letter habits to word habits; then another plateau is followed by a new rise in the curve, from word habits to phrases and eventually to short sentences. The plateau is often a period of discouragement for the student who seems unable to make any progress. But, given the motivation to improve, the new level of mastery appears, and the learning curve shoots up again.

The expert's higher-order units are different from the lower-order units, not by being executed more rapidly—the difference is not a matter of degree but of quality—the expert has better, more abstract units at her command. She also has an increased time span, illustrated by anticipation and copying behind.

The key to the formation of higher-order units lies in two features, *higher units* and *overlap*. As cognons are formed in the cognitive centers of the brain, they themselves take part in providing the stimuli for still higher-order cognons. These represent increasingly abstract and sophisticated percept qualities or concepts in the central cortical fields of the analyzers that are capable of discrimination learning or concept formation. The most numerous and conceptually sophisticated percepts are associated with vision and audition, because these analyzes are represented by the greatest amount and complexity of cortical tissue in the brain. We create subtle visual qualities and auditory nuances and harmonies in the higher levels of these analyzers. Such cognons link with kinesthetic cognons to form dance and music.

THE ROLE OF REINFORCEMENT

Sheer repetition fails to improve performance. Students often hear the phrase, "you learn by doing." That statement is incomplete; it should be "you learn by doing and getting results."

The higher levels of skill demand more than half-hearted practice. The critical factor is reinforcement or knowledge of results. Learning cannot be achieved by repetition alone.

Fred Keller (1943) discovered a very simple way to improve radically the mastery of telegraphy. Immediately after writing the letter tapped out by the instructor, the student heard the letter repeated. The procedure differed from the traditional one in which the student got feedback only at the end of a lesson, if at all. In the Keller method, after receiving a pattern of clicks sent by the instructor, the student wrote the corresponding letter and was immediately informed, not only of the correctness or incorrectness of his response, but what the correct response should have been. The key to rapid improvement in any skill is reinforcement—immediate, swift, and revealing.

Under ordinary circumstances of learning a new skill, pupils remain in ignorance of the correctness of their performance for some time. They receive a good grade or a poor grade, but what the pupil did that was right is a mysterious secret. Yet that information is more important for improving performance than the evaluation, and it is usually far more difficult to discover than that they did something wrong. Our current educational system is geared to periodic testing and grading of students. Yet long delays occur between student performances on tests and the results of those performances. Usually all they are told is their grade or rank in class; they may learn that they did poorly or well; but what they did *correctly* is rarely specified. Consequently, many reach only a moderate level of skill and never acquire expert technique at anything. Evidently, feedback, knowledge of results, or reinforcement, whatever name you call it, is important in human learning. The much-publicized failure of our schools to teach basic skills, much less mastery of language and science, is often attributable to the lack of attention to this factor (Skinner, 1965; 1968).

The processes of development of higher-order skills and complex cognitive functions have necessarily been described in psychological terms. The underlying physiological processes are still unknown. Yet recently, progress in understanding the neural mechanisms that mediate behavioral modifications has been achieved and may be applied to the problem of recovery following brain damage.

RECOVERY FROM BRAIN DAMAGE

With the new understanding of the importance of connections between different parts of the brain for complex behavior, it has become clear that neither equipotentiality nor vicarious functioning can explain the recovery of function following brain lesions. Indeed, with a part of the brain scooped out, certain circuits are no longer transmissible. Complex functions, speech, or memory may return, but their ability to do so rests on the possibility of educating potential new paths to accomplish the same ends as before the injury occurred.

Nowhere is this more dramatically illustrated than in the disconnection syndrome produced by commissurotomy. The split brain patient is characterized by an unbridgeable chasm between the consciousness of the two hemispheres (Chapter Three). Although both cerebral hemispheres can learn, both can remember, and both can feel joy, anguish, disgust, or fear, neither one can communicate to the other, and only the left hemisphere can talk to us.

The callosal syndrome was induced in these patients deliberately as a therapeutic procedure to relieve intractable epilepsy. Other patients may suffer permanent disconnection between a small number of functional regions in the brain caused by strokes or tumors. A stroke, or cerebral vascular accident (CVA), results from occlusion or hemorrhage in a blood vessel. If the blood supply to the brain is insufficient, and the condition is severe and prolonged, neurons die and the resulting disconnection is termed *infarction*.

Geschwind and Kaplan (1962) describe a remarkable case of a patient whose writing with the right hand was linguistically correct, but, with the left hand, aphasic. His left hand could not type, nor calculate normally, but was able to function well on nonverbal tasks, (tactile localization, for example). Behavior was competent in all tasks in which both the stimuli and the responses required the use of a single hemisphere, whether right or left. But the patient performed poorly when the stimulus required processing by one half of the brain, and the response was controlled by the other. The patient was found to have an *infarction* near the anterior cerebral artery that prevented the crossing over of the information from one hemisphere to the other.

Another syndrome is called "isolation of the speech area" (Geschwind, 1970). A woman patient was left helpless by an episode of carbon monoxide poisoning and never uttered a sentence of propositional speech during the nine years in which her case was studied.

Language performance in other areas was all the more amazing because she would repeat, perfectly, sentences said to her by the examiner, even complete jingles. For example, if he said "Roses are red," she would say, "violets are blue, sugar is sweet, and so are you." She articulated normally, and even astonished everyone by singing songs that had not existed before her illness. Her instructor was a record player—after several repetitions of a song, the record player had merely to start, and she would continue to sing the words and music to the end. Postmortem examination showed that both Broca's and Wernicke's areas, the classic speech areas, were intact. The damage had affected the regions surrounding the speech areas (either in the cortex or the underlying white matter) thus isolating the speech area itself, and that accounted for the strange dissociation of functions. Language comprehension was disrupted because the association areas that support and interpret verbal inputs were disconnected from the speech areas. Her remarkable ability to learn new songs can be attributed to the preservation of the hippocampal region, which, as dramatically shown by the anterograde amnesic case of Henry M. and the other patients studied by Milner (1970), is indispensable for the new learning of verbal material.

The examples cited in this and earlier chapters are profoundly pessimistic with regard to the recovery of functions lost as a result of brain damage. Are there not also cases in which disturbed functions recover?

The answer, of course, is yes, preeminently so following brain injuries to very young children. Below five years of age, there is good evidence that speech can transfer from left to right hemispheres. Even the loss or agenesis of a complete left hemisphere may result in the development of normally functional language centers in the right hemisphere, if the child is young enough.

One of the most important discoveries for understanding the capacity of the central nervous system to recover impaired function following brain injury comes from studies of the morphological consequences of prenatal injury to the primate brain. Since in primates the crucial events underlying the migration of nerve cells and the differentiation of their axons and dendrites occur before birth, such studies provide unique information on the limits of neuronal plasticity necessary for understanding and treating brain-damaged human patients. Modern neurobiological methods now available to analyze fetal brain development can be combined with prenatal surgery in infrahuman primates. The combination provides a well-controlled experimental approach to the study of the brain's adaptive capabilities.

Patricia Goldman-Rakic and members of her laboratory at the Yale University School of Medicine have pioneered in developing techniques and conducting investigations for this purpose (Goldman & Galkin, 1978; Goldman-Rakic, 1981). They have studied young monkeys that had sustained cortical ablations at some point in their embryonic development and subsequently survived to term to become available for postnatal examination. The prenatal surgery necessary to preserve pregnancy and produce viable offspring is incredibly delicate. Recently Goldman-Rakic has developed a neurosurgical procedure that enables her to remove the fetus temporarily from the uterus, maintaining contact with the mother via the umbilical cord, resect parts of the fetal cortex, and then return the fetus to the uterus where its intrauterine development continues uninterrupted until delivery. (See Figure 14.7.)

The results were dramatic. The most obvious change is in the external surface of the cerebrum. The configuration of sulci and gyri is radically altered as compared with unoperated monkeys or monkeys operated after birth. A striking feature of the abnormal fissural pattern is its bilateral symmetry, even

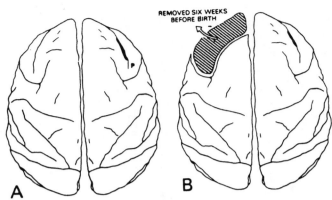

Figure 14.7. Diagram showing plan of experiment designed to reveal alterations in prefrontal cortex. The dorsolateral prefrontal cortex of the monkey fetus was resected before birth. After birth, tritiated amino acids were injected in both (A) normal and (B) prenatally operated monkeys for the purpose of autoradiographically examining projections from site (P) shown in black in control and experimental cases. P.S. Goldman. Neuronal plasticity in primate telencephalon: Anomalous crossed cortico-caudate projections induced by prenatal removal of frontal association cortex. *Science*, 1978, *202*, 768–770. Copyright © 1978 by AAAS.

following unilateral resection. Since no new neurons are generated to compensate for the loss of cells, it appears that many of the spared neurons actually change their course to populate regions adjacent to the ablated area. (See Figures 14.8 and 14.9.) Such redistribution is made possible by the absence of radial glial fibers that normally guide cortical neurons to their appropriate positions and also pose restraints to their lateral movement. (See Figures 14.1, 14.2, and 14.3.)

These studies provide valuable insight into the critical periods during gestation in which fissural patterns develop and thalamic and corticocortical afferents invade various parts of the cortex.

The most revealing finding is the extraordinary malleability of the primate brain in response to external forces. It thus displays a degree of neural plasticity far greater than that shown by numerous nonprimate animals. The finding has major significance for understanding pediatric neuropathological disorders as well as the normal development of the human brain.

Cerebral vascular accidents typically afflict older persons. Can they recover from an aphasia that leaves them little speech, uttered only with great effort and poor articulation? In contrast to this nonfluent aphasia, what is the prognosis for the fluent aphasic who will speak rapidly but with so many paraphasias (incorrect or nonsense words) that the listener finds it meaningless jargon?

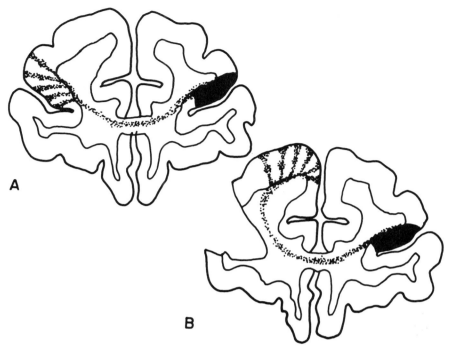

Figure 14.8. Drawing of prefrontal cortex in the left and right hemispheres of the rhesus monkey. (A) Normal animal showing the pattern of alternating callosal fiber bundles in the homotopic cortex of the left hemisphere. (B) Monkey in which the dorsolateral prefrontal cortex was resected in the left hemisphere three months earlier at 8 weeks of age. Callosal fibers deprived of their normal target in the contralateral hemisphere pass by the resected area and become redistributed in the cortex dorsal and medial to the resected area. Note that they retain their pattern of spatial periodicity. Goldman-Rakic, 1981. Copyright © 1981 by the Massachusetts Institute of Technology. Photographs courtesy of Dr. Patricia Goldman-Rakic.

The answer to these questions depends upon a number of factors, the site and extent of brain damage, the age and motivation of the patient, and the nature of the syndrome.

If a patient remains hemiplegic as a result of vascular disease for three weeks, the chances for recovery are thought to be minimal (Geschwind, 1971). Still, some patients recover spontaneously even after longer periods of disorder. Specific therapy has been shown to be especially effective in cases of Broca's and in conduction aphasia.

The more completely we understand the various disorders of the higher functions of the brain, the more rationally we can devise therapies for them.

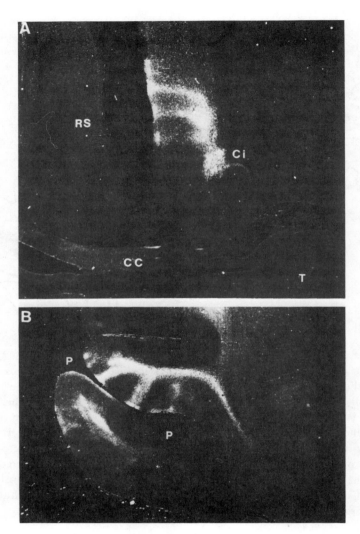

Figure 14.9. Dark-field autoradiograms illustrating columnar mode of distribution of two classes of cortico-cortical projections emanating from the dorsal back of the principal sulcus in one hemisphere. (A) Associational (ipsilateral) connections terminating in the retrosplenial cortex (RS). (B) Callosal (contralateral) projections terminating in the homotopic dorsal bank of the principal sulcus (P) in the opposite hemisphere. These fibers are distributed through all layers of the cortex and interdigitate widely with other fiber systems. Goldman-Rakic, 1982. Photographs courtesy of Dr. Patricia Goldman-Rakic. Copyright © 1982 by Academic Press, Inc. All rights of reproduction reserved.

CAN BRAIN GRAFTS CORRECT BRAIN DAMAGE?

Brain transplants might seem like the wild idea of a science fiction writer. Yet, recently, neurobiologists have successfully grafted fetal brain tissue directly into the mammalian host brain. This work is proving to be enormously helpful to investigators for tackling the unsolved problems of brain development. Even more exciting is the potential clinical application to treatments for brain damage.

The remarkable studies conducted by Patricia Goldman-Rakic and her associates at Yale University School of Medicine have provided evidence that biological mechanisms exist for aiding recovery after early brain injury in primates. Whereas lesions in frontal cortex in adult monkeys irreversibly impair performance on the delayed response task, the same lesions induced early in the life of the monkey have no deleterious effect on capacity to perform the task.

The prospect of grafting in the area of the brain known to participate in learning and memory—the hippocampus—offers promise of a therapy for memory loss that occurs with aging, especially with Alzheimer's disease, caused by a lack of acetylcholine in the brain. Dorothy Krieger (1980) and her associates at Mount Sinai School of Medicine have begun still another sort of grafting experiment to study transplants that produce hypothalamic gonado-tropin-releasing hormones. In male mice, the lack of this hormone, caused by a mutation, results in immature reproductive organs and small, undescended testes. Krieger and Hughes (1980) were able to correct this mutation by fetal transplants from the preoptic area which makes this hormone. Early fetal tissue works best, probably because these nerve cells are able to divide—an ability that is lost with age. The particular neurotransmitter that the tissue secretes seems to stimulate nerve growth and to direct the migrating fibers to just the right location.

Perhaps the most intriguing research is that which grafts genes directly into developing host embryos. The next step is to make gene grafts work in monkeys. Only then can clinically significant work on humans be confidently undertaken.

SUMMARY

We have seen that all behavior depends on the foundation created by heredity and ontogenetic development. External environmental factors, however, exert profound effects on the development of the brain beginning before birth and during early critical periods of maturation. These environmental influences can produce morphological or structural changes in the central nervous system that leave permanent and irreversible aftereffects. Other behavioral modifications as the result of experience can produce functional or plastic alterations at synapses that can be transformed by conditioning processes and are thus reversible. Whether a given interaction with the environment produces a temporary or stable long-term effect on the individual's behavior and experience must be determined in each case by appropriate experimentation.

The forces that at one time shaped limbs were translated into developmental instructions about limb making that are now part of our genetic heritage, but the instructions are fulfilled by use. The principle of natural selection is as much under the control and direction of the forces to which the system is exposed as it is to genetic preformation. Heredity proposes and environment disposes. In the particular case of greatest concern to us, the human mind, natural selection gives us, not one principle, but two principles that shape and direct our behavior. Our evolutionary heritage has selected a tightly organized structure whose precise arrangement still leaves vast opportunities for plastic or functional change under the impact of environmental forces. The effectiveness of the connections within the central nervous system and the properties of the individual neurons themselves between which these connections exist are created by the individual's own experience and interaction with the environment.

Some remarkable new advances in knowledge and technology are making possible environmental, chemical, and surgical manipulations to relieve perceptual and motor disorders caused by damage to the brain. Even brain grafts could become a scientific reality for treatment of some neurological diseases.

Studies of the development of complex performance skills reveal the formation of higher-order cognons as the result of the integration of lower-level cognons. This integrative activity of the brain reaches its highest level in the creative contributions of individuals as writers, artists, musicians, scientists, and humanitarians.

In the development of complex skills, maturation and learning are not different processes. They are different yet closely intertwined facets of one and the same process. Your heredity is contained in the chromosomes present in every cell of your body. It thus continues to exert an effect on your behavior throughout the course of your life even as new experiences and activities lead to your continued growth and change.

SUGGESTED READINGS

Blakemore, C. Developmental factors in the formation of feature extracting neurons. In F.O. Schmitt & F.G. Worden (Eds.), *The neurosciences: Third study program* (105–113). Cambridge: MIT Press, 1974.

Blakemore, C. Maturation and modification in the developing visual system. In R. Held, H.W. Leibowitz & H.-L. Teuber (Eds.), *Handbook of sensory physiology* (Vol. VIII) *Perception.* New York: Springer-Verlag, 1978.

Blakemore, C., Garey, L.J., & Vital-Durand, F. The physiological effects of monocular deprivation and their reversal in the monkey's visual cortex. *Journal of Physiology,* 1978, **283,** 223–262.

Cooper, W.E. (Ed.). *Cognitive aspects of skilled typewriting.* New York: Springer-Verlag, 1983.

Darwin, C. *On the origin of species by means of natural selection.* New York: Appleton-Century-Crofts, 1860.

Fiorentini, A., & Maffei, L. Change of binocular properties of the simple cells of the cortex in adult cats following immobilization of one eye. *Vision Research,* 1974, **14,** 217–218.

Goldman, S.A., & Nottebohm, F. Neuronal production, migration, and differentiation in a vocal control nucleus of the adult female canary brain. *Proceedings of the National Academy of Science,* 1983, **80,** 2390–2394.

Gould, S.J. *Ontogeny and phylogeny.* Cambridge: Harvard University Press, 1977.

Hirsch, H.V., & Spinelli, D.N. Visual experience modifies distribution of horizontally and vertically oriented receptive fields in cats. *Science,* 1970, **168,** 869–871.

McGraw, M.B. *The neuromuscular maturation of the human infant.* New York: Hafner, 1963.

Maffei, L., & Fiorentini, A. Geniculate neural plasticity in kittens after exposure to periodic gratings. *Science,* 1974, **186,** 447–449.

Maffei, L., & Fiorentini, A. The visual cortex as a spatial frequency analyzer. *Vision Research,* 1973, **13,** 1255–1267.

Newton, G., & Levine, S. (Eds.). *Early experience and behavior: The psychobiology of development.* Springfield, Ill.: Thomas, 1968.

Rosenzweig, M.R., Krech, D., Bennett, E.L., & Diamond, M.C. Modifying brain chemistry and anatomy by enrichment or impoverishment of experience. In G. Newton & S. Levine (Eds.), *Early experience and behavior: The psychobiology of development.* Springfield, Ill.: Thomas, 1968.

Tighe, T.J., & Leaton, R.N. *Habituation: Perspectives from child development, animal behavior, and neurophysiology.* Hillsdale, N.J.: Erlbaum, 1976.

CHAPTER FIFTEEN
General Summary

The structural design of the whole neocortex is such that it should be conceived as a mosaic of overlapping columns each possessing its own functional specificity on the basis of its tangential articulation with incoming fibers and each processing this information up and down within the column for a significant output.

Colonnier, 1966, p. 18.

ARCHITECTURE OF INTEGRATIVE MIND-BRAIN FUNCTION

One of the most remarkable new concepts of how the brain is organized is that the major cortical and subcortical regions are further divided into partially isolated local modular units—columns of neurons—united by a common task.

The columns serve as anatomical devices for bringing cells together, much like integrated circuit chips in sophisticated microcomputers. Interconnections between these neurons can integrate discrete, but convergent, sensory inputs and can generate complex higher-order information necessary for recognition of patterns and objects. Individual command cells exert a control over an entire behavioral sequence, causing the heart to beat faster, the pulse to quicken, or the many pairs of muscles in the legs to execute an intricate dance.

An important recent neurophysiological discovery was the columnar organization of not only the somesthetic, visual, and other sensory and motor projection cortex but also of the prefrontal association areas (Goldman-Rakic & Schwartz, 1982). Figure 5.17 illustrates how callosal (contralateral) terminals alternate with associational (*ipsilateral) terminals in side-by-side, mutually exclusive columns, linking the two hemispheres, and underlying our spatiotemporal integration.

There is good reason to believe that the central nervous system extends the same columnar principle to the entire cortex. As a result, the architecture of the association cortex, like the visual striate and somesthetic cortex, may be supposed to consist of a columnar organization, modular blocks or hyper-columns, each consisting of a uniform array of minicolumns, but with columns of identical neurons now representing, not features or specific submodalities of sensory input, but identical configurations representing recognizable objects or relations with spatial, temporal, or drive-related significance.

At the very highest levels of representation, however, a new process seems to occur. The mechanism of transformation of afferent messages changes from a topographic, or metric, form of mapping to a topological and categorical one. Whereas the primary sensory and motor areas of the projection cortex have a precise topographic mapping of the effectors and receptive surfaces of the body, the association cortex seems to have a *categorical structure* in which neural units are distributed according to their common biological task or consummatory significance. Instead of a point-for-point representation of the visual field or the bodily surface, single units now represent relations between features. Evolution gave the mammalian brain its competitive edge by bringing together all the analyzers in a single and comparatively homogeneous structure—the neocortex. The neocortical ad-vantage lies in facilitating the integration of information from different sensory modalities about particular objects and events. Thus a predator might be recognized by its sight, sound, or smell, or by any one of these senses in the absence of the others, if there has been prior cross-indexing of this information. Such cross-modal matching is believed to furnish the basis for language. The same word or name can be used to refer to the same object, whether it is encountered by sight, touch, or other sense, or simply imagined before or after its actual appearance. At a cognitive level, any given configuration can be processed in more than one way.

Donald MacKay (1970) makes the point: you may perceive the contents of this page as ink marks on paper, as letters, as words, as sentences, or as arguments with which you may or may not disagree. The meaning of the contents is not confined to any single level, but is your internal response to the relations between the elements considered as belonging to a given level. If you have been paying attention to my arguments, you may be startled to be asked a question about the color of the ink, or the typefont, or the frequency of the letter *t*. Indeed you may have to look again in order to respond at a very different level than your current mental set can provide.

In terms of neural organization, this phenomenon points to a heterarchical structure. Responses are initiated and processed at different levels. One level is not necessarily higher or lower, more elementary, nor more complex and sophisticated than another. Children may learn to read by processing whole words before they are able to identify individual letters; and certainly the ability to identify typefont comes later than either reading or discriminating letters. Our limited channel capacity simply means that information must be processed at different levels. Even if more than one level is attended to at one time, they cannot be equally available to consciousness, but priorities differ and may shift.

THE HETERARCHICAL PRINCIPLE IN MIND-BRAIN ACTIVITY

The various components of a complete system can be combined in different ways. In particular, programs can be combined serially, hierarchically, or heterarchically.

Serial combination is a form of chaining; data from one program are taken over by the next in line; then another takes over, and so on—always in a linear, step-by-step progression. Hebb's (1949) "cell-assembly," described earlier, is a classic example of a strictly serial chain of neural reactions. Although Hebb emphasized the maintenance of activity in a self—re-exciting circular loop, a "reverberating circuit," the result is an intractable rigidity, a carousel going round and round in place. No direct evidence for a reverberating circuit appears to exist, and Hebb later retracted the idea.

In a *hierarchy*, the vicious circle appears to be broken. One program has overall control; others are subordinate to it—mere subroutines of the master program. The flow of control passes in one direction only—from the top down—but that has no certain advantage over the bottom-up procedure of the serial cell assembly.

Evolution has provided the human brain with a biological solution that is clearly superior in flexibility, the *heterarchy*, first named, I believe, by the well-known neurophysiologist, Warren S. McCullough.

The advantages of the heterarchical form of organization are described by Margaret Boden in her remarkable book, *Artificial Intelligence and Natural Man* (1977). Boden, professor of philosophy and psychology at the University of Sussex, explains how heterarchical thinking enhances the problem-solving and decision-making ability of computers. Unlike the serial or the hierarchical forms or organization, both of which suffer from the fixed progression of responsibility through successive levels of the system, the heterarchical arrangement offers varied and flexible arrangements: bottom-up and top-down, feedforward and feedback, serial and parallel processing.

In a heterarchical organization, the responsibility for control can be equally distributed throughout the system. Internal communication can be increased. Boden writes:

> Programs that are related heterarchically can address or call upon each other either "up," "down," or "sideways." Moreover, they can do this at many different points in their (potentially independent) functioning. The human analogy is a group of intercommunicating specialists contributing their several skills to a cooperative enterprise, rather than a troop of servants each unquestioningly obeying their mistress—or her butler, cook, and house-keeper. (1977, p. 127)

Our heterarchical brain is a dynamically organized, interconnected set of systems and subsystems that can pass control from one to another in many different directions. Earlier units in a heterarchy can be modified by the activity of later ones, later units can undo mistakes, and units at any point can forestall adverse contingencies. This is the power of intelligence responsible for the highest reaches of human thought.

The image of the central nervous system as a heterarchy is not a bad model for a social organization, even an entire society. The concept of a heterarchy expresses the orderliness with which a smoothly functioning democracy, composed of many autonomous units serving in specialized capacities on different levels of the system, can be made to work toward common goals.

As a model for human society, a heterarchy emphasizes three ideas—harmony, mutual respect, and unity of purpose. In our model of the human brain, the survival of its owner depends on the cooperation of subcortical units with cortical pattern or object recognition mechanisms called cognons.

THE ROLE OF COGNONS IN MIND-BRAIN ACTIVITY

Situated in the cognitive fields of the visual, auditory and other analyzers, cognons are high-level trigger units that finally analyze the coded converging messages and decide whether a predetermined criterion has been met. When excited by messages coming from sense receptors, cognons give rise to unitary perceptions; excited by association (interneurons within the brain), cognons produce images. Unitary perceptions are accompanied by the targeting reflex adjusting the sense organs to the optimal reception of a stimulus. This reflex gives perception its mark of external reality. In contrast, the absence of the targeting reflex makes even the most vivid image seem to reside within the head.

Hallucinations arise when sensory input is cut off by sleep, drugs, or bypassed by direct brain stimulation or strong emotional states. The flow of neural traffic downstream from cognitive to projective areas gives the hallucination the quality of an incoming perception.

The cognon has a place in the brain's anatomy that is most simply conceived as a single neural unit although many equivalent cells or synapses may be brought into existence at the time of initial formation. Packed in narrow vertical columns, the cognons integrate and store biologically significant information obtained from the outside world and the organism's own activity.

In nonhuman animals, single neural units in the sense organs and motor centers react to complex stimulus patterns that ethologists call *releasers* or *trigger features*. These potentially reactive neural units are laid down by the genetic inheritance of a species and imprinted by releasers during a critical period of development. In humans, the genes program and maturation develops potential recipient neurons and connecting pathways for the formation of pattern recognition units. These are cognons. Cognons are located not in the sensory or motor projection areas but between them, in the newly developed regions of association cortex. These neocortical nerve cells in the human brain integrate and store mental representations of objects, action programs, and events as the result of a process, not unlike imprinting, of perceptual learning.

Experiments on the effects of early experience and early deprivation of particular kinds of stimulation show clearly that certain kinds of perceptual learning demand exposure to adequate stimuli at sensitive periods of development. Tantalizing recent evidence (Goldman & Nottebohm, 1983; Nottebohm, 1980; 1981) reveals that adult male canaries learn to sing and females to recognize new and different songs every year, and there is good reason to suppose that human adults continue to learn well into old age. The critical conditions for the formation of new perceptual and motor skills are a place in the brain for their control centers and motivation sufficient to sustain attention to the new song or word or face. In the canary, brain space and the mating drive are jointly triggered each season by sex hormones; the plastic substrate for vocal learning is renewed yearly, "a growing, then shedding of synapses, much the way trees grow leaves in the spring and shed them in the fall" (Nottebohm, 1981, p. 1370).

The much larger human brain may not require the shrinking or shedding of old brain nuclei in order to make room for new cognons. Still, forgetting or some retraction of neurites may be, Nottebohm suggests, the indispensable first step for their rejuvenation. Whether brain space is the prerequisite or the result of new learning, the relation itself, regardless of its direction, is clear.

Brain nuclei and neural pathways must be available if behavior is to be modified by experience.

The existence of cognons in the human brain is supported by neurological and psychological evidence. The single most dramatic example is the "monkey paw" cell discovered by Gross and co-workers in monkey inferotemporal cortex. Anatomical localization of particular categories of cognons in different analyzers is shown by the selective impairment of functions following lesions to specific cortical areas. The disorder may be highly selective, disturbing only one particular category, such as the ability to recognize human faces or the comprehension of spoken words, but with all other visual or auditory functions intact.

Many of the symptoms of brain damage are produced by the disconnection of two essential areas. A dramatic example is the loss of connection between the speech hemisphere and the visual receiving area in the other hemisphere, which makes it impossible for the patient to read, although he can write and spell (alexia without agraphia). The severing of the corpus callosum has disconnected the angular gyrus, the visual centers, and the motor speech area needed to convert written language to speech.

A frequent associated difficulty is the failure to name colors presented by the examiner. The patient is able to match two colors and talk about the green grass but cannot match the color name to the color stimulus because color and printed words are confined to vision.

The psychological properties of unitary perceptions are tied to their supposed anatomical and physiological bases. The principles of cognon activity derived from psychological experiments reveal striking parallels between their psychological and physiological properties. These are:

1. *Pattern or object recognition.* The cognon represents the stored model or standard form of the familiar stimulus object and evokes immediate recognition following selective attention to that object.

2. *Categorization.* The organization of cognons into modular blocks consisting of minicolumns representing similar sorts of things is consistent with the anatomical and behavioral evidence for well-structured natural categories.

3. *Integrity.* The cognon is an indivisible unit. Its all-or-none character insures the invariance of the unitary perception or unitary image and accounts for the constancies of color, size, and shape of perceived objects, and the flashback stereotypy of images and hallucinations. The alternative percepts produced by ambiguous figures do not mix but remain, like antagonistic motor acts, mutually exclusive.

4. *Selectivity.* The cognon is a highly selective pattern detector that extracts essential elements and rejects or ignores irrelevant aspects of a stimulus pattern. Since we respond to relations rather than to absolute

properties, the cognon sorts out the higher-order variables, say, the few lines of a caricature that one recognizes at a glance. The topological integration of the sensory input makes possible a simple and economical code for perception and action.

5. *Complementarity.* Both on-units and off-units converge their input onto cognons. This results in both the stability and the lability of perception and voluntary movements.

In reversible perspective drawings, figure and ground change places; in monocular or binocular rivalry, the advantage shifts from one competing orientation, color, or spatial frequency domain to another. Simultaneous and successive contrasts and negative aftereffects are the well-known perceptual phenomena resulting from intracategory coupling of positive and negative spaces or elements.

6. *Mutual antagonism.* A related consequence of the above properties is the proactive, retroactive, and lateral inhibition found between cognons of the same category. This accounts for interference effects in recognition and memory found especially in recall of lists of similar materials and the limits of information processing shown by the immediate memory span, attention span, and various judgment functions. Perceptions from cognons belonging to different categories show no antagonism, but complement each other, as in looking and listening concurrently. The interesting outcome is the formation of cross-modal associations—the essential foundation for language, hand-eye coordination, and the development of higher-order cognons for abstract conceptual thinking and skilled performance.

MODULARITY IN MIND-BRAIN ACTIVITY

The human brain's organization makes important use of two features: modularity and multilevel packaging. Modularity, small compact units distributed throughout an area, and multilevel packaging, heterarchical systems in which control of a function passes back and forth from subcortical to cortical sites in overlapping sequences, have many advantages. The modular and heterarchical nature of cerebral organization are now being introduced into computer architecture with resultant economy, diversity, and power (Birnbaum, 1982). The quest for smallness, realized in increasingly tiny, integrated circuit chips, and the partitioning of tasks for parallel processing in the present generation of microcomputers, increases their versatility, lowers their price, and makes them faster, more reliable, and easy to use. Miniaturization improves speed, and dense packaging improves reliability, because unreliability comes from the number and spacing of connections. (See Figure 15.1.)

In the brain, a significant amount of computation can proceed simultane-

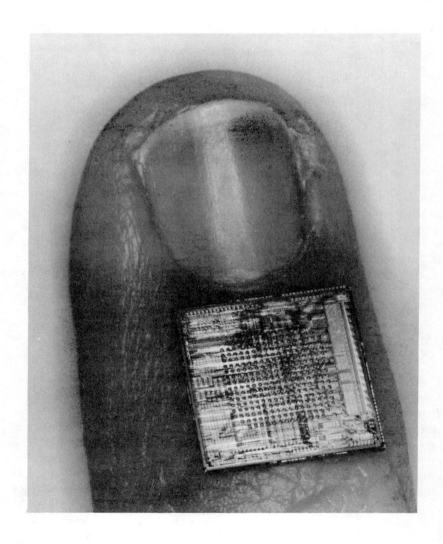

Figure 15.1. Experimental computer memory chips combine high density with very fast operating speeds. (A) This experimental chip, shown here on a child's finger, combines the equivalent of 4,208 logic circuits with 13,000 bits of read only memory. The finger and chip (7-millimeter square) are magnified 13 times. Photograph courtesy of IBM Corporation. (B) This new chip—capable of storing 72,000 bits of data—achieves its high operating speeds through the use of bipolar transistor technology. Photograph courtesy IBM Corporation.

465

ously by partitioning tasks and integrating results. A single dramatic discovery may be used to illustrate the point. Since direct evidence gained by penetrating single brain cells is unattainable in human subjects, experiments on monkeys make it possible to find the neural substrates of higher intellectual functions.

In an elegant series of studies, Lynch (1980), Motter and Mountcastle (1981), and their associates investigated the functional organization of the parietal association areas of the cortex. Macaque monkeys are particularly suitable for such experiments; their similarities to humans, especially in their hand and eye coordinations, and in the general anatomy of their nervous systems, make them a good model for understanding human higher nervous function.

Mountcastle and his associates carried out experiments on the inferior parietal lobule of waking, behaving monkeys. They identified 1,616 parietal neurons and studied 781 of them intensively in order to define precisely what effect different visual stimuli had on them when the animal was behaving in one specific way rather than another. For example, they trained monkeys to reach and to manipulate in the light and also in total darkness. Most of the cells were sensitive to light and were classified as light-sensitive (LS) neurons. "The most striking dynamic property of these (LS) neurons is their sensitivity to movement of light stimuli, and to the direction of that movement"(Motter & Mountcastle, 1981, p. 21).

Those cells fired over a wide range of velocities of movement, from 10° per second to 800° per second. They responded to opposite directions of movement, pointing toward or away from the central line of gaze—an "opponent vector organization" that could play significant roles in guiding hand and eye movements and in attracting visual attention to objects and to events that were outside, as well as within, the center of foveal vision in the immediately surrounding space.

The scientists were enthusiastic about their success in identifying these crucial functions in single neurons for representing and for coordinating reaching and visual fixations during movements of the body in space. But they were even more impressed by their ability, gained through these experiments, to determine how the animal's behavioral "set," or internal state of attention, affected the excitability of the parietal cells. This required preliminary training.

They trained the monkeys to:

1. fixate a target light intently so as to respond as quickly as possible to its dimming, for which the monkey received a reward;

2. keep watching a uniform field for the onset of that target light in between rewarded trials; and

3. simply sit quietly gazing at a noneventful field.

The three behavioral states gave straightforward results. The recorded responses of the single parietal cells depended on *what the monkey was doing at that moment.* Under conditions 1 and 2, a particular cell would fail to respond if its owner was simply sitting quietly, or even if it was monitoring the uniform field. But under condition 1 with the monkey intently fixating the target light and *set* to detect and to react to a decrement in brightness with a reward in the offing, the identical cell gave a vigorous response.

The importance of this finding is that scientists now have an *objective measure of expectant attention or mental set.* One single brain cell tells us *in advance* of an overt response, whether the monkey is actively paying attention or not. Now we can look at the computer analysis of microelectrode recordings of the activity of single brain cells and *predict* whether the monkey will make a correct or an incorrect response to the target light. It depends on his state of expectant or trained *attention.* This work represents a significant breakthrough, for it provides a handle on the problem of central concern to the student of *mind*—how is directed thought (set) represented in the nervous tissue of the brain.

Clearly, goal set has a distinctive effect on the activity of single neural units, depending on whether drive reduction (reward or reinforcement) follows. The ability to anticipate the impending arrival of the unconditioned stimulus is, as we have seen, the key to classical and instrumental conditioning. This is the way we learn about causal relations in the environment and our own ability to produce the unconditioned stimulus.

The conclusion is inescapable that the cognitive and emotive systems do not function in isolation from each other. Their joint collaboration is essential for directing behavior.

Although cognition and emotion are intimately intertwined in normal behavior, marked distinctions between what we know and what we feel often emerge under extraordinary conditions.

THE EMOTIVE AND THE COGNITIVE BRAIN SYSTEMS

Electrical stimulation of the emotive system and the cognitive system produces completely different effects. Direct stimulation of the sensory and motor areas in the cognitive neocortex produces either sensations or passive movements, depending upon the localization, and is devoid of any emotional aspects. In contrast, stimulation of the subcortical emotive brain gives rise to strong emotional experiences and autonomic responses. Self-stimulation by electrodes implanted in the hypothalamic-limbic structures produces in animals fantastic extremes of response—evidently of extreme pleasure or severe pain—depending on the exact location of the stimulating electrode.

Comparable effects have been reported by conscious humans suffering from epilepsy, brain tumors, or mental illness. Reward centers are found in the human brain by implanted electrodes, but punishment areas also appear, as observed in other animals.

Implantation of electrodes in the brain of human patients has been used for diagnostic and therapeutic purposes in several neurosurgical medical centers around the world. There is considerable agreement that electrical brain stimulation (EBS) can be helpful in selected classes of disorders, such as epilepsy and intractable pain. As therapy for behavior dysfunctions— uncontrollable aggression, for example—the use of EBS is highly controversial. In contrast to neurosurgery, one cited advantage is its reversibility. Electrical stimulations can be withdrawn, whereas destruction of parts of the brain after a critical early age is irreversible (see review of debates in Valenstein, 1980). The major conclusion to emerge from depth-electrographic studies in the human brain is that the investigations so far have resulted in more new questions than answers (Sem-Jacobsen, 1976).

The best evidence for the effect of direct EBS on human consciousness comes from work on epileptic patients undergoing surgery (see Chapter Seven). Human subjects who have had epileptic discharges in the temporal region are remarkably susceptible to hallucinations produced by direct electrical stimulation of the temporal lobes. Penfield and Jasper (1954) describe dramatic examples in which electrical stimulation causes patients to relive past experiences; for example, hear voices or music or experience vivid emotions.

Penfield and Jasper conclude that the brain is "a storehouse of potential recollections." These are highly specific and discretely localized but accessible via temporal stimulation. It is as though the stimulating electrode could actuate one memory record without reawakening others—suggesting a mechanism of reciprocal inhibition of adjacent patterns when one of them is activated. The startling aspect of these findings is the ability of the stimulus to evoke realistic memories of events that may combine visual, auditory, and emotional images as they were experienced at the time of the original event.

Direct brain stimulation shows that not only recall of long-past events but recent memories are highly localized in the cortex. In patients undergoing neurosurgery under local anesthesia, the electrical stimulus has a disruptive effect on specific categories that may be quite discretely localized in the cortex. Ojemann and his group (1983) found, in a series of experiments, that short-term memory for the orientation of lines, and also for the recognition of faces, has quite specific localization in the parieto-occipital junction of the right hemisphere. An unexpected result showed that judgments of the emotional expression of faces can be altered markedly by direct stimulation of the posterior portion of the middle temporal gyrus of the right hemisphere. This dissociation in the right hemisphere is analogous to that found for the anterior and posterior regions of the left hemisphere for separate verbal functions.

THE RIDDLE OF MENTAL ILLNESS

There is reason to believe that lesions of the emotive system can produce alterations in personality. Damage to the orbital region of the frontal lobes or temporal epilepsy can totally change the easygoing, likable, and cheerful Dr. Jekyll into someone completely opposite—a Mr. Hyde who is aggressive, hypersexual, and violently hostile, or fearful, humorless, and withdrawn (see Chapter Nine).

Lesions sustained in the cognitive system give a completely different picture of disordered behavior. The symptoms of cognitive damage are often profound disturbances of perception, language, or memory functions, but the patient's personality does not change. The particular syndrome depends upon the site and the extent of the lesion, its cerebral lateralization, and the involvement of the commissures. Damage confined to the sensory projection areas will produce field defects of vision or other sensory modalities, impairing sensory discrimination, but it will not affect *images* belonging to the injured modality. On the other hand, as we have seen, an injury affecting the association cortex may abolish an entire category of object recognition, but leave sensation unimpaired. Extreme disturbances of thought, motivation or affect, and social misconduct are seen in the so-called *functional psychoses, schizophrenia* and *manic depression.*

The nineteenth century distinction between the *organic* mental illnesses (dementias and toxic psychoses) and the *functional* mental illnesses (including the neuroses and various affective or depressive disorders and the schizophrenic syndromes) is now believed to be artificial. The experiments reviewed in this book, especially those showing the profound effects of sensory deprivation and learning, show that the social and functional determinants of behavior have *biological* consequences. These are no less real, no less powerful, no less disruptive, than those labeled as demonstrably *organic* or anatomical disturbances. As Kandel concludes, "Even in the most socially determined mental disturbances, the end result is biological. Insofar as social intervention, such as psychotherapy or counseling works, it must work by acting on the brain, and quite likely on the connections between nerve cells" (1981a, p. 631).

Although the causes of these disorders are still unknown, *schizophrenia* and *manic depression* are thought to be manifestations of genetically predisposed neurochemical diseases of the brain. The evidence for a hereditary basis comes from studies of twins and of adopted children. Studies of schizophrenia in monozygotic twins show a concordance (or coincidence) rate that is two to six times as high as that in dizygotic twins or siblings (Kety, 1970; 1978). Since the former are genetically identical and may be expected to share no more of their environment with each other than dizygotic twins or siblings, this is a fairly good argument for genetic factors. More compelling evidence based on 57 twin pairs in which one member was schizophrenic in the clinical judgment of 6 independent raters of different backgrounds yielded a concordance of 40–50 percent in the monozygotic and 9–10 percent in the dizygotic twin pairs (Kety, 1979). Obviously these data do not exclude the operation of environmental factors that must have contributed to the discordance in half the identical twin pairs. What these factors are remains to be established.

The significant epigenetic role of biochemical factors in psychosis is generally agreed upon since specific drugs do have powerful effects in both schizophrenia and the affective disorders (Sachar, 1981). But none has proven *therapeutically* effective for the complex psychotic syndromes. In particular, drugs do not work on the poor social adjustments that develop during schizophrenia. Most alarming are the harmful side effects that antipsychotic drugs commonly produce. Much more research is required to develop a truly rational therapy for psychotic and emotional disorders.

It is remarkable that the best predictor of whether you will develop schizophrenia is to have an identical schizophrenic twin—the chances are 40–50 percent. But even more remarkable is the equal or greater probability that you will not develop schizophrenia; this probability suggests that most of us possess mechanisms for successfully resisting the expression of bad genetic programs. If we could discover what these mechanisms are, we might be able to accomplish the same result at will.

THE IMPORTANCE OF DRIVES (EMOTIONS) IN LEARNING AND MEMORY

Drives are recognized by consciousness as specific emotions—pain, fear, hunger, sex, or curiosity. Although their centers in the limbic system and hypothalamus are subcortical, they can emerge into awareness to form direct associations with situational stimuli represented by cognons in the cognitive centers.

Drives are essential for the formation of associations between affective stimuli and various perception units, and also between the sensory and motor centers. Two forms of cross-modal associations are thus established by experience—limbic-perceptual associations and nonlimbic or cross-perceptual associations. Motor-programming units are also linked with perception units via the mediation of the emotive system. They may form associations in different subcortical structures: the hippocampus, the cerebellum, and others still to be discovered. There is now a solid body of evidence that the hippocampus and the cerebellum serve as memory loci (engrams) for conditioned motor responses (Thompson et al., 1983).

In classical conditioning, the arousal of drive (e.g., fear) and the synchronous excitation of cognons representing each of the paired stimuli provide the preconditions for linking the CS and the US. An important distinction separates preparatory or drive CRs from consummatory CRs. The drive CRs are identical with the drive URs; in the case of the consummatory CRs this is not so—they are dissociable. The learned CR can occur in the absence of the unlearned performance, the UR, as Thompson and his co-workers have shown. Consummatory CRs tend to be connected to the sporadic stimuli that appear just before the onset of the US—they therefore appear anticipatory in character and differ in latency, form and degree from the consummatory UR.

Instrumental conditioning, as we have seen, requires the arousal of the drive center, and the active movement that produces the US. The synchronous excitation of the CS—whether or not it "elicits" or simply sets the occasion for the response, the motor act—and the US is essential. The indispensable factor is the temporal contiguity of activation of the CS cognon and the kinesthetic cognon of the instrumental movement. The termination of drive (antidrive state or relief) reinforces the successful response and eliminates all preceding unsuccessful movements by the process of retroactive inhibition. A special strength of this theory is its ability to satisfy both the hedonic requirement that an instrumental movement is learned because it produces an anticipated reward and also because it leads to the termination of drive. Extinction of a response may be viewed most simply as the depression of the association between a CS and a response as the result of its nonreinforcement (no US). The locus of the connection and its reversal is the same—a change in the synaptic efficacy of the cognon representing the CS. Recovery of a CR either spontaneously or as a result of renewed reinforcement by the US may rapidly establish the original linkage.

We are led to the realization that emotion colors all our cognitive life as a result of the involvement of cellular mechanisms in all associative learning—intersensory and sensorimotor connections. Every object that we perceive, every voluntary movement, and their associated images, are tinged by various shades of emotional coloration.

The two systems, the emotive and the cognitive, intermesh like two cogwheels in gear. This interplay results in successive cycles of preparatory and consummatory reflexes, greatly modified by learning. Our adaptability reflects this continuous intermingling of drive, perceptual and motor behavior, of forward-oriented goal seeking and feedback reinforcement.

These concepts contrast "upward causality" and "downward causality," and, as Douglas Hofstadter (1981) vividly explains, they "have to do with how events on different time scales...and different size scales in space determine each other."

FREE WILL AND THE PROBLEM OF NEUROPSYCHOLOGICAL CAUSATION

Can conscious decisions and intentions play a causal role in behavior, as adherents of "free will" claim, or can the firing of a neuron be caused only by the firing of another neuron as the "hard-nosed" determinists insist? Does no physical or anatomical point exist that can be influenced by a thought?

Hofstadter suggests that the problem has to do with the way we use words. Everyday terms like "cause" and "effect" have different meanings in different contexts. We need to be able to shift back and forth between a purely physiological language and one in which ideas, beliefs, desires, do indeed exert effects on overt behavior.

A shift from one set of terms to another can induce a shift of point of view and with it an entirely new way of perceiving. In Chapter One, I used Woodworth's metaphor of maps drawn to different scales, each corresponding to a different science—physics, biology, and psychology—each with its own concepts and levels of emphasis and detail, but with no one map more valid or necessary than another. Here, I am reminded again of the need to take different levels into account, and I ask you to consider the desirability of taking a fresh perspective from time to time. The present flows into the future, but the future projects backward in time in a very real sense to guide and to direct our course of action. One comes closest to the *space-binding* and the *time-binding* power of maps at different levels and to the feedforward and feedback streams of causality with one very special neural symbol, the *self-cognon*. Here the various streams converge, past and future meet in the present moment, the cognon of self provides the bridge between retrospective and prospective memory.

THE FUNCTION OF CONSCIOUSNESS

Of what use is consciousness? It can often be graceless and awkward, as when we are embarrassingly self-conscious, and then again it can be mere excess baggage, as when we think about how to shift gears, instead of simply doing it. What is it in the brain that makes some things, but not others, known to consciousness?

Just as no rigid distinction can be made between sensory and motor functions, no line can be drawn between a conscious mental side and an unconscious physical side in the organization of the brain. All neural structures, including those representing conscious experience—feelings, percepts, and emotions—are involved in the programming and guidance of behavior. The essential function of the nervous system is to help the organism to survive. In carrying out this function, as organisms became increasingly complex, capable of a vast set of possible actions, evolution must have favored the development of consciousness. Confronted with changing environments calling for radically different adaptations, consciousness is needed to select the appropriate action. If women and men are more complex than oysters and toads, then our feelings and ideas must have come about because they are valuable tools in the processes of our nervous system and improve its overall efficacy.

William James was the pioneer champion of this idea. James wrote "[By] bringing a more or less constant pressure to bear in favor of *those* of its performances which make for the most permanent interests of the brain's owner [and]...a constant inhibition of the tendencies to stray aside... consciousness serves *real* ends" (1890, Vol. 1, p. 140).

James adds still another bit of circumstantial evidence:

> Consciousness is only intense when nerve-processes are hesitant. In rapid, automatic, habitual action it sinks to a minimum. Nothing could be more fitting than this, if consciousness has the teleological function we suppose; nothing more meaningless, if not.... Where indecision is great, as before a dangerous leap, consciousness is agonizingly intense. (1890, Vol. 1, p. 142)

The attempt to correlate conscious experience with complex decisions and problem solving encountered a rude shock when it became known that many difficult solutions appeared full blown in their creator's minds without any intervening consciousness whatever. Although some people reported vivid images, others insisted that at the moment of a clear flash of thought, they had no true images at all, but only an awareness of some relation, if that. So arose the "imageless thought" controversy (Woodworth, 1938, pp. 784–789).

Still another setback to the effort to correlate conscious experience with the underlying cerebral events appeared when commissurotomy patients behaved as if they now saw things through two quite separate and distinct perceiving systems, one in each hemisphere, neither having any conscious connection to the other (see Chapter Three).

These patients are unable to name objects flashed to the left visual field and to the right hemisphere, although they can do so readily when the same item is shown to the right visual field and to the left hemisphere. Still, the right brain is not blind, as shown by nonverbal instead of verbal response. When a picture is exposed to the right brain, the split brain patient consistently denies having seen anything except perhaps a flash of light; but he can select by hand from a collection of test objects the one object that matches the picture. Even more interesting, he can simultaneously retrieve the two different objects (each of which matches the separate sample, or word, flashed to the corresponding visual half-field) with his two hands. Sperry (1970) compares this double retrieval to two separate people searching through the collection of objects with no communication between them. Neither hand seems to know what the other is looking for.

What are the implications for neural mechanisms of consciousness? The intact brain fails to detect any discontinuity in its visual experience, even though the optic image, on its way to the brain, gets split down the middle— one half being sent to the right and one half to the left hemisphere. Indeed, the right-left doubling of most sensory input seems to be the rule of the neural traffic. But as far as conscious awareness is concerned, unity prevails. Of course, we usually explore the visual scene by scanning with both eyes so that the same input goes to both hemispheres. Studies of the split brain patients had to take care to control this visual input and other cues.

In his Nobel Prize address, Sperry (1982) said that one of the more important results of the split brain work is a revised concept of the nature of consciousness and its fundamental causal role in brain function and behavior. The switch is from a reductionist view that writes off cognitive introspective psychology, Sperry concluded, to a new view of inner experience as a major explanatory construct in a causal account.

THE MIND'S I: EMERGENCE OF SELF-CONSCIOUSNESS

Autoimmunity occurs when the immune system begins to attack the body's own tissues, and the severely diseased conditions to which it leads result from the failure to distinguish self from not-self. Thus it is not surprising that self-consciousness evolved in the primate brain; it has a physiological basis and undoubtedly confers an adaptive advantage for a highly developed nervous system "grown too complex to regulate itself" (James, 1890).

But, just what advantage consciousness itself confers, and by which mechanism it enables its possessor to steer its own nervous system, has remained a matter of speculation and controversy. Some light on this problem might be expected from an investigation of the quality and the level of self-awareness in the disconnected minor hemisphere of patients who have undergone surgical section of the forebrain commissures. The left, talking, brain provides direct verbal communication concerning its subjective experience. What can the mute, agraphic right hemisphere tell us about its social awareness and self-consciousness? Does the right brain have an "I," and, if so, is it a different "I" from that which its verbal left brain possesses?

SELF-RECOGNITION IN THE DISCONNECTED MUTE HEMISPHERE

One might contend that, without language, the right brain is simply a high-order, unconscious, computerlike automaton whose "self" is nonexistent or else is centered in the left brain or in the brainstem. At the other extreme, we learned in Chapter Three that two "separate, but equal" consciousnesses might coexist even in the intact brain of the normal person. Thus the discovery of two independent conscious minds in the split brain patient could readily be predicted.

To investigate these possibilities, Sperry, Zaidel, and Zaidel (1979) undertook a study of two split brain patients with visual input lateralized to the left or to the right half of the visual field (see Chapter Three). The stimuli were chosen to represent key personal and affect-laden meanings among neutral control stimuli. The critical items included pictures of the subject's self, relatives, pets, and belongings, and another group of public, historical, and religious figures and personalities intended to evoke characteristic social and personal awareness.

A social knowledgeability test was also presented. Selective manual and emotional responses from the right hemisphere were obtained and could be compared with those from the verbal left hemisphere of the same subject.

The results were astonishingly clearcut. The awareness in each hemi-sphere of the split brain subjects was essentially identical. The concept of self was present and as well developed in the disconnected mute right hemisphere as in the left hemisphere. Except for the fact that the subject cannot talk about them, consciousness of self and general social awareness in the right brain are much like that found in the speaking left brain. The right brain of these subjects could find a portrait of themselves inserted among similar photo-graphs as readily with one as with the other hemisphere. Pictures of pets and other personal belongings were also easily recognized by either hemisphere.

Appropriate emotional responses, particularly to key items that appeared unexpectedly, were also obtained from the nonspeaking right hemisphere, as well as evaluative judgments expressed by pointing, and thumbs-up or thumbs-down gestures in response to various items. For instance, a picture of Hitler flashed to the right hemisphere received an unmistakeable thumbs down; the same hemisphere gave the patient's own family a thumbs-up response. The emotional (protopathic) tone of these responses often crossed over into the left hemisphere, presumably through the subcortical systems, but not the item in its cognitive (epicritic) aspect, as shown by the questions: "Who are they?" or "Was it me?"

Some subtle cognitive auras did seem to permit categorical distinctions to cross over, like that between the government versus the private sector, or domestic versus foreign, or historical versus entertainment. Such auras haunt normal everyday experience, as when we attempt to recall dreams or to fish out buried memories, or when we experience the tip of the tongue phenomena and other instances of generic recall, perhaps to play an important role in creative imagination and productive thinking.

The participation of subcortical structures in conscious awareness thus continues to find support. Yet we look to the neocortex and the integrity of the midline commissures increasingly for the unity of self-consciousness and also for social awareness and the development of altruism, or the ability to take the other fellow's point of view.

CONSCIOUSNESS AND THE NEOCORTEX

Sperry and his colleagues place the recognition of self as a factor of consciousness in the cerebral cortex, at or above the level of the development of the brain in the great ape. They write:

> Self-consciousness appears to be almost strictly a human attribute, according to present evidence drawn mainly from mirror self-recognition tests.... It seems not to be found in animals below the primates, and only to a limited extent in the great apes. In human childhood, self-consciousness makes its appearance relatively late in development, appearing first at around eighteen months of age.... Thus, ontogenetically as well as phylogenetically, self-consciousness can be rated as a relatively advanced stage of conscious awareness. (Sperry, Zaidel & Zaidel, 1979, p. 153)

Yet Harvard psychologists find that the pigeon can look into a mirror and recognize spots on its feathers that are hidden from direct view and peck at them if rewarded for doing so (Epstein, Lanza, & Skinner, 1981).

Thomas Nagel (1981) urges the view that conscious experience is a widespread phenomenon at many levels of animal life. The essence of the belief that bats, for example, have experience is that "there is something that it is like, to be a bat. *What is it like,*" he asks, "from the bat's own perspective, *to be a bat?*"

Of special interest in Nagel's analysis is that it enables us to make a general observation about the subjective character of experience. There appear to be facts that embody a particular point of view. It is often possible, he states, to take up a point of view other than one's own. Premack and Woodruff's (1978) ingenious attempts to show that the chimpanzee has a "theory of mind" used pictures of human actors in various predicaments, (such as being locked in a cage, or shivering because of a malfunctioning heater, etc.) and pictures showing various possible solutions—finding a key or plugging a machine into an electrical outlet, etc. The chimpanzee Sarah's consistent choice of the correct solution to the human problem demonstrated an empathy, if not a "theory of mind,"showing that the animal recognized the scene as representing another individual's problem and imputed a mental state or purpose to that individual, which led to an inference about that purpose that could be used to predict the human actor's behavior. The animal is able to impute to a human actor a state of intention and an experienced obstacle to the fulfillment of that intention. The chimpanzee, Sarah, has, in a perfectly objective way, ascribed a state of experience to another creature. Sarah has shown that she can adopt his human point of view.

This bears directly on the mind-brain problem. Consider once again the fascinating outcome of the human split brain experiments. There is behavioral evidence of double awareness. Yet from the commissurotomy patient's own point of view there is neither splitting nor doubling of consciousness but a persistent unity.

We are led to conclude that the apparent unity of consciousness is a deceit of artful nature. We are protected from the knowledge of our own conflicts and frequent inconsistencies by this wonderful mechanism.

No aspect of mind is more obvious, no mechanism of brain more mysterious, than self-consciousness. I know what it is like to be me and that what I call myself, my body, or my experience, is different from everything else in the universe.

SELF-CONSCIOUSNESS AS A BRIDGE BETWEEN PAST, PRESENT, AND FUTURE

What we call *reality*—"this is it"; "I am here"; "this is happening to me"—is a certain relationship between memories and sensations that surround us at the same time. That is the only true relationship that marks the distinction between self and not-self. *I* am the bridge between past and present, and also between present and future. This linkage demands something more than memory. It must contain a combination of a present sensation (especially a taste, a sound, a smell, or a touch) with recollection, a remembrance of the sensuous past. It was just this experience, where sensation and memory came together that Proust, in his monumental work, *À la recherche du temps perdu*, sought, and lost time was found again.

I raised to my lips the teaspoonful of the tea in which I had soaked a morsel of the cake. No sooner had the warm liquid and the crumbs with it, touched my palate than a shudder ran through me, and I stopped, intent upon the extraordinary changes that were taking place in me.... And suddenly the memory returns. The taste was that of the little bit of madeleine which on Sunday mornings at Combray...when I went to say good day to her in her bedroom, my Aunt Leonie used to give me, dipping it first in her own cup of tea or of lime-flower infusion. (Proust, 1927, p. 224)

Other sensations, standing on two uneven stones in the baptistry of Saint Mark's in Venice, the tinkle of a spoon against a plate, the feeling of a starched napkin, the jangling twinkle of the little bell, bring to him floods of memories of similar sensations in the past. "I heard the sounds again, the very identical sounds themselves, although situated so far back in the past...I could recapture it, go back to it, merely by descending more deeply within myself."

Lost time can be captured only by the intensely conscious *self* experiencing a hallucination—a conditioned drive response.

If we are deceived by consciousness, how can it be useful to us? My hunch is that the utility of consciousness resides in its apparent simplicity, unity, and integrity. Complex work involving millions of neurons and billions of synapses takes place at a level that proceeds effectively without our conscious intervention. Consciousness is thus freed to concentrate on the priorities of the moment, and by its selective emphasis can direct our behavior to our self-selected ends. The ability of the brain to construct a representational system, an internal model of the world outside, provides a means of manipulating the environment without actually suffering the pains of physical action or the consequences of wrong moves. Consciousness enables us to select the most effective program of behavior by relieving us of the need to do more than sit and think. The "idea of a beefsteak" is effective if it enables a person to decide that a trip to the butcher shop is necessary—and, at another level, if it enhances the effectiveness of a synaptic connection between two cognons. The key is *continuity,* the thread on which we string the past and the future. The problem to be solved is to keep these impressions from vanishing under the constantly changing pressures of the present and to be able to anticipate the future. The solution of that problem is the functional significance of the consciousness of self and others.

AN OVERALL VIEW

In this chapter, I have tried to present a general summary of the major principles and concepts of neuropsychology from the viewpoint of the theory advanced in this book. I have underscored the idea that human behavior is under the control of an emotive as well as a cognitive brain. No function is uninfluenced by the pressure of drives and emotions; cognition and emotion are interwoven in the way we move, speak, love, and communicate with one another. Interactions between ourselves and the environment are inevitably colored by our emotions and our beliefs. They make learning and memory possible. These processes are now being studied effectively with the techniques of molecular biology in animal species with fewer but larger and more readily identifiable nerve cells than are found in humans.

The realization that the cellular and biochemical mechanisms that underlie conditioning, learned skills, and even long-term memory are universal in all nervous systems enables us to examine these functions at different levels of analysis: experiential, behavioral, neurophysiological, molecular, and genetic.

We can now approach the problem of central importance to both neurobiology and psychology—how we learn, how we remember, and how we forget—in terms of both behavior and cellular biochemistry.

Psychologists generally accept a sharp distinction between short-term memory and long-term memory. Is there a biochemical basis for such a distinction? What we find is that the short-term process grades into the long-term process. Yet, in long-term memory, the terminals of the sensory neurons undergo striking morphological and functional changes. Could these changes be mediated by the formation of a new regulatory subunit—a unique molecular event that marks the curious discontinuity we examined in Chapter Ten? Some distinctive molecular events involving the synthesis of new proteins is essential to produce these changes and to convert the limited short-term to the stable long-term process. Recent advances have brought scientists close to their identification.

Self-consciousness and the ability to recognize one's self in a mirror have been thought to demand a neocortex, a late phylogenetic development, shared by humans with the great apes. Yet pigeons can look into a mirror to locate and examine spots painted on their feathers. The search for a model of the nature of intelligence based on human-valued behaviors is being replaced by evolutionary principles of divergence along a multiplicity of roads and by adaptation to whatever environment these diverging roads lead. Behaviors that have been classified as "intelligent" (adaptive) include habituation, conditioning, delayed response, the formation of learning sets, and complex problem solving. These appear to be universal phenomena in some form in all organisms that possess a central nervous system. The formation of cognons, including the cognon of self, shows continuity throughout the evolutionary series. Our most spectacular human achievements may eventually be understood by pursuing the study of mind as the functions of a brain shaped by its owner's genes and environment at every level of the animal kingdom.

The neural and behavioral sciences are undergoing a revolution that is changing our conception of the nature of intelligence, a revolution no less profound than the Darwinian conception of our origins or the Einsteinian conception of the physical world. The next few decades, years, perhaps even months, will bring a new understanding of our inner world and its expression in our behavior.

SUGGESTED READINGS

Eccles, J.C. (Ed.), *Brain and conscious experience.* New York: Springer-Verlag, 1966.

Goldman-Rakic, P.S. Development and plasticity of primate frontal association cortex. In F.O. Schmitt, F.G. Worden, & S.G. Dennis (Eds.), *The organization of the cerebral cortex.* Cambridge: MIT Press, 1981, 69–97.

Hofstadter, D.R., & Dennett, D.C. (Eds.). *The mind's I: Fantasies and reflections on self and soul.* New York: Basic, 1981.

Kety, S.S. Disorders of the human brain. *Scientific American,* 1979, *241,* 201–214.

McGeer, P.L., Eccles, J.C., & McGeer, E.G. *Molecular neurobiology of the mammalian brain.* New York: Plenum, 1978.

Mayr, E. *The growth of biological thought.* Cambridge: The Belknap Press of Harvard University Press, 1982.

Mountcastle, V.B. An organizing principle for cerebral function: The unit module and the distributed system. In G.M. Edelman & V.B. Mountcastle (Eds.). *The mindful brain.* Cambridge: MIT Press, 1978.

Oakley, D.A., & Plotkin, H.C. (Eds.). *Brain, behavior, and evolution.* London: Methuen, 1979.

Parsons, H.L. Minding as a material force. In D.H. DeGrood, D. Riepe, & J. Somerville (Eds.), *Radical currents in contemporary philosophy.* St. Louis, MO: Green, 1971.

Premack, D., & Woodruff, G. Does the chimpanzee have a theory of mind? *The Behavioral and Brain Sciences,* 1978, *4,* 515–526.

Sachar, E. Psychobiology of schizophrenia. In E.R. Kandel & J.H. Schwartz (Eds.), *Principles of neural science.* New York: Elsevier/North Holland, 1981b.

Scheflin, A.W., & Opton, E.M., Jr. *The mind manipulators; A non-fiction account.* New York: Paddington Press, 1978.

Schmitt, F.O., Worden, F.G., Adelman, G., & Dennis, S.G. (Eds.), *The organization of the cerebral cortex.* Cambridge: MIT Press, 1981.

Snyder, S.H. The dopamine hypothesis of schizophrenia. *American Journal of Psychiatry,* 1976, *133,* 197–202.

Szentagothai, J. Local neuron circuits of the neocortex. In F.O. Schmitt & F.G. Worden (Eds.), *The neurosciences: Fourth study program.* Cambridge: MIT Press, 1978.

Valenstein, E.S. (Ed.), *The psychosurgery debate: Scientific, legal, and ethical perspectives.* San Francisco: W.H. Freeman, 1980.

BIBLIOGRAPHY

Adams, P.A., & Haire, M. The effect of orientation on the reversal of one cube inscribed in another. *American Journal of Psychology,* 1959, *72,* 296–299.

Akert, K., Peper, K., & Sandri, C. Structural organization of motor end plate and central synapses. In P.G. Waser (Ed.), *Cholinergic mechanisms.* New York: Raven Press, 1975.

Akelaitis, A.J. A study of gnosis, praxis, and language following section of the corpus callosum. *Journal of Neurosurgery,* 1944, *1,* 94–102.

Albert, M.L., & Obler, L.K. *The bilingual brain.* New York: Academic Press, 1978.

Albrecht, D.G., DeValois, R.L., & Thorell, L.G. Visual cortical neurons: Are bars or gratings optimal stimuli? *Science,* 1980, *207,* 88–90.

Angevine, J.B., Jr., & Cotman, C.W. *Principles of neuroanatomy.* New York: Oxford University Press, 1981.

Anstis, S.M. Luminance profiles demonstrate non-linearities of brightness perception. *Behavioral Research Methods and Instrumentation,* 1976, *8,* 427–436.

Anstis, S.M. Apparent movement. In R. Held, H.W. Leibowitz, & H.-L. Teuber (Eds.), *Handbook of sensory physiology: Perception* (Vol. VIII). Berlin: Springer-Verlag, 1978.

Arnheim, R. *Art and visual perception.* Berkeley: University of California Press, 1974.

Aserinski, N.E., & Kleitman, N. Regularly occurring periods of eye motility and concomitant phenomena during sleep. *Science,* 1955, *118,* 273–274.

Attneave, F. Multistability in perception. *Scientific American,* 1971, *225,* 62–71.

Baack, J., de Lacoste-Utamsing, C., & Woodward, D.J. Sexual dimorphism in human fetal corpora collosa. Society for *Neuroscience,* 1982. (Abstract)

Bailey, C.H., & Chen, M. Morphological basis of long-term habituation and sensitization in *Aplysia. Science,* 1983, *220,* 91–93.

Balint, R. Die Seelenlahmuns des "Schauens," *Mitschrift für Psychologie und Neurologie* 1909, *1,* 51–81.

Barlow, H.B. Summation and inhibition in the frog's retina. *Journal of Physiology,* 1953, *119,* 69–88.

Barlow, H.B. Single units and sensation: A neuron doctrine for perceptual psychology? *Perception,* 1972, *1,* 371–394.

Barlow, H.B. Linking features and Gestalt perception. *Proceedings of the Royal Society B,* 1981, *212,* 1–34.

Barlow, H.B., Blakemore, C., & Pettigrew, J.D. The neural mechanism of binocular depth discrimination. *Journal of Physiology,* 1967, *193,* 327–342.

Barlow, H.B., & Hill, R.M. Evidence for a physiological explanation of the waterfall illusion. *Nature,* 1963, *200,* 1934–1935.

Barlow, H.B., & Mollon, J.D. *The senses.* Cambridge: Cambridge University Press, 1982.

Barlow, H.B., Narasimhan, R., & Rosenfield, A. Visual pattern analysis in machines and animals. *Science,* 1972, *177,* 567–575.

Barron, F., Jarvik, M.E., & Bunnell, S., Jr. The hallucinogenic drugs. *Scientific*

American, 1964, *210,* 29–37.

Beach, F.A., Hebb, D.O., Morgan, C.T., & Nissen, H.W. (Eds.). *The neuropsychology of Lashley.* New York: McGraw-Hill, 1960.

Bear, D.M. The temporal lobes: An approach to the study of organic behavioral changes. In M.S. Gazzangia (Ed.), *Handbook of behavioral neurobiology* (Vol. 2). New York: Plenum Press, 1979.

Beck, J. *Surface color perception.* Ithaca, N.Y.: Cornell University Press, 1972.

Békésy, G.v. *Experiments in hearing* (E.G. Wever, Ed. and trans.). New York: McGraw-Hill, 1960.

Bender, M.B. *Disorders in perception.* Springfield, Ill.: Thomas, 1952.

Bender, M.B., & Teuber, H.L. Spatial organization of visual perception following injury to the brain. *Archives of neurology and psychiatry,* 1947, *58,* 721–739.

Benson, D.F., & Blumer, D. *Psychiatric aspects of neurologic disease.* New York: Grune & Stratton, 1975.

Berger, T.W., Clark, G.A., & Thompson, R.F. Learning-dependent neuronal responses recorded from limbic system brain structures during classical conditioning. *Physiological Psychology,* 1980, *8,* 155–167.

Berger, T.W., & Thompson, R.F. Identification of pyramidal cells as the critical elements in hippocampal neuronal plasticity during learning. *Proceedings of the National Academy of Sciences of the U.S.A.,* 1978, *75,* 1572–1576.

Berlucchi, G. Cerebral dominance and interhemispheric communication in normal man. In F.O. Schmitt & F.G. Worden (Eds.), *The neurosciences: Third study program,* Cambridge: MIT Press, 1974.

Bernstein, N. *The co-ordination and regulation of movements.* London: Pergamon, 1967.

Betz, V. Quelques mots sur la structure de l'écorce cérébrale. *Revue Anthropologique,* 2ᵉ series, 1881, *4,* 426–438.

Bever, T.G., & Chiarello, R.J. Cerebral dominance in musicians and nonmusicians. *Science,* 1974, *185,* 137–139.

Birnbaum, J.S. Computers: A survey of trends and limitations. *Science,* 1982, *215,* 760–765.

Black, A.H., & Prokasy, W.F. *Classical conditioning II: Current research and theory.* Englewood Cliffs, N.J.: Prentice-Hall, 1972.

Blakemore, C. Developmental factors in the formation of feature extracting neurons. In F.O. Schmitt & F.G. Worden (Eds.), *The neurosciences: Third study program* (105–113). Cambridge: MIT Press, 1974.

Blakemore, C. Central visual processing. In M.S. Gazzaniga & C. Blakemore (Eds.), *Handbook of psychobiology.* New York: Academic Press, 1975.

Blakemore, C. *Mechanics of the mind.* Cambridge, Engl.: Cambridge University Press, 1977.

Blakemore, C. Maturation and modification in the developing visual system. In R. Held, H.W. Leibowitz, & H.-L. Teuber (Eds.), *Handbook of sensory physiology: Perception* (Vol. VIII). Berlin: Springer-Verlag, 1978.

Blakemore, C., & Campbell, F.W. On the existence in the human visual system of neurones selectively sensitive to the orientation and size of retinal images. *Journal of Physiology,* 1969, *203,* 237–260.

Blakemore, C., & Cooper, G.F. Development of the brain depends on the visual environment. *Nature,* 1970, *228,* 477–478.

Blakemore, C., Garey, L.J., & Vital-Durand, F. The physiological effects of monocular deprivation and their reversal in the monkey's visual cortex. *Journal of Physiology,* 1978, *283,* 223–262.

Blakemore, C., Nachmias, J., & Sutton, P. Perceived spatial frequency shift: Evidence of frequency-selective neurones in the human brain. *Journal of Physiology,* 1970, *210,* 727–750.

Blakemore, C., & Sutton, P. Size adaptation: A new aftereffect. *Science,* 1969, *166,* 245–247.

Blakemore, C., & Van Sluyters, R.C. Reversal of the physiological effects of monocular deprivation in kittens: Further evidence for a sensitive period. *Journal of Physiology,* 1975, *237,* 195–216.

Blodgett, H.C. The effect of the introduction of reward upon the maze performance of rats. *California University Publications in Psychology,* 1929, *4,* 113–134.

Bloom, F.E. Dynamics of synaptic modulation: Perspectives for the future. In F.O. Schmitt & F.G. Worden (Eds.), *The neurosciences: Third study program.* Cambridge: MIT Press, 1974.

Bloom, L. *One word at a time: The use of single word utterances before syntax.* The Hague: Mouton, 1975.

Boden, M. *Artificial intelligence and natural man.* New York: Basic Books, 1977.

Book, T. *The psychology of skill.* Missoula, Montana Press, 1908. (Cited in R.S. Woodworth, *Experimental psychology,* 1938.)

Boring, E.G. A new ambiguous figure. *American Journal of Psychology,* 1930, *42,* 444–445.

Boring, E.G. *Sensation and perception in the history of experimental psychology.* New York: Appleton-Century-Crofts, 1942.

Boring, E.G., Langfeld, H.S., & Weld, H.P. *Psychology: A factual textbook.* New York: Wiley, 1935.

Bossy, J. *Atlas of neuroanatomy and special sense organs.* Philadelphia: Saunders, 1970.

Braddick, O., Campbell, F.W., & Atkinson, J. Channels in vision: Basic aspects. In R. Held, H.W. Leibowitz, & H.-L. Teuber (Eds.), *Handbook of sensory physiology: Perception* (Vol. VIII). New York: Springer-Verlag, 1978.

The brain: A Scientific American book. San Francisco: Freeman, 1979.

Braine, M.D.S. On learning the grammatical order of words. *Psychological Review,* 1963, *70,* 323–348.

Breese, B.B. On inhibition. *Psychological Monographs,* 1899, *3,* 1–65.

Bregman, A.S. Asking the "what for" question in auditory perception. In M. Kubovy & J.R. Pomerantz (Eds.), *Perceptual organization.* Hillsdale, N.J.: Erlbaum, 1981.

Brion, S. Korsakoff's syndrome: Clinico-anatomical and physiopathological considerations. In G.A. Talland & N.C. Waugh (Eds.), *The pathology of memory.* New York: Academic Press, 1969.

Broadbent, D.E. The role of auditory localization in attention and memory span. *Journal of Experimental Psychology,* 1954, *47,* 191–196.

Broadbent, D.E. *Perception and communication.* London: Pergamon, 1958.

Broca, P. Rémarques sur le siège de la faculté du language articule. *Bulletin Société d'Anthropologie,* 1861.

Brodmann, K. *Vergleichende Lokalisationslehre der Grosshirnrinde.* Leipzig: J.A. Barth, 1909.

Brown, J.L. Sensory systems. In *Best and Taylor's Physiological basis of medical practice* (9th ed.). Baltimore: Williams & Wilkins, 1973.

Brown, R. The acquisition of language. In *Disorders of communication.* D. McK. Rioch & E.A. Weinstein (Eds.), *Research publications: Association for research in nervous and mental disease (Vol. 42).* New York: Hafner, 1969.

Brown, R. *Psycholinguistics: Selected papers.* New York: Free Press, 1970.

Brown, R. *A first language: The early stages.* Cambridge: Harvard University Press, 1973.

Brown, R., & Fraser, C. The acquisition of syntax. In C.N. Cofer & B.X. Musgrove (Eds.), *Verbal behavior and learning: Problems and processes.* New York: McGraw-Hill, 1963.

Brown, R., & McNeil, D. The "tip of the tongue" phenomenon. *Journal of Verbal Learning and Verbal Behavior,* 1966, *5,* 325–337.

Bruner, J.S., Goodnow, J.J., & Austin, J.G. *A study of thinking.* New York: Wiley, 1956.

Bruner, J.S. On perceptual readiness. *Psychological Review,* 1957, *64,* 123–152.

Bryan, W.L., & Harter, N. Studies in the physiology and psychology of telegraphic language. *Psychological Review,* 1897, *4,* 27–53.

Bullock, T.H., Orkand, R., & Grinnell, A. *Introduction to nervous systems.* San Francisco: Freeman, 1977.

Butler, R.A. Discrimination learning by Rhesus monkeys to visual exploration motivation. *Journal of Comparative and Physiological Psychology,* 1953, *46,* 95–98.

Cajal, S.R. *[Neuron theory or reticular theory? Objective evidence of the anatomical unity of nerve cells]* (M.U. Purkiss & C.A. Fox, trans.). Madrid: Consejo Superior de Investigaciones Cientificas Instituto Ramon y Cajal, 1908.

Cajal, S.R. [A new concept of the histology of the central nervous system.] In D.A. Rottenberg (Ed. & trans.), *Neurological classics in modern translation.* New York: Hafner, 1977.

Campbell, F.W. The transmission of spatial information through the visual system. In F.O. Schmitt & F.G. Worden (Eds.), *The neurosciences: Third study program.* Cambridge: MIT Press, 1974.

Campbell, F.W., Gilinsky, A.S., Howell, E.R., Riggs, L.A., & Atkinson, J. The dependence of monocular rivalry on orientation. *Perception,* 1973, *2,* 123–125.

Campbell, F.W., & Maffei, L. Electrophysiological evidence for the existence of orientation and size detectors in the human visual system. *Journal of Physiology,* 1970, *207,* 635–652.

Campbell, F.W., & Robson, J.G. Application of Fourier analysis to the visibility of gratings. *Journal of Physiology,* 1968, *197,* 551–566.

Cannon, W.B. *Bodily changes in pain, hunger, fear and rage* (2nd ed.). New York: Appleton-Century-Crofts, 1929.

Carew, T.J., Hawkins, R.D., & Kandel, E.R. Differential classical conditioning of a defensive withdrawal reflex in *Aplysia californica. Science,* 1983, *219,* 297–400.

Carlson, A.J. *The control of hunger in health and disease.* Chicago: University of Chicago Press, 1916.

Carroll, Lewis. *Through the looking class and what Alice found there.* Philadelphia: Jacobs, 1872.

Castellucci, V., & Kandel, E.R. Presynaptic facilitation as a mechanism for behavioral sensitization in *Aplysia. Science,* 1976, *194,* 1176–1178.

Cattell, J. McK. The time it takes to see and name objects. *Mind,* 1886, *11,* 63–65. (a)

Cattell, J. McK. The time taken up by cerebral operations, I. Apparatus and methods; II. The reaction time. *Mind,* 1886, *11,* 220–242. (b)

Cerella, J. Visual classes and natural categories in the pigeon. *Journal of Experimental Psychology: Human Perception and Performance,* 1979, *5,* 68–77.

Chomsky, N. *Cartesian linguistics.* New York: Harper & Row, 1966.

Chomsky, N. *Language and mind.* New York: Harcourt, Brace, Jovanovich, 1972.

Chomsky, N. *Reflections on language.* New York: Pantheon, 1975.

Clark, E.V. On the child's acquisition of antonyms in two semantic fields. *Journal of Verbal Learning and Verbal Behavior,* 1972, *11,* 750–758.

Clark, E.V. What's in a word? On the child's acquisition of semantics in his first language. In T.E. Moore (Ed.), *Cognitive development and the acquisition of language.* New York: Academic Press, 1973.

Cohen, H.H., Bill, J.C., & Gilinsky, A.S. Simultaneous brightness contrast: Variations on Koffka's ring. *Proceedings of the 76th Annual Meeting of the American Psychological Association,* 1968, pp. 99–100.

Colonnier, M.L. Structural design of the neocortex. In J.C. Eccles (Ed.), *Brain and conscious experience.* New York: Springer-Verlag, 1966.

Cooper, W.E. (Ed.). *Cognitive aspects of skilled typewriting.* New York: Springer-Verlag, 1983.

Corbit, J.D. Behavioral regulation of hypothalamic temperature. *Science,* 1969, *166,* 256–258.

Corbit, J.D. Voluntary control of hypothalamic temperature. *Journal of Comparative and Physiological Psychology,* 1973, *83,* 394–441.

Corsi, P.M. *Human memory and the medial temporal region of the brain.* Thesis, McGill University, Canada, 1972.

Côté, L. Basal ganglia, the extrapyramidal motor system, and diseases of transmitter metabolism. In E.R. Kandel & J.H. Schwartz (Eds.), *Principles of neural sciences.* New York: Elsevier/North Holland, 1981.

Courant, R., & Robbins, H. Topology. In J.R. Newman (Ed.), *The world of mathematics.* New York: Simon & Schuster, 1956.

Cowey, A., & Weiskrantz, L. Demonstration of cross-modal matching in rhesus monkeys, Macaca mulatta. *Neuropsychologia,* 1975, *13,* 117–120.

Craig, W. Appetites and aversions as constituents of instincts. *Biological Bulletin of the Marine Biological Laboratory (Woods Hole),* 1918, *34,* 91–107.

Craik, K.J.W. *The nature of explanation.* Cambridge, Engl.: The Cambridge University Press, 1943.

Crick, F.H.C. Thinking about the brain. In *The brain: A Scientific American book,* San Francisco: Freeman, 1979.

Critchley, M. *The parietal lobes.* New York: Hafner, 1966. (Originally published, 1953.)

Darwin, C. *On the origin of species by means of natural selection.* New York: Appleton-Century-Crofts, 1860.

Davis, C.M. Self-selection of diet by newly weaned infants. *American Journal of Diseases of Children,* 1928, *36,* 651–679.

Dax, M. Lésions de la moitié gauche de l'encéphale coincidant avec trouble des signes de la pensée (lu à Montpellier en 1836), *Gazette hebdomadaire,* deuxiem serie, 1865.

Deaux, E., & Gormezano, I. Eyeball retraction: Classical conditioning and extinction in the albino rabbit. *Science,* 1963, *141,* 630–631.

Déjerine, J. Sur un cas de récite verbale avec agraphie, suivi d' autopsie, *Memoires Societé Biologie,* 1891, *3,* 197–201.

Déjerine, J. *Séméiologie du système nerveux.* Paris: Masson, 1901.

Delcomyn, F. Neural basis of rhythmic behavior in animals. *Science,* 1980, *210,* 492–98.

Delgado, J. *Physical control of the mind.* New York: Harper & Row, 1969.

Delgado, J.H.R. New orientations in brain stimulation in man. In A. Wauquier & E.T. Rolls (Eds.), *Brain-stimulation reward.* New York: American Elsevier Publishing Co., 1976. Copyright Janssen Research Foundation.

Della-Fera, M.A. Cholecystokinin octapeptide: Continuous picomole injections into the cerebral ventricles suppress feeding. *Science,* 1979, *206,* 471–473.

Dement, W.C. *Some must watch while some must sleep.* San Francisco: San Francisco Book Company, 1976.

Dement, W., Halper, C., Pivik, T., Ferguson, J., Cohen, H., Henriksen, S., McGarr, K., Gonda, W., Hoyt, G., Ryan, L., Mitchell, G., Barchas, J., & Zarcone, V. Hallucinations and dreaming. In D.A. Hamburg, K.H. Pribram, & A.J. Stunkard (Eds.), *Perception and its disorders.* Baltimore: Williams & Wilkins, 1970.

Dement, W.C., & Kleitman, N. The relation of eye movements during sleep to dream activity: An objective method for the study of dreaming. *Journal of Experimental Psychology,* 1957, *53,* 339–46.

Denenberg, V.H. Hemispheric laterality in animals and the effects of early experience. *The Behavioral and Brain Sciences,* 1981, *4,* 1–49.

Denny-Brown, D. Discussion Fourth Session, (pp. 246–247). In V.B. Mountcastle (Ed.), *Interhemispheric relations and cerebral dominance.* Baltimore: Johns Hopkins University Press, 1962.

Descartes, R. *[The philosophical works of Descartes.]* (E.S. Haldane & G.R.T. Ross, trans.) Cambridge, Mass.: Cambridge University Press, 1967.

DeWeid, D. Hormonal influences on motivation, learning, memory and psychosis. In D.T. Krieger and J.C. Hughes (Eds.), *Neuroendocrinology: A Hospital Practice Book.* Sunderland, Mass.: Sinauer, 1980.

Dirac, P.A.M. *The principles of quantum mechanics* (4th ed.). Oxford: Clarendon Press, 1958.

Drees, O. Üntersuchungen über die angeborenen Verhaltensweisen bei Springspinnen (Salticidae). *Zeitschrift für Tierpsychologie,* 1952, *9,* 169–207.

Duncan, C.P. The retroactive effect of electroshock on learning. *Journal of Comparative and Physiological Psychology,* 1949, *42,* 32–44.

Ebbinghaus, H. *Über das Gedachtnis.* Leipzig: Duncker, 1885. *[Memory, a contribu-*

tion to experimental psychology] (H.A. Ruger & C.E. Bussenius trans.). New York: Dover, 1964.

Eccles, J.C. (Ed.). *Brain and conscious experience*. New York: Springer-Verlag, 1966.

Eccles, J.C. *The understanding of the brain*. New York: McGraw-Hill, 1973.

Eccles, J.C., Ito, M., & Szentagothai, J. *The cerebellum as a neuronal machine*. Berlin: Springer-Verlag, 1967.

Eddington, A.S. The theory of groups. In J.R. Newman (Ed.), *The world of mathematics* (Vol. 3). New York: Simon & Schuster, 1956.

Edwards, B. *Drawing on the right side of the brain*. Los Angeles: J.P. Tarcher, 1979.

Ehrenfels, C.v. Über Gestaltqualitaten. *Vierteljahrschrit für Wissenschaftliche Philosophie*, 1890, *14*, 249–292.

Ehrhardt, A.A., & Meyer-Bahlburg, H.F.L. Effects of prenatal sex hormones on gender-related behavior. *Science*, 1981, *211*, 1312–1318.

Eibl-Eibesfeldt, I. *[Ethology: the biology of behavior]* (E. Klinghammer, trans.). New York: Holt, Rinehart, & Winston, 1970.

Enroth-Cugell, C., & Robson, J.G. The contrast sensitivity of retinal ganglion cells of the cat. *Journal of Physiology*, 1966, *187*, 517–552.

Entus, A.K. Hemisphere asymmetry in processing of dichotically presented speech and nonspeech by infants. In S.J. Segalowitz & F. Gruber (Eds.), *Language development and neurological theory*. New York: Academic, 1977.

Epstein, A. The physiology of thirst. In D.W. Pfaff (Ed.), *The physiological mechanisms of motivation*. New York: Springer-Verlag, 1982.

Epstein, R., Lanza, R.P., & Skinner, B.F. "Self-awareness" in the pigeon. *Science*, 1981, *212*, 695–696.

Estes, W.K. Memory and conditioning. In F.J. McGuigan & D.B. Lumsden (Eds.), *Contemporary approaches to conditioning and learning*. Washington, D.C.: Winston, 1973.

Estes, W.K. Structural aspects of associative models for memory. In C.N. Cofer (Ed.), *The structure of human memory*. San Francisco: Freeman, 1975.

Evans, R.M. *An introduction to color*. New York: Wiley, 1948.

Evarts, E.V. Brain mechanisms in movement. *Scientific American*, 1973, *229*, 96–103.

Evarts, E.V. Motor cortex reflexes associated with learned movement. *Science*, 1973, 501–503.

Evarts, E.V. Brain mechanisms of movement. *Scientific American*, 1979, *241*, 164–179.

Evarts, E.V. Brain mechanisms in voluntary movement. In D. McFadden (Ed.), *Neural mechanisms in behavior: A Texas symposium*. New York: Springer-Verlag, 1980.

Evarts, E., & Tanji, J. Reflex and intended responses in motor cortex pyramidal tract neurons of monkey. *Journal of Neurophysiology*, 1976, *39*, 1069–1080.

Favreau, O.E., & Corballis, M.C. Negative aftereffects in visual perception. *Scientific American*, 1976, *235*, 42–48.

Ferrier, D. Experiments on the brain of monkeys—No. 1. *Proceedings of the Royal Society*, (23) 409–430. London, 1875.

Feuchtwanger, E. Die Funktionen des Stirnhirns, ihre Pathologie und Psychologie. O. Foerster & K. Williams (Eds.), *Monographien aus dem Gesamtgebiete der*

Nerologie und Psychiatrie. Berlin: Springer-Verlag, 1923, *38*, 4–194.

Fiorentini, A., & Maffei, L. Change of binocular properties of the simple cells of the cortex in adult cats following immobilization of one eye. *Vision Research,* 1974, *14*, 217–218.

Fiorentini, A., Pirchio, M., & Spinelli, D. Electrophysiological evidence for spatial frequency selective mechanisms in adults and infants. *Vision Research,* 1983, *23*, 119–127.

Fisher, G.H. Ambiguity of form: Old and new. *Perception and Psychophysics,* 1968, *4*, 189–192.

Fisher, H.E. *The sex contract: The evolution of human bonding.* New York: Morrow, 1982.

Fitzsimons, J.T. *The physiology of thirst and sodium appetite.* New York: Cambridge University Press, 1979.

Fletcher, H. *Speech and hearing in communication.* New York: Van Nostrand, 1953.

Flourens, P. *Recherches experimentales sur les propriétes et fonctions du système nerveux, dans les animaux vertébrés.* Paris: Chèz Crérot, 1824.

Freeman, N.H., & Hargreaves, S. Directed movements and the body proportion effect in pre-school children's human figure drawing. *The Quarterly Journal of Experimental Psychology,* 1977, *29*, 227–235.

Freud, S. *[The psychopathology of everyday life]* (A. Tyson, trans.). New York: Norton, 1971. (Originally published, 1901.)

Frisch, K. von. *[The dance language and orientation of bees]* (L. Chadwick, trans.). Cambridge: Harvard University Press, 1967.

Fritsch, G., & Hitzig, E. [Über die electrische Erregbarkeit des Grosshirn 1870.] In G. von Bonin (trans.). *Some papers on the cerebral cortex.* Springfield, Ill.: Thomas, 1960, pp. 73–96.

Gall, F.J., & Spurzheim, G. Recherches sur le systeme nerveux en general, et sur celui du cerveau en particulier, 1809. Cited in E.G. Boring, 1942.

Gallistel, C.R. The incentive of brain stimulation reward. *Journal of Comparative and Physiological Psychology,* 1969, *69*, 713–721.

Gallistel, C.R. Self-stimulation: The neurophysiology of reward and motivation. In J.A. Deutsch (Ed.), *The physiological basis of memory.* New York: Academic Press, 1973.

Gallistel, C.R. *The organization of action: A new synthesis.* Hillsdale, N.J.: Erlbaum, 1980.

Gallistel, C.R., Stellar, J.R., & Bubis, E. Parametric analysis of brain stimulation reward in the rat. I. The transient process and the memory-containing process. *Journal of Comparative and Physiological Psychology,* 1974, *87*, 848–859.

Garcia, J., & Ervin, F.R. Gustatory-visceral and telereceptor-cutaneous conditioning— adaptation in internal and external milieus. *Communica. Behav. Biology,* 1968. Part A, *1*, 389–415.

Garcia, J., & Koelling, R.A. The relation of cue to consequence in avoidance learning. *Psychonomic Science,* 1966, *4*, 123–124.

Gardner, E. *Fundamentals of neurology: A psychophysiological approach* (6th Ed.). Philadelphia: Saunders, 1975.

Gardner, H. *Artful scribbles: The significance of children's drawings.* New York: Basic Books, 1980.

Gardner, J. *The art of living and other stories.* New York: Knopf, 1981.

Gardner, B.T., & Gardner, R.A. Teaching sign language to a chimpanzee. *Science,* 1969, *165,* 664–672.

Gazzaniga, M.S. (Ed.). *Handbook of behavioral neurobiology,* (Vol. 2). *Neurophysiology.* New York, Plenum, 1979.

Gazzaniga, M.S. The split brain in man. *Scientific American,* 1967, *217,* 24–29.

Gazzaniga, M.S. *The bisected brain.* New York: Plenum, 1970.

Gazzaniga, M.S., & Blakemore, C. *Handbook of psychobiology.* New York: Academic Press, 1975.

Gazzaniga, M.S., & Ledoux, J.E. *The integrated mind.* New York: Plenum, 1978.

Geschwind, N. Disconnexion syndromes in animals and man. I. *Brain,* 1965, *88,* 237–294. II. *Brain,* 1965, *88,* 585–644.

Geschwind, N. The organization of language and the brain. *Science,* 1970, *170,* 940–944.

Geschwind, N. Current concepts: Aphasia. *New England Journal of Medicine,* 1971, *284,* 654–656.

Geschwind, N. Language and the brain. *Scientific American,* 1972, *226,* 76–83.

Geschwind, N. *Selected papers on language and the brain.* Boston: Reidel, 1974.

Geschwind, N. The apraxias: Neural mechanisms of disorders of learned movement. *American Scientist,* 1975, *63,* 188–195.

Geschwind, N. Specializations of the human brain.

Geschwind, N. Specializations of the human brain. *Scientific American,* 1979, *241,* 180–199.

Geschwind, N. The perverseness of the right hemisphere (commentary/Puccetti: Mental duality). *The Behavioral and Brain Sciences,* 1981, *4,* 106–107.

Geschwind, N., & Behan, P. Left-handedness: Association with immune disease, migraine, and developmental learning disorder. *Proceedings of the National Academy of Sciences,* 1982, *79,* 5097–5100.

Geschwind, N., & Kaplan, E. A human cerebral deconnection syndrome: A preliminary report. *Neurology,* 1962, *12,* 675–685.

Geschwind, N., & Levitsky, W. Human brain: Left-right asymmetries in temporal speech region. *Science,* 1968, *161,* 186–187.

Gesell, A., & Ilg, K.L. *The child from five to ten.* New York: Harper & Brothers, 1946.

Ghent, L. Developmental changes in tactual thresholds on dominant and nondominant sides. *Journal of Comparative and Physiological Psychology,* 1961, *54,* 670–673.

Gilbert, C.D., & Wiesel, T.N. Laminor specialization and intracortical connections in cat primary visual cortex. In F.O. Schmitt, F.G., Worden, G. Adelman, & S.G. Dennis (Eds.), *The organization of the cerebral cortex.* Cambridge: MIT Press, 1981.

Gilinsky, A.S. Perceived size and distance in visual space. *Psychological Review,* 1951, *58,* 460–482.

Gilinsky, A.S. The effect of attitude upon the perception of size. *American Journal of Psychology,* 1955, *68,* 173–192.

Gilinsky, A.S. The span and the scale: A bridge between attention and memory. *IBM Research Report RC,* 1964, *1214,* 1–65.

Gilinsky, A.S. Masking of contour detectors in the human visual system. *Psychonomic*

Science, 1967, *8,* 395–396.

Gilinsky, A.S. Orientation-specific effects of patterns of adapting light on visual acuity. *Journal of the Optical Society of America,* 1968, *58,* 13–18.

Gilinsky, A.S. The paradoxical moon illusions. *Perceptual and Motor Skills,* 1980, *50,* 271–283.

Gilinsky, A.S. Reorganization of perception: A Konorskian interpretation of the Innsbruck experiments. *Acta Neurobiologiae Experimentalis,* 1981, *41,* 491–508.

Gilinsky, A.S., & Doherty, R.S. Interocular transfer of orientational effects. *Science,* 1969, *164,* 454–455.

Gilinsky, A.S., & Mayo, T.H. Inhibitory effects of orientational adaptation. *Journal of the Optical Society of America,* 1971, *61,* 1710–1714.

Ginsburg, A.P. Visual perception based on spatial filtering constrained by biological data. (Dissertation for PhD, Cambridge University, 1978) (Published as AFAMRLTR-78-129).

Gleitman, H., & Jonides, J. The cost of categorization in visual search: Incomplete processing of targets and field items. *Perception and Psychophysics,* 1976, *20,* 281–288.

Gleitman, H., & Jonides, J. The effect of set on categorization in visual search. *Perception and Psychophysics,* 1978, *24,* 361–368.

Goffman, E. Mental symptoms and social order. In D. Rioch & E.A. Weinstein (Eds.), *Disorders of communication.* New York: Hafner, 1969.

Goldman, P.S. Neuronal plasticity in primate telenecphalon: Anomalous crossed cortico-caudate projections induced by prenatal removal of frontal association cortex. *Science,* 1978, *202,* 768–770.

Goldman, P.S., & Galkin, T.W. Prenatal removal of frontal association cortex in the rhesus monkey: Anatomical and functional consequences in postnatal life. *Brain Research,* 1978, *52,* 451–485.

Goldman, S.A., & Nottebohm, F. Neuronal production, migration, and differentiation in a vocal control nucleus of the adult female canary brain. *Proceedings of the National Academy of Science,* 1983, *80,* 2390–2394.

Goldman-Eisler, F. On the variability of the speed of talking and on its relation to the length of utterances in conversations. *British Journal of Psychology,* 1954, *45,* 94–107.

Goldman-Rakic, P.S. Development and plasticity of primate frontal association cortex. In F.O. Schmitt, F.G. Worden, G. Adelman, & S.G. Dennis (Eds.), *The organization of the cerebral cortex.* Cambridge: MIT Press, 1981, 69–97.

Goldman-Rakic, P.S. Organization of frontal association cortex in normal and experimentally brain-injured primates. In M.A. Arbib (Ed.), *Neural models of language processes.* N.Y.: Academic Press, 1982.

Goldman-Rakic, P.S., & Schwartz, M.L. Interdigitation of contralateral and ipsilateral columnar projections to frontal association cortex in primates. *Science,* 1982, *216,* 755–757.

Goldschmidt, R. Einiges vom feineren Bau des Nervensystems. [Proceedings of the German Zoological Association] *Verh. Dtsh. Zool. Ges.,* 1907, pp. 130–132.

Gombrich, E.H. *Art and illusion: A study in the psychology of pictorial representation.* Princeton: Bollingen Series, Princeton University Press, 1972.

Goodall, J. van L. The behavior of the chimpanzee. In G. Kurth & I. Eibl-Eibesfeldt (Eds.), *Hominisation und Verhalten.* Stuttgart: Gustav Fischer, 1975.

Goodnow, J. *Children drawing*. Cambridge: Harvard University Press, 1977.

Gordon, H.W. Hemispheric asymmetries in the perception of musical chords. *Cortex,* 1970, *6,* 387–398.

Gordon, H.W., & Sperry, R.W. Lateralization of olfactory perception in the surgically separated hemispheres of man. *Neuropsychologia,* 1969, *7,* 111–120.

Gormezano, I. Classical conditioning. In J.B. Sidowski (Ed.), *Experimental methods and instrumentation in psychology*. New York: McGraw-Hill, 1966, 385–420.

Gormezano, I. Investigations of defense and reward conditioning in the rabbit. In A.H. Black & W.F. Prokasy (Eds.), *Classical conditioning II: Current research and theory*. Englewood Cliffs, N.J.: Prentice-Hall, 1972.

Gormezano, I., Kehoe, E.J., & Marshall, B.S. Twenty years of classical conditioning research with the rabbit. In J.M. Sprague & A.N. Epstein (Eds.), *Progress in psychobiology and physiological psychology* (Vol. 10). New York: Academic, 1983.

Gormezano, I., Schneidermann, N., Deaux, E., & Fuentes, I. Nictitating membrane: Classical conditioning and extinction in the albino rabbit, *Science,* 1962, *138,* 33–34.

Gottschaldt, K. Über den Einfluss der Eifahrung auf die Wahrnehmiung von Figuren. *Psychologische Forschung,* 1926, *8,* 261–317.

Gould, S.J. *Ontogeny and phylogeny*. Cambridge: Harvard University Press, 1977.

Graham, C.H. (Ed.). *Vision and visual perception*. New York: Wiley, 1965.

Granit, R. *The purposive brain*. Cambridge: MIT Press, 1977.

Greenberg, J.H., Reivich, M., Alavi, A., Hand, P., Rosenquist, A., Rintelman, W., et al. Metabolic mapping of functional activity in human subjects with the [18F] Fluorodeoxyglucose technique, *Science,* 1981, *212,* 678–680.

Greengard, P., & Kebabian, J.W. Role of cyclic AMP in synaptic transmission in the mammalian peripheral nervous system. *Federal Proceedings,* 1974, *33,* 1059–1067.

Gregory, R.L. *Eye and brain*. New York: McGraw-Hill, 1966.

Gregory, R.L. Visual illusions. *Scientific American,* 1968, *219,* 66–76.

Gregory, R.L. *The intelligent eye*. London: Woldenfeld & Nicholson, 1970.

Griffin, D.R. *The question of animal awareness*. New York: Rockefeller University Press, 1976.

Groot, A. de. *Thought and choice in chess*. The Hague: Mouton, 1965.

Gross, C.G., Rocha-Miranda, C.E., & Bender, D.B. Visual properties of neurons in inferotemporal cortex of the macaque. *Journal of Neurophysiology,* 1972, *35,* 96–111.

Gross, C.G., & Weiskrantz, L. Some changes in behavior produced by lateral frontal lesions in the macaque. In J.M. Warren & K. Akert (Eds.), *The frontal granular cortex and behavior*. New York: McGraw-Hill, 1964.

Groves, P.M., & Thompson, R.F. Habituation: A dual process theory. *Psychological Review,* 1970, *77,* 419–450.

Haith, M.M. Visual scanning in infants. In L.J. Stone, H.T. Smith, & R.B. Murphy (Eds.), *The competent infant: A handbook of readings*. New York: Basic Books, 1973.

Haith, M.M. *Rules that babies look by: The organization of newborn visual activity*. Hillsdale, N.J.: Erlbaum, 1980.

Hamburg, D.A., Pribram, K.H., & Stunkard, A.J. (Eds.). *Perception and its disorders.* Baltimore: Williams & Wilkins, 1970.

Harmon, L.D. The recognition of faces. *Scientific American,* 1973, *229,* 70–82.

Harmon, L.D., & Julesz, B. Masking in visual recognition: Effects of two-dimensional filtered noise. *Science,* 1973, *180,* 1194–1197.

Harnad, S., Doty, R.W., Goldstein, L., Jaynes, J., & Krauthamer, G. *Lateralization in the nervous system.* New York: Academic Press, 1977.

Hawkins, R.D., Abrams, T.W., Carew, T.J., & Kandel, E.R. A cellular mechanism of classical conditioning in *Aplysia.* Activity-dependent amplification of presynaptic facilitation. *Science,* 1983, *219,* 397–400.

Heath, R.G., & Mickle, W.A. Evaluation of seven years experience with depth electrode studies in human patients. In E.R. Ramey & D.S. O'Doherty (Eds.), *Electrical studies on the unanesthetized brain.* New York: Hoeber, 1960.

Hebb, D.O. On the nature of fear. *Psychological Review,* 1946, *53,* 259–275.

Hebb, D.O. *The organization of behavior: A neuropsychological theory.* New York: Wiley, 1949.

Hebb, D.O. Distinctive features of learning in the higher animal. In J.F. Delafresnaye (Ed.), *Brain mechanisms and learning.* Oxford: Blackwell, 1961.

Hécaen, H. Clinical symptomatology in right and left hemisphere lesions. In V.B. Mountcastle (Ed.), *Interhemisphere relations and cerebral dominance.* Baltimore: Johns Hopkins Press, 1962.

Hécaen, H., & de Ajuriaguerra, J. *Troubles mentaux au cours des tumeurs intracraniennes.* Paris: Mason, 1956.

Hécaen, H., & Albert, M.L. Disorders of mental functioning related to frontal lobe pathology. In D.F. Benson & D. Blumer (Eds.), *Psychiatric aspects of neurologic disease.* New York: Grune & Stratton, 1975.

Hécaen, H., & Albert, M.L. *Human neuropsychology.* New York: Wiley, 1978.

Heilman, K.M. Neglect and related disorders. In K.M. Heilman & E. Valenstein (Eds.), *Clinical neuropsychology.* New York: Oxford University Press, 1979.

Heilman, K.M., Scholes, R., & Watson, R.T. Auditory affective agnosia. Disturbed comprehension of affective speech. *Journal of Neurology, Neurosurgery, and Psychiatry,* 1975, *38,* 69–72.

Heilman, K.M., & Valenstein, E. Frontal lobe neglect in man. *Neurology,* 1972, *22,* 660–664.

Heilman, K.M., & Watson, R.T. The neglect syndrome—a unilateral defect of the orienting response. In S. Harnad, R.W. Doty, L. Goldstein, J. Jaynes, & G. Krauthamer (Eds.), *Lateralization in the nervous system.* New York: Academic Press, 1977.

Held, R. Plasticity in sensory-motor systems. *Scientific American,* 1965, *213,* 84–90.

Held, R., & Hein, A. Movement-produced stimulation in the development of visually guided behavior. *Journal of Comparative and Physiological Psychology,* 1963, *56,* 872–876.

Held, R., Ingle, D., Schneider, G.E., & Trevarthen, C.B. Locating and identifying: Two modes of visual processing. *Psychologishe Forschung,* 1967–1968, *31,* 44–62; 299–348.

Held, R., Leibowitz, H.W., & Teuber, H.-L. (Eds.). *Handbook of sensory physiology: Perception* (Vol. VIII). Berlin: Springer-Verlag, 1978.

Helmholtz, H. von. *[On the sensations of tone]*(2nd English ed.). New York: Dover, 1954. (Originally published, 1877.)

Heron, W. The pathology of boredom. *Scientific American*, 1957, *196*, 52–56.

Hess, E.H. Imprinting in animals. *Scientific American*, 1958, *198*, 81–90.

Hess, E.H. Imprinting in birds. *Science*, 1964, *146*, 1128–1139.

Hess, W.R. *Diencephalon: Autonomic and extrapyramidal functions.* New York: Grune & Stratton, 1954.

Hinde, R.A. Intraspecific communication in animals. In D. Rioch & E.A. Weinstein (Eds.), *Disorders of communication.* New York: Hafner, 1964.

Hinde, R.A. *Animal behavior: A synthesis of ethology and comparative psychology* (2nd ed.). New York: McGraw-Hill, 1970.

Hirsch, H.V., & Jacobson, M. The perfectible brain: Principles of neuronal development. In M.S. Gazzaniga & C. Blakemore (Eds.), *Handbook of psychobiology* (107–137). New York: Academic Press, 1975.

Hirsch, H.V., & Spinelli, D.N. Visual experience modifies distribution of horizontally and vertically oriented receptive fields in cats. *Science*, 1970, *168*, 869–871.

Hirsch, H.V., & Spinelli, D.N. Modification of the distribution of receptive field orientation in cats by selective visual exposure during development. *Experimental Brain Research*, 1971, *13*, 509–527.

Hoebel, B.G., & Novin, D. (Eds.). The neural basis for feeding and reward. *Proceedings of a symposium, Los Angeles, 1981.* Brunswick, Me: Haer Institute for Electrophysiological Research, 1982.

Hoebel, B.G., & Teitelbaum, P. Hypothalmic control of feeding and self-stimulation. *Science*, 1962, *135*, 375–377.

Hofstadter, D.R. Comments in D.R. Hofstadter & D.C. Dennett (Eds.). *The mind's I: Fantasies and reflections on self and soul.* New York: Basic, 1981.

Hollister, L.E., Davis, K.L., & Davis, B.M. Hormones in the treatment of psychiatric disorders. In D.T. Krieger & J.C. Hughes (Eds.), *Neuroendocrinology.* Sunderland, Mass.: Sinauer, 1980.

Holst, E. von. Relative coordination as a phenomenon and as a method of analysis of central nervous function. In E. von Holst (Ed.), *The behavioral physiology of animals and man: Selected papers.* Coral Gables, Fla.: University of Miami Press, 1973.

Hrdy, S.B. *The woman that never evolved.* Cambridge: Harvard University Press, 1981.

Hubel, D.H. The visual cortex of the brain. *Scientific American*, 1963, *209*, 54–62.

Hubel, D.H., The brain. In *The brain: A Scientific American book.* San Francisco: Freeman, 1979.

Hubel, D.H., & Wiesel, T.N. Receptive fields, binocular interaction and functional architecture in the cat's visual cortex. *Journal of Physiology* (London), 1962, *160*, 106–154.

Hubel, D.H., & Wiesel, T.N. Receptive fields of cells in striate cortex of very young, visually inexperienced kittens. *Journal of Neurophysiology*, 1963, *26*, 994–1002.

Hubel, D.H., & Wiesel, T.N. Receptive fields and functional architecture of monkey striate cortex. *Journal of Physiology* (London), 1968, *195*, 215–243.

Hubel, D.H., & Wiesel, T.N. Anatomical demonstration of columns in the monkey striate cortex. *Nature*, 1969, *221*, 737–750.

Hubel, D.H., & Wiesel, T.N. The period of susceptibility to the physiological effects of unilateral eye closure in kittens. *Journal of Physiology*, 1970, *206*, 419–436.

Hubel, D.H., & Wiesel, T.N. Brain mechanisms of vision. *Scientific American*, 1979, *241*, 150–162.

Hubel, D.H., Wiesel, T.N., & Stryker, M.P. Anatomical demonstration of orientation columns in macaque monkey. *Journal of Comparative Neurology*, 1978, *177*, 361–380.

Hughes, A. *Aspects of neural ontogeny.* London: Logos Press, 1968.

Hull, C.L. *Principles of behavior.* New York: Appleton-Century-Crofts, 1943.

Humphrey, N.K. The social function of intellect. In P.P.G. Bateson & R.A. Hinde (Eds.), *Growing points in ethology.* Cambridge, Engl.: Cambridge University Press, 1976.

Hunter, W.S. The delayed reaction in animals and children. *Behavior monographs*, 1913, *2*, 21–30.

Hunter, W.S., & Sigler, M. The span of visual discrimination as a function of time and intensity of stimulation. *Journal of Experimental Psychology*, 1940, *26*, 160–179.

Hurvich, L.M. The range of apprehension and sensory discrimination. *Journal of Experimental Psychology*, 1940, *27*, 313–317.

Hurvich, L., & Jameson, D. *The perception of brightness and darkness.* Boston: Allyn and Bacon, 1966.

Huxley, A. *The doors of perception and heaven and hell.* New York: Penguin, 1959.

Ingle, D., Schneider, G., Trevarthen, C., & Held, R. Locating and identifying: Two models of visual processing (A Symposium). *Psychologische Forschung*, 1967, *31*, 42–62; 1968, *32*, 299–337.

Jacob, F. *[Logic of life: A history of heredity.]* B.E. Spillman (trans. from French). New York: Random, 1976.

Jackson, J.H. *Selected writings of John Hughlings Jackson* (2 vols.). J. Taylor (Ed.). London: Hodder & Stoughton, 1931–1932. (Originally published, 1896.)

Jacobsen, C.F. Functions of frontal association area in primates. *Archives of neurology and psychiatry*, 1935, *33*, 558–569.

Jacobson, M. *Developmental neurobiology* (2nd Ed.). London: Plenum, 1978.

James, H. The tone of time, 1900. In H. James, *Affairs of the heart.* London: Pan Books, 1975. (Originally published in 1900.)

James, W. *Principles of psychology* (Vols. 1 & 2). New York: Dover, 1950. (Originally published, 1890.)

James, W. *Psychology: The briefer course* (G.W. Allport, Ed.). New York: Harper Torchbooks, The Academy Library, 1961.

Jenkins, G., & Dallenbach, K.M. Oblivescence during sleep and waking. *American Journal of Psychology*, 1924, *35*, 605–612.

Jensen, E.M., Reese, E.P., & Reese, T.W. The subitizing and counting of visually presented fields of dots. *Journal of Psychology*, 1950, *30*, 363–392.

Jerne, N.K. Antibodies and learning: Selection versus instruction. In G.C. Quarton, T. Melnechuk, & F.O. Schmitt (Eds.), *The Neurosciences.* New York: Rockefeller

University Press, 1967.

Jersild, A.T. Emotional development. In L. Carmichael (Ed.), *Manual of child psychology* (Chap. 15, p. 762). New York: Wiley, 1946.

Jonides, J., & Gleitman, H. A conceptual category effect in visual search: O as letter or digit. *Perception & Psychophysics,* 1972, *12,* 457–460.

Jouvet, M. Monoaminergic regulation of the sleep-waking cycle in the cat. In F.O. Schmitt & F.G. Worden (Eds.), *The Neurosciences: Third study program.* Cambridge: MIT Press, 1974.

Jouvet, M. The function of dreaming: A neurophysiologist's point of view. In M.S. Gazzaniga & C. Blakemore (Eds.), *Handbook of psychobiology.* New York: Academic Press, 1975.

Julesz, B. *Foundation of cyclopean perception.* Chicago: University of Chicago Press, 1971.

Kaas, J.H., Merzenich, M.M., & Killackey, H.P. The reorganization of somato-sensory cortex following peripheral nerve damage in adult and developing mammals. In W.M. Cowan (Ed.), *Annual Review of Neuroscience 1983* (Vol. 6). Palo Alto, Calif.: Annual Reviews, 1983.

Kaas, J.H., Nelson, R.J., Sur, M., & Merzenich, M.M. Multiple representations of the body within the primary somatosensory cortex of primates. *Science,* 1979, *204,* 521–523.

Kaas, J.H., Nelson, R.J., Sur, M., & Merzenich, M.M. Organization of somato-sensory cortex in primates. In F.O. Schmitt, F.G. Worden, G. Adelman, & S.G. Dennis (Eds.), *The organization of the cerebral cortex.* Cambridge: MIT Press, 1981.

Kandel, E.R. *Cellular basis of behavior: An introduction to behavioral neurobiology.* San Francisco: Freeman, 1976.

Kandel, E.R. (Ed.). Cellular biology of neurons. *Handbook of physiology. The nervous system* (Vol. 1). Baltimore: Williams & Wilkins, 1977.

Kandel, E.R. *Behavioral biology of Aplysia.* San Francisco: Freeman, 1979.

Kandel, E.R. Small systems of neurons. *Scientific American,* 1979, *241,* 66–76.

Kandel, E.R. Brain and behavior, 1–13; Nerve cells and behavior, 14–23. In E.R. Kandel & J.H. Schwartz, (Eds.), *Principles of neural science.* New York: Elsevier/ North Holland, 1981. (a)

Kandel, E.R. Somatic sensory system III. In E.R. Kandel & J.H. Schwartz (Eds.), *Principles of neural science.* New York: Elsevier/North Holland, 1981. (b)

Kandel, E.R., & Schwartz, J.H. (Eds.). *Principles of neural science.* New York: Elsevier/North Holland, 1981.

Kandel, E.R., & Schwartz, J.H. Molecular biology of learning: Modulation of transmitter release. *Science,* 1982, *218,* 433–442.

Kanisza, G. Subjective contours. *Scientific American,* 1976, *234,* 48–52.

Kanisza, G. *Organization in vision: Essays on Gestalt perception.* New York: Praeger, 1979.

Katz, D. *[The world of colour.]* (R.B. MacLeod & C.W. Fox, trans.) London: Kegan Paul, Trench, Trubner, 1935.

Kaufman, E.L., Lord, M.W., Reese, T.W., & Volkmann, J. The discrimination of visual number. *American Journal of Psychology,* 1949, *62,* 498–525.

Kaufman, L. *Sight and mind.* New York: Oxford University Press, 1974.

Keller, F.S. Studies in International Morse Code, I. A new method of teaching code reception. *Journal of Applied Psychology,* 1943, *27,* 407–415.

Kelly, D.D. Physiology of sleep and dreaming. In E.R. Kandel & J.H. Schwarz (Eds.), *Principles of neural science.* New York: Elsevier/North Holland, 1981. (a)

Kelly, D.D. Somatic sensory system IV. In E.R. Kandel & J.H. Schwartz (Eds.), *Principles of neural science.* New York: Elsevier/North Holland, 1981. (b)

Kennedy, D., Evoy, W.H., & Hanawalt, J.T. Release of coordinated behavior in crayfish by single central neurons. *Science,* 1966, *154,* 917–920.

Kent, G.H., & Rosanoff, A.J. A study of association in insanity. *American Journal of Insanity,* 1910, *67,* 37–96; 317–390.

Kepler, J. *The six-cornered snowflake.* C. Hardie (Ed. and trans.) from the Latin. Oxford: Clarendon, 1966. (Originally published, 1611.)

Kertesz, A. Anatomy of jargon. In J. Brown (Ed.), *Jargon aphasia.* New York: Academic Press, 1980.

Kety, S.S. The biogenic amines in the central nervous system: Their possible roles in arousal, emotion, and learning. In F.O. Schmitt (Ed.), *The neurosciences: Second study program.* New York: Rockefeller University Press, 1970.

Kety, S.S. Genetic and biochemical aspects of schizophrenia. In A.M. Nicholi, Jr. (Ed.), *The Harvard guide to modern psychiatry.* Cambridge, Mass.: The Belknap Press, 1978.

Kety, S.S. Disorders of the human brain. *Scientific American,* 1979, *241,* 201–214.

Keyser, C.J. The group concept. In J.R. Newman (Ed.), *The world of mathematics* (Vol. 3). New York: Simon & Schuster, 1956.

Kim, S. *Inversions.* Peterborough, N.H.: Byte Books, a division of McGraw-Hill, 1981.

Kimura, D. Cerebral dominance and the perception of verbal stimuli. *Canadian Journal of Psychology,* 1961, *15,* 166–171.

Kimura, D. Functional asymmetry of the brain in dichotic listening. *Cortex,* 1967, *3,* 163–178.

Kimura, D. The asymmetry of the human brain. *Scientific American,* 1973, *228,* 70–78.

King, F.L., & Kimura, D. Left-ear superiority in dichotic perception of vocal nonverbal sounds. *Canadian Journal of Psychology,* 1972, *26,* 111–116.

Kinsey, A.C., Pomeroy, W.B., Martin, C.E., & Gebhard, P.H. *Sexual behavior in the human female.* Philadelphia: Saunders, 1953.

Klüver, H. *Mescal and mechanisms of hallucinations.* Chicago: University of Chicago Press, 1966.

Klüver, H., & Bucy, P.C. Preliminary analysis of functions of the temporal lobes in monkeys. *Archives of neurology and psychiatry,* 1939, *42,* 979–1000.

Koffka, K. *Principles of Gestalt psychology.* New York: Harcourt Brace, 1935.

Kohler, I. Experiments with goggles. *Scientific American,* 1962, *206,* 62–72.

Kohler, I. [The formation and transformation of the perceptual world] (H. Fiss, trans.). *Psychological Issues,* 1964, *3,* 1–175.

Köhler, W. *The mentality of apes.* London: Kegan Paul, 1924.

Köhler, W. *Gestalt psychology.* New York: Liveright, 1947.

Kolata, G. Grafts correct brain damage. *Science,* 1982, *217,* 342–344.

Kolb, B., & Whishaw, I.Q. *Fundamentals of human neuropsychology.* San Francisco: Freeman, 1980.

Konorski, J. The physiological approach to the problem of recent memory. In J.F. Delafresnaye (Ed.), *Brain mechanisms and learning: A symposium.* Oxford: Blackwell Science Publication, 1962, pp. 115–132.

Konorski, J. *Integrative activity of the brain: An interdisciplinary approach.* Chicago: University of Chicago Press, 1967.

Konorski, J. *Conditioned reflexes and neuron organization.* Cambridge, Engl.: Cambridge University Press, 1968. (Originally published, 1948.)

Konorski, J. Developmental pathways of research on brain-behavior interrelations in animals. *Acta Biologiae Experimentalis,* 1969, *29,* 239–249.

Konorski, J. Pathophysiological mechanisms of speech on the basis of studies on aphasia. *Acta Neurobiologie Experimentalis,* 1970, *30,* 189–210. (a)

Konorski, J. The problem of the peripheral control of skilled movements. *International Journal of Neuroscience,* 1970, *1,* 39–50. (b)

Konorski, J. Classical and instrumental conditioning: The general laws of connections between "centers." *Acta Neurobiologiae Experimentalis,* 1974, *34,* 5–13.

Konorski, J., & Lawicka, W. Analysis of errors by prefrontal animals on the delayed-response test. In J.M. Warren & K. Akert (Eds.), *The frontal granular cortex and behavior.* New York: McGraw-Hill, 1964.

Konorski, J., & Miller, S. Nouvelles recherches sur les reflexes conditionnels moteurs. *Comptes Rendus des Séances de la Société de Biologie,* 1933, *115,* 91–96.

Kornhuber, H.H. Neural control of input into long-term memory: Limbic system and amnestic syndrome in man. In M.P. Zippel (Ed.), *Memory and transfer of information.* New York: Plenum, 1973.

Kornhuber, H.H. Cerebral cortex, cerebellum, and basal ganglia: An introduction to their motor functions. In F.O. Schmitt & F.G. Worden (Eds.), *The neurosciences: Third study program.* Cambridge: MIT Press, 1974.

Kral, U.A. Memory disorders in old age and senility. In G.A. Talland & N.C. Waugh, *The pathology of memory* (41–48). New York: Academic Press, 1969.

Krieger, D.T., & Hughes, J.C. (Eds.). *Neuroendocrinology.* Sunderland, Mass.: Sinauer, 1980.

Kuffler, S.W., & Nicholls, J.G. *From neuron to brain: A cellular approach to the functions of the nervous system.* Sunderland, Mass.: Sinauer, 1976.

Kulikowski, J.J., & Tolhurst, D.J. Psychophysical evidence for sustained and transient detectors in human vision. *Journal of Physiology,* 1973, *232,* 149–162.

Kubovy, M., & Pomerantz, J.R. (Eds.). *Perceptual organization.* Hillsdale, N.J.: Erlbaum, 1981.

Kupfermann, I. Hypothalamus and limbic system. I. Peptidergic neurons, homeostasis, and emotional behavior; II. Motivation. In E.R. Kandel & J.H. Schwartz (Eds.), *Principles of neural science.* New York: Elsevier/North Holland, 1981.

Kupfermann, I. Localization of higher functions. In E.R. Kandel & J.H. Schwartz (Eds.), *Principles of neural science.* New York: Elsevier/North Holland, 1981.

Kupfermann, I., & Weiss, K.R. The command neuron concept. *The Behavioral and Brain Sciences,* 1978, *1,* 3–39.

Lacoste-Utamsing, C., & Holloway, R.L. Sexual dimorphism in the human corpus callosum. *Science*, 1982, *216*, 1431–1432.

Ladd-Franklin, C. *Colour and colour theories*. New York: Harcourt, Brace, 1929.

Land, E.H. Experiments in color vision. *Scientific American*, 1959, *200*(5), 84–97.

Land, E.H. The retinex. *American Scientist*, 1964, *52*, 247–264.

Lansdell, H. A sex difference in effect of temporal lobe neurosurgery on design preference. *Nature*, 1962, *194*, 852–854.

Lashley, K.S. *Brain mechanisms and intelligence*. Chicago: University of Chicago Press, 1929.

Lashley, K.S. In search of the engram. *Symposium of the Society for Experimental Biology*, 1950, *4*, 454–482.

Lashley, K.S. The problem of serial order in behavior. In L.A. Jeffress (Ed.), *Cerebral mechanisms in behavior: The Hixon symposium*. New York: Wiley, 1951.

Lashley, K. Dynamic processes in perception. In J.F. De la Fresnaye (Ed.), *Brain mechanisms and consciousness*. Springfield, Ill.: Thomas, 1954.

LeMay, M. Asymmetries of the skull and handedness. *Journal of the Neurological Sciences*, 1977, *32*, 243–253.

LeMay, M., & Culebras, A. Human brain: Morphologic differences in the hemispheres demonstrable by carotid-angiography. *New England Journal of Medicine*, 1972, *287*, 168–170.

Lenneberg, E.H. *Biological foundations of language*. New York: Wiley, 1967.

Lenneberg, E.H., Nichols, I.A., & Rosenberger, E.F. Primitive stages of language development in mongolism. In D. Rioch & E.A. Weinstein (Eds.), *Disorders of communication* (Vol. 42). New York: Hafner, 1969.

Lennie, P. Sustained or X and transient or Y ganglion cells. *Vision Research*, 1980, *20*, 561–

Lettvin, J.Y., Maturana, H.R., McCulloch, W.S., & Pitts, W.H. What the frog's eye tells the frog's brain. *Proceedings of the Institute of Radio Engineers*, 1959, *47*, 1940–1951.

LeVay, S., Hubel, D.H., & Wiesel, T.N. The pattern of ocular dominance columns in macaque visual cortex revealed by a reduced silver stain. *Journal of Comparative Neurology*, 1975, *159*, 559–576.

LeVay, S., Wiesel, T.N., & Hubel, D.H. The postnatal development and plasticity of ocular-dominance in the monkey. In F.O. Schmitt, F.G. Worden, G. Adelman, & S.G. Dennis (Eds.), *The organization of the cerebral cortex*. Cambridge: MIT Press, 1981.

Levin, H., & Addis, A.B. *The eye-voice span*. Cambridge: MIT Press, 1979.

Levy, J. Cerebral asymmetries as manifested in split-brain man. In M. Kinsbourne & W.L. Smith (Eds.), *Hemispheric disconnection and cerebral function*. Springfield, Ill.: Thomas, 1974.

Levy, J., Trevarthen, C., & Sperry, R.W. Perception of bilateral chimeric figures following hemispheric deconnexion. *Brain*, 1972, *95*, 61–78.

Liepmann, H. *Über Storungen des Handelns bei Gehirn Kranken*. Berlin: Karger, 1905.

Lindauer, M. *Communication among social bees* (Rev. ed.). Cambridge: Harvard University Press, 1971.

Lorente de Nó, R. Cerebral cortex: architecture, intracortical connections, motor projections. In J. Fulton (Ed.), *Physiology of the nervous system* (3rd ed.). New York: Oxford University Press, 1949.

Lorenz, K. The comparative method in studying innate behavior patterns. *Symposium of the Society for Experimental Biology,* 1950, *4,* 221–268.

Luria, A.R. *Higher cortical functions in man.* New York: Basic Books, 1966. (a)

Luria, A.R. *Human brain and psychological processes.* New York: Harper & Row, 1966. (b)

Luria. A.R. *The mind of a mnemonist.* New York: Basic Books, 1968.

Lynch, J.C. The command function concept in studies of the primate nervous system. *The behavioral and brain sciences,* 1978, *1,* 31–32.

Lynch, J.C. The functional organization of posterior parietal association cortex. *The Behavioral and Brain Sciences,* 1980, *3,* 485–534.

McCollough, C. Color adaptation of edge-detectors in the human visual system. *Science,* 1965, *149,* 1115–1116.

McCormick, D.A., Clark, G.A., Lavond, D.G., & Thompson, R.F. Initial localization of the memory trace for a basic form of learning. *Proceedings of the National Academy of Science,* 1982, *79,* 2731–2735.

McEwen, B.S., Davis, P.G., Parsons, B., & Pfaff, D.W. The brain as a target for steroid hormone action. *Annual Review of Neuroscience,* 1979, *2,* 65–112.

McGarvey, H.R. Anchoring effects in the absolute judgment of verbal materials. *Archives of Psychology,* 1943, No. 281.

McGeer, P.L., Eccles, J.C., & McGeer, E.G. *Molecular neurobiology of the mammalian brain.* New York: Plenum, 1978.

McGlone, J. Sex difference in functional brain asymmetry. *Cortex,* 1978, *14,* 122–128.

McGraw, M.B. *The neuromuscular maturation of the human infant.* New York: Hafner, 1963.

Mach, E. *[The analysis of sensations and the relation of the physical to the psychical]* (C.M. Williams, trans.). Dover, 1959.

MacKay, D.M. Moving visual images produced by regular stationary patterns. *Nature,* 1957, *180,* 849–850.

MacKay, D.M. Perception and brain function. In F.O. Schmitt (Ed.), *The Neurosciences: Second study program.* New York: Rockefeller University Press, 1970.

MacLean, P.D. Psychosomatic disease and the "visceral brain." *Psychosomatic medicine,* 1949, *11,* 338–353.

MacLean, P.D. New fundings relevant to the evolution of psychosexual functions in the brain. *Journal of Nervous and Mental Disease,* 1962, *135,* 289–301.

MacLean, P.D. The internal-external bonds of the memory process. *Journal of Nervous and Mental Disease,* 1969, *149,* 40–47.

MacLean, P.D. The triune brain, emotion, and scientific bias. In F.O. Schmitt (Ed.), *The neurosciences: Second study program.* New York: Rockefeller University Press, 1970.

MacLean, P.D. A triune concept of the brain and behavior. *The Clarence M. Hincks Memorial Lectures.* Toronto: University of Toronto Press, 1973.

Maffei, L., & Fiorentini, A. The visual cortex as a spatial frequency analyser, *Vision Research,* 1973, *13,* 1255–1267.

Maffei, L., & Fiorentini, A. Geniculate neural plasticity in kittens after exposure to periodic gratings. *Science,* 1974, *186,* 447–449.

Magoun, H.W. *The waking brain.* Springfield, Ill.: Thomas, 1958.

Maier, S.F., & Seligman, M.E.P. Learned helplessness: Theory and evidence. *Journal of Experimental Psychology,* 1976, *105,* 3–46.

Marr, D. A theory of cerebellar cortex. *Journal of Physiology,* 1969, *202,* 437–470.

Maruszewski, M. *[Language communication and the brain: A neuropsychological study]* (G.W. Shugar, trans.). Hawthorne, N.Y.: Mouton, 1975.

Marx, J.L. Transplants as guides to brain development, *Science,* 1982, *217,* 340–342.

Masters, W., & Johnson, V. *Human sexual response.* Boston: Little, Brown, 1966.

Mauk, M.D., Warren, J.T., & Thompson, R.F. Selective naloxone-reversible morphine depression of learned behavioral and hippocampal responses. *Science,* 1982, *216,* 434–436.

Mayr, E. *The growth of biological thought.* Cambridge: The Belknap Press of Harvard University Press, 1982.

Medawar, P.B. *The art of the soluble.* London: Methuen, 1967.

Meller, K., & Tetzlaff, W. Neuronal migration during the early development of the cerebral cortex: A scanning electron microscopic study. *Cell Tissue Research,* 1975, *163,* 313–325.

Meltzoff, A.N., & Moore, M.K. Imitation of facial and manual gestures by human neonates. *Science,* 1977, *198,* 75–78.

Menzel, E.W. Chimpanzee spatial memory organization. *Science,* 1973, *182,* 943–945.

Mervis, C.B., & Pani, J.R. Acquisition of basic object categories. *Cognitive Psychology,* 1980, *12,* 496–522.

Mervis, C.B., & Rosch, E. Categorization of natural objects. *Annual Review of Psychology,* 1981, *32,* 89–115.

Merzenich, M.M., & Kaas, J.H. Principles of organization of sensory-perceptual systems in mammals. In J.M. Sprague & A.N. Epstein (Eds.), *Progress in psychobiology and physiological psychology* (Vol. 9). New York: Academic Press, 1980.

Mesulam, M.-M., & Geschwind, N. On the possible role of neocortex and its limbic connections in the process of attention and schizophrenia: Clinical cases of inattention in man and experimental anatomy in monkey. *Journal of Psychiatric Research,* 1978, *14,* 249–259.

Miller, G.A. Information and memory. *Scientific American,* 1956, *195,* 42–46. (a)

Miller, G.A. The magical number seven, plus or minus two: Some limits on our capacity for processing information. *Psychological Review,* 1956, *63,* 81–96. (b)

Miller, N.E. Studies of fear as an acquirable drive I. Fear as motivation and fear-reduction as reinforcement in the learning of new responses. *Journal of Experimental Psychology,* 1948, *38,* 89–101.

Miller, N.E. Learning of visceral and glandular responses. *Science,* 1969, *163,* 434–435.

Miller, N.E. Motivation and psychological stress. In D.W. Pfaff (Ed.), *The physiological mechanisms of motivation.* New York: Springer-Verlag, 1982.

Miller, N.E., & Dollard, T. *Social learning and imitation.* New Haven: Yale University Press, 1941.

Miller, S., & Konorski, J. Sur une forme particuliere des réflexes conditionnels. *Comptes Rendus des Séances de la Société de Biologie,* 1928, *99,* 1155–57.

Miller, S., & Konorski, J. [On a particular form of conditioned reflex] (Postscript by Konorski.) (B.F. Skinner, trans.). *Journal of the Experimental Analysis of Behavior,* 1969, *12,* 187–189. (Originally published in French, 1928.)

Milner, B. Laterality effects in audition. In V.B. Mountcastle & M.D. Mountcastle (Eds.), *Interhemispheric relations and cerebral dominance.* Baltimore: Johns Hopkins Press, 1962, pp. 177–195.

Milner, B. Amnesia following an operation on the temporal lobe. In C.W.M. Whitty & O.L. Zangwill (Eds.), *Amnesia.* London: Butterworth, 1966.

Milner, B. Brain mechanisms suggested by studies of temporal lobes. In F.L. Darley (Ed.), *Brain mechanisms underlying speech and language.* New York: Grune & Stratton, 1967.

Milner, B. Visual recognition and recall after right temporal-lobe excisions in man. *Neuropsychologia,* 1968, *6,* 191–210.

Milner, B. Memory and the medial temporal regions of the brain. In K.H. Pribram & D.E. Broadbent (Eds.). *Biology of memory* (29–50). New York: Academic Press, 1970.

Milner, B. Hemispheric specialization: Scope and limits. In F.O. Schmitt & F.G. Worden (Eds.), *The neurosciences: Third study program* (75–89). Cambridge: MIT Press, 1974.

Mitchell, D.E. The influence of early visual experience on visual perception. In C.S. Harris (Ed.), *Visual coding and adaptability.* Hillsdale, N.J.: Erlbaum, 1980.

Monod, J. *[Chance and necessity: An essay on the natural philosophy of modern biology]* (A. Wainhouse, trans.). London: Collins, 1972. (Originally published under the title *Le hasard et la necessité,* Paris: Editions du Seuil, 1970.)

Moore, T.E. (Ed.). *Cognitive development and the acquisition of language.* New York: Academic Press, 1973.

Morrison, A.R. Brainstem regulation of behavior during sleep and wakefulness. In J.M. Sprague & A.N. Epstein (Eds.), *Progress in psychobiology and physiological psychology* (Vol. 8). New York: Academic Press, 1979.

Morrison, A.R. Central activity states: Overview. In A.L. Beckman (Ed.), *The neural basis of behavior,* Jamaica, N.Y.: Spectrum, 1982.

Morrison, A.R. A window on the sleeping brain. *Scientific American,* 1983, *248,* 94–102.

Moruzzi, G., & Magoun, H.W. Brain stem reticular formation and activation of the EEG. *Electroencephalography and Clinical Neurophysiology,* 1949, *1,* 455–473.

Moskowitz, B.A. The acquisition of language. *Scientific American,* 1978 (November).

Motter, B.C., & Mountcastle, V.B. The functional properties of the light-sensitive neurons of the posterior parietal cortex studied in waking monkeys: Foveal sparing and opponent vector organization. *Journal of Neuroscience,* 1981, *1,* 3–26.

Mountcastle, V.B. Modality and topographic properties of single neurons of cat's somatic sensory cortex. *Journal of Neurophysiology,* 1957, *20,* 408–434.

Mountcastle, V.B. The view from within: Pathways to the study of perception. *Johns Hopkins Medical Journal,* 1975, *136,* 109.

Mountcastle, V.B. An organizing principle for cerebral function: The unit module and the distributed system. In G.M. Edelman & V.B. Mountcastle (Eds.), *The mindful brain.* Cambridge: MIT Press, 1978.

Mountcastle, V.B., & Mountcastle, M.D. (Eds.). *Interhemispheric relations and cerebral dominance.* Baltimore: Johns Hopkins Press, 1962.

Muir, D.W., & Mitchell, D.E. Visual resolution and experiences. Acuity deficits in cats following early selective visual deprivation. *Science,* 1973, *180,* 420–422.

Müller, G.E., & Pilzecker, A. Experimentelle Beitrage zur Lehre vom Gedachtniss. *Zeitschrift fur Psychologie Ergbd.* No. 1, 1900.

Nabokov, V. *Speak, memory: An autobiography revisited.* Middlesex, England: Penguin, 1969. Originally published under the title *Conclusive evidence.* Great Britain: Weidenfeld & Nicolson, 1967.

Nagel, T. What is it like to be a bat? In D.R. Hofstadter & D.C. Dennett (Eds.), *The mind's I.* New York: Basic Books, 1981.

Nauta, W.J.H., & Freitag, M. The organization of the brain. *Scientific American,* 1979, *241,* 78–91.

Neisser, U. *Cognitive psychology.* New York: Appleton-Century-Crofts, 1967.

Newton, G., & Levine, S. (Eds.). *Early experience and behavior: The psychobiology of development.* Springfield, Ill.: Thomas, 1968.

Nicholi, A.M., Jr. *The Harvard guide to modern psychiatry.* Cambridge, Mass.: Belknap Press, 1978.

Norman, D.A. (Ed.). *Perspectives on cognitive science.* Norwood, N.J.: Ablex, 1981.

Noton, D.N., & Stark, L. Eye movements and visual perception. *Scientific American,* 1971, *224,* 34–43.

Noton, D., & Stark, L. Scanpaths in eye movements during pattern perception. *Science,* 1971, *171,* 308–311.

Nottebohm, F. Ontogeny of bird song, *Science,* 1970, *167,* 950–956.

Nottebohm, F. Brain pathways for vocal learning in birds: A review of the first 10 years. In J.M. Sprague & A.N. Epstein (Eds.), *Progress in psychology and physiological psychology* (Vol. 9). New York: Academic Press, 1980.

Nottebohm, F. A brain for all seasons: Cyclical anatomical changes in song control nuclei of the canary brain. *Science,* 1981, *214,* 1368–1370.

Oakley, D.A., & Plotkin, H.C. (Eds.). *Brain, behaviour, and evolution.* London: Methuen, 1979.

Oakley, D.A., & Russell, I.S. Subcortical storage of Pavlovian conditioning in the rabbit. *Physiology and Behavior,* 1977, *18,* 931–937.

Ojemann, G.A. Organization of short-term verbal memory in language areas of human cortex: Evidence from electrical stimulation, *Brain and Language,* 1978, *5,* 331–340.

Ojemann, G.A. Brain organization for language from the perspective of electrical stimulation mapping. *Behavioral and Brain Sciences,* 1983, *6,* 189–206.

Olds, J. Pleasure centers in the brain. *Scientific American,* 1956, *195,* 105–116.

Olds, J. Self-stimulation of the brain. *Science,* 1958, *127,* 315–324.

Olds, J. Reward and drive neurons: 1975. In A. Wauquier & E.T. Rolls (Eds.), *Brain-stimulation reward.* New York: Elsevier/North Holland, 1976.

Olds, J., & Milner, P. Positive reinforcement produced by electrical stimulation of septal areas and other regions of rat brains. *Journal of Comparative and Physiological Psychology,* 1954, *47,* 419–427.

Olson, C.R., & Freeman, R.D. Progressive changes in kitten striate cortex during monocular vision. *Journal of Neurophysiology,* 1975, *38,* 26–32.

Orbach, J. (Ed.). *Neuropsychology after Lashley: Fifty years since the publication of brain mechanisms and intelligence.* Hillsdale, N.J.: Erlbaum, 1982.

Overmeier, J.B., & Seligman, M.E.P. Effects of inescapable shock on subsequent escape and avoidance learning. *Journal of Comparative and Physiological Psychology,* 1967, *63,* 23–33.

Papez, J.W. A proposed mechanism of emotion. *Archives of Neurology and Psychiatry,* 1937, *38,* 725–743.

Parsons, H.L. Minding as a material force. In D.H. DeGrood, D. Riepe, & J. Somerville (Eds.), *Radical currents in contemporary philosophy.* St. Louis, Mo.: Green, 1971.

Paterson, A., & Zangwill, O.L. Disorders of visual space perception associated with lesions of the right cerebral hemisphere, *Brain,* 1944, *67,* 331–348.

Pavlov, I.P. *[Conditioned reflexes: An investigation of the physiological activity of the cerebral cortex]* (C.G. Anrep, Ed. and trans.). New York: Dover, 1960. (Originally published, 1927.)

Peiper, A. *[Cerebral function in infancy and childhood]* (H. Nagler, trans.). New York: Consultants' Bureau, 1963.

Penfield, W. Speech, perception and the uncommitted cortex. In J.C. Eccles (Ed.), *Brain and conscious experience.* New York: Springer-Verlag, 1966.

Penfield, W., & Jasper, H. *Epilepsy and the functional anatomy of the human brain.* Boston: Little, Brown, 1954.

Penfield, W., & Perot, P. The brain's record of auditory and visual experience. *Brain,* 1963, *86,* 595–696.

Penfield, W., & Rasmussen, T. *The cerebral cortex of man: A clinical study of localization of function.* New York: Macmillan, 1950.

Penfield, W., & Roberts, L. *Speech and brain mechanisms.* Princeton, N.J.: Princeton University Press, 1959.

Perky, C.W. An experimental study of imagination. *American Journal of Psychology,* 1910, *21,* 422–452.

Pfaff, D.W. *Estrogens and brain function.* New York: Springer-Verlag, 1980.

Pfaff, D.W. (Ed.). *The physiological mechanisms of motivation.* New York: Springer-Verlag, 1982.

Pfaffmann, C. Taste: A model of incentive motivation. In D.W. Pfaff (Ed.), *The physiological mechanisms of motivation.* New York: Springer-Verlag, 1982.

Piaget, J., Inhelder, B., & Szeminska, A. *[The child's conception of geometry]* (E.A. Lunzer, trans.). New York: Harper & Row, 1964.

Pillsbury, W.B. A study in apperception. *American Journal of Psychology,* 1897, *8,* 315–393.

Pittenger, J.B., & Shaw, R.E. Aging faces as viscalelastic events: Implications for a theory of nonrigid shape perception. *Journal of Experimental Psychology: Human Perception and Performance,* 1975, *1,* 374–382.

Pittenger, J.B., Shaw, R.E., & Mark, L.S. Perceptual information for the age level of faces as a higher order invariant of growth. *Journal of Experimental Psychology: Human Perception and Performance,* 1979, *5,* 478–493.

Pollack, I., & Ficks, L. Information of elementary multidimensional auditory displays. *Journal of the Acoustical Society of America,* 1954, *26,* 155–158.

Premack, A.J., & Premack, D. Teaching language to an ape. *Scientific American,* 1972, *227,* 92–97.

Premack, D. Reversibility of the reinforcement relation. *Science,* 1962, *136,* 235–237.

Premack, D. Language in chimpanzee? *Science,* 1971, *172,* 808–822.

Premack, D. *Intelligence in ape and man.* Hillsdale, N.J.: Erlbaum, 1976.

Premack, D., & Woodruff, G. Does the chimpanzee have a theory of mind? *The Behavioral and Brain Sciences,* 1978, *4,* 515–526.

Pribram, K.H. Some dimensions of remembering: Steps toward a neuropsychological model of memory. In J. Gaito (Ed.), *Macromolecules and behavior* (2nd ed.). New York: Appleton-Century-Crofts, 1972. Originally published, 1966.

Pribram, K.H., & Broadbent, D.E. (Eds.). *Biology of memory.* New York: Academic Press, 1970.

Proust, M. *A la recherche du temps perdu.* Paris: Gallimard, 1927.

Puccetti, R. The case for mental duality: Evidence from split-brain data and other considerations. *The Behavioral and Brain Sciences,* 1981, *4,* 93–123.

Rakic, P. Developmental events leading to laminar and areal organization of the neocortex. In F.O. Schmitt, F.G. Worden, G. Adelman, & S.G. Dennis (Eds.), *The organization of the cerebral cortex.* Cambridge: MIT Press, 1981.

Rakic, P. Neuronal migration and contact guidance in primate telencephalon. *Postgraduate Medical Journal,* 1978, *54,* 25–40.

Rakic, P. Prenatal development of the visual system in rhesus monkey. *Transactions of the Royal Society.* London, 1977, *B278,* 245–260.

Ranson, S.W. The hypothalamus: its significance for visceral innervation and emotional expression. *Transactions College Physicians,* Philadelphia (Series 4) 1934, *2,* 222–242.

Ratliff, F. *Mach bands: Quantitative studies on neural networks in the retina.* San Francisco: Holden-Day, 1965.

Reese, E.P., Reese, T.W., Volkmann, J., & Corbin, H.H. (Eds.). *Psychophysical Research Summary Report,* 1946–1952. NAVE-XDS P1104, Technical Report Number SDC–131–1–5.

Ribot, T.A. *The psychology of emotions* (2nd ed.). New York: Walter Scott, 1911.

Richards, W. The fortification illusions of migraines. *Scientific American,* 1971, *224,* 88–96.

Riesen, A.H. Plasticity of behavior: Psychological aspects. In H.F. Harlow & C.N. Woolsey (Eds.), *Biological and biochemical bases of behavior.* Madison: University of Wisconsin, 1958.

Riesen, A.H. Sensory deprivation. In E. Stellar & J.M. Sprague (Eds.), *Progress in physiological psychology* (Vol. 1). New York: Academic Press, 1966.

Rioch, D. McK. Group discussion, following Fessard, A.E. Mechanisms of nervous integration and conscious experience. In J.F. Delafresnaye (Ed.), *Brain mechanisms and consciousness.* Springfield, Ill.: Thomas, 1954.

Rioch, D., & Weinstein, E.A. (Eds.). *Disorders of communication.* (Research publications: Association for research in nervous and mental disease, Vol. 42.) New York: Hafner, 1969.

Rockel, A.J., Hiorns, R.W., & Powell, T.P.S. Numbers of neurons through full depth of neocortex. *Proceedings of the Anatomical Society of Great Britain and Ireland,* 1974, *118,* 371.

Rogers, S. The anchoring of absolute judgments. *Archives of Psychology,* 1941, No. 261.

Rolls, B.J., Wood, R.J., & Rolls, E.T. Thirst: The initiation, maintenance, and termination of drinking. In J.M. Sprague & A.N. Epstein (Eds.), *Progress in psychobiology and physiological psychology* (Vol. 9). New York: Academic Press, 1980.

Rosch, E.H. Natural categories. *Cognitive Psychology,* 1973, *4,* 328–350. (a)

Rosch, E.H. On the internal structure of perceptual and semantic categories. In T.E. Moore (Ed.), *Cognitive development and the acquisition of language.* New York: Academic Press, 1973. (b)

Rosch, E.H. Human categorization. In N. Warren (Ed.), *Advances in cross-cultural psychology.* New York: Academic, 1977.

Rosch, E.H. Principles of categorization In E.H. Rosch & B.B. Lloyd (Eds.), *Cognition and categorization.* Hillsdale, N.J.: Erlbaum, 1978.

Rosch, E.H., & Mervis, C.B. Family resemblances: Studies in the internal structure of categories. *Cognitive Psychology,* 1975, *7,* 573–605.

Rosch, E.H., Mervis, C.B., Gray, W., Johnson, D., & Boyes-Braem, P. Basic objects in natural categories. *Cognitive Psychology,* 1976, *8,* 382–439.

Rosenblith, W. (Ed.). *Sensory communication.* Cambridge: MIT Press, 1961.

Rosenzweig, M.R. Evidence for anatomical and chemical changes in the brain during primary learning. In K.H. Pribram & D.E. Broadbent (Eds.), *Biology of memory.* New York: Academic Press, 1970.

Rosenzweig, M.R., & Bennett, E.L. (Eds.). *Neural mechanisms of learning and memory.* Cambridge: MIT Press, 1976.

Rosenzweig, M.R., Krech, D., & Bennett, E. Heredity, environment, brain biochemistry, and learning. In *Current trends in psychological theory.* Pittsburgh: University of Pittsburgh, 1961.

Rosenzweig, M.R., Krech, D., Bennett, E.L., & Diamond, M.C. Modifying brain chemistry and anatomy by enrichment or impoverishment of experience. In G. Newton and S. Levine (Eds.), *Early experience and behavior: The psychobiology of development.* Springfield, Ill.: Thomas, 1968.

Rosenzweig, M.R., & Leiman, A.L. *Physiological psychology.* Lexington, Mass.: Heath, 1982.

Ross, E.D. The aprosodias: Functional-anatomical organization of the affective components of language in the right hemisphere. *Archives of Neurology,* 1981, *37.*

Ross, E.D. Disorders of recent memory in humans. *Trends in Neurosciences,* 1982, *5,* 170–173.

Ross, E.D., & Mesulam, M.M. Dominant language functions of the right hemisphere. *Archives of Neurology,* 1979, *36,* 144–148.

Rowe, W.W. *Nabokov's deceptive world.* New York: University Press, 1971.

Rubin, E. *Synsoplevede Figuren.* Copenhagen: Gyldendalska, 1915.

Rubin, E. *Visuell wahrgenommene Figuren.* Copenhagen: Gyldendalska, 1921.

Rumbaugh, D.M. (Ed.). *Language learning by a chimpanzee: The Lana project.* New York: Academic Press, 1977.

Russell, I.S. Brain size and intelligence: A comparative perspective. In D.A. Oakley & H.C. Plotkin (Eds.), *Brain, behavior and evolution.* London: Methuen, 1979.

Ryle, G. *The concept of mind.* London: Hutchinson, 1949.

Sachar, E.J. Psychobiology of affective disorders. In E.R. Kandel & J.H. Schwartz (Eds.), *Principles of neural science.* New York: Elsevier/North Holland, 1981. (a)

Sachar, E. Psychobiology of schizophrenia. In E.R. Kandel & J.H. Schwartz (Eds.), *Principles of neural science.* New York: Elsevier/North Holland, 1981. (b)

Saltzman, I.J., & Garner, W.R. Reaction time as a measure of span of attention. *Journal of Psychology,* 1948, *25,* 227–234.

Satinoff, E. Are there similarities between thermoregulation and sexual behavior? In D.W. Pfaff (Ed.), *The physiological mechanisms of motivation.* New York: Springer-Verlag, 1982.

Schachter, S., & Singer, J. Cognitive social and physiological determinants of emotional state. *Psychological Review,* 1962, *69,* 379–399.

Scheflin, A.W., & Opton, E.M., Jr. *The mind manipulators: A non-fiction account.* New York: Paddington Press, 1978.

Schmechel, D.E., & Rakic, P. Arrested proliferation of radial glial cells during midgestation in rhesus monkey. *Nature,* 1979, *277,* 303–305.

Schmitt, F.O., & Worden, F.G. *The Neurosciences: Third study program.* Cambridge: MIT Press, 1974.

Schmitt, F.O., & Worden, F.G. (Eds.), *The Neurosciences: Fourth study program.* Cambridge: MIT Press, 1978.

Schmitt, F.O., Worden, F.G., Adelman, G., & Dennis, S.G. (Eds.). *The organization of the cerebral cortex.* Cambridge: MIT Press, 1981.

Schoenfeld, N. An experimental study of some problems relating to stereotypes. *Archives of Psychology,* 1942, No. 270.

Scoville, W.B., & Milner, B. Loss of recent memory after bilateral hippocampal lesions. *Journal of Neurology, Neurosurgery, and Psychiatry.* 1957, *20,* 11–21.

Selfridge, O.G., & Neisser, U. Pattern recognition by machine. *Scientific American,* 1960, *203,* 60–68.

Seligman, M.E.P. Learned helplessness. *Annual Review of Medicine,* 1972, *23,* 407–412.

Seligman, M.E.P., & Maier, S.F. Failure to escape traumatic shock. *Journal of Experimental Psychology,* 1967, *74,* 1–9.

Sem-Jacobsen, C.W. Electrical stimulation and self-stimulation in man with chronic implanted electrodes. In A. Wanquier & E.T. Rolls (Eds.), *Brain-stimulation reward.* Amsterdam: Elsevier Press, 1976.

Sem-Jacobsen, C.W., & Torkildsen, A. Depth recording and electrical stimulation in the human brain. In E.R. Ramey & D.S. O'Doherty (Eds.), *Electrical studies on the unanesthetized brain.* New York: Hoeber, 1960.

Senden, M. von. *[Space and sight]* (P. Heath, trans.). Glencoe, Ill.: Free Press, 1960.

Shepherd, G.M. *Neurobiology.* New York: Oxford University Press, 1983.

Sherrington, C.S. *The integrative action of the nervous system* (1st ed.). New York: Charles Scribner's Sons, 1906.

Siegel, R.K. Hallucinations. *Scientific American,* 1977, *237,* 132–140.

Siegel, R.K., & West, L.J. *Hallucinations: Behavior, experience and theory.* New York: Wiley, 1975.

Simon, H.A. *The science of the artificial.* Cambridge: MIT Press, 1969.

Simon, H.A. How big is a chunk? *Science,* 1974, *183,* 482–488.

Sinz, R., Grechenko, T.N., & Sokolov, Y.N. The memory neuron concept: A psychophysiological approach. In R. Sinz & M.R. Rosenzweig (Eds.), *Psychophysiology*. 1980. Amsterdam: North Holland, 1982.

Sinz, R., & Rosenzweig, M.R. *Psychophysiology 1980: Memory, motivation and event-related potentials in mental operations. Symposia from the XXIInd International Congress of Psychology*, Amsterdam: North Holland, 1982.

Skinner, B.F. *The behavior of organisms: An experimental analysis.* New York: Appleton-Century-Crofts, 1938.

Skinner, B.F. *Science and human behavior.* New York: Macmillan, 1953.

Skinner, B.F. Why teachers fail. *Saturday Review,* October 16, 1965, *48,* 80–81; 98–102.

Skinner, B.F. *The technology of teaching.* New York: Appleton-Century-Crofts, 1968.

Snyder, S.H. The dopamine hypothesis of schizophrenia. *American Journal of Psychiatry,* 1976, *133,* 197–202.

Snyder, S.H. Opiate receptors and internal opiates. *Scientific American,* 1977, *236,* 44–56.

Snyder, S.H., & Childers, S.R. Opiate receptors and opioid peptides. *Annual Review of Neuroscience,* 1979, *2,* 35–64.

Sokoloff, L. Circulation and energy metabolism of the brain. In R.W. Albers, G.J. Siegel, R. Katzman, & B.W. Agranoff, (Eds.), *Basic neurochemistry.* Boston: Little, Brown, 1972, pp. 299–325.

Sokoloff, L. Measurement of local glucose utilization and its use in mapping local functional activity in the nervous system. In W.H. Sweet (Ed.), *Neurosurgical treatment in psychiatry.* Baltimore: University Park Press, 1976.

Sokolov, E.N. *[Perception and the conditioned reflex.]* (S.W. Waydenfeld, trans.). New York: Pergamon, 1963.

Spellacy, F., & Blumstein, S. The influence of language set on ear preference in phoneme recognition. *Cortex,* 1970, *6,* 430–440.

Spence, K.W. Theoretical interpretations of learning. In S.S. Stevens (Ed.), *Handbook of experimental psychology.* New York: Wiley, 1951.

Sperry, R.W. Problems outstanding in the evolution of brain function. *James Arthur Lecture on the evolution of the human brain.* New York: The American Museum of Natural History, 1964.

Sperry, R.W. Brain bisection and mechanisms of consciousness. *Pontificiae Academiae Scientiarum Scripta Varia,* 1965, *30,* 1–16.

Sperry, R.W. Mental unity following surgical disconnection of the cerebral hemispheres. *The Harvey Lectures,* Series 62, New York: Academic Press, 1968.

Sperry, R.W. Perception in the absence of the neocortical commissures. In D.A. Hamburg, K.H. Pribram, & A.J. Stunkard (Eds.), *Perception and its disorders* (123–138). Baltimore: Williams & Wilkins, 1970.

Sperry, R.W. Lateral specialization in the surgically separated hemispheres. In F.O. Schmitt & F.G. Worden (Eds.), *The neurosciences: Third study program.* Cambridge: MIT Press, 1974.

Sperry, R.W. Some effects of disconnecting the cerebral hemispheres. *Science,* 1982, *217,* 1223–1226.

Sperry, R.W., Gazzaniga, M.S., & Bogen, J.E. Interhemispheric relationships; the neocortical commissures; syndromes of hemisphere disconnection. In P.J. Vinkin & G.W. Bruyen (Eds.), *Handbook of clinical neurology* (Vol. 4). Amsterdam: North Holland, 1969.

Sperry, R.W., Zaidel, E., & Zaidel, D. Self recognition and social awareness in the deconnected minor hemispheres. *Neuropsychologia,* 1979, *17,* 153–166.

Spitz, R.A. Hospitalism: An inquiry into the genesis of psychiatric conditions in early childhood. *Psychoanalytic Study of the Child,* 1945, *1,* 53–74. Hospitalism: A follow-up report on investigation described in Volume 1, 1945. *Psychoanalytic Study of the Child,* 1946, *2,* 113–117.

Sprague, J.M., & Epstein, A.N. (Eds.). *Progress in psychobiology and physiological psychology* (Vols. 1–10). New York: Academic Press, 1973–1983.

Spurzheim, J.C. *Phrenology, or the doctrine of the mind* (3rd ed.). London: Knight, 1825.

Stavrianos, B.K. The relation of shape perception to explicit judgments of inclination. *Archives of Psychology,* 1945, No. 296.

Steinman, A.R. Reaction time to change, compared with other psychophysical methods. *Archives of Psychology,* NY, 1944 (Monograph no. 292).

Steinman, D.B. (In W. Ratigan, biography), *Highways over broad waters: Life and times of David B. Steinman, bridge builder.* Grand Rapids, Mich.: Erdmans, 1959.

Stellar, E. The physiology of motivation. *Psychological Review,* 1954, *61,* 5–22.

Stellar, E. Drive and motivation. In J. Field, H.W. Magoun, & V.E. Hall (Eds.), *Handbook of physiology.* I: *Neurophysiology* (Vol. 3). Washington, D.C.: American Physiological Society, 1960.

Stellar, E. Brain mechanisms in hunger and other hedonic experiences. *Proceedings of the American Philosophical Society,* 1974, *118,* 276–282.

Stellar, E. Brain mechanisms in hedonic processes. *Acta Neurobiologiae Experimentalis,* 1980, *30,* 313–324.

Stellar, E. Brain mechanisms in hedonic processes. In D.W. Pfaff (Ed.). *The physiological mechanisms of motivation.* New York: Springer-Verlag, 1982.

Stellar, J.R., Brooks, F.H., & Mills, L.E. Approach and withdrawal analysis of the effects of hypothalamic stimulation and lesions in rats. *Journal of Comparative and Physiological Psychology,* 1979, *83,* 446–466.

Stellar, E., & Jordan, H.A. Perception of satiety. In D.A. Hamburg, K.H. Pribram, & A.J. Stunkard (Ed.), *Perception and its disorders.* Baltimore: Williams & Wilkins, 1970.

Stent, G.S. A physiological mechanism for Hebb's postulate of learning. *Proceedings of the National Academy of Sciences of the U.S.A.,* 1978, *70,* 997–1001.

Stevens, C.F. The neuron. *Scientific American,* 1979, *241,* 54–65.

Stratton, G.M. Vision without inversion of the retinal image. *Psychological Review,* 1897, *4,* 341–360.

Straus, E., & Yalow, R.W. Cholecystokinin in the brains of obese and non-obese mice. *Science, 203,* 68–69.

Stromeyer, C.F. Form-color aftereffects in human vision. In R. Held, H.W. Leibowitz, & H.-L. Teuber (Eds.), *Handbook of sensory physiology: Perception* (Vol. VIII). Berlin: Springer-Verlag, 1978.

Studdert-Kennedy, M., & Shankweiler, D. Hemispheric specialization for speech perception. *The Journal of the Acoustical Society of America,* 1970, *48,* 579–594.

Sur, M., Wall, J.T., & Kaas, J. Modular segregation of functional cell classes within the postcentral somatosensory cortex of monkeys. *Science,* 1981, *212,* 1059–1061.

Sutherland, N.S. Outlines of a theory of visual pattern recognition in animals and man. *Proceedings of the Royal Society;* Series B: Biological Sciences, (London), 1968, *171,* 297–317.

Swanson, L.W., & Sawchenbo, P.E. Hypothalamic integration: Organization of the paraventricular and supraoptic nuclei. *Annual Review of Neuroscience,* 1983, *6,* 269–324.

Szentagothai, J. The "module concept" in cerebral cortex architecture. *Brain Research,* 1975, *95,* 475–496.

Szentagothai, J. Local neuron circuits of the neocortex. In F.O. Schmitt & F.G. Worden (Eds.), *The neurosciences: Fourth study program.* Cambridge: MIT Press, 1978.

Talland, G., & Waugh, N. *Pathology of memory.* New York: Academic Press, 1969.

Taves, E.H. Two mechanisms for the perception of visual numerousness. *Archives of Psychology,* 1941, No. 265.

Taylor, J. (Ed.). *Selected Writings of John Hughlings Jackson* (Vol. 2). (Evolution and dissolution of the nervous system. Affections of speech. Various papers, addresses, and lectures). London: Staples Press, 1958.

Taylor, L.B. Perception of digits presented to right and left ears in children with reading difficulties. Paper read at meeting of the *Canadian Psychological Association,* Hamilton, Canada, 1962.

Terman, L.M., & Merrill, M.A. *Stanford-Binet intelligence scale—Manual for the third revision.* Boston: Houghton Mifflin, 1972.

Teuber, H.-L. Perception. In J. Field, H.W. Magoun, & V.E. Hall (Eds.), *Handbook of physiology. I: Neurophysiology.* (Vol. 3). Washington, D.C.: American Physiological Society, 1960.

Teuber, H.-L. The riddle of frontal lobe function in man. In J.M. Warren & K. Akert (Eds.), *The frontal granular cortex and behavior.* New York: McGraw-Hill, 1964.

Teuber, H.-L. The brain and human behavior. In R. Held, H.W. Leibowitz, & H.-L. Teuber (Eds.), *Handbook of sensory physiology: Perception* (Vol. VIII). Berlin: Springer-Verlag, 1978.

Thomas, E.L. Movements of the eye. *Scientific American,* 1968, *219,* 88–95.

Thompson, D.W. *On growth and form.* (J.T. Bonner, Ed., abridged edition). Cambridge, Mass.: Cambridge University Press, 1961.

Thompson, P. Margaret Thatcher: A new illusion. *Perception,* 1980, *9,* 438–484.

Thompson, R.F. The engram found? Initial localization of the memory trace for a basic form of associative learning. In J.M. Sprague & A. Epstein (Eds.), *Progress in psychobiology and physiological psychology.* New York: Academic Press, 1983.

Thompson, R.F., Berger, T.W., Berry, S.D., Hoehler, F.K., Kettner, R.E., & Weisz, D.J. Hippocampal substrate of classical conditioning. *Physiological Psychology,* 1980, *8,* 262–279.

Thompson, R.F., Berger, T.W., Cegavske, C.F., Patterson, M.M., Roemer, R.A., Teyler, T.J., & Young, R.A. The search for the engram. *American Psychologist,* 1976, *31,* 209–227.

Thompson, R.F., Berger, T.W., & Madden, J. IV. Cellular processes of learning and memory in the mammalian CNS. In W.M. Cowan (Ed.), *Annual Review of Neuroscience* (Vol. 6). Palo Alto, Calif.: Annual Reviews, 1983.

Thompson, R.F., Hicks, L.H., & Snvyrok, V.B. (Eds.). *Neural mechanisms of goal-directed behavior and learning.* New York: Academic Press, 1980.

Thompson, R.F., McCormick, D.A., Lavond, D.G., Clark, G.A., Kettner, R.E., & Mauk, M.D. The engram found? Initial localization of the memory trace for a basic form of associative learning. In J.M. Sprague & A. Epstein (Eds.), *Progress in psychobiology and physiological psychology* (Vol. 10). New York: Academic Press, 1983.

Thompson, R.F., & Spencer, W.A. Habituation: A model phenomenon for the study of neuronal substrates of behavior. *Psychological Review,* 1966, *73,* 16–43.

Thorndike, E.L. Animal intelligence: An experimental study of the association process in animals. *Psychological Monographs,* 1898, *2*(8).

Thorndike, E.L. *Animal intelligence, experimental studies.* New York: Macmillan, 1911.

Thorndike, E.L. *Human learning.* Cambridge: MIT Press, 1931.

Thorpe, W.H. *Learning and instinct in animals.* London: Methuen, 1956.

Tighe, T.J., & Leaton, R.N. (Eds.). *Habituation: Perspectives from child development, animal behavior, and neurophysiology.* Hillsdale, N.J.: Erlbaum, 1976.

Tinbergen, N. *The study of instinct.* Oxford: Clarendon Press, 1951.

Tinbergen, N. The curious behavior of the stickleback. *Scientific American,* 1952, *187,* 22–38.

Tootell, R.B., Silverman, M.S., & DeValois, R.L. Spatial frequency columns in primary visual cortex. *Science,* 1981, *214,* 813–815.

Valenstein, E.S. (Ed.). *The psychosurgery debate: Scientific, legal, and ethical perspectives.* San Francisco: Freeman, 1980.

Van der Velde, Th. H. *Ideal marriage.* New York: Random House, 1926.

Van Sluyters, R.C., & Blakemore, C. Experimental creation of unusual neuronal properties in visual cortex of kittens. *Nature,* 1973, *246,* 506–508.

Volkmann, J. Anchoring of absolute scales, *Psychological Bulletin,* 1936, *33,* 742–743.

Von Szeliski, V. Relation between the quantity perceived and the time of perception. *Journal of Experimental Psychology,* 1924, *7,* 135–147.

Vygotsky, L.S. *Mind in society: The development of higher psychological processes.* M.C. Cole, V. John-Steiner, S. Scribner, & E. Souberman (Eds.). Cambridge: Harvard University Press, 1978.

Wada, J., & Rasmussen, T. Intracarotid injection of sodium amytal for the lateralization of cerebral speech dominance. *Journal of Neurosurgery,* 1960, *17,* 266–282.

Walk, R.D., & Gibson, E.J. A comparative and analytic study of visual depth perception. *Psychological Monographs,* 1961, *75,* (Whole No. 519).

Walke, R.D., Shepherd, J.D., & Miller, D.R. Attention to an alternative to self-induced motion for perceptual behavior of kittens. *Society for Neuroscience Abstracts,* 1978, *4,* 129.

Walsh, K.W. *Neuropsychology: A clinical approach.* Edinburgh: Churchill Livingstone, 1978.

Walters, E.T., & Byrne, J.H. Associative conditioning of single sensory neurons suggests a cellular mechanism for learning. *Science,* 1983, *219,* 405–408.

Warren, J.M. Learning in vertebrates. In D.A. Dewsbury & D.A. Rethlingshafer (Eds.), *Comparative psychology: A modern survey.* Tokyo: McGraw-Hill Kogakusha, 1974.

Warrington, E.K., & Weiskrantz, L. Amnesic syndrome: Consolidation or retrieval? *Nature* (London), 1970, *228,* 628–630.

Watson, J.B. *Behaviorism.* New York: Norton, 1930.

Waugh, N.C. Serial position and the memory-span. *American Journal of Psychology,* 1960, *73,* 68–79.

Waugh, N.C., & Norman, D.A. Primary memory, *Psychological Review,* 1965, *72,* 89–104.

Webster, W.G. Territoriality and the evolution of brain asymmetry. *Annals of the New York Academy of Sciences,* 1977, *299,* 213–221.

Weimer, W.B. Manifestations of mind: Some conceptual and empirical issues. In G.C. Globus, G. Maxwell, & I. Savodnik (Eds.), *Consciousness and the brain.* New York: Plenum, 1976.

Weinstein, E.A., & Friedland, R.P. (Eds.), *Hemi-inattention and hemispheric specialization.* New York: Raven Press, 1977.

Weinstein, E.A. Clinical features of hemi-inattention. *The Behavioral and Brain Sciences,* 1980, *3,* 518–520.

Weinstein, E.A. Extinction and hemi-inattention: Their relation to commissurotomy. (Commentary/Pucetti: Mental duality). *The Behavioral and Brain Sciences,* 1981, *4,* 114–115.

Weinstein, E.A., Kahn, R.L., & Slote, W. Withdrawal, inattention and pain asymbolia. *AMA Archives of Neurology and Psychiatry,* 1955, *74,* 235–248.

Weiskrantz, L. The interaction between occipital and temporal cortex in vision: An overview. In F.O. Schmitt & F.O. Worden (Eds.), *The neurosciences: Third study program.* Cambridge: MIT Press, 1974.

Weiskrantz, L., Cowey, A., & Passingham, C. Spatial responses to brief stimuli by monkeys with striate cortex ablations. *Brain,* 1977, *100,* 655–670.

Weiss, J.M., Goodman, P.A., Losito, B.G., Corrigan, S., Charry, J.M., & Bailey, W.H. Behavioral depression produced by an uncontrollable stressor. Relationship to norepinephrine, dopamine, and serotonin levels in various regions of rat brain. *Brain Research Reviews,* 1981, *3,* 167–205.

Wernicke, K. The symptom-complex of aphasia. In A. Church (Ed.), *Diseases of the nervous system.* New York: Appleton-Century-Crofts, 1908.

Wertheimer, M. Experimentelle Studien über das Sehen von Bewegung. *Zeitschrift für Psychologie,* 1912, *61,* 161–625.

Wertheimer, M. *Productive thinking.* New York: Harper, 1945.

Whitaker, H.A., & Ojemann, G.A. Lateralization of higher cortical functions: A critique. In S.J. Dimond & D.A. Blizard (Eds.), *Evolution and lateralization of the brain.* New York: Annals of the New York Academy of Sciences, 1977.

White, E.B. *Charlotte's web.* New York: Harper & Row, 1952.

Wickelgren, W.A. Sparing of short-term memory in an amnesic patient: Implications for strength theory of memory. *Neuropsychologia*, 1968, *6*, 235–244.

Wiersma, C.A.G. Function of the giant fibers of the central nervous system of the crayfish. *Proceedings of the Society of Experimental Biology and Medicine*, 1938, *38*, 661–662.

Wiesel, T.N., & Hubel, D.H. Single-cell responses in striate cortex of kittens deprived of vision in one eye. *Journal of Neurophysiology*, 1963, *26*, 1003–1017.

Wiesel, T.N., & Hubel, D.H. Comparison of the effects of unilateral and bilateral eye closure on cortical unit responses in kittens. *Journal of Neurophysiology*, 1965, *28*, 1029–1040. (a)

Wiesel, T.N., & Hubel, D.H. Extent of recovery from the effects of visual deprivation in kittens. *Journal of Neurophysiology*, 1965, *28*, 1060–1072. (b)

Wiesel, T.N., & Hubel, D.H. Ordered arrangement of orientation columns in monkeys lacking visual experience. *Journal of Comparative Neurology*, 1974, *158*, 307–318.

Wilson, D.M. Insect walking. *Annual review of entomology*, 1966, *11*, 103–122.

Wittgenstein, L. *Philosophical investigations*. New York: Macmillan, 1953.

Woodworth, R.S. *Dynamic psychology*. New York: Columbia University Press, 1918.

Woodworth, R.S. Gestalt psychology and the concept of reaction stages. *American Journal of Psychology*, 1927, *39*, 62–69.

Woodworth, R.S. Situation-and-goal set. *American Journal of Psychology*, 1937, *50*, 130–140.

Woodworth, R.S. *Experimental psychology*. New York: Henry Holt, 1938.

Woodworth, R.S. *Psychological issues*. New York: Columbia University Press, 1939, p. 740.

Woodworth, R.S. *Psychology* (4th ed.). New York: Henry Holt, 1940.

Woodworth, R.S. Reënforcement of perception. *American Journal of Psychology*, 1947, *60*, 119–124.

Woodworth, R.S., & Marquis, D.G. *Psychology* (5th ed.). New York: Henry Holt, 1947.

Woodworth, R.S., & Schlosberg, H. *Experimental psychology* (Rev. ed.). New York: Holt, Rinehart and Winston, 1954.

Wunderlich, K., & Gloede, W. *Nature as constructor*. New York: Arco, 1981.

Wurtz, R.H., Goldberg, M.E., & Robinson, D.L. Behavioral modulation of visual responses in the monkey: Stimulus selection for attention and movement. In J.M. Sprague & A.N. Epstein (Eds.), *Progress in psychobiology and physiological psychology* (Vol. 9). New York: Academic Press, 1980.

Yarbus, A.L. *Eye movements and vision*. New York: Plenum, 1967.

Yates, F.A. *The art of memory*. Chicago: University of Chicago Press, 1966.

Yin, R.K. Looking at upside-down faces. *Journal of Experimental Psychology*, 1969, *81*, 141–145.

Young, J.Z. *Programs of the brain*. Oxford: Oxford University Press, 1978.

Zeki, S. The representation of colours in the cerebral cortex. *Nature*, 1980, *284*, 412–418.

Zola-Morgan, S., Squire, L.R., & Mishkin, M. The neuroanatomy of amnesia: Amygdalahippocampus versus temporal stem. *Science*, 1982, *218*, 1337–1339.

GLOSSARY

ablation   Surgical excision or removal of any part of the brain or spinal cord.

absolute judgment   A categorical response, absolute in form, but relative to the range of stimuli considered along one dimension. A rating or estimate of magnitude.

acalculia   Inability to identify numerals or symbols for mathematical operations.

acetylcholine (ACh)   A neurotransmitter found in the central nervous system and in the parasympathetic division of the autonomic nervous system.

action codes   Neural representations of unitary acts or voluntary movements thought to be encoded as topological formulae in kinesthetic programming units. (See **kinesthetic cognon.**)

action potential   Brief electrochemical impulse along a neuron resulting from depolarization of the cell membrane.

active movements   Acts performed voluntarily as instrumental responses. (Contrast **passive movements.**)

actual connection   Strengthening of a potential connection as the result of learning resulting in the formation of an association. (See **associative learning.**)

adaptation   Decline in response or increase in threshold for a repeated or continuing stimulus or its categorical equivalent. Generally, a regulatory change in responsiveness of the nervous system appropriate to the environment.

adenine   One of the nucleotide bases of RNA and DNA.

adenosine triphosphate (ATP)   A molecule important to cellular energy metabolism. ATP converts to cyclic AMP, an intermediate messenger in the production of postsynaptic potential by some neurotransmitters.

adenylate cyclase   An enzyme that catalyzes the production of cyclic AMP.

adipsia   Complete lack of drinking caused by brain damage.

adrenalin   A hormone secreted by the adrenal medulla that serves the sympathetic division of the autonomic nervous system.

affect   (n.) An emotional or mood state. Manifest feelings. (v.) To influence or move.

afferent   Conducting from receptors toward the central nervous system.

aftereffect   An illusion resulting from intense or persistent inspection of a stimulus, often opposite or complementary to the original perception; a negative afterimage or negative aftereffect.

agnosia   Inability to recognize or imagine a category of perceptual stimuli. A selective brain disorder not attributable to a sensory defect.

agraphia   Loss of ability to write following brain damage.

akinesia   Inability to initiate movement, as in Parkinsonism, resulting from degeneration of the dopamine-containing cells of the nigrostriate pathways in the basal ganglia.

alexia   Loss of ability to read following brain damage.

all-or-none law   An action potential, if started, continues without decrement or change in amplitude to the end of the fiber.

alpha rhythm   A regular wave pattern (about 10 Hz) recorded by EEG during relaxation with eyes closed.

alpha waves   Fairly regular EEG waves (between 8 and 12 Hz) recorded during a relaxed waking state with eyes closed.

Alzheimer's disease   Progressive dementia produced by brain damage located in the basilar nucleus of Maynert just above the optic chiasm.

ambient   In the immediately surrounding space. Peripheral vision needed for space perception.

ambivalence   Alternation between two antagonistic forms of response.

amnesia   Partial or total loss of memory following brain injury or electroconvulsive shock.

amygdala   Nuclei of the limbic system in the base of the temporal lobe.

analyzer   The entire sensory-perceptual system for obtaining and sorting information from the receptors belonging to that system: visual, auditory, somatosensory, kinesthetic, emotive, olfactory, gustatory, or vestibular system. The subdivision by means of which the CNS differentiates and selects significant stimuli out of the complex environment, e.g., the visual analyzer selects vibrations of light; the acoustic analyzer selects vibrations of sound, and so on. The structure of each analyzer includes the peripheral receptor with all its afferent nerves, and at the other extreme, the nerve cells at the central termination of the fibers.

anarthria   Loss of coordination of the mouth and speech muscles.

angular gyrus   Gyrus in the parietal lobe in Brodmann's area 39 that serves major language functions. Converts visual to auditory words and vice versa. Also stores rules of grammar and spelling.

anomia   Loss of ability to name objects following brain damage.

anosmia   Loss of ability to recognize odors.

antagonist   Opponent or opposite in effect to an agonist.

anterograde amnesia   Loss of memory for posttraumatic events with little effect on memory for information acquired prior to brain trauma.

antidrive   Inhibition or reduction of drive resulting from consummatory activity (reinforcement or reward). (See **mood**.)

aphagia   Inability to eat resulting from a lesion of the lateral hypothalamus.

aphasia   A disorder of language caused by lesions of certain regions of the language-dominant (usually left) hemisphere of the brain. (See **Broca's area** and **Wernicke's area**.)

aplysia   Large marine mollusk (snail) that serve as an effective model for cellular biological studies of learning and memory.

appetitive   A desirable stimulus object or goal, eliciting an approach or preservative drive.

apraxia   Loss of ability to execute learned movements following brain damage but with no elementary paralysis or defect of muscular coordination.

aprosody   Lack of emotional expression or its perception in verbal communication often caused by damage to the right cerebral hemisphere.

arcuate fasciculus   Bundle of nerve fibers in the left hemisphere that connects Wernicke's and Broca's areas. Damage to the arcuate fasciculus disconnects these language centers and results in conduction aphasia.

arousal   In neurophysiology, a process that brings large groups of neurons into a state of increased responsiveness. An important cause is stimulation of a nonspecific activating system. In psychology, heightened motivation facilitating learning.

asomatognosia Loss of perceptual awareness of one's body or parts of one's body. (See **hemi-inattention**.)

association Link between two ideas or perceptions corresponding to a physiological connection or synaptic contact between cognons.

association areas Regions of the brain that integrate information and interconnect sensory and motor processes originating in the projection areas.

association cortex A vast area of granular six-layered cortex, occupying most of the frontal lobe, and extensive parts of the parietal, occipital and temporal lobes. Neither sensory nor motor, this noncommitted cortex is essential to integration, cognitive functions, and voluntary movement skills.

associative learning Formation of an association or conditioned response linking two stimuli or a stimulus and a response as the result of their temporal pairing in experience.

astereognosia Loss of ability to recognize objects by touch following brain damage.

asymbolia Inability to recognize or manipulate symbols as a result of brain damage.

ataxia Disorder of muscular action resulting from lesions in the central nervous system.

attention Selective perceiving or tuning of a sensory analyzer for optimal reception of particular stimuli. (See **targeting reflex**.)

auditory Transmits sound information from the environment to the brain of the hearer.

autoimmune Self-protective mechanism that resists invading cells or foreign tissue.

aversive A painful, noxious, or threatening stimulus object eliciting a protective reflex.

axial movements Learned movements of the bilateral midline structures: eyes, trunk, neck.

axon Part of a neuron that transmits impulses to other neurons or effectors.

basal ganglia A group of large nuclei in the forebrain with important functions in regulating bodily movements.

Betz cells Giant pyramidal cells in layer IV of primary motor cortex. Important in voluntary movements.

bilateral Occurring on, or applied to both sides of the body.

brain Head part of the central nervous system that integrates and coordinates all behavior and experience. (See **mind**.)

Broca's area A region of the left frontal lobe (frontal opercullum) involved in speech functions. Damage to this area results in Broca's aphasia, a disorder of speech articulation.

Brodmann's map A cytoarchitectonic mapping devised by Brodmann showing the anatomical areas of the cerebral cortex.

callosal Pertaining to the corpus callosum.

camouflage Disguising or hiding an object by adding masking noise that renders its contours or frequencies less visible or audible.

capacity Potential ability for performance.

catecholamines A family of neurotransmitters including epinephrine, norepinephrine, and dopamine.

categorization   A recoding of stimulus input in terms of those features of the object or event perceived that permit the reconstruction of the remainder of the object or event.

category   A class of nonidentical members that are treated as equivalent to each other and as different from members of a contrasting category.

category scale   A rating scale that divides stimuli into classes of similar or equivalent members. Category labels may be numbers or names of classes along some dimension of magnitude or value.

cell assembly   Hebb's (1949) neuropsychological theory of directed thought based on presumed reverberating electrical circuits maintained in a closed loop of neurons in the brain.

center   A more or less circumscribed region of the central nervous system, consisting of a few or many cells of special importance in some function (e.g., initiating, integrating, or receiving).

central action program   The schema or structure of a motor act stored in a kinesthetic cognon.

central motor behavioral system   Whole set of behavioral acts that a subject has available for execution. Repetoire of active movements or skills.

central nervous system (CNS)   Brain and spinal cord.

cerebellum   Specialized part of hindbrain. Preprograms and stores learned motor patterns.

cerebral hemispheres   Two major parts of the forebrain in mammals. Integrative, coordinating structures of the nervous system.

cerebral vascular accident (CVA)   (See **stroke**.)

cerebrum or cerebral cortex   Outermost layer of gray matter of the cerebral hemispheres.

channel   An actual connection or series of synaptic contacts between neurons that act in parallel with other insulated channels of neural activity.

cingulate gyrus   Strip of limbic cortex just above the corpus callosum along the medial walls of the cerebral hemispheres.

classical conditioning   Learned relation between two stimuli (or cognons) as the result of their temporally paired activity in the past experience of the individual.

clone, clonal   Replication of a particular cell by cell division resulting in identical progeny.

cognitive field   A region of the association cortex containing the cognons belonging to a particular category system in a given analyzer.

cognize   To perceive, know, or recognize.

cognon   Basic neural unit of mind and brain that participates in perception, imagination, thought, learning, and voluntary movement. (See **unitary perception, unitary image**.)

cogwheel   A gear with teeth or cogs that meshes with adjacent mechanisms and moves them synchronously. Metaphorically, an information processing system constrained by six cogs or cognons in the mind-brain.

columnar organization   Arrangement of cells in the cerebral cortex in modular blocks of macro- or hypercolumns consisting of thin vertical minicolumns of neurons with identical or complementary functions.

command cell A neuron that can initiate and maintain a program of coordinated movements involving a set of muscles and pathways with no peripheral feedback. (See **kinesthetic cognon.**)

commissure A bundle of fibers connecting corresponding points on the two sides of the brain or spinal cord.

commissurotomy Surgical disconnection of the two hemispheres by cutting the corpus callosum. (See **split brain syndrome.**)

complementarity Apposition of opposite processes in close spatial proximity in the central nervous system.

complementary colors Two colors that when mixed additively cancel each other and appear gray.

computerized axial tomography (CAT) (CT) scan An x-ray procedure for mapping the brain in three dimensions.

conditioned discrimination A process of learning in which one stimulus is followed, and another not followed, by an unconditioned stimulus.

conditioned reflex See **conditioned response.**

conditioned response (CR) A response elicited by some originally neutral stimulus, a conditioned stimulus (CS), as the result of its temporal pairing with an unconditioned stimulus (US) that produces a biologically significant effect.

conditioned stimulus (CS) In classical conditioning, the originally neutral stimulus that assumes the role of the eliciting natural or unconditioned stimulus (US) for a response as the result of temporal pairing. The CS evokes the image of the US—a kind of hallucination.

cones Visual receptors concentrated in the fovea of the retina that process fine detail and color vision. (See **rods.**)

consciousness Subjective awareness of ongoing experience.

constancy Tendency to perceive objects as relatively stable and unaltered despite wide changes in the environmental conditions in which they appear.

consummatory conditioned responses Discrete phasic responses evoked by brief stimuli in conditioning experiments.

consummatory phase or activity Phasic second stage of drive-produced behavior in which the food or other goal object is ingested or possessed.

contiguity Paired presentation of two stimuli or a stimulus and a response that leads to their learned association or connection.

contralateral Opposite side of the body.

contrast detector Response of a neuron not to absolute stimulus intensity but to the degree of difference between two contiguous stimuli (e.g., light and dark).

corollary discharge Postulated neural messages sent to sensory areas by command centers that initiate voluntary or active movements.

corpus callosum Massive cable of nerve fibers connecting the right and left hemispheres of the brain.

cortex Bark or outer layer of an organ such as the cerebrum, cerebellum, or adrenal gland.

cortical columns (columnar organization) Vertical, cylindrical modules of 100–300 cortical neurons, efferent and afferent fibers, and intrinsic connections. Programming units for input and output data that comprise the elementary working units (cognons) of the cerebral cortex.

cortical layers A major organizing feature of the cerebral cortex; together with the cortical columns, such lamination provides for orderly circuitry, progressive analysis, and cross–integration of information between adjacent columns.

critical band A cluster or category of adjacent temporal sound or visual-spatial frequencies that are sufficiently close to mask each other, thus interfering with clear signal detection.

critical period An ontogenetic stage of heightened sensitivity to a particular class or category of environmental stimuli.

cross-modal Connection between two modalities or analyzers, for example, seeing and touching.

cytoarchitectonic map A map of the cortex showing the organization and structure of the cells.

decorticate Surgical removal of the cortex of the brain.

déjà vu (French, already seen). Illusion that one has already experienced something before.

delayed reaction A cue that indicates the location of a goal object is removed and the subject is prevented from approaching the goal for a shorter or longer period of time.

dementia Irreversible deterioration of intellectual faculties resulting from organic brain damage.

dendrites Treelike branches at the receiving end of a neuron and conduct impulses toward the cell body and axon.

dichopic An experimental procedure for presenting a different stimulus to each eye simultaneously. Consistent with microscopic, telescopic, stereoscopic, etc., although often written as *dichoptic*.

dichotic listening An experimental procedure for separating different messages to each ear simultaneously.

diencephalon A region of the brain that includes the hypothalamus, thalamus and epithalamus.

differentiation Ability to respond differently to two discriminated stimuli.

disconnection Severing of one region of the brain from another by surgery, tumor, or other insult to nervous tissue that disrupts communication between regions.

disconnection syndrome A disorder of perception or movement resulting from the severing of neural connections in the association cortex or between the neocortex and the limbic system.

discrimination Ability to perceive distinctions between two or more stimuli. (See **conditioned discrimination**.)

dissociation A differential response based on selective facilities or disorders.

dopamine (DA) A catecholamine that is the neurotransmitter in various brain structures important in motor action. Its depletion is a cause of Parkinson's disease.

dreams Hallucinations during a period of paradoxical sleep characterized by PGO spikes and REMs. (See **hallucinations**.)

drive A specific physiological state of arousal that motivates (energizes and directs) activity toward a specific antidrive (drive reduction or consummatory goal). (See **emotion**.)

drive reduction   Any movement that is followed by the inhibition of drive by its antidrive (e.g., pressing a bar results in getting food, escaping to a safe place).

dynamic change   Hypothesis that a stimulus activates a reverberating circuit to maintain short-term memory in the nervous system.

dysarthria   A disorder of articulation distinguished from aphasia.

dysfunction   Any impairment or disorder of behavior.

dyslexia   Difficulty in learning to read with no single cause.

effectors   Muscles and glands that produce environmental effects.

efferent   Nerves that conduct impulses to the effectors (muscles or glands).

electroconvulsive shock therapy (ECT or ECS)   Controversial "treatment" for affective disorders by application of massive electric shock across the brain. Induces amnesia.

electroencephalogram (EEG)   A record of electrical potentials from the surface of the scalp that measures brain wave activity.

emotion   Psychological, hedonic, or subjective counterpart of drive (e.g., fear, pain, hunger, curiosity, etc.). (See **drive**.)

endocrine   System of ductless glands that secrete chemical products directly into the blood stream.

endocrine glands   Ductless glands, such as the thyroid, adrenals, and gonads that secrete directly into the blood stream.

endorphins   Hormones secreted by the brain that have pain-killing and tranquilizing abilities.

enkephalin   A protein occurring in the brain and having opiate qualities.

enzyme   A protein whose synthesis is controlled and directed by a specific gene. Acts as a catalyst directing major chemical reactions in the living organism.

epilepsy   A seizure of convulsive disorder caused by brain lesions, often preceded by an aura and hallucinations.

ethology   A branch of biology that studies the behavior of animals under natural conditions.

excitatory postsynaptic potentials (EPSPs)   Depolarizations that increase the probability of firing of the postsynaptic neuron.

experimental extinction   Gradual disappearance of the CR as a result of repeated nonreinforced trials.

exteroceptors   Distance receptors located in the eye and ear, and on the surface of the body, skin, tongue, nostrils.

extinction   Weakening or loss of a conditioned response as the result of nonreinforcement. (See **habituation**.)

facilitation   A first stimulus alone fails to activate a synapse but adds to the effectiveness of a second stimulus.

feature detector   Neuron in the retina or brain that responds only to specific aspects of stimuli, such as orientation, movement, or spatial frequency.

feedback   Consequence of an action affects (feeds back on) the action. May be positive (facilitating the action) or negative (inhibitory) as in a thermostatically controlled furnace.

firing   A nerve cell or part is said to fire when it initiates an impulse. Excitation or activation of a single fiber.

fixed action pattern   Ethologist's term for stereotyped, species-specific behavior triggered by a key stimulus or genetically programmed releaser. (See **consummatory act.**)

forebrain   In mammals the cerebral hemispheres, thalamus and hypothalamus.

gamma-aminobutyric acid (GABA)   A major inhibitory neurotransmitter.

gene   Functional unit of the chromosome that directs protein synthesis.

generalization   Tendency to make a similar response to a new stimulus that resembles (belongs in the same category as) a familiar stimulus.

Gestalt   An organized whole or perceptual pattern such as a familiar face or melody.

Gestalt psychology   German-American school of psychology headed by Max Wertheimer, Kurt Koffka, and Wolfgang Köhler. According to their view, the perception of relations, patterns, and organized wholes is primary and cannot be analyzed into constituent elements.

glia   Supportive cells of the central nervous system.

glucose   Major source of energy for most bodily tissues. Of great importance in brain metabolism.

gnosis   Knowledge, cognition.

gnostic unit   Konorski's (1967) term for a single cognitive neuron, here called a cognon.

goal set   A drive that arouses and directs behavior toward a selected consummatoy act. (See **drive, emotion.**)

graded potential   Summed activity of excitatory and inhibitory impulses at the dendrites of a postsynaptic neuron that determines its firing rate. See **EPSPs** and **IPSPs.**

gustation   Sense of taste—taste detecting analyzer.

gyrus   A convolution or mound of the cerebral cortex separated by sulci or fissures.

habituation   Gradual decrease of response to a maintained or repeated stimulus of little biological importance. (See **extinction.**)

hallucinations   Images falsely believed to be perceptions of actually present stimuli. (See **dreams.**)

hemi-inattention   Neglect or loss of ability to pay attention to one side of space or to one side of the body, usually the left side, as a result of damage to the right hemisphere.

heredity   Genetic programs that determine the variance of a trait in a given population.

hertz   International unit of frequency, equal to one cycle per second.

heterarchy   A democratic organization in which control may be top-down, bottom-up, sideways (e.g., a smoothly functioning football team or a human brain).

hierarchy   A vertical organization in which control passes from top to bottom (e.g., Army, Navy, or Catholic Church.)

hindbrain   Primitive parts of the mammalian brain that include the cerebellum and the medulla.

hippocampus   A forebrain structure of the temporal lobe, important in learning and memory.

homotypical cortex Uniform six-layered pattern displayed by much of cerebral cortex, as distinguished from agranular and granular areas of heterotypical cortex.

homunculus A diminutive man or mannikin used to represent the proportions of bodily parts active in sensory or motor functioning by the cortex. Derived from direct electrical stimulation of the cerebral cortex. (See **topography**.)

hormone A chemical substance released by an endocrine gland that affects target cells on other organs of the body.

Huntington's chorea A disease of the basal ganglis characterized by excessive involuntary movements.

Huntington's disease A disturbance of movement characterized by wild flailing wrought by GABA derangements in brain.

hypercolumn (macrocolumn) A large functional unit of the cerebral cortex built up of overlapping and intermixing cortical columns (e.g., ocular dominance, orientation, columns in primary visual cortex; hemispheric dominance and pressure or touch sensitive columns in somatic sensory cortex; unitary perceptions (cognons) in association cortex).

immune system Body's protection against foreign proteins and infections.

imprinting A learned attachment or perception unit that is formed at a critical or sensitive period in life and is difficult to reverse.

infarct An area of dead or dying tissue resulting from obstruction of the blood vessels that normally supply the region.

inferior colliculi Protrusions of the midbrain that relay auditory information to other parts of the brain.

inferotemporal cortex In monkeys, the highest level of visual associative cortex located on the inferior surface of the temporal lobe. Integrates pattern information and object recognition.

inhibitory postsynaptic potentials (IPSPs) Hyperpolarizations that decrease the probability of neural firing.

insight Learning by perceiving the relations between elements of the problem in contrast to "blind trial and error."

insightful learning Perception of the relations of elements to a goal may lead to the sudden appearance of a solution to a problem and its transfer to new situations. Stressed by Gestalt psychology.

instrumental (operant) conditioning Formation of an association (connection) between a conditioned response (CR) and an unconditioned stimulus (US) produced by or contingent upon the response.

intention A program or design for a specific purpose.

interoceptors Receptors located within the recesses of the body (lungs and viscera) that provide information about the internal milieu (digestion, heart rate, respiration, etc.).

interocular transfer Crossover of information received by one eye to affect the visual pathways served by the other eye.

ipsilateral Same side of the body.

kinesthesis Information provided by proprioceptors about the movements of various parts of the body. Feedback from the body's own activity. (See **proprioceptors**.)

kinesthetic cognon   A single nerve cell in the central premotor association area that controls a program for active or voluntary movements.

labeled line   A neural pathway identified by specific function with known origin and destination in the CNS.

labeled line code   Origin and destination of a neuron conveys the specific quality of a sensation.

lateralization   Asymmetry of function of the two cerebral hemispheres with a probable anatomical basis.

lateral geniculate nucleus   A group of cell bodies within the thalamus that receive impulses frrm the retina and project fibers to the primary visual area in the cortex.

lateral hypothalamus (LH)   A region of the hypothalamus that contains cell bodies and diffuse fibers. Important in spontaneous movement, eating and drinking.

lateral inhibition   Inhibitory effects of adjacent neural units upon each other's activity. Underlies brightness contrast and negative aftereffects.

L-dopa   A precursor of dopamine, effective in relieving symptoms of striatal lesions, such as Parkinsonism.

learned helplessness   A condition created by exposure to intense uncontrollable stress.

lesion   A circumscribed pathological alteration of tissue, wound or injury.

limbic system   A group of subcortical structures including the anterior thalamus, amygdala, hippocampus, and parts of the hypothalamus that mediate drive-related behavior and transmit emotional information to the cortex and other parts of the brain.

lobectomy   Surgical removal of a lobe from the brain.

lobotomy   Surgical division of a lobe, usually the frontal lobe, from other parts of the brain; disconnecting cerebral nerve tracts.

locus coeruleus   A blue-colored group of noradrenergic cell bodies located near the rostral end of the floor of the fourth ventricle in the brain stem. Important in arousal, mood, recovery from depression.

long-term memory   Relatively stable retention of nonassociative or associative learning. (See **short-term memory**.)

magnet effect   Von Holst's term for the dominance of one rhythm upon another movement.

maturation   Process of natural development of the individual as the result of environmental facilitation of the genetic programs.

medulla oblongata   Nervous tissue at the base of the brain that controls respiration, circulation, and other vital functions.

memory span   Number of items one can recall after a single presentation.

microelectrode   A very fine electrode used to record activity of individual nerve cells.

midbrain   Part of the brain that includes centers for sensation, movement, and arousal. Contains the superior and inferior colliculi, important in processing visual and auditory signals.

mind   Functions of the brain manifested in feeling, perceiving, imagining, thinking, learning, remembering, and voluntary movements. (See **brain**.)

mnemonics   Artful devices for aiding memory.

modality   Selective division or subsystem of an analyzer with its own specialized function (e.g., color vision, space perception, etc.).

mood Psychological, hedonic, or subjective counterpart of antidrive (e.g., relief, satiety, peace, calm, etc.). (See **antidrive**.)

motor task Bernstein's term for a kinesthetic action program.

neocortex Newest, most recently developed part of the cerebral cortex surrounding the hemispheres.

nerve fiber An axon (the principal branch) of a nerve cell that may extend for long distances.

neural codes Spatial and temporal arrangements of neural impulses that convey quality and intensity information to the brain.

neuron A nerve cell with its processes. The basic functional unit of the central nervous system, specialized to receive and conduct excitation, contacts with other neurons and with effectors or receptors.

neuron doctrine Theory that the nervous system is composed of individual neurons biologically independent but communicating by synapses.

neurophysiology Interdisciplinary sciences of neurology and physiology. The study of the functions of the nervous system in all organisms.

neuropsychology An interdisciplinary synthesis of psychology and neural sciences that attempts to elucidate neural mechanisms underlying behavior and conscious experience.

neurotransmitters Chemical substances released at the terminals of axons that travel across synapses and may excite or inhibit postsynaptic target neurons.

nonassociative learning Habituation, sensitization, and perceptual learning are nonassociative because they do not require pairing between two active pathways. They are forms of learning because they show progressive changes in behavior resulting from experience.

nonadrenergic A family of chemical neurotransmitters including norepinephrine (NE) whose depletion by stress causes behavioral depression.

norepinephrine A neurotransmitter found in the brain and the sympathetic branch of the autonomic nervous system.

olfaction Sense of smell—odor detecting analyzer.

ontogeny Development of an individual by maturational processes guided by genetic programs.

opponent process A reciprocal inhibitory connection between two pathways in the CNS.

organism A highly organized living system with the capacity to respond to external stimuli, metabolize, grow, learn, and to differentiate responses, depending on feedback from the environment.

orientation reflex (See **orienting response**.)

orienting response Initial investigatory reaction to a new or threatening stimulus. (See **attention**.)

oscillator (pacemaker) A dual action cell that produces cyclical activity governed by reciprocal interaction.

paradoxical (deep) sleep Characterized by dreaming and a profound relaxation of peripheral muscle accompanied by rapid eye movement (REM) and activation of the cortical EEG.

parasympathetic system A division of the autonomic nervous system that serves vegetative functions and conserves energies. Its action is antagonistic to that of the sympathetic system.

Parkinson's disease A neurological disorder of movement, characterized by tremor and rigidity. A degeneration of the nigrostriatal bundle and depletion of dopamine.

passive movements Movements forced by an external agent such as direct electrical brain stimulation, or pulling or lifting a limb. (Contrast **active movements**.)

perception unit A unitary neural representation of an external object or event in the brain. (See **cognon**.)

perseveration Continued or repetitive activity or actions.

phasic A transitory or brief period of activity in contrast to a sustained tonic state. (See **fixed action pattern**.)

phenylketonuria (PKU) A severe form of mental retardation determined by a single gene. If detected early enough, the disorder can be treated by special diet.

phylogeny Processes of evolutionary development guided by natural selection.

plastic Capable of building or shaping tissue; altering synaptic transmissability and encoding memories.

plastic change Functional and structural modifications of synaptic efficacy as a result of experience.

positron emission tomography A technique for examining regional differences in brain metabolism by injecting radioactive substances into the bloodstream. The result is a color-coded dynamic picture of regional activity in the intact brain.

postsynaptic Follower or target neuron that receives neurotransmitter from a presynaptic sensory neuron or interneuron.

potential connection Prefunctional genetically programmed arrangement of neurons and synapses underlying their actual connection as the result of experience and learning.

praxis Habitual or established actions and coordinated motor skills.

preparatory conditioned responses (CRs) Drive conditioned responses, usually tonic and prolonged (e.g., hunger CRs to time of day).

preparatory reflex Tonic first stage of drive arousal, including restless searching motor behavior (e.g., hunger, thirst, sexual arousal, etc.).

proactive inhibition Disturbance of memory caused by previously learned material.

projection area Primary cortical receiving areas of an analyzer such as visual areas 17, 18, and 19 in the striate cortex.

proprioceptors Receptors located in the muscles, tendons, and joints that provide information about the organism's own motor activities. (See **kinesthesis**.)

prosopagnosia Loss of the ability to recognize familiar faces as the result of brain damage.

protein kinase Any protein that catalyzes the transfer of a phosphate group from ATP to form a phosphoprotein.

prototype An exemplar or "best" instance of membership in a category. A robin is more "birdlike" than an ostrich or penguin, hence protytypical.

psychosis A broad category of severe mental disorders including schizophrenia, manic depression, and other affective disorders.

psychosurgery Surgical disconnection or removal of brain tissue for which no organic pathology can be demonstrated. Controversial "therapy" for mental disorders that may eliminate troublesome symptoms but at risk of reduced emotive and cognitive capacities.

psychotherapy   Any form of treatment that uses verbal or behavioral methods rather than medicinal approaches for emotional or behavioral dysfunctions.

pyramidal cells   One of the two main types of cerebral cortical neurons, shaped in the form of a pyramid with a single apical dendrite and numerous basal dendrites.

quiet sleep   Stages of non-REM sleep in which the EEG shows progressively less cortical arousal.

rapid eye movement sleep (REM sleep)   Paradoxical or dream sleep.

reaction stages   Progressive transformations of stimulus input by successively newer integrative levels of neural processing.

recall   A task in which some absent item must be imagined or reproduced from memory. The arousal of a cognon via associative pathways.

receptive field   Portion of a sensory receptor, such as the retina, that affects the firing rate of an individual cell.

receptor   A specialized type of sensory cell that transduces physical stimuli into slow, graded receptor potentials that alter the rate of firing in postsynaptic neurons.

reciprocal inhibition   Excitation of neural system is accomplished by the inhibition of the system's antagonist (e.g., flexor muscles contract when extensors relax).

recognition   Perceptual identification of a familiar object or event.

reflex   A stereotyped muscular or glandular response that is the direct result of a particular stimulus.

refractory period   If absolute, no further impulses can arise in a particular nerve fiber during this period of time.

reinforced trial   A trial in classical conditioning in which the CS is followed by the US. In operant conditioning the CR is followed by the US.

reinforcement   Pavlov's term for the strengthening of the tendency of the CS to elicit the CR by repeatedly pairing the CS and the US.

reticular activating system   A system emanating from the reticular formation of the brainstem with a powerful recruiting influence on other parts of the brain.

reticular formation   A large network of neural tissue located in central regions of the brainstem, from the medulla to the diencephalon.

retina   Photoreceptive inner surface of the posterior portion of the eye.

retrieval   Process by which memories stored in the brain are brought to affect behavior. The active firing of cognons in recognition and recall.

retroactive inhibition   Disturbance of memory caused by material learned subsequent to the lesson desired for retrieval.

retrograde amnesia   Loss of memory for past events or information stored prior to trauma to the brain, such as injury or electroconvulsive shock.

ribonucleic acid (RNA)   A complex macromolecule composed of a sequence of nucleotide bases.

rods   Retinal photoreceptors that transduce luminous energy and convey light and dark information to the visual analyzer. (See **cones**.)

saturation   Mode of color perception. The purity of a color unmixed with black or white.

schizophrenia   A family of severe psychotic disorders with no known organic basis but evident inherited predisposition, variously characterized by disturbances of thought, hallucinations, delusions, inappropriate affect, withdrawal, or antisocial behavior.

sensitization   Prolonged enhancement of the investigatory response as the result of the arousal of the orientation reflex by the stimulus itself or another stimulus. A facilitatory form of nonassociative learning.

serotonin   A neurotransmitter (5-hydroxytryptamine) that has a constricting effect on blood vessels. Important in *Aplysia* learning and memory.

servoloop   Automatic control by feedback pathways.

servomechanism   Apparatus designed for feedback control operation.

short-term memory   Relatively brief or temporary retention of information, also referred to as immediate, recent, or transient memory. (See **long-term memory**.)

slow wave (light) sleep   Characterized by slow, synchronized cortical EEG activity and muscle tone not greatly reduced from the waking state.

somatosensory system   Analyzer that receives many projection fibers from the exterior and interior surfaces of the body serving tactile, joint, and pain sensitivity.

spatial frequency   Spacing of alternate light and dark bands of luminance across the visual field. Measured in cycles per degree of visual angle, hence increasing with distance of a grating pattern from the eye.

species   A reproductive community or population in which no member mating outside the community can produce fertile offspring.

split brain syndrome   Alterations of behavior following the surgical disconnection of the two hemispheres of the brain.

stellate cells   A type of cerebral cortical neuron, usually with small cell bodies in the form of a star or polygon; their axons form intracortical circuits.

striate cortex   Primary projection areas of the visual cortex.

stroke   Sudden onset of neurological symptoms as a result of arterial interruption of blood flow to the brain. (See **cerebral vascular accident** (CVA).)

subitizing   Unitary perception of the number of items in a display. Upper limit is six.

sulcus   A fissure of the convoluted surface of the cerebral cortex.

superimposition   Additive mixture of sound waves of spatial frequencies that produces complex wave forms.

superior colliculi   Protrusions on top of the midbrain serving to provide spatial information. Part of the light sensitive visual and other analyzers.

sympathetic system   A division of the autonomic nervous system that mobilizes the body's energies for protective reactions. Its action is antagonistic to that of the parasympathetic division.

synapses   Gaps or junctions between neurons across which signals that modify behavior are transmitted.

synaptic transmission   Communication between the axon of a presynaptic neuron and the dendrites of a postsynaptic neuron by chemical or (rarely) electrical contact.

synaptic vesicle   A small container of transmitter substance found in terminal buttons of axons.

syndrome   A pattern of symptoms that underlie a common pathology.

tardive dyskinesia   A disease of the basal ganglia characterized by rigidity and inability to control body movements.

targeting reflex   Sensory and motor adjustments of the particular analyzer for optimal reception of a stimulus. Fine tuning. (See **attention**.)

teleology   The study of the existence of some endpoint or goal that is preserved in the program that regulates behavior. (See **teleonomic**.)

teleonomic A physiological process or a behavior that owes its goal—directedness—to the operation of a genetic program and depends on the existence of some endpoint or consummatory act. (See **teleology**.)

thalamus A large ovoid mass of gray matter that relays sensory impulses to the cerebral cortex and acts in integrative and nonspecific functions.

tonic Characterized by continuous tension until normal tone is produced. (See **preparatory reflex**.)

topography Graphic description of a particular place such as the map of points on the skin or retina of the eye. (See **homunculus**.)

topologist A specialist in the properties of knots, pretzels, and other forms that can be pulled, squeezed, bent, or otherwise distorted without essential alteration of topological properties.

topology A branch of mathematical geometry that describes the invariant feaures of an object or pattern despite transformations of size, distance, etc.

transduce Convert from one form of energy to another, as visual receptors convert light photons into photochemical products for stimulating retinal nerve cells.

triune brain Paul MacLean's term for the unified reptilian, paleomammalian, and neomammalian parts of the human brain.

unconditioned reflex (UR) Natural or unlearned response to a particular stimulus or pattern.

unconditioned stimulus (US) A biologically important stimulus that elicits an unlearned reflex such as salivation or leg flexion.

unitary image A single act of retrieval of a stimulus from memory without necessarily naming or labeling the stimulus. (See **cognon**.)

unitary motor acts Kinesthetically programmed movements that require no peripheral feedback for their instrumentalization.

unitary perception A single act of immediate recognition without necessarily naming or labeling the stimulus. (See **cognon**.)

ventricles Cavities of the brain that contain cerebrospinal fluid.

ventromedial hypothalamus (VMH) A region of the hypothalamus located near the walls of the third ventricle. Important in hunger and satiety.

voluntary movement Instrumental, active motor behavior under the influence of a drive. Distinguished from a passive movement.

Wernicke's aphasia Inability to comprehend speech or to produce meaningful speech after lesions to posterior cortex.

AUTHOR INDEX

SUBJECT INDEX